Symbol	Definition	Chapter First Introduced
M^d	Money demand (nominal)	Chapter 4
MPK	Marginal product of capital	Chapter 5
MPN	Marginal product of labor	Chapter 5
M^s	Money supply (nominal)	Chapter 4
M^s/P	Real supply of money balances	Chapter 4
N	Employment	Chapter 5
N^d	Labor demand	Chapter 5
N^s	Labor supply	Chapter 6
P	Price level for output	Chapter 4
P^e	Expected future price of output	Chapter 5
P_k^e	Expected future price of capital	Chapter 5
P_f	Price level for output in foreign country	Chapter 6
P_k	Price of capital	Chapter 5
π	Rate of inflation	Chapter 12
π^e	Expected rate of inflation	Chapter 5
r	Money or nominal interest rate	Chapter 5
R	Expected real rate of interest $(r - \pi^e)$	Chapter 6
r_f	Foreign interest rate (nominal)	Chapter 6
r^*	Return to lending in foreign country	Chapter 6
S	Saving	Chapter 4
t	Tax rate on income	Chapter 9
T	Net taxes (total taxes net of government transfer payments: $T_b + T_h - TR$)	Chapter 4
T_b	Business taxes	Chapter 4
T_h	Household taxes	Chapter 4
TR	Government transfer payments	Chapter 4
U	Unemployment rate	Chapter 2
U_n	Natural rate of unemployment	Chapter 7
V	Income velocity of money	Chapter 8, 16
W	Money wage	Chapter 5
X^d	Export demand	Chapter 4
Y	Real gross national product (GNP)	Chapter 4
Y^d	Economy-wide output demand	Chapter 5
YD	Real disposable income $(Y\text{-}CCA\text{-}T)$	Chapter 4
YD_f	Foreign country real disposable income	Chapter 6
Y^*	Full employment level of real GNP	Chapter 7
Z^d	Import demand	Chapter 4

MACROECONOMICS

MACROECONOMICS

John M. Barron
Purdue University

Mark A. Loewenstein
Virginia Polytechnic Institute and State University

Gerald J. Lynch
Purdue University

Addison-Wesley Publishing Company

Reading, Massachusetts   Menlo Park, California   New York   Don Mills, Ontario
Wokingham, England   Amsterdam   Bonn   Sydney   Singapore   Tokyo   Madrid   San Juan

Sponsoring Editor: Barbara Rifkind

Senior Production Supervisor: Kazia Navas

Production Coordinator: Sarah Hallet

Text Designer: C.J. Petlick/Hunter Graphics

Cover Designer: Marshall Henrichs

Technical Art Consultant: Dick Morton

Illustrators: Horvath and Cuthbertson

Copyeditor: Stephanie Argeros-Magean

Permissions Editor: Mary Dyer

Manufacturing Supervisor: Roy Logan

LIBRARY OF CONGRESS
Library of Congress Cataloging-in-Publication Data

Barron, John M.
    Macroeconomics / John M. Barron, Mark Loewenstein, Gerald Lynch.
    p. cm.
    Includes bibliographical references and index.
    ISBN O-201-13623-6
    1. Macroeconomics. I. Loewenstein, Mark. II. Lynch, Gerald J.
III. Title.
HB172.5.B375 1988
339--dc19   88-6071
                                                                          CIP

Preface

It is said that macroeconomic analysis is in an unsettled state, in part because economists often have conflicting opinions about the direction of the macroeconomy. Macroeconomists have adopted competing approaches for analyzing the performance of the economy, and they modify or even discard these approaches in favor of new theories more often than other economists seem to change their models. But one should not make too much of all this for two reasons.

First, it is important to recognize that there is a large common body of macroeconomic analysis that is generally accepted as useful for understanding the performance of an economy. One aim of this book is to present this widely accepted body of macroeconomic analysis. Second, even though there remain important areas in which there are conflicting ideas about how the macroeconomy performs, these conflicts are not necessarily unproductive. In fact, in this regard macroeconomics displays its character as a science. Philosopher I. Lakatos has noted, ". . . the history of science has been and should be a history of competing research programmes . . . the sooner competition starts, the better for progress."[1] These very competing ideas are evidence of a field of study that is alive, interesting, and undergoing change.

The touchstone of any science is its ability to empirically test alternative theories. Accordingly, a critical part of macroeconomic research is testing to see which of the competing theories best agrees with the facts. In this book we aim to show how the available evidence accords with the various macroeconomic theories introduced in the text. To reiterate, the two major goals of this book are to present a widely accepted body of macroeconomic analysis and to relate evidence that highlights the applicability as well as the limitations of the various macroeconomic models.

Content Coverage

To achieve our aims, we stress the following aspects of macroeconomics:

The Microeconomic Foundations of Macroeconomics. By the microeconomic foundations of macroeconomic analysis we simply mean describing the behavior of the various participants in the economy. A key element in our discussion is that we explicitly develop and utilize the budget and financing constraints that the individual participants face. Structuring the book so that

---

[1] I. Lakatos, *The Methodology of Scientific Research Programmes*, (1978), p. 69. Lakatos is joined in this view by the noted philosopher of science Karl Popper, who considers all theories tentative and subject to dismissal.

the microeconomic foundations precede the macroeconomic analysis lets students understand the critical elements that underlie macroeconomic analysis. Our discussion of microeconomic foundations provides students with an appreciation of both the nature of the decisions made by the individual participants in the economy and how these decisions impact others. The analysis of microfoundations thus anticipates the general equilibrium analysis that follows. In particular, we have found that explicitly specifying individual budget constraints makes it easier for students to grasp the general equilibrium considerations that lie at the core of macroeconomics.

The Integration of Financial Markets into Macroeconomic Analysis. A number of economic events converged in the early 1980's and led to the high interest rates that affected many portions of the economy. A modern analysis of the macroeconomy must be able to explain and account for these forces. Yet in most textbook treatments, financial markets lurk in the background, and are not explicitly introduced into the analysis. In contrast, we give financial markets prominent attention, explicitly introducing them into the discussion. This allows for a direct analysis of how the decisions of households, government, firms, and foreigners combine to determine interest rates. It also makes it easier to discuss topics such as "crowding out." We have found that our approach helps students to see more clearly how the financial markets they actually observe fit into macroeconomic analysis.

The Integration of International Topics Throughout the Text. The dominant economic news of the 1980s has been the balance of trade deficit and the large inflows of foreign capital into the United States. These occurrences have highlighted the growing economic interdependencies among countries that must be accounted for if actual events are to be fully understood. We therefore weave international considerations throughout the analysis instead of waiting until late in the book. This helps the student see how an open economy differs from a closed economy at each phase of the analysis.

Early Discussion of the Neoclassical Macroeconomic Model. The neoclassical model is our term for the macroeconomic model that assumes prices are flexible and agents are well informed. Economists widely agree that the neoclassical model is useful for analyzing the performance of the economy over the long run. We find it pedagogically advantageous to discuss the neoclassical model before models with a short-run orientation. After working through the neoclassical model, the student really gets a feel for developing a model and using it to carry out economic analysis systematically. Further, after studying the neoclassical model, students can more fully appreciate the crucial features of macroeconomic models with a short-run orientation. These short-run models include the Keynesian model with its fixed price level as well as models with sticky wages and asymmetric price information.

Pedagogical Features

In addition to presenting a modern and unified theory of macroeconomics, this text incorporates many pedagogical features to help students learn. Within each chapter we have included margin definitions and summary boxes. At the end of each chapter we include a summary list of key terms and equations, and a section entitled "Looking Ahead," which describes the topics explored in the following chapters. There are also numerous review questions that range from straightforward to challenging. Working through these study questions will help students as they are introduced to new macroeconomic terms and concepts. Also, a complete glossary is found at the end of the book.

We have incorporated a number of case studies that give the student a macroeconomic framework for analyzing recent world events and issues, including case studies on "Junk Bonds" (Chapter 3), "Black Monday, Blue Consumers: The Effect of Wealth on Consumption Demand" (Chapter 5), and "Differences in Unemployment Rates Among Demographic Groups (Chapter 15).

Another feature of the text is one that students will probably appreciate the most. A conscientious attempt has been made throughout the book to write lucid explanations of macroeconomic theory and, as an aid in understanding, to link the theory at each step to supporting empirical evidence. This helps students understand not only the logic of macroeconomic analysis but also the relevance of the theory. A feature of the book that will serve the serious student well is the extensive use of footnotes to indicate additional references on various topics.

Finally, a word concerning notation. We make use of symbols and equations because these aid immeasurably in making the discussion more precise and in summarizing the main lines of analysis. However, because we deal with so many variables, students may initially be a little bewildered by the abundance of symbols. With this in mind, we have taken several steps to help students become comfortable with the notation in very little time. First, we make frequent use of mnemonics. For example AD stands for aggregate demand, G^d for government demand for goods and services, I^d for investment demand, X^d for export demand, M^s for money supply, and so forth. Second, for the sake of consistency we adopt certain conventions throughout the text. For example, the only superscripts we use are d, for demand and s, for supply. Third, for the student's convenience, all symbols used in the text are listed in the inside front and back covers of the book. Finally, we state things in simple English as much as possible. When there is an equation we often write the descriptions of the various terms right below the equation.

So far, we have listed the book's advantages from the point of view of the student. Yet the text is also designed to give flexibility to the instructor with regard to the sequencing of topics. In this regard, the following two features of the text are relevant:

1. Some instructors would prefer to delay coverage of the more detailed microeconomic foundations topics (Chapters 5 and 6) until after they have covered the core chapters on macroeconomic models (Chapters 7 through 12). These later core chapters have been written to include all the key microeconomic analysis that is required if the early chapters are skipped.

2. Pedagogically, it is easier for the student to understand the analysis of the open economy if he or she first understands the closed economy. Thus the analysis in each chapter is introduced in the context of a closed economy, then expanded to include an open economy. This flexibility allows the instructor to postpone or omit coverage of international topics by simply bypassing those sections in each chapter.

Supplements

Accompanying the textbook is an excellent study guide written by Professor Scott Fuess of the University of Nebraska. Professor Fuess has class tested the book in manuscript form several times and developed many of the exercises in the study guide out of his classroom experience with the book. Students will likely benefit greatly from the use of his study guide. The authors have prepared an Instructor's Manual that includes an overview of each chapter, answers to the chapter-end review questions, and new, additional discussion and multiple-choice questions with answers.

Acknowledgments

Many long hours and many hands and minds are involved in writing a textbook. The people associated with Addison-Wesley College Publishing have been most supportive and encouraging throughout. We thank Will Ethridge, Steve Mautner, Kazia Navas, Stephanie Argeros-Magean, Christine O'Brien, Dick Morton, Liz King, Mary Dyer, and Sarah Hallet for their attention to detail—they were all great.

We benefited tremendously from insightful comments reviewers offered throughout the writing process. They gave much more time and effort than we anticipated and demonstrated that they genuinely cared about how macroeconomics is taught today. They are:

Bruce Bolnick (Northeastern University)

Wayne Carroll (University of Wisconsin, Eau Claire)

Donald Dutkowsky (Syracuse University)

Steven Fazzari (Washington University)

Luis Fernandez (Oberlin College)

John Flanders (Central Methodist University)

Charles Garrison (University of Tennessee, Knoxville)

Aliya Hashmi (University of Illinois, Chicago)

Emile Mullick (University of Texas, Arlington)

Richard Pollock (University of Hawaii)

Michael K. Salemi (University of North Carolina, Chapel Hill)

Steven M. Sheffrin (University of California, Davis)

David E. Spencer (Brigham Young University)

Case Sprenkle (University of Illinois, Champaign)

Sheldon Stein (Cleveland State University)

Donald G. Tailby (University of New Mexico)

David VanHoose (Indiana University, Bloomington)

Additionally another group of professors reviewed the prospectus of this project and offered valuable suggestions at this early but crucial state:

Betty C. Daniel (State University of New York at Albany)

John C. Haltiwanger (University of Maryland)

David E. Spencer (Brigham Young University)

Sheldon H. Stein (Cleveland State University)

Various versions of the textbook have been class tested at a number of institutions including the University of Kentucky, University of Nebraska, Purdue University, and Virginia Polytechnic Institute and State University. Directly or indirectly we have received much information from a number of students that has served to improve the text. The following professors used early versions of the text and also made very helpful comments and suggestions: Professors Dan Black, Scott Fuess, Sheng Hu, Doug McTaggart, and Bill Smith.

In the case of two of us, this textbook forced us to neglect among other things our wives, Cathy and Therese, and our children, Jeff, Julie, Mike, Daniel, John, Patrick and Angela. The third of us just neglected other things.

West Lafayette, IN   J. M. B.
Blacksburg, VA   M. A. L.
West Lafayette, IN   G. J. L.

Brief Contents

Contents

_____

* Advanced topics that can be skipped without loss of continuity.

Part One

Measuring and Modeling the Macroeconomy

Chapter 1

An Introduction to Macroeconomics

MACROECONOMICS looks at the big picture in terms of what can happen to the economy and why. It is important that you understand how the economy works for at least two reasons. On a personal level, the health of the economy affects your ability to find a job, the interest rate you receive as a return to saving or pay when you borrow, and the rate of increase in the prices of goods and services you buy. On an intellectual level, studying how the economy operates will help you put often conflicting discussions of economic conditions and policies into perspective.

We begin our examination of macroeconomics by isolating the key concerns of macroeconomic analysis and considering, at least briefly, the historical background that both motivates these concerns and highlights their relevance.

1.1 THE CONCERNS OF MACROECONOMICS

During the Great Depression of the 1930s, nearly 25 percent of the labor force was unemployed. So many workers were idle that by 1933 the amount of goods and services produced by the U.S. economy was less than two thirds the level of production in 1929. One in five commercial banks closed its doors, never to reopen. A 1934 survey of home mortgage lenders in major cities showed that in every city no fewer than 21 percent of homeowners,

Figure 1.1   **Real GNP: Growth and Rate of Change Over Time**

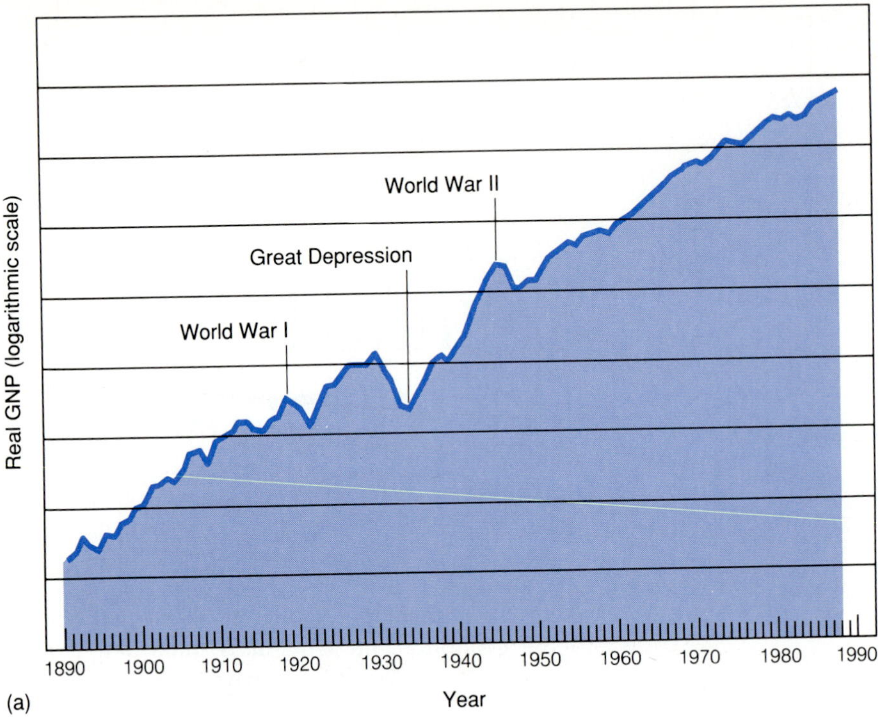

(a)

continued

and as many as 62 percent of homeowners in Cleveland, Ohio, had defaulted on their home loans.[1] Many of those who defaulted were forced to live in makeshift settlements of plywood and cardboard houses.[2]

As one surveys the litany of economic failures during the Great Depression, one begins to realize why this period is considered such a pivotal historical event in the twentieth century. The Great Depression focused the attention of economists, politicians, and the public on questions concerning the causes of downturns in the economy as well as the corrective actions that governments could take to prevent future recurrences of such fluctuations. In fact, because of the Depression, a key element of macroeconomic analysis is the study of why fluctuations in output, employment, and unemployment occur and the role of government in stabilizing the economy.

[1] Lester V. Chandler, *America's Greatest Depression 1929–1941* (New York: Harper and Row, 1970), p. 73.

[2] Herbert Hoover, the president at that time, was often blamed for the depressing economic conditions, and these settlements were thus frequently referred to as ''Hoovervilles.''

Figure 1.1   continuing

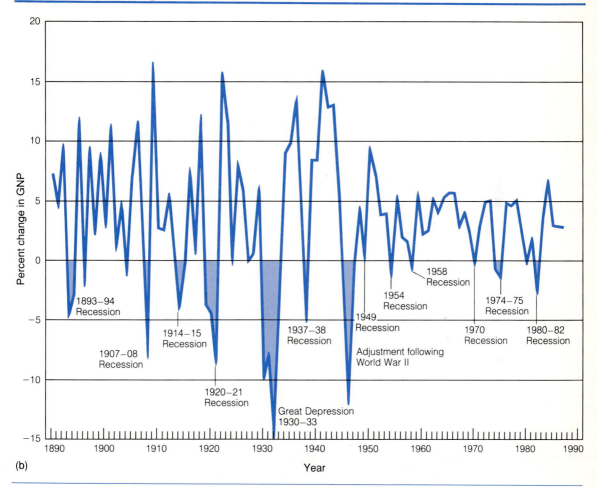

(b)

Source: Figures for real GNP from 1889 to 1928 are based on data reported in *Historical Statistics of the United States: Colonial Times to 1970*, U.S. Department of Commerce, 1975. The more recent figures are from the *Economic Report of the President* (1988).

Growth in GNP

A look at how production in the U.S. economy has varied in recent history indicates the severity of the Depression. The total amount of goods and services produced annually is generally referred to as the real gross national product, or *real GNP*. Figure 1.1 (a and b) shows how real GNP has varied since 1890. Figure 1.1(a) simply plots the trend in real GNP over time.[3] Figure 1.1(b) indicates yearly percentage changes in real GNP.

---

[3] In Figure 1.1(a), a logarithmic scale is used to graph the trend in real GNP. Doing so means that equal proportionate changes in real GNP (e.g., 100 to 200 and 500 to 1000) are shown as covering equal distances.

Clearly, the Great Depression is the most severe downturn in output over the last 100 years. Between 1929 and 1933, real GNP fell at an average annual rate of 8.5 percent. However, there have been other less severe downturns in production. These downturns, called *recessions*, occurred during the following periods: 1893–1894, 1907–1908, 1914–1915, 1920–1921, 1937–1938, 1949, 1954, 1958, 1970, 1974–1975, and 1980–1982.[4] A recession is typically defined as two or more consecutive quarters of negative growth in real GNP.

Although recessions receive a great deal of attention in the press, Figure 1.1(a) indicates that reductions in output are not typical; real GNP is usually rising. Even during times of rising real GNP, however, the rate of growth in real GNP varies. For example, although the average annual rate of growth in real GNP between 1983 and 1987 approximated 3.9 percent, this reflected a growth in real GNP of 6.8 percent between 1983 and 1984, 3.0 percent between 1984 and 1985, and 2.9 percent between 1985 and 1986 and also between 1986 and 1987.

Unemployment

Slow growth in real GNP, and in the extreme the decreases in real GNP that characterize recessions and depressions, attract so much attention in large part because of the rise in unemployment that inevitably accompanies them. Figure 1.2 illustrates the wide fluctuations that have occurred in the U.S. unemployment rate over the last 100 years. The unemployment rate is defined as the ratio of the total number of unemployed workers to the total number of employed workers plus unemployed workers. A comparison of Figures 1.1 and 1.2 shows that when real GNP is growing rapidly, the unemployment rate tends to decline; when real GNP is declining or growing slowly, the unemployment rate tends to rise.

Another interesting feature of Figure 1.2 is that there is an apparent upward trend in the unemployment rate beginning in 1970. This rise in unemployment presents a puzzle: On the one hand, there has been no apparent change in consumers' desires for ever-increasing amounts of goods and services; on the other hand, the pool of unemployed resources seemingly available to expand the production of goods and services has been growing. Why has unemployment shown an upward trend? More fundamentally,

---

[4] The apparent downturn from 1945 to 1948 primarily reflects the adjustments in the economy to peacetime following World War II. It should be noted that data for the period prior to World War I are not strictly comparable with data following World War II. Thus the apparent reduction in the volatility of real GNP (as well as unemployment and industrial production) that is suggested by Figure 1.1 is at least partly an artifact of the way the data are measured. See Christina Romer's papers: "Spurious Volatility in Historical Unemployment Data," *Journal of Political Economy* (February 1986), pp. 1–37; "Is the Stabilization of the Postwar Economy a Figment of the Data," *American Economic Review* (June 1986), pp. 314–334; and "The Prewar Business Cycle Reconsidered: New Estimates of Gross National Product, 1872–1918" (Unpublished manuscript, Princeton University, 1985).

Figure 1.2 **Unemployment Rates**

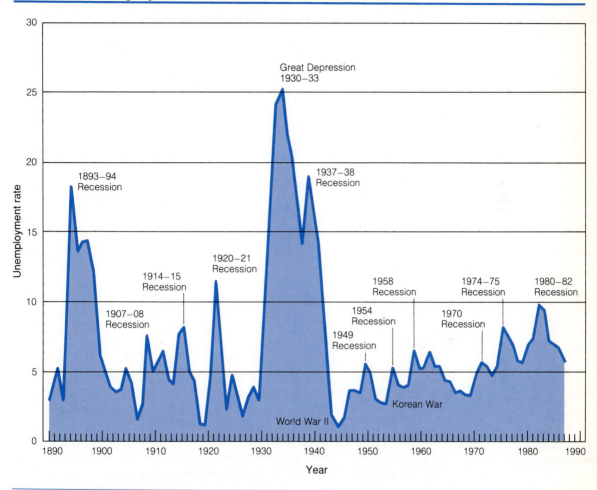

Source: Unemployment rate data are reported in various publications issued by the U.S. Bureau of Labor Statistics. Values before 1940 are from Stanley Lebergott. *Manpower in Economic Growth* (New York: McGraw Hill, 1964). Recent unemployment data are from the *Economic Report of the President* (Washington, D.C.: 1988).

why is there any unemployment at all? These questions, like those concerning fluctuations in output, are addressed by macroeconomics.

Inflation

There are yet other important questions addressed by macroeconomics. Throughout history there have been numerous instances not only of falling output and rising unemployment but also of runaway inflation. A vivid example is the German hyperinflation of the 1920s. From August 1922 to November 1923, the prices of German goods rose by over one *billion* times. After World War II, Hungarians had a similar experience, as prices rose by over one *octillion* times in the space of 13 months.[5] Nations that more recently have had very high rates of inflation include Bolivia (1,281.4 percent from 1983 to 1984), Brazil (196.7 percent from 1983 to 1984), Israel (373.8 percent from 1984 to 1985), and Zaire (96.2 percent from 1986 to 1987).[6]

Even the United States—which is not in the major leagues of the hyperinflaters—surprised many people with near double-digit inflation in the late 1970s and early 1980s. Of course, the inflationary experience of the United States is not directly comparable with the hyperinflations of the sort mentioned above since hyperinflations generally have cataclysmic effects on the economies in which they occur. However, these foreign episodes of hyperinflation are directly relevant to understanding the inflationary experience of all countries, including the United States, because they serve to isolate the critical causes of inflation.

Figure 1.3 depicts the rate of change in the general level of prices for the United States over the last 100 years. Up to World War II, there were recurring periods of rising prices (inflation) and falling prices (deflation). In contrast, the postwar era has been characterized by rising prices, although the rate of inflation has varied considerably. Until the early 1970s, inflation rates were typically below 4 percent except during and immediately after periods of war. In the late 1970s, however, prices rose at a more rapid rate, with the average rate of inflation being over 7 percent. Although at this point some forecasters expected a pattern of ever-increasing inflation, the rate of inflation fell in the 1980s.

Interest Rates

By the early 1980s, both the U.S. inflation rate and the rate of unemployment were receding from their previous high levels. It was at that time that high interest rates started receiving most of the attention. Figure 1.4 illustrates how the interest rate on mortgages rose dramatically during this period, peaking at close to 17 percent in 1981. As Figure 1.4 indicates, since World War II only the late 1970s and the 1980s have seen a mortgage rate above 10 percent.

Trade and Foreign Exchange Rates

On October 19, 1987, in what has come to be referred to as "Black Monday," the Dow Jones Industrial Index fell by 508 points. Initial reports as to why the market fell by so much pointed, in part, to a record balance of payments

---

[5] An octillion is 10 taken to the 27th power—or 10 with 27 zeros tacked on. These figures are reported in William Poole, *Money and the Economy: A Monetarist View* (Reading, Mass.: Addison-Wesley, 1978), p. 11.

[6] Various issues of *International Financial Statistics,* International Monetary Fund.

Figure 1.3 Percent Change in U.S. Price Level

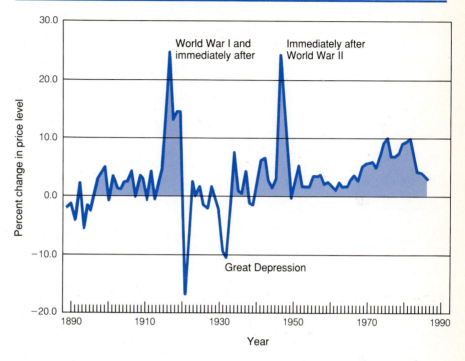

Source: The rate of change in the U.S. price level is measured by a price index known as the GNP deflator, as reported in various issues of the *Survey of Current Business*. A discussion of how the GNP deflator is constructed appears in the next chapter.

deficit for August of 1987. Six months later, reports of continuing trade deficits were widely cited when the Dow plunged over 100 points on April 14, 1988. The fact that the stock market can react so strongly to news about the trade deficit demonstrates the extent to which the economy has become internationalized.

The trade deficits of 1987–1988 were not a one-time phenomenon. In fact, the balance of trade was last in surplus (exports exceeded imports) in 1982. As Figure 1.5 indicates, starting in 1983 there was a growing imbalance between exports and imports so that for 1987, the balance of trade deficit was $134.3 billion in 1982 dollars, almost seven times higher than it had been just four years earlier.

At the same time that the balance of trade was running significant deficits, the value of the dollar in terms of foreign currency—the dollar foreign exchange rate—was fluctuating widely. Between 1980 and the first quarter of 1985, the dollar rose, on average, by 64 percent against the currencies of U.S. trading partners. In the next two years, the value of the dollar plummeted 31 percent.

Figure 1.4   **U.S. Interest Rate for Mortgages**

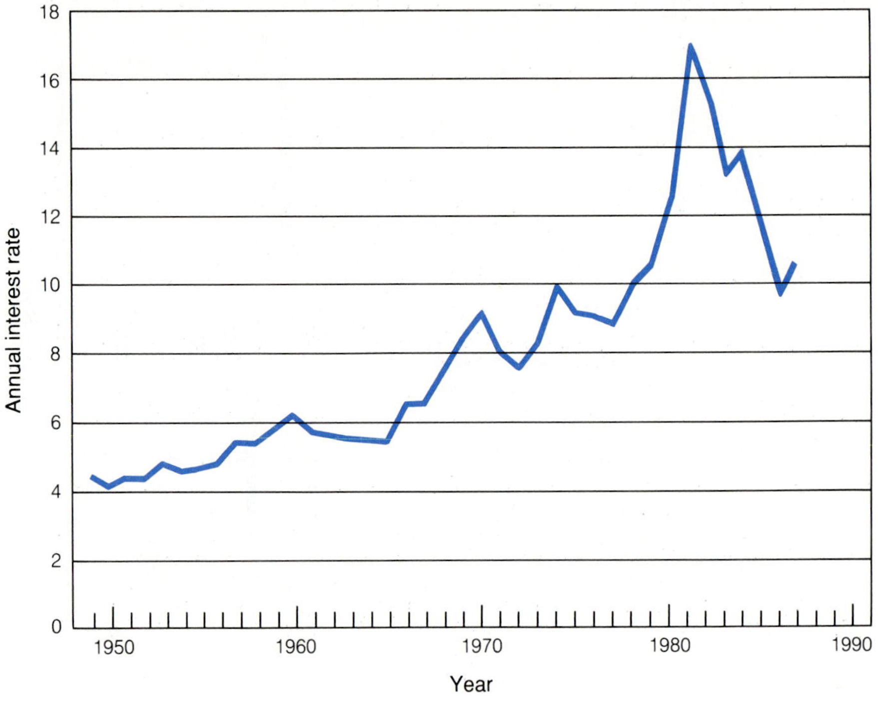

Source: The mortgage rate is the interest rate charged on FHA home mortgages in July of each year, as reported in various issues of *Business Conditions Digest.*

1.2   THE QUESTIONS OF MACROECONOMICS

Macroeconomics: The branch of economics that studies the determinants of such aggregate economic variables as total output, employment and unemployment, the level of prices, interest rates, and foreign exchange rates.

Several important questions arise from the discussion so far. What causes booms and recessions in the economy? Why does unemployment exist when the desire for goods and services is insatiable? What affects the trend in the growth rate of output? Why has the unemployment rate been rising over the past two decades? What determines the rate of inflation? Why have interest rates been relatively high and volatile in the last few years? Why have U.S. trade balances and exchange rates experienced such dramatic swings in recent years? In short, why does the economic landscape seem to be, as W.C. Fields would say, "fraught with imminent peril"?

Attempting to answer such questions is the "stuff" of **macroeconomics.** The purview of macroeconomics is the overall performance of the economy. Macroeconomics studies the determinants of aggregate economic variables such as total output, the overall level of prices and wages, total employment,

Figure 1.5   Exports, Imports, and the Balance of Trade

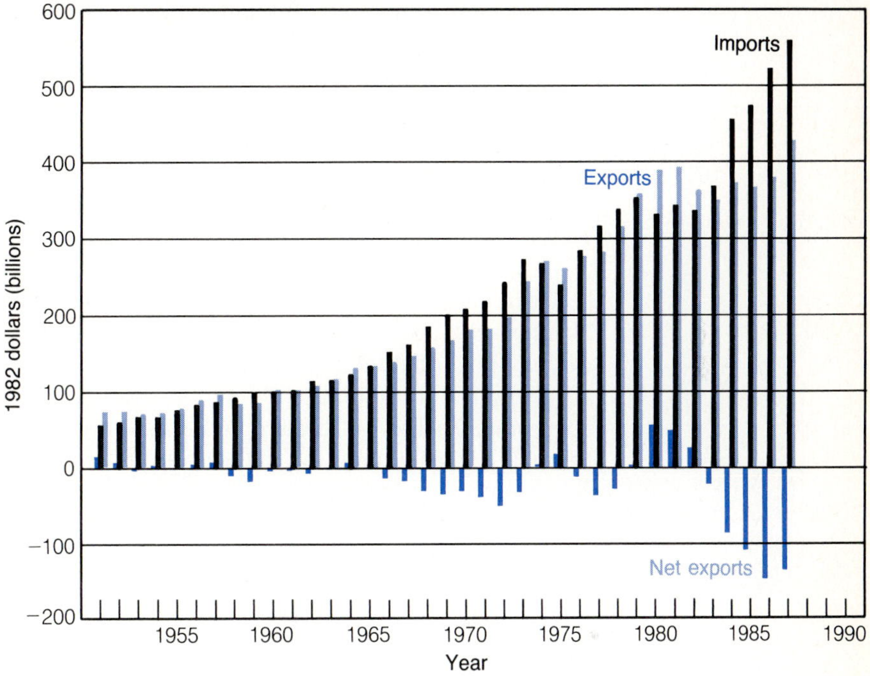

Source: Economic Report of the President (1988).

the national rate of unemployment, interest rates, and foreign exchange rates. The importance of understanding the macroeconomy cannot be over-estimated. Knowing why events such as the Great Depression and hyper-inflations occurred can help us predict and avoid such events in the future. As Carlos Santayana, historian and philosopher, stated, ''Those who cannot remember the past are condemned to repeat it.''

The key macroeconomic variables—growth in output, unemployment rates, inflation, interest rates, wages, and foreign exchange rates—are all potentially affected by the behavior of the government. For this reason, macroeconomics concerns itself with policy issues such as the effects that government spending, taxation, borrowing, and money creation have on the economy. Economists are not entirely in agreement concerning these effects, and this is reflected in the differing views among politicians about the way in which government policies affect the performance of the economy. For example, the Kennedy administration proposed a tax cut in 1963 to stimulate consumer demand for goods and services. It was this administration's view that ''the most important single thing we can do to stimulate investment in today's economy is to raise consumption by a major reduction of individual income tax rates.''[7]

Eighteen years later, President Reagan proposed a similar tax cut, but this time the stated rationale was to stimulate production and supply, not demand. In his 1981 State of the Union Address, he stated that ''it is time to create new jobs, build and rebuild industry, and give the American people room to do what they do best. And that can only be done with a tax program which provides incentives to increase productivity for both workers and industry.''[8] The supply-side orientation of Reagan's policy prescription contrasts with the demand-side view of tax cuts taken by the Kennedy administration.

An important macroeconomic policy question concerns the differences between demand-oriented government policies and supply-oriented policies. This text will also examine many other important policy questions: To what extent does inflation reflect government policies? Do government policies affect the economy differently in the short run and the long run? Can the government achieve a desired combination of inflation and unemployment through active intervention in the economy, or is the appropriate government role a more passive one?

To the Point

THE QUESTIONS OF MACROECONOMICS

- Macroeconomics attempts to discover the reasons for fluctuations in production and real GNP, employment, unemployment, inflation, interest rates, foreign exchange rates and other variables that measure the overall activity in an economy.

- Macroeconomics can help also answer questions having to do with the appropriate role of government policy actions in achieving such goals as full employment and stable prices. The effects of fiscal policy changes (changes in government taxation, spending, and borrowing) and monetary policy changes (changes in the economy's supply of money) are of particular interest.

1.3   THE USE OF MODELS

In order to obtain satisfactory answers to the important questions of macroeconomics, we must develop a simple model of the economy. A model captures the essential features of the real world for the questions at hand

---

[7] The Economic Report to Congress presented by President John F. Kennedy on January 21, 1963.

[8] *New York Times*, 19 February 1981.

by reducing the number of complex details to consider. One economic model with which you are likely already familiar is the interaction of demand and supply to explain market exchange. Macroeconomic analysis expands upon this supply and demand model. It examines the behavior in, and the interactions among, four types of markets that play a crucial role in the economy's overall performance. These markets are as follows:

1. **Output markets,** where newly produced goods and services are bought and sold.

2. **Financial markets,** where securities like stocks and bonds are bought and sold.

3. **Labor and other input markets,** where the factors of production such as labor services, raw materials, and other inputs into the production process are bought and sold.

4. **Foreign exchange markets,** where the currency of one country is exchanged for the currency of other countries.

In looking at these four types of markets, we often disregard many complex details of the real world in order to concentrate on the essential macroeconomic features. For example, in discussing the output market, we often do not distinguish between such varied products as automobiles, houses, and vegetables. Thus when a macroeconomic model predicts that output will increase, this does not necessarily mean that the production of each and every product in the economy will increase. It simply means that total production will increase, although the production of some goods may actually decrease. In the next chapter, we will explain how real GNP measures this "net" change in total output.

Similarly, when discussing the financial market, our concern is with the general movement in interest rates, and thus we frequently simplify by not distinguishing between equity shares (stocks), short-term bonds, and long-term bonds. This lumping together of interest rates would not have served our purpose if our concern were to explain differences in specific rates of return on various financial instruments. However, since our concern is with the movements of more aggregate variables, we lose little insight by not distinguishing between different types of financial assets.

Finally, when discussing the labor market, we often do not distinguish between the services provided by a janitor and those provided by a business executive. Nor do we distinguish between the wages that each earns since our concern is with the total level of employment, the national unemployment rate, and the overall level of wages. Again, if our focus were on a different problem, for instance career choice, then we would have to incorporate the difference in wages between janitors and business executives to obtain a satisfactory model. But such detail is not especially important for explaining business cycles.

How can we know that the models that we construct to explain macroeconomic events are not overly simplified? "To know the wisdom of an act, study its results."[9] This statement reminds us that to test the usefulness of any macroeconomic model, one must examine the model's ability to explain actual changes in the macroeconomy. The empirical evaluation of macroeconomic models is an integral part of macroeconomics. If real world events conflict with the predictions of a model, the model is discarded or revised. For instance, the emergence of the "new classical" macroeconomic models in the last 15 years represents a response to the perceived inability of earlier models to explain the acceleration in inflation that occurred during the late 1960s and the simultaneous high inflation and unemployment rates of the 1970s.

1.4   A PREVIEW OF THE TEXT

In order to discover the causes and cures of macroeconomic fluctuations, it is essential to understand how macroeconomic variables are measured and how they interrelate. The next two chapters address the topic of measuring macroeconomic variables. Chapter 2 examines the aggregate measures of activity in the output and labor markets. Among the measures discussed are real GNP, the rate of inflation, and the unemployment rate. Chapter 3 looks at various aggregate measures of activity in the financial and foreign exchange markets as well as measures of the money supply.

Changes in macroeconomic variables are the result of actions by numerous individuals in the economy. A common element facing all individuals is the fact that there is a limit or constraint on their economic activities. For example, household spending and saving is constrained by the income households earn. Similarly, government spending is constrained in that it cannot exceed revenues raised from taxes and the sale of government bonds. Consideration of these budget constraints in Chapter 4 makes it easier to understand the important interactions that occur among macroeconomic variables determined in the various markets in the economy. For instance, the fact that an increase in government spending on goods and services must be financed means that changes in government spending generally affect not only the output market but also the financial markets.

In Part II, we investigate the determinants of individual behavior in the economy. In Chapter 5, our focus is on the hiring and investment decisions of firms and the creation of the money supply by the Federal Reserve. In Chapter 6, we look at the labor supply, consumption, and saving behavior of households. That chapter also considers the behavior of foreigners in the

---

[9] Chinese fortune cookie, Eggroll Express, West Lafayette, Indiana, October 22, 1986.

output, financial, and foreign exchange markets. Taken together, Chapters 5 and 6 contain the microeconomic underpinnings or foundations of macroeconomics.

Full-blown macroeconomic models are developed in Part III. Chapter 7 introduces the useful graphical tools of aggregate demand and aggregate supply curves. The aggregate demand curve depicts the inverse relationship between the level of prices and the total amount of output that firms find they can sell. As we shall see, an analysis of the output, financial, and foreign exchange markets underlies the aggregate demand curve. The aggregate supply curve depicts the relationship between the level of prices and the production of total output; an analysis of the labor and other input markets is the underpinning for the aggregate supply curve.

The aggregate demand/aggregate supply model developed in Chapter 7 assumes that all prices fully adjust. By fully adjusting prices, we mean that (a) the prices in the various markets in the economy adjust so as to equate demand and supply (flexible prices) and (b) participants in the various markets are fully informed about prices in all markets (complete information). We call this model of fully adjusting prices the neoclassical model since it is a modern version of the writings of the classical economists of the 1800s and early 1900s.

The neoclassical model is useful in the analysis of the long-run effects of unexpected shocks to the economy such as changes in government policy or oil supply disruptions. By the long-run we mean a time sufficiently long for participants in the economy to obtain full information and for prices to adjust. In addition, the neoclassical model is useful in analyzing the immediate effect of fully anticipated changes in the economy. Chapter 8 determines what, if any, long-run changes in output, employment, prices, and interest rates result from changes in government fiscal and monetary policies. Chapter 9 employs the neoclassical model to highlight the effects of supply-side shocks such as an oil embargo or harvest failure as well as to focus on the determinants of long-run growth in an economy.

Although the neoclassical model is a good predictor of how the economy responds in the long run to both demand-side and supply-side shocks, it is not particularly well suited for analyzing the macroeconomy in the short run. Chapter 10 introduces one alternative view of the macroeconomy. This alternative view presumes that prices are inflexible or "predetermined" in the short run. As we will see in Chapter 11, the macroeconomic model with predetermined prices is useful in explaining the impact in the short run of changes in government fiscal and monetary policies, as well as the impact of other demand-side shocks. A second alternative to the neoclassical model that offers insight into the short run behavior of the economy is offered in Chapter 12. This view presumes that input prices, such as wages, do not fully adjust because of incomplete information.

Part IV considers some recent controversies with respect to monetary and fiscal policy. Chapter 13 takes a more detailed look at monetary policy effects and the role of the central bank. Chapter 14 looks more closely at the impact of fiscal policy and the national debt.

The final part of the book, Part V, discusses several special topics in macroeconomics. It will become apparent as we go through the book that the labor market and money markets are critical markets in the economy. Thus Chapter 15 offers a more detailed discussion of labor market activity, including unemployment, job search, and labor contract theory. Chapter 16 explores in more depth the factors behind the demand for and supply of money. Chapter 17 completes the book with a consideration of international finance and trade, with particular emphasis on the consequences of government intervention in the foreign exchange markets to fix exchange rates. Earlier chapters presume flexible exchange rates in their discussions of macroeconomic analysis in an open economy.

Chapter 2

Measuring Activity: Output and Labor Markets

ALMOST every evening on the news Dan Rather, Tom Brokaw, Peter Jennings, and the other television news anchors report some statistics on the health of the economy. They may report that real GNP rose by a meager 1.2 percent from the previous year, that the national unemployment rate increased by .5 percent, that the prime interest rate fell from 10 to 9.5 percent, or that the value of the dollar fell in foreign exchange markets. Newspapers and newsmagazines also faithfully report these statistics. For many, these measures of the overall performance of the economy have a mystery that is undeserved.

How can we make sense of all these different measures of an economy's performance? One way is to categorize the measures of activity by the four major types of markets in the economy—output, labor, financial, and foreign exchange. In this chapter, we examine the macroeconomic variables that summarize activity in the output and labor markets. The first part of the chapter examines real GNP and price indexes and how they measure changes in total output and the average price level over time. The second part of the chapter looks at the various measures of labor market activity, such as employment, work hours, unemployment, labor force participation, and the real wage rate. In Chapter 3, we will examine measures of activity in the financial and foreign exchange markets.

Recall that our main objective in this book is to develop macroeconomic models that explain why the levels of total output or real GNP, the overall price level, unemployment, interest rates, and foreign exchange rates vary over time in an economy like that of the United States. This chapter and the next begin that process by explaining how we construct the key measures of the performance of an economy.

2.1 MEASURING ACTIVITY IN OUTPUT MARKETS: REAL GNP

In an economy like that of the United States, a tremendous variety of goods and services are produced and sold each year. In any given year, the production of some goods may increase, while the production of other goods may decrease. Similarly, in any given year the prices of some goods rise rapidly, the prices of other goods rise less rapidly, and the prices of some goods fall. In order to ascertain the overall performance of the economy, we must have a way of measuring changes over time in both total output and the average level of prices. The government publishes statistics on activity in the output market under the general heading of the National Income and Product Accounts. We begin by discussing the statistics in the national income accounts known as nominal gross national product and real gross national product. As we will see, the rate of change in real GNP provides us with a measure of the rate of growth in total output.

Nominal Gross National Product

To understand the difficulties that can arise in attempting to measure changes in the economy's total output, consider the fairly typical example of 1984. In 1984, 3.6 billion square feet of new structures and additions were constructed in the U.S., an increase of 6.5 percent over 1983. Passenger car production rose from 6.78 million cars in 1983 to 7.77 million in 1984. In contrast, U.S. production of wine fell from 813 million gallons in 1983 to 691 million gallons in 1984 and the 1984 production of pork fell 2 percent, from 15.2 billion pounds produced in 1983 to 14.9 billion pounds in 1984. What happened to *total* output in the economy in 1984 as compared to 1983? Was it higher or lower? If total output was higher, by how much did it increase?

The inherent problem in answering these questions is that we cannot simply sum the physical quantities of the various goods and services produced in the economy to obtain total output. Adding square footage, cars, gallons of wine, and pounds of pork, along with the multitude of other goods and services produced during 1987, would make no sense. We need a common yardstick for measuring the output of these goods and services. The yardstick that we generally use is price or market value. We determine how total output changes over time by comparing the total market value of the goods produced—the gross national product—in different periods.

For example, suppose that the U.S. economy produced only two goods last year—8.5 million cars and 1 million homes. If the prices of cars and new homes were $6,000 and $60,000 respectively, then last year's gross national product (GNP) equaled ($6,000 × 8,500,000) + ($60,000 × 1,000,000) or $111 billion. If during the current year, 7.5 million cars are produced and 2 million homes are constructed and prices do not change, then the GNP will rise to $165 billion. These computations illustrate how GNP is computed in general. Specifically, **nominal gross national product** is the current market value of all final goods and services produced by an economy over a specified period of time, usually one year. The three key phrases in this definition are: market value, final goods and services, and produced over a specified period of time. Let's examine each of these phrases.

Nominal gross national product: The current market value of all final goods and services produced by an economy in a specified period of time.

The *market value* of goods and services is determined by the prices at which they sell in the marketplace. Utilizing market values enables us to aggregate the output of vastly different types of goods and services. Unfortunately, problems arise when goods are not exchanged in the market and consequently have no explicit market price. The values of some of these goods are imputed by the U.S. Department of Commerce. For example, the goods and services provided by government employees, such as police protection, are not sold in the marketplace. Therefore in computing GNP, the value of the goods and services produced by government employees is imputed as equal to the wages that they earn.

Other goods and services, such as the services of homemakers and the output of home gardens, are simply omitted from GNP. The output of the "underground economy" is also often overlooked, although the compilers of GNP statistics continually adjust and revise the statistics in an attempt to account for such activity. For instance, in 1985 the Department of Commerce revised its estimates of GNP because of an improvement in its "underground economy adjustments." (See *Case Study: The Underground Economy* later in this chapter.) The effect was a significant increase in the Department's estimates of GNP. For example, the improved measures of the underground economy led to an increase in estimated GNP in 1977 of $21.8 billion or 1.1 percent. This revision reflects the discovery of a more extensive underreporting or failure to report income on tax returns than had been previously thought.[1]

The second key phrase in the GNP definition is that GNP is calculated by using the market values of *final goods and services*. Final goods are goods that are not resold during the period. By including only final goods in GNP, we avoid double counting. For example, suppose that one firm produces and sells leather to a second firm that uses the leather in the same period to manufacture shoes. GNP is not the sum of the market value of the leather

---

[1] See Robert P. Parker, "Improved Adjustments for Misreporting of Tax Return Information Used to Estimate the National Income and Product Accounts, 1977," *Survey of Current Business* (June 1984). The Commerce Department makes extensive use of tax return information provided by the IRS in estimating the gross national product and its components.

plus the market value of the shoes produced from the leather. This would count the value of the leather twice, since the price of the shoe incorporates the value of the leather. Only the market value of the shoes, the final good, is counted as part of GNP.

Finally, the third key phrase indicates that GNP refers to only those goods and services *produced over a specified period of time*. Market transactions involving the exchange of previously produced goods are excluded. The sale of a used home, for example, is not included in current GNP. Likewise, the sale of a stock on the New York Stock Exchange is not included in GNP since this sale, like the sale of a used home, simply involves a transfer of ownership and not the production of a new good or service. The value of the services of the broker who facilitates the sale of the stock or the real estate agent who helps sell the used home would be included in current GNP, however, since these activities constitute the production of services. Note also that because GNP measures production over a specified period of time, GNP is a "flow" variable. Just like water flowing out of a faucet, GNP can only be measured by first specifying the length of time over which the production (the flow of output) occurs. In the case of GNP, the standard length of time used is one year.

Case Study   THE UNDERGROUND ECONOMY

The term underground economy refers to the activity of individuals who work "off the books," usually for cash, in an attempt to avoid detection by the government because they want to avoid taxes or because their activity is illegal. The existence of the underground economy poses an obvious problem in calculating GNP since in practice this calculation relies in part on information from tax returns. Without additional adjustments by the Department of Commerce, income that individuals do not report in order to avoid taxes is not included in GNP.[2]

An article by Peter Gutman entitled "The Subterranean Economy" represents one of the first attempts by an economist to estimate the size of the underground economy.[3] Gutman's estimate that the underground economy was approximately 10 percent of total (uncorrected) GNP spurred additional research on both the accuracy of his measurement and the implications of his findings. In a detailed study released in 1979, the IRS estimated that the

---

[2] Not all activity in the underground economy belongs in GNP. Income from illegal activity, such as prostitution and the sale of drugs, is excluded by definition from GNP.

[3] Peter Gutman, "The Subterranean Economy," *Financial Analysts Journal* (November/December 1977): 23–26, 34.

underground economy comprised no more than 5 percent of total GNP.[4] Another economist, Edward Feige, has suggested that the underground economy is as high as 20 percent of total GNP.[5]

In practice, it is difficult to measure something that obviously seeks to avoid detection. There are no cash register receipts to look at to see how much underground activity exists. The way that Feige, Gutman, and others have approached the problem is to look at what has been happening to currency holdings over time. The fact that a lot of currency seems to be floating around is undeniable. At the end of 1986 the amount of currency per capita in the United States was $846. Even allowing for the fact that a lot of kids have penny collections, this is more currency than it would seem normal to hold. Part of the currency holdings undoubtedly finance activity in the underground economy.

A recent attempt to estimate the size of the underground economy takes a different tack. Frank deLeeuw notes that "although there is little agreement about the size of the underground economy, there is widespread agreement about the industries in which much underground activity takes place." Such industries include the service industries, construction, and farming. By comparing growth rates in the "suspect" industries with those of other industries, deLeeuw estimated the rate at which the underground economy has been growing over time.[6] He finds evidence that the underground economy grew from 1949 to 1982, causing the growth in natural income to be understated by one quarter of 1 percent per year during this period.

A study by David Blau on the effects of taxes on self-employment offers some insight into determinants of the size of the underground economy.[7] Blau found that the trend to increased self-employment during the late 1970s, a reversal of the previous downward trend over the preceding century, could be attributed in part to higher tax rates. During the 1970s, overall marginal tax rates rose from 32 percent to over 39 percent. Such an increase in tax rates shifts individuals to self-employment since it is relatively easier to underreport self-employment income. For the same reasons, some economists argue that one effect of the tax bills of 1981 and 1986 has been to reduce the size of the underground economy. With these two tax bills, the top

---

[4] U.S. Internal Revenue Service, *Estimates of Income Unreported on Individual Income Tax Returns* (Washington, D.C.: Government Printing Office, 1979).

[5] Edward Feige, "How Big Is the Irregular Economy," *Challenge* (November/December 1979): 5–13. Other estimates of the underground economy include Gerald J. Lynch, "Currency, Marginal Tax Rates, and the Underground Economy," *Journal of Economics and Business* (February, 1985): 59–67; Vito Tanzi, "The Underground Economy in the United States: Estimates and Implications," *Banca Nazionale del Lavoro Quarterly Review* no. 135 (December 1980): 427–53.

[6] Frank deLeeuw, "An Indirect Technique for Measuring the Size of the Underground Economy," *Survey for Current Business* 65 (April 1985): 64–72.

[7] David Blau, "A Time-Series Analysis of Self-Employment in the United States," *Journal of Political Economy* 95 (June 1987): 445–467.

marginal tax rate on federal income fell from 70 percent down to around 30 percent.

The reason why lower taxes might lead to less underground activity is not difficult to see. Suppose that an employee initially falls into a 70 percent marginal tax bracket. Because every additional dollar earned is taxed at a 70 percent rate, a $10 per hour pre-tax income becomes a $3 per hour after-tax income. Both employer and employee have an incentive to not report the employee's income. If the employee works for cash, say at a rate of $7 per hour, he or she takes home more money and the employer pays out less. Although there is the risk of detection and prosecution for both employer and employee, the monetary gain from not reporting the income may well be sufficiently large to induce them to take this risk. If the worker were in a lower tax bracket, then the monetary gain to not reporting this income would be lower. A lower marginal tax rate, therefore, makes it less likely that the employer and employee will be willing to incur the risk associated with operating in the underground economy.

While not significant, the underground economy in the United States seems relatively small by international comparisons. Using the currency demand approach, Friedrich Schneider and Markus Hoftreither have estimated the size of the underground economies in 17 developed countries in 1978. Their estimates, reported in *The Economist*, appear in Table 2.1.

Among the countries in the table, Italy checks in with largest estimated underground economy, a whopping 30 percent of GNP. With the exception of Switzerland, all of the countries in the table appear to have larger underground economies than the United States, something that should not be all that surprising in light of the fact that most of these countries have higher tax rates than the United States. The underground economies of less developed countries seem to be even higher than those of developed countries. For example, India's underground economy has been estimated as being equal to about 35 percent of its GNP as has Taiwan's, while Burma's underground economy is thought to be about as large as its officially recognized one.

What are the implications for macroeconomic policy of an underground economy of the size suggested by the various researchers? If the underground economy in the United States is 10 percent of GNP, then economic activity totaling over $400 billion dollars went untaxed in 1987. If the federal government had been able to tax that income at a 30 percent rate, it would have generated an additional $120 billion worth of tax revenue. That additional revenue could have significantly reduced the 1987 budget deficit, thus enabling the government to reduce its borrowing in the credit markets.

Growth of the underground economy also means that real GNP would understate the true growth of the economy. Sluggish growth was a hallmark of the U.S. economy in the 1970s. Yet, if a larger portion of real activity was carried on in the underground economy, it may simply mean that a large part of real economic activity was not being measured. This has potentially important policy implications. If efforts are aimed at stimulating growth when

Table 2.1 **Estimated Size of the Domestic Underground Economy as a Percent of Total Output in 1978**

Austria	10	Ireland	8
Belgium	21	Italy	30
Britain	7	Norway	11
Canada	11	Spain	23
Denmark	9	Sweden	13
West Germany	11	Switzerland	7
France	7	United States	5

Source: The Economist (September 19–25, 1987).

in reality there is significant growth but it is not measured, then government policy is misdirected. This problem of understating the economy's growth, however, may not be severe since revised GNP estimates appear to be much more successful in incorporating the growth of the underground economy.

Real Gross National Product

From 1977 to 1987, nominal gross national product rose from 1.99 trillion dollars to 4.49 trillion dollars. This 256 percent increase in nominal GNP does not indicate, however, that the economy produced more than two and one-half times as much output in 1987 as in 1977. Having seen how nominal GNP is computed, we know that changes in nominal GNP do not necessarily reflect simply increased production, for every time the prices of products rise, nominal gross national product also rises.

For many purposes, we need a measure of changes in output alone. A simple way to obtain such a measure is to calculate what GNP would have been had there not been any price changes. We do this by valuing the goods and services produced by the economy in various years using "constant" or "base year" prices rather than current year prices. This output measure is called **real gross national product** or **real GNP.** Thus, real GNP is output in terms of constant dollars, whereas nominal GNP is output in terms of current dollars.

Real gross national product: Nominal gross national product adjusted for price changes.

An example may clarify how real GNP is computed and the relationship between real and nominal GNP. Suppose that only three goods are produced in the economy: radios, apples (in bushels), and shirts. The hypothetical outputs and prices of these goods are listed in Table 2.2 for the years 1982 and 1989. Note that, according to our example, nominal GNP rose from $120 in 1982 to $155 in 1989, a 29 percent increase. Part of this increase, however, was due to an increase in prices. By how much did total output change

Table 2.2   Prices and Output for a Hypothetical Economy

	1982			1989			1989		
	Output	*Price*	*Dollar Value*	*Output*	*Price*	*Dollar Value*	*Output (1989)*	*Price (1982)*	*Real Value*
Radios	5	$14	$70	4	$20	$80	4	$14	$56
Shirts	3	10	30	5	9	45	5	10	50
Apples	4	5	20	5	6	30	5	5	25
	Nominal GNP (1982):		$120	Nominal GNP (1989):		$155	Real GNP (1989):		$131

in *real* terms? Letting 1982 be the base year (that is, using 1982 prices to calculate real GNP), real GNP for 1982 is the same as nominal GNP, or $120. Real GNP in 1989 is obtained by summing 1989 quantities valued at 1982 prices. Thus, as Table 2.2 indicates, real GNP in 1989 is ($14 × 4) + ($10 × 5) + ($5 × 5) = 131 (1982) dollars. From 1982 to 1989, real GNP therefore increased by 11 (1982) dollars or by 9 percent in our hypothetical economy.

Real GNP is a more useful statistic than nominal GNP since, unlike nominal GNP, it enables us to measure changes in output. In fact, changes in nominal GNP are among the most uninteresting statistics reported by the government since one does not know whether such changes reflect price level changes or changes in output produced. Even television news anchors do not report changes in nominal GNP but rather changes in real GNP. As we saw in Chapter 1, real GNP is typically rising. However, there have been periods when real GNP has declined. **Recessions** are defined as periods when real GNP has fallen.

Recession: A period showing a fall in real GNP, typically spanning at least two quarters.

The Purchasers of Real GNP

Each quarter of the calendar year, the Department of Commerce computes and publishes the National Income and Product Accounts. These accounts report not only nominal and real GNP, but also a breakdown of real GNP by type of output buyer. There are four types of market participants purchasing the economy's output: households, firms, governments, and foreigners.

Consumption expenditures: Household purchases of final output.

Household purchases of final output are called real **consumption expenditures.** Household consumption includes purchases of services (such as haircuts and medical care), nondurable goods (such as food and clothing), and durable goods (such as automobiles and televisions). New homes are the one consumer durable good *not* included in consumption spending. When it comes to housing, households are treated as "firms." Thus, as we discuss below, households' purchases of new homes are considered to be investment spending rather than purchases for consumption. Table 2.3 and the accom-

Table 2.3   The Components of GNP (all figures in billions of 1982 dollars)

Year	Real GNP	=	Real Consump-tion Expen-ditures	+	Real Invest-ment Expen-ditures	+	Real Government Expenditures	+	Real Net Exports
1976	2,826.7	=	1,803.9	+	453.5	+	580.3	+	−11.0
1977	2,958.6	=	1,883.8	+	521.3	+	589.1	+	−35.5
1978	3,115.2	=	1,961.0	+	576.9	+	604.1	+	−26.8
1979	3,192.4	=	2,004.4	+	575.2	+	609.1	+	3.6
1980	3,187.1	=	2,000.4	+	509.3	+	620.5	+	57.0
1981	3,248.8	=	2,024.2	+	545.5	+	629.7	+	49.4
1982	3,166.0	=	2,050.7	+	447.3	+	641.7	+	26.3
1983	3,279.1	=	2,146.0	+	504.0	+	649.0	+	−19.9
1984	3,501.4	=	2,249.3	+	658.4	+	677.7	+	−84.0
1985	3,607.5	=	2,352.6	+	636.1	+	726.9	+	−108.2
1986	3,713.3	=	2,450.5	+	654.0	+	754.5	+	−145.8
1987	3,819.6	=	2,495.2	+	685.4	+	773.3	+	−134.3

Components of GNP—1987

panying bar chart indicate that consumption is by far the largest component of GNP. In 1987, for example, real consumption spending accounted for 65.3 percent of total real GNP.

The purchase of final output by firms is called real **investment.** Real investment constitutes one of the most volatile components of GNP; indeed, some economists consider it to be a major source of instability in the economy. Investment spending is generally divided into two categories. The first of these is *fixed investment,* which constituted 94 percent of total investment in 1987. This component of investment is further divided into nonresidential fixed investment and residential fixed investment. Nonresidential fixed investment, approximately two thirds of total fixed investment in 1987, includes spending by firms to construct new plants and to purchase machinery and other capital equipment. Residential fixed investment consists of the afore-mentioned spending for the construction of new homes and apartments.

The second type of investment spending is net *inventory investment,* which is the difference between production and sales. If production exceeds sales, then firms' inventories increase and firms in essence purchase some of their own output. Since this addition to inventories is a purchase of final output by firms, it is part of the total investment spending of firms. In contrast, if sales exceed production, inventories decrease and net inventory investment is negative. In 1987, inventory investment was positive, equalling 6 percent of total gross investment.

A caution about the term investment is warranted at this point. When individuals add stocks or bonds to their portfolio, they often say they are

Investment: The pur-chase of final output by firms.

"investing." However, in macroeconomics we call these purchases of financial assets part of saving if they are financed from current income. If the purchases are financed by the sale of other assets, then this change in the composition of their holdings of assets is simply referred to as a portfolio adjustment. In either case, such purchases are *not* counted as investment. Investment in macroeconomics refers only to purchases of capital goods such as new houses, industrial plants, and machinery.

Not surprisingly, the National Income and Product Accounts refer to the purchases of final output by federal, state, and local governments as real **government purchases of goods and services.** As can be seen from Table 2.3, in recent years government purchases of final output have hovered at about 20 percent of real GNP. It is important to note that government expenditures such as welfare benefits, unemployment compensation, interest payments on government debt, and social security benefits are not included in government purchases of goods and services since they do not represent a demand for currently produced output by the government. Such payments are called **transfer payments** because they simply involve the redistribution or transfer of income among households.

Government transfer payments have fluctuated substantially over time, although an upward trend is evident in the last 45 years. In 1940, transfer payments in total represented 23.2 percent of total government outlays. After World War II, due to the GI Bill and other such programs, the percentage of government expenditures going to transfer payments peaked at 39.1 percent in 1947. By 1955, transfer payments had fallen back to 23.5 percent of total government outlays. However, with the expanding welfare and social security programs and the servicing of an increasing debt, the proportion of total government outlays going to transfer payments has grown steadily since then, rising to 41.2 percent in 1987.

Purchases of domestic output by foreigners are called real **exports.** Export purchases are significant, equaling 425.8 billion (1982) dollars in 1987, or over 11 percent of real GNP. Reported household consumption, firm investment, and government purchases of goods and services typically include not only purchases of domestically produced output but also purchases of output produced abroad, or real **imports.** Consequently, to obtain total purchases of real GNP, we must not only add in real exports to foreigners but also subtract out real imports from the reported purchases of households, firms, and government. In 1987, real imports equaled 560.1 billion (1982) dollars, or 14.7 percent of GNP. The difference between real exports and real imports is termed real **net exports.** In 1987, real net exports equaled −134.3 billion (1982) dollars (425.8 − 560.1). This means that in 1987 the United States exported 134.3 (1982) billion dollars fewer goods and services than it imported.

Summing the purchases by households, firms, governments, and foreigners, and subtracting out imports in order to measure purchases of domestically produced goods, we obtain real GNP:

Government purchases of goods and services: Purchases at all government levels (federal, state, and local). Does not include government transfer payments.

Transfer payments: Government outlays such as social security payments that simply involve the redistribution or transfer of income among households.

Exports: The goods and services produced by an economy that are sold to foreigners.

Imports: The goods and services produced abroad and purchased for domestic consumption.

Net exports: The difference between exports and imports.

$$\text{Real GNP} = \begin{array}{c}\text{Real}\\\text{consumption}\\\text{(including}\\\text{foreign goods)}\end{array} + \begin{array}{c}\text{Real}\\\text{investment}\\\text{(including}\\\text{foreign goods)}\end{array} + \begin{array}{c}\text{Real}\\\text{government}\\\text{purchases}\\\text{(including}\\\text{foreign goods)}\end{array} + \begin{array}{c}\text{Real net}\\\text{exports}\\\text{(exports minus}\\\text{imports)}\end{array} \quad \textbf{(2.1)}$$

Net Investment and Net National Product

As we have seen, the National Income and Product Accounts divide the investment component of GNP into two categories: fixed investment and net inventory investment. These accounts also divide investment expenditures a second way. Since capital equipment such as plants or machinery *depreciates,* or loses value, as it wears out with use or becomes obsolete over time, some investment spending is required just to maintain the economy's existing stock of capital. The remaining investment spending constitutes an addition to the economy's stock of capital and is therefore called **net investment.** In other words, we can divide total or gross investment into net investment and depreciation. Depreciation is generally reported in the national income accounts as the **capital consumption allowance** (CCA). Table 2.4 on page 28 reports values for net investment and the capital consumption allowance in recent years.

Net investment: Gross investment minus the capital consumption allowance. A measure of the change in the capital stock.

Capital consumption allowance: The measure of capital depreciation reported in the National Income and Product Accounts.

In any given year, net investment can be either positive or negative. If net investment is positive, then gross investment exceeds depreciation and firms are making net additions to the economy's stock of capital. If net investment is negative, then gross investment is not sufficiently high to replace the capital that is used up during the period and the capital stock falls. As Table 2.4 indicates, net investment, although quite volatile, has been positive in recent years, which indicates a growing capital stock.[8] For instance, in 1987 net investment was $226.7 billion, or 33.1 percent of gross investment. Thus the capital stock grew by $226.7 billion in 1987. The capital consumption allowance figure for 1987 indicates that $458.7 billion of capital was used up in the production process that year.

Net national product: GNP minus the capital consumption allowance.

Just as real gross investment overstates the net addition to the economy's stock of capital, real GNP overstates the economy's net output. Net output in the economy is called real **net national product** (NNP) and is obtained by subtracting measured depreciation from real GNP. That is,

$$\text{Real NNP} = \text{Real GNP} - \text{Capital consumption allowance} \quad \textbf{(2.2)}$$

Since net investment equals the difference between gross investment and depreciation, NNP can be written as the sum of consumption expenditures, net investment expenditures, government expenditures (on output), and net

---

[8] In fact, net investment has been positive every year since the end of World War II in 1945.

Table 2.4   **The Components of Investment (all figures
in billions of 1982 dollars)**

Year	Real GNP	Gross Investment	Capital Consumption Allowance	Net Investment	Real NNP
1976	2,826.7	453.5	297.3	156.2	2,529.4
1977	2,958.6	521.3	309.6	211.7	2,469.0
1978	3,115.2	576.9	323.7	253.2	2,791.5
1979	3,192.4	575.2	341.3	233.9	2,851.1
1980	3,187.1	509.3	356.1	153.2	2,831.0
1981	3,248.8	545.5	369.7	175.8	2,879.1
1982	3,166.0	447.3	383.2	64.1	2,782.8
1983	3,279.1	504.0	394.4	109.6	2,884.7
1984	3,501.4	658.4	407.2	251.2	3,094.2
1985	3,607.5	636.1	426.3	209.8	3,181.2
1986	3,713.3	654.0	442.0	212.0	3,271.3
1987	3,819.6	685.4	458.7	226.7	3,360.9

exports. Table 2.4 shows that real gross national product was $3,819.6 billion in 1987, while real net national product was $3,360.9 billion given depreciation (as measured by the capital consumption allowance) of $458.7 billion.

Conceptually, net national product is preferred to GNP as a measure of the economy's performance since it captures the net addition to output produced by the economy in a given year. However, given current accounting practices, measuring depreciation is more of an art than a science, so that in practice real GNP is often the more useful measure.

A Value-Added Approach to Measuring Real GNP

As we have seen, we can obtain real GNP by summing up the expenditures on total output made by households, firms, government, and foreigners. This is often called the "expenditure approach" to measuring GNP. An alternative approach is to measure GNP from the production side. In this approach, we calculate the contribution to total output made by every producer in the economy. The contribution of each producer to total output is termed the producer's *value added*. GNP is obtained by summing the values added by all producers. Although either method obtains the same estimate of GNP, the value-added approach has the advantage of identifying the various contributors to output.

One way of measuring the value added by a particular producer is to take the difference between receipts from sales and purchases from outside suppliers. For example, suppose that the struggling ABC Bookstore sells just one book in 1989 (we said it was struggling). Let's say ABC purchased the book from a publisher for $75 and sold the book for $100 (it was a large

Table 2.5   An Example of Value Added by a Particular Producer

Supplier	Proceeds from Sale (1)	Purchases from Suppliers (2)	Value Added (1) − (2)
ABC Bookstore	$100	$75	$ 25
A & W Publishers	75	40	35
Paper company	40	15	25
Lumber company	15	0	15
Total value added			$100

book). The value added is simply the value that ABC added to the inputs it purchased from other firms, in this case the publisher. Since the total cost of these inputs was $75, ABC added $25 of value.

As Table 2.5 indicates, there are a number of stages in the process of bringing the book to the public. At each stage, value is added by some producer. The publisher purchased paper and materials for the book from a paper company, paying $40. Thus, the value added by the publisher is $35. The paper company, in turn, purchased pulp from a lumber company for $15. Thus the value added by the paper company is $25. Of course, the lumber company that produced the pulp also purchased supplies such as chain saws and trucks from other companies. However, to keep the example simple, we have assumed that the lumber company represents the first stage of production. Thus the value added by the lumber company is the sale price of the pulp, or $15.

By summing up the value added by ABC Bookstore and the other producers who contributed to the production and marketing of the book, we arrive at a figure of $100. This is, of course, equal to the market value of the final good that was produced. The "value-added approach" to measuring GNP thus arrives at the same GNP figure as that obtained by the "expenditure approach."

Table 2.6 lists the value added to GNP by the various industries in the economy in 1986. Although Table 2.6 indicates that manufacturing contributed 21.9 percent to GNP in 1986, this is a decline from the 25 percent manufacturing contributed in 1948. Agriculture has had a relatively greater decline over the same time period, its value added falling from 6 percent of GNP in 1948 to slightly less than 2.7 percent of GNP in 1986. The service sector, in contrast, has grown in importance, as its value added has risen from 11.6 percent of GNP in 1948 to 15.2 percent in 1986.

The Relationship of GNP to Income

Every purchase of output creates income for the seller. Viewed in this way, income and output are interchangeable macroeconomic concepts. We have already pointed out that part of the income raised from the sale of output

Table 2.6   **Value Added by Industry
in 1986 (all figures in billions
of 1982 dollars)**

Agriculture, forestry, and fisheries	$ 100.4
Mining	118.1
Construction	168.3
Manufacturing	812.2
Transportation and public utilities	328.3
Wholesale and retail trade	644.7
Finance, insurance, and real estate	551.3
Services	564.9
Government and government enterprises	405.4
Other	19.8
Gross national product	$3,713.3

Source: *Economic Report of the President* (1988). Table B-11.

goes to replacing the capital used up in the production process. Subtracting the capital consumption allowance from GNP leaves the net national product. After corporate profit taxes and indirect business taxes such as sales, excise, and property taxes are paid out of NNP, the remainder is distributed to households. Households receive this income in the form of wages, dividends, interest payments, and rental payments.[9]

Table 2.7 highlights the distribution of the net national product in 1987. Of total net national product, 9.3 percent or $370.9 billion went directly to federal, state, and local governments as payment for indirect business taxes such as sales and excise taxes. Government collected an additional $137.5 billion from firms in the form of taxes on corporate profits. The remainder, $3,498.4 billion was the gross income (before personal taxes) received by households in 1987. Seventy-six percent of this income took the form of employee compensation for labor services.

Table 2.7 allows us to illustrate an important principle: Even if the government levies taxes directly on firms, for instance by imposing a profits tax, the ultimate effect is to reduce the income of households. As we reiterate in later chapters, household income after taxes (disposable income) is below net national product not only because of direct personal taxes such as income taxes but also because of taxes levied on firms. Thus, ultimately, only households pay taxes.

---

[9] In practice, not all firm profits are distributed to households as dividends. Some are "undistributed," that is, kept as retained earnings. Conceptually, however, we can think of households as receiving this money as income and then using it to purchase additional (constant value) equity shares. We will say more about this in Chapter 3.

Table 2.7   **1987 NNP and Household Income (all figures in billions of current dollars)**

Gross national product	4,486.2
less capital consumption allowance	479.4
Net national product	4,006.8
less indirect business taxes	370.9
(and other minor items)	
National income	3,635.9
less corporate profit taxes	137.5
Household gross income	3,498.4
Compensation of employees	$2,647.5
Proprietors' income	327.8
Dividends (includes undistributed)	167.8
Rent	18.5
Net interest	336.7

Source: *Economic Report of the President* (1988), Tables B-23 and B-24.

Problems with GNP as a Measure of Welfare

Although real GNP tells us a lot about the performance of the economy, GNP does not fully reflect the welfare of society for a number of reasons. First, it is simply not possible to accurately record all market output produced each year in an economy the size and complexity of the U.S. economy. This is especially true given the many goods and services that are produced and exchanged in the underground economy. (However, as we have seen, the Department of Commerce does attempt to adjust GNP to include a measure of goods and services produced and traded in the underground economy.)

Even if we could measure all market production, however, we would still not be counting goods affecting welfare that are not exchanged. For example, services that are performed in the home are not counted as part of GNP. If someone prepares his own Chinese dinner, the value of his labor services is not recorded as part of real GNP. However, if he orders a Chinese dinner from the Eggroll Express, GNP will be higher. This example is particularly relevant given the increased participation by women in the labor force since World War II. Many services that were previously performed by women in their own homes such as cooking and housekeeping, and thus not recorded in real GNP, are now being purchased in the market and thus recorded in real GNP. Consequently, the increase in measured real GNP since, say, prior to World War II, overstates the increase in the goods and services actually produced.

There are other examples of goods that affect welfare but are not exchanged in the market, and thus are not measured by real GNP. For instance in measuring GNP no allowance is made for such goods affecting welfare as clean air and safe streets. While GNP rises with increased automobile production, it does not fall with the loss of clean air due to the increase in car exhaust. A trend to a more violent society may result in an increased employment of police that raises real GNP, but the streets may still be less safe. Leisure is another example of a good whose value is not measured in real GNP. Suppose there is an improvement in technology that allows individuals to work less—to enjoy more leisure time—with no loss in production. Although this increase in technology leads to no measured change in the level of real GNP, there is clearly an improvement in welfare from the increase in leisure time.

Finally, since GNP is an aggregate measure, it does not give us information about changes in the distribution of total output among the various households in the economy. For instance, one might view a more equal distribution of income as welfare improving. If this were the case, a change in government policy that leads to a more equal distribution of income could be perceived as improving the welfare of society even though it might also lead to a fall in real GNP.

To the Point

DIFFERENT PERSPECTIVES ON GNP

- Nominal gross national product is the current market value of the final goods and services produced by an economy each year. Real GNP, in contrast, values the goods and services produced by the economy in various years by using "constant" or "base year" prices, rather than valuing goods by using current prices. Changes in real gross national product thus provide a measure of changes in the economy's aggregate output.

- One perspective on real GNP is provided by the expenditure approach. Real GNP can be divided into categories on the basis of the type of buyer: household consumption, firm gross investment, government purchases of goods and services, and exports. Gross investment is the sum of the capital consumption allowance (purchases that replace depreciated capital) and net investment. The net national product is GNP minus the capital consumption allowance.

- A second perspective on real GNP is provided by the value-added approach. Real GNP is the sum of each producer's contribution to total output or value added.

- A third perspective on real GNP is that it reflects the income earned by the factors of production. Each purchase of output creates income for those who contributed to its production, so that income and output are basically interchangeable macroeconomic concepts.

- A fourth perspective on real GNP is that it is a welfare measure. However, real GNP is an imperfect measure of welfare since changes in the production of a variety of goods that affect the well-being of individuals in the economy are not taken into account in measuring real GNP.

2.2   MEASURING ACTIVITY IN OUTPUT MARKETS: PRICE INDEXES

Inflation: A rise in the general level of prices.

Deflation: A fall in the general level of prices.

Price index: A ratio of the expenditure on a basket of goods and services in some given period to the expenditure in some base period.

When we started our analysis of GNP, we noted that there were problems involved in measuring output since in any given period, the production of some goods increases, while the production of other goods falls. Yet, we have seen how to correct for that problem and how real GNP measures changes in total output over time. Likewise, over any period of time, some prices are rising while others are falling. In such a setting, can we say whether prices are rising or falling *on average,* and by how much? Price indexes attempt to measure increases and decreases in the average level of prices. If prices in general are rising, we have **inflation;** if prices in general are falling, we have **deflation.** The rate of inflation or deflation is defined as the percentage change in an economy-wide price index over some period of time.

A **price index** for the current period is the ratio of the total expenditure on a group of goods and services computed using current prices to the total expenditure on the same group of goods computed using some prior, or base, period prices. What a price index in essence indicates is the change in expenditures required to buy a particular basket of goods over time. Since the basket of goods does not change, changes in the index must solely reflect price changes. There are two important price indexes for the U.S. economy: the GNP implicit price deflator and the consumer price index (CPI). These two price indexes differ in two fundamental ways.

First, the indexes differ as to the types of goods and services included in the basket of goods and services used to compute expenditures for various periods. The GNP deflator, which is the more comprehensive price index, uses all the goods and services included in the computation of gross national product. The consumer price index's basket of goods consists of goods and services purchased by the typical urban family of four.

The second way that the two price indexes differ is that they answer different questions. The consumer price index answers the question of how much it costs today to buy the same basket of goods purchased in some prior, or base periods. The GNP implicit price deflator answers the question of how much it would have cost in the base period to buy the basket of goods purchased in the current period.[10] Although these two approaches may seem remarkably similar, an example illustrating how each of the indexes is calculated will help clarify the difference.

The GNP Deflator

GNP deflator: The price index used to measure changes in the overall level of prices for the goods and services that make up the GNP.

The **GNP deflator** is a price index constructed by the U.S. Department of Commerce to measure changes in the overall level of prices for the goods and services that make up the GNP. Suppose that production in the economy consists of only the three goods that were listed in Table 2.2, reproduced on page 35 for convenience.

We see that in 1989 the total expenditure required to purchase the three goods is $155 $[(4 \cdot \$20) + (5 \cdot \$9) + (5 \cdot \$6)]$. How much would be required to purchase this basket of goods in 1989 if prices were the same as in 1982, the base year? The answer is $131 $[(4 \cdot \$14) + (5 \cdot \$10) + (5 \cdot \$5)]$. This $131 is the value of the 1989 quantities in terms of 1982 prices. If 1982 is used as the base period, the GNP deflator in 1989 is therefore the ratio of $155 (the expenditure in the current year on the current year's basket of goods) to $131 (what the expenditure on this basket would have been at base year prices). Convention dictates that we multiply this ratio by 100, so that the GNP deflator in 1989 is given by

$$\begin{array}{l} \text{GNP} \\ \text{deflator} \\ \text{in 1989} \end{array} = \frac{(4 \cdot \$20) + (5 \cdot \$9) + (5 \cdot \$6)}{(4 \cdot \$14) + (5 \cdot \$10) + (5 \cdot \$5)} \times 100$$

$$= (155/131) \times 100$$

$$= 118.3$$

Because of the way the GNP deflator is constructed, the GNP deflator for the base period will always equal 100. In our example, the GNP deflator of 118.3 in 1989 means that an 18.3 percent greater expenditure is required to purchase the economy's goods in 1989 than would have been the case had prices remained at their 1982 levels. In other words, prices have, on average, risen by 18.3 percent between the base year, 1982, and the current year, 1989.

---

[10] The consumer price index is an example of a Laspeyres price index, while the GNP deflator is an example of a Paasche index.

	1982			1989			1989		
	Output	*Price*	*Dollar Value*	*Output*	*Price*	*Dollar Value*	*Output (1989)*	*Price (1982)*	*Real Value*
Radios	5	$14	$70	4	$20	$80	4	$14	$56
Shirts	3	10	30	5	9	45	5	10	50
Apples	4	5	20	5	6	30	5	5	25
	Nominal GNP (1982):		$120	Nominal GNP (1989):		$155	Real GNP (1989):		$131

Nominal GNP, Real GNP, and the GNP Deflator

There is a simple relationship between nominal GNP, real GNP, and the GNP deflator. In the preceding example, we calculated nominal GNP for 1989 to be $155 and real GNP for 1989 to be $131. The GNP deflator for 1989 is simply the ratio of these values multiplied by 100. In general then, the GNP deflator can be written as

$$\begin{matrix} \text{GNP} \\ \text{deflator} \\ \text{in year } t \end{matrix} = \frac{\text{Nominal GNP in year } t}{\text{Real GNP in year } t} \times 100 \qquad \textbf{(2.3)}$$

Since the values of nominal and real GNP implicitly define the GNP deflator, this price index is sometimes referred to as the GNP *implicit* price deflator. We can rearrange the equation above to show that real GNP is simply nominal GNP divided by the GNP deflator. That is,

$$\begin{matrix} \text{Real GNP} \\ \text{in year } t \end{matrix} = \frac{\text{Nominal GNP in year } t}{(\text{GNP deflator in year } t)/100}$$

Recent annual values of nominal GNP, real GNP, and the GNP deflator are reported in Table 2.8.

As the figures in Table 2.8 demonstrate, increases in real GNP are typically less than increases in nominal GNP due to rising prices. For instance, between 1986 and 1987, nominal GNP rose by 5.9 pecent. Real GNP, however, rose by only 2.9 percent during the same period. Thus, half of the increase in nominal GNP was due to rising prices, as indicated by the 3 percent increase in the GNP deflator between 1986 and 1987. Note that since nominal GNP equals real GNP multiplied by the GNP deflator, the percentage increase in nominal GNP (5.9 percent) is approximately equal to the sum of the percent change in real GNP (2.9 percent) and the percent change in the GNP deflator (3 percent).[11]

---

[11] As illustrated by our example, this summation is only an approximation. In actuality, since nominal GNP equals the product of two variables (GNP deflator and real GNP), the percent

Table 2.8   **Real GNP, the GNP Deflator and Nominal GNP***

Year	Real GNP (in billions of 1982 dollars)		Nominal GNP (in billions of dollars)		GNP deflator divided by 100
1980	3,187.1	=	2,731.3	÷	.857
1981	3,248.8	=	3,053.9	÷	.940
1982	3,166.0	=	3,166.0	÷	1.000
1983	3,279.1	=	3,405.7	÷	1.039
1984	3,501.4	=	3,771.0	÷	1.077
1985	3,607.5	=	4,011.5	÷	1.112
1986	3,713.3	=	4,236.9	÷	1.141
1987	3,819.6	=	4,488.0	÷	1.175

* Nominal GNP figures differ slightly from published figures due to rounding errors.

The Consumer Price Index

Consumer price index: A measure of the changes in the level of consumer prices.

The U.S. Bureau of Labor Statistics (BLS) constructs the **Consumer Price Index** (CPI) to measure general changes in the level of consumer prices. The BLS surveys urban households to determine what goods the "typical urban family" purchased in some particular period, denoted the base period. At the same time, surveyors visit approximately 18,000 establishments to determine the prices of these various goods. By multiplying prices times quantities, the BLS determines the total expenditure of the typical household in the base period. Each month in succeeding years, the price surveyors determine the current prices of the goods purchased in order to calculate the new total expenditure required to buy the same basket of goods. The consumer price index in any month is simply the expenditure required that month to purchase the base-period basket of goods divided by the expenditure on that basket in the base period. An example should help clarify how the CPI is computed.

Suppose that the three goods listed in Table 2.2 are the goods that the typical urban household purchases.[12] We see that the total expenditure required

---

change in nominal GNP equals the percent change in real GNP (β) plus the percent change in the GNP deflator (θ) plus the product of the percent changes in real GNP and the GNP deflator divided by 100 ($\beta\theta/100$). That is, the percent change in nominal GNP equals β + θ + $\beta\theta/100$. For example, between 1986 and 1987 the percent change in nominal GNP (5.926) exactly equaled the percent change in real GNP (2.862) plus the percent change in the GNP deflator (2.979) plus the product of these two changes divided by 100 [(2.862 × 2.979)/100 = .084]. The product of the percent changes in real GNP and the GNP deflator divided by 100 is of a small order of magnitude (in our example, it accounts for only .084 percentage points of the total percent change in nominal GNP). Thus we often neglect it.

[12] As noted earlier, in reality the set of goods included in computing the GNP deflator is not identical to that used in computing the CPI. We choose to use the same set of goods in our example in order to highlight the second conceptual difference between the two indexes—the use of base period quantities (CPI) versus current period quantities (GNP deflator).

to purchase these three goods in 1982 was $120 [(5 · $14) + (3 · $10) + (4 · $5)]. Purchasing the same basket of goods at 1989 prices requires an expenditure of $151 [(5 · $20) + (3 · $9) + (4 · $6)]. If 1982 is used as the base period, the CPI is the ratio of $151 to $120, or the expenditure in the current year required to buy the base period basket divided by the expenditures on this basket in the base year. Multiplying this number by 100, the CPI in 1989 is given by

$$\frac{\text{CPI}}{\text{in 1989}} = \frac{(5 \cdot \$20) + (3 \cdot \$9) + (4 \cdot \$6)}{(5 \cdot \$14) + (3 \cdot \$10) + (4 \cdot \$5)} \times 100$$

$$= (151/120) \times 100$$

$$= 125.8$$

As with the GNP deflator, the CPI will always equal 100 in the base period. In our example, the CPI of 125.8 in 1989 means that a 25.8 percent increase in expenditure is required in 1989 to buy the same basket of goods as purchased in the base period, 1982. In other words, prices have, on average, risen by 25.8 percent since the base period.[13]

These CPI figures are, of course, hypothetical. In 1987, the actual CPI reported by the Bureau of Labor Statistics was 113.6, with 1982–84 being the base period. This means that, on average, the prices of consumer goods rose by 13.6 percent from the base period to 1987. More generally, the percent change in prices between any two years is given by the percent change in the CPI between those years. For example, in 1986 the CPI was 109.6. Thus from 1986 to 1987 the prices of consumer goods rose on average by 3.6 percent [(113.6 − 109.6)/109.6 multiplied by 100].

The consumer price index is a widely used measure of price changes. For instance, many government payments are tied to the CPI. As of 1987, if the CPI increases by more than 3 percent, indicating an inflation rate exceeding 3 percent, then the government increases social security and other government payments to reflect the rise in the consumer price index. It has been estimated that in times of high inflation, a 1 percentage point increase in the consumer price index leads to an automatic increase in federal expenditures of $1 billion to $2 billion.[14] Union wage contracts also often have

---

[13] Computing the rate of inflation by using the CPI is like taking a weighted sum of the rate of change in the prices of each of the n goods included in the index, where the weight for each good equals the proportion of total expenditures in the base period spent on that good. To see this, let us formally define the CPI in period t, CPI_t as equal to 100 times the expression $\sum_{i=1}^{n}(P_t^i Q_0^i)/\sum_{i=1}^{n}(P_0^i Q_0^i)$, where P_t^i is the price of the good i in period t, Q_t^i is the quantity of the good i purchased, and period 0 is the "base year." The rate of inflation between period t and the base year is given by $\pi = (CPI_t - 100)/100$. Substituting the expression for the CPI_t into this inflation expression and rearranging, we obtain $\pi = \sum_{i=1}^{n}\alpha^i \pi^i$, where $\alpha^i = (P_0^i Q_0^i)/\sum_{i=1}^{n}(P_0^i Q_0^i)$ is the proportion of the total expenditures on good i in the base period and $\pi^i = (P_t^i - P_0^i)/P_0^i$ is the rate of inflation for good i.

[14] Testimony by Lawrence deMilner at the Hearings of the Task Force on Inflation, on December 14, 1979.

cost of living adjustment clauses (COLA's) that tie wages increases to changes in the CPI.

The rationale for tying payments to changes in the CPI is the notion that such adjustments in income are necessary if consumers are to keep pace with changes in the "cost of living." These adjustments suggest that increases in income equal to the change in the consumer price index are necessary for individuals to maintain the same level of well-being. Is this true?

The consumer price index indicates the change in expenditure (and thus income) required for individuals to be just able to purchase the same basket of goods in the current year as in the base period. However, individuals will generally be able to do *better* in the current year since they can take advantage of *relative* price changes. If prices do not all change by the same proportion, then individuals will switch away from goods that become relatively more expensive and toward goods that become relatively cheaper. In other words, the quantities of goods that consumers demand change when relative prices change.[15] Yet the CPI is calculated assuming that the same basket of goods is consumed in the current year as in the base period. As a consequence, the CPI *overstates* the true increase in the cost of living by giving too much weight to those goods whose prices rise by the most. This means that if individuals' incomes rise by the same percentage as the change in the CPI, they will be better off.

The late 1960s and 1970s provide a prime example of this bias in the CPI. From 1967 to 1978, the price of a gallon of gasoline increased by more than 300 percent. During the same period, the CPI increased 95.4 percent from 100 to 195.4. These figures indicate that the price of gasoline rose relative to the price of other goods during this period. Accordingly, as we would expect, consumers substituted small, fuel-efficient cars for large gas-guzzlers, reducing their per capita consumption of gasoline. Since the 1978 CPI calculated total expenditures on gasoline by using the amount purchased in the then base year of 1967, it gave too much weight to the increase in gasoline prices and overstated the true increase in the "cost of living."

Other problems also arise from using the base-year market basket to compute the CPI. For instance, although economists and statisticians at the Bureau of Labor Statistics try to make appropriate adjustments, it is difficult to adjust the CPI for both new goods and quality changes in existing goods.

At regular intervals, the Bureau of Labor Statistics resurveys households to update the base-year basket of goods to reflect shifts in purchasing patterns. Beginning in January 1987, the CPI was revised using a market basket reflecting 1982–1984 buying patterns. With the update of the base period from 1967 to 1982–1984, new goods have been included to reflect shifting consumption patterns. For instance, indoor plants, fresh cut flowers, video

---

[15] For example, in Table 2.2 the price of radios increased from \$14 to \$20, or by 42.8 percent, from 1982 to 1989 while the price of good apples increased from \$5 to \$6, or 20 percent. Thus, the price of apples fell relative to the price of radios. As the table indicates, in 1989 individuals purchased more apples and fewer radios in response to this change in relative prices.

rentals, and cemetery lots are now included. The CPI also adjusts prices of goods to reflect quality changes. For example, a color TV in the late 1950s priced at $350 often made everyone look like they suffered from jaundice. A comparably priced color TV in the 1980s offers a truer color picture. In this example, the statisticians at the Bureau of Labor Statistics record a fall in the price of color TVs after adjusting for quality. Similarly, adjustments are made for improvements in cars since "each car purchased now has more to it—radial rather than bias-ply tires, for example."[16]

Comparing the GNP Deflator to the CPI

The CPI and the GNP deflator generally yield different estimates of the increase in the average price level for two reasons. First, the two indexes are computed using different bundles of goods. In particular, the GNP deflator is based on a much broader range of goods and services. Second, the CPI weights prices by base year purchases while the GNP deflator weights prices by current year purchases. This is why in our calculation based on Table 2.2, the estimated increase in the average price level provided by the GNP deflator (18.3 percent) is lower than that provided by the CPI (25.8 percent). Our gasoline example suggests why these different figures occur. The CPI overstates the increase in inflation since it puts too much weight on those goods with the largest percentage price increases. In contrast, the GNP deflator tends to understate the increase in inflation because it puts too little weight on these goods.

To focus on the difference that results from using base period rather than current purchases in computing a price index, Table 2.9 compares the CPI with the personal consumption deflator. The personal consumption deflator is that part of the GNP deflator that measures average price changes in the personal consumption component of GNP. The personal consumption deflator is similar in the goods covered to the CPI except that it includes rural as well as urban households. The major difference in these two indexes is that the personal consumption deflator (like the GNP deflator) is weighted to reflect current consumption patterns. As is apparent from Table 2.9, for the period between 1967 and 1987 the CPI rose by 240.4 percent while the personal consumption deflator rose by 216.2 percent.

To the Point

PRICE INDEXES TO MEASURE PRICE CHANGES

- Price indexes attempt to measure increases and decreases in the average level of prices. The GNP deflator is the price index that measures changes

---

[16] Charles Mason and Clifford Butler, "New Market Basket for the Consumer Price Index," *Monthly Labor Review* (January 1987): 15.

Table 2.9   **Price Indexes and Rates of Inflation or Deflation**

Year	Personal Consumption Deflator (base 1982)	Annual Percent Change in the PCD	CPI (base 1967)	Annual Percent Change in the CPI
1967	37.6		100.0	
1971	44.9		121.3	
1972	46.7	4.0	125.3	3.3
1973	49.6	6.2	133.1	6.2
1974	54.8	10.4	147.7	11.0
1975	59.2	8.0	161.2	9.1
1976	62.6	5.7	170.5	5.8
1977	66.7	6.5	181.5	6.5
1978	71.6	7.3	195.4	7.7
1979	78.2	9.2	217.4	11.3
1980	86.6	10.7	246.8	13.5
1981	94.6	9.2	272.4	10.4
1982	100.0	5.7	289.1	6.1
1983	104.1	4.1	298.4	3.2
1984	108.1	3.8	311.1	4.3
1985	111.8	3.4	322.2	3.6
1986	114.3	2.2	328.4	1.9
1987	118.9	4.0	340.4	3.7

in the average level of prices for the goods and services that make up the gross national product.

- The GNP deflator is so named because real GNP equals the nominal GNP deflated by (divided by) the GNP deflator.

- The consumer price index (CPI) measures changes in the cost of the basket of goods purchased by the typical urban family of four. The CPI is widely used in calculating cost of living adjustments in union wage contracts and social security benefits.

2.3   MEASURING ACTIVITY IN LABOR MARKETS

Up to this point we have been discussing measures of activity in the output markets. Another type of market that provides key measures of how the economy is performing is the labor market. The quantity and price variables that best summarize the performance of the labor market are employment, average number of hours worked per week, and wages. The unemployment rate and the participation rate are also critical variables capturing unique aspects of labor market performance.

Table 2.10 **Employment and Hours**

Year	Civilian Employment (in thousands)	Average Hours (weekly)	
1965	71,088	38.8	
1970	78,678	37.1	
1971	79,367	36.9	
1972	82,153	37.0	
1973	85,064	36.9	
1974	86,794	36.5	(recession)
1975	85,846	36.1	(recession)
1976	88,752	36.1	
1977	92,017	36.0	
1978	96,048	35.8	
1979	98,824	35.7	
1980	99,303	35.3	
1981	100,397	35.2	(recession)
1982	99,526	34.8	(recession)
1983	100,834	35.0	
1984	105,005	35.2	
1985	107,150	34.9	
1986	109,597	34.8	
1987	112,440	34.8	

Source: Department of Labor, Bureau of Labor Statistics. Note that average weekly hours are for production and nonsupervisory workers in private, nonagricultural industries. These individuals comprise 91 percent of total civilian employment. Not counted in computing average hours are such individuals as proprietors, self-employed persons, and domestic servants.

Employment, Work Hours, and Real Wages

If we were to measure the total employment of labor in terms of the number of individuals employed, we would not distinguish between a given number of employed individuals working 35 versus 40 hours per week. Yet the first situation clearly involves a smaller total supply of labor services. Therefore we measure total labor services by total work hours, which is the number of people employed multiplied by the average number of hours worked. Table 2.10 lists the number of people employed and average hours worked per week for recent years.

Table 2.10 indicates that during the recessions of 1974–1975 and 1980–1982, there was a dip not only in employment but in average hours worked as well. Both types of reductions generally contribute to the fall in total work hours during recessions. Subsequent recoveries are accompanied by expanding employment and a rise in average hours worked. Table 2.10 also indicates that over time there has been a long-term upward trend in employment and a long-term downward trend in average hours worked per week. The fall in average hours occurring during the 23 years covered in the table does not fully capture the long-term trend to a shorter workweek. For example, compare the close to 39 hours worked on average each week in 1965 with the average hours worked per week in 1890 (between 55 and 60 hours) and in 1914 (close to 50 hours).

Although replacing employment with total work hours improves our measure of the use of labor, it is still an imperfect measure of an economy's use of labor since it does not take into account changes in the amount of output each worker produces. The increase in real GNP during an economic recovery reflects not only an increase in work hours but also a more intensive use of employees. Thus output per work hour, or **labor productivity,** typically increases more rapidly during a recovery. In contrast, labor productivity growth is typically less rapid when the growth in total output slackens. This is due in part to employers' hoarding labor in slack times so that they do not lose trained employees whom they will want when there is an upturn in demand. Hoarding labor means that employers keep on more workers than necessary to produce the current output, so that each worker has less work to do than normal.[17]

Labor productivity: A measure of output per work hour.

National employment figures are also incomplete in that they neglect the supply of volunteer labor. Volunteer labor is quantitatively important: According to one survey, more than 80 million individuals in the United States volunteered 8.4 billion hours of labor to organizations in 1980.[18] This equals 5 percent of the total paid work hours recorded in 1980. Even though volunteer workers, by definition, are not paid, they are still influenced by wages. In fact, it has been estimated that a 10 percent increase in wages reduces the supply of volunteer labor by 4 percent, other things equal, as higher wages raise the opportunity costs to volunteering labor services.[19]

Naturally, wage changes can directly affect the traditional measures of paid employment. Given that work hours measure the quantity of labor services exchanged, the hourly wage measures the price of labor. By hourly wage we mean the total compensation that workers receive per hour; compensation includes not only wages but also the value of fringe benefits such as pension plans and health insurance.

Just as we divided nominal GNP by a price index to obtain real GNP, we can also divide the money wage by a price index to obtain what is known as the **real wage.** A change in the real wage tells us how the hourly payment received by labor in terms of actual real goods and services has changed.

Real wage: The money wage divided by the level of output prices.

---

[17] The labor hoarding phenomenon, also referred to as the labor reserve hypothesis, has been interpreted as a lower output per work hour during periods of slack demand. Among those who have examined this phenomenon are J. Taylor, "The Behavior of Unemployment and Unfilled Vacancies: Great Britain, 1958–1971. An Alternative View," *The Economic Journal* (December 1972) and Robert Hall, "Employment Fluctuations and Wage Rigidity," *Brookings Papers on Economic Activity* (1980).

[18] Virginia Hodgkinson and Murray Weitzman, *Dimensions of the Independent Sector: A Statistical Profile,* Independent Sector, Washington, D.C., 1984.

[19] Paul Menchik and Burton Weisbrod, "Volunteer Labor Supply," *Journal of Public Economics* 32 (1987): 159–183.

Figure 2.1 **Real Compensation per Hour**

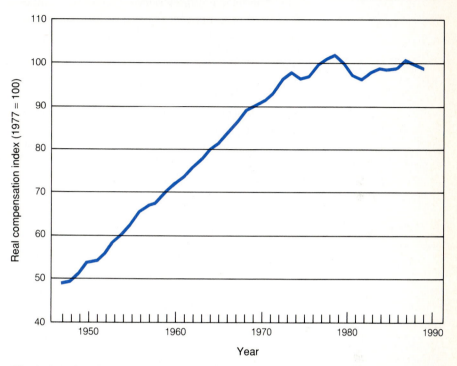

The index of real compensation equals total wages, including fringe benefits, divided by the consumer price index. Note that the index measures compensation before taxes.

Source: *Business Conditions Digest*, various isses.

For example, if the money wage increases by 10 percent and prices rise by 5 percent, then the resulting 5 percent increase in the real wage means that the wage earner has an increased command over goods and services. In contrast, if the money wage increases by 10 percent and prices rise by 15 percent, the resulting 5 percent reduction in the real wage signals a loss in workers' purchasing power. Figure 2.1 indicates that the real wage, as measured by real hourly compensation, has been rising over time, with the notable exception of the ten-year period from 1974 to 1983.

Even though the changes in hourly compensation indicated in Figure 2.1 are adjusted to reflect changes in prices, the resulting measure of *real* hourly compensation may still not accurately reflect how the reward to working has varied over time. Households supply labor, giving up their leisure, in order to gain command over real goods and services. Thus labor suppliers look not so much at the real wage but at the real wage *net* of taxes. This is sometimes referred to as real "take-home" compensation. In some years, the net real wage has not risen as fast as the real wage due to rising tax rates. The impact of high tax rates on labor supply is one of the issues raised by supply-side economics, as we will see in later chapters.

Unemployment, the Labor Force, and Participation

Unemployment rate: The number of unemployed workers expressed as a percentage of the total number of workers in the labor force.

The **unemployment rate** is a statistic faithfully reported in the news every month. The U.S. Census Bureau obtains the data on unemployment rates from a monthly household survey that it conducts. The survey covers approximately 60,000 households from across the country. The Census Bureau generates the survey data, and the Bureau of Labor Statistics then analyzes that data.

To be counted as *unemployed* in the Census Bureau survey, an individual not only must be currently without a job but also must be either actively searching for work, laid off and awaiting recall from an employer, or waiting to start a new job within 30 days. Adding up the number of individuals in all three categories yields the total number unemployed.

There are two alternatives to being unemployed. One obvious one is to be employed. The sum of the number of people employed and the number unemployed equals the total number of people in the **labor force.** The

Labor force: The sum of the number of people employed and the number unemployed.

unemployment rate is simply the number of unemployed workers expressed as a fraction or percentage of the total number of workers in the labor force.

In 1983, the government proposed including the military as part of the employed labor force. The proposal was initiated to reflect the voluntary nature of the armed forces but had the added impact of reducing the unemployment rate. In subsequent years, two unemployment rates ("all workers" and "civilian workers") were published, with the civilian workers' unemployment rate slightly above the unemployment rate for all workers. For example, in 1987 while the unemployment rate for civilian workers was 6.2 percent, the unemployment rate for all workers was 6.1.

Participation rate: The proportion of the noninstitutionalized population over age 16 in the labor force.

The other alternative to being unemployed is to be out of the labor force. Those not in the labor force may be persons engaged in their own housework, retired, in school, unable to work because of long-term physical or mental illness, or persons, sometimes referred to as discouraged workers, who do not look for work because they believe no suitable jobs are available in their area. Of the total civilian, noninstitutionalized population over age 16, the fraction who are in the labor force defines the **participation rate.** Table 2.11 records recent employment, unemployment, and labor force participation figures.

The data reported in Table 2.11 reinforce the point made in Chapter 1, that a striking feature of the recent path of unemployment rates was the upward trend in unemployment after 1970. The high unemployment rates of the 1980s contrast sharply with the low unemployment rates of the mid-

Table 2.11   **Unemployment Rate, Labor Force, and Participation Rate**
             (Numbers in thousands)

Year	Civilian noninstitutionalized population	Civilian labor force	Participation rate (percent)	Civilian number employed	Number unemployed	Unemployment rate (percent)
1965	126,513	74,455	58.85	71,088	3,367	4.52
1967	129,874	77,347	59.56	74,372	2,975	3.85
1969	134,335	80,734	60.10	77,902	2,832	3.51
1970	137,085	82,771	60.38	78,678	4,093	4.94
1971	140,216	84,382	60.18	79,367	5,015	5.94
1972	144,126	87,034	60.39	82,153	4,881	5.61
1973	147,096	89,429	60.80	85,064	4,365	4.88
1974	150,120	91,949	61.25	86,794	5,155	5.61
1975	153,153	93,775	61.23	85,846	7,929	8.46
1976	156,150	96,158	61.58	88,752	7,406	7.70
1977	159,033	99,009	62.26	92,017	6,992	7.06
1978	161,919	102,251	63.15	96,048	6,203	6.07
1979	164,863	104,962	63.67	98,824	6,138	5.85
1980	167,745	106,940	63.75	99,303	7,637	7.14
1981	170,130	108,670	63.87	100,397	8,273	7.61
1982	172,130	110,670	64.29	99,526	11,144	10.07
1983	174,215	111,550	64.03	100,834	10,716	9.61
1984	176,383	113,544	64.37	105,005	8,539	7.52
1985	178,206	115,461	64.79	107,150	8,312	7.20
1986	180,587	117,834	65.25	109,597	8,237	6.99
1987	182,753	119,865	65.59	112,440	7,425	6.19

Source: Economic Report of the President (1988), Table B-33.

and late 1960s. Table 2.11 also indicates the rise in the labor force participation rate between 1965 and 1987, an increase attributable to the entrance of women into the labor force in ever-increasing numbers.

Figure 2.2 vividly portrays the increase in the female participation rate that occurred from 1965 to 1987. In 1965, the labor force participation rate for females was 39.3 percent. By 1987, it had increased to 56 percent. In contrast, the labor force participation rate for males fell from 80.7 percent in 1965 to 76.2 percent in 1987, primarily because men stayed in school longer and retired earlier. Interestingly, as we will see in Chapter 15, these trends in labor force participation were not unique to the United States, but were also experienced by other developed countries.

Perhaps the major factor behind the increased participation of women was the introduction of laborsaving devices in the household. A second factor was a rise in the divorce rate. According to a recent study, "the effect of actual divorce on the probability of participation is about 20 percentage points (from .68 to about .88). Since the fraction of all women currently divorced

Figure 2.2   Labor Force Participation Rates of Men and Women

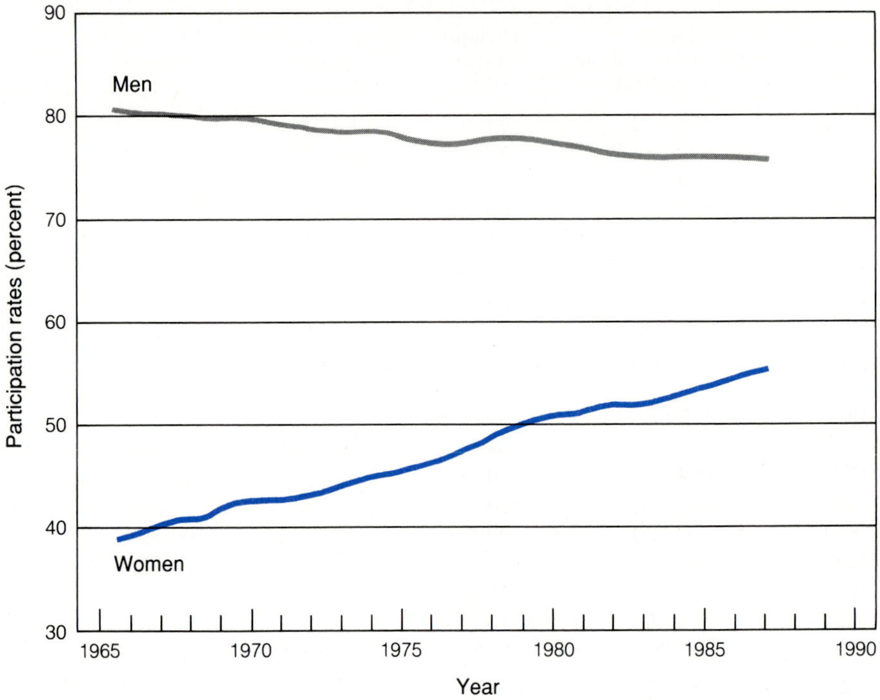

In contrast to the labor force participation rate for men, the participation rate for women has risen steadily in recent years.

Source: Economic Report of the President (1988), Table B-36.

rose from 2.3 to 6.7 percent from 1960 to 1980, the direct effect of the rise in divorce is to increase women's labor force participation by .8 percentage points."[20] Later we will analyze how the changing participation rate of women has influenced the overall unemployment rate in the economy.

International Comparison of Unemployment Rates

The U.S. unemployment rate is often compared to the rates in other countries. Sometimes the comparison is favorable, as was the case in the late 1980s when the U.S. rate was far below Spain's unemployment rate of around 20

[20] William R. Johnson and Jonathan Skinner, "Labor Supply and Marital Separation," *American Economic Review* 76 (June 1986): 468.

percent. Yet during this same period, the comparison was not so favorable between the U.S. rate and the unemployment rates of Switzerland and Japan, which were 1 and 3 percent, respectively. What might surprise you is that such comparisons can be misleading since the methods of measuring unemployment differ from one country to another.

There are two basic ways in which unemployment can be measured. As we have seen, one way that is carried out not only by the United States but also by Japan, Canada, and Sweden, is to base the figures on monthly surveys of households. An alternative that is used by all major European countries, with the exception of Sweden, is to rely on the number of individuals claiming unemployment benefits. One thing that makes comparisons difficult is that not all people who would be counted as unemployed by a survey actually register for benefits. For instance, one study found that for Italy, only 63 percent of those recorded as unemployed in a labor force survey were registered as unemployed.

In contrast, there are cases in which individuals who would not have been counted as unemployed by a survey may show up on the unemployment register and be counted as unemployed. For instance, in 1987 when Britain began its "restart scheme" that required everyone unemployed for more than one year to report to the local government "Job Centre" for an interview, it was discovered that many on the unemployed register were not really available for work.

Another problem in international comparisons is that even if two countries had the same "standardized" unemployment rate, there might be quite different underlying conditions in their labor markets. For example, when faced with declining production, many large companies in Japan extend holidays, cut overtime, or give early retirement rather than cut employment. As the *Economist* noted, "The true level of Japanese unemployment—in terms of those without proper work—is estimated to be at least twice the official rate of 3 percent."[21]

To the Point

A BREAKDOWN OF LABOR MARKET MEASURES

- That part of the population that is over 16 and neither institutionalized nor in the armed forces has the potential to participate in the civilian labor force.

- Of those who have the potential to participate in the labor force, the fraction that does participate defines the civilian participation rate. Those who participate are either employed or unemployed.

---

[21] *The Economist* (27 June 1987).

- ▪ Of those who participate in the labor force, the fraction who are un-employed defines the unemployment rate.

- ▪ Variations in employment do not entirely capture changes in the utilization of labor. Total work hours, which is the product of the number of workers employed and the average number of hours worked, is a better measure of the quantity of labor services utilized.

SUMMARY

Nominal GNP is the current market value of all final goods and services produced in an economy over a specified period of time, usually one year. However, changes in nominal GNP reflect not only changes in output but also changes in prices. To measure output changes alone, we must control for price changes. We do this by computing real GNP, which is the value of final goods and services produced each year in terms of base period, or constant, prices.

Real GNP can be divided into four components according to the type of output buyer: consumption expenditures (purchases of final output by households), investment (purchases of final output by firms), government purchases of goods and services, and net exports (net purchases of output by foreigners). We further divide investment into the capital consumption allowance and net investment. The capital consumption allowance reflects purchases of capital to replace capital used up in the production process (capital that has depreciated or become obsolete). Net investment is that part of investment that constitutes an addition to the capital stock.

A second measure of activity in the output market is the change in the level of prices in the economy. Changes in the price level are measured by various price indexes, such as the GNP deflator and the consumer price index. The GNP deflator measures changes in the prices of goods that are included in the computation of GNP. Nominal GNP divided by the GNP deflator equals real GNP. The consumer price index indicates the average change in the prices of commodities purchased by the typical urban family of four.

In addition to measuring the activity in the output market, we are also interested in how labor markets are performing. There are measures of labor market activity that are analogous to the measures for the output market. Whereas in the output market we look at output produced (real GNP) and the price level (GNP deflator), in the labor market we look at total work hours (employment multiplied by average hours) and average compensation. From the point of view of the seller of labor services, money wages must be deflated by a price index and taxes must be subtracted (to obtain the real wage net of taxes) in order to express compensation in terms of its command over goods and services.

Other important measures of labor market activity are the unemployment rate and the labor force participation rate. The unemployment rate equals the number unemployed divided by the labor force (the number unemployed plus the number employed). The labor force participation rate is the number in the labor force divided by the total noninstitutionalized adult population.

LOOKING AHEAD

To judge the performance of an economy, we must look at variables associated with each of four critical markets. This chapter has explored the measurement of activity in two of these markets, the output market and the labor market. In the next chapter, we discuss measures of activity in the remaining two markets, the financial market and the foreign exchange market. For financial markets, interest rates are important indicators of the state of an economy. In the foreign exchange markets, foreign exchange rates and the volume of exports, imports, and international capital flows are critical.

With the background of how to measure activity in the various markets in the economy, in subsequent chapters we will develop a model of the economy with the aim of explaining the past changes in the economy's performance. An equally important goal, however, is to develop an analytical framework so that you can understand future changes in such variables as GNP, interest rates, prices, or the unemployment rate.

KEY TERMS

Nominal gross national product, 19

Real gross national product, 23

Recession, 24

Consumption expenditures, 24

Investment, 25

Government purchases of goods and services, 26

Transfer payments, 26

Exports, 26

Imports, 26

Net exports, 26

Net investment, 27

Capital consumption allowance, 27

Net national product, 27

Inflation and deflation, 33

Price index, 33

GNP deflator, 34

Consumer price index, 36

Labor productivity, 42

Real wage, 42

Unemployment rate, 44

Labor force, 44

Participation rate, 44

REVIEW QUESTIONS

1. Consider the following figures:

GNP	4,800
Gross investment	800
Net investment	300
Consumption	2,960
Government purchases	1,000

   What is

   a. the net national product?
   b. the capital consumption allowance?
   c. net exports?

2. According to the *Wall Street Journal* (April 23, 1986), "Falling oil prices led to a 0.4 percent decline in the government's consumer price index in March, the same as in February . . . It was the first two-month drop in the index since July and August 1965. . . . Consumer prices for all items except energy rose by 0.3 percent in March." Suppose that the actual prices and purchases by consumers for 1985 were those indicated below.

	Energy Good		Other Goods	
	Price	Quantity	Price	Quantity
1985	1.00	50	1.10	40
1986	.90	60	1.20	30

   a. Letting 1985 be the base period, calculate the CPI in 1986.
   b. According to your computed CPI, what is the rate of inflation or deflation between 1985 and 1986?

3. In a recent *Wall Street Journal* article (April 23, 1986), it was stated that "the fall in the wage-earner index (the consumer price index for urban wage earners and clerical workers) increases the likelihood that, under current law, Social Security recipients won't receive a cost-of-living boost next year. The law provides for such an increase only if the wage-earner index rises more than 3 percent from the third quarter of one year to the third quarter of the next." Assume that last year was the base period for the wage-earner index and that the wage-earner index this year is 102. If Congress wishes to change the law in order to leave the welfare of those receiving Social Security payments constant, should social security

payments be increased by more or less than 2 percent? Why is the answer not an increase in payments by exactly 2 percent?

4. A recent *Wall Street Journal* article (April 18, 1986) indicated that, "the economy expanded at a healthy 3.2 percent annual rate in the first quarter, according to a preliminary estimate by the Commerce Department. The increase in the real gross national product, the inflation-adjusted value of the nation's output of goods and services, was stronger than many economists expected. It followed a paltry 0.7 percent growth rate in the fourth quarter. A GNP-based price measure, known as the _____, rose at a 2.5 percent annual rate in the latest quarter, the smallest increase since the measure showed no price change in the second quarter of 1967. The inflation measure increased at a 3.3 percent rate in the fourth quarter."

   a. To what "GNP-based price measure" does the above quote refer? Indicate the relationship between the "GNP-based price measure," the "inflation-adjusted value of the nation's output of goods and services," and nominal gross national product.

   b. What does the above quote imply was the percentage change in nominal GNP for the first quarter of 1986?

5. If depreciation (the capital consumption allowance) exceeds gross private domestic investment, the following can be concluded:

   a. The economy is expanding.

   b. The economy is importing more than it exports.

   c. Net investment is negative.

   d. Nominal GNP is rising but real GNP is declining.

6. Suppose that the noninstitutionalized population of Lower Slobovia over the age of 16 is 112,000. The participation rate is 60 percent and the unemployment rate is 8 percent. How many people are unemployed in Lower Slobovia?

7. If Ms. Smith marries her butler, who continues to perform the same services as a butler although now without payment, what happens to GNP?

8. Which of the following individuals would be classified as employed, unemployed, or out of the labor force?

   a. Mark is about to start a job at a university in Virginia and has decided to hike across America during the next two months while he is waiting to begin his new job.

   b. Robert E. Lee is a full-time college student but works at night at the local disco.

   c. Steve was laid off from his job at a publishing company and there are no prospects of his being recalled for work by his former employer. Depressed, Steve sits in front of the TV all day, watching soap operas.

d. Liz recently had a baby and works fifteen hours a week out of her home as an "editor for hire." Is she employed?

e. Therese is a full-time student at a local college taking a smattering of courses with no specified career objective. She does, however, plan to "get her act together" next year and look for a job.

9. During a particular year, farmer Smith grows wheat, which she sells to Miller the miller for $100. Miller grinds the flour into wheat, which he sells to Baker the baker for $175. Baker bakes 150 loaves of bread from the flour, and sells 100 of them during the current year for $2 per loaf. The other 50 loaves are frozen for future sale. What is the total contribution to gross national product this year from all of these transactions? What are the values added by Smith, Miller, and Baker?

10. If nominal GNP in 1990 is $3 trillion dollars and the GNP price deflator is 240 (with 1982 as the base year), what will real GNP be in 1990?

11. Consider the following information:

	1987		1988	
	Price	*Quantity*	*Price*	*Quantity*
Good 1	$10	10	$9	11
Good 2	5	4	5	5
Good 3	5	4	3	7

a. Compute nominal GNP for 1987 and 1988.

b. Taking 1987 as the base period, compute real GNP for 1987 and 1988.

c. Taking 1987 as the base period, compute the GNP deflator for 1987 and 1988.

d. Taking 1987 as the base period and assuming that only Goods 1 and 2 are purchased by the typical urban household, compute the CPI for 1988.

What is the rate of inflation between 1987 and 1988 according to the GNP deflator?

12. According to the *Wall Street Journal* (February 26, 1988), "The Commerce Department increased its estimate of fourth-quarter economic growth to a strong 4.5 percent annual rate. . . . After the revisions, the government put fourth-quarter GNP at an annual rate of $3.878 trillion, up from $3.836 trillion in the third quarter. Before adjusting for inflation, GNP was 4.604 trillion, up from $4.524 trillion." According to the quote, the implied GNP deflator for the third and fourth quarter of 1987 were _____ and _____, respectively. The implied rate of change in the GNP deflator between the third and fourth quarter is thus _____. (You need not explicitly calculate these numbers as long as you show exactly how they would be computed.)

Chapter 3

Measuring Activity: The Financial Market, the Foreign Exchange Market, and Money

IN 1980, when voters went to the polls to choose between the incumbent president, Jimmy Carter, and the challenger, Ronald Reagan, the prime interest rate was 21 percent, the highest it had been in this century.[1] This factor doubtlessly contributed to Ronald Reagan's sweeping victory. Interest rates influence presidential elections because they affect the well-being of businesses, home buyers, students taking out loans to finance their educations, and individuals saving for retirement and other purposes. In evaluating the economy's overall performance, interest rates are thus among the important variables we must consider.

In the first part of this chapter, we discuss interest rates as they relate to bonds and stocks, the financial assets issued by firms and governments. In the process, we explain several issues: how macroeconomics simplifies the activity in the financial markets; why bond prices and interest rates move in opposite directions; why we make the distinction between the money or nominal interest rate; and what is termed the real interest rate.

---

[1] The prime rate is the interest rate that banks publicize as charged on short-term loans they make to their largest, most dependable customers.

In addition to the dramatic rise in interest rates in the late 1970s and the 1980s, there were also substantial changes in dollar foreign exchange rates (the price of a dollar in terms of foreign currency) as well as huge trade deficits in the 1980s. The second part of this chapter discusses measures of activity in the international markets. We examine the international balance of payments accounts in order to identify the sources of the demand for and supply of dollars in the foreign exchange markets. These sources include exports, imports, and international capital flows.

The chapter concludes by introducing measures of a key macroeconomic variable—the money supply. We will find throughout the book that the money supply is a critical macroeconomic variable and that monetary policy is one of the most controversial macroeconomic issues.

3.1 MEASURING THE ACTIVITY IN THE FINANCIAL MARKETS

When governments, firms, or households borrow money, they enter into contracts that spell out the terms of their loan agreements. Every loan agreement can be distinguished by three features:

1. *Maturity* of the loan, or the agreed upon schedule for repayment of the loan.

2. *Uncertainty* concerning repayment, or the perceived probability that the borrower will not pay back the loan on schedule.

3. *Tax status* of the loan's interest income, or the extent to which the loan's interest income is tax-free.

Interest rate: The specified charge per dollar per period that borrowers pay or lenders receive.

These three features affect the **interest rate** or yield—the per period specified charge per dollar borrowed—associated with the loan. In order to gain some understanding of how these three features affect interest rates, let's consider some examples of various types of debt instruments that differ in maturity, tax status, and likelihood of default.

A Sampling of Various Loan Agreements

Firms issue many different types of debt instruments that reflect their varied borrowing activities. Short-term instruments that mature in less than one year and are issued by large corporations are called *commercial paper*. Long-term debt instruments that have a maturity of between one year and ten years are called *corporate notes* and obligations with maturities exceeding ten years are called *corporate bonds*. Announcements of note and bond sales by firms appear daily in the *Wall Street Journal* and other financial publications. By way of example, Figure 3.1 presents an announcement by Ryder System,

Figure 3.1 **A Sample Announcement of a Bond Sale**

This announcement is neither an offer to sell nor a solicitation of an offer to buy these securities.
The offer is made only by the Prospectus Supplement and the related Prospectus.

RYDER SYSTEM   New Issue / March 21, 1988

$200,000,000

Ryder System, Inc.

9.20% Notes, Series M, Due March 15, 1998

Price 100% and accrued interest from March 15, 1988

Copies of the Prospectus Supplement and the related Prospectus may be obtained
in any State in which this announcement is circulated only from such of the
undersigned as may legally offer these securities in such State.

Salomon Brothers Inc	Morgan Stanley & Co.
	Incorporated
The First Boston Corporation	Goldman, Sachs & Co.
Merrill Lynch Capital Markets	Shearson Lehman Hutton Inc.
Bear, Stearns & Co. Inc. Daiwa Securities America Inc.	Deutsche Bank Capital
	Corporation
Dillon, Read & Co. Inc. Donaldson, Lufkin & Jenrette	Drexel Burnham Lambert
	Securities Corporation Incorporated
Kidder, Peabody & Co. Lazard Freres & Co.	The Nikko Securities Co.
Incorporated	International, Inc.
Nomura Securities International, Inc.	PaineWebber Incorporated
Prudential-Bache Capital Funding	L.F. Rothschild & Co.
	Incorporated
SBCI Swiss Bank Corporation	Smith Barney, Harris Upham & Co.
Investment banking	Incorporated
UBS Securities Inc.	Wertheim Schroder & Co.
	Incorporated
Dean Witter Capital Markets	Yamaichi International (America), Inc.

This is a typical example of an announcement by a firm to sell corporate notes. It appeared in the *Wall Street Journal* on March 21, 1988. The firms listed in bottom half of the announcement are brokerage firms that will be selling the notes.

Inc., in the *Wall Street Journal* that it is issuing notes with a 10-year maturity to borrow $200 million on which it will pay 9.2 percent interest.

As noted in Chapter 2, when it comes to the construction of new homes, households are treated as "firms" in the National Income and Product Accounts. That is, the construction of new homes is counted as part of investment rather than consumption spending. Loans to finance the construction of homes, as well as farm and business property, are called *mortgages*.

The financial assets that the government sector issues vary in both their maturity and in the level of government at which they are issued. Short-term obligations of the federal government, which mature in three months to one year, are called *treasury bills*. Treasury bills, which are sold at weekly auctions, typically pay the holder (the "bearer") a single payment of $10,000 (the bill's "face value") on maturity. Naturally, the buyer of the new bill pays less than that when it is initially issued, with the difference determining the bill's interest payment. For instance, on April 19, 1988 the *Wall Street Journal* reported the results of the Monday, April 18, 1988 auction of short-term U.S. government bills, in which the bills "sold at a discount of 5.78 percent from face value in units of $10,000 to $1 million."

Treasury notes and bonds constitute longer term obligations of the federal government. *Treasury notes* are obligations of the federal government that, like corporate notes, have maturities of between one and ten years. *Treasury bonds* are obligations of the federal government that have maturities longer than ten years.

Unlike treasury bills, treasury notes and bonds make payments to the bearer before they mature. Such payments are called coupon payments. For example, a five-year treasury note with a face value of $10,000 will specify payment during the five-year period of, say, $700 per year as well as the payment of the $10,000 principal at the end of the five year period. The $700 annual payments are the bond's coupon payments. Most long-term loan agreements make coupon payments, not just the treasury notes and bonds issued by the federal government. Loan agreements that make a single payment upon maturity are often called "zero-coupon bonds." The treasury bills cited above are examples of zero-coupon bonds.

In addition to the federal government, states, cities, and other local government entities also borrow. The long-term debt obligations of local governments are called *municipal bonds.* An important aspect of municipal bonds is that their interest earnings are generally not subject to the federal income tax. This tax-free status allows municipalities to sell bonds at lower interest rates than corporations and still offer the same after-tax return to lenders.

Most of us are familiar with firms and governments as issuers of bonds since we see GM and Uncle Sam selling bonds to raise money. We are less familiar with the fact that many households also issue what can be called in a generic sense "bonds." Although you may not think of households as supplying bonds, upon reflection you will realize that whenever a household takes out a loan from a bank, it is selling a bond. That is, in exchange for the money borrowed, the household in essence issues a piece of paper—a "bond"—that spells out its agreement to repay the loan over a specified period of time. Thus one way to view a household borrowing $13,000 from the First National Bank to buy a new car is that it is really just issuing a bond. Throughout the book we will use the term "bond" in the generic sense to refer to loan agreements.

Of course, other households purchase rather than issue bonds. In this capacity, they act as lenders in the financial market. An obvious example is the $25 Series E Government Savings Bond that your grandmother might have given you on your birthday. Less obviously, contributions made by your parents into a retirement plan typically go to the purchase of bonds and other financial assets. In later chapters, we will focus on households as buyers of financial assets (lenders) rather than sellers of financial assets (borrowers) because when taken as a group, total household saving exceeds total borrowing.

Maturity, Risk, and Interest Rate Differentials

Term structure of interest rates: The relationship between interest rates on bonds that are similar in all characteristics except maturity.

The relationship between interest rates on bonds that are similar in all characteristics except maturity is known as the **term structure of interest rates.** The term structure of interest rates describes differences in interest rates related not to such factors as default risk or tax treatment but rather to differences based solely on variations in maturity. Figures 3.2a and 3.2b depict how interest rates have varied for bonds of different maturity and for bonds issued by the government as opposed to firms.

Figure 3.2(a) compares the interest rate on short-term government treasury bills ("T-bills") with the interest rate on long-term treasury bonds ("T-bonds"). Generally, longer term bonds have higher interest rates than shorter term bonds. For example, for almost the entire 38-year period from 1948 to 1986, the interest rate on long-term treasury bonds was higher than the interest rate on short-term treasury bills. But this relationship does not always hold. As Figure 3.2(a) indicates, during the early 1980s the short-term interest rate on treasury bills was higher than the long-term rate on treasury bonds. We will see later that the reason for this was that individuals anticipated higher inflation in the immediate future than they did over the long run.

Differences among interest rates also reflect differences in the market's assessment of the relative riskiness of the various assets. The interest rates offered on riskier bonds must be sufficiently high to compensate lenders for assuming a higher risk. For example, debt instruments issued by the federal government are generally viewed as being the least risky because there are no instances of the federal government ever defaulting on a treasury bill, note, or bond. Because commercial paper issued by firms is viewed as being more risky than government bonds of similar maturity, the commercial paper rate exceeds the T-bill interest rate as indicated in Figure 3.2(b). Likewise, we would find that if we were to compare the interest rate on long-term corporate bonds to the treasury bond rate, the corporate bond rate would be higher.

Even among debt instruments offered by firms, there are wide differences in the uncertainty of repayment of the debt. One reason is that some corporate debt is backed by real assets owned by the issuing firm. In such cases, the debt is said to be *secured,* and the assets that secure the loan are termed collateral. These assets can include merchandise, plant and equipment, and, in some instances, even accounts receivable (payments due to the borrower). Mortgages are loans secured by real estate. If the borrower fails to repay the loan on schedule, the lender may sell the collateralized assets to recover losses. Because the lender has claim to something of value (the collateral) if the borrower defaults, secured loans are considered less risky than unsecured loans, and thus typically have a lower interest rate.

Figure 3.2   U.S. Interest Rates

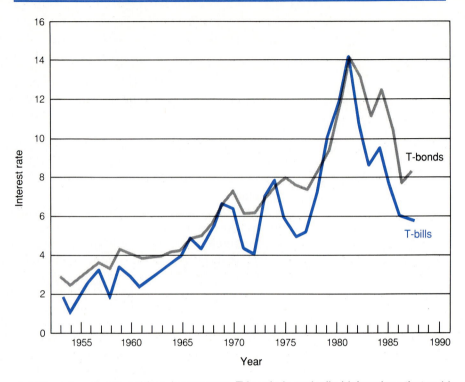

(a) The interest rate paid on longer term T-bonds is typically higher than that paid on T-bills.

(continued)

Among government bonds, at least at the state and local levels, some bonds are more likely to default than others. Two widely publicized examples of default occurred in the 1970s when New York City and Cleveland suspended interest payments on some of their debt issues. Concern about municipal borrowing increased in the early 1980s as a result of the largest single default on tax-exempt debt in U.S. history.[2] The Washington Public Power Supply System (WPPSS) ceased interest payments on $2.5 billion of debt issued to finance the construction of nuclear power plants.

To help the potentially bewildered investor differentiate between bonds, rating services such as Standard and Poor's and Moody's rate both corporate

---

[2] Lynn Asinof, "Possible Effects of a WPPSS Bond Failure Are Visible in Past U.S. Municipal Defaults," *Wall Street Journal*, July 13, 1983.

Figure 3.2 *continuing*

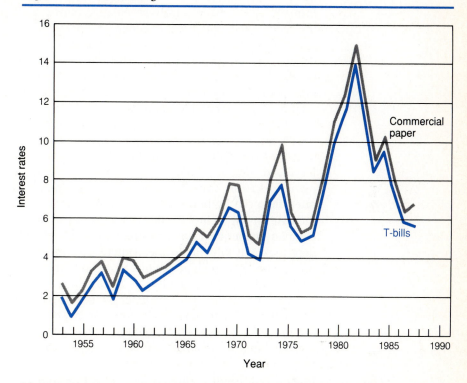

(b) Because there is a lower risk of default on T-bills, they typically pay a lower interest rate than privately issued financial assets of a similar maturity.

Source: *Economic Report of the President*, 1988, Table B-71.

and municipal bonds, from least risky (Standard and Poor's AAA or Moody's Aaa rated bonds) to speculative (Standard and Poor's and Moody's B rated bonds) to high probability of default (Standard and Poor's CCC and Moody's Caa rated bonds).

Case Study

JUNK BONDS

Among the fastest growing types of bonds traded in recent years have been the so-called "junk bonds." Like junkyard and junk food, the term junk bonds conjures up the vision of inferior quality—and in a real sense this is a correct view of junk bonds. Junk bonds, or high-yield bonds as they are formally called, have a truly speculative nature, with a significant risk that the lender will not repay the loan. It has been estimated that the rate of default on high-yield bonds is more than 15 times higher than the rate of default on total corporate debt.[3] This is the reason for the high yields of these bonds, since buyers must be compensated for this risk. In fact, yields on junk bonds averaged between 2.5 and 5 percent above yields of government securities of comparable maturity.

High-yield debt, an insignificant part of financial markets in the mid 1970s, was estimated to be close to 20 percent of total newly issued corporate debt by 1985. One reason for this is the increased use of junk bonds in the leveraged buyout (LBO). In a leveraged buyout, a company purchases its own stock; this conversion of a public company to a private company is often financed by bonds issued by the company. The result is a substantial increase in the debt that the company must service from earnings. If the company experiences a subsequent shortfall in earnings, this high level of debt makes it difficult to meet interest payments on the debt, and default can occur. The real possibility of default makes the bonds issued for a leveraged buyout speculative, and thus they must offer a high-yield.

Junk bonds are also sometimes used for highly leveraged hostile takeovers of companies. Often in these cases, a smaller company is attempting to acquire a much larger company; the smaller company issues bonds to finance the purchase of the larger company's stock, planning to repay the bonds by using the earnings and assets of the larger, target firm. As with a leveraged buyout, the result is often a firm with substantial debt and sizable interest payments that it may not be able to meet should there be an economic downturn. This high risk of default means that the bonds used to finance such hostile takeovers are high yield, i.e. junk, bonds. Two recent examples of hostile takeovers that used junk bonds were Pantry Pride's offer for Revlon and Mesa Petroleum's bid for Unocal (directed by the infamous takeover artist T. Boone Pickens), both of which occurred during the second half of 1985.

3.2   COMMON ELEMENTS OF DEBT INSTRUMENTS

The dizzying array of debt instruments listed above is almost overwhelming. Yet we have not yet mentioned another critical type of financial instrument. Firms raise funds not only by selling bonds but also by issuing new equity shares, more commonly known as stocks. Stocks differ from bonds in that

---

[3] The source of these and other figures on the market for junk bonds is Edward Almon and Scott Nammacher, *Investing in Junk Bonds* (New York: John Wiley, 1987).

they entitle their owners to a share of the earnings of a corporation. Earnings paid out to stockholders are called dividends. Unlike bonds, stocks do not promise specific money payments at specific times in the future; rather the future money payments (dividends) that stockholders receive depend on realized future earnings of the company.

As with bonds, there is a variety of different types of equity shares. For instance, there is preferred stock and common stock, with holders of preferred stock having a claim on dividend distribution before any dividends are paid to holders of common stock.

Faced with the above diversity of financial instruments, it is simply not possible for macroeconomics analysis to consider in detail the market for each type of financial asset. Consequently, macroeconomics simplifies the analysis of financial markets by focusing on the common elements of these financial assets and collapsing the financial sector of the economy into a single market for financial assets.

Simplifying the Financial Markets: Lumping Together Bonds and Stocks

The essential common feature of the various types of bonds and equity shares that we focus on is that all are lending agreements: When they are issued, the sellers receive a money payment in return for a commitment to repay the loan in the future. For bonds, the commitment involves a particular schedule for repayment (coupon payments and repayment of principal on maturity). For equity shares, the commitment to repayment in the form of dividends is a commitment contingent on the fortunes of the firm. In either case, however, the buyers expect to receive future money payments in return for their loan. Both bonds and equity shares add to the buyer's portfolio of earning assets.

Given the similarity among bonds and between stocks and bonds, macroeconomics typically lumps together equity shares and the variety of different bonds. As indicated above, most analysis in this book assumes a single, representative debt instrument and associated interest rate. We will refer to this generic debt instrument as a **financial asset.**

Financial asset: A contract between a borrower and a lender that specifies the terms of a loan agreement.

Of course, bonds and equity shares do differ. By not considering the differences between such financial assets, we will not address certain real-world details—such as the differences between short-term and long-term interest rates and the differences between the return on equity shares and bonds. This loss of real-world details is offset, however, by the gain of a clearer picture of financial markets. As Figure 3.2 illustrated, interest rates for different types of financial assets historically tend to move together. Macroeconomics seeks to explain this general trend in interest rates and rates of return on equity shares over time. That is why we can ignore some details of the differences among bonds and between bonds and equity shares and focus on a representative financial asset.

The representative financial asset of macroeconomic analysis has two important features. First, there is an inverse relationship between the price of a financial asset, such as a bond, and its interest rate. This relationship, examined in the next section, reflects the fact that the current price of the bond equals the present value of its future money payments. The second important feature of financial assets is that there is a distinction between the nominal, or money, interest rate and the real rate of interest.

Interest Rates and Bond Prices: The Concept of Present Value

If you follow the yields and prices on various financial assets in the financial section of the newspaper, you may discover what seem like conflicting reports. For example, you may read in the *Wall Street Journal* that on the same day bond prices have risen and interest rates have fallen. As we demonstrate in this section, the *Wall Street Journal* is merely reporting the same event, for there is an inverse relationship between a bond's price and its interest rate.

To understand this inverse relationship, consider a simple bond that makes a single payment one year from the date it is issued. Let's look again at our previous example of the $10,000 T-bill offered for sale on April 18, 1988 with an interest rate of 5.78 percent. As a one-year T-bill, it promises to pay the face value of $10,000 one year from today. But the $10,000 payment one year from today is not the T-bill's current price, for an individual would be unwilling to pay $10,000 today to receive $10,000 a year later. If individuals are unwilling to pay $10,000 today, how much will they pay today in order to receive in return $10,000 one year from today? That is, what is the "present value" of the $10,000 future payment?

The present value of a money payment, say $1, received one year from today is the amount that, if set aside today and allowed to earn interest, would grow to $1 in one year. Clearly, then, the present value (PV) of $1 one year from now depends upon the market interest rate (r). If the interest rate is 10 percent ($r = .10$), then 90.9 cents set aside today will yield $1 one year from now. That is because the 90.9 cents plus the interest earnings of 9.1 cents (90.9 × .10) sum to $1. If the interest rate is 12 percent ($r = .12$), then 89.3 cents will have to be set aside in order to have $1 one year from today [89.3 + .12(89.3) = $1].

In general, letting PV denote the amount of dollars that, if set aside today earning interest rate r, will grow to $1 in one year, PV is determined by the equation

$$PV + r \cdot PV = \$1 \text{ or } PV \cdot (1 + r) = \$1$$

Present value: The amount that one is willing to give up today in order to obtain a future sum.

PV is called the **present value** of a dollar received one year from today. We can simply rearrange the above equation to obtain the general expression for this present value of a future dollar:[4]

$$PV = \$1/(1 + r) \qquad\qquad (3.1)$$

Earlier we asked how much individuals are willing to pay for a $10,000 T-bill. When the market interest rate is 5.78 percent, the present value of $10,000 to be received in one year is $9,453.58, or $10,000/(1 + .0578). This present value of the T-bill's future money claim is exactly the current price of the T-bill. A higher interest rate would mean a lower T-bill price since less has to be set aside today in order to have $10,000 one year from today. For example, if the interest rate rose to 6.78, the price of the T-bill would drop to $9,365.05 or $10,000/(1 + .0678). The lower the interest rate, the greater the present value of the $10,000, and thus the higher the T-bill price. From this simple example, it is apparent that the interest rate and the current price of a bond are by necessity inversely related.

The example we have just worked through is an unusually simple one, for the T-bill we considered matured in one year and offered no coupon payments. However, the same principles apply if we consider a treasury bond that matures in ten years and makes coupon payments in the intervening years. For a treasury bond, the government agrees to pay the holder a specified amount of money each year until maturity, called the *coupon payment.* On maturity, the government makes a lump-sum payment that retires the bond. The general principle is that the price of a bond is the present value of future coupon and principal payments and that the bonds price and interest rate are inversely related.[5]

Perpetuity: A financial instrument that yields a perpetual stream of payments.

An interesting type of bond is a **perpetuity,** which is a financial instrument that yields a perpetual stream of coupon payments. If a perpetuity lasts for an infinite number of years, does that mean you would pay an infinite sum to have it? The answer, of course, is no. Suppose that you buy a financial asset that will pay you $100 per year in perpetuity. How much is it worth? The answer is simple. If we assume an interest rate of 10 percent, then someone with $1000 earning the market interest rate of 10 percent can get $100 per year forever without ever touching the principle. This is precisely what the previously described perpetuity would be worth. In general, the present value of a perpetuity that pays a coupon payment (C) in every subsequent period equals C/r, where r is the market rate of interest. Put differently, the present value of the perpetual stream of payments of amount

---

[4] In general, if a bond promises to pay X dollars after a period of n years, then its present value is given by $PV = X/(1 + r)^n$, where r denotes the constant market interest rate for the coming n periods.

[5] Similarly, the price of a stock equals the present value of expected future dividends. The appendix to this chapter provides a detailed exposition of the relationship between rates of return and prices for long-term bonds and for stocks.

C each period is C/r. In our example, where $C = \$100$ and $r = .10$ (or 10 percent), the present value of the perpetuity is $1,000 ($100/.10).

Interest Rates and Inflation: The Concept of the Real Interest Rate

Real rate of interest: The nominal or money rate of interest minus the rate of inflation.

The interest rates discussed above are what are often referred to as nominal or money interest rates because they indicate the rates of return of bonds in dollar terms. Yet the money interest rate measures neither the real cost to borrowers nor the real return to lenders. The real cost and return are measured by what economists call the **real rate of interest.** The real rate of interest can be approximated by the money interest rate minus the rate of inflation. The following discussion illustrates the importance of the real rate of interest to lenders and borrowers.

If you pay $100 today for a bond and receive $110 one year from now, then the nominal interest rate is 10 percent. If the inflation rate is 10 percent over the next year, however, the *ex post,* or after the fact, real rate of interest is zero. The $110 dollars received next year will purchase exactly what the initial $100 could purchase today. Thus borrowers pay back in real terms exactly what they borrowed and lenders receive a zero real return on their loans. On the other hand, if the rate of inflation were 6 percent, a nominal interest rate of 10 percent means a real interest rate of approximately 4 percent.

Figure 3.3 illustrates the difference between the nominal and actual real interest rate for 3-month treasury bills over the last 36 years. This actual real rate of interest is termed the *ex post* real rate of interest since it is the nominal interest rate minus the actual or *ex post* rate of inflation. Although the real rate of interest on treasury bills for this period has averaged 1 percent, it has ranged from a negative 3.9 percent during 1974 and 1979 to highs of over 5 percent in the early 1980s.

Expected real rate of interest: The nominal interest rate minus the expected rate of inflation.

When borrowers and lenders buy and sell bonds, they do not, of course, know for certain what the inflation rate will be during the time period to maturity of the loan. Consequently, both lenders and borrowers interpret the market interest rates in light of their expectations of future inflation. In other words, they have in mind an **expected real rate of interest** equal to the nominal interest rate minus the *expected* rate of inflation. This expected real rate of interest is referred to as the *ex ante* real rate of interest. If their anticipation of inflation turns out to be correct, then the expected (*ex ante*) real interest rate and actual (*ex post*) real interest rate will not differ. Since Figure 3.3 is based on actual inflation rates, it reports actual, not expected, real interest rates. As we will see later, however, firms' decisions with respect to investment and households' decisions with respect to saving depend on the expected real interest rate.

Figure 3.3   U.S. Real and Nominal Interest Rates

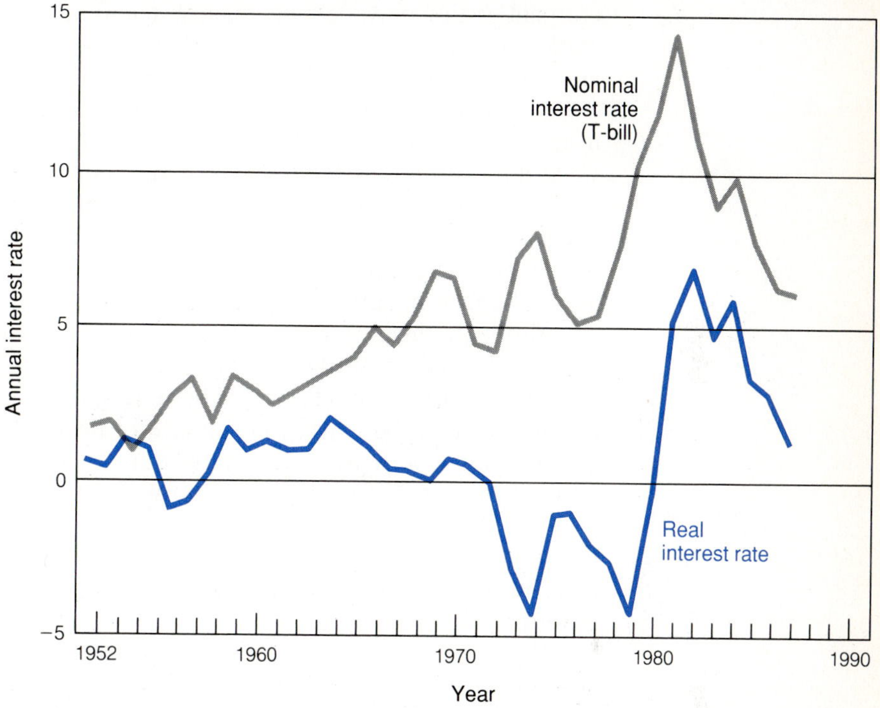

The real interest is the nominal interest rate minus the rate of the inflation during the year. The rate of inflation computed using the consumer price index.

Source: *Economic Report of the President* (1988).

Financial assets such as bonds and equity shares are traded in the financial markets. In the next section, we discuss primary and secondary markets, markets in which new debt issues and prior issues, respectively, are traded.

The Primary and Secondary Financial Markets: The Stock/Flow Distinction

The bulk of exchanges in the stock market are transfers of previously issued stocks, not new issues. Similarly, many exchanges in the bond market are transfers of previously issued bonds rather than sales of newly issued bonds. We distinguish conceptually between exchanges of previously issued stocks and bonds and exchanges of new issues in the following manner. Newly issued financial assets are said to be exchanged in the *primary financial market*.

For instance, when a firm issues bonds to finance the purchase of new machinery or plants, it enters the primary market. Similarly, when the government issues new debt to finance spending, it also enters the primary market. On the other hand, financial assets that have been previously issued are said to be traded in the *secondary financial market.*

By way of an example, on April 11, 1988 Gould's Pumps, Inc., announced in the *Wall Street Journal* that it would be selling 2.3 million new shares of stock during the remainder of 1988 at a price per share of $18.75. These new shares were sold in the primary financial market when issued in 1988. The shares of stock currently trade in the secondary financial market. Similarly, newly issued treasury bonds that were sold in the primary market in 1988 are exchanged in subsequent years in the secondary market.

Although there is a great deal of activity in the secondary financial market, the activity in the primary market is of crucial importance in macroeconomics because it reflects firm borrowing to finance new capital purchases and government borrowing in the face of deficits. Figure 3.4 indicates the real amount of new financial assets issued by firms and government in the primary market during the last 37 years. Note that the relative proportion of newly issued financial assets from government has grown substantially in the last ten years, reflecting large federal government deficits that more than offset recent surpluses (and debt retirements) of state and local governments.

The distinction between primary and secondary financial markets can be stated in another way. The primary financial market concerns flow variables. A variable is a **flow variable** if it is measured over a period of time. For example, the real dollar value of financial assets issued during a particular year in the primary market is a flow variable. We cannot measure this or any other flow variable without specifying a time period over which the flow is measured. Other important examples of flow variables are the real output produced in the economy over a year (real GNP) and the amount of capital equipment purchased by firms in a given year (real investment spending). On a personal note, the income the authors earn in a year is a flow variable.

In contrast to flow variables, there are **stock variables.** A stock variable is one that can be measured at a specific point in time. For example, at any point in time we can measure the real dollar value of financial assets previously issued. Other examples of stock variables are the amount of capital in the economy and the amount of money in the hands of households. In all these cases, the variable can be measured at a point in time. Like economists, accountants distinguish between stock variables and flow variables. When they report on the health of a firm, they offer both an income statement (which lists the flow of income and expenses over a given period of time) and a balance sheet (which lists the stock of assets and liabilities of the firm at a particular point in time).

Flow variable: A variable that is measured over a period of time.

Stock variable: A variable that is measured at a specific point in time.

Figure 3.4 New Issues of Financial Assets in the Primary Market

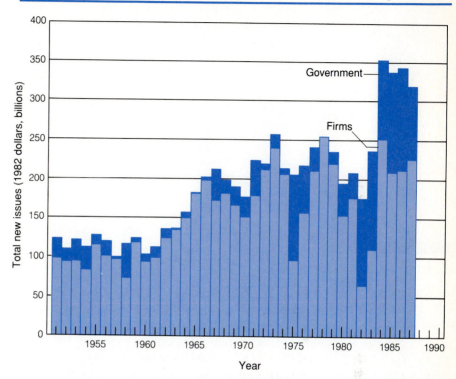

The figures for the government are the total of federal, state, and local governments in 1982 dollars (billions). For firms, as our discussion in Chapter 4 will show, our estimate of the new real amount of financial assets issued by firms relies on published figures on net real investment.

A flow of newly issued stocks and bonds are sold in the primary market each year. This flow adds to the stock of existing financial assets that are subsequently traded in the secondary market.

To the Point

THE VARIETY OF FINANCIAL INSTRUMENTS

- There are numerous financial instruments that fall into one of two categories: bonds and equity shares. These financial instruments vary by maturity, uncertainty of future payments, and the tax status of the return.

- Bonds are sold by firms and by the government, and they promise specified money payment(s) in the future. The buyers of bonds—households, depository institutions, and foreigners—are lenders in the financial market. Equity shares, commonly called stocks, are issued by firms and entitle the holder to a share of the earnings of the corporation.

- Macroeconomics simplifies the financial market by lumping together stocks and bonds in order to consider a single, representative financial asset. Two features common to all financial assets are the inverse relationship between the price of the financial asset and its interest rate and the distinction between the money interest rate and the real interest rate (the money interest rate minus the rate of inflation).

- Newly issued stocks and bonds are sold in the primary market. They represent borrowing by firms and government to finance investment and government spending, respectively. The stock of previously issued bonds and equity shares is exchanged in the secondary financial market.

3.3   MEASURING THE ACTIVITY IN THE FOREIGN EXCHANGE MARKETS

Foreign exchange rate: The price of one country's currency in terms of a second country's currency.

International trade has played an increasingly important role in the world economy in the last two decades. From 1972 to 1987, U.S. exports of goods and services more than doubled so that by 1987 exports equalled 11.1 percent of GNP. U.S. imports increased at a similar rate during the same period. The increased integration of the United States into the world economy has meant that changes in **foreign exchange rates** have a greater impact on the U.S. economy. A foreign exchange rate for the dollar is simply the price of the dollar in terms of a foreign currency. For example, in early 1987 the price of a U.S. dollar was .65 of a British pound, which is equal to 65 pence. One year later, in April 1988, the price of the dollar had fallen to 53 pence. A fall in this price, other things equal, means that U.S. goods become cheaper for foreigners to buy and foreign goods become more expensive for Americans to buy.

Recent U.S. experience provides dramatic evidence of the impact of a change in the foreign exchange rate. During the period from late 1980 to early 1985, the price of the dollar in terms of other currencies rose by over 60 percent. For U.S. companies selling abroad, this meant that even if they did not change the price of their product in domestic markets, the cost of their product to foreigners would have risen by over 60 percent. In the ensuing two years, the price of the dollar fell back by two thirds of the previous rise, to the relief of U.S. exporters (and the chagrin of U.S. importers).

Underlying these substantial fluctuations in foreign exchange rates are changes in the demand for and supply of dollars in the foreign exchange markets. In the next section, we will show how the balance of payments accounts link the demand and supply of dollars in the foreign exchange markets to exports, imports, and international capital flows. In addition, we will examine the recent changes in U.S. exports, imports, international capital flows, and foreign exchange rates.

The Balance of Payments Accounts

A U.S. car retailer who plans to buy a new Toyota for later resale in the United States is an example of someone who demands a foreign good but begins with dollars. An individual with U.S. dollars who decides to buy stocks and bonds in the West German financial markets is another example of an individual starting with dollars who seeks to purchase in a foreign market.

Of course, sellers of Toyotas and West German stocks and bonds seek payment in their own currencies. For sellers of Toyotas, this currency is the yen, while for sellers of West German financial assets, it is the mark. Thus demanders of Japanese and West German goods who begin with U.S. dollars must first exchange their dollars for yen and marks, respectively. Such individuals enter the foreign exchange market for the U.S. dollar as *suppliers of dollars*.

In contrast, there are individuals who demand U.S. goods but begin with foreign currency. The owner of a restaurant in West Germany who wants to purchase 300 pounds of prime Texas beef is one such individual. The Japanese investor who wants to purchase 1000 shares of IBM stock is another. Naturally, sellers of U.S. goods such as Texas beef and U.S. financial assets seek payment in U.S. dollars. Thus demanders of U.S. goods who begin with foreign currency must exchange their yen or marks for dollars. Such individuals enter the foreign exchange markets for the U.S. dollar as *demanders of dollars*.

The U.S. Department of Commerce keeps a record of the various sources of the demand for and supply of dollars in the foreign exchange markets. This record of international transactions is called the *balance of payments accounts*. Table 3.1 lists its major components. These transactions are categorized as either sources of the demand for or the supply of dollars in the foreign exchange market for the U.S. dollar.

The balance of payments accounts separate the sources of the demand for and supply of dollars in the foreign exchange markets into three categories. The first of these is the current account, which measures the amount of dollars exchanged in conjunction with the trade of goods and services between Americans and foreigners (U.S. exports and imports), the transfer of interest and dividend payments to U.S. holders of foreign assets and foreign holders of U.S. assets, and other transfer payments such as grants and gifts.

Balance of trade: The difference between exports and imports.

The net demand for dollars associated with the first component of the current account—exports and imports—is called the **balance of trade.** If the balance of trade is negative, as it was in 1987, then the United States is said to experience a balance of trade deficit. If it is positive, as was the

Table 3.1   **The U.S. Balance of Payments Accounts in 1987**

Demand for Dollars (in billions)		Supply of Dollars (in billions)		Net Demand for Dollars
Current Account				
(1) U.S. exports of goods and services	250.8	U.S. imports of goods and services	410.0	−159.2
(2) Transfers (interest and dividends to U.S. holders of foreign financial, government grants, and gifts)	169.3	Transfers (interest and dividends to foreign holders of U.S. financial assets, government grants, and gifts)	170.8	−1.5
Total (current account)	420.1		580.8	−160.7
Capital Account				
(3) Foreign purchases of U.S. financial assets (capital inflow)	155.1	U.S. purchases of foreign financial assets (capital outflow)	73.0	82.1
Total (current and capital account)				−78.6
Statistical discrepancy				21.9
Total (current and capital accounts and statistical discrepancy				−56.7
Official Reserve Transaction Balance				56.7

Source: Survey of Current Business, (March 1988) Table 1-2. Figures reported are preliminary estimates which are typically revised by the U.S. Department of Commerce over the year.

case for 106 consecutive years from the end of the Civil War to 1971 as well as through most of the 1970s, then a balance of trade surplus is said to exist. In contrast to this earlier period, the 1980s were a period when the United States typically had a balance of trade deficit. Not coincidentally, the trade surplus Japan and other countries experienced grew in the 1980s. For instance, Japan's trade surplus increased 2.1 billion dollars in 1980 to 92.8 billion dollars in 1986.

The second category of the demand for and supply of dollars in the balance of payments accounts is the capital account. The capital account measures the dollars exchanged when foreigners buy U.S. financial assets

International capital flows: The sale and purchase of financial assets among different countries.

Capital inflows: The purchase of U.S. financial assets by foreigners.

Capital outflows: The purchase of foreign financial assets by Americans.

and Americans buy foreign financial assets. These currency exchanges are called private **international capital flows.** Private international capital flows associated with the demand for dollars are referred to as U.S. **capital inflows,** since they reflect the inflow of foreign currency due to foreigners' purchases of U.S. financial assets. Private international capital flows associated with the supply of dollars are referred to as U.S. **capital outflows,** since they reflect the outflow of dollars due to U.S. purchases of foreign financial assets.

In measuring the exports, imports, and international capital flows, a number of items are often missed. For instance, the clandestine transfer of funds from the Philippines to a U.S. bank account would generate a demand for dollars. On the other side, secretive imports of heroin from Turkey results in a supply of dollars in international markets. The net of such unmeasured transactions are lumped under the heading of "Statistical discrepancy" in the balance of payments accounts.

Balance of payments: The difference between the private demand for and supply of dollars in the foreign exchange markets.

Summing the net demand (demand minus supply) for dollars associated with the capital and current accounts and adjusting for measurement errors (the discrepancy term) we obtain what is called the U.S. **balance of payments.** In 1987, the balance of payments was a negative 56.7 billion dollars. Such a negative balance of payments account is referred to as a balance of payments deficit. A positive balance of payments is called a balance of payments surplus.

When there is a surplus or deficit in the balance of payments accounts, then equality between the demand for and supply of dollars is brought about by an offsetting deficit or surplus on the official reserve transaction balance. The official reserve transaction balance reflects the intervention into the foreign exchange market by the U.S. Federal Reserve and/or foreign central banks. Since there was a balance of payments deficit in the U.S. in 1987, on net, central banks demanded 56.7 billion U.S. dollars in the foreign exchange markets. That is, in 1987 central banks on net exchanged other currencies for 56.7 billion U.S. dollars.

U.S. Trade, International Capital Flows and Foreign Exchange Rates

In the past several years, the United States has had a persistent balance of trade deficit, as the U.S. has imported more than it has exported. Offsetting the resulting deficit in the current account has been a large surplus in the capital account, as foreigners have flocked to the U.S. financial markets to take advantage of the high yields on relatively safe U.S. assets. These two events are related; the flocking of foreigners to the U.S. financial markets has led to a fleecing of U.S. exporters. As reported in the *Wall Street Journal*, the capital influx ". . . pushes up the exchange rate and costs Americans jobs in the foreign trade sector." In other words, as foreigners have increased their demand for dollars to purchase U.S. financial assets, they have pushed up the price of the dollar in foreign exchange markets. With a rising price of the dollar, U.S. goods have become more expensive for foreigners, resulting in a decline in their purchases of U.S. goods. At the same time, there has been a shift in U.S. purchases toward foreign goods as foreign goods have become relatively cheaper to U.S. citizens. Both changes have resulted in a fall in demand for U.S. goods.

This discussion highlights an important relationship between the current and capital accounts and the balance of payments. If the balance of payments equals zero, then a surplus in the current account, reflecting, say, a U.S. balance of trade surplus (U.S. exports are greater than U.S. imports), implies an offsetting deficit in the capital account (the capital outflow from the United States is greater than the capital inflow into the United States). In other words, the fact that Americans are selling more goods and services to foreigners than they are buying from foreigners means that foreigners are financing the difference by on net selling more financial assets to (or on net borrowing more from) the United States. On the other hand, a deficit in the current account, reflecting, say, a U.S. balance of trade deficit, must be offset by a surplus in the capital accounts. In this case, the excess in U.S. spending on imports over exports is financed by the United States on net borrowing from foreigners (the capital outflow from the United States is less than its capital inflow).

Figure 3.5 depicts the changes that occurred from 1960 to 1987 in the U.S. balance of trade and in total net capital inflows (private capital inflows minus outflows, plus net capital inflows reflecting changes in governments' reserve assets as summarized by the official reserve balance). As one would expect from our discussion of the balance of payments accounts, there is a strong inverse relationship between the balance of trade and total net capital inflows, sometimes referred to as net foreign investment.

While the recent large deficits on current account and large surpluses on capital account by the United States have received much attention, the tables were turned in the early 1960s. The United States then had a trade surplus, and the concern was over potentially large capital outflows. To avoid a flow of U.S. capital abroad, an interest equalization tax was initiated in 1963. When U.S. citizens tried to take advantage of higher interest rates abroad by purchasing foreign financial assets, they were taxed at a rate equal to the interest differential between foreign and domestic financial assets. With the onset of the 1980s, imports grew dramatically relative to exports. As Figure 3.5 indicates, the result was a steep rise in net capital inflows. At this time, some called for exactly the opposite of the 1963 remedy, to wit, a Reverse Interest Equalization Tax.

Coincident with the large U.S. net capital inflows of the early 1980s was a substantial rise in the price of a dollar in terms of foreign currency. Figure 3.6 indicates the pattern of the exchange rate for the dollar in the last 15 years. As previously indicated, the dollar rose dramatically between 1980 and early 1985, leading to a significant upheaval among U.S. man-

Figure 3.5   **U.S. Balance of Trade and Total Net Capital Inflows**

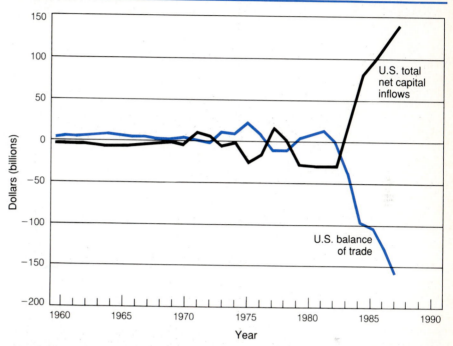

In concept, the balance of trade equals exports minus imports as reported in the GNP accounts. However the series differ due to the different way certain items are handled in the balance of payments accounts. Total net capital inflows equal private capital inflows minus outflows plus the official reserve balance, which reflects the net capital inflows associated with changes in the U.S. and foreign governments' official reserves.

Source: Economic Report of the President (1988), Table B-102.

ufacturers exporting to other countries. After that time, the foreign exchange rate for the dollar fell, and by 1988 there were signs of a lessening of the balance of trade deficit.

To the Point

THE FOREIGN EXCHANGE MARKETS

- A foreign exchange rate for the dollar is simply the price of the dollar in terms of a foreign currency.

- U.S. exports and foreign purchases of U.S. financial assets constitute the

Figure 3.6   U.S. Exchange Rate

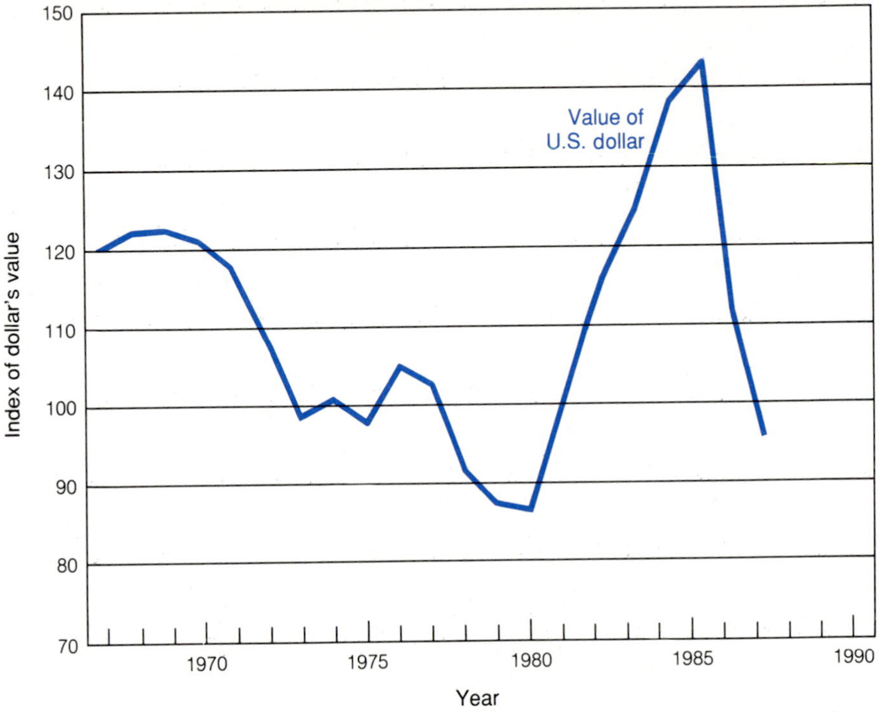

The exchange rate for the dollar is the multilateral trade-weighted value of the U.S. dollar, with the base period being March 1973 (i.e., March 1973 = 100).

Source: *Economic Report of the President* (1987), Table B-108.

demand for dollars in the foreign exchange market. U.S. imports and U.S. purchases of foreign financial assets are behind the supply of dollars.

- The difference between U.S. exports and U.S. imports is called the U.S. balance of trade. The balance of payments also takes into account the difference between U.S. capital inflows and outflows. The balance of payments is the net demand (demand minus supply) for dollars associated with the capital and current accounts in the international accounts.

3.4   THE MONEY SUPPLY

Money: A medium of exchange, a store of value, and a unit of account.

So far, we have examined measures of the activity in the output, labor, financial, and foreign exchange markets. A critical common feature of all these markets is that all involve the exchange of **money.** Before we begin our study of the macroeconomy, there are some crucial questions that must be answered. What are the characteristics of money? What are the various measures of money? How have these measures of money changed over time?

In this section, we will begin by discussing the properties of money, for money is defined by its properties, not by how it looks or tastes. We will then look at what serves as money in the U.S. economy and review how the various measures of money have changed.

Money as a Medium of Exchange

Throughout history, numerous artifacts have served as money. Examples include rice in Japan, beaver pelts in Canada, tobacco in the southern American colonies, goats in British Africa, cigarettes in the prisoner of war camps of World War II, and butter in fourteenth-century Norway. For nearly 2000 years, inhabitants of the Yap Islands close to the Philippines have used 6600 large stone wheels as money. What do these various goods all have in common? They each serve as a medium of exchange.

A medium of exchange facilitates trade. Without such a medium, all trades would have to take the form of barter. In a barter economy, if you want your car fixed and have a spare watch, you have to find a car mechanic who wants a watch. In other words, in a barter economy exchange requires a "double coincidence of wants." In an economy with a medium of exchange, however, you can sell your watch to any taker for "money" and then use the money to purchase repairs for your car. Societies adopt money because it reduces the cost of making exchanges.[6]

Money has two other characteristics that stem naturally from its role as a medium of exchange. First, money is a unit of account. That is, since money is involved in every exchange, prices are typically quoted in money terms.[7] Second, money is a store of value. If individuals do not have confidence in the future purchasing power of a good, then it will not be used as a medium of exchange. For instance, in cases of extreme inflation, called hyperinflation, currency no longer becomes a store of value and exchanges often revert to barter.

At the end of World War I, as we previously mentioned, inflation in Germany reached incredible proportions. During this period, prices were constantly increasing. Goods that could be purchased for one German mark in August 1922 had a price of 10.2 billion marks in November 1923. People often burned German marks in fires for warmth since the currency had more value in Btu's than as a medium of exchange. Perhaps the most interesting feature of such periods of hyperinflation is not that individuals finally stop

---

[6] An interesting article by Robert Jones, "The Origin and Development of the Media of Exchange," *Journal of Political Economy* 84 (August 1976): pp. 757–776, discusses the role of money in reducing the costs of exchange.

[7] One rare exception has been the guinea as a unit of account in present-day England. See Don Patinkin, *Money, Interest, and Prices* (New York: Harper and Row, 1965).

accepting currency as money but that they continue to use currency as money for such a long time. This suggests the substantial gains to using a medium of exchange rather than resorting to a system of barter.

With our understanding of the properties of money, let us turn to the question of what is counted as money in the United States. What simultaneously fulfills the roles of medium of exchange, unit of account, and a store of value in the present day U.S. economy?

Measures of the Money Supply

M1: A measure of the money supply, consisting of currency, travelers checks, and checkable deposits held by the nonbank public.

Assets that can be *directly* used to purchase goods and services comprise the money supply measure denoted **M1.** Specifically, M1 consists of coins, currency, travelers checks, and checkable deposits held by the nonbank public. Checkable deposits include checking accounts, or "demand deposits," at commercial banks. The term "demand deposits" signifies that such deposits are payable upon demand.

Until 1980, M1 consisted only of currency and checking accounts at commercial banks. On March 31, 1980, the Depository Institutions Deregulation and Monetary Control Act was signed into law. One of the key provisions of the act was to authorize nationwide the offering of "checkable" deposits at depository institutions other than commercial banks. Thus since 1980 the M1 measure of money has included such checkable deposits as negotiable order of withdrawal (NOW) accounts, share draft accounts at credit unions, and automatic transfer of savings accounts (ATS).[8] Each of these new types of accounts, like demand deposits at commercial banks, serve as media of exchange.

M1 may be thought of as a "transactional" measure of money since it includes only assets that can be directly used as media of exchange in transactions. **M2** provides a broader measure of the money supply. M2 includes all assets included in M1 plus all assets that can be quickly converted into a medium of exchange at little or no cost. Such assets are said to be *highly liquid,* and include noncheckable savings accounts at depository institutions, small time deposits (less than $100,000), money market deposit accounts, and money market mutual funds.[9] Table 3.2 lists recent levels of M1 and M2. Note that less than one fourth of M2 are direct media of

M2: A measure of the money supply, consisting of all assets included in M1 plus all assets that can be quickly converted into a medium of exchange.

---

[8] Some NOW accounts existed before 1980, primarily in New England, but they were not included in the measure of the money supply known as M1.

[9] Time deposits are certificates of deposit that impose penalties if the deposit is withdrawn prior to some specified period of time. Note that money market mutual fund accounts (accounts at brokerage houses) and money market deposit accounts (accounts at banks) have an element of checkability. These are not counted in the M1 measure of the money supply, however, since there are typically restrictions on such things as the number of checks that can be written and the minimum size of a check.

Table 3.2 **Money Supply Measures**
            (as of January 1988, in billions)

Currency in hands of the nonbank public	197.1	
Traveler's checks	6.6	
Demand deposits	295.8	
Other checkable deposits	265.3	
M1	764.8	
M1		764.8
Money market deposits (at commercial and thrift institutions)		524.1
Savings deposits		411.2
Small time deposits		929.8
Money market mutual funds and other components		307.4
M2		2,937.3

Source: Federal Reserve Bulletin (April, 1988). Figures are not seasonally adjusted.

exchange (counted in M1). The other three fourths are often termed near money, with the largest single component being small time deposits.[10]

Corresponding to each of the components of the money supply are financial asset holdings of either private depository institutions or the Federal Reserve, the central bank of the United States. The next chapter explains this relationship between the money supply and the holdings of financial assets by depository institutions. This link is important because changes in the money supply mirror equivalent changes in the financial asset purchases of depository institutions.

A Comparison of Money Measures

The distinction between the M1 and M2 measures of the quantity of money has been blurred by the Monetary Decontrol Act of 1980. The act opened the door for a type of account that had already been creeping through the transom since the late 1970s—an interest-bearing checkable account. It would really be more correct to say reopened the door since this type of account had been in existence prior to the mid-1930s.[11] From that time until the late 1970s, there was a clear distinction between the two measures of the money supply. The old M1 included only noninterest-bearing demand

---

[10] Overnight repurchase agreements at commercial banks and overnight Eurodollars at Caribbean branches are also included as part of M2.

[11] Interest payments on demand deposits were outlawed in the 1930s in the face of lobbying by bankers' associations that claimed that allowing interest payments on demand deposits was not in the public interest since it led to "unsound, ruinous competition."

Figure 3.7   **Money Supply Measures over Time**

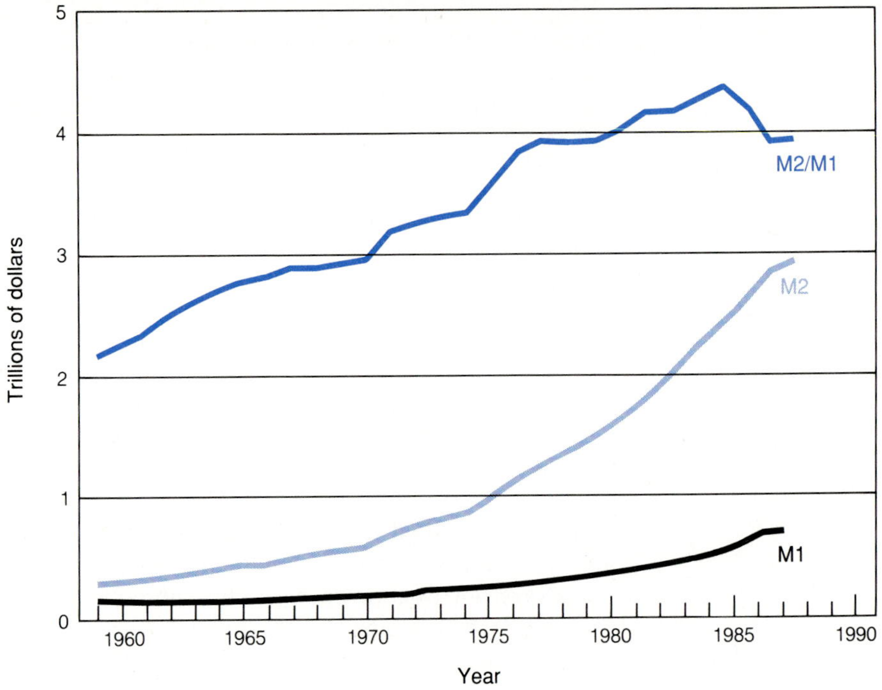

As the graph suggests, M2 has grown more rapidly than M1 in the last 30 years so that the ratio M2/M1 has risen from slightly over 2 in 1960 to nearly 4 in the late 1980s.

Source: *Economic Report of the President* (1988), Table B-67.

deposits at commercial banks. The old M2 was M1 plus time and saving deposits that were not checkable.

The distinction that remains between the two measures of money is that M1, unlike M2, involves solely transactional assets. But not everyone is in agreement that this distinction is relevant. Some in fact have argued that a better criterion for selecting a measure of money is the ability of that measure to predict economic activity.[12] If M1 and M2 moved in concert, the debate about the appropriate measure of the money supply would not be important. However, coincident movements are not always the case. Figure 3.7 illustrates the paths of M1 and M2 over the last 30 years. A recent development was a sudden increase in M1 relative to M2. During 1986, for example, M1 grew

---

[12] Nobel laureate economist Milton Friedman is one of the foremost advocates of this view.

by some 17 percent while M2 rose by less than 10 percent. This raises some potentially serious policy questions for the Federal Reserve, the governmental body that controls the money supply.[13] Which measure of money should the Federal Reserve have been controlling? Should they have looked at M1, concluded that money was growing at too rapid a rate, and choked off the rate of growth of the money supply? Or should the Federal Reserve have taken M2 as the barometer of economic activity and not acted so severely? As we will discuss later, answers to such questions are not always clear-cut.

To the Point

MONEY SUPPLY MEASURES

- Money is a medium of exchange, a unit of account, and a store of value.
- There are two basic measures of the money supply: M1, which is a transactional measure that includes only coin, currency, traveler's checks, and checkable deposits; and M2, which is comprised of M1 plus other highly liquid assets.

SUMMARY

Firms, governments, and households enter into the financial markets when they supply financial assets: firms to finance new investment, government to pay off a deficit, and households to purchase consumer goods. Households, foreigners, and depository institutions are the key buyers of financial assets. Government issues bonds such as T-bills, treasury notes, treasury bonds, and municipal bonds. Firms issue not only bonds, such as commercial paper and corporate bonds, but also stocks. Those households taking out loans from banks are also issuing financial assets. Bonds can differ according to maturity (for example, a one-year T-bill versus a 20-year treasury bond), risk of default (a riskless T-bill versus riskier commercial paper), and tax status (for example, municipal bonds with tax-free interest income versus corporate bonds with taxable interest income).

In macroeconomics, we typically simplify our analysis of financial markets by lumping debt instruments such as stocks and bonds together into the category "financial assets" and view these financial assets as traded in a single financial market. Common to financial assets is an inverse relationship between their price and the interest rate and a yield in nominal terms that

---

[13] Chapter 4 discusses in more detail the nature of the Federal Reserve and how it implements changes in the money supply.

is converted to a real interest rate by subtracting the rate of inflation. The single financial market of macroeconomics can be subdivided into primary and secondary financial markets. When firms issue stocks and bonds to finance investment and the government issues bonds to finance spending, these bonds are initially sold in the primary market. The primary market involves the exchange of this flow of new financial assets. The flow adds to the stock of existing financial assets that are traded in the secondary financial market.

In the last two to three decades, the world's economy has become increasingly integrated. The U.S. economy has seen a rapid growth in both exports and imports. This trend has accentuated the importance of foreign trade and foreign exchange rates. A foreign exchange rate is the price of one country's currency in terms of another country's currency. As we will see in Chapter 7, the foreign exchange rate of, say, the dollar, is determined by the interaction of the demand for and supply of dollars in the foreign exchange market. U.S. exports and capital inflows (foreigners' purchases of U.S. financial assets) result in a demand for dollars in the foreign exchange market. U.S. imports and capital outflows (U.S. purchases of foreign financial assets) result in a supply of dollars to the foreign exchange market. If the balance of payments is zero, then a balance of trade surplus (exports greater than imports) corresponds to a deficit in the capital account (capital outflow greater than inflow). Similarly, a current account deficit reflecting a balance of trade deficit (exports less than imports) indicates a surplus in the capital account (capital outflow less than inflow).

Money serves as a medium of exchange and thus facilitates trade. Two other characteristics of money stem naturally from its role as a medium of exchange: It is a unit of account and a store of value. There are two major measures of the money supply. The narrower measure is M1. It includes coins, currency, travelers checks, and all checkable deposits. These assets are all readily accepted as media of exchange. M2 is a broader measure of the money supply and includes all the components of M1 plus other highly liquid assets such as money market funds and savings accounts.

LOOKING AHEAD

In measuring the activity of an economy, we have looked at variables associated with each of the four types of markets that are critical to macroeconomic analysis. With respect to the output markets, we have examined real GNP and various price indexes; for the labor market, we have reviewed the measures of employment, work hours, unemployment, labor force participation, and real wages; for the financial market, the important indicators of activity discussed were interest rates, the quantities of newly issued stocks and bonds;

for the foreign exchange markets, the key variables were exchange rates, exports, imports, and international capital flows. Finally, we have considered two measures of the money supply: M1 and M2.

In the chapters that follow, we develop a macroeconomic model that will explain past variations in these critical measures of an economy's performance. Equally important is the development of an analytical framework that will enable us to understand the forces leading to future changes in variables such as GNP, interest rates, prices, foreign exchange rates, and the unemployment rate. We begin this task in the next chapter by looking at some elements common to macroeconomic models.

KEY TERMS

Interest Rate, 54
Term structure of interest rates, 57
Financial asset, 61
Present value, 62
Perpetuity, 63
Real rate of interest, 64
Expected real rate of interest, 64
Flow variable, 66
Stock variable, 66

Foreign exchange rate, 68
Balance of trade, 69
International capital flows, 71
Capital inflow, 71
Capital outflow, 71
Balance of payments, 71
Money, 74
M1, 76
M2, 76

REVIEW QUESTIONS

1. Which of the following represent stocks and which represent flows:
   a. IBM's computer sales this year
   b. Gross National Product
   c. The value of all capital in the United States
   d. The output of rice produced in China in 1986
   e. Larry Bird's field-goal percentage
   f. The national debt
   g. A government deficit

2. On January 1, a T-bill is issued with a $10,000 face value. The T-bill matures on December 31 of that year, at which time the $10,000 will be paid.
   a. If the interest rate is 10.4 percent, what is the price of the T-bill on January 1?

b. If the interest rate is 12 percent, what is the price of the T-bill?

c. If individuals expect a 7 percent rate of inflation between January 1 to December 31, what will be the expected real rate of interest if the money interest rate is 10.4 percent?

d. If the CPI is 140 on January 1 and 150 on December 31, what is the actual real rate of interest?

3. Beaver Manufacturing issued a one year zero coupon bond with a promised payment at the end of the year of $10 to finance its entry into a new line of business, making cleavers.

a. What would be a good name for this business?

b. If bonds of the same maturity and risk (Graded Aaa by Moody's) are currently paying a 12 percent interest rate, what will individuals pay for Beaver bonds?

c. Suppose that Beaver announces that Eddie Haskel will be the new president of the corporation. Reflecting on Eddie's high school record, Moody's decides to downgrade Beaver bonds to C. What will happen to the price individuals are willing to pay for the same bond that promises a payment of $10?

4. What considerations account for the fact that interest rates differ greatly on various types of financial assets? Use these considerations to predict how interest rates will vary in each of the following situations.

a. A long-term $1000 government bond versus a $1000 pawnshop loan.

b. A Federal Housing Association (FHA) mortgage loan of $67,000 versus a $67,000 loan from the E-Z Credit Company.

5. Suppose that the interest rate has risen from 8 percent to 10 percent over a three-year period. During that time, expected inflation has risen from 3 percent to 6 percent. What has happened to the real interest rate over time?

6. When Stephanie decides to forego present consumption for future consumption, she has the choice of putting her money into either an equity share or a bond. We would expect that if the equity share pays a higher expected rate of return than the bond initially, then investors like Stephanie will switch their funds from bonds to equity shares. This would bid up the price of an equity share until the dividend that is paid on the equity share would translate into a rate of return that is equal to that on a bond. Yet we observe a long-term higher yield on equity shares than on bonds. Can you explain this phenomenon?

7. Are sales of stocks on the New York Stock Exchange recorded in GNP? Does it make any difference whether or not you look at stocks issued in the primary or secondary market?

8. A bond is issued that pays a fixed coupon payment. If, after the bond is issued, the interest rate that is paid on a comparable, newly issued bond rises, what will happen to the price of the previously issued bond in the primary market? In the secondary market?

9. We have stated that money has value only in exchange. If that is the case, why did Germans burn money during the hyperinflation of the 1920s?

10. Suppose that a group of people switch their deposits from checking accounts at commercial banks to checking accounts at their local savings and loan.

   a. Does that have any effect on M1? On M2?

   b. Suppose that they switch their deposits from their local savings and loan to a money market fund. Does that have any effect on M1 and M2?

11. Which of the following serve as money in the U.S. economy?

   a. Deposits at savings and loan institutions

   b. Large certificates of deposit at commercial banks

   c. American Express traveler's checks that Karl Malden has convinced you to leave in a drawer at home for over two years

   d. Japanese yen

   e. Canadian dollars

   f. Mastercards

12. For more than 100 years following the Civil War, the United States ran balance of trade surpluses. What does this necessarily imply about the capital account in the absence of central bank intervention?

13. Suppose that the United States runs a balance of trade deficit simultaneously with a zero net private capital inflow. If the central bank of the United States intervenes to offset the resulting balance of payments (deficit, surplus), what will it have to do?

14. Tom Traynor is considering the purchase of an apartment building. He discounts the future flow of profits from owning that apartment building at the current market rate and calculates that the present value of the stream of future profits is $195,000. Tom Faith, the owner of the building, is asking $200,000 and buyer and seller have reached an impasse. The next week the market interest rate falls and the buyer decides to pay the owner's asking price. Is this because the future stream of payments has changed or because the present value of the future stream has changed? What does this tell you about present value and interest rates?

15. On December 29, 1987, Mexico proposed a solution to its current "debt crisis." As described by Wendell Wilkie Gunn in *The Wall Street Journal*

(January 14, 1988), Mexico asked the banks to whom it owes money to forgive $4 billion of the $14 billion that is currently due and to extend the maturity on the remaining $10 billion by 20 years. In return, Mexico offered to provide collateral for the $10 billion loan extension by using $2 billion of its foreign currency reserves to buy U.S. treasury bonds that mature in 20 years, paying $10 billion upon maturity. Since the bonds pay $10 billion at the same time that the principal on Mexico's $10 billion loan is due, the bonds are touted as an effective U.S. government guarantee of the loan principal. Much of the news media and some in the financial community have hailed the proposal as "innovative."

a.   What are banks getting in return for forgiving the $4 billion debt and extending the maturity on the remaining debt? Use the concept of present value to determine your answer.

b.   Is Mexico able to provide collateral for all of its $10 billion debt through the "magic of compound interest" as suggested by the *Washington Post*? What is the present value of the collateral provided by Mexico?

Rates of Return on Long-term Bonds and Equity Shares

In the text we considered the relationship between the interest rate and the price of a bond for a simple bond with a one year maturity. In this appendix, we will show how the rate of return would be calculated for a multi-year bond and an equity share. If someone buys a long-term bond when it is issued, holds it for only one year, and then sells the bond in the financial market, what is the return? The first-year return to the buyer of the bond has two parts—the coupon payment and an appreciation or depreciation in the price of the bond.

More precisely, the expected dollar payment one year from now to buying the bond and holding it for one year (R_b) is the sum of the future coupon payment (C) and the price the bond is expected to sell for next year (P_b^e). Subtracting the current price from this expected future dollar payment defines the expected dollar return to holding the bond for one year. Dividing this future dollar return by the current price, we obtain the bond's expected rate of return. That is, the expected rate of return for this long-term treasury bond (r_b) is given by

$$r_b = \frac{R_b - P_b}{P_b} = \frac{C + P_b^e - P_b}{P_b} \tag{A3.1}$$

Note that the future dollar return to holding the bond is the sum of the coupon payment (C) plus the expected appreciation (if $P_b^e - P_b > 0$) or depreciation (if $P_b^e - P_b < 0$) in the price of the bond.

Equation (A3.1) summarizes the relationship between a long-term bond's current price (P_b) and its expected rate of return (r_b). If we hold constant the expected future price of the bond, an increase in the interest rate is associated with a reduction in the current price of a bond. To show this explicitly, let's rearrange the expression for the expected rate of return. First, adding one to both sides, we obtain

$$1 + r_b = \frac{R_b}{P_b} = \frac{C + P_b^e}{P_b}$$

where r_b is the expected rate of return, C is the future coupon payment, P_b^e is the expected future price of the bond, and P_b is the current market price of the bond. Solving for P_b, we obtain the expression for the current price of the bond:

$$P_b = \frac{C + P_b^e}{1 + r_b} = \frac{R_b}{1 + r_b} \tag{A3.2}$$

The above expression simply states that the current price of a bond equals the present value of its future expected dollar payment. This is the same conclusion that we arrived at in our discussion of the T-bill, which was a one-year zero-coupon bond. The only difference here is that a longer-term bond's future dollar return incorporates a coupon payment as well as the bond's expected future price. As before, there is an inverse relationship between the bond's market interest rate and its current price.

Equity Shares as Financial Assets

The rate of return on equity shares is computed in a fashion similar to that for long-term bonds. In particular, let P_s denote the current price of a stock, let D denote the dividend payment that a purchaser of the stock expects to receive next period, and let P_s^e denote the price the purchaser expects the stock to sell for one period from now.[14] The purchaser's expected dollar payment one period hence (R_s) is the sum of future dividends (D) plus the expected price of the stock next period. Subtracting from this the current price of the stock, we obtain the expected dollar return to buying the stock and holding it for one period:

$$R_s - P_s = D + P_s^e - P_s$$

The purchaser's expected rate of return on an equity share is equal to the ratio of the expected dollar return ($R_s - P_s$) to the current price of the equity share (P_s). That is, the expected rate of return on equity (r_s) is

$$r_s = \frac{R_s - P_s}{P_s} = \frac{D + P_s^e - P_s}{P_s} \tag{A3.3}$$

Note that the expected return to holding an equity share depends not only on dividend payments but also on the expected appreciation ($P_s^e - P_s > 0$) or depreciation ($P_s^e - P_s < 0$) in the price of the stock.

Equation (A3.3) summarizes the relationship between an equity share's current price (P_s) and its expected rate of return (r_s). If the expected dividend payment and expected future price of the stock are held constant, then a lower current price of the stock implies a higher expected rate of return on the equity share. Note that this result is analogous to that concerning the inverse relationship between the rate of return on a bond and the bond's current price.

---

[14] The expected price of equity one period from now depends on the dividends that are expected to be received in all future periods other than the next.

Chapter 4

Macroeconomic Modeling: Markets, Participants, and Constraints

O UR major objective in this book is to understand the determinants of changes in the overall level of activity in the economy. It is not an easy task to determine why the levels of aggregate output, employment, prices, interest rates, and foreign exchange rates vary over time. One reason for this is that there are some important disagreements among macroeconomists with respect to how the economy responds to such changes as an increase in government spending or a rise in the money supply. A variety of macroeconomic models are developed in later chapters to highlight the diverse views of how the economy operates. An important result of studying these various models is that we gain an understanding of what underlies the different views concerning the impact of government policies on the economy.

In this chapter, however, we begin our task of modeling the economy not by emphasizing the differences between macroeconomic models but by identifying the elements that they all have in common. We have already noted one similarity between various macroeconomic models—that they simplify the economy by grouping markets into four broad categories (the output, financial, labor, and foreign exchange markets) and by grouping the participants in these markets into five categories (households, firms, government, depository institutions, and foreigners). The first part of this chapter outlines this stylized view of how the economy works and, in the process, identifies the activity of the five participants in the various markets.

**Partial equilibrium
analysis:** This analysis focuses on a single market
and does not fully con-
sider the implications for
other markets.

**General equilibrium
analysis:** This analysis
considers the interaction
of supply and demand
across all markets in the
economy.

A second similarity between macroeconomic models is their emphasis
on the interdependencies of markets. Macroeconomics recognizes that events
in one market imply changes in other markets as well. This contrasts with
microeconomics, which is less concerned with how changes in one market
affect other markets. For instance, if consumers decrease their demand for
cars, microeconomics would typically focus on the effect in the automobile
market without fully considering the implications for other markets. This is
referred to as **partial equilibrium analysis.** In contrast, macroeconomics
carries on what economists call a **general equilibrium analysis.** Suppose
that the fall in the demand for cars reflects a shift by households to increased
saving in the form of financial assets. Macroeconomics analyzes not only
the fall in the demand for cars in the output market but also the increase
in the demand for stocks and bonds in the financial market. The sources of
such links across markets, which are so important in macroeconomic analysis,
are the spending "constraints" faced by the participants in the various markets.

Our discussion of spending constraints begins with firms. The fact that
firms' purchases of capital goods in the output markets are constrained by
the amount of funds they can borrow in the financial markets to finance
these purchases provides one link between the output and the financial
markets. A second link between these two markets arises when we consider
the budget constraint faced by households.

Depository institutions also face a very important constraint that links
changes in monetary policy to the financial market. Developing this constraint
requires understanding the balance sheets of the Federal Reserve and private
depository institutions. Our discussion of constraints concludes with a look
at the fiscal constraint faced by government. This constraint highlights the
fact that government spending on output is limited by the funds raised by
taxes and by borrowing in the financial markets.

The constraints facing firms, households, depository institutions, and the
fiscal side of government can be summed to obtain the aggregate budget
constraint that further illustrates the interdependencies across markets so
essential to macroeconomics. In the final part of this chapter, we obtain the
aggregate budget constraint for the closed economy as well as for an open
economy, which includes a foreign sector.

4.1 A STYLIZED VIEW OF HOW THE
ECONOMY OPERATES

There are literally thousands of markets in the economy. Since we would
be hard pressed to keep track of so many individual markets in modeling
the economy, macroeconomic models simplify by reducing the number of

markets considered to four key types of markets: output, financial, labor, and foreign exchange.

Not only are there thousands of distinct markets in a modern economy, but there are also literally millions of participants in these various markets. To grasp the implications of the diverse behavior of so many individuals, macroeconomic models simplify further by categorizing participants in the economy's markets as members of one of five broad groups of participants: firms, households, governments, depository institutions, and foreigners.

The Participants and the Markets

The five types of economic participants are distinguished by the roles they play in the various markets in the economy. Each group enters certain markets as purchasers (demanders) and other markets as sellers (suppliers). Table 4.1 lists the demanders and the suppliers in each of the four markets as well as the aggregate variables that measure the activity in the various markets.

According to Table 4.1, the five participants in the economy can be described as follows:

1. **Firms** demand labor services when they hire workers, supply output when they sell the goods and services they produce, demand output when they purchase capital goods such as machinery and plants, and supply financial assets when they issue stocks and bonds to raise funds to finance their capital purchases. As Table 4.1 indicates, firms are the only buyers or demanders in the labor market and the sole suppliers in the output market, while they are one of several demanders of goods in the output market and one of several suppliers of stocks and bonds in the financial markets.[1] When firms supply new stocks and bonds, they act as borrowers and, hence, demanders of loanable funds in the financial market.

2. **Households** supply labor services and demand output when they purchase durable and nondurable consumption goods. As Table 4.1 indicates, households are the sole suppliers in the labor market but one of several demanders in the output and financial markets. When households demand new stocks and bonds, they act as lenders and, hence, suppliers of loanable funds in the financial market. When purchasing foreign goods and foreign financial assets, households supply dollars (in return for foreign currencies) in the foreign exchange markets.

   It may surprise you that Table 4.1 does not list households as suppliers of financial assets since we pointed out in Chapter 3 that some households

---

[1] To simplify macroeconomic analysis, government is viewed as a purchaser of final output produced by firms. Government employees can be viewed as being employed by "firms" who then sell their output to the government.

Table 4.1   Participants in the Markets of an Economy

	Demanders	Suppliers	Key macroeconomic variables
Output markets	Firms Households Government Foreigners	Firms	Real output Output prices
Labor markets	Firms	Households	Employment Unemployment Wages
Financial markets	Depository institutions Households Foreigners (lenders)	Firms Government (borrowers)	New issues of financial assets Interest rates
Foreign exchange market (dollars)	Foreigners	Households Depository institutions	Trade Foreign exchange rates

do issue financial assets when they borrow to finance their consumption expenditures. However, taken as a group, households historically have been net demanders of financial assets. That is, total lending of households exceeds total borrowing, so that households are net lenders. This net position of households in the financial market is the one depicted in Table 4.1, with households appearing only as demanders of financial assets.

3. *Government* demands output when it purchases goods and services and supplies financial assets when it issues bonds to finance deficits. Government also taxes households and firms and makes social security, unemployment insurance, and other transfer payments to households. As seen in Table 4.1, the government joins firms as suppliers of financial assets in the financial market and joins households, firms, and foreigners as demanders in the output market. Like firms, when the government supplies new bonds, it acts as a borrower and, hence, a demander of loanable funds in the financial market.

4. *Depository institutions* demand financial assets when they purchase bonds from (make loans to) households, firms, government, and foreigners. As we will discuss in some detail later in this chapter, the category depository institutions encompasses not only private depository institutions such as commercial banks and savings and loan associations but also the Federal Reserve. When depository institutions demand financial assets, they, like

households, act as lenders and, hence, suppliers of loanable funds in the financial market. When purchasing foreign securities, depository institutions supply dollars (in exchange for foreign currencies) in the foreign exchange markets.

When we talk about "depository institutions," we focus on the role of the Federal Reserve and private depository institutions as creators of checkable deposits. We ignore those activities of private depository institutions that solely reflect their role as financial intermediaries. In fact, much of the activity of private depository institutions falls under the heading of financial intermediation, in which these institutions purchase financial assets and then repackage them for households in the form of savings deposits, time deposits, and certificates of deposit. In this role, depository institutions will be lumped together with other financial intermediaries as facilitators of household saving in the form of financial assets.

5. *Foreigners* demand output when they buy our goods and services and demand financial assets when they buy our bonds and stocks. To finance these purchases, foreigners supply foreign currency and thus demand dollars in the foreign exchange markets.

The Workings of the Economy

How do the five types of participants in the economy interact in the four markets to determine the key macroeconomic variables? A complete answer to this question must await further developments in later chapters. However at this point we can begin to tackle this question by considering a stylized view of how markets work. To keep things simple, let's look at an economy that is not open to international trade—in the jargon of macroeconomics, a "closed" economy.

In the stylized view of the economy taken by macroeconomic models, firms and households meet in the labor market to exchange labor services at the start of each period. At that time, wages and employment are determined. During the subsequent period, firms combine the labor hired with their capital stock (machines, plants, etc.) to produce goods. At the end of this period of production, the goods produced are offered for sale in the output market to households (for consumption), firms (for investment), and the government (for the good of all).[2] At that time, firms pay wages, interest payments, and dividends to households.

An important result emerges from the fact that production takes time. When firms decide on how much labor to hire and commit to wage payments and production plans at the start of the period, they must estimate the prices

---

[2] Recall that we are looking at a closed economy, so that the demand for output by foreigners (for export) is not considered.

at which they will be able to sell their output at the end of the period. Or, if output prices are predetermined at the start of the period, firms must estimate how much output they will be able to sell at the end of the period at these fixed prices. In other words, a firm's decision concerning employment at the start of the period, and the resulting output produced during the period, is based upon either its *expectations of future prices*, or, if prices are fixed, upon *expectations of the future demand* for its products. As a consequence, forecasting errors by firms concerning the level of output prices or the adequacy of demand will have important effects on labor demand and output.

Like firms, when households decide on how much labor to supply they must also base their decisions on their predictions or expectations of the level of output prices that will prevail at the end of the period when wages are paid. As we discussed in Chapter 3, workers are concerned not so much with money wages but rather with the real purchasing power of their wages, which depends on the level of output prices. If households err in their forecasts of prices, this misperception of future real wages will affect the supply of labor, with potential effects on economy-wide employment and output.

As with output, the exchange of newly issued financial assets in the financial market takes place at the end of each period. On the supply side of this market are firms selling bonds and stocks to finance their investment expenditures and possibly the government selling bonds to finance a deficit. On the demand side of the financial market are households, who typically acquire bonds and stocks with part of their savings. Buyers of financial assets may also include depository institutions if they are expanding their outstanding loans.

The above discussion suggests two key aspects of macroeconomic analysis. One has to do with the expectations held by households and firms at the start of each period with respect to the nature of the output market at the end of the period. In fact, different assumptions with respect to these expectations distinguish the alternative macroeconomic models considered in Part III of this text. A second key aspect is that macroeconomics analyzes a number of markets in the economy simultaneously. To get a better feel for how these markets interrelate, we will examine in the next section what is termed the "circular flow" diagram.

The Circular Flow

Figure 4.1 illustrates the nature of the interaction among the participants in the economy and how money "circulates" through the economy in what is referred to as a "circular flow" diagram. Many students may find this figure to be a morass of lines, arrows, boxes, and circles making about as much sense as the plumbing system in a renovated seventeenth-century Parisian hotel. There is a way, however, to make sense of all this. Participants in the economy are enclosed in boxes. The arrows leading into each of these boxes indicate the sources of revenues for that participant, while the arrows

Figure 4.1 The Circular Flow Diagram

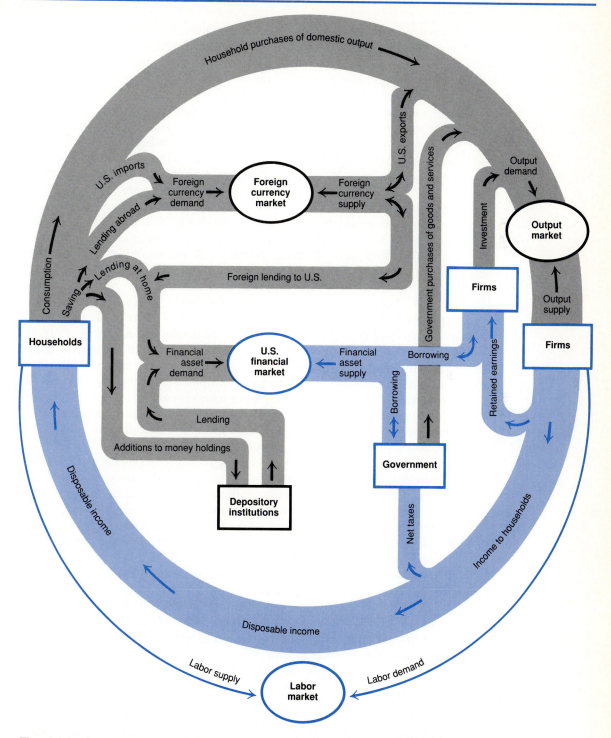

The circular flow diagram demonstrates the relationships between the participants in the four markets of the economy.

leading out of each box indicate expenditures. Since most revenues and expenditures reflect activity in the various markets in the economy, the markets are enclosed in circles. To decipher what is going on, let's start with the box for households (located on the far left side of the figure).

Households receive income from firms largely as payments for their labor services. As you can see, not all income generated by firms goes to households since part of it is retained by firms and part is taxed by the government. The income received by households after taxes is called disposable income. Out of disposable income received, households make expenditures for consumption and for saving. Consumption can be broken down into consumption of domestically produced output and consumption of goods produced abroad (imports), which creates a demand for foreign currency. Saving takes the form of additions to households' money holdings, additions to their holdings of domestic financial assets, and additions to their holdings of foreign financial assets. This final form of saving, denoted U.S. capital outflows, contributes to the demand for foreign currency.

On the right side of the diagram are firms. Firms receive income from the sale of output and pay most of it out. Firms do retain some of their earnings, however, to purchase capital. Thus there is an arrow from firms as suppliers of output to the box inside the circle that represents firms as demanders of output. Note that firms enter our circular flow diagram twice since, unlike other participants in the market, they are both suppliers and demanders of output. As demanders of output, firms' total expenditure on capital goods is financed not only from retained earnings but also from the sale of financial assets. When firms sell financial assets, they are borrowing. Thus there is a double arrow between the financial market and firms (as purchasers of capital goods), indicating that when firms enter the financial asset market as suppliers, they are borrowing money to help finance investment.

Government expenditures on output are financed in two ways. The bulk of the expenditures is financed by taxes; the remainder is financed by borrowing. Thus there is an arrow from the financial market to the government indicating the government as a seller of financial assets. Like firms, government borrowing involves the supply of financial assets. Thus there is the double arrow between the financial market and government, indicating that government supply of financial assets and government borrowing to finance expenditures are two ways of describing the same event.

The fourth participant, the depository institutions, receive part of household saving and purchase financial assets. Finally, although not explicitly identified, foreigners are involved in the market for foreign currency as suppliers of foreign currency in order to finance purchases of U.S. output (U.S. exports) and U.S. financial assets (U.S. capital inflows).

Tracing around the upper half of the circular flow, we can see that the demand for domestically produced output comes from households' consumption demand minus imports, foreigners' demand for U.S. exports, firms' purchases of capital goods (their gross investment demand), and government demand for goods and services. In this respect, the circular flow diagram provides a pictorial representation of Equation (2.1) in Chapter 2, which equated real GNP to the sum of purchases by households, firms, government, and foreigners.

A compelling feature of the circular flow diagram is that the value of the revenues or income for each participant *must* equal the value of its expenditures. Another way of saying this is that each participant's expenditures are constrained by its revenues. The remaining sections of this chapter further develop the links between these various markets by examining in more detail the constraints that the participants in these markets face. We start by describing the constraint facing firms, which purchase goods for investment in the output market and issue financial assets in the financial market.

4.2 FIRMS: INVESTMENT AND THE FINANCING CONSTRAINT

Although a firm's capital is fixed in the current period, it can change over time. Current purchases of capital add to the capital stock available for use in subsequent periods. At the same time that capital purchases are adding to the capital stock, the existing capital is depreciating, as plants and machinery wear out or become obsolete. This depreciation, measured in the National Income and Product Accounts by the capital consumption allowance, has the effect of reducing the capital stock. As we discussed in Chapter 2, the net change in the capital stock, or *net investment*, is simply the difference between total capital purchases, or gross investment, and capital depreciation.

Gross investment typically exceeds depreciation, so that net investment is positive and the capital stock is growing. For instance, it has been estimated that between 1965 and 1984, the stock of capital in the U.S. economy grew at an average annual rate of 3.76 percent; the stock of fixed private capital attained a real (1982 dollar) value of $6,519.8 billion in 1984.[3] Accompanying these net additions to the capital stock and associated demand for output by firms is a supply of new financial assets in the financial market, as we will see below.

How Firms Finance Real Investment Purchases

Firms use the revenue they receive from the sale of their output in a variety of ways. Some of the revenue is used to pay wages to workers for their labor services, some is used to make interest payments to holders of bonds issued by that firm in the past, some is used to purchase new capital to

---

[3] The growth in the stock of capital is taken from E. F. Denison, "The Interruption of Productivity Growth in the United States," *Economic Journal* 93 (March 1983): 56–77. Estimates of the size of the capital stock are in John C. Musgrave, "Fixed Reproducible Tangible Wealth in the United States: Revised Estimates," *Survey of Current Business* (January 1986): 51–75.

Figure 4.2   The Distribution of Firm Revenues for 1987

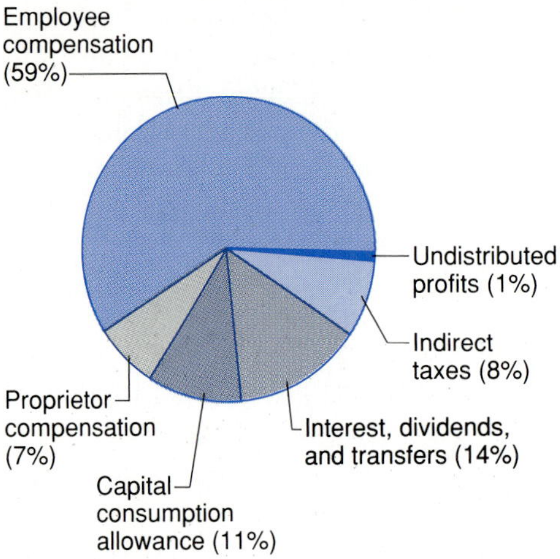

Employee compensation (59%)

Undistributed profits (1%)

Indirect taxes (8%)

Interest, dividends, and transfers (14%)

Proprietor compensation (7%)

Capital consumption allowance (11%)

Source: Economic Report of the President (1988).

replace depreciated capital, and some is used to pay taxes to government. Whatever revenue remains from the sale of output after all of these payments have been made is either distributed as dividends to shareholders or kept as "retained earnings."

Figure 4.2 illustrates the actual distribution of firm revenues in 1987. Note that the bulk of these revenues goes to households as wages, interest payments, and dividends or to the government as taxes. Most of the rest is used by firms to replace capital used up in the production process. Firms seeking to finance a given level of net investment demand are left with one of three alternatives: to issue new bonds, to issue new equity shares (stocks), or to use retained earnings (undistributed corporate profits). As we explain below, all three financing methods are similar because they all can lead to an identical increase in the value of the financial assets issued by the firm.[4]

---

[4] Franco Modigliani and Merton Miller were the first to formally demonstrate this equivalence proposition in their classic article "The Cost of Capital, Corporation Finance, and the Theory of Investment," *American Economy Review* (June 1958). See also Eugene Fama and Merton Miller, *The Theory of Finance* (New York: 1972) and Eugene Fama, "The Effects of a Firm's Investment and Financing Decisions on the Welfare of its Security Holders," *American Economic Review* (September 1978), where this proposition is expanded on and clarified. We may note that the proposition abstracts from tax considerations; differences in tax treatments between bond and equity financing will generally affect the optimal form of financing capital purchases, so that owners of firms (the stockholders) would no longer be indifferent as to whether capital purchases are financed by issuing new stock, by issuing bonds, or by using retained earnings.

Suppose that a firm adds $100 to its capital stock by buying a new piece of machinery. If the firm issues a $100 bond to pay for the machinery, then there is a direct $100 increase (the new bond) in the value of the financial assets issued by the firm. Note that the value of the current shareholders' stock is unchanged in this case of bond-financed investment. While it is true that the tangible assets of the firm have increased by the $100 addition to capital, this benefit to shareholders is exactly offset by the fact that the firm's debt has also increased by $100.

If the firm finances the $100 net investment by issuing new shares of stock equal to $100, again there is a $100 increase (the new equity shares) in the value of the financial assets issued by the firm. As with bond financing, however, the value of the initial shareholders' stock is unchanged when the firm finances its capital purchases by issuing new equity shares. The new shares do not dilute the value of the shares of the initial shareholders since the capital purchase increases the firm's tangible assets by $100, which is exactly the value of the new equity shares issued.

Finally, if the firm finances the $100 net investment through retained earnings, there is, in essence, a $100 increase in the value of the financial assets issued by the firm for the following reason. When a firm retains earnings in order to finance a capital purchase, the current stockholders own the right to the income generated from the additional capital. As a consequence, the value of their equity shares rises to reflect the value of the new capital owned by the firm. We can equivalently view this as the firm paying out $100 in dividends to its initial shareholders who then use the dividends to buy additional "constant value" equity shares equal to the value of the capital purchased by the firm. In other words, when the firm uses retained earnings to finance its investment spending, it is implicitly issuing new financial assets—equity shares.

Case Study

FINANCING CHOICES AND DIFFERENT CAPITAL STRUCTURES

We have just seen that, at least as a first approximation, we need not distinguish between firms financing capital purchases by selling bonds or by issuing stock. The view that the method of financing capital purchases is largely irrelevant is a very useful simplification for macroeconomic analysis. However, you should be aware of some complicating factors that we are ignoring, factors that can cause firms to care about the method by which capital purchases are financed.

From the point of view of an individual firm, financing capital purchases using bonds will increase what is known as its debt-to-equity ratio as the value of outstanding debt issued by the firm rises. However, on the other hand, financing capital purchases using equity shares (explicitly or implicitly by using retained earnings) will reduce a firm's debt-to-equity ratio, as the value of outstanding equity shares issued rises. Thus the method of financing capital purchases affects the firm's debt-to-equity ratio. What factors might influence a firm's choice of a debt-to-equity ratio, also known as its "capital structure?" Two factors are tax considerations and bankruptcy costs.

The corporate taxes that firms pay are calculated as a percent of earnings. For tax purposes, corporate earnings are equal to total revenues net of costs, where costs include not only wages and payments for raw materials but also interest payments to bondholders. Thus if a firm finances its purchase of capital using bonds, the future interest payments will reduce its taxable earnings and fewer taxes will have to be paid in the future. This means that a firm can lower its future tax liability by raising its debt-to-equity ratio—that is by financing new capital purchases by using bonds rather than equity shares.

There are potential costs, however, to raising the debt-to-equity ratio that relate to what are known as "bankruptcy costs." Unlike equity shares which promise shareholders dividend payments if profits are sufficiently high, bonds promise *fixed* payments to their holders. (Recall that with equity shares firms pay unspecified dividends that depend on earnings.) Greater debt thus increases the fixed obligations that firms must meet in the future. This means that a fall in future revenues is more likely to force a firm to bankruptcy.

Bankruptcy occurs when a firm's revenues do not cover its costs and it is forced to default on its obligations to bondholders. With bankruptcy comes

Table 4.2   Debt-to-Equity Ratios Across Various Industries

| | Mean Debt-to-Equity Ratios* | |
	Book Value of Equity	Market Value of Equity
Steel	1.973	1.665
Petroleum refining	1.548	1.117
Textiles	1.405	1.296
Motor vehicles	.922	.594
Plastics	.843	.792
Machine tools	.472	.425
Pharmaceuticals	.194	.079

* The book value of equity is computed by using accounting sources, while the market value of equity is the value determined by the current market price of the outstanding shares. The ratios are computed by using data collected over the 1981–1982 period.

Source: W. Carl Kester, "Capital Ownership Structure: A Comparison of the United States and Japanese Manufacturing Corporations," *Financial Management* 15, no. 1, Spring 1986, pp. 5–16.

bankruptcy costs, the most obvious being hefty legal costs associated with going to court and reorganizing. The existence of bankruptcy costs serves to limit the amount of borrowing a firm will undertake. It will hesitate to increase its debt-equity ratio beyond some level since the gain in tax savings will be offset by the costs associated with an increased likelihood of incurring bankruptcy.

To summarize, if we take into account the twin effects of taxes and bankruptcy costs, the result is that every firm has an optimal debt-to-equity ratio that reflects a trade-off of these two factors. Table 4.2 lists the general level of debt-to-equity ratios for a sample of different industries. Note that debt-to-equity ratios vary widely. The debt-to-equity ratio for steel firms, with a value of debt close to 1.7 times the market value of the outstanding equity shares, is the highest. But in many industries the ratio is below one.

The Firm Financing Constraint

As the foregoing discussion indicates, we can speak of firms financing net investment demand entirely by issuing new financial assets even though some capital purchases are actually financed out of retained earnings. If we let A_f^s denote the real value of the new financial assets that firms plan to supply and I^d denote firms' net investment demand, then the relationship between net investment demand and the value of the new financial assets is given by

$$
\underset{\substack{\text{Net investment} \\ \text{demand}}}{I^d} \quad = \quad \underset{\substack{\text{Firms' supply of} \\ \text{additional financial assets}}}{A_f^s} \qquad \textbf{(4.1)}
$$

Firm financing constraint: This constraint ($I^d = A_f^s$) indicates that firms' desired net investment purchases (I^d) must be financed by their real supply of financial assets (A_f^s).

We shall refer to Equation 4.1 as the **firm financing constraint.** This constraint indicates that firms' investment purchases (I^d) are constrained by the amount of funds raised through the issuance or supply of new financial assets (A_f^s).

In interpreting Equation 4.1, recall from Chapter 3 that the issuance of new financial assets by firms in the current period (A_f^s) takes place in the primary financial market and is a flow variable. The amount of new capital that firms purchase in the current period (I^d) is also a flow variable. Thus unlike the existing stocks of financial assets and capital that can be measured at a point in time, these flow variables are measured over a period of time. Also recall that we simplify our analysis of financial markets by ignoring the considerable diversity among the various types of financial assets that are issued in practice. Instead, we assume that firms issue a "representative" financial asset that offers the interest rate r.

The firm financing constraint illustrates one of the links between the financial and output markets. As the constraint demonstrates, the amount of capital goods that firms purchase depends on their sale of financial assets in the financial market. In the financial market, firms find themselves in competition with other borrowers in the market, particularly government. One of the major concerns of the business sector throughout the 1980s has been the pressure put on financial markets by the large federal deficits. When firms and the government compete for a scarce amount of loanable funds, some borrowers may be crowded out of the market. If firms are crowded out, that lowers investment and thus the future stock of private capital. The possibility of a less productive economy in the future due to large federal deficits has been emphasized by those legislators who have called for a balanced budget amendment.

Although the impact of government deficits is not as clear-cut as the above discussion suggests, more complete discussions of government deficits and investment in later chapters will still rely on the insights provided by the firm financing constraint as well as the constraints facing the other participants in the economy. A recurrent theme throughout this book is the important links between financial and output markets stemming from the financing constraints facing firms and the other market participants.

4.3   HOUSEHOLDS: CONSUMPTION, SAVING, AND THE BUDGET CONSTRAINT

As we have just seen, firms use part of the revenue they receive from the sale of output to replace depreciated capital. Some revenue is used to pay taxes to the government. The remainder of the revenue is distributed to households in the form of wages, interest payments, and dividend payments. Thus all revenue from the sale of output that remains after depreciated capital has been replaced and business taxes paid ultimately goes to households.[5] This means that household *real gross income* equals real GNP (Y) minus depreciation (the capital consumption allowance, or CCA) and business taxes (T_b). In other words, household real income equals $Y - CCA - T_b$.

Household Real Disposable Income

Anyone who has disappointedly noted the difference between gross pay and take-home pay on payday or who has listed the amount of interest and dividend income earned on any tax form knows that households do not keep all the income that they earn. Part of this income is taxed away by federal, state, and local government. Let's denote the total real tax payments that households make by T_h.

The government not only taketh income but it also giveth income away

---

[5] Business taxes include both indirect taxes (such as sales and excise taxes) and taxes on corporate profits.

in the form of transfer payments. Government transfer payments include welfare payments, social security payments, and interest payments on government debt. Let TR denote total real government transfer payments made to households. Aggregating across all households, we can denote households' net real taxes (T_n) as the difference between total household taxes (T_h) and transfer payments (TR) or $T_n = T_h - TR$.

Subtracting net real taxes from real income, we obtain the total amount of real income available to households to either purchase consumption goods or increase their savings. This amount is generally referred to as **real disposable income** (YD). That is, real disposable income equals total output minus the capital consumption allowance and total net taxes:

Real disposable income: Total output (Y) minus the capital consumption allowance (CCA) and total net taxes (T).

$$
\begin{array}{ccccccc}
YD & = & Y & - & CCA & - & T_b & - & T_n \\
\text{Real} & & \text{Real} & & \text{Capital} & & \text{Business} & & \text{Household taxes} \\
\text{disposable} & & \text{income} & & \text{consumption} & & \text{taxes} & & \text{net of transfer} \\
\text{income} & & & & \text{allowance} & & & & \text{payments}
\end{array}
\tag{4.2}
$$

The above expression for real disposable income has an important implication for policy discussions concerning who should be taxed. Although it is often suggested that the government raise revenue by taxing firms, we see from Equation 4.2 that households ultimately pay these taxes. This insight allows us to simplify both our discussion of household disposable income and our notation. Specifically, let T denote the total net taxes paid by households and firms (i.e. $T = T_b + T_n$). Then real disposable income is given by

$$
YD = Y - CCA - T
\tag{4.3}
$$

In future discussions, when we refer to the effect of a change in taxes, we will often not bother to distinguish between a change in "taxes on business" and a change in "taxes on households," for both taxes are ultimately borne by households.

We should note one discrepancy between our measure of real disposable income and that found in the National Income and Product Accounts. As mentioned above, firms sometimes use retained earnings to finance purchases of new capital. In the National Income and Product Accounts, retained earnings are called "undistributed corporate profits" and are not included in its definition of personal income. However, households ultimately have a claim on these undistributed profits since households are the owners of firms (by virtue of their being the holders of equity shares). Thus unlike the National Income and Product Accounts, our measure of household income includes these undistributed profits. Not only does this capture the true state of affairs but it also simplifies the analysis.

The Household Budget Constraint

As we are fond of telling our students, you can do only two things with an after-tax dollar: spend it or save it. Let C^d denote household planned real consumption expenditures, or consumption demand. Let S denote real household saving, which can take the form of either additions to financial asset holdings (bonds and stocks) or additions to money holdings. The fact that household consumption and saving decisions are constrained by their real disposable income is captured by the **household budget constraint:**

Household budget constraint: A constraint that equates the sum of consumption and saving (C^d + S) to households' real disposable income (Y − CCA − T).

$$C^d \quad + \quad S \quad = \quad Y \quad - \quad CCA \quad - \quad T$$

Consumption demand	Saving	Real income	Capital consumption allowance	Net taxes	**(4.4)**

The household budget constraint equates the sum of desired consumption and saving (C^d + S) to households' real disposable income (Y − CCA − T).

Figure 4.3 illustrates the actual division of GNP into household real disposable income and the capital consumption allowance plus taxes for 1967 in part (a) and for 1987 in part (b). This figure also shows how real disposable income is divided between consumption and saving. Figure 4.3 indicates that there has been an increase in disposable income (consumption plus saving) as a proportion of GNP between 1967 and 1987, which is due to a fall in taxes as a proportion of GNP. A second change between these two years is that in 1987 the percent of disposable income that households devoted to saving declined from the 1967 level, as households shifted away from saving to consumption during this period.

There are three points we wish to make with respect to household saving. First, although many households have consumption that exceeds their disposable income and thus have negative saving (that is, there are many households that are net borrowers), it is important to remember that when we aggregate across households to obtain the household budget constraint (Equation 4.4), households as a group have positive saving.

The fact that total household saving is positive may seem at odds with your perception that most individuals you know typically borrow to purchase new cars, appliances, or stereo systems. But keep in mind an often overlooked part of household disposable income that is channeled directly into saving—namely, the payments by firms and workers into workers' private pension funds. Individuals who borrow to finance consumer goods often in fact are net savers as the amount of funds they borrow is often less than their contributions to pension plans.

A second point about household saving is that it encompasses some items that are frequently overlooked in discussions in the popular press concerning household saving. For instance, during the mid-1980s concern was often expressed about the low saving rates, a view often supported by the observation that the "personal saving rate" was 2.7 percent of GNP in 1987.[6] However, as Figure 4.3 indicates, total household saving as a proportion of GNP was substantially greater. Remember that total saving includes "business

---

[6] *Economic Report of the President*, (January 1988).

Figure 4.3   GNP, Real Disposable Income, Consumption, and Saving for 1967 and 1987

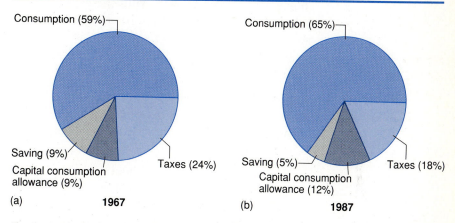

By comparing parts (a) and (b), note the rising portion of disposable income going to consumption over the last twenty years.

Source: Economic Report of the President (1988).

saving" as well as "personal saving." When firms retain earnings as undistributed corporate profits, we may think of these undistributed profits as part of households' disposable income that goes directly to saving, as these undistributed profits raise the value of household stock holdings. Nevertheless, the concern about saving is somewhat justified since total saving as a proportion of GNP fell from 9 percent in 1967 to approximately 5 percent in 1987, as Figure 4.3 indicates.

The final point we wish to make concerning saving is that household saving can be divided into two broad categories: the accumulation of money and the accumulation of financial assets. When households save in the form of money, they are accumulating assets that can be readily used as media of exchange. Such assets include coins, currency, and checking accounts, all of which can be used directly to purchase goods and services. The amount of money balances that households want to accumulate over a period is simply equal to the difference between their desired money holdings at the end of the period (M^d) and their prior money balances ($\overline{M}$).[7]

Dividing by the price level, we can express this portion of desired saving in the form of the accumulation of *real* money balances. Specifically, let L^d

---

[7] To simplify our analysis of money demand, we ignore the fact that businesses as well as individuals hold money balances. This simplification does not affect our results since the factors that affect the money demand of individuals are similar to the factors that affect the desired money holdings of businesses, a point we return to in Chapters 6 and 16.

Real money demand
(L^d): Households' desired
holdings of real money
balances.

denote household desired real money balances or **real money demand** at
the end of the period, so that $L^d = M^d/P.$[8] Similarly, initial real money
holdings are given by $\overline{M}/P$. Thus the expression $L^d - \overline{M}/P$ denotes desired
additions to money balances in terms of the goods and services that these
additional money balances can purchase.

Besides adding to their real holdings of money, saving by households
can take the form of additions to their financial assets holdings—that is, the
purchase of additional stocks and bonds. Let A_h^d denote the amount by which
households want to increase their real holdings of financial assets. Total
desired saving can then be written as desired real accumulation of money
balances plus desired accumulation of financial assets, or

$$
\underset{\text{Saving}}{S} = \underset{\substack{\text{Household demand} \\ \text{for additional} \\ \text{financial assets}}}{A_h^d} + \underset{\substack{\text{Demand for} \\ \text{additional real} \\ \text{money balances}}}{L^d - \overline{M}/P}
\tag{4.5}
$$

Substituting Equation (4.5) into Equation (4.4), we can express the household
budget constraint in the following form:

$$
\underset{\substack{\text{Consumption} \\ \text{demand}}}{C^d} + \underset{\substack{\text{Household demand} \\ \text{for additional} \\ \text{financial assets}}}{A_h^d} + \underset{\substack{\text{Demand for} \\ \text{additional real} \\ \text{money balances}}}{L^d - \overline{M}/P} = \underset{\substack{\text{Real} \\ \text{disposable} \\ \text{income}}}{Y - CCA - T}
\tag{4.6}
$$

Comparing Equation (4.6) with (4.4), we see that the household budget
constraint equates real disposable income ($Y - CCA - T$) to consumption
(C^d) plus saving in the form of additions to real holdings of money ($L^d - \overline{M}/P$) and financial assets (A_h^d).

To the Point

CONSTRAINTS FACING FIRMS AND HOUSEHOLDS

- Firms finance net investment demand either from retained earnings or
  by issuing new financial assets. In either case, the total value of firms
  outstanding financial assets increases by the value of capital purchased.
  In fact, the firm financing constraint indicates that firms' net investment
  demand equals their supply of new financial assets.

- The household budget constraint indicates that household consumption
  plus saving is constrained by real disposable income (income minus the
  capital consumption allowance and net taxes); that is, $C^d + S = Y - CCA - T$. Household saving is divided into the accumulation of financial
  assets and money (i.e., $S = A_h^d + L^d - \overline{M}/P$).

---

[8] The term L^d, popularized by noted economist John Maynard Keynes, represents households'
"liquidity" preference.

4.4 DEPOSITORY INSTITUTIONS: BALANCE SHEETS AND THE FINANCING CONSTRAINT

The participants in the economy that we are labeling "depository institutions" can in fact be divided into two categories. One category contains private depository institutions such as commercial banks, savings and loan associations, credit unions, and mutual savings banks. These familiar institutions provide general banking services to the public. The other type of depository institution— the central bank—is less familiar. In the United States, the central bank is the Federal Reserve.

Monetary policy: Decisions relating to actions by the Federal Reserve (the U.S. central bank) that determine the rate of change in the money supply.

The Federal Reserve determines **monetary policy,** the most important aspect of which is setting the rate of growth in the money supply. As we will see in this section, changes in the money supply are accompanied by equivalent changes in the financial asset holdings of depository institutions. We call this relationship, which is important in linking monetary policy decisions to the financial markets, the depository institution financing constraint. In order to demonstrate the link between the money supply and depository institutions' holdings of financial assets, we start with some critical background material on the structure of the Federal Reserve System and its balance sheet. We also consider the balance sheets of private depository institutions.

The Federal Reserve System

The Federal Reserve System or the "Fed" was established by Congress in 1913 as an independent agency of the federal government. The Fed consists of twelve regional Federal Reserve banks, each of which regulates and supervises the private depository institutions in its district and provides banking services for the U.S. Treasury, other government agencies, and private depository institutions. Two bodies share in the governing of the twelve Federal Reserve banks: the Federal Reserve Board of Governors and the Federal Open Market Committee.

The Federal Reserve Board of Governors consists of seven individuals, each appointed by the president for 14-year terms. Every four years, the president names one member of the Board of Governors as chairman of the Board. In the summer of 1987, Paul Volcker stepped down after two terms as chairman to be replaced by Alan Greenspan. The chairman of the Board of Governors is widely viewed as the primary architect and spokesman of the Fed's monetary policy. The Federal Open Market Committee (FOMC) is a group that includes the seven members of the Board of Governors as well as five representatives from five of the 12 Federal Reserve banks. This committee determines the day-to-day purchases and sales of government securities in the open market by the Federal Reserve. As we will find out in Chapter 5, these "open market" operations are critical to determining the money supply.

The banking services provided by the Fed include clearing checks between banks, making loans to private depository institutions, and providing currency. Note, however, that the Fed does not provide banking services to private individuals or businesses. The character of the Fed may best be understood by examining the combined balance sheet of the twelve Federal Reserve banks.

Assets of the Fed. Table 4.3 summarizes in a simplified form the balance sheet of the Fed as of January 1988.[9] Note that the bulk of the Fed's assets are financial assets in the form of government security holdings and loans made by the Fed to private depository institutions. The Fed's government security holdings include treasury bills, notes, and bonds as well as other federal agency obligations. In fact, Federal Reserve banks are largely restricted to holding government securities as opposed to private securities. An exception is the loans the Fed makes to private depository institutions. These loans are an outgrowth of the Fed's responsibility as a lender of last resort to private depository institutions faced with mass withdrawals of their deposits. Included under other assets held by the Fed are gold certificates, or claims on gold, and international reserves such as foreign currency holdings.

Liabilities of the Fed. According to Table 4.3, the liabilities of the Fed include currency in the hands of the nonbank public, which is one component of the money supply. At first glance, counting this as a liability may seem strange, but when we recognize that currency is an asset for individuals, it makes sense that it is a liability for the Fed. Prior to 1933, it was more apparent that currency was a Fed liability since holders of currency could redeem it at the Fed for gold. As recently as the early 1970s, the Fed issued silver certificates that could, ostensibly, be redeemed for silver. Today, however, if you are fortunate enough to have folding money in your pocket, you will notice that there is no mention of what you can redeem that currency for at the Fed. Instead, these "Federal Reserve notes" are simply denoted as "legal tender for all debts, public and private."

Although the bulk of the currency issued by the Fed is held by the nonbank public and thus makes up part of the M1 measure of the money supply, some currency is held by private depository institutions. These currency holdings, called vault cash, constitute a second liability of the Fed. The liability side of the Fed's balance sheet also includes the deposits of private depository institutions at the Fed. These deposits plus vault cash make up the reserves of the private depository institutions, as we will see in the next section when we examine the combined balance sheet of private depository institutions. Other deposits at the Fed, which include deposits of the U.S. Treasury, are the final category of the Fed's liabilities.

---

[9] A more complete listing of the assets and liabilities of the Fed may be found in various issues of the *Federal Reserve Bulletin*.

Table 4.3   **The Fed's Balance Sheet (End of Month, January 1988)**

Assets (in billions of dollars)		Liabilities (in billions of dollars)	
Financial assets (e.g., government securities, loans to private depository institutions)	226	Currency in hands of the nonbank public	180
		Vault cash	26
Other assets (e.g., international, reserves, gold certificates)	39	Deposits of private depository institutions at Fed	35
		Other deposits	24
Total	265		265

Monetary base or high-powered money: The sum of currency held by the nonbank public plus bank reserves (vault cash and deposits of private depository institutions at the Fed).

The **monetary base** is defined as the sum of bank reserves (vault cash and deposits of private depository institutions at the Fed) and currency in the hands of the nonbank public. As we can see in Table 4.3, the monetary base is essentially the liability side of the Fed's balance sheet.[10] As such, the Fed controls the size of the monetary base. In subsequent chapters, we will show how the Fed determines the money supply through its control of the monetary base. But first, let us examine the balance sheet of the private depository institutions and then derive the depository institution financing constraint from this balance sheet and the balance sheet of the Fed.

Private Depository Institutions

As the balance sheet of the Fed indicates, the Fed can pay for purchases of additional financial assets from the nonbank public simply by printing additional currency. In this case, it is clear that both the financial asset holdings of depository institutions (the Fed in particular) and the money supply increase by equivalent amounts. Recall that currency in the hands of the nonbank public makes up one third of the money supply (M1). Thus we are part way to an understanding of the depository institution financing constraint, a constraint that links money supply changes to changes in depository institutions' holdings of financial assets. We have not yet considered why changes in the other major component of the money supply, specifically checkable deposits, are linked to changes in depository institutions' financial asset holdings. To see why, we must look at the balance sheets of private depository institutions.

---

[10] This is not exactly correct. Also included in the monetary base are coins issued by the U.S. Treasury and held by the nonbank public and by private depository institutions. These coins constitute approximately five percent of the total monetary base. For simplicity, we will ignore them in our analysis. In addition, it may be noted that "other deposits" are not counted as part of the monetary base.

Assets and Liabilities of Private Depository Institutions. There are many different types of private depository institutions and a variety of different types of accounts. To simplify our analysis here, Table 4.4 presents the combined balance sheet for private depository institutions as of January 1988. The major liability of private depository institutions is in the form of deposits. These deposits include not only the checkable deposits counted in the M1 measure of the money supply but also savings and time deposits, and other noncheckable accounts that are counted in the M2 measure of the money supply. Completing the liability side are private depository institutions borrowings from the Fed, which typically are of small magnitude, and capital accounts. The capital accounts show the amount originally invested by the owners (shareholders), modified by retained profits and losses thereafter.

As Table 4.4 indicates, the assets of private depository institutions can be divided into two groups—reserves and financial asset holdings. Most bank reserves, held either as vault cash or as deposits at the Fed, are what are termed **required reserves.** Required reserves are reserves held by the private depository institutions in order to meet reserve requirements set by the Fed. For example, in 1988 the Fed required 3 to 12 percent of checkable deposits to be held as reserves, with the lower requirement applying to the first $40.5 million of deposits at any one depository institution. For increments in deposits over $40.5 million, the required reserve to deposit ratio was .12, or 12 percent. Reserves held in excess of required reserves are termed **excess reserves.** Excess reserves are held to pay off unexpected withdrawals of deposits.

Few reserves are typically held in excess of what is required by the Fed. For instance, during the early 1980s less than two percent of reserves were excess reserves. However, this has not always been the case. During the period of the Great Depression from 1929 to 1933 a number of banks failed, unable to meet the onslaught of withdrawal demands by their customers. As a consequence, by 1935 close to 50 percent of the reserves held by the surviving banks were excess reserves. With the experience of the early 1930s fresh in their minds, banks wanted to be prepared in case of a repeat performance of the banking panics, when depositors rushed en masse to convert their deposits into currency.

As Table 4.4 indicates, reserves do not make up the bulk of the assets of private depository institutions. The majority of their assets are in the form of financial assets that include both government bonds and loans made to the private sector—firms and households. Interest earnings on their financial asset holdings constitute the revenues of depository institutions.

Depository Institutions as Financial Intermediaries. Embedded in the combined balance sheet of the private depository institutions is the link we seek between changes in the money supply—specifically checkable deposits—and depository institutions' demand for financial assets. However, this link is obscured by the role banks play as financial intermediaries. Patinkin describes

---

Required reserves: Reserves held by private depository institutions to meet reserve requirements set by the Fed.

Excess reserves: Reserves held by private depository institutions in excess of required reserves.

Table 4.4   **Combined Balance Sheet for Private Depository**
Institutions

Assets (in billions of dollars)		Liabilities (in billions of dollars)	
Bank reserves	61	Checkable deposits	550
Vault cash	26	Other deposits	2200
Deposits of private depository institutions at Fed	35	Loans from Fed	10
Financial assets	2899	Capital accounts	200
Total	2960		2960

financial intermediaries "as processing plants whose effective function is to transform the bonds issued by firms (and government) into securities which the ultimate lenders (households) consider more suitable for their needs."[11]

Part of the activity of private depository institutions is indeed indistinguishable from the activity of other financial intermediaries such as life insurance companies, pension funds, and brokerage firms. Private depository institutions act solely as financial intermediaries when they accept such noncheckable deposits from lenders as time and savings accounts, certificates of deposit, and money market deposits (these fall into the category "other deposits" in Table 4.4), and use the funds raised from these deposits to purchase financial assets.

Private depository institutions, however, are unique among financial intermediaries in that they have "money" as part of their liabilities. In particular, private depository institutions checkable deposit liabilities are counted in the M1 measure of money since they are directly used as media of exchange. To isolate the unique role that private depository institutions play in the money supply process, when we talk about "depository institutions" we will mean the Fed and private depository institutions in their role as creators of checkable deposits. We exclude those activities of private depository institutions solely reflecting their role as financial intermediaries, a role indicated by such liabilities as savings deposits, time deposits, and certificates of deposit. In this role, depository institutions will be lumped together with other financial intermediaries as facilitators of household saving in the form of financial assets. With this simplification in mind, we are now ready to explicitly state the financing constraint for depository institutions.

---

[11] Don Patinkin, *Money, Interest and Prices* (New York: Harper and Row, 1963), p. 301.

The Depository Institution Financing Constraint

The two components of the money supply—currency in the hands of the nonbank public and checkable deposits—are both matched by equivalent holdings of financial assets by depository institutions. This can be readily seen by examining the balance sheets of the Fed and private depository institutions, which are reproduced in simplified form in Table 4.5.

Consider first the currency component of the money supply. As Table 4.5 indicates, offsetting the Fed's liabilities in the form of currency in the hands of the nonbank public are holdings of financial assets. In fact, the currency in the hands of the nonbank public has paid for financial assets purchased by the Fed. Thus one can argue that the currency component of the money supply is matched by an equivalent dollar value of financial asset holdings by depository institutions, namely the Fed.

Either directly or indirectly, the deposit component of the money supply is also matched by an equivalent dollar value of the financial asset holdings by depository institutions. As Table 4.5 illustrates, some of the deposit liabilities of private depository institutions are directly offset by their holdings of financial assets. The remainder of the deposits are offset by bank reserves. Yet even the fraction of the deposits backed by reserves is ultimately matched by financial asset holdings of a depository institution, in this case the Fed. For, as Table 4.5 indicates, bank reserves are a liability of the Fed, and as such are offset by the Fed's financial asset holdings. In summary, then, the deposit component of the money supply, like the currency component, is linked, either directly or indirectly, to the financial asset holdings of depository institutions.

To formalize this relationship, let M^s denote the depository institutions' nominal supply of money at the end of the current period and let $\overline{M}$ denote initial money balances. Then the change in the money supply from last period equals the current money supply M^s minus the prior level of money balances $\overline{M}$. To convert this change to real terms, we simply divide by the price level (P). Thus the real change in the money supply is $(M^s/P) - \overline{M}/P$. The banking system financing constraint indicates that this real change in the money supply equals depository institutions' real additions to their holdings of financial assets. Denoting this real demand for additional financial assets by the "banking system" by A_b^d, the **depository institution financing constraint** takes the form

Depository institution financing constraint: A constraint that equates the depository institutions' real flow demand for financial assets (A_b^d) to the change in the real supply of money [$(M^s - \overline{M})/P$].

$$A_b^d \quad = \quad M^s/P - \overline{M}/P$$

"Banks" demand   Supply of

for additional   additional real

financial assets   money balances

(4.7)

Equation 4.7 indicates that money supply changes have a direct impact on the financial markets. An increase in the money supply means an increase in the demand for financial assets by depository institutions. As we will see in later chapters, this expansion in lending that accompanies the higher real

Table 4.5   The Balance Sheets of the Depository Institutions

Fed		Private Depository Institutions (combined)	
Assets	*Liabilities*	*Assets*	*Liabilities*
Financial assets	Currency in hands of the nonbank public	Bank reserves Financial assets	Deposits
	Bank reserves		

money supply can drive down interest rates, stimulating output demand. In light of the potentially pervasive influence of money on the economy, it is important to be able to pinpoint the source of most monetary changes. Chapter 5 will highlight what this section has suggested: that the Fed is that source.

4.5   GOVERNMENT: THE FINANCING CONSTRAINT AND FISCAL POLICY

The 1980s started with the election of a president, Ronald Reagan, who promised the advent of what has become known as "supply-side" economics, a policy that proposes cutting tax rates. Critics responded that the policy would simply result in higher government deficits, as the government would have to compensate for the decrease in tax revenue with higher borrowing. The administration's response was twofold. First, the cut in tax rates would stimulate output in the economy; as output rose, tax revenues would rise, offsetting the effect on tax revenues of the cut in tax rates. Second, any shortfall in revenue that did occur could be met with cuts in government spending rather than higher borrowing. Underlying this exchange of ideas is the government financing constraint. We must understand this government financing constraint if we are to analyze fully the effects on the economy of government tax and spending decisions.

The Government Financing Constraint

In making its decisions on spending, taxing, and borrowing, the government, like firms, households, and depository institutions, faces a financing constraint.[12]

---

[12] As we saw in the national income accounts presented in Chapter 2, rather than distinguishing between federal, state, and local government, macroeconomics typically refers to the government as though it were a single entity.

Specifically, the government must finance its expenditures either by levying taxes or by borrowing. Recall from Chapter 2 that the government makes two types of expenditures: It purchases goods and services and it makes transfer payments such as social security, welfare payments, and interest payments to holders of government bonds. Denoting real government demand for final output by G^d and real government transfer payments by TR, total government expenditures are thus given by $G^d + TR$.

The government raises money for its expenditures in part by levying taxes. Recall that we use T_h and T_b to denote real government tax receipts from households and businesses, respectively. In addition to taxes, the government finances expenditures by borrowing (issuing bonds). For instance, in 1987 the government (federal, state, and local combined) borrowed 91.2 billion (1982) dollars. Just as firms borrow by issuing bonds, the government also borrows by issuing bonds. When the government issues bonds, it is supplying financial assets to the financial market. We will denote the real value of financial assets that the government supplies to help finance its expenditures by A_g^s.

Since the government's tax revenues and borrowing must be sufficient to finance its total expenditures, the government financing constraint is given by

$$
\underset{\substack{\text{Government} \\ \text{demand for} \\ \text{goods and} \\ \text{services}}}{G^d}
+
\underset{\substack{\text{Government} \\ \text{transfer} \\ \text{payments}}}{TR}
=
\underset{\substack{\text{Total taxes} \\ \text{on} \\ \text{businesses}}}{T_b}
+
\underset{\substack{\text{Total taxes} \\ \text{on} \\ \text{households}}}{T_h}
+
\underset{\substack{\text{Government's supply} \\ \text{of additional} \\ \text{financial assets}}}{A_g^s}
\qquad \textbf{(4.8)}
$$

In the household budget constraint, we identified net real taxes paid by households (T) as the difference between total taxes ($T_b + T_h$) and transfer payments (TR). The net real tax term is embedded in Equation 4.8, as you can see if you subtract transfer payments TR from both sides of the equation. Doing so, one can rewrite the **government financing constraint** as

Government financing constraint: A constraint that equates real government spending (G^d) to real net taxes (T) and real government borrowing (A_g^s).

$$
\underset{\substack{\text{Government} \\ \text{demand}}}{G^d}
=
\underset{\substack{\text{Net real} \\ \text{taxes}}}{T}
+
\underset{\substack{\text{Government's supply of} \\ \text{additional financial assets}}}{A_g^s}
\qquad \textbf{(4.9)}
$$

where net real taxes (T) equals $T_b + T_h - TR$. Note from Equation 4.9 that the government's real financial asset supply equals the difference between real government spending on goods and services and net real taxes. If real government spending on output exceeds net real taxes, then A_g^s is positive and the government runs a *deficit*. In contrast, if net real taxes exceed real government spending, then the government runs a *surplus* and A_g^s is negative. Finally, if in any year government purchases of goods and services equal net real taxes, the government budget is balanced for that year and A_g^s is zero.

Figure 4.4   A Breakdown of Government Outlays and Sources of Revenue for 1987

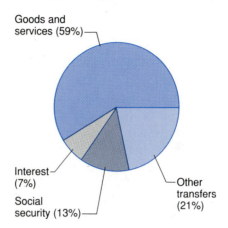

Goods and services (59%)

Interest (7%)

Social security (13%)

Other transfers (21%)

Government outlays are broken down into purchases of goods and services and transfers. The components of transfers are: interest payments, social security, and other transfers.

Source: Economic Report of the President (1988).

Figure 4.4 highlights the extent to which government outlays consist largely of transfer payments. In 1987, 41 percent of total government outlays are transfer payments, with approximately 49 percent of these transfer payments involving either federal social security payments (32 percent) or interest payments on outstanding government debt (17 percent). The remainder of government outlays are government demand for goods and services (G^d), financed either through net taxes (T) or government borrowing (A_g^s). In 1987, 11.6 percent of government purchases were financed by borrowing.

Every recent president has come into office with the promise to eliminate the deficit and balance the budget. This is commonly confused with eliminating the national debt. The confusion is a result of the difference between a stock and a flow. The deficit is a flow measure, the national debt is a stock measure. The extent to which government spending over any given year exceeds tax receipts (a deficit) determines the size of the *increase* in the debt. The following example illustrates this stock/flow distinction.

In 1987, the real federal deficit was 129.9 billion (1982) dollars. (The last time the federal government ran a surplus was in 1969.) The sum of all past nominal deficits and surpluses is the nominal value of the debt, a stock measure. Dividing this by the price level yields the real national debt. In October 1987, the real federal debt equaled $2,005 billion. When presidents talk about balancing the budget, they mean the flow measure. That is, they propose that in a given year, federal receipts from taxes should equal government expenditures. There are few people, Lyndon Larouche being an exception, who seriously consider eliminating the national debt.

Government Fiscal Policy

Fiscal policy: Decisions dealing with changes in government real spending on output, net real taxes, and the real supply of government bonds to influence the direction of the economy.

The government's **fiscal policy** decisions deal with its real spending on output, its net real taxes, and its real supply of government bonds. Since this book undertakes an examination of macroeconomics and not political science, we will not try to explain government behavior. Instead, we take government behavior as given and focus our attention on how changes in the government's behavior affect the economy.

Fiscal policy decisions cannot be made independently, since they must satisfy the government financing constraint, as shown in Equation 4.9. For example, if government demand for goods and services (G^d) increases and net taxes (T) do not change, then the supply of government bonds (A_g^s) *must* increase. If transfer payments increase with no change in total taxes, then the reduction in net taxes (T) means the government must either decrease its spending on goods and services (a fall in G^d) or issue additional bonds (a rise in A_g^s).

Missing from the government financing constraint is the possibility that the government will "print" money to finance its expenditures. If Congress decides to increase government spending, it does not have the power to increase the money supply to finance that spending; such power rests with the Federal Reserve. There is one way in which government expenditures can, however, be financed by newly created money. If the government finances expenditures by issuing new bonds, and if the Federal Reserve simultaneously increases the money supply, then new money is essentially substituted for the newly issued bonds.

To see how changes in the money supply can be introduced into the government financing constraint, define A_p^s as the supply of government of financial assets to the nonbank public. Then the total amount of newly issued government financial assets (A_g^s) equals that acquired by depository institutions (A_b^d) plus that supplied to the nonbank public (A_p^s)—that is, $A_g^s = A_b^d + A_p^s$. Substituting this breakdown of the total supply of newly issued government securities into the government financing constraint, we have

$$G^d = T + A_p^s + A_b^d$$

Substituting the depository institution financing constraint ($A_b^d = (M^s/P) - \overline{M}/P$) into the above equation, we obtain

$$G^d \quad = \quad T \quad + \quad A^s_p \quad + \quad (M^s/P) - \overline{M}/P$$

| Government demand | Net real taxes | Government supply of financial assets to nonbank public | Supply of additional real money balances |

Thus we can view part of government purchases of goods and services as essentially financed by an expansion in the real money supply, with the remainder financed from taxes and the sale of bonds to the nonbank public. However, we will find it more useful to distinguish between fiscal actions, with the corresponding government financing constraint ($G^d = T + A^s_g$), and monetary actions, with the corresponding depository institution financing constraint ($A^d_b = (M^s/P) - (\overline{M}/P)$).

In the chapters that follow, we explore how the government's fiscal policy decisions affect output, interest rates, prices, and employment in the economy. When we examine the effects of fiscal policy changes on the various markets in the economy, we must be careful to take into account the interrelationships between fiscal policy variables dictated by the government financing constraint. In addition, as we see in the concluding section of this chapter, the government financing constraint, along with the constraints faced by firms, households, and depository institutions, are important in understanding the interrelationships between the various markets in the economy.

To the Point

CONSTRAINTS FOR MONETARY AND FISCAL POLICY

- The fact that purchases of financial assets by private depository institutions are financed by the creation of deposits is summarized by the depository institution financing constraint, which equates the real change in the money supply to depository institutions' real demand for additional financial assets.

- The government financing constraint demonstrates that government spending is constrained to equal the amount collected in taxes and through borrowing. If the government spends exactly what it collects in taxes during the year, then the budget is balanced and government does not borrow during that year. Deficits occur when spending exceeds taxes.

- The government financing constraint links together its fiscal policy decisions concerning the choice of real spending on output, net real taxes, and real supply of government bonds.

4.6   THE AGGREGATE BUDGET CONSTRAINT: THE CLOSED ECONOMY

From our analysis of the various participants in the economy, we know that all economic agents face constraints in making their demand and supply decisions. The importance of understanding these financing constraints cannot be overemphasized. The financing constraints are what link the various markets in the economy together and illustrate the general equilibrium nature of macroeconomic analysis. To show this, let's start by reviewing these constraints.

The firm financing constraint (Equation 4.1) equates firms' real net investment demand (I^d) to their real supply of new financial assets A_f^s. In other words, according to the firm financing constraint,

$$I^d = A_f^s \tag{4.10}$$

The household budget constraint (Equation 4.4) equates household consumption (C^d) and saving (S) to real disposable income ($Y - CCA - T$). As shown by Equation 4.5, households save by adding to their real holdings of money ($L^d - \overline{M}/P$) and to their holdings of financial assets (A_h^d). Thus we can write the household budget constraint as

$$C^d + A_h^d + L^d - \overline{M}/P = Y - CCA - T \tag{4.11}$$

The depository institution financing constraint (Equation 4.7) equates depository institutions' real demand for additional financial assets (A_b^d) to the increase in the real supply of money (M^s/P) $- \overline{M}/P$. According to the depository institution financing constraint

$$A_b^d = (M^s/P) - \overline{M}/P \tag{4.12}$$

Finally, the government financing constraint (Equation 4.11) equates real government spending (G^d) to real net taxes (T) and real government borrowing (A_g^s). That is, according to the government financing constraint

$$G^d = T + A_g^s \tag{4.13}$$

Deriving the Aggregate Budget Constraint

Aggregate budget constraint: A constraint that is obtained by summing the constraints faced by each of the individual participants in the economy. Indicates that the excess demands in the various markets in the economy must sum to zero.

To simplify macroeconomic analysis, we sometimes consider the U.S. economy in isolation from the rest of the world. We refer to such an economy, one without foreign trade, as a "closed" economy. If we sum the budget constraints faced by each of the four participants in a closed economy, we obtain the closed economy **aggregate budget constraint.** Specifically, summing equations (4.10) through (4.13) and rearranging terms, the aggregate budget constraint for a closed economy is given by

$$\underbrace{[C^d + I^d + CCA + G^d - Y]}_{\substack{\text{Excess demand} \\ \text{output market}}} + \underbrace{[A_h^d + A_b^d - (A_f^s + A_g^s)]}_{\substack{\text{Excess demand} \\ \text{financial market}}} + \underbrace{[L^d - M^s/P]}_{\substack{\text{Excess demand} \\ \text{money "market"}}} = 0 \qquad \textbf{(4.14)}$$

The aggregate budget constraint tells us that the demands and supplies for output, financial assets, and money are interdependent. To obtain better insight into this interdependency, we will denote the economy-wide demand for output by Y^d. Since the total demand for output in a closed economy is equal to the sum of consumption demand, gross investment demand (I^d + CCA), and government demand, we have

$$Y^d \equiv C^d + I^d + CCA + G^d \qquad \textbf{(4.15)}$$

where the symbol $\equiv$ indicates that Y^d is identical to or defined by $C^d + I^d + CCA + G^d$.

In a similar fashion, let A^d denote the total real demand for financial assets. This demand is simply the sum of the demands of households and the depository institutions or

$$A^d \equiv A_h^d + A_b^d \qquad \textbf{(4.16)}$$

Finally, let A^s denote the real supply of financial assets. Since firms and the government are the net issuers of financial assets (borrowers of loanable funds),

$$A^s \equiv A_f^s + A_g^s \qquad \textbf{(4.17)}$$

Substituting Equations 4.15, 4.16, and 4.17 into Equation 4.14, the aggregate budget constraint, we can rewrite the aggregate budget constraint as

$$\underbrace{(Y^d - Y)}_{\substack{\text{Excess demand} \\ \text{output market}}} + \underbrace{(A^d - A^s)}_{\substack{\text{Excess demand} \\ \text{financial market}}} + \underbrace{(L^d - M^s/P)}_{\substack{\text{Excess demand} \\ \text{money "market"}}} = 0 \qquad \textbf{(4.18)}$$

Equation 4.18 consists of terms that describe the difference between demand and supply for output, financial assets, and money. If quantity of a good demanded exceeds the quantity supplied, we say there is "excess demand" for that good. Conversely, if the quantity of the supplied exceeds the quantity demanded, there is a negative excess demand or an "excess supply" of the good. For example, if the quantity of output demanded (Y^d) exceeds the output produced (Y), then an excess demand for output exists. Similarly, the excess demands for financial assets and money are defined by the terms $A^d - A^s$ and $L^d - M^s/P$, respectively. In the financial market, an excess demand for financial assets means that quantity of financial assets demanded by buyers of financial assets (the lenders) exceeds the quantity supplied by sellers (the borrowers). An excess demand for money means that the desired real holdings of money exceed the quantity of real money balances supplied.

Equation (4.18) helps us identify the aggregate budget constraint as equating the sum of "excess demands" for output, financial assets, and money to zero. We can rephrase this statement in terms of markets instead of goods by stating that the *excess demands in the output, financial, and money markets must sum to zero*. In this context, the use of the term money "market" differs from its usage in everyday language. The common usage of the term money market, as reported for example in the *Wall Street Journal*, refers to the market for short-term financial assets. As we saw in Chapter 3, this market is part of what macroeconomics calls the financial market. In contrast, the term money "market" in macroeconomics refers to the relationship between the demand for and supply of money balances. For example, if the quantity of money balances demanded exceeds the quantity supplied, we say there is an excess demand in the money market.

As we discuss below, the relationship between excess demands in the various markets highlighted by the aggregate budget constraint helps us to understand the important links among the various markets in the economy.

The Interrelationships Between the Output, Financial, and Money Markets

The fact that the sum of excess demands across all markets equals zero is often referred to as Walras' Law, in honor of León Walras, who first derived the result in his book, *Eléments d'économie Politique Pure*.[13] Walras' Law simply reflects the budget constraints faced by the various participants in the economy. It is important to note that our application of Walras' Law ignores activity in the labor market. The outcome of the labor market—employment and the resulting output production—is summarized by the actual output (Y) that appears in household budget constraint. Our approach follows Patinkin, who notes that this simplification makes later discussions of comparative statics easier and also makes possible the use of certain helpful graphical devices.[14] In particular, we will later use an "aggregate supply" curve to summarize events in the labor market, and an "aggregate demand" curve to summarize events in the output, financial, and money markets. Given this qualification, let's look at some of the implications of Walras' Law.

Suppose that the real quantity of money demanded is less than the real quantity of money supplied ($L^d < M^s/P$) and that the quantity of financial assets demanded equals the quantity supplied ($A^d = A^s$). The aggregate budget constraint, Equation 4.18, tells us that output demand must exceed the quantity produced ($Y^d > Y$). Thus in the case of equilibrium in the financial market, an excess supply of money implies an excess demand for

---

[13] León Walras, *Elements d'économie Politique Pure* (Lausanne: 1874–77, issued in two consecutively paginated volumes).

[14] Don Patinkin, *Money, Interest, and Prices* (New York: Harper and Row, 1965), p. 205.

output. Intuitively, the excess demand in the output market is a reflection of the fact that individuals' money holdings exceed what they desire, and these excess holdings are chasing after goods if the quantity of financial assets demanded equals the quantity supplied.

Let's take another example. Suppose that the quantity of output demanded equals that produced (that is, $Y^d = Y$), and that the demand for financial assets equals the supply of financial assets (that is $A^d = A^s$). Then the aggregate budget constraint tells us that the demand for money *must* equal the supply of money.

This second example illustrates an important principle: Since excess demands in the output, financial, and money markets must sum to zero, *if any two of these markets are in equilibrium, then the third one must also be in equilibrium.* This result simplifies our analysis of economy-wide equilibrium because we can confine our analysis to the labor market and two of the other three markets. Convenience is the sole determinant of which two markets we choose (output and financial, output and money, or financial and money).[15]

4.7   THE AGGREGATE BUDGET CONSTRAINT: THE OPEN ECONOMY

Up until now, our discussion of the aggregate budget constraint considered a closed economy. To include a foreign sector means modifying our analysis to take into account the foreign exchange constraints faced by both households and foreigners. Specifically, households need foreign currency to purchase foreign goods and financial assets. Foreigners must supply foreign currency to finance their purchases of U.S. goods and financial assets. Note that we have simplified our analysis of the open economy by assuming that firms neither sell financial assets in foreign financial markets nor purchase foreign output. A second simplifying assumption we make is that U.S. depository institutions do not purchase foreign financial assets. We do not lose any important insights by making these two simplifications since the critical issue is that at least one U.S. participant in the economy, in our case households, is purchasing foreign goods and foreign financial assets.

The next section develops the constraints faced by households and foreigners associated with their activities in the foreign exchange market. We then use these constraints to derive the aggregate budget constraint in the open economy. As we will see, in an open economy the aggregate budget constraint includes the excess demand in the foreign exchange market.

---

[15] If you have taken a previous course in macroeconomics, your analysis was probably confined to the output and money markets.

Household and Foreigner Financing Constraints in the Foreign Exchange Market

Expanding our discussion of the aggregate budget constraint to include the open economy requires us to broaden the choices facing U.S. households. Household consumption expenditures now include purchases of foreign goods (U.S. imports), and household financial asset purchases now include the purchase of foreign financial assets (U.S. capital outflows). Let import demand be denoted by Z^d and let household demand for foreign financial assets be denoted by AF_h^d. U.S. household purchases of imports and foreign financial assets constitute a demand for foreign currency since foreign currency is required to make these purchases. Letting FC^d denote U.S. households' real demand for foreign currency in the foreign exchange market, this **household foreign exchange constraint** can be written as

Household foreign exchange constraint: A constraint that equates households' real demand for foreign currency (FC^d) to the sum of import demand (Z^d) plus households' real desired purchases of foreign financial assets (AF_h^d).

$$
\underset{\substack{\text{Real demand} \\ \text{for foreign} \\ \text{currency}}}{FC^d} \quad = \quad \underset{\substack{\text{Real U.S.} \\ \text{import} \\ \text{demand}}}{Z^d} \quad + \quad \underset{\substack{\text{Household demand for} \\ \text{additional foreign} \\ \text{financial assets}}}{AF_h^d}
\tag{4.19}
$$

As we saw in Chapter 3, foreigners demand dollars in the foreign exchange markets in order to purchase U.S. goods and financial assets. In order to purchase dollars in the foreign exchange markets, they must supply their own currency. In other words, foreigners' demand for U.S. goods and financial assets is ultimately financed by the supply of their own currency. This relationship is summarized by the foreigner financing constraint. Specifically, letting FC^s denote foreigners' *real* supply of foreign currency to the foreign exchange market, we can write **foreigner foreign exchange constraint** as

Foreigner foreign exchange constraint: A constraint that indicates that the sum of X^d and A_{for}^d foreigners' demand for U.S. goods and services (U.S. exports) and for U.S. financial assets (A_{for}^d) equals their real supply of foreign currency (FC^s).

$$
\underset{\substack{\text{Real Supply} \\ \text{of foreign} \\ \text{currency}}}{FC^s} \quad = \quad \underset{\substack{\text{Real U.S.} \\ \text{export} \\ \text{demand}}}{X^d} \quad + \quad \underset{\substack{\text{Foreign demand} \\ \text{for additional U.S.} \\ \text{financial assets}}}{A_{for}^d}
\tag{4.20}
$$

Equation 4.20 indicates that the sum of X^d and A_{for}^d, foreign demand for U.S. output (U.S. exports) and for financial assets (U.S. capital inflows), respectively, equals their real supply of foreign currency.

The right-hand side of Equation 4.20 is foreigners' demand for U.S. goods and financial assets in real terms. Thus their supply of foreign currency to finance these purchases must also be real terms, that is in terms of U.S. goods and services. The real supply of foreign currency (FC^s) is computed as follows. The nominal amount of foreign currency supplied by foreigners is first converted to dollars by multiplying by the price of the foreign currency in terms of dollars. For instance, a German supplying 100 marks is, if the foreign exchange rate is .5 dollars per mark, supplying $50 worth of marks. This supply of foreign currency in terms of U.S. dollars is then converted into U.S. real goods and services by dividing by the U.S. price level.

Deriving the Open Economy Aggregate Budget Constraint

Adding the foreign exchange constraints (Equations 4.19 and 4.20) to the financing constraints facing households, firms, government, and depository institutions (Equations 4.14 to 4.17) and rearranging terms, we obtain the aggregate budget constraint for the open economy:

$$[C^d + I^d + CCA + G^d + (X^d - Z^d) - Y] + [A_h^d + A_b^d + (A_{for}^d - AF_h^d) - (A_f^s + A_g^s)] + [L^d - M^s/P] + [FC^d - FC^s] = 0 \quad (4.21)$$

Excess demand output market	Excess demand financial market	Excess demand money "market"	Excess demand foreign currency market

Four distinct terms, each included in a bracket, appear in Equation (4.21). The first three reflect excess demands in the U.S. output, financial, and money markets, respectively. The fourth term reflects the real excess demand for foreign currency in the foreign exchange market.

Several differences become obvious when we compare the terms in the aggregate budget constraint for the open economy (Equation 4.21) with those in the aggregate budget constraint for the closed economy (Equation 4.14). The expression for excess demand in the output market, the first term in both aggregate budget constraints, now includes net export demand ($X^d - Z^d$). The expression for excess demand for U.S. financial assets, the second term in both aggregate budget constraints, now includes net international capital inflows ($A_{for}^d - AF_h^d$)—that is, foreigners' demand for U.S. financial assets A_{for}^d (capital inflows) minus U.S. households' demand for foreign financial assets AF_h^d (capital outflows). Finally, the aggregate budget constraint for the open economy introduces the term, $[FC^d - FC^s]$. This term represents the real excess demand for foreign currency, which equals the difference between U.S. households' real demand for foreign currency and foreigners' real supply of foreign currency.

SUMMARY

We simplify our task of modeling the overall economy by dividing the economy's participants into five major categories. This chapter looked at how these participants take part in the workings of the economy. An essential feature of each participant's activity in the economy is that each faces a spending constraint. For instance, firms are constrained to finance net investment demand out of retained earnings or by issuing new financial assets—bonds and equity shares (borrowing). In either case, the total value of firms' outstanding financial assets (stocks and bonds) increases by the value of capital purchased. Thus we can speak as though firms finance net investment demand entirely by issuing additional financial assets. The equality between firms' desired investment spending and the value of new financial assets issued is summarized by the firm financing constraint.

Households use the fruits of their labor, or their labor income, for consumption and saving. Additional sources of income are the interest and dividend payments households receive from firms. Firms, however, do not distribute all of the revenue earned from production (Y) back to households. Firms use some of their revenues to pay taxes and some to replace the capital consumed in the production process (CCA); the rest is distributed to households in the form of wages, dividends, and interest. Households pay additional taxes to the government from the income received from firms. Thus, as the household budget constraint indicates, consumption and saving ($C^d + S$) is constrained by household's disposable income ($YD = Y - CCA - T$), where T stands for total taxes paid by households and firms net of government transfer payments.

There are two basic types of depository institutions in the United States: private depository institutions and the central bank. Among the various private depository institutions are commercial banks and thrift institutions, such as savings and loan associations, mutual savings banks, and credit unions. The central bank in the United States is the Federal Reserve, commonly called the "Fed." Depository institutions play a unique role in the economy; when they purchase financial assets, they create money. In fact, for every dollar of the money supply, there is a dollar's worth of financial assets held either by the Fed or by private depository institutions. This relationship is summarized by the depository institution financing constraint.

The government financing constraint relates changes in government spending to the government's sources of revenue: tax revenue and borrowing. If the government spends only what it collects in tax revenue in a given year, it is said to have a balanced budget. If spending exceeds taxes, the government is said to run a deficit; a surplus occurs when tax revenues exceed government expenditures.

The aggregate budget constraint is arrived at by summing the budget constraints of the various participants in the macroeconomy—firms, households, government, depository institutions, and, in an open economy, foreigners. The aggregate budget constraint indicates that the sum of the excess demands in the various markets must equal zero. As we will see more clearly in subsequent chapters, this result is important because it simplifies our analysis of economy-wide equilibrium.

LOOKING AHEAD

The reason we study macroeconomics is to understand what determines changes in output, employment, prices, interest rates, and other aggregate variables. As we will see in later chapters, these changes occur as the various markets adjust to excess demands or supplies. While the presence of excess demand in any of the markets leads to equilibrating adjustments within that market, the aggregate budget constraint reminds us that the markets are interrelated. Excess demand in one market implies excess supply in at least one other market. The aggregate budget constraint, derived from agents' financing constraints that were developed in this chapter, thus constitutes the backbone of macroeconomic analysis.

Although our ultimate interest is in understanding how the key aggregate variables are determined, we must always keep uppermost in our mind that these aggregate variables are the outcome of a multitude of decisions made by the individual economic actors in the economy. To understand the whole or "macroeconomy," we must start by looking at the behavior of the individuals that comprise it, or its microeconomic foundations. Chapter 5 begins our analysis of the "microeconomic foundations of macroeconomics" by looking at the investment, employment, and production decisions of firms.

SUMMARY OF KEY EQUATIONS

Firm financing constraint

$$I^d = A_f^s \tag{4.1}$$

Household budget constraint

$$C^d + A_h^d + L^d - \overline{M}/P = Y - CCA - T \tag{4.6}$$

Depository institution financing constraint

$$A_b^d = (M^s/P) - \overline{M}/P \tag{4.7}$$

Government financing constraint

$$G^d = T + A_g^s \tag{4.9}$$

Aggregate budget constraint (closed economy)

$$(Y^d - Y) + (A^d - A^s) + (L^d - M^s/P) = 0 \tag{4.18}$$

Household foreign exchange constraint

$$FC^d = Z^d + AF_h^d \tag{4.19}$$

Foreigner foreign exchange constraint

$$FC^s = X^d + A_{ion}^d \tag{4.20}$$

Aggregate budget constraint (open economy)

$$[C^d + I^d + CCA + G^d + (X^d - Z^d) - Y] + [A_h^d + A_b^d + (A_{for}^d - AF_h^d) - (A_f^s + A_g^s)] + [L^d - M^s/P] + [FC^d - FC^s] = 0 \tag{4.21}$$

KEY TERMS

Partial equilibrium analysis, 88
General equilibrium analysis, 88
Firm financing constraint, 99
Real disposable income, 101
Household budget constraint, 102
Real money demand, 104
Monetary policy, 105
Monetary base, 107

Required reserves, 108
Excess reserves, 108
Depository institution financing
   constraint, 110
Government financing constraint, 112
Fiscal policy, 114
Aggregate budget constraint, 116
Household foreign exchange
   constraint, 120
Foreigner foreign exchange constraint,
   120

REVIEW QUESTIONS

1. What is the difference between a change in investment and a change in the capital stock of a firm?

2. The return that an investor receives from holding an equity share can come in one of two forms—dividends or appreciation. If a firm earns large profits in a year and, rather than distributing that profit, decides to reinvest in net investment for the company, does the shareholder earn

   (a) no return?

   (b) return in the form of dividends?

   (c) return in the form of the appreciation of his share? Explain your answer.

3. Give the equation for the household budget constraint. Interpret this equation.

4. Is the following statement true or false? "By increasing taxes on firms, we can lower taxes on households, thereby raising their real disposable income." Explain your answer.

5. Suppose that someone estimates that in 1988, real GNP in small, peace-loving Fredonia was $200, real depreciation of capital was $20, real net taxes were $20, real consumption spending was $150, and real saving was $50. Can these estimates be correct?

6. What are the two forms that household saving can take?

7. What items constitute the monetary base? For whom are these items liabilities? For whom are they assets?

8. What do we mean when we say that depository institutions serve as "financial intermediaries"?

9. What are required reserves? What are excess reserves? If a bank has deposits of $400,000 and financial asset holdings of $315,000 and its required reserve to deposit ratio is .10, what are its excess reserves?

10. What is the depository institution financing constraint? Interpret this constraint.

11. A November 26, 1984 *Wall Street Journal* article reported the following: "The latest Fed figures showed that the basic money supply, known as M1, declined by $1.3 billion in the week ending November 12. The Fed estimated M1 averaged seasonally adjusted $545.5 billion in the latest week, down from $546.7 billion the previous week. That left M1 only $1.1 billion above the lower end of the Fed's target range, which calls for 4 percent to 8 percent growth this year." If the money supply is lower, what do we know about depository institutions' financial asset demand? Why?

12. Interpret the government financing constraint.

13. Suppose that real government spending is $80 billion and real net taxes are $60 million.

   (a) Is the government running a deficit or a surplus? How much is it?

   (b) What is the government's real financial asset supply equal to?

   (c) Suppose that government spending increases to $85 billion. What happens to real net taxes and the government's real supply of financial assets?

14. In what sense can we speak of the government "printing money" to finance its expenditures?

15. Consider a closed economy.

   (a) State the aggregate budget constraint.

   (b) Where does the aggregate budget constraint come from?

   (c) Suppose that the demand for money equals the supply of money and that the demand for financial assets equals the supply of financial assets. What do we know about the demand for and supply of output?

   (d) Suppose that there is an excess supply of output. What do we know about the demand and supply of money and the demand for and supply of financial assets?

16. Compare the aggregate budget constraint for the open economy with that of the closed economy.

17. For a closed economy, derive the aggregate budget constraint for the following situation:

   (a) Household income is explicitly defined as equal to wage income $[(W/P)N^s]$, dividends (D), and interest payments (I) from firms (i.e., $Y - CCA - T$ is replaced with $(W/P)N^s + D + I - T$).

(b) A firm distribution constraint is added that states that firms' revenues other than those used to purchase depreciated capital are distributed to households (i.e., $(W/P)N^d + D + I + CCA - Y = 0$). Note that N^s and N^d in the above expressions refer to labor supply by households and labor demand by firms. Express your result in terms of excess demands in the various markets in the economy.

18. Using the budget constraints for the various participants in the economy:

(a) In the context of an open economy, algebraically express equilibrium in the loanable funds market in terms of household saving, net capital inflow, investment, and government deficit spending. To do so, assume money demand and supply are equal.

(b) Express equilibrium in the foreign exchange market in terms of exports, imports, and net capital inflow. Combining this with part a, show how equilibrium in the output market is implied by equilibrium in the other three markets.

Part Two

Behavior of the Participants in the Economy

Chapter 5

Firms and Depository Institutions

ALTHOUGH we look at the overall performance of the economy in macroeconomics, we must recognize that this overall performance reflects the aggregation of individual actions in the various markets. Thus we cannot discuss investment for the economy as a whole unless we know what motivates the investment decisions of individual firms. Likewise, in order to understand what motivates changes in the unemployment rate and the overall level of employment, we need to analyze the hiring decisions of firms. In general, our understanding of the workings of the macroeconomy is only as complete as our understanding of its microfoundations, i.e. the theory predicting the behavior of the individuals that participate in the economy.

In the first part of this chapter, we develop the theory of the behavior of firms in the labor market as demanders of labor and in the output market as purchasers of capital. Since the economic output of a nation depends critically on both the labor and capital inputs, it is important to understand the factors that motivate firms to hire labor and to add to their capital stock.

The second part of this chapter looks at how the actions of the depository institutions determine changes in the money supply. The Federal Reserve is the key player in initiating money supply changes; these changes can have profound impacts on the economy. Given the power of the Fed, it is critical that we fully understand exactly how the Federal Reserve instigates changes in the money supply, as well as how changes in the money supply can affect the economy. This chapter addresses the first of these questions—how the Fed determines the money supply. In subsequent chapters, we explore how monetary changes can affect the economy under different circumstances.

While this chapter looks at firms and depository institutions, Chapter 6 examines the behavior of households and foreigners, thereby completing the microeconomic foundations of the macroeconomic models to be developed in subsequent chapters. Understanding the material in these two micro-foundation chapters, along with the spending constraints presented in Chapter 4, will make it easier to grasp the views of the economy presented by the different macroeconomic models.

Before we start our development of the microfoundations of macroeconomics, one clarifying statement should be made about our approach. Our discussions of the microfoundations move from analyzing an individual firm or household to analyzing the behavior of all firms and all households. To ease this transition between individual agents and the aggregate, we often consider the individual household or firm as the "representative" agent. The representative agent is essentially an average unit; it differs from the aggregate only in size, not in behavior. Consequently we can move freely between discussions of the individual agent and the aggregate, and we can use the same notation for both. For example, we can use the symbol Y to denote not only the output of the representative firm but also aggregate output in the economy—real GNP.

5.1   PRODUCTION TECHNOLOGY

Firms, whether they are set up as corporations, proprietorships, or partnerships, are the economic agents that organize production in the economy. Firms combine the economy's productive inputs, such as labor and capital, to produce output. As we discussed in Chapter 2, the total output produced by firms in an economy over a specified time period is called real gross national product. Below we examine the factors that affect output decisions (how much to produce) and input decisions (how much labor to employ and how many capital goods to purchase). We begin by introducing the concept of a production function; the production function summarizes the relationship between the amount of output that a firm produces and the quantities of inputs it employs.

The Production Function

The amount of output that a firm produces depends directly on the amounts of capital and labor it employs. For example, consider the representative firm in the economy producing the output Y during the current period. Let K denote the size of the firm's capital stock (plants, machinery, etc.) and let N denote the firm's current employment level measured in work hours.[1]

---

[1] Recall from Chapter 2 that work hours are the product of the number of workers employed and the average number of hours worked.

Production function:
The relationship between a firm's output and its use of capital, labor, and other inputs.

The relationship between a firm's output and its capital and labor inputs is called the firm's **production function.** Denoting the production function by $f(\cdot)$, we obtain

$$Y = f(N,\ K,\ ...)$$
$$\quad\quad +\quad +$$

$$\text{(5.1)}$$

Economic models often represent relationships between variables as functions; the production function is an example of this. Since we will often see functions throughout this book, let's explain exactly what Equation 5.1 tells us. The equation indicates that Y, the output produced, is determined by the levels of the inputs of labor (N) and capital (K). The positive signs under the quantities of labor and capital indicate that output rises with the increased use of either input. The three dots indicate that such important inputs as raw materials and energy have been left unspecified. For the present, the fact that we omit these inputs is unimportant. Later, when we analyze the effects of such events as "energy crises" and "raw material shortages," we will accordingly expand our view of the production function.

There are three observations that should be made concerning our specification of the production function. First, we measure the labor input solely in terms of work hours. This means, for example, that we implicitly assume that ten employees who work 40 hours each produce exactly the same output as eight employees who work 50 hours each. Thus we are not taking into account such factors as worker fatigue or the possibility that the intensity with which workers are used may vary over time.[2]

The second observation to be made about the production function is that the labor input encompasses the supply of labor by individuals of vastly different skill levels. The units of labor are those of the representative worker and, as such, reflect an average skill level. The third observation about the production function is that it depends on the current level of technology. If technology changes, the production function, which simply summarizes the relationship between output and the capital and labor inputs, also changes. The increasingly widespread use of computers and the resulting revolution in processing information is an example of a major technological change. One consequence of this technological change has been an increase in the efficiency of office workers, and thus a rise in output per worker. Later in the text we discuss the effect of technological change on the long run growth of the economy's output.

Capital and Labor as Fixed and Variable Inputs

The production function, as it is characterized by Equation 5.1, indicates that firms can change their output level by altering either employment or

---

[2] As we discussed in the previous chapter, labor utilization (and hence labor productivity) is frequently greater during an economic recovery than during a recession, when labor hoarding occurs. The appendix to this chapter formally develops a model of labor hoarding.

the size of their capital stock. Although firms can change the level of employment almost instantaneously, changing the size of the capital stock generally takes more time.[3] Expressed differently, labor is a "variable" input while capital is, in a sense, a "fixed" input in the short run. To lower output, a firm's initial response would be to reduce work hours and lay off workers rather than to reduce its capital stock by selling off plants and machinery. Similarly, to increase output, a firm's initial response would be to recall laid-off workers, hire new workers, and increase hours, rather than to build new plants and purchase additional equipment. Thus with capital essentially fixed in the short run, changes in a firm's output are closely tied to changes in its employment of labor.

The relative fixity of capital in the short run is exemplified by a recent decision by General Motors to build a new plant for the production of a new line of cars. In the spring of 1984, GM announced that it would locate its new plant to manufacture Saturns in Tennessee. Two years later, GM broke ground for the new plant. Production of the Saturn is scheduled to begin in 1990. It thus took GM six years to implement a planned increase in its capital stock. In the interim, any increase in car production was achieved primarily through an increase in the employment of labor and not by an expansion in the firm's stock of capital.

The Marginal Product of Labor

As the discussion above suggests, we can view a firm's capital stock (K) as essentially fixed in the current period. For this *fixed* capital stock, the production function (Equation 5.1) tells us the output that firms can produce at any employment level. Figure 5.1(a) depicts the relationship between a firm's labor input and output for a given fixed level of capital ($\overline{K}$). As you might expect, increases in employment result in increases in output. For instance, an increase in employment from two work hours to three leads to an increase in a firm's output by the amount ΔY_1. This change in output associated with a one-unit increase in the labor input is called the **marginal product of labor** (*MPN*). A firm's marginal product of labor curve is graphed in Figure 5.1(b).

The concave shape of the production function in Fig. 5.1 indicates that although increases in employment lead to increases in output, output increases at a diminishing rate as employment rises. The marginal product of labor for the increase in employment from three to four work hours (ΔY_2) is smaller than the marginal product of labor for an increase in employment from two work hours to three, (ΔY_1). Similarly, the marginal

Marginal product of labor: The increase in output associated with a one-unit increase in the employment of labor, holding other inputs constant.

---

[3] We say *almost* instantaneously because labor also has some attributes of a fixed input. Since there are hiring and training costs associated with increasing employment, firms are less willing to change employment in response to changes in the demand for the product the firm produces than if labor can be varied without such costs. The appendix at the end of this chapter develops the nature of labor demand when it is costly for employers to adjust the size of their work force.

**Figure 5.1 The Production Function and the Marginal
Product of Labor**

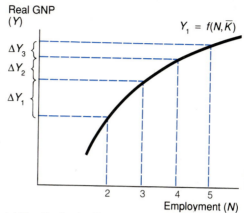

(a) The Production Function with Fixed Level of Capital $\bar{K}$

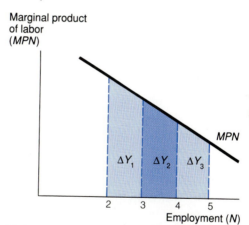

(b) The Marginal Product of Labor

The graph of the production function holding capital fixed depicts how output rises with increased employment. The graph of the marginal product of labor indicates that the increase in output associated with equal increases in employment is smaller as more of the labor input is used, other inputs fixed. This diminishing marginal product of labor is reflected in the downward slope of the marginal product of labor curve. The shaded areas under the marginal product curve denote the increases in output (ΔY_1, ΔY_2, and ΔY_3, respectively) shown on the vertical axis of the production function graph above.

product of labor for an increase in employment from four work hours to five (ΔY_3) is smaller than the marginal product of labor when employment increases from three to four (ΔY_2).

The falling marginal product of labor in Figure 5.1 captures the fact that most real-world production processes are characterized by the well-known

Law of diminishing marginal returns: A law stating that as more units of labor are added to a fixed amount of capital, the resulting increases in output tend to diminish.

law of diminishing marginal returns. This law states that as more units of labor are added to a fixed amount of capital, the resulting increases in output tend to diminish. The law of diminishing marginal returns dictates that the marginal product of labor curve depicted in Figure 5.1 is downward-sloping.

5.2   FIRM BEHAVIOR IN THE LABOR MARKET

As discussed above, a firm's output is determined by its level of employment in the short run. How much labor firms choose to employ depends, in turn, on the value and cost of additional labor services. The cost in dollars of a unit of labor is simply the wage that has to be paid. The dollar value of an additional unit of labor to firms is simply the revenues generated from the sale of the additional output that is produced. As we will see in this section, a firm's optimal employment of labor is the level at which the value of the last unit of labor hired just equals its cost. This optimal level of employment for various levels of real wages is graphically depicted by the demand for labor curve.

The Real Wage and Labor Demand

When making decisions about hiring additional labor, firms are motivated by a desire to maximize profits. If firms increase employment by one unit, output will increase by the marginal product of labor (MPN). The increase in revenue from producing the additional output depends on the nature of the market in which firms are selling their product. We assume for the moment the standard "competitive" or "price taker" market of microeconomics, in which individual firms can sell whatever output they produce at the prevailing market price.[4] In this type of market, firms receive the market price of P dollars for each unit of output sold, so that increasing employment by one unit raises revenue by the amount $P \cdot MPN$. The quantity $P \cdot MPN$ is referred to as the **value of the marginal product of labor.**

Value of the marginal product of labor ($P \cdot MPN$): The marginal product of labor multiplied by the price of output.

Firms must pay the prevailing money wage of W dollars for each unit of labor that they employ. If the value of the marginal product of labor exceeds the wage rate, then firms can increase profits by hiring more labor since the resulting increase in revenue will exceed the increase in cost. In contrast, if the value of the marginal product of labor is less than the wage

---

[4] This assumption is the standard one underlying the supply and demand analysis of microeconomics. It is often the case, however, that firms cannot sell all they wish at prevailing prices. Confronted with this situation and unsure of how much they can sell at various prices, firms must search for an optimal price as well as the optimal output and employment. For present purposes, using the standard supply and demand framework instead of these more complex, albeit realistic, market settings allows us to isolate in a simple way a set of factors that can be critical for the determination of employment and output in the economy.

rate, then firms can increase profits by reducing employment since the resulting reduction in revenue will be less than the reduction in cost. Only if the value of the marginal product of labor equals the wage rate will firms be unable to increase profits by changing the level of employment. Therefore, if firms are to maximize profit, their choice of employment must be such that

$$P \cdot MPN = W$$

<table>
<tr><td>Value of the
marginal product
of labor</td><td>Money
wage</td><td>**(5.2)**</td></tr>
</table>

In other words, at the profit-maximizing employment level the value of the marginal product of labor just equals the wage rate.

As Equation 5.2 indicates, employment decisions depend upon two money prices: the money wage (W), which is the price of labor, and the price of output (P). The net effect of these two prices on labor demand is summarized by what is known as the **real wage.** The real wage equals the money wage divided by the price of output. To see the role played by the real wage in determining employment decisions, divide both sides of Equation 5.2 by the output price (P) to obtain the following alternative way of stating the profit-maximizing employment rule:

Real wage: The money wage divided by the level of output prices.

$$MPN = W/P$$

<table>
<tr><td>Marginal product
of labor</td><td>Real
wage</td><td>**(5.3)**</td></tr>
</table>

According to Equation 5.3, if firms are to maximize profits, then they must employ labor up to the point where the marginal product of labor (MPN) just equals the real wage (W/P).

Conceptually, the real wage is simply the cost of labor to firms in terms of the amount of output that must be sacrificed. For example, suppose for the sake of concreteness that a firm produces tweezers. If each tweezer sells for $2 and if the hourly wage rate is $10, then the real wage is five tweezers. When the firm hires one additional hour of labor, the firm is paying the equivalent of five tweezers for the additional labor. If the firm is initially producing 2000 tweezers per hour, and if at that level of output the marginal product of an additional hour of labor is more than five tweezers, then the firm will hire additional labor. As more labor is hired, the marginal product of labor falls. The firm will hire labor up to the point where the marginal product of an additional hour of labor just equals the real wage of five tweezers. Equation 5.3 states this profit-maximizing condition.

The Labor Demand Curve

According to Equation 5.3, firms hire labor up to the point where the marginal product of labor equals the real wage. If the real wage falls, the quantity of labor demanded will be greater. In Figure 5.2, the labor demand

Figure 5.2 The Real Wage and the Demand for Labor

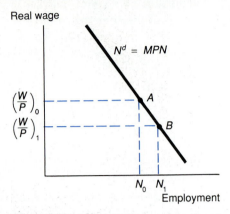

The downward-sloping marginal product of labor curve (the demand for labor curve) indicates that the increase in output from an additional unit of labor falls as employment increases. If the real wage falls from $(W/P)_0$ to $(W/P)_1$, firms will increase the quantity of labor demanded from N_0 to N_1.

curve labelled N^d illustrates this inverse relationship between the quantity of labor demanded and the real wage. According to Figure 5.2, if the real wage falls from $(W/P)_0$ to $(W/P)_1$, then a firm's desired employment rises from N_0 to N_1. At this higher level of employment the marginal product of labor will again equal the new lower real wage. Since at each real wage the quantity of labor demanded equates the marginal product of labor to the real wage, the labor demand curve is simply the marginal product of labor curve.

The fall in real wage depicted in Figure 5.2 can be the result of either a fall in the money wage or a rise in the price level. The wage givebacks of the early 1980s provide an example of the inverse relation between the real wage rate and the amount of labor firms demand. At that time, members of both the United Auto Workers (UAW) and the United Rubber Workers (URW) were experiencing substantial layoffs and high unemployment. Consequently, the UAW and the URW negotiated lower money wages and hence lower real wages for their members. The reason that these unions were willing to accept lower wages is demonstrated by Figure 5.2: A lower real wage has the effect of increasing the quantity of labor demanded and thus employment. At least in this instance, the unions were willing to trade off a reduced wage in order to increase the employment of their members.

A rise in the price of output, like a fall in the money wage, also means a fall in the real wage and thus an increase in the profit-maximizing level of employment. During the early 1980s, although the price level (P) was increasing at double-digit rates, some labor unions accepted a wage freeze—

which meant that these unions thus took a cut in their real wage. If wages are not actually frozen, but they increase by less than prices, then the real wage still falls, leading to an increase in the quantity of labor demanded. Graphically, this is shown by the movement down the labor demand curve from point A to point B in Figure 5.2. The resulting increase in the quantity of labor demanded is shown by the movement from N_0 to N_1 on the horizontal axis.

We can summarize the effect on labor demand N^d of changes in wages and the price level by the equation

$$N^d = N^d(\underset{-}{W/P}, ...)$$

(5.4)

where N^d equals labor demand and W/P equals the real wage. The negative sign below the real wage indicates that the aggregate demand for labor is inversely related to the real wage. In other words, a rise in the real wage reduces the amount of labor that firms demand.

Case Study

HIRING AND TRAINING COSTS—LABOR AS A QUASI-FIXED INPUT

In our analysis of labor demand, we have assumed (at least implicitly) that firms can adjust the size of their labor force costlessly. Upon further reflection, however, it is obvious that the real world is typically more complicated than this; firms generally incur significant costs when changing the size of their labor force because adding new employees often entails substantial hiring and training costs. By way of illustration, a *Wall Street Journal* article on December 1, 1987 reported that the new Toyota plant in Georgetown, Kentucky, spends a great deal of time screening applicants: "Even someone applying for the lowest paying job on the shop floor goes through at least 14 hours of testing . . . . Only one applicant in 20 makes it to an interview which is conducted by a panel representing various Toyota departments." In addition to hiring costs, employers also incur a cost of training new employees. The article went on to report that "Nissan Motor Company, which has been operating in Smyrna, Tennessee, since the early 1980s, prefers to give probable hires at least 40 hours of "pre-employment" training."

Labor economists have devoted considerable effort both to ascertaining the magnitude of hiring and training costs and to analyzing the consequences for labor market behavior. Firm hiring costs include the costs involved in advertising job openings and in screening and evaluating job applicants. Evidence that these costs are not trivial is provided by Barron and Bishop in a study that finds that when hiring for a job vacancy, employers on average interview nine applicants, in the process devoting an average of close to ten hours to recruiting and screening to fill a position.[5]

Once hired, the new employee must generally receive some training, both formal and informal. Training programs are often required to teach new skills, such as how to use a particular piece of equipment, and also to provide background information on the firm and the various employee benefits. In a recent study, Barron, Black, and Loewenstein provide evidence on the importance of these training activities.[6] They find that for a sample of entry level positions, "approximately 30 percent of a newly hired employee's time is typically spent in on-the-job training activities during the first three months of employment. Thus on-the-job training constitutes a significant investment by worker and employer."

How does the existence of hiring and training costs affect labor input decisions? Recall the simple profit-maximizing employment rule that emerged under the assumption that firms can costlessly add new workers to their labor force: Always employ labor just up to the point where the marginal product of labor (MPN) equals the real wage (W/P). This rule must be altered once we take hiring and training costs into account. Such costs mean that firms should be less willing to change employment in response to changes in output demand; in other words, as noted by Walter Oi, the presence of hiring and training costs make labor a "quasi-fixed factor of production."[7]

In the appendix to this chapter, we analyze exactly how hiring and training costs can alter labor input decisions. For current purposes, it suffices to note that when hiring a worker today, a firm expects to receive a future return sufficiently large enough to justify the hiring and training costs it incurs. This future return takes the form of an expected value of marginal product of the worker that exceeds his or her future wage.

Suppose, however, that the value of the worker's labor services turns out to be lower than the firm initially expected, say due to a future price of output below that which had been expected. Will the firm dismiss the worker during the next period? Not necessarily; if the price of output is not too low, then the value of marginal product of labor may still exceed the wage. In this case, the firm has no reason to dismiss any of its workers. Although the firm will not earn enough to make back all of its past hiring and training costs, these costs are sunk and are therefore irrelevant. As long as the firm's currently trained workers have a value of the marginal product that is greater than the current wage, it will still be worthwhile for the firm to continue employing all of them.

Our discussion so far has stressed how employer-specific hiring and training costs can make labor a less variable input than would be the case

---

[5] John M. Barron and John Bishop, "Extensive Search, Intensive Search, and Hiring Costs: New Evidence on Employer Hiring Activity," *Economic Inquiry* (July 1985): 370.

[6] John M. Barron, Dan A. Black, and Mark A. Loewenstein, "Job Matching and On-the-Job Training," *Journal of Labor Economics*, January 1989.

[7] Walter Oi, "Labor as a Quasi-fixed Factor," *Journal of Political Economy* (November, 1972).

if such costs were zero. Perhaps equally important in tying workers to firms is the fact that it generally takes time for employers to determine the true productivity of their individual workers and for workers to discover the various attributes of a job.

Employers are generally uncertain about the abilities and work habits of their newly hired workers because such information is usually obtained only by monitoring a worker's performance over time. Employers can thus do better by continuing to employ experienced workers whom they have already observed to be productive rather than hiring new workers who may turn out to be unproductive.[8] Similarly, when first taking a job, workers face uncertainty with respect to whether or not they will like their co-workers, the conditions under which they must work, and the types of tasks that they will have to perform.[9] Workers who, over time, have found jobs to be of their liking can do better by staying with their current employer rather than moving elsewhere.

Incentives for long-term employment relations between firms and workers are created not only by employer-specific training but also by employer-specific information. The importance of these long-term employment relations is underscored by Robert Hall's finding that for workers aged 30 and above, about 40 percent are in a job which will eventually last at least 20 years. The macroeconomic consequences of these long-term employment relations, particularly as they pertain to temporary layoffs, are discussed in Chapter 15.

To the Point

FIRMS AS BUYERS IN THE LABOR MARKET

- A production function specifies the relationship between output and inputs such as labor and capital. In the short run, most changes in output reflect changes in the labor input. The capital input is typically viewed as fixed in the short run.

---

[8] Of course, on the other side of the coin, workers who are found out to be unproductive are dismissed, something that would not happen if ties between workers and firms resulted only from costly training. Further comparison of the roles played by costly training and costly information in creating long-term employment relations between employers and workers can be found in John Barron and Mark Loewenstein, "On Employer-Specific Information and Internal Labor Markets," *Southern Economic Journal* (October 1985). The authors provide evidence that dismissals and fires are indeed substantial.

[9] William Johnson in "A Theory of Job Shopping," *Quarterly Journal of Economics* (May 1978) notes that the fact that workers can learn about many of a job's attributes only by working on the job for a period of time causes them to shop around for jobs by trying them out. Evidence that workers and employers obtain information on each other only belatedly is provided by Robert Hall, "The Importance of Lifetime Jobs in the U.S. Economy," *American Economic Review* (September 1982). Hall's results indicate that many employer-worker matches are unsuccessful and thus only of short duration. The typical pattern is for individuals to hold a number of very brief jobs in the first few years of participation in the labor force. Eventually one job turns out to be a good match and lasts for a number of years.

- The change in output that is associated with a one-unit change in the labor input, holding capital fixed, is termed the marginal product of labor. Due to diminishing marginal returns, the marginal product of labor declines as employment increases.

- The value to a firm of an additional unit of labor equals the marginal product of labor times the price of output. To maximize profits, firms hire labor up to the point where the value of the marginal product equals the wage.

- An equivalent statement of the profit-maximizing employment condition is that labor is hired up to the point where the marginal product of labor equals the real wage. The real wage, which is the money wage divided by the price of output, defines the cost of labor in terms of output forgone. The labor demand curve depicts the inverse relationship between the real wage and the quantity of labor demanded.

- With hiring costs and training costs, labor becomes a quasi-fixed input, and firms adjustments in employment given changes in the real wage are less pronounced. Such costs, as well as firm-specific information on the capabilities of current employees, can lead to long-term employment relations between particular firms and workers.

5.3   FIRM BEHAVIOR IN THE OUTPUT AND FINANCIAL MARKETS

Changes in an economy's stock of capital—its net real investment—are important because they affect the rate at which the economy's productive capacity grows. Expressed differently, increases in the capital stock increase the output that can be produced by any given amount of labor. The relationship between capital and productivity was highlighted in the 1983 *Economic Report of the President,* which noted that during the 1970s "no other major industrial nation devote[d] as small a fraction of total output to new investment as [did] the United States." As a consequence, the United States had "the lowest growth rate of productivity." For example, Japan devoted 34 percent of its gross domestic product to investment between 1971 and 1980, and had an average growth rate of output per hour in manufacturing of 7.4 percent. In contrast, U.S. gross investment was 19.1 percent of gross domestic product over the same time period, and the average annual rate of growth of output per hour in manufacturing was only 2.5 percent.[10]

Because investment is so important in determining the future productive capability of an economy, as well as being a key component of output demand, we want to investigate the factors that determine firms' investment demand. In the following section, we show how purchases of new capital

---

[10] *Economic Report of the President* (1983), p. 81.

goods in the output market depend on what is called the user, or rental, cost of capital. We then discuss an important implication of the firm financing constraint developed in Chapter 4: that the factors determining a firm's investment demand are the same ones determining a firm's supply of financial assets, or equivalently its demand for loanable funds, in the financial market.

Factors Determining Net Investment Demand: A Simple Example

Firms purchase new capital as long as the gains exceed the costs—as is the case when they hire labor. To understand what motivates the investment demand decision of firms, let us consider the gains and costs to an increase in investment for a firm in the business of producing tweezers.

Suppose that the tweezer firm increases its net real investment by one unit. The extra unit of capital—an automatic punch press that stamps out tweezers—costs P_k dollars today. If the firm issues a one-year bond to pay for this purchase of capital, then the firm agrees to pay $1 + r$ dollars next year for each dollar borrowed today, where r is the nominal interest rate. Thus the cost to the firm of purchasing the unit of capital in the current period is the $P_k(1 + r)$ dollars it must pay next year. This is the marginal cost of the investment in terms of dollars next year.

Marginal product of capital (*MPK*): The increase in output associated with a one-unit increase in capital, other inputs being held constant.

The firm's capital investment yields a future marginal gain to the firm that is made up of two components. First, revenue will be higher next year because a larger capital stock will enable it to produce, and consequently sell, more tweezers next year. The increase in the firm's output of tweezers next year resulting from an additional unit of capital is the **marginal product of capital** (*MPK*). To obtain the increase in the firm's expected revenue, we multiply the increase in its output by the price at which the firm expects to sell this output next year (P^e). Thus the expected increase in the firm's revenue next year from the extra unit of investment this period is $P^e \cdot MPK$.[11]

The second component of the firm's marginal gain from the capital purchase in the current period is its saving on capital spending next year. The machine bought today will be around tomorrow, although it will have depreciated somewhat. If the machine depreciates at the annual rate d, then after one year of use the amount $(1 - d)$ will still be available for use in the future. Whatever amount of capital the firm planned to purchase next year can be reduced by $1 - d$ because of the unit of capital it bought today. If we let P_k^e denote the expected price of the automatic punch press next year, then the expected dollar savings in capital purchases next year from the extra unit of investment today is $P_k^e \cdot (1 - d)$.

Combining the two components of the marginal gain to investment, we

---

[11] This increase in revenue from the additional future output that the investment provides presumes that the firm can sell all it wishes at the expected future market price P^e. As we see later, if this is not the case, then an additional factor affecting investment demand must be taken into account, namely expected future output demand.

find that a one-unit increase in net real investment increases the firm's expected future revenue by $P^e \cdot MPK + P_k^e \cdot (1 - d)$, where $P^e \cdot MPK$ is the expected revenue from increased output next period and $P_k^e \cdot (1 - d)$ is the expected savings from reduced spending on investment next year. Note that this marginal gain to investment is in terms of dollars next year.

Recall from our previous discussion that the marginal cost of investment in terms of dollars next year is the current price of capital multiplied by one plus the interest rate, or $P_k(1 + r)$. If the firm is to maximize its profit, it must invest up to the point where the gain from an extra unit of investment just equals the cost. Consequently, the optimal level of investment satisfies

$$P^e \cdot MPK \quad + \quad P_k^e \cdot (1 - d) \quad = P_k(1 + r)$$

Expected future value of marginal product of capital	Expected future saving from reduced capital spending in future	Cost of a unit of capital (in terms of dollars in future) **(5.5)**

As the firm purchases more capital, the marginal product of capital falls and the gain to additional capital purchases is reduced. This is a reflection of the law of diminishing marginal returns, albeit for the capital rather than the labor input. As Equation 5.5 indicates, the firm purchases capital to the point where the marginal gain to buying one more unit of capital just equals the marginal cost.

The Expected Real Rental Cost of Capital and Investment Demand

In deciding on the amount of labor to employ, we saw that firms hire labor up to the point where the marginal product of labor equals the real wage. Firms' investment decisions are similar, as can be seen by rewriting Equation 5.5. In order to isolate the marginal product of capital, we first move the term $P_k^e \cdot (1 - d)$ to the right side of the equation and then divide both sides by the expected future price of output P^e. Our equation now looks like this:

$$MPK = \frac{P_k(1 + r) - P_k^e \cdot (1 - d)}{P^e}$$

Factoring out P_k/P, the price of capital in terms of output, we obtain[12]

---

[12] In our example, the real price of capital to the tweezer producer is the price of the particular piece of capital purchased (the punch press) divided by the price of the particular output produced (tweezers). This tells us how many tweezers the firm sacrifices today in order to obtain a punch press. This real price has to be compared with the increased production of tweezers in the following year that results from the purchase of a unit of capital (MPK). (As we see below, this comparison will require adjustments for the interest rate and the rate of depreciation.) To simplify our discussion, we do not distinguish between the price of tweezers and the general level of output prices denoted by P. Nor do we distinguish between the price of a punch press and the general level of prices of capital goods. In essence, we are considering the investment decision of the "representative" firm.

$$MPK = \frac{P_k}{P} \cdot \left\{ \frac{(1+r) - (1-d)P_k^e/P_k}{P^e/P} \right\} \tag{5.6}$$

In Equation 5.6, the ratio of the expected price of output next year to the current price of output (P^e/P) simply equals one plus the expected rate of change in the output price. Similarly, the ratio of the expected price of capital next year to its current price (P_k^e/P_k) equals one plus the expected rate of change in the price of capital. For simplicity, let us assume that the expected rates of change in the prices of output and capital are the same, and let us denote this **expected rate of inflation** by π^e.[13] In practice, this has in the past turned out to be a fairly good approximation. For example, during the period 1950 to 1985, the average annual rate of inflation in consumption goods was 3.4 percent, which approximately equaled the 3.6 percent average annual rate of change in the prices of capital goods.

Substituting $1 + \pi^e$ for P^e/P and P_k^e/P_k into Equation 5.6, we obtain

$$
\begin{aligned}
MPK &= \frac{P_k}{P} \cdot \left\{ \frac{(1+r) - (1-d)(1+\pi^e)}{(1+\pi^e)} \right\} \\
&= \frac{P_k}{P} \cdot \left\{ \frac{(1+r) - (1+\pi^e) + d(1+\pi^e)}{(1+\pi^e)} \right\}. \\
&= \frac{P_k}{P} \cdot \left\{ \frac{r - \pi^e}{(1+\pi^e)} + d \right\}
\end{aligned}
$$

Simplifying the above equation by letting $r - \pi^e$ approximate $(r - \pi^e)/(1 + \pi^e)$, we obtain[14]

$$MPK = (P_k/P)(r - \pi^e + d) \tag{5.7}$$

Marginal product   Expected real
of capital   user or rental
                 cost of capital

The left side of Equation 5.7, the marginal product of capital, denotes the firm's gain in output (tweezers) next period from the employment of one additional unit of capital (a punch press). The right side of Equation 5.7 is the cost in output next period from using one additional unit of capital. Equation 5.7 indicates that firms will purchase additional capital up to the point where the gain in output from using an additional unit of capital next period just equals the cost.

This cost of using a unit of capital, called the **expected real user, or rental, cost of capital,** is made up of two components. First, there is the cost today of purchasing the machine. Expressed in terms of output foregone,

Expected rate of inflation (π^e): The rate of inflation expected to occur in the future.

Expected real user, or rental, cost of capital (P_k/P)($r - \pi^e + d$): The cost of using or renting capital for one period. It rises with an increase in the interest rate r and the rate of depreciation of capital d, falls with an increase in the expected rate of inflation π^e, and rises with an increase in the real price of capital P_k/P.

---

[13] In other words, if π^e denotes the expected rate of change in the output price and the price of capital, then $P^e = P(1 + \pi^e)$ and $P_k^e = P_k(1 + \pi^e)$. Rearranging, we obtain $P^e/P = P_k^e/P_k = (1 + \pi^e)$, so that we are substituting $(1 + \pi^e)$ for P^e/P and P_k^e/P_k in Equation 5.6.

[14] For instance, if $r = .07$ and $\pi^e = .04$, then $r - \pi^e = .03$. This is approximately equal to $(r - \pi^e)/(1 + \pi^e)$, which equals .029.

this cost equals P_k/P. If the punch press has a price of $100 and if the price of a pair of tweezers is $1, then the real cost of a machine today in terms of output is 100 pairs of tweezers. Thus when the firm borrows today to buy the machine, it borrows the equivalent of 100 pairs of tweezers.

The second component of cost $(r - \pi^e + d)$ is the cost of using a "tweezer's worth" of capital for one period. To interpret this component of the expected real user cost of capital, we can divide it into two parts: the expected real rate of interest $(r - \pi^e)$ and the rate of depreciation (d). Although we encountered the concept of the expected real rate of interest in Chapter 3, let's review the concept in the context of the investment decision.

Recall that the expected real rate of interest is the nominal, or money, interest rate (r) minus the expected rate of inflation (π^e). For the borrower, the expected real rate of interest is the expected real cost of borrowing in terms of the amount of goods and services actually forgone. We can use our example of borrowing for the punch press to illustrate the concept of the expected real rate of interest. If the price of the punch press is $100, the firm must borrow $100 today to buy the machine. If the money interest rate (r) is .10, or 10 percent, then the firm must pay back $1.10 next year for each dollar borrowed today. Contrary to what one might think, however, it is not how many dollars it costs the firm for each dollar borrowed today that is critical in its investment and borrowing decisions. What matters is the borrowing cost in terms of *real goods forgone*, a cost that depends not only on the money rate of interest but also on the expected rate of inflation.

When the firm borrows $1 today, if the price of a tweezer is $1, it borrows the equivalent of one tweezer. As we have seen, a money interest rate of 10 percent implies that the firm must pay back $1.10 next year. But in real terms what must the firm pay back? If the expected rate of inflation is .10, or 10 percent, then the price of tweezers next year is expected to be $1.10. Although the firm must pay back $1.10 next year for each dollar borrowed today, in real terms this is exactly one tweezer. Since the firm expects to pay back in real goods (tweezers) exactly what it borrows, the *expected real interest rate* is zero. That is, the money interest rate r (.10) minus the expected rate of inflation π^e (.10) equals zero. If the expected rate of inflation is .06 or 6 percent, then the expected real rate of interest will be .04, or 4 percent $(.10 - .06)$.

With our review of the expected real rate of interest, we can now interpret the real user cost of capital, $(P_k/P)(r - \pi^e + d)$. The real price of capital (P_k/P) tells us the cost of a unit of capital today in terms of real output. When P_k/P is multiplied by the expected real rate of interest $(r - \pi^e)$, we have the expected real cost of borrowing to purchase a unit of capital for one year's use. We add to this cost the real price of capital multiplied by the depreciation rate in order to capture the real cost arising from the fact that capital wears out with use.

Our example of the tweezer producer may help you gain a better understanding of the real user cost of capital. With a $100 price tag on a punch press and a $1 current price tag on a pair of tweezers, the real cost of purchasing the machine is 100 tweezers (P_k/P). A nominal interest rate (r) of .10, an expected rate of inflation (π^e) of .06, and a rate of depreciation (d) of, say, .10 means that the expected real user cost of capital $(P_k/P)(r - \pi^e + d)$ is 14 tweezers. With a real interest rate of .04 or 4 percent, the firm expects to pay back four tweezers when it borrows the money to purchase the machine for one year's use $[(P_k/P)(r - \pi^e)]$. In addition, if the rate of depreciation (d) is .10, then the firm will also lose 10 percent of the machine, or ten tweezers, through depreciation, $[(P_k/P)d]$. Borrowing 100 tweezers to purchase the machine will therefore cost the firm 14 tweezers next year. Only if the marginal product of the punch press is greater than this user cost of 14 tweezers will the firm buy this piece of capital.

The importance of the expected real user cost of capital in determining the demand for one form of capital, namely inventory holdings, is highlighted by the following comment from the *Wall Street Journal* (September 18, 1984): "Analysts say that high interest rates and low inflation, which increase the cost of carrying inventories, have encouraged companies to keep their (inventory) stocks low." As the quote suggests, both a high market interest rate and a low expected inflation rate lead to reduced investment since both tend to raise the expected real rate of interest and hence the real user cost of capital. In interpreting the quote, be sure to realize that it is not the past low inflation rate that directly encourages companies "to keep their (inventory) stocks low." Rather, the past experience of low inflation indirectly reduces investment in inventories by reducing firms' *expectations of future inflation.*

The Investment Demand Curve of Firms

A change in any of the components of the real user cost of capital affects net investment demand by altering the marginal cost of capital purchases. Figure 5.3 illustrates the relationship (implied by Equation 5.7) between one of these components, the money interest rate, and net real investment demand (I^d). In interpreting this figure, note that we have plotted net real investment on the horizontal axis and the money interest rate on the vertical axis.

As Figure 5.3 illustrates, the quantity of capital that firms choose to purchase today is inversely related to the current interest rate. For example, at the interest rate r_0, real investment demand is I_0 units of capital. If the interest rate falls to r_1, then desired investment spending will increase to I_1 since the fall in the interest rate reduces the expected real user cost of capital.

New housing construction is one type of investment that is highly sensitive to changes in the interest rate. For example, in 1977–1978, the average interest rate on new home mortgages was 9.25 percent and private housing starts averaged 1.75 million per year. During the interest rate peak of 1981–1982, the average new home mortgage rate was 15 percent and housing starts plummeted to less than 1 million per year. In 1983–1984, the average

Figure 5.3   The Investment Demand Curve of Firms

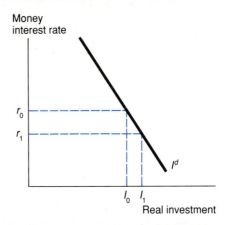

A fall in the interest rate from r_0 to r_1 reduces the expected real user cost of capital, and thus leads to an increase in the quantity of investment demanded from I_0 to I_1. The downward slope of the investment demand curve reflects diminishing marginal returns to capital.

interest rate dropped to 12.5 percent and housing starts recovered to an average of 1.63 million per year.

Although the effect of a change in the money interest rate can be shown graphically as a movement along the investment demand curve in Figure 5.3, changes in other factors will cause the curve to shift. For instance, if the real price of capital rises or the expected rate of inflation falls, investment demand will decrease since either event implies a rise in the real user cost of capital. Since either change means investment demand is lower at each interest rate, either change will be shown graphically by a shift to the left in the investment curve depicted in Figure 5.3.

We summarize our investment demand discussion with the following equation:

$$I^d = I^d[(P_k/P)(r - \pi^e + d), \overline{K}, ...] \qquad (5.8)$$

Equation 5.8 indicates that the expected real user cost of capital and the existing stock of capital are both determinants of investment demand. A rise in the real user cost of capital $[(P_k/P)(r - \pi^e + d)]$ raises the cost of capital, and thus reduces investment demand. The existing capital stock $(\overline{K})$ also has an effect of investment demand. A larger capital stock lowers the marginal product of additional capital and thus reduces the gain to additional purchases of capital. The minus sign under the $\overline{K}$ term in Equation 5.8 indicates this inverse relationship between the existing capital stock and investment demand.

Table 5.1 **The Balance Sheets of the Depository Institutions**

Fed		Private Depository Institutions (combined)	
Assets	Liabilities	Assets	Liabilities
Financial assets	Currency in hands of the nonbank public Bank reserves	Bank reserves Financial assets	Deposits

in particular changes in bank reserves—can lead to changes in the money supply equal to a multiple of the change in the monetary base—thus its alternative name of "high-powered money." As we show below, integral to this role of the monetary base is the fractional reserve nature of the banking system.

The Fractional Reserve Banking System

When an individual adds $1000 to his or her checking account, that deposit simultaneously creates an asset and a liability for the bank. The deposit is a liability of the bank since its owner can demand payment of it at any time; it is a demand deposit. At the same time, the $1000 is an asset for the bank. If the $1000 sits in the vault, however, it earns no interest. Banks want to turn their assets into earning assets, so they make loans (buy bonds). If you were the president of a bank, how much of the $1000 deposit would you loan out? Before you answer "All of it," remember that the person who made the deposit may want some money back tomorrow in the form of currency. You would not stay in the banking business long if, when depositors came to withdraw some of their deposits, you apologetically explained that you had lent their money out the previous day.[16] Thus, you have an incentive to hold some of your deposits in the form of reserves.

The proportion of deposits that you would hold as reserves would depend on your forecast of future deposits and withdrawals. On any given day, some individuals withdraw funds from their deposits and others add to their deposits. If a bank knew with certainty the pattern of withdrawals and deposits it faced each day, it could plan accordingly and start each day with an amount no more than the net amount to be withdrawn on that day. Since banks are uncertain about the amount of withdrawals and deposits on any given day, however, they maintain part of their assets as reserves.

---

[16] This once happened in an episode of "The Beverly Hillbillies." Jed Clampett, on finding out that his banker, Mr. Drysdale, did not have his $10 million available as cash, threatened to close his account.

To some extent, the burden of deciding exactly how much to hold as reserves has been lifted from private depository institutions. The Fed requires private depository institutions to hold specified minimum amounts of their checkable deposits in the form of reserves. Recall that these are termed *required reserves*. Reserves above those required by the Fed are called *excess reserves*. Evidence that the reserve holdings required by the Fed are above the level of reserve depository institutions would otherwise hold is reflected by the fact that, as a general rule, depository institutions keep their excess reserve holdings quite small.

An important point to note is that reserves held by depository institutions equal only a fraction of deposits. In 1988, the required reserve ratio on transaction deposits at large banks was 12 percent. Such a banking system, where private depository institutions hold only a fraction of their deposits as reserves, is called a **fractional reserve banking system.** As we discuss below, in a fractional reserve banking system, a change in reserves can result in a change in deposits of a much greater magnitude.

Fractional reserve banking system: A banking system in which private depository institutions hold only a fraction of their deposits as reserves.

The Deposit Creation Process

Let us now examine how a change by the Fed in the monetary base, specifically in bank reserves, leads to an even greater change in the money supply in the form of deposits. Suppose that the Fed purchases $10 worth of government bonds. This Federal Reserve transaction is termed an open-market purchase. In general, **open-market operations** refer to the sale or purchase of government securities such as treasury notes and bills. Suppose that the $10 worth of government bonds are bought from a small time bond dealer named John McConnell. McConnell puts the $10 check from the Fed in his checking account at Bank A. Bank A, in turn, redeems the check at the Fed, and the Fed credits Bank A deposits at the Fed, thereby adding $10 to Bank A's reserves.

Open-market operations: The buying and selling of government bonds by the Federal Reserve. Such activity alters the size of the monetary base.

The effects of the above open-market operations on the Fed's and Bank A's balance sheets are depicted as Step 1 in Table 5.2. As Step 1 indicates, the initial result of the Fed's open-market purchase is that Bank A's deposits and reserves have both increased by $10.

In Step 1, Bank A's reserves and deposits have both increased by $10. The $10 increase in Bank A's reserves constitutes a $10 increase in the monetary base, while the $10 increase in deposits is a $10 increase in the economy's money supply. The increase in the money supply is accompanied by an equal increase in the total financial assets held by the depository institutions (the Fed plus private depository institutions), as we know it must from the depository institutions financing constraint.

In Step 1, the Fed's increase in the monetary base through the purchase of financial assets from the bond dealer has led not only to the *creation of money* in the form of checkable deposits at Bank A but also to increased demand for financial assets by depository institutions. The deposit creation process does not stop here, however. Let's assume that the Fed requires

Table 5.2 The Deposit Creation Process

	Step 1			
	Assets		*Liabilities*	
Federal Reserve	Financial assets (purchase from bond dealer)	+10	Deposits of depository institution at Fed (Bank A's deposits)	+10
	Assets		*Liabilities*	
Bank A	Reserves (deposits at Fed)	+10	Deposits (bond dealer)	+10

private depository institutions to hold 10 percent of their deposit liabilities in the form of reserves (either as vault cash or as deposits at the Fed). With its $10 increase in deposits, Bank A's required reserves rise by $1. The remaining $9 increase in Bank A's reserves are thus excess reserves.

For simplicity, we will assume that depository institutions do not wish to hold any reserves above those required. As a consequence, Bank A will use its entire $9 in excess reserves to purchase interest-earning financial assets. Suppose, for example, that Bank A loans the $9 to firm XYZ, which wants to purchase an automatic punch press. The effects of the loan transaction are shown as Step 2 in Table 5.3. Firm XYZ issues a $9 financial asset (a bond) to the bank, and in exchange Bank A increases the firm's deposits by $9. The money supply has now increased by an additional $9, in the form of additional deposits at Bank A. At the same time, depository institutions' holdings of financial assets have also increased by $9, since Bank A created the deposit in return for the bond issued by firm XYZ.

Recall that firm XYZ borrowed the $9 to finance the purchase of a machine. It pays for the machine by writing a $9 check. The seller, Bodine's Machines, then deposits the check in its bank, Bank B. Bank B credits Bodine's account and sends the check to the Fed. The Fed, in turn, clears the check by crediting $9 to Bank B's deposits at the Fed and subtracting $9 from Bank A's deposits at the Fed. Finally, when Bank A receives the check, it subtracts $9 from firm XYZ's deposits. Step 3 in Table 5.4 depicts the effects on the balance sheets of Banks A and B. Note that when the check clears, Bank A's deposits and reserves both fall by $9 while Bank B's deposits and reserves both increase by $9.

Assuming a required reserve ratio of .10 or 10 percent, Bank B's required reserves have increased by $.90 as a result of the $9 increase in its deposits. Since Bank B's actual reserves have increased by $9, it now has excess reserves in the amount of $8.10. Bank B, like Bank A, uses its excess reserves to make a loan (that is, purchase financial assets). This, in turn, results in

Table 5.3   The Deposit Creation Process

	Step 2			
	Assets			Liabilities
Bank A	Financial assets (loan to XYZ)	+9	Deposits (XYZ's deposit)	+9

Table 5.4   The Deposit Creation Process

	Step 3			
	Assets			Liabilities
Bank A	Reserves (transferred to Bank B)	−9	Deposits (reduction in XYZ's deposit)	−9
	Assets			Liabilities
Bank B	Reserves (transferred from Bank A)	+9	Deposits (Bodine's deposit)	+9

Table 5.5   The Deposit Creation Process

	Step 4			
	Assets			Liabilities
Bank B	Financial assets	+8.10	Deposits	+8.10

an $8.10 increase in the money supply, since Bank B's purchase of financial assets is financed by the creation of deposits. This is shown as Step 4 in Table 5.5.

Recall that total reserves in the banking system increased by $10 as a result of the Fed's open-market purchase. Thus far, the deposits at depository institutions have risen by $27.10—$10 at a Bank A and $17.10 ($9 + $8.10) at Bank B—which means that total required reserves have risen by $2.71. There thus remain excess reserves in the banking system of $7.29. Since we have assumed private depository institutions have no desire to hold excess reserves, additional loans will be made and the deposit creation process continues. When deposits have increased sufficiently to raise required

Table 5.6 The Deposit Creation Process

	Final Outcome			
	Assets		*Liabilities*	
Combined private depository institutions	Reserves	+10	Deposits	+100
	Financial assets	+90		

reserves by the $10 increase in actual reserves initiated by the Fed's open-market purchase, the deposit creation process stops. Since the required reserve ratio is .10 or 10 percent, the deposit creation process is thus complete when total deposits in the banking system increase by $100.

The final step in Table 5.6 illustrates the total effect on the *combined* balance sheet of all depository institutions after the deposit creation process has been completed. Total deposits at depository institutions, and thus the money supply, increase by $100 as a result of the Fed's $10 open-market purchase. The financial asset holdings of private depository institutions increase by $90. If we recall that it was the $10 increase in the Fed's holdings of financial assets that initiated the deposit creation process, we see that the total increase in the financial asset holdings of all depository institutions is $100, the same amount by which the money supply increases. This reflects the fact that depository institutions finance purchases of financial assets by the creation of deposits.

Naturally, the above discussion could be done in reverse. A fall in bank reserves brought on by an open-market sale by the Fed would lead to a reduction in the money supply by a multiple of the fall in reserves.

The Simple Money Multiplier

Money multiplier: The ratio of the total change in the money supply to an initial change in the monetary base.

In the previous example, we saw that a $10 increase in the monetary base led to an increase in the total money supply greater than $10. This is a characteristic of a fractional reserve banking system. The magnitude of the increase in the money supply resulting from a $1 increase in the monetary base (banking system reserves plus currency in the hands of the nonbank public) is called the **money multiplier.** In the example above, the simple money multiplier was ten: a $10 increase in bank reserves led to a 10-fold, or $100 increase, in the money supply.

The money multiplier obtained in the above example has a simple formula because of two assumptions: that the public does not change its holdings of currency and that private depository institutions do not change their holdings of excess reserves. Under these two assumptions, when the monetary base or high-powered money (H) changes by the amount ΔH dollars, the money supply will increase until depository institutions' required reserves rise by exactly ΔH dollars. Letting ΔM^s denote the change in the money supply in the form of deposits, and letting rr denote the required reserve-to-deposit ratio, the increase in required reserves will equal $rr \cdot \Delta M^s$. Equating this increase in required reserves to the change in the monetary base, we have

$$rr \cdot \Delta M^s = \Delta H \qquad \qquad \textbf{(5.9)}$$

Solving Equation 5.9 for the simple money multiplier ($\Delta M^s/\Delta H$) yields

$$\Delta M^s/\Delta H = 1/rr \qquad \qquad \textbf{(5.10)}$$

Equation 5.10 tells us that the money supply changes by $1/rr$ dollars for every \$1 change in the monetary base. In other words, the simple money multiplier is equal to the reciprocal of the required reserve ratio.

A required reserve ratio less than one means a simple money multiplier greater than one. In the previous example, with a required reserve ratio of .1, the simple money multiplier was $1/.1$, or 10. Each \$1 change in the monetary base led to a \$10 change in the money supply in the form of deposits. Note that a higher required reserve ratio (say .2) will result in a lower simple money multiplier (5).

Our analysis of the deposit creation process has abstracted from several important factors that affect the size of the money multiplier. First, as noted above we assumed all the increase in the monetary base took the form of an increase in bank reserves. Yet, households may want to hold part of the increase in their money holdings in currency. To see how this affects the money multiplier, let's consider again John McConnell, the individual who sells the bond to the Fed. This time McConnell deposits only \$8 of the \$10 payment from the Fed at Bank A and converts the rest into currency. Bank A will have fewer excess reserves (in Step 2) and, consequently, will loan out less money. Similarly, each depository institution involved in the deposit creation process will find that it has fewer excess reserves to make additional loans. Consequently, the total increase in the money supply resulting from the Fed's open-market purchase will be less and the money multiplier will be smaller.[17]

There is another factor affecting the money multiplier: Private depository institutions may want to hold some fixed fraction of additional deposits as excess reserves. This means that a \$1 increase in the monetary base results in a smaller expansion in bank loans and deposits, as an increase in deposits increases banks desired holdings of excess reserves. In other words, the money multiplier is smaller.

---

[17] If households' desired currency-to-deposit ratio is denoted by cd, then the money multiplier will equal $(1 + cd)/(rr + cd)$. In the case where $cd = 0$, the money multiplier simplifies to $1/rr$. Chapter 16 examines in more detail the factors that affect the money multiplier.

Figure 5.5   The Money Multiplier

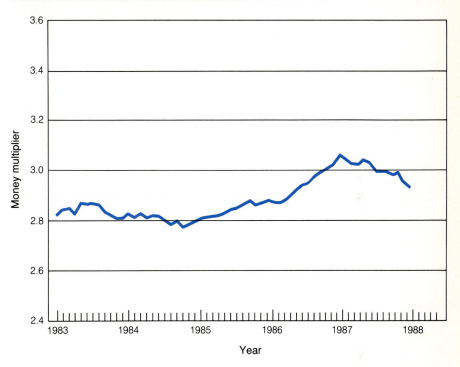

The graph indicates the average money multiplier calculated by dividing the money supply (M1) by the monetary base. In the text we discuss what might be termed a "marginal" money multiplier that looks at the impact on the money supply of small changes in the monetary base.

Source: *Federal Reserve Bulletin*, various issues.

Given that reserve requirements have not exceeded 12 percent, we would expect the simple money multiplier ($1/rr$) to have been at least equal to eight or nine. Due to the leakages from the deposit creation process of currency holdings by the public and excess reserves held by banks, the actual money multiplier has been around three. That is, on average, a change in the monetary base results in a threefold change in the money supply.

The fact that the money multiplier can vary with currency holdings, which are determined by the public, and excess reserves, which are determined by banks, means that the Fed does not have *complete* control of the money supply. Nevertheless, as Figure 5.5 demonstrates, the variability in the money multiplier is not extreme. In addition, some of the variability is predictable. As a consequence, as we discuss further in Chapter 16, as a first approximation the Federal Reserve can be viewed as determining the money supply.

CHANGES IN BANK RESERVES AND THE CREATION OF MONEY

- The liabilities of the Federal Reserve, currency in the hands of the nonbank public and bank reserves (vault cash and the deposits of private depository institutions at the Fed) make up the monetary base.

- Open-market operations that lead to changes in the monetary base, specifically bank reserves, induce changes in lending by depository institutions. Changes in lending by depository institutions are accompanied by changes in the money supply (specifically deposits), as indicated by the depository institution financing constraint introduced in Chapter 4.

- In a fractional reserve banking system, only a fraction of deposits are held as reserves. Thus a dollar increase in reserves supports a multiple-dollar increase in the money supply. The money multiplier equals the change in the money supply divided by the change in the monetary base.

SUMMARY

Firms are the economic agents that coordinate production in the economy. The relationship between the output and the inputs of firms is called the production function. Because firms can adjust their employment of labor quite quickly, we treat labor as a "variable" input; because changes in the capital stock generally take considerable time, we treat capital as a "fixed" input.

Firms are motivated by profit maximization when making decisions about hiring additional labor. To maximize profit, firms hire up to the point where the value of marginal product of labor ($P \cdot MPN$) equals the wage rate (W). Alternatively, we can say that firms hire labor up to the point where the marginal product of labor (MPN) equals the real wage (W/P). We thus see that hiring decisions depend on the real wage and the marginal product of labor. An increase in the real wage decreases the quantity of labor demanded, as shown by a movement up the labor demand curve.

As is the case with the hiring of labor, firms purchase new capital as long as the gain to purchasing an additional unit of capital exceeds the cost. Firms purchase capital up to the point where the marginal product of capital equals its marginal cost, which is the expected real user cost of capital. The expected real user cost of capital equals the real price of capital multiplied by the expected real interest rate ($r - \pi^e$) plus the rate at which capital depreciates (d). The expected real rate of interest (the money interest rate

(r) minus the expected inflation π^e) measures the expected real cost of borrowing. If we plot the nominal interest rate on the vertical axis and the net investment demand of firms on the horizontal axis, their investment demand curve is downward-sloping. A lower interest rate reduces the real user cost of capital and thus increases the quantity of investment demanded.

When firms supply financial assets to finance investment, they equivalently demand loanable funds in the marketplace. We can represent graphically the relationship between the interest rate and firms' borrowing by the demand for loanable funds curve. An increase in the interest rate reduces the quantity of loanable funds demanded by firms since the higher interest rate reduces desired investment spending. In other words, the demand for loanable funds curve is downward-sloping.

The Fed has direct control of the monetary base, which consists of currency in the hands of the nonbank public, vault cash at private depository institutions, and the deposits of private depository institutions at the Fed. By changing the monetary base, the Fed can alter the money supply. An open-market purchase of financial assets by the Fed that increases bank reserves induces depository institutions to expand their lending. This lending is accompanied by the creation of deposits and hence an increase in the money supply. Since only a fraction of deposits must be held as reserves, the lending and deposit creation that follows an increase in bank reserves is such that each dollar increase in reserves supports more than a one-dollar increase in the money supply. The ratio of the change in the money supply to the change in the monetary base is termed the money multiplier. As the deposit creation process highlights, changes in bank lending (depository institutions' purchases of financial assets) are accompanied by changes in the money supply. This relationship is summarized by the depository institution financing constraint.

LOOKING AHEAD

In this chapter, we have examined the role of firms in the economy by developing simple behavioral postulates with respect to the demand for labor and investment by firms. We have also looked at depository institutions and the money supply process. Firms and depository institutions are just two of the five types of participants in the economy. The next chapter turns to a discussion of two other participants, namely households and foreigners. In particular, we look at households' labor supply decision in the labor market, their consumption demand decision in the output market, and their saving decisions, which affect the financial market. We also consider the demand for U.S. goods and financial assets by foreigners.

SUMMARY OF KEY EQUATIONS

Production function

$$Y = f(N, K, ...)$$

$$\overset{+}{}\ \overset{+}{}$$

(5.1)

Profit-maximizing condition for the employment of labor

$$MPN = W/P$$

(5.3)

Labor demand function

$$N^d = N^d(W/P, ...)$$

(5.4)

Profit-maximizing condition for the purchase of capital

$$MPK = (P_k/P)(r - \pi^e + d)$$

(5.7)

Investment demand function

$$I^d = I^d[(P_k/P)(r - \pi^e + d), \overline{K}, ...]$$

(5.8)

Simple money multiplier

$$\Delta M^s/\Delta H = 1/rr$$

(5.10)

KEY TERMS

Production function, 131
Marginal product of labor, 132
Law of diminishing marginal returns, 134
Value of the marginal product of labor, 134
Real wage, 135
Marginal product of capital, 141
Expected rate of inflation, 143
Expected real user, or rental, cost of capital, 143

Loanable funds, 147
Monetary base, or high-powered money, 148
Bank reserves, 148
Fractional reserve banking system, 150
Open-market operations, 150
Money multiplier, 153

REVIEW QUESTIONS

1. What effect does a technological improvement that raises the productivity of labor have on the demand for labor? At a given real wage, what will happen to the quantity of labor firms seek to hire?

2. Suppose that there is no change either in the production function or the wage. How will a change in output prices change labor demand?

3. Ugo Pagano owns a garlic-making factory that has the following relationship between the labor input and output.

Number of Laborers	1	2	3	4	5	6	7	8	9	10
Output	20	42	66	90	112	132	150	166	180	190

   a. If the money wage is $36 and the firm sells its product for $2, how many workers will the firm employ?

   b. Assuming that nothing else changes from (a) but the money wage rises to $60, how many workers will the firm employ?

   c. How many workers will the firm employ if nothing else changes from (a) but the firm now sells its product for $3? For $1.80?

   d. How many workers will the firm employ if nothing else changes from (a) but the technical production function of the firm changes so that each worker can now produce twice that produced in the initial situation?

   e. In which of these instances (b, c, and d) did the real wage vary from the real wage cited in (a)?

   f. What can you conclude are determinants of the number of workers that a firm employs?

4. In 1986, the Daniel B. Manufacturing Company had a capital stock with a value of $10,000. During the year, 35 percent of the capital stock was consumed in production. The firm purchased $5000 worth of new equipment that year. What was the net investment for the firm in that year? What was the size of the capital stock for the firm at the end of the first year?

5. A survey of economists by the American Economic Association in the mid-1970s indicated that the major concern economists foresaw for the economy was a lack of capital investment. From 1978 to 1981, the productivity of labor in the United States actually fell. Is there any relation between these two events? Do these events show that economists are clever or dimwitted? (Do not let your emotions color this answer.)

6. What causes shifts in the investment demand function?

7. A boat that you are thinking of buying costs $12,000 and will, after one year, have a resale value of $10,000. The rate of interest on the bank loan you would take if you did buy the boat is 10 percent. The local boat distributor will lease you the identical boat for one year for $3600 on the condition that you incur all operating expenses (gas, maintenance, boat storage, etc.). Should you lease the boat from the dealer or should you buy? What is the rental rate that the boat dealer is asking? What is the user cost of capital if you buy? Have you expressed these rates in real terms or in nominal terms? Given your answer, what would you need to know in order to express it in the other terms?

8. On the day that you enter college suppose that you agree to lend money to a classmate at what you expect to be a zero real rate of interest. Payment is to be made at graduation, with interest at a fixed money rate. If inflation proves to be lower during your four years in college than you both had expected, who will gain and who will lose?

9. Suppose that a labor union enters into a contract that increases the nominal wage at 10 percent per year for the next three years. The expectation is that prices will increase by 10 percent for each of the next three years. In the ensuing time period, prices do not rise as rapidly as expected. What will happen to the real wage of the workers at this firm and what will happen to their level of employment?

10. When firms finance net investment they (supply/demand) financial assets, which is the same as saying they (borrow/lend) or (demand/supply) loanable funds.

11. A new lubricant is invented that reduces wear and tear on machinery. What does this do to the user cost of capital? What does it do to investment demand? How would you classify this change in terms of the firm production function?

12. Suppose that the Fed sells $20 worth of government bonds to small-time bond dealer Don Jankowski.

   a. Assume Don pays for the bonds by writing a check on his account at Purdue National Bank. Show the resulting effects on the balance sheets of the Fed and of Purdue National.

   b. Suppose that Purdue National's excess reserves were initially zero. What are they now? What will Purdue National Bank be forced to do as a result? Show the resulting effect on its balance sheet.

   c. Suppose that the required reserve ratio of depository institutions is 20 percent. Assuming that depository institutions do not wish to hold excess reserves and that all money in the economy takes the form of deposits, what will be the total change in the money supply when the deposit expansion (or contraction) process is completed? What is the simple money multiplier equal to? Illustrate the effect that the Fed's bond sale has had on the combined balance sheet of all private depository institutions.

13. What does the simple money multiplier tell us?

   a. Is the simple money multiplier greater, equal to, or less than one? Why?

   b. Suppose that instead of assuming that households hold all of their money in the form of deposits, we assume instead that they also hold some money in the form of currency. What will happen to the simple money multiplier? Why?

14. Depository institutions find it necessary to hold some assets in the form

of vault cash in order to pay customers who wish to withdraw funds from their deposits. From 1917 through December 1959, vault cash did not count toward satisfying the Federal Reserve's reserve requirements. This was changed in 1959 and 1960 so that after 1960 vault cash did count toward reserve requirements.

a. Suppose that the required reserve ratio is 10 percent. Consider a bank that initially has deposits of $500,000, reserve holdings in the form of deposits at the Fed of $50,000, and vault cash of $1250. After the law changes, does the bank have excess or insufficient reserves?

b. What effect will the change in the law have on the total money supply? Why?

15. Another way that the Fed can affect the money supply is by making loans to private depository institutions. When these institutions borrow from the Fed, the Fed simply credits their deposit account by the amount of the loan. The interest rate charged on these loans is called the discount rate.

a. Suppose that the Fed lowers the discount rate. What effect will this policy have on desired borrowing by banks?

b. Suppose that borrowing by banks changes by $10. Illustrate the immediate effect on the Fed's balance sheet and on the combined balance sheet of private depository institutions.

c. Do depository institutions have excess reserve or insufficient reserves? How much do they amount to?

d. What has happened to the monetary base? Suppose that the required reserve ratio is 10 percent. When the deposit expansion (or contraction) process ends, what will be the total change in the money supply. Indicate the effect that the change in the discount rate has on the combined balance sheet of depository institutions after the deposit expansion (or contraction) process is completed.

16. Trace through the first several steps in the deposit creation process if households desire to increase their currency holdings by an amount equal to 10 percent of any increase in deposits. Assume that the required reserve to deposit ratio is 10 percent, that banks do not desire to change their holdings of excess reserves, and that the initial Fed purchase is a $100 Treasury bond from a bond dealer.

17. In a recent *Wall Street Journal*, it is stated that "In a narrow technical sense, one can tell whether the Fed's been buying or selling by looking directly at its own balance sheet. The statistic Federal Reserve Bank Credit measures the Fed's own assets, principally government securities and loans to banks. The Fed _____ the money supply by buying
                                   expands, contracts

government securities, thus providing banks with _____ reserves on

more, less

which to base loans."

a. Indicate for the balance sheets of the Fed and Bank A the effect if the Fed, say, buys $100 worth of government securities from Bank A. Label the changes.

Federal Reserve		Bank A	

b. According to (a), there is initially _____ in

an increase, a decrease, no change

bank excess reserves equal to _____ dollars. Assuming a reserve-to-deposit ratio of .25 and no change in either banks' desired holdings of excess reserves or individuals' holdings of currency, the result of this will ultimately be a _____ dollar change in the money supply and a _____ dollar change in the dollar amount of loans made by depository institutions (private plus the Fed). Implied is a money multiplier equal to _____.

Labor Demand When It Is Costly to Adjust Workforce Size

In this chapter, we noted that firms generally incur significant costs when changing the size of their labor force since adding new employees often entails substantial hiring and training costs. In this appendix, we analyze exactly how such hiring and training costs alter the labor input decisions of firms and thus lead to the view that labor is a "quasi-fixed" input.

Hiring and training costs are generally concentrated early in a worker's employment tenure with a firm; later, after the initial hiring and training period, these investments can be expected to show up as future increases in worker productivity. Thus when deciding how many workers to hire today, employers have to consider the effects of hiring on future as well as current revenues and costs; the presence of hiring and training costs means that hiring decisions must take into account future as well as current considerations. For example, consider a firm that has a two-period planning horizon (below we will discuss the implications of a longer planning period). If the firm is to maximize its profit over this two-year period, how many new workers should it hire today given hiring and training costs?

Suppose that it costs the firm C dollars to hire and train a new employee. This hiring and training cost includes not only explicit monetary costs, such as the costs of employing workers to provide formal training to the new employee, but also implicit hiring and training costs, such as the value of the output that is lost because capital equipment is used by the new worker rather than an experienced worker or because an experienced worker devotes time to providing informal training to the new worker. If the new worker is paid the wage rate W_1 in the first period, then the first-period cost of hiring a new worker is simply $C + W_1$, the sum of the hiring and training cost (C) and the first period wage rate (W_1). Assuming that all hiring and training costs are incurred in the first period, the only cost incurred by the employer in the second period is the wage payment in the second period, which we may denote by W_2. The total present discounted cost incurred by the employer when hiring an additional worker today to be employed for this period and the next is therefore simply $C + W_1 + W_2/(1 + r)$.

When deciding how many workers to hire, the employer must compare the cost of hiring an additional worker with the gain. The gain consists of the increase in revenue from employing that worker for the two-period horizon. Thus let P_1 and P_2 denote the price of the employer's output in periods 1 and 2, respectively, and let MPN_1 and MPN_2 denote a worker's marginal product in each of the two periods. Then the increase in the employer's present discounted revenue from hiring an additional worker today and employing that worker for this period and the next is simply $P_1MPN_1 + P_2MPN_2/(1 + r)$, the discounted sum of the value of the marginal product of labor in periods 1 and 2. For convenience, we will denote this discounted sum of the value of marginal product in the two periods by the term discounted *VMPN*.

Equating the marginal cost of hiring an additional worker to the marginal gain, we see that in order to maximize its profit, the firm should hire new workers up to the point where

$$C + W_1 + W_2/(1 + r) = P_1MPN_1 + P_2MPN_2/(1 + r)$$

$$\underset{\text{an additional worker}}{\underbrace{\text{Discounted costs of}}} \qquad \underset{\text{marginal product of labor}}{\underbrace{\text{Discounted value of the}}} \qquad \textbf{(A5.1)}$$

Simplifying terms and rearranging, we can express Equation A5.1 in a more useful form:

$$\text{Discounted } VMPN - \text{Discounted wages} = C > 0 \qquad \textbf{(A5.2)}$$

According to Equation A5.2, to maximize profit the firm should hire new workers until the sum of the discounted differences between the worker's value of marginal product and wage payments equals the cost of hiring and training an additional worker (C). The return to the firm's investment in hiring and training new workers takes the form of the workers' value of marginal product exceeding their wage (at least in some periods).

Our analysis of the firm hiring decision given hiring and training costs has an important implication with respect to the variability of the firm's labor input. Recall that when hiring costs are absent, firms hire workers until the value of the marginal product equals the wage or

$$VMPN = W \qquad \textbf{(A5.3)}$$

Since the value of the marginal product of labor (*VMPN*) equals the price level P multiplied by the marginal product of labor *MPN*, we can divide Equation A5.3 through by the price level P to obtain

$$MPN = W/P \qquad \textbf{(A5.4)}$$

This equating of the marginal product of labor to the real wage was the profit-maximizing condition derived in the text (Equation 5.3).

The presence of hiring and training costs introduces a wedge between the value of marginal product and the wage. Equation A5.2 defines this wedge by the positive difference between the discounted value of the marginal product of labor and wages, a difference equal to hiring and training costs. The existence of this wedge has important implications for how firms respond to changes in output prices.

When hiring workers today, a firm expects to receive a sufficiently large addition to its revenue next period so as to justify its current hiring and training investment. That is, the firm expects the future value of marginal product of labor to exceed future wage payments by a sufficiently large amount for the firm to make up for the cost of its hiring and training investment. Suppose, however, that the price of the firm's output next period turns out to be lower than the firm initially expected. Will the firm dismiss workers next period? Not necessarily. If the price of output is not too low, then the value of marginal product of labor may still exceed the wage rate. In this case, the firm has no reason to dismiss any of its workers. Although the firm will not recoup all of its past hiring and training investment, this cost is sunk and is therefore irrelevant. As long as the firm's currently trained workers have a value of marginal product that is greater than the current wage, it will still be worthwhile for the firm to continue employing all of them.

If the firm has a planning period that is longer than two periods, then even if next year's price of the firm's output turns out to be so low that the value of marginal product of trained workers falls below their wage rate, the firm still may not dismiss any of its workers. To see why, suppose that the price of output increases in the future. Then in order to increase employment in the future, the firm will have to hire new workers to replace those whom it dismissed today, in the process incurring hiring and training costs all over again. In summary then, if the firm anticipates that the price of its output will rise in the future, then it may not dismiss workers today even though their current value of marginal product is below their wage rate. What the firm may do is to lay off some workers temporarily with the understanding that they will be the first to be employed should output demand recover. However, since laid-off workers are more likely than employed workers to find jobs elsewhere, the firm may even be reluctant to lay off workers temporarily.[18]

In summary, as Figure A5.1 illustrates, the existence of hiring and training costs introduces a degree of fixity in a firm's labor input decisions. A firm will hire new workers only if current and anticipated future prices of its output are sufficiently high that it can recoup its hiring and training costs. If next period's price is lower than expected, the firm will tend to hoard these workers, laying them off only if the price of output is sufficiently low that the value of marginal product of trained workers actually falls below their wage.

In Chapter 3, we noted that labor productivity has a pronounced cyclical tendency, tending to fall during recessions and to rise during recoveries. This is, of course, perfectly consistent with our current analysis of the quasi-fixity of the labor input. When experiencing a fall in output demand, firms tend to hang on to workers in whose training they have invested. This hoarding of excess labor means a reduction in output per worker or "labor productivity." In contrast, when experiencing an increase in output demand, firms are slow to hire new workers since doing so requires that they incur hiring and training costs. In order to economize on these costs, firms tend to work their existing employees harder, which results in an increase in output per worker.

---

[18] The point is made by Barron, Black, and Loewenstein ("On Recalls, Layoffs, Variable Hours, and Labor Adjustment Costs," *Journal of Economic Dynamics and Control*, December 1984).

Figure A5.1   **The Effect of Hiring and Training Costs on a Firm's Hiring and Dismissal Decisions**

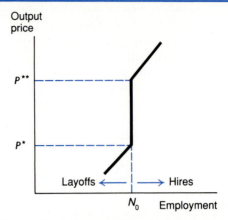

The existence of hiring and training costs introduces a degree of fixity into a firm's labor input decisions. The firm will be willing to hire new workers, thereby increasing its employment level, only if the price of output exceeds the critical value P^{**} since only then can the firm expect to make a sufficiently high return on its hiring and training investment so as to make hiring worthwhile. The firm will lay off workers, thereby reducing its employment level, only if the price of output falls below the critical value P^* since only then will the value of marginal product of labor fall below the wage rate so that dismissals are worthwhile. If the price of output is between P^* and P^{**}, the firm will neither hire new workers nor lay off current ones.

Chapter 6

Households and Foreigners

FROM Chapter 2, we know that household consumption spending is by far the largest component of gross national product. For that reason, traditional macroeconomic analysis has focused considerable attention on the consumption decisions of households.[1] This tendency to focus on households as buyers of output has, perhaps, led to too little attention being paid to the roles of households in other markets in the economy. Besides being a purchaser of output, households also play important roles as suppliers of labor, demanders of financial assets, and suppliers of dollars in the foreign exchange markets. In this chapter, we examine the behavior of households in each of the various markets.

We begin the chapter by examining the labor supply decisions of households, both in terms of whether to participate in the labor market and, if choosing to participate, how many hours of labor services to provide. We then move to a discussion of how households divide their income between consumption and saving. We introduce a consumption function to summarize the impacts of disposable income and other variables on consumption demand.

Just as households have to decide how to allocate their disposable income between consumption demand and saving, they also have to decide how to allocate their saving. Households can save in two ways: They can increase their holdings of financial assets such as stocks and bonds, or they can increase their holdings of money. In this chapter, we examine the factors affecting household's real demand for money. With an understanding of the determinants of money demand and consumption demand, we can then use the household budget constraint to infer the determinants of household

---

[1] Noted economist John Maynard Keynes, in his then revolutionary book, *The General Theory of Employment, Interest and Money* (London: Harbinger Press, 1936), considered his theory of consumption as the linchpin of his new theory of income and employment determination.

saving in the form of financial assets and thus their supply of loanable funds in the financial market.

Reports on the large U.S. trade deficit have often focused on U.S. imports of foreign goods and services. Often neglected in these reports is a rise in U.S. exports and foreign purchases of U.S. financial assets during the same time period. The final part of this chapter examines the behavior of households and foreigners in an open economy. We first consider household behavior as suppliers of dollars in the foreign exchange market and their underlying decisions with respect to U.S. imports and purchases of foreign financial assets. We then consider the behavior of foreigners as demanders of dollars in the foreign exchange market and their underlying decisions with respect to U.S. exports and purchase of U.S. financial assets.

6.1   HOUSEHOLD BEHAVIOR IN THE LABOR MARKET

In Chapter 5 we analyzed the behavior of firms as demanders in the labor market. On the other side of the labor market are households who supply labor services. Recall from Chapter 2 that we measure the supply of labor not only by the number of workers who are employed but also by the average number of hours worked per week. In this section, we examine what factors motivate individuals to participate in the labor force and to what extent.

The Supply of Labor and the Net Real Wage

Throughout time, people have debated whether work is a self-fulfilling experience or the bane of their existence. This debate notwithstanding, the majority of adults in the United States trudge off to work each day and "offer" their labor services in the market. What motivates households to supply these labor services? To a large extent, people work to finance their consumption; labor supply and the consumption of output are inextricably intertwined. Households ultimately are interested in the real purchasing power of the compensation they receive for the labor services they offer.

As payment for working, an individual receives an hourly wage (W).[2] The individual does not get to keep all of this payment, however, as the government takes part of it in the form of taxes. If the government taxes income at the average rate t, then the after tax, or net, wage received for

---

[2] The term "wage" should be viewed as the total compensation paid workers. This compensation involves not only an explicit money payment but also payments in the form of "fringe" benefits, such as private retirement systems and life and health insurance. Stephen Woodbury, "Substitution Between Wage and Nonwage Benefits," *American Economic Review* (March 1983), estimates that the share of total compensation paid as fringe benefits rose from .082 in 1966 to .115 in 1974.

working one additional hour equals $(1 - t)W$. The net wage is not the final determinant of a household's ability to purchase output for consumption, however. The final determinant is the **net real wage.** With a price of output P, the net real wage is $(1 - t)(W/P)$ units of output.

Net real wage
$[(1 - t)(W/P)]$:
The money wage after taxes divided by the level of output prices.

If the money wage and the tax rate remain the same, then an increase in the price of output results in a reduction in the net real wage. For example, if the money wage is $5 per hour and the tax rate is 20 percent, then the net wage rate is $4 per hour $[(1 - .2) \cdot \$5]$. Suppose that the only good our seller of labor services consumes is Big Macs priced at $1 each. In real terms, then, the individual is compensated the equivalent of four Big Macs for every hour of leisure given up. If the price of Big Macs rises to $2, the net real wage is halved and the individual now is paid on net only two Big Macs per hour. Likewise, the net real wage also falls if the money wage falls or the tax rate rises.

Not surprisingly, the net real wage plays an important part in determining the supply of labor. A rise in the net real wage does not automatically result in an increase in an individual's labor supply, however. Individuals make two types of labor supply decisions. The first decision is whether to participate in the labor market at all. A rise in the net real wage unambiguously increases the likelihood that an indvidual will join the labor force. Consider, for example, a housespouse who does not currently participate in the labor market. When deciding whether to participate, the housespouse weighs the potential gain to working—the net real wage payment—against the cost of working—the value of the leisure forgone.[3] An increase in the net real wage raises the gain to participating in the labor force, which causes the number of individuals who choose to participate in the labor market to increase. Through its effect on labor force participation, an increase in the net real wage increases the supply of labor.

A second type of labor supply decision, how many hours to work, is made by those who are already in the labor market. Will a rise in the net real wage induce an individual already in the labor market to work an additional hour, or perhaps to take a second job? Not necessarily. An increase in the net real wage has two offsetting effects on the number of hours an individual chooses to work. First, if the net real wage increases, then the gain to working an additional hour increases, inducing the individual to work more hours (i.e., supply *more* labor). This effect of a higher wage on labor supply is referred to as the *substitution effect* since the increased gain to working an additional hour leads individuals to substitute labor for leisure. Offsetting the substitution effect, however, is the *income effect*. A higher net real wage means that an individual can choose to increase *both* the amount of output purchased and the amount of leisure enjoyed. If leisure is a normal good, and there is much evidence to indicate that it is for most people, then

---

[3] Leisure is a very broad term, encompassing all non-labor-market activity. Nonmarket activity includes such varied activities as producing child-rearing services, watching the soaps, preparing meals, and spending time in bed.

the income effect induces the individual to work fewer hours (i.e., supply *less* labor and demand more leisure).[4]

In sum, then, an increase in the net real wage has an ambiguous effect on the number of hours an individual chooses to work. If the substitution effect outweighs the income effect, then an increase in the net real wage causes an increase in an individual's labor supply. If the income effect outweighs the substitution effect, then an increase in the net real wage causes labor supply to fall.[5] The available evidence suggests that for many workers, the income effect tends to dominate slightly. Estimates are that for men, an increase of 10 percent in the real wage results in approximately a 1.5 percent reduction in the hours worked. This reduction in hours worked reflects an income effect of approximately −2.5 percent and a substitution effect of about 1 percent. Recent evidence suggests a similar pattern for working women.[6]

The Aggregate Supply of Labor

In the aggregate, the supply of labor is directly related to the net real wage. Although an increase in the net real wage reduces the number of hours that some individuals work, this is more than offset by the number of individuals who are induced to participate in the labor market by the higher net real wage and by those who increase the hours they work. Thus the aggregate labor supply curve, depicted in Figure 6.1, slopes upward. In interpreting this figure note that we have plotted aggregate employment (measured in work hours) on the horizontal axis and the real wage on the vertical axis.

According to Figure 6.1, an increase in the real wage from $(W/P)_0$ to $(W/P)_1$, due either to a rise in the money wage or a fall in the price level, increases the net real wage and thus the aggregate quantity of labor supplied from N_0 to N_1. In general, we can express this relationship by

$$N^s = N^s[(1 - t)W/P, ...]$$
$$+$$

(6.1)

---

[4] A good is said to be normal if an increase in income causes an increase in demand for that good.

[5] As we saw above, for an individual deciding whether to participate in the labor force, there is only a substitution effect and not an income effect. However, there is another indirect way in which a rising wage can affect an individual's labor force participation decision. If the individual is part of a household decision-making unit and is supported by the income generated by a second person, a rise in the wage of the *second* person and accompanying increase in his or her income may reduce the likelihood of the first person joining the labor force.

[6] George Borjas and James Heckman, "Labor Supply Estimates for Public Policy Evaluation," *Proceedings of the Industrial Relations Research Association (1978)*, pp. 320–31. See also John Pencavel, "Labor Supply of Men: A Survey" in *Handbook of Labor Economics*, ed. Orley Ashenfelter (Amsterdam: North-Holland, 1985) for a survey of recent estimates. For evidence on the effect of wage increases on the labor supply of working women, see A. Nakamura and M. Nakamura, "A Comparison of the Labor Force Behavior of Married Women in the U.S. and Canada, with Special Attention to the Impact of Income Taxes," *Econometrica* 49 (1981): 451–89, and Chris Robinson and Nigel Tomes, "More on the Labour Supply of Canadian Women," *Canadian Journal of Economics* (February 1985) 18, 156–63.

Figure 6.1 Labor Supply

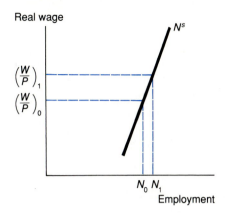

For a given tax rate, an increase in the money wage or a decrease in the price level will result in an increase in the real wage from $(W/P)_0$ to $(W/P)_1$. As the positively sloped aggregate labor supply curve indicates, the result is an increase in the quantity of labor supplied from N_0 to N_1.

where N^s is aggregate labor supply and $(1 - t)W/P$ is the real wage net of taxes. The plus sign below the net real wage indicates that the aggregate supply of labor increases with an increase in the net real wage.

Note that while the effect on labor supply of a change in the real wage is shown graphically in Figure 6.1 by a movement along the labor supply curve, a change in the tax rate would cause a shift in the labor supply curve. For example, a decrease in the tax rate will raise the net real wage and hence increase the supply of labor at any given real wage. This will cause the labor supply curve to shift to the right. In contrast, an increase in the tax rate will reduce the net real wage and thus lower the amount of labor supplied at any given real wage. This means the labor supply curve will shift to the left.

The Intertemporal Substitution of Labor

There is a potentially important consideration that has thus far been missing from our discussion of household labor supply—the allocation of work and leisure over an individual's lifetime. The fact that individuals work and consume goods and leisure over a time period spanning many years means that a household's labor supply decision has an intertemporal element to it. By working more hours today, saving some of its increased earnings, and using this saving to buy consumption goods in the future, the household can reduce its labor supply in the future without any loss in future consumption.

Conversely, if it so desires, the household can substitute increased work hours in the future for decreased work hours today.

To see how the introduction of intertemporal considerations affects the labor supply decision, suppose that the net real wage increases in the current period. If households expect the increase in wages to be temporary, then the increase in their long-run earning prospects will be negligible. Consequently, the income effect of the real wage change should be relatively small.[7] In contrast, the substitution effect should be large because households will find it worthwhile to work more hours in the current period at a relatively high real wage and fewer hours in other periods at a relatively low real wage.

Intertemporal substitution hypothesis: A hypothesis indicating that labor supply responds positively to transitory increases in the real wage.

The idea that labor supply responds positively to transitory increases in the real wage is known as the **intertemporal substitution hypothesis.** This hypothesis was introduced by Robert Lucas and Leonard Rapping in their influential paper, "Real Wages, Employment, and Inflation."[8] The hypothesis is important for macroeconomics because it implies that year-to-year fluctuations in the real wage will lead to significant year-to-year changes in the amount of labor that households supply. Thus as noted by Alogoskoufis, the intertemporal substitution hypothesis "is a central hypothesis of modern, competitive models of the business cycle."[9]

Lucas and Rapping's empirical results are quite supportive of the intertemporal substitution hypothesis. Using time series data, they estimate a short-run labor supply real wage elasticity of approximately 1.50 and a long-run elasticity close to zero.[10] This result—that labor supply is responsive to a change in the real wage in the short run but not in the long-run—is in agreement with the above reasoning; unlike the case with a long-run wage increase, with a short-run wage increase the income effect should be small and the intertemporal substitution effect dominant. Note also that Lucas and

---

[7] If the current period increase in the real wage was completely anticipated beforehand, then there should be no income effect at all since households will have no reason to revise their view of how well off they are.

[8] The paper, first published in the *Journal of Political Economy* (September/October 1969), is reprinted in *Microeconomic Foundations of Employment and Inflation Theory,* Phelps et al., (W. W. Norton, 1970), p. 257–305.

[9] George Alogoskoufis, "On Intertemporal Substitution and Aggregate Labor Supply," *Journal of Political Economy* (October 1987). Actually, there is another element to the intertemporal substitution hypothesis. According to the hypothesis, labor supply responds positively not only to transitory changes in the real wage but also to transitory changes in the real interest rate. A higher real interest rate today means that the labor (as well as other) income that is saved today can be converted into increased amounts of future consumption. (In the next section, we will examine the relationship between saving, the real interest rate, and future consumption more closely). Households thus find it worthwhile to work more hours today and fewer hours in the future. In other words, they substitute leisure in the future for leisure today.

[10] Recall from your previous economics courses that the term "real wage elasticity of labor supply" is simply a shorthand expression for the percentage change in the quantity of labor supplied that results from a one percent change in the real wage. Also, note that time-series data involves observations on an individual or a group of individuals at different points in time. Cross-section data involves observations on different individuals at a point in time.

Rapping's estimated short-run labor supply elasticity is much larger than the labor supply elasticities that we reported earlier. This result is also consistent with the intertemporal substitution hypothesis since the results that we reported earlier were for cross-section studies; to the extent that cross-section variations in wages correspond to permanent differences in wages across individuals, intertemporal substitutions of labor will be absent in cross-section data.

Other evidence concerning the intertemporal substitution hypothesis is mixed. Time series estimates obtained by Hall for the United States and Andrews and Nickell for Great Britain are in accord with the hypothesis.[11] In contrast, the labor supply real wage elasticities obtained by Altonji are statistically insignificant.[12] Mankiw, Rottemberg, and Summers also obtain results that contradict the hypothesis.[13] The most recent word on the subject is provided by Alogoskoufis, who finds that transitory changes in the real wage have a significant effect on the number of individuals who choose to work (with an elasticity of about 1), but an insignificant effect on the average number of hours that employees work.[14]

To the Point

HOUSEHOLDS AS SELLERS IN THE LABOR MARKET

- Households supply labor services to finance consumption. The extent to which the wage payment gives households command over goods and services is reflected in the net real wage, which is the after-tax money wage divided by the price level.

- An increase in the net real wage will lead to an increase in the number of individuals who choose to participate in the labor force. However, a rise in net real wage has an ambiguous effect on the labor supply of those already in the labor force, as the substitution effect and the income effect related to a change in the net real wage work in opposite directions.

- The aggregate labor supply curve encompasses the effects of a change in the net real wage on both labor force participation and on the hours worked by those already in the labor force. The aggregate labor supply curve is upward-sloping.

[11] Robert Hall, "Labor Supply and Aggregate Fluctuations," *Carnegie-Rochester Conference Series Public Policy* 12 (Spring 1980); Martyn Andrews and Stephen Nickell, "Unemployment in the United Kingdom since the War," *Review of Economic Studies* 49, no. 5 (supplement, 1982), 731–59; Martyn Andrews, "The Aggregate Labour Market: An Empirical Investigation into Market Clearing," Discussion Paper No. 154, London School of Economics (1983).

[12] Joseph Altonji, "The Intertemporal Substitution Model of Labour Fluctuations: An Empirical Analysis," *Review of Economic Studies* 49, no. 5 (supplement, 1982), 783–824.

[13] Gregory Mankiw, Julio Rottemberg, and Lawrence Summers, "Intertemporal Substitution in Macroeconomics," *Quarterly Journal of Economics* 100 (February 1985), 225–251.

[14] Alogoskoufis also obtains similar results for the effects of changes in the real interest rate, namely that a transitory change in the expected real interest rate has a significant effect on the number of individuals who work but not on the average number of hours worked.

6.2   HOUSEHOLD BEHAVIOR IN THE OUTPUT MARKET

Prior to the development of the modern exchange economy, consumption was largely constrained by the goods each individual produced. A distinguishing feature of a market economy is the exchange of goods among individuals. This breaks the link between what each individual consumes and produces, but only to an extent. Although in the modern exchange economy we are not limited to consuming only the goods that we produce, over our lifetime we are limited in that we can consume other goods of no greater value than the value of the goods we produce. This idea is captured by the household budget constraint.

Recall from Chapter 4 that the household budget constraint expresses the fact that household expenditures cannot exceed their real disposable income. Remember that real disposable income (YD) equals real GNP (Y) minus the capital consumption allowance (CCA) and total net taxes (T) paid by households and firms. That is,

$$YD = Y - CCA - T \qquad (6.2)$$

In this section, we examine the factors that determine the fraction of disposable income households devote to purchases of goods and services in the output market. In other words, we look at what affects the division of a household's real disposable income between consumption and saving. In subsequent sections, we then consider household behavior with respect to the division of saving between financial assets and money. Finally, we look at the division of consumption between purchases of domestic and foreign output and the division of financial asset purchases between purchases of domestic and foreign financial assets. Figure 6.2 summarizes our breakdown of various household consumption and saving decisions. You may find it useful to refer to this figure as you go through the remainder of this chapter.

A Simplified View of the Consumption Function

Economists summarize the determinants of consumption behavior by what is referred to as the consumption function. Nobel prize–winning economist Franco Modigliani motivates our concern for this topic when he notes that "the study of the consumption function has undoubtedly yielded some of the highest correlations as well as some of the most embarrassing forecasts in the history of economics. Yet the interest in the subject continues unabated since, if it were possible to establish the existence of a stable relation between consumption, income, and other relevant variables and to estimate its parameters, such a relation would represent an invaluable tool for economic policy and forecasting."[15]

[15] Franco Modigliani and Richard Brumberg, "Utility Analysis and the Consumption Function:

Figure 6.2   The Household Decision Tree

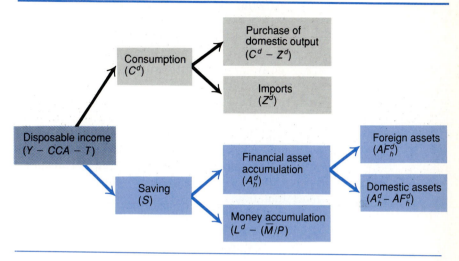

The various theories of consumption and saving behavior share a common theme—the choice between current and future consumption. The sole purpose of saving is to finance consumption in future periods. Or, as John Maynard Keynes noted, "Consumption—to repeat the obvious—is the sole end and object of all economic activity." This common theme is evident in the major theories of consumption proposed by Keynes (the propensity to consume), Nobel prize–winner Milton Friedman (the permanent income hypothesis), and Modigliani (the life-cycle hypothesis).

An important element in Keynes' *The General Theory of Employment, Interest, and Money* was a theory of consumption that emphasized the effects of changes in current income on consumption demand. Following Keynes, we can "define what we shall call *the propensity to consume* as the functional relationship between a given level of income (and) the expenditure on consumption. . . . Given the general economic situation, the expenditure on consumption depends in the main on the volume of output and employment. . . . Whilst the other factors are capable of varying (and this must not be forgotten), the aggregate income . . . is, as a rule, the principal variable upon which the consumption-constituent of the aggregate demand function will depend."[16]

Consumption function:
The relationship between total household consumption spending and the total disposable income of all households.

Keynes proposed a **consumption function** that relates each household's desired consumption spending to its real disposable income. One obtains the aggregate consumption function by relating total household consumption

---

An Interpretation of Cross-section Data," in *Post-Keynesian Economics,* ed. Kenneth K. Kurihara (New Brunswick: Rutgers University Press, 1954), p. 388.
[16] Keynes, *General Theory,* p. 96.

spending to the total disposable income of all households. Keynes proposed the following specific form for this aggregate consumption function:

$$C^d = a + b \cdot (Y - CCA - T) \tag{6.3}$$

where a and b are positive parameters, C^d is consumption demand, and $Y - CCA - T$ is real disposable income.

Marginal propensity to consume (MPC): The ratio of the increase in the real consumption demand of households to the increase in their real disposable income.

In Equation 6.3, the parameter b is called the **marginal propensity to consume.** The marginal propensity to consume (MPC) is the ratio of the increase in the real consumption demand of households to the increase in their real disposable income that induces the increase in consumption. The marginal propensity to consume is positive but less than one, because an increase in real disposable income causes consumption spending to rise, but by an amount smaller than the total increase in income.[17] This reflects the fact that households generally respond to an increase in real disposable income by increasing not only consumption spending but also saving.

To clarify the relationship between income and consumption, consider a numerical example of Equation 6.3. Suppose that the value of a is 10 and the value of b, the marginal propensity to consume, is .9. That is, suppose

$$C^d = 10 + .9 \cdot (Y - CCA - T)$$

If real disposable income is \$400 billion, then consumption demand is \$370 billion. If income rises to \$500 billion, then consumption demand increases to \$460 billion. Note that the \$100 billion increase in disposable income results in a \$90-billion increase in consumption. This change in consumption is simply the product of the marginal propensity to consume (.9) and the change in income (\$100 billion). Empirical studies generate a "customary estimate of the marginal propensity to consume of .7 to .9"[18]

Figure 6.3 represents graphically the linear consumption function specified above. The consumption function slopes upward since a higher income leads to increased consumption demand. The slope of the consumption function indicates the change in consumption demand per unit change in disposable income. Thus the slope equals the marginal propensity to consume.

The relationship between desired saving and real disposable income is called the *saving function.* Using the linear consumption function (Equation 6.3), we can obtain the saving function in a straightforward fashion since we know from the household budget constraint that saving equals real disposable income minus consumption, or

$$S = (Y - CCA - T) - C^d$$

---

[17] According to Keynes, "The fundamental psychological law, upon which we are entitled to depend with great confidence both *a priori* from our knowledge of human nature and from the detailed facts of experience, is that men are disposed, as a rule and on the average, to increase their consumption as their income increases, but not by as much as the increase in their income." p. 96.

[18] Franco Modigliani and Arlie Sterling, "Government Debt, Government Spending, and Private Sector Behavior: Comment," *American Economic Review* (December 1986), p. 1173.

Figure 6.3   The Consumption Function

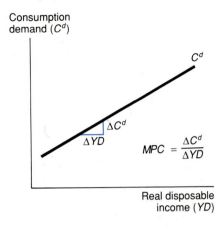

The consumption function slopes upward, indicating that a rise in real disposable income leads to a rise in consumption demand. The slope of the consumption function equals the marginal propensity to consume (MPC) and is between zero and one.

Substituting the expression for consumption demand as given by Equation 6.3 into the above equation, we have

$$S = (Y - CCA - T) = [a + b \cdot (Y - CCA - T)]$$

Combining terms and rearranging, we obtain the saving function:

$$S = -a + (1 - b) \cdot (Y - CCA - T) \tag{6.4}$$

Marginal propensity to save (MPS): The ratio of the increase in real saving of households to the increase in their real disposable income.

The **marginal propensity to save** (MPS) is the ratio of the increase in real saving of households to the increase in their real disposable income that induces the increase in saving. From Equation 6.4, we see that the marginal propensity to save equals $1 - b$. Note that the marginal propensity to consume (b in Equation 6.3) and the marginal propensity to save ($1 - b$ in Equation 6.4) sum to one. Intuitively this makes sense since that fraction of an increase in real disposable income that does not go to increased consumption spending must, according to the household budget constraint, go to increased saving.

The term a in Equation 6.3 summarizes the influence on consumption spending of variables other than current disposable income. Among the variables that affect the division of a given amount of real disposable income between consumption and saving is the expected real rate of interest. The expected real interest rate (the nominal rate r minus the expected rate of inflation π^e) affects current consumption because it affects the cost of consumption today in terms of the consumption foregone next year. By purchasing financial assets, households can exchange one unit of consumption today for $1 + (r - \pi^e)$ units of real consumption next year.[19] Since an increase in the expected real rate of interest raises the cost of consumption today in terms of the amount of consumption forgone next year, we would expect it to reduce real consumption spending and to increase real saving.[20] In fact, we observe precisely this as household purchases of consumer durables such as refrigerators and cars do typically fall with an increase in the expected real rate of interest.

A more general form of the consumption function than Equation 6.3 that identifies not only real disposable income $(Y - CCA - T)$ but also the expected real rate of interest $(r - \pi^e)$ as a determinant of current consumption demand is

$$C^d = C^d(\underset{+}{Y - CCA - T}, \underset{-}{r - \pi^e}, ...) \tag{6.5}$$

As the three dots in Equation 6.5 indicate, in addition to real disposable income and the expected real rate of interest, there are additional factors that affect aggregate consumption demand. One of these is the distribution of real disposable income across households. For example, if income is transferred from households with low marginal propensities to consume to households with high propensities to consume, aggregate consumption demand will rise and saving will fall even though total real disposable income remains unchanged.

Another factor that can influence current consumption spending is anticipated future income. We highlight this idea in our discussions below of the intertemporal household budget constraint and the related **life-cycle hypothesis** and **permanent income hypothesis**.[21] Both hypotheses indicate that current consumption demand depends directly on anticipated future income as well as current income. As such, the life-cycle and permanent income hypotheses lead to the proposition that current consumption demand is not very responsive to changes in disposable income that are considered temporary or transitory.

In contrast, a change in current disposable income that is not transitory, but is instead anticipated to be permanent, will lead to a more dramatic change in current consumption demand since both current and anticipated future income are altered. Cast in terms of the marginal propensity to consume,

Life-cycle hypothesis: Like the permanent income hypothesis, this hypothesis examines the implications of household choices of consumption across time.

Permanent income hypothesis: A hypothesis suggesting that consumption is based on the individual's perception of permanent income.

---

[19] Recall from our discussion of the investment decisions of firms that $(r - \pi^e)$ is an approximation for $(r - \pi^e)/(1 + \pi^e)$. The exact amount of real consumption next year that a household can obtain by giving up one unit of consumption today is $(1 + r)/(1 + \pi^e) = 1 + (r - \pi^e)/(1 + \pi^e)$. Given that anticipated inflation π^e is typically a small fraction (less than .10), we approximate this expression by $1 + (r - \pi^e)$.

[20] Irving Fisher provides the classic analysis of the effect of the expected real interest rate on consumption in his book *The Theory of Interest* (New York: 1930).

[21] Keynes was aware of the potential effect of future income on current consumption. However, in the *General Theory,* Keynes argued that future income "is a matter about which there is, as a rule, too much uncertainty for it to exert much influence." (p. 95) Given individuals' uncertainty with respect to future income, Keynes perceived them as typically relying on current income as a predictor of future income. Similarly, Keynes downplayed the role of the interest rate in affecting consumption, stating that a "fluctuation in the rate of interest is not likely, however, to have much *direct* influence on spending." (p. 93)

these hypotheses suggest that the *MPC* is lower for income changes that are considered transitory in nature than it is for changes in income that are considered permanent. Both the permanent income hypothesis and the life-cycle hypothesis indicate that the consumption component of output demand will be relatively stable since erratic temporary changes in income will not be translated into large changes in consumption.

*The Intertemporal Nature of the Household Budget Constraint

Keynes' view that the key factor affecting consumption is current disposable income fits nicely with the simple way in which we have written the household budget constraint: $C^d + S = YD$. The constraint indicates that the sum of consumption and saving are constrained to be no greater than current disposable income, making it natural to focus on current disposable income as an important determinant of current consumption demand.

The household budget constraint as so stated, however, does not make explicit the link between current saving and future consumption and income. In this section, we restate the budget constraint with this link made explicit in order to identify a number of factors other than current disposable income that can affect current consumption demand. We start by examining the typical or representative household's consumption and saving decisions for the simple case in which there is only a two-year time horizon—the current year zero and the subsequent year one. We then generalize to the case of households with an *N* period lifetime. In the subsequent two sections, we use this expanded view of the household budget constraint to highlight the implications of the life-cycle and permanent income hypotheses.

As before, let C^d denote the representative household's consumption demand during the current year and let *S* denote saving. While saving reduces consumption in the current year 0, the income saved helps finance planned consumption in year 1, denoted by C_1^d. Specifically, if saving is used to purchase financial assets such as stocks and bonds, the household can anticipate $1 + R$ units of consumption next year for each unit of saving in the current period, where *R* is the expected real rate of interest (the nominal interest rate *r* minus the expected rate of inflation π^e). Thus saving of the amount *S* in the current year is expected grow in real terms to $S(1 + R)$ one year later.

For our simple example with a two-year time horizon, planned consumption in year 1 (C_1^d) is constrained to be no greater than the expected real income derived from saving in the current year 0 $[S(1 + R)]$ plus expected disposable labor income in year 1 (YD_1^e) plus the real income from cashing in the value of assets acquired from all previous saving before year 0 $(\overline{A})$.[22] Since the stock of financial asset holdings is expected to increase

---

[22] The term disposable labor income (YD_1^e) refers to expected income earned from labor minus total expected taxes. We refer explicitly to labor income so as to distinguish it from the other sources of income, specifically dividends and interest earnings from household asset holdings. Total expected future taxes include taxes on anticipated future interest and dividend income from the household's holdings of stocks and bonds as well as taxes on labor income.

in value by the factor $(1 + R)$ because of real interest and dividend payments between year 0 and year 1, real income from cashing in the initial asset holdings equals $\overline{A}(1 + R)$. The anticipated constraint on consumption in year 1 may thus be expressed as

$$C_1^d \quad = \quad YD_1^e \quad + \quad S(1 + R) \quad + \quad \overline{A}(1 + R)$$

| Consumption spending in year 1 | Disposable labor income in year 1 | Value in year 1 of savings in year 0 | Value in year 1 of initial asset holdings | (6.6) |

Note that a two-year time horizon means that the household does not plan on consuming beyond year 1. As a consequence, there is no reason to hold on to savings beyond year 1, so that all available resources in year 1 are used to finance consumption.

We can rearrange Equation 6.6 to express current saving in terms of future planned consumption, future expected disposable labor income, and current financial asset holdings. Specifically, using Equation 6.6 to solve for current saving S, we have

$$S = C_1^d/(1 + R) - [YD_1^e/(1 + R) + \overline{A}]$$

This equation indicates that current saving finances consumption spending in the next period in excess of future after-tax income obtained from working plus liquidating financial asset holdings. Substituting this expression for saving into the simple household budget constraint $C^d + S = YD$, we obtain

$$C^d + [(C_1^d - YD_1^e)/(1 + R) - \overline{A}] = YD$$

which, upon rearranging, becomes

$$C^d + C_1^d/(1 + R) = YD + YD_1^e/(1 + R) + \quad \overline{A}$$

| Present value of consumption | Present value of income | Initial asset holdings |

The above restatement of the household budget constraint for a two-year time horizon indicates that the present value of the household's consumption stream during year 0 and year 1 (the left side of the equation) is constrained by the household's current disposable income (YD), initial financial asset holdings $(\overline{A})$, and the present value of future expected labor income net of taxes $[YD_1^e/(1 + R)]$ (the right side of the equation). In general, for a time horizon of $N + 1$ years, the household budget constraint can be expressed as[23]

$$C^d + C_1^d/(1 + R) + C_2^d/(1 + R)^2 + \cdots + C_N^d/(1 + R)^N =$$

$$YD + YD_1^e/(1 + R) + YD_2^e/(1 + R)^2 + \cdots YD_N^e/(1 + R)^N + \overline{A}$$

---

[23] Note that the length of the time horizon need not coincide with individuals' anticipated lifetimes. If individuals care about their descendants (have a "bequest" motive for saving), then the fact that weight is placed on the expected future incomes and expenses of offspring can be interpreted as extending individuals' time horizon beyond their anticipated lifetimes.

where C^d is current consumption demand, YD is current disposable income, C_t^d is planned consumption demand in year t, and YD_t^e is expected real labor income after taxes in year t.[24] Using the term $\Sigma_{t=0}^N$ to denote a summing of terms from $t = 0$ to $t = N$, the above intertemporal budget constraint can be rewritten more compactly as

$$C^d + \sum_{t=1}^N C_t^d/(1 + R)^t = YD + \sum_{t=1}^N YD_t^e/(1 + R)^t + \quad \overline{A}$$

(6.7)

| Present value of consumption | Present value of income | Initial asset holdings |

If we retrace the steps taken to derive Equation 6.7, it should be clear that this form of the household budget constraint is merely a more detailed expression of the statement that household consumption plus saving equals current disposable income. However, unlike the simpler expression for the household budget constraint, Equation 6.7 makes explicit that besides current disposable income, the initial financial asset holdings, the anticipated future labor income net of taxes, and the expected real rate of interest may also affect current consumption demand.

*The Life-Cycle Hypothesis and Consumption Smoothing

Equation 6.7 indicates that an individual's consumption in any period is not constrained by the income received during that period but rather that lifetime consumption is constrained by the income accruing to an individual over his or her lifetime. While income tends to rise and fall during the lifetime of an individual, through appropriate saving and borrowing the individual can maintain a smooth or constant rate of consumption over his or her lifetime. This smoothing of consumption across time plays a critical role in Franco Modigliani's "life-cycle hypothesis" of consumption.[25]

Figure 6.4 indicates a stylized pattern of income and consumption expenditures over an individual's lifetime. Prior to retirement, wage income

---

[24] The present value of future labor income has been termed the value of "human capital." The term human capital, popularized by University of Chicago economist Gary Becker, refers to the fact that individuals, like physical capital, offer productive services over an extended period of time. See Gary S. Becker, *Human Capital: A Theoretical and Empirical Analysis with Special Reference to Education* (New York: National Bureau of Economic Research, Columbia University Press, 1964). Human capital can be increased by investments in such things as education and on-the-job training.

[25] As Modigliani has stated, "the consumption and saving decisions of households at each point of time reflect a more or less conscious attempt at achieving the preferred distribution of consumption over the life cycle, subject to the constraint imposed by the resources accruing to the household over the lifetime." Franco Modigliani, "Life Cycle Hypothesis of Saving, the Demand for Wealth and the Supply of Capital," *Social Research* (June 1966). Modigliani summarizes his contribution to the analysis of consumption behavior in his Nobel lecture of December 1985, reprinted as "Life Cycle, Individual Thrift, and the Wealth of Nations," *American Economic Review* (June 1986).

Figure 6.4   The Life Cycle of Consumption, Income, and Wealth

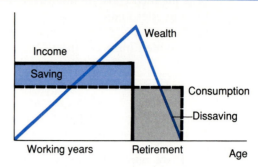

During working years, consumption is less than income, saving is positive, and household wealth increases. Dissaving occurs during retirement to finance consumption and household wealth falls. This pattern of saving and dissaving results in an inverted V-shaped wealth-age profile.

exceeds consumption and saving is positive.[26] During this period saving increases household wealth. On retirement, wage income drops to zero, and consumption is financed by dissaving. As Figure 6.4 shows, during the retirement period household wealth falls as people draw on their accumulated savings to finance consumption during their "golden" (a euphemism for waning) years.

The inverted V-shaped wealth-age profile predicted by the standard life-cycle model (saving during preretirement years and dissaving or running down the stock of accumulated wealth in the years following retirement) is supported by a number of studies of aggregate household consumption and saving behavior.[27] However, what happens in the aggregate does mask different behavior among subgroups of the populations. For instance, Burbidge and Robb find for Canadian data that while an inverted V-shaped profile exists for the "average" Canadian household, "white collar" households do appear to continue to accumulate wealth years after both husband and wife have left the labor force.[28]

To make clearer the implications of consumption smoothing for the consumption function, we will make the simplifying assumption that the typical household seeks to completely smooth out consumption spending across time, so that its desired consumption is the same every year. This

---

[26] Although firms often directly contribute to the pension funds of their workers, these payments are in essence made by workers, since such contributions reduce workers' wages in the form of explicit salary payments and other fringe benefits.

[27] See, for example, P. A. Diamond and J. A. Hausman, "Individual Retirement and Savings Behavior," *Journal of Public Economics* 23, (1984): 81–114 and Michael Hurd, "Savings of the Elderly and Desired Bequests," *American Economic Review* (June 1987): 298–312.

[28] J. B. Burbidge and A. L. Robb, "Evidence on Wealth-Age Profiles in Canadian Cross-Section Data," *Canadian Journal of Economics* (November 1985): 854–875.

means that planned consumption demand for any year t equals current consumption demand, or $C_t^d = C^d$ for all t. In this case, we can rewrite Equation 6.7 as

$$C^d = \Omega \cdot \left\{ YD + \sum_{t=1}^{N} YD_t^e / (1 + R)^t + \overline{A} \right\} \tag{6.8}$$

where the Greek letter omega (Ω), which equals $1/\sum_{t=0}^{N} 1/(1 + R)^t$, is what Modigliani has called the "proportionality factor." The proportionality factor (Ω) indicates the proportion of total household resources—consisting of initial assets, current income and anticipated future income—devoted to consumption each year.[29] Comparing Equation 6.8 to the simpler consumption function of Keynes (Equation 6.3), we see that in addition to current income, anticipated future disposable labor income and the expected real rate of interest, as well as current holdings of financial assets, also affect consumption demand.

An important implication of Modigliani's life-cycle hypothesis is that the marginal propensity to consume—the fraction of an increase in current disposable income that goes toward increased current consumption—will vary depending on whether the increase in current disposable income (YD) signals an increase in future after-tax income as well. If a change in current income is viewed as transitory, most of the increase in income will go to saving in order to finance increased consumption during future years. This idea that the effect of a change in current disposable income on consumption demand depends on the degree to which the change in income is viewed as temporary or permanent lies at the heart of Milton Friedman's permanent income hypothesis, which we explore in the next section.

*The Permanent Income Hypothesis

The permanent income hypothesis is like the life-cycle hypothesis in that it emphasizes the fact that current consumption demand depends not only on current income, but also on anticipated income in the future. More specifically, the permanent income hypothesis states that a household's current consumption spending depends on its "permanent" income, which is in essence a weighted average of its current and expected future income.

A more precise definition of permanent income would be the following. Permanent income is that income which if received each year over a household's time horizon will yield an income stream with a present value exactly equal to the present value of the household's actual income stream. Since the present value of the household's actual income stream equals the household's current disposable income (YD) plus the present value of future expected

---

[29] To see how Ω is obtained, note that if $C_t^d = C^d$ for every year t, then the left side of Equation 6.9 can be written as

$$C^d + \sum_{t=1}^{N} C^d / (1 + R)^t = C^d \left(\sum_{t=0}^{N} 1/(1 + R)^t \right) = C^d \cdot (1/\Omega)$$

labor income after taxes $[\Sigma_{t=1}^{N} YD_t^e/(1 + R)^t]$ plus the household's initial financial asset holdings $(\bar{A})$, permanent income Y_p is defined by the following equation:

$$Y_p + \sum_{t=1}^{N} Y_p/(1 + R)^t = YD + \sum_{t=1}^{N} YD_t^e/(1 + R)^t + \bar{A} \qquad (6.9)$$

Factoring out Y_p in the left side of Equation 6.9, we obtain

$$Y_p\left[\sum_{t=0}^{N} 1/(1 + R)^t\right] = YD + \sum_{t=1}^{N} YD_t^e/(1 + R)^t + \bar{A}$$

Let's solve the above equation for permanent income Y_p. Multiplying through by $[1/\Sigma_{t=0}^{N} 1/(1 + R)^t]$, we obtain

$$Y_p \quad = \quad \Omega \quad \cdot \left\{ YD + \sum_{t=1}^{N} YD_t^e/(1 + R)^t + \bar{A} \right\} \qquad (6.10)$$

Permanent income	Proportionality factor	Present value of disposable income	Initial asset holdings

where the proportionality factor Ω equals $1/[\Sigma_{t=0}^{N} 1/(1 + R)^t]$.

To understand the intuition behind Equation 6.10, suppose that the real rate of interest (R) is zero. When R equals zero, Ω equals $1/(N + 1)$. In this case, we can rewrite Equation 6.10 as

$$Y_p = (1/N + 1)\left(YD + \sum_{t=1}^{N} YD_t^e + \bar{A} \right) \qquad (6.11)$$

From Equation 6.11 we see that permanent income has a very simple interpretation when the real interest rate is zero. In this case, permanent income is simply the household's average income level over time. When the real interest rate is not zero, permanent income is still a weighted average of current and future incomes, but in this case incomes in the more distant future are weighted less heavily since they are discounted more highly.

Recall that if households completely smooth their consumption spending across time, then their current consumption is given by Equation 6.8. Substituting Equation 6.10, which defines permanent income, into Equation 6.8, we obtain the following equation for current consumption demand:

$$C^d = Y_p \qquad (6.12)$$

Equation 6.12 captures Friedman's view that current consumption demand depends not on current income but on permanent income (Y_p). In fact, given our assumption that households completely smooth their consumption spending across time, then Equation 6.12 tells us that current consumption demand exactly equals permanent income. The reason is simple. Since permanent income is the "average income" that the household expects to earn over its lifetime, if consumption is to be held constant, it must just equal permanent income.

The permanent income hypothesis as represented by Equation 6.12 implies that a change in current disposable income affects consumption demand only if the change alters permanent income. For instance, if an increase in current income signals a similar increase in disposable income in all future years, then from Equation 6.10 we know that permanent income increases by approximately the same amount as current disposable income. As Equation 6.12 indicates, current consumption will in turn rise by this same amount. In other words, the marginal propensity to consume out of a change in current income that is perceived as permanent is equal to one.

In contrast, the marginal propensity to consume out of a change in current disposable income that is perceived as entirely transitory is small. Following Friedman, we may define the transitory component of current income as equal to the difference between current disposable income YD and permanent income Y_p. Given that current consumption depends on permanent rather than current income, the transitory component of income is almost entirely saved if positive, or borrowed if negative. This transitory component of current income can reflect such events as a temporary layoff, a short-run opportunity to work overtime, or a temporary tax rebate.

In summary, the life-cycle and permanent income hypotheses both predict that consumption spending will not be very responsive to transitory changes in income. This prediction has important implications for the macroeconomic impacts of such fiscal policy actions as tax changes. For instance, it provides an explanation as to why policymakers significantly overestimated the negative effect that the Johnson administration's temporary tax surcharge in 1968 would have on consumption spending. Given this important policy implication of both the life cycle/permanent income hypothesis, substantial research has been devoted to testing this hypothesis against the simple Keynesian consumption function.

One way to test the life-cycle/permanent income hypothesis is to consider the effect on consumption of anticipated versus unanticipated changes in income. In the simple Keynesian consumption function, consumption demand depends solely on current disposable income. Thus a change in income would have the same effect on consumption demand whether or not it had been anticipated. In contrast, the life-cycle/permanent income hypothesis would predict that previously anticipated changes in income have no effect on consumption demand since consumption plans have already incorporated this income. The recent evidence offers mixed support for the life-cycle/permanent income hypothesis.

On the one hand, there is little impact on consumption when changes in current income are anticipated. Yet most recent empirical studies reject the notion that consumption demand depends *solely* on permanent income, as Equation 6.12 indicates.[30] Equation 6.12 is clearly too simple a representation of the household consumption decision. In particular, note that one of the key assumptions made in deriving Equation 6.12 is that households can freely lend or borrow to maintain consumption equal to permanent income. A "liquidity constraint" may exist for many households, however, as they likely have limited ability to borrow to finance current consumption during periods when their current income falls below their permanent income.

Taking into account a potential liquidity constraint facing some households, the modified life cycle/permanent income hypothesis would no longer predict that current consumption is unaffected by changes in transitory income but rather that consumption is less sensitive to transitory than to permanent changes in income. In other words, the marginal propensity to consume out of changes in transitory income would be less than out of changes in permanent income, but it would not equal zero. This modified life cycle/permanent income hypothesis is supported by available evidence.[31] In particular, liquidity constraints seem to be especially important in explaining the consumption behavior of young households.

Case Study

BLACK MONDAY, BLUE CONSUMERS? THE EFFECT OF WEALTH ON CONSUMPTION DEMAND

From our discussion of consumption spending it should be clear that a household's financial wealth is a potentially important determinant of its consumption demand. For example, according to the life-cycle hypothesis, a household's consumption spending is proportional to their total wealth, which is simply the sum of the present value of their anticipated labor income and the value of their financial asset holdings. And according to the permanent income hypothesis, a household's consumption spending is equal to its permanent income, which is itself dependent on the value of its financial asset holdings and its anticipated labor earnings.

---

[30] See, for example, Joseph Altonji and Alyosius Siow, "Testing the Response of Consumption to Income Changes with (Noisy) Panel Data," *Quarterly Journal of Economics* (1987): 293–328; Robert Hall and Frederick Mishkin, "The Sensitivity of Consumption to Transitory Income: Estimates from Panel Data on Households," *Econometrica* (March 1982): 261–281; Majorie Flavin, "The Adjustment of Consumption to Changing Expectations About Future Income," *Journal of Political Economy* 89 (1981): 974–1009.

[31] For example see Majorie Flavin, "Excess Sensitivity of Consumption to Current Income: Liquidity Constraints or Myopia," *Canadian Journal of Economics* (February 1985): 117–136 and Fumio Hayashi, "The Effect of Liquidity Constraints on Consumption: A Cross-Sectional Analysis," *Quarterly Journal of Economics* (February 1985): 183–206.

The value of households' financial asset holdings is simply the value placed by the market on the earnings that are expected to accrue on these assets. During the early and mid-1980s, this value rose appreciably. From a low of 776.42 in 1982, the Dow-Jones average rose to 2,722.42 in August 1987. In terms of 1982 dollars, this corresponded to an increase in the value of stocks of close to 200 percent over this 5 year period. The increases in the stock prices that occurred in the mid-1980s have been given some of the credit for the high level of consumption demand that existed during the period.

A couple of months after stock prices peaked in August 1987, they came tumbling down. In fact, on October 19, 1987—now known as Black Monday— the stock market crashed so hard it made the 1929 crash that is popularly viewed as ushering in the Great Depression sound like a pin drop. The 508.32 drop in the Dow-Jones average represented a 23.2 percent decline, close to double the 12.8 percent fall on that notorious day of October 28, 1929.

The fall in the market value of U.S. securities on Black Monday was enormous, amounting to approximately $500 billion. In light of our theory of consumption, this can be expected to lead to a fall in consumption demand. Empirical studies do confirm that consumption spending is directly related to stock prices. After the crash, there was concern that the fall in consumption would be large enough to cause a recession, bringing to an end the expansion of the prior five years. However, through other stimulative factors such as increasing export demand and a more expansionary monetary policy by the Fed, a fall in aggregate demand in the ensuing months did not materialize.

To the Point

HOUSEHOLDS AS BUYERS IN THE OUTPUT MARKET

- The household budget constraint indicates that household consumption plus saving is constrained by real disposable income YD (income minus the capital consumption allowance and taxes net of transfer payments)— that is, $C^d + S = YD$.

- Keynes' consumption function relates consumption demand to current disposable income. The change in consumption and the change in saving resulting from a one-unit change in real disposable income are, respectively, the marginal propensity to consume and the marginal propensity to save.

- Modigliani's life-cycle hypothesis and Friedman's permanent income hypothesis relate current consumption not only to current disposable income but also to anticipated future income. As a consequence, a change in current disposable income is predicted to have a greater impact on current consumption if it is perceived as being permanent rather than temporary.

6.3   THE DEMAND FOR MONEY

As was illustrated by the household decision tree in Figure 6.2, there are only two things households can do with their after-tax income: consume it or save it. In the previous section, we looked at factors that affect the division of disposable income between consumption and saving. After a household has decided how much income to allocate to saving, however, it must then decide how to divide the saving among various assets. In other words, the household must select the composition of its portfolio. The next two sections examine this household portfolio decision.

Saving and the Implied Portfolio Choices

Individuals can purchase a wide variety of assets as a means of saving, including currency, checking accounts, stock in General Motors or Nova Concepts, U.S. treasury bills, mutual funds, and Penn Central bonds. As noted earlier, payments by firms into workers' private pension funds are also part of household saving. Although the forms of household saving vary greatly, recall from Chapter 4 that we group saving into two broad categories: the accumulation of money and the accumulation of financial assets.

When households save in the form of money, they add to their stock of real money balances. We denote this desired accumulation of real money balances by $L^d - \overline{M}/P$. Household desired saving in the form of financial assets through the accumulation of stocks and bonds is denoted by A_h^d. Thus as we saw in Chapter 4, total desired saving can be written as desired real accumulation of money balances plus desired accumulation of financial assets, or

$$S \quad = \quad A_h^d \quad + \quad L^d - \overline{M}/P$$

| Saving | Household demand for additional financial assets | Demand for additional real money balances | **(6.13)** |

Equation 6.13 offers an important insight into household saving behavior. The equation indicates that for a given level of saving (S), households' portfolio decisions concerning their desired end-of-period stock of real money balances (L^d) have implications not only for their accumulation of real money balances ($L^d - \overline{M}/P$) but also for the desired accumulation of financial assets (A_h^d). For instance, if there is no change in saving, an increase in households' desired stock of real money balances means a fall in their planned accumulation of financial assets by an equivalent amount.

In summary, when households choose a level of saving and how much of that saving to hold in the form of money, they in essence also decide how much to hold in the form of financial assets. Below we examine the factors that affect households' desired money holdings. The next section then combines this analysis with our previous analysis of the saving decision to derive household demand for financial assets.

Variables Affecting Household Demand For Real Money Balances

Economists refer to a household's decision as to how much money to hold (L^d) as its real money demand. To be more precise, the "demand for money" refers to how much wealth individuals are willing and able to hold in the form of money at a particular point in time. Consequently, when we speak of the demand for money, we are talking about a stock variable.

When households hold wealth in the form of money, they give up the opportunity to put it into financial assets that offer higher interest earnings.[32] Why, then, do households hold any money? When households receive their income, they can of course immediately buy financial assets and then later convert these financial assets back to money right before they purchase consumption goods. Such a procedure would enable households to maximize their interest earnings, but it would be costly in terms of both the time and the brokerage fees required. By keeping money balances on hand, households can reduce these conversion costs.

An increase in the volume of transactions households engage in will increase the average amount of money balances that they want to hold. It is intuitive that a household that now purchases $3000 worth of real goods and services per month will on average hold more real money balances than that same household when it purchased $1000 worth of real goods and services per month. This relationship holds in the aggregate as well; an increase in the real value of GNP, which reflects a rise in the real value of transactions in the economy, leads to an increase in real money demand. In other words, real money demand is directly related to real GNP (Y). At times it will be convenient to express this relationship between real money demand and real GNP by the simple linear equation

$$L^d = k \cdot Y \tag{6.14}$$

where k is a positive parameter. According to this equation, an increase in real income, other things being equal, leads to an increase in real money demand equal to k multiplied by the change in income.

Be sure to note that the money demand appearing in Equation 6.14 is a demand for *real* money balances. That is, this equation tells us that *real* money demand (L^d) is directly related to real output (Y). The demand for money is a demand for real balances because households hold money for

---

[32] Remember that, unlike financial assets, coins, currency, and checking accounts pay no interest. Although other forms of money, such as checkable deposits at depository institutions, pay some interest, this interest rate on monetary assets is typically less than that available on financial assets and only partially adjusts in response to changes in the market interest rate on financial assets.

Figure 6.5   The Demand for Money

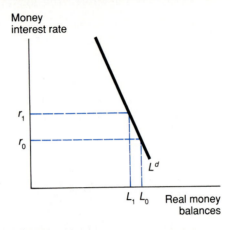

The inverse relationship between the interest rate and real money demand results in a downward-sloping demand for money curve. As the interest rate falls from r_0 to r_1, the quantity of real money demanded increases from L_0 to L_1.

the purchasing power it gives them over output. Thus as Equation 6.14 indicates, changes in the price level result in equiproportionate changes in the dollar value of money demand, leaving real money demand (L^d) unaffected.

An increase in the interest rate induces households to economize on their money holdings, since it raises the cost of holding money in terms of the forgone interest on financial assets. To economize on their money holdings, households make more frequent conversions between money balances and financial assets. These more frequent conversions reduce households' average money balances and increase their average holdings of financial assets. In terms of Equation 6.14, a higher interest rate would reduce k, the ratio of real money demand to real output.[33]

Summarizing, real money demand (L^d) is directly related to real GNP (Y), but inversely related to the interest rate (r). That is, the general form of the money demand function is

$$L^d = L^d(\underset{+}{Y}, \underset{-}{r}, ...) \tag{6.15}$$

This relationship is represented graphically in Figure 6.5. With the interest rate on the vertical axis, the money demand curve is downward-sloping,

---

[33] For simplicity, we do not give households the option of holding inventories of commodities. If we did, then the expected rate of inflation as well as the nominal interest rate would affect the desired holding of money balances, as an increase in the expected rate of inflation would induce households to economize on money balances in favor of holding inventories of commodities. A more detailed discussion of the factors affecting money demand is contained in Chapter 16.

indicating that a lower interest rate increases households' desired holdings of real money balances. An increase in real income (Y) shifts the money demand curve to the right since at every interest rate, households desire to hold a higher level of real money balances to facilitate their increased quantity of transactions.

6.4 HOUSEHOLD BEHAVIOR IN THE FINANCIAL MARKET

Household saving decisions influence the demand for financial assets in the financial markets, which, in turn, has an important influence on interest rates. An understanding of the factors affecting households' financial asset demand will thus help us in future discussions of the determinants of the interest rate. In the next section, we explore what our previous analyses of consumption demand and money demand imply for the demand for financial assets.

Variables Affecting Household Demand for Financial Assets

Rearranging Equation 6.13, we see that households' desired accumulation of financial assets (stocks and bonds) equals saving minus the desired accumulation of real money balances. That is,

$$A_h^d = S - (L^d - \overline{M}/P)$$

$$\begin{array}{ccc} \text{Household demand} & \text{Saving} & \text{Demand for} \\ \text{for additional} & & \text{additional real} \\ \text{financial assets} & & \text{money balances} \end{array} \qquad \textbf{(6.16)}$$

As Equation 6.16 highlights, households determine their desired saving, planned money holdings, and financial asset demand simultaneously. For a given level of real money demand, an increase in saving means an increase in a household's demand for financial assets. And, for a given level of saving, an increase in real money demand means a decrease in financial asset demand.

We know that the expected real rate of interest and real disposable income affect household consumption demand and thus saving. We also know that real GNP and the nominal interest rate affect households' real money demand (L^d). From this information, we can identify four determinants of household financial asset demand: real GNP, taxes, the nominal interest rate, and the expected rate of inflation. Let's consider the effect that each of these variables has on household demand for financial assets.

An increase in real GNP leads to a higher disposable income, which, according to our earlier discussion, causes households to increase their desired saving. According to Equation 6.16, this rise in saving would imply an increase in financial asset demand if there were no change in the real demand for money. As we have just seen, however, an increase in real income results in an increased real money demand on the part of households. For a given level of saving, this increase in real money demand (L^d) would imply according to Equation 6.16 a fall in household demand for financial assets. Thus the net effect of an increase in real income on household financial asset demand is, in general, ambiguous.

Households' desired accumulation of financial assets is inversely related to taxes. An increase in taxes lowers disposable income and thus reduces household consumption and saving. We make the simplifying assumption, common to macroeconomic models, that changes in taxes do not affect real money demand. With no change in household demand for money balances, the fall in saving due to a tax increase thus results in a fall in household demand for financial assets equal to the reduction in saving.[34]

For a given nominal interest rate, the demand for financial assets is inversely related to the expected inflation rate. For a given nominal interest rate, a decrease in the expected inflation rate raises the expected real rate of interest. As we have discussed, this increase in the expected real rate of interest leads to a decrease in consumption and consequently a rise in saving. The increase in saving means an increased demand for financial assets.

Finally, household demand for financial assets is positively related to the nominal interest rate. There are two reasons for this. First, for a given expected rate of inflation, a higher interest rate on financial assets means a higher expected real rate of interest. As noted above, this reduces consumption and increases saving in the form of financial assets. Second, as we noted in our discussion of real money demand, an increase in the money interest rate induces households to reduce their holdings of money and increase demand for financial assets.

To summarize, household real desired accumulation of financial assets (A_h^d) depends directly on the nominal interest rate (r) and inversely on taxes (T) and the expected rate of inflation (π^e). The effect of changes in real GNP (Y) on financial asset demand is ambiguous. That is, household real financial asset demand can be represented by

$$A_h^d = A_h^d(\,r\,,\ T\,,\ \pi^e,\ Y,\ ...) $$
$$+\ \ -\ \ -\ \ ?$$

$$(6.17)$$

The Household Supply of Loanable Funds Curve

Recall that when households purchase financial assets, they are lenders. To be more exact, the value of the financial assets that households purchase equals the value of the loanable funds they supply. Thus we can speak

---

[34] For simplicity, our discussion of the effect of a change in taxes on financial asset demand does not take into account the fact that some tax changes can affect the incentive to save, thereby affecting the marginal propensity to save. For instance, a *temporary* increase in a sales or value added tax raises the gain to postponing consumption.

Figure 6.6 Aggregate Household Supply of Loanable Funds

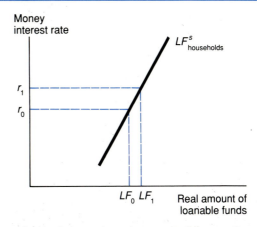

A rise in the interest rate from r_0 to r_1 increases the quantity of loanable funds supplied by households from LF_0 to LF_1, reflecting both the increase in household saving and the substitution of financial assets for money in household portfolios.

interchangeably of household demand for financial assets and supply of loanable funds.

As mentioned in Chapter 5, it is easier to work graphically with the financial market when it is presented in terms of loanable funds rather than financial assets. In anticipation of this, Figure 6.6 illustrates the effect of a change in the interest rate on household supply of loanable funds for a given level of real income (Y), expected inflation (π^e), and net taxes (T). A rise in the interest rate increases the quantity of loanable funds that households supply since the higher interest rate increases their demand for financial assets, as Equation 6.17 states. Thus the household supply of loanable funds curve slopes upward.

Although a change in the interest rate will cause a movement along the supply of loanable funds curve in Figure 6.6, changes in real income, taxes, and the expected rate of inflation will cause shifts in the curve. For example, consider a decrease in the expected rate of inflation (π^e). This means an increase in the expected real rate of interest ($r - \pi^e$) at each money interest rate (r). The result will be an increase in the supply of loanable funds at each interest rate, which is shown graphically by a shift to the right in the supply of loanable funds curve.

To the Point

HOUSEHOLD SAVING BEHAVIOR

- Households save in order to attain a desired stock of money and financial assets. Since money is held to facilitate transactions, the desired stock of money, or real money demand, rises with an increase in the real value of GNP. Real money demand falls with an increase in the interest rate.

- Financial asset demand is the difference between total household saving and the desired accumulation of money balances. An increase in the interest rate means a rise in financial asset demand since it both reduces desired money holdings and increases saving.

- A rise in the interest rate raises the quantity of loanable funds households supply in the financial market. This is shown graphically by a supply of loanable funds curve that slopes upward.

6.5   HOUSEHOLD BEHAVIOR IN THE FOREIGN EXCHANGE MARKET: IMPORTS AND CAPITAL OUTFLOWS

In the summer of 1985, U.S. tourists flocked to Europe in record numbers for vacations, filling airlines and jamming hotels. At the same time, U.S. hotels were well below capacity due to the exodus of U.S. tourists and to the fact that few Europeans came to sightsee in such garden spots as Newark, New Jersey, and Gary, Indiana. What caused this mass expatriation? The purchasing power of the U.S. dollar in foreign markets increased, which caused a fall in the relative price of foreign goods.

In the first part of this section, we examine how a rise in the foreign exchange rate for the U.S. dollar can reduce the relative price of foreign goods, and thus lead to a change in household consumption away from the purchase of domestic goods and toward the purchase of foreign goods. We also examine other factors that influence U.S. imports of goods and services and thus the supply of U.S. dollars in the foreign exchange markets.

As the household decision tree in Figure 6.2 illustrates, in addition to deciding how to divide consumption between foreign and domestic goods and services, households must also decide how to divide their accumulation of financial assets between U.S. stocks and bonds and the financial assets of foreign countries. As we saw in Chapter 3, household purchases of foreign financial assets constitute capital outflows, since households must supply dollars in the foreign exchange market in order to make these purchases. In the second part of this section, we see how differences in foreign and domestic interest rates and the expected appreciation or depreciation of the U.S. dollar determine the relative returns on foreign and domestic financial assets. These relative returns in turn affect household portfolio choices between foreign and domestic financial assets and the supply of dollars in the foreign exchange market.

Variables Affecting Household Demand for Imports

When deciding whether to purchase foreign or domestic goods, households look at relative prices. The *relative* price of a foreign good is the real quantity of a U.S. good that must be sacrificed to purchase the foreign good. For example, if the price of a Japanese car is $6000 and the price of a U.S. computer is $1500, then the relative price of a Japanese car in terms of U.S. computers is four computers. If the relative price of Japanese cars rises, the United States will import fewer Japanese cars. It is the relative price of foreign goods, sometimes referred to as the *terms of trade,* that affects the quantity of imports.

The relative prices of foreign goods depend on (1) the dollar prices of U.S. goods, (2) the prices of foreign goods in their own currency, and (3) foreign exchange rates (the price of one currency in terms of a second currency). The simple example that follows illustrates this point. Suppose that the price of a U.S. computer is $1500 and that in Japan the price of a Japanese car is 600,000 yen. The third "price" that we need to know in order to compute the relative price of a Japanese car in terms of U.S. computers is the foreign exchange rate, in particular the price of a yen in terms of dollars.

Suppose that it takes E yen to buy one dollar in the foreign exchange markets. This means that it will take $1/E$ dollars to buy one yen. For example, if E is 100, then the price of a dollar is 100 yen and the price of a yen will be $1/100$ dollars, or one cent. Returning to our example of Japanese cars and U.S. computers, a Japanese car with a yen price of 600,000 would in this case have a dollar price of 600,000 yen times $1/100$ dollars per yen, or $6000. More generally, the calculation of the relative price of a Japanese car is given by

$$\begin{array}{l}\text{Relative price of} \\ \text{a Japanese car} \\ \text{(in terms of} \\ \text{U.S. computers)}\end{array} = \frac{\begin{array}{l}\text{Yen price of} \\ \text{Japanese car}\end{array} \times \begin{array}{l}\text{Price of yen in} \\ \text{terms of dollars } (1/E)\end{array}}{\begin{array}{l}\text{Dollar price of} \\ \text{U.S. computers}\end{array}}$$

$$= \frac{(600{,}000 \text{ yen}) \times (1/100 \text{ dollars per yen})}{(1500 \text{ dollars per computer})}$$

$$= 4 \text{ U.S. computers}$$

According to this equation, a rise in the yen price of Japanese cars raises the relative price of Japanese cars. Similarly, a fall in the dollar price of U.S. computers raises the relative price of Japanese cars. Finally, a rise in the price of a yen in terms of dollars (or, equivalently, a fall in the price of a dollar in terms of yen) also increases the relative price of Japanese cars. Since all three changes mean a higher relative price of Japanese cars, and thus an increase in the cost to U.S. buyers of Japanese cars in terms of U.S. goods foregone, all three changes reduce U.S. imports of Japanese cars.

Discussions of trade between countries usually focus not on a single good but instead on a basket of traded goods. We have just shown how the relative or "real" price of a single foreign good depends on its price in foreign currency, the exchange rate, and the money price of a domestic good. In general, we will denote P_f as the general level of prices for a basket of foreign goods, with these prices denominated in terms of the foreign currency (yen in our example). Let P denote the price level in the United States and let $(1/E)$ denote the exchange rate for the foreign currency (in our example, dollars per yen). Then the relative price of the foreign country's goods can be expressed as $P_f \cdot (1/E)/P$. In our example, if only Japanese cars and U.S. computers are included in the basket of goods for each country, then P_f equals 600,000 yen, $(1/E)$ equals .01 dollars or 1 cent per yen, and P equals 1500 dollars, so that the relative price of the foreign good is four U.S. computers ($600{,}000 \times .01/1500$).

This relative price expression for a basket of foreign goods is sometimes termed the **real exchange rate** for foreign goods. That is,

Real exchange rate for foreign goods [$P_f/(P \cdot E)$]: A measure of the real amount of domestic goods and services that must be given up to obtain a foreign good.

$$\frac{\text{Real exchange rate}}{\text{(foreign goods)}} = \frac{\text{Dollar price of foreign goods}}{\text{Dollar price of U.S. goods}} = \frac{P_f(1/E)}{P} = \frac{P_f}{P \cdot E}$$

The real exchange rate for foreign goods is a measure of the average amount of U.S. goods and services that must be given up to obtain foreign goods. In this sense, it is the real price of imports.

Our expression for the real exchange rate for foreign goods indicates that if U.S. and foreign price levels (P and P_f, respectively) change in a similar fashion, then changes in the real exchange rate will largely reflect changes in exchange rates (E). In particular, a dollar that is depreciating (its price in terms of foreign currency is falling) implies rising real prices of imports. This naturally follows since a depreciating dollar (E falling) means a rising price for foreign currency in terms of dollars ($1/E$ rising), and thus in the dollar prices of foreign goods.

This inverse relationship between the dollar exchange rates and the real exchange rate for foreign goods is depicted in Figure 6.7. The color line indicates how the real exchange rate for foreign goods has changed over the past 15 years, while the black line is an index of dollar exchange rates. During the late 1970s, the dollar exchange rate fell in value such that real import prices rose. In contrast, the dollar rose sharply between 1980 and 1984 and, as a consequence, real import prices declined significantly. This trend was reversed in 1985; from 1985 to early 1988 the dollar declined and relative import prices rose.

The real exchange rate or relative price of foreign goods is a key long-run determinant of U.S. import demand, which we have denoted Z^d. A rise in the relative price of foreign goods will lead to a reduction in the quantity of foreign goods bought, while a fall in the relative price will increase the quantity of foreign goods demanded. However, we have to be careful to not infer from this that U.S. import demand will necessarily be inversely related

**Figure 6.7   The Real Exchange Rate for Foreign Goods (the real
price of imports) and the Dollar Exchange Rate**

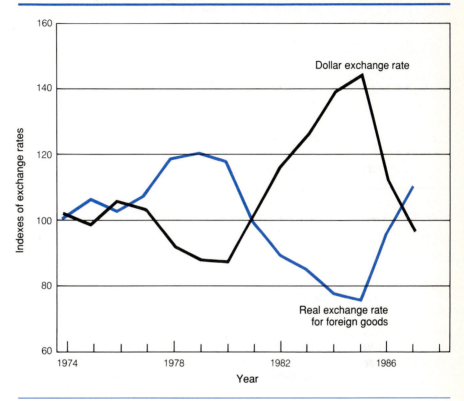

Source: Economic Report of the President (1987).

to the relative or real price of imports. The reason for this is that our measure
of U.S. import demand is in terms of U.S. goods and services, not in terms
of foreign goods. An example will highlight this distinction.

Let's say the dollar depreciates (E falls). With the implied appreciation
of foreign currency ($1/E$ rises), the price of foreign goods in terms of U.S.
goods increases, as our expression for the real exchange rate for foreign
goods ($P_f/P \cdot E$) indicates. With a higher price, fewer foreign goods will be
purchased—this is clear. By itself, this would suggest a fall in the value of
imports into the U.S. But a higher price also means that each foreign good
purchased will cost more in terms of U.S. goods that must be sacrificed. This
by itself would suggest a rise in the value of U.S. imports (measured in terms
of U.S. goods that must be paid to obtain the imports). The net impact of
a change in the relative price of foreign goods on U.S. imports depends on
which of these two effects is stronger.

It is usually assumed that over time the rise in the relative prices of
imports leads to a large fall in the quantity of imports purchased, so that

the value of imports in terms of U.S. goods (Z^d) falls with a rise in the relative price of imports. This is what we will assume for the moment. Later, in particular in Chapter 17, we will look at the situation in which, in the short-run, a rise in the relative price of imports due to a depreciation of the dollar can, in fact, lead to a rise in the value of imports as well. This short-run phenomenon, referred to as the J-curve phenomenon, occurred for the U.S. during the depreciation of the dollar between 1985 and 1987.

Besides the relative prices of imports, real disposable income affects U.S. import demand. Recall from our discussion of consumption that an increase in disposable income leads to a rise in household consumption demand. In an open economy with foreign trade, a rise in consumption demand means an increase in purchases not only of domestically produced goods but also of foreign goods. Thus household import demand is directly related to disposable income.

To summarize, household real import demand (Z^d) depends on the relative price of foreign goods, $P_f(1/E)/P$, and disposable income, $Y - CCA - T$. We write this as follows:

$$Z^d = Z^d[P_f(1/E)/P, Y - CCA - T, ...] \tag{6.18}$$

Capital Outflows: Household Demand for Foreign Financial Assets

When deciding whether to purchase U.S. or foreign financial assets, households compare domestic and foreign rates of return. The rate of return on U.S. financial assets is simply the money interest rate r. The comparable rate of return on foreign financial assets is not so simple to identify. To explain how to compute this return, which we will denote r^*, let's suppose that a household lends one dollar in the foreign financial market.

If the price of a dollar is E units of the foreign currency, say yen, then in terms of the foreign currency, the household lends E yen. If foreign financial assets offer the interest rate r_f, then one year from now the household will have $E(1 + r_f)$ yen. At the end of the year, the household will convert these yen holdings back to dollars at the exchange rate that exists then. At the time the money is lent, this future exchange rate is not known; households however have an expectation of what this future exchange rate will be. Letting next year's expected exchange rate for the dollar (number of yen per dollar) be denoted by E^e, the household expects to convert its $E(1 + r_f)$ yen next year into $E(1 + r_f)/E^e$ dollars. Subtracting the one dollar with which the household started, the rate of return to lending in foreign financial markets equals $[E(1 + r_f)/E^e] - 1$, or

$$r^* = [E(1 + r_f)/E^e] - 1 = \{E(1 + r_f) - E^e\}/E^e \tag{6.19}$$

We can simplify Equation 6.19 by noting that the expected future dollar exchange rate of E^e yen per dollar equals the current exchange rate of E yen times $(1 + \theta^e)$, where θ^e is the expected rate of change in the price of a dollar in terms of yen. Substituting the expression $E(1 + \theta^e)$ for the expected future dollar exchange rate E^e into Equation 6.19, we obtain

$$r^* = \{E(1 + r_f) - E(1 + \theta^e)\}/E(1 + \theta^e) = \{r_f - \theta^e\}/\{1 + \theta^e\} \quad \textbf{(6.20)}$$

Since the expected rate of appreciation of a dollar (θ^e) is usually small, we can approximate Equation 6.20 by

$$r^* \approx r_f - \theta^e \qquad\qquad \textbf{(6.21)}$$

Equation 6.21 has a straightforward interpretation. The return to lending in the foreign financial market equals the difference between the foreign interest rate and the expected rate of change in the price of the dollar. The return to lending in foreign financial markets increases with a higher foreign interest rate (r_f) and decreases with a higher expected rate of increase in the price of the dollar (θ^e). The higher the expected rate of increase in the price of the dollar, the lower the expected return to lending in foreign financial markets. This is because for a given number of dollars sold for foreign currency at the start of the period, fewer dollars can be bought back at the end of the period.

An example will help clarify Equation (6.21). Let's say r_f is .10 or 10 percent. Lending in foreign financial markets will increase one's holding of foreign currency by 10 percent, but as Equation 6.21 indicates, this does not by itself tell us the expected return to such lending. If θ^e is .10, indicating a 10 percent expected appreciation in the dollar, the 10 percent increase in foreign currency due to interest earnings will simply allow the lender to buy back the same number of dollars that are initially loaned out. In this case, the expected return to lending in foreign financial markets ($r_f - \theta^e$) is zero. This return will be positive only if the expected change in the price of the dollar is less than the foreign interest rate. For example, if the expected change in the price of the dollar (θ^e) is .06, then the return to lending abroad ($r_f - \theta^e$) will be .04, as the 10 percent increased holdings of foreign currency can now purchase approximately 4 percent more dollars than were initially lent out.

When households choose between purchasing domestic and foreign financial assets, they compare the domestic interest rate (r) with the rate of return to lending in the foreign financial markets ($r_f - \theta^e$). We can thus express the demand for foreign financial assets as

$$AF_h^d = AF_h^d(\underset{-}{r}, \underset{+}{r_f - \theta^e}, ...) \qquad\qquad \textbf{(6.22)}$$

We see from Equation 6.22 that an increase in the U.S. interest rate or a fall in the rate of return on foreign financial assets each imply a reduction in households' real demand for foreign financial assets. As before, the "dots" in the equation represent factors that have been left unspecified. For instance, a change in the political stability of foreign governments is one unspecified factor that would likely impact on U.S. household demand for foreign financial assets.

Equation 6.22 suggests that we should add another facet to our previous discussion on household demand for U.S. financial assets (Equation 6.17). In addition to real income, taxes, the U.S. money interest rate, and the expected rate of inflation, household demand for U.S. financial assets depends on the expected return to lending abroad ($r_f - \theta^e$).

The Foreign Exchange Market: The Supply of Dollars Curve

Figure 6.8 shows graphically how a change in the price of a dollar (in terms of a second currency) affects the real quantity of dollars supplied in the foreign exchange market. We start with the price of a dollar set at E_0, let's say 100 yen. If the price of a dollar now falls to E_1, say 50 yen, then this **depreciation** of the dollar (or *appreciation* of the yen) leads to a reduction in the real quantity of dollars supplied from Q_0 to Q_1.[35]

Depreciation of a currency: A fall in the price of one currency in terms of other currencies. A rise in the price of a currency is termed an appreciation of the currency.

A fall in the price of a dollar from 100 to 50 yen per dollar means a rise in the dollar price of a yen, from .01 to .02 dollars, or from 1 cent to 2 cents. Even though there is no increase in the yen price of Japanese goods, the dollar price of Japanese goods rises. For example, a 600,000 yen Japanese car that formerly cost 6000 dollars (600,000 times .01) now costs 12,000 dollars (600,000 times .02). If the dollar prices of U.S. goods have not changed, then the *relative* or *real* prices of Japanese cars have risen. In our example, this means that U.S. households must give up an increased amount of U.S. goods to obtain one more Japanese car.[36]

The depreciation of the dollar, and resulting higher relative price for Japanese goods, leads U.S. households to reduce their demand for Japanese goods. However, as we discussed above, the fact that there is a fall in the quantity of Japanese goods purchased does not necessarily mean that there is also a fall in the quantity of dollars supplied. There are two countervailing forces at work here. Although the purchase of fewer Japanese goods reduces the quantity of dollars supplied, the fact that each Japanese good has a higher dollar price increases the quantity of dollars supplied. By assuming that the first effect outweighs the second effect, we conclude that a depreciation of the dollar causes the real quantity of dollars supplied in the foreign exchange market to fall. This is shown in Figure 6.8 by the upward sloping supply of dollars curve.[37]

---

[35] Note that the real quantity of dollars supplied in the foreign exchange market is the value of the (nominal) quantity of dollars supplied in terms of U.S. goods. It is obtained by taking the number of dollars that households offer to exchange for foreign currency and then dividing by the U.S. price level.

[36] Recall from our discussion in Chapter 4 that although firms also participate in the foreign exchange market to finance the purchase of foreign capital and financial assets, we simplify our analysis by lumping such activity under households.

[37] Formally, this condition required that the price elasticity of demand for Japanese goods be greater than one. That is, a 1 percent increase in the price of Japanese goods must cause a greater than one percent reduction in the amount of Japanese goods that U.S. households demand.

Figure 6.8   **The Supply of Dollars in the Foreign Exchange
Market**

A depreciation in the price of a dollar from E_0 to E_1 leads to a reduction in the real quantity of dollars supplied from Q_0 to Q_1.

As the above discussion suggests, if U.S. buyers of foreign goods do not reduce their purchases significantly following a depreciation of the dollar (appreciation of foreign currency) and the resulting higher real prices of import, then the supply of dollars curve may in fact be negatively sloped. That is, a depreciation of the dollar could lead to an increase in the quantity of dollars supplied in the foreign exchange market. This occurrence is more likely in the short-run than in the long-run for two reasons. First, it often takes time for U.S. buyers of imports to discover substitutes for foreign goods when there is a change in relative prices. Second, the prices of domestic goods that are close substitutes for the imported goods can rise significantly in the short-run if domestic producers hit short-run production constraints.

For the time being, we abstract from such short-run considerations, although this is not to lessen their importance, as the experience from 1985 to 1987 indicates. Even though the dollar depreciated, the dollar value of imports grew as the United States had to supply more dollars for each imported good while there was initially little reduction in the quantity of goods imported.

There is another complication that has the effect of making the supply of dollars curve steeper—that is, making the supply of dollars curve less responsive to changes in the exchange rates. Foreign producers, at least in the short-run, often adjust the prices of goods they export to partially offset the impact of exchange rate changes. For instance, Michael Knetter finds that with a depreciation of the dollar (appreciation of the West German mark), West German exporters often reduce the mark price of their exports so as to minimize the rise in the dollar price of German goods that would result from the appreciation of the mark.[38] Similarly, the *Wall Street Journal* (April 18, 1988) reports that "Japanese car and light-truck (dollar) prices didn't go up as much as they should have to fairly reflect the (rise) in the value of the yen. So now U.S. manufacturers have accused the Japanese of dumping trucks; that is, illegally selling them here for less than in Japan."

Naturally, behind the supply of dollars in the foreign exchange market is not only U.S. import demand but also U.S. demand for foreign financial assets. As we saw in Chapter 4, the sum of the U.S. import demand (Z^d) and household demand for foreign financial assets (AF_h^d) can be interpreted as representing not only a supply of dollars but also a demand for foreign currency. Recall from Chapter 4 that FC^d denotes household real demand for foreign currency in the foreign exchange market, so that the *household foreign exchange constraint* is written as

$$
\begin{array}{ccccc}
FC^d & = & Z^d & + & AF_h^d \\
\text{Real demand} & & \text{Real U.S.} & & \text{Household demand} \\
\text{for foreign currency} & & \text{import} & & \text{for additional foreign} \\
\text{(real supply of dollars)} & & \text{demand} & & \text{financial assets}
\end{array}
\qquad \textbf{(6.23)}
$$

Note that the variables in Equation 6.23, like all real variables, are defined in terms of "base year" dollars. Thus FC^d is computed by taking the foreign currency demanded by U.S. households, using the exchange rate to convert this to dollars, and then dividing by the price level to express it in real dollar terms.

It is important to remember that while we talk of households as being the only demanders of foreign goods and financial assets, this is purely a simplifying device. Firms also demand foreign goods and depository institutions demand foreign financial assets. The analysis would be more complex if we explicitly recognized these demands, but our conclusions would be unchanged since we can subsume in the household actions the actions of firms and depository institutions in foreign markets.

To the Point

U.S. HOUSEHOLDS AS BUYERS OF FOREIGN GOODS AND FINANCIAL ASSETS

- Household purchases of foreign goods and services (U.S. imports) depend on the relative price of foreign goods and U.S. disposable income. To households, the relative price of foreign goods equals the price (in foreign currency) of foreign goods (P_f) times the price in dollars of the foreign currency ($1/E$) divided by the price of U.S. goods (P).

---

[38] Michael Knetter, "Export Prices and Exchange Rates: Theory and Evidence," Unpublished manuscript, Stanford University, November 1987.

- A depreciation of the dollar (E falls, $1/E$ rises) reduces the quantity of goods imported since it raises the relative price of foreign goods. We assume that this fall in the quantity imported dominates the rise in the dollar price of imports, so that quantity of dollars supplied in the foreign exchange market falls with a depreciation. Graphically, this is given by an upward-sloping supply of dollars curve.

- Household purchases of foreign financial assets depend on a comparison of the rate of return available on financial assets in the United States (r) with the return to lending abroad ($r_f - \theta^e$). The return to lending abroad equals the foreign interest rate (r_f) minus the expected rate of change in the price of the dollar (θ^e).

- Household purchases of foreign goods and financial assets require foreign currency. Since households start with dollars, they supply dollars (demand foreign currency) in the foreign exchange market. The household foreign exchange constraint equates households' real demand for foreign exchange (real supply of dollars) to their real demand for foreign goods and financial assets.

6.6 THE BEHAVIOR OF FOREIGNERS IN THE FOREIGN EXCHANGE MARKET: EXPORTS AND CAPITAL INFLOWS

Large U.S. foreign trade deficits tend to receive a great deal of attention in the press. What does not receive as much attention is the tremendous foreign demand for U.S. goods and services and for U.S. financial assets. Foreigners have a significant impact on the U.S. macroeconomy. For example, foreigners play an important role in the financial market. In 1987, foreigners supplied more than 132 billion (1982) dollars of loanable funds in the U.S. financial market, more than one-third of the total supply (with households and depository institutions supplying the rest).

We talked about the foreign sector above in our discussion of household behavior and their choices of imports and purchases of foreign financial assets. We now turn to the opposite side of this coin as we examine foreigners' purchases of U.S. goods and services and of U.S. financial assets. In this section, we discuss factors affecting foreigners' demand for U.S. goods (U.S. exports) and for U.S. financial assets. We then show how these two sum together to equal the real demand for dollars in the foreign exchange market, as summarized by the foreign financing constraint.

Variables Affecting Foreign Demand for U.S. Goods

Just as U.S. demand for foreign goods depends on relative prices, so too is foreign demand for U.S. goods based on the relative prices of those goods.

The relative prices of U.S. goods to foreigners are determined by what foreigners have to give up of their own goods in order to purchase U.S. goods. We have seen that these relative prices depend on the money prices of U.S. goods, the money prices of foreign goods, and the exchange rate, as the following example illustrates.

Returning to our example of Japanese cars and U.S. computers, let's assume again that the price of a Japanese car is 600,000 yen and the price of a U.S. computer is $1500. For a given exchange rate, we can determine the relative price of a U.S. computer in terms of a Japanese car. If the exchange rate E is 100 yen per dollar, then a Japanese buyer needs 150,000 yen ($1500 times 100 yen/dollar) in order to buy a U.S. computer. In real terms, the cost of a computer to the Japanese is one fourth of a Japanese car (150,000 yen/600,000 yen). Note that this is the reciprocal of the cost of a Japanese car (in terms of computers) to a U.S. citizen.

More generally, the relative price of a U.S. computer is given by

$$\frac{\text{Relative price of a U.S. computer (in terms of Japanese cars)}}{} = \frac{\text{Dollar price of U.S. computer} \times \text{Price of dollar in terms of yen } (E)}{\text{Yen price of Japanese car}}$$

$$= \frac{(\$1500) \times (100 \text{ yen per dollar})}{(600,000 \text{ yen per car})}$$

$$= 1/4 \text{ Japanese car}$$

Naturally, if we consider the basket of goods exported, we can compute a real exchange rate for U.S. goods or a real price of U.S. exports. This relative price of U.S. goods to foreigners is given by

$$\frac{\text{Real exchange rate (U.S. goods)}}{} = \frac{\text{Dollar price of U.S. goods}}{\text{Dollar price of foreign goods}} = \frac{P}{P_f(1/E)} = \frac{P \cdot E}{P_f}$$

Note that the real exchange rate for U.S. goods is simply the inverse of the previously obtained real exchange rate for foreign goods.

We see from the above equation that the prices that determine foreign demand for U.S. goods and services are the same as those that determine the U.S. demand for foreign goods and services. As we would expect, the demand for U.S. goods decreases if the real price of U.S. goods rises. This occurs if the dollar prices of U.S. goods (P) rise, if the prices of foreign goods (P_f) fall, or if the price of a dollar in terms of foreign currency (E) rises. As mentioned before, the price of a dollar in terms of an index of foreign currencies rose by 70 percent from 1981 to 1985. The resulting rise in the relative prices of U.S. goods contributed significantly to a reduction in foreign demand for U.S. goods and the large U.S. trade deficit of the mid-1980s. Similarly, the dramatic fall in the price of a dollar in the subsequent period from late 1985 to 1988 led to an increase in exports.

We know from our previous discussion that an increase in U.S. disposable income leads to a rise in household purchases of both domestically produced output and foreign goods and services. Similarly, an increase in foreigners' disposable income leads to a rise in their purchases of U.S. goods. Summarizing, real export demand (X^d) depends on the relative price of U.S. goods ($P \cdot E/P_f$) and foreign disposable income (YD_f) or

$$X^d = X^d(\underset{-}{P \cdot E/P_f}, \underset{+}{YD_f}, ...) \tag{6.24}$$

Capital Inflows: Foreign Demand for Financial Assets

In 1960, purchases of U.S. financial assets by foreigners were approximately one half the amount of purchases of foreign financial assets by U.S. citizens. In the U.S. financial markets, foreign purchases of new U.S. financial assets were less than 5 percent of household and depository institution purchases. Twenty-five years later, foreign purchases of U.S. financial assets were over two times more than purchases of foreign financial assets by U.S. individuals. In the U.S. financial markets, approximately one-third of new U.S. financial assets were being purchased by foreigners. This dramatic change in capital inflows to the U.S. is one indication of the growing importance to the U.S. economy of international trade not only in goods but also in financial assets.

As with U.S. households, foreigners decide to purchase either U.S. assets or financial assets of their own country by comparing the rates of return on the two types of financial assets. For foreigners, the rate of return on domestic assets is the money interest rate in their own country (r_f). The expected rate of return to foreigners on U.S. financial assets equals the U.S. interest rate plus the expected change in the price of the dollar in the foreign exchange market (i.e., $r + \theta^e$).

Not surprisingly, the expected return to foreigners lending in U.S. financial markets increases when the U.S. interest rate (r) increases. Not as obvious is that the return also increases with an increase in the expected rate of change in the price of the dollar θ^e. This is because foreigners lending in U.S. financial markets convert their currency to dollars to make the loans. When the loans are repaid, they then convert dollars back to their own currency. If the dollar is anticipated to appreciate during the course of the year, then part of their expected return to lending in the United States is the increase in the value of the dollars (in terms of their own currency).[39]

The extent of lending by foreigners in the United States also depends on the interest rates available in their own country. In the summer of 1987, rising interest rates on Japanese bonds led the Japanese to purchase fewer U.S. financial assets.[40] As we will see in our subsequent analysis, this reduced capital inflow contributed to rising interest rates in the United States during this period.

---

[39] You should recognize that this discussion is similar to our earlier discussion about the return to U.S. citizens from lending in the foreign financial markets.

[40] *Wall Street Journal,* 24 August 1987.

Summarizing, we can express the foreign demand for U.S. financial assets as

$$A_{\text{for}}^d = A_{\text{for}}^d(\underset{-}{r_f},\ \underset{+}{r\ +\ \theta^e},\ ...) \tag{6.25}$$

This equation indicates that foreign demand for U.S. financial assets increases if the U.S. interest rate (r) rises, or the expected rate of change in the price of the dollar (θ^e) increases or the foreign interest rate (r_f) falls.

The Foreign Exchange Market: The Demand for Dollars Curve

Figure 6.9 illustrates the effect of a change in the price of a dollar (in terms of a second currency) on the quantity of dollars demanded in the foreign exchange market. Suppose that the price of a dollar is E_0, say 100 yen. If the price of a dollar now falls to E_1, say 50 yen, then this *depreciation* of the dollar (or *appreciation* of the yen) leads to an increase in the real quantity of dollars demanded from Q_0 to Q_1.[41]

This fall in the price of the dollar increases the quantity of dollars demanded because it lowers the relative price of U.S. goods to foreigners. A fall in the price of a dollar from 100 yen to 50 yen per dollar causes a rise in the dollar price of the yen from 1 cent to 2 cents. Even though there has been no increase in the dollar price of U.S. goods, the yen price of U.S. goods falls, and the Japanese increase their demand for U.S. goods. As a consequence, the real quantity of dollars demanded in the foreign exchange market rises.

Naturally, behind the demand for dollars in the foreign exchange market is not only foreigners' export demand but also their demand for U.S. financial assets. As we saw in Chapter 4, this sum of the export demand (X^d) and foreigners' demand for U.S. financial assets (A_{for}^d) can be interpreted as representing not only a demand for dollars but also a supply of foreign currency. Recall that FC^s denotes foreigners' real supply of foreign currency in the foreign exchange market, so that the *foreigner foreign exchange constraint* is written as

$$
\underset{\substack{\text{Real supply of}\\ \text{foreign currency}\\ \text{(real demand for dollars)}}}{FC^s}
=
\underset{\substack{\text{Real U.S.}\\ \text{export}\\ \text{demand}}}{X^d}
+
\underset{\substack{\text{Foreign demand for}\\ \text{additional U.S.}\\ \text{financial assets}}}{A_{\text{for}}^d}
\tag{6.26}
$$

As elsewhere, all terms in the equation are denominated in "base year" dollars or real dollars.

---

[41] Recall that the real quantity of dollars demanded in the foreign exchange market is simply the value of the (nominal) quantity of dollars demanded in terms of U.S. goods. It is obtained by taking the number of dollars that foreigners demand in the foreign exchange market and then dividing by the U.S. price level.

Figure 6.9 The Demand for Dollars in the Foreign Exchange Market

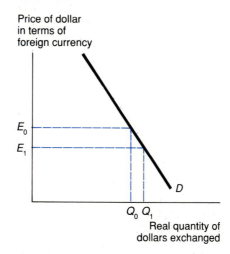

A depreciation in the price of a dollar from E_0 to E_1 leads to an increase in the real quantity of dollars demanded from Q_0 to Q_1.

To the Point

FOREIGNERS AS BUYERS OF U.S. GOODS AND FINANCIAL ASSETS

- Foreign purchases of U.S. goods and services (U.S. exports) depend on the relative price of U.S. goods and foreign disposable income. To foreigners, the relative price of U.S. goods equals the dollar price of U.S. goods (P) multiplied by the foreign exchange rate for the U.S. dollar (E) divided by the price (in foreign currency) of foreign goods (P_f).

- A depreciation of the dollar (E falls) raises U.S. exports since it reduces the relative price of U.S. goods. The result is an increase in the quantity of dollars demanded in the foreign exchange market with an appreciation. Graphically, this is given by a downward-sloping demand for dollars curve.

- Foreign purchases of U.S. financial assets depend on a comparison of the rate of return available on financial assets in their own country (r_f) with the return to lending in the United States. The return to lending in the United States equals the U.S. interest rate (r) plus the expected rate of change in the price of the dollar (θ^e).

- Foreign purchases of U.S. goods and financial assets require dollars. Since foreigners start with foreign currency, they demand dollars (supply foreign currency) in the foreign exchange market. The foreign exchange constraint equates foreigners' real supply for foreign exchange to their real supply for foreign goods and financial assets.

SUMMARY

This chapter has examined the behavior of households and foreigners in the macroeconomy. We started by noting that the net real wage determines the household supply of labor. A rise in the net real wage unambiguously increases the labor force participation rate but can reduce the labor supply of someone already working if the income effect outweighs the substitution effect. In the aggregate, however, the supply of labor is directly related to the net real wage.

Households use their income for consumption, paying taxes, and saving. Keynes suggested that current disposable income is the major factor affecting current consumption demand. He also noted that people consume a fraction of any increase in income (the marginal propensity to consume) and save a fraction (the marginal propensity to save). In Modigliani's life-cycle hypothesis and Friedman's permanent income hypothesis, the fraction of any increase in current income that is consumed depends on whether the increase in current income signals an increase in future income as well. If a change in current income is viewed as transitory, most of the increase in income will go to higher saving.

In addition to deciding how to divide after-tax income between consumption and saving, households must decide how to allocate saving between the accumulation of money or the accumulation of financial assets. Households' desired stock of money, or real money demand, is directly related to real GNP and inversely related to the interest rate.

Household demand for real money balances together with desired saving imply a particular demand for financial assets (supply of loanable funds). A higher interest rate increases household supply of loanable funds since it both increases saving and reduces real money demand. Taxes, real income, and the expected rate of inflation also affect household supply of loanable funds.

When we open the economy to include a foreign sector, we must take into account how households allocate consumption spending between foreign and domestically produced goods and services and how they allocate their financial purchases between domestic and foreign financial assets. The amount of foreign goods that U.S. citizens import depends on their disposable income and the relative prices of foreign goods. The relative prices of foreign goods in turn depends on the dollar price of U.S. goods, the price of foreign goods in terms of their own currency, and foreign exchange rates. A rise in the price of the dollar reduces the relative price of foreign goods, which causes U.S. imports to rise. In deciding between foreign and domestic financial assets, U.S. citizens compare the domestic interest rate with the return to lending abroad. The return to lending abroad is the foreign interest rate minus the expected rate of change in the price of the dollar.

When purchasing foreign goods and financial assets, U.S. households supply dollars in the foreign exchange market. The supply of dollars curve is upward-sloping since an increase in the price of the dollar causes import demand to rise.

Introducing a foreign sector also means that we must incorporate into our macroeconomic analysis the behavior of foreigners in their purchases of U.S. goods and services and U.S. financial assets. Foreign demand for U.S. exports falls with an increase in the relative price of U.S. goods to foreigners and with a fall in their disposable income. The expected rate of return to foreigners from purchasing a U.S. financial asset equals the U.S. interest rate plus the expected rate of change in the price of the dollar in the foreign exchange market.

When foreigners purchase U.S. goods and services and financial assets, they must do so with U.S. dollars. Merchants will usually not accept Hungarian zlotys or other foreign currencies. Thus foreigners demand dollars when purchasing U.S. goods and financial assets. The real demand for dollars curve is downward-sloping—a fall in the price of the dollar lowers the relative price of U.S. goods to foreigners and thus increases foreign demand for U.S. goods and services.

LOOKING AHEAD

The last three chapters have explored the microfoundations of macroeconomics. We have considered the constraints of each of the five market participants (Chapter 4), the behavior of firms and depository institutions in the various markets (Chapter 5), and the behavior of households and foreigners (Chapter 6). We do not examine the behavioral decisions of government since the government's behavior is taken to be given and exogenous to the analysis. The mortar and bricks are now in place, and we are ready to show how the various agents interact in the economy to determine changes in such aggregate variables as output, employment, interest rates, inflation, and foreign exchange rates.

SUMMARY OF KEY EQUATIONS

Labor supply function $$N^s = N^s[(1 - t)W/P, ...]$$ **(6.1)**
$$\underset{+}{}$$

Keynes' consumption function $$C^d = a + b \cdot (Y - CCA - T), a > 0, 1 > b > 0$$ **(6.3)**

General consumption function

$$C^d = C^d(\underset{+}{Y - CCA - T}, \underset{-}{r - \pi^e}, ...)$$ (6.5)

Division of saving

$$S = A_h^d + L^d - (\overline{M}/P)$$ (6.13)

Linear money demand function

$$L^d = k \cdot Y, \; k > 0$$ (6.14)

General money demand function

$$L^d = L^d(\underset{+}{Y}, \underset{-}{r}, ...)$$ (6.15)

Financial asset demand function

$$A_h^d = A_h^d(\underset{+}{r}, \underset{-}{T}, \underset{-}{\pi^e}, \underset{?}{Y}, ...)$$ (6.17)

Import demand function

$$Z^d = Z^d[\underset{-}{P_f(1/E)/P}, \underset{+}{Y - CCA - T}, ...)$$ (6.18)

Return to lending abroad

$$r^* \approx r_f - \theta^e$$ (6.21)

Demand function for foreign assets

$$AF_h^d = AF_h^d(\underset{-}{r}, \underset{+}{r_f - \theta^e}, ...)$$ (6.22)

Export demand function

$$X^d = X^d(\underset{-}{P \cdot E/P_f}, \underset{+}{YD_f}, ...)$$ (6.24)

Foreign financial asset demand function

$$A_{for}^d = A_{for}^d(\underset{-}{r_f}, \underset{+}{r + \theta^e}, ...)$$ (6.25)

KEY TERMS

Net real wage, 169
Intertemporal substitution hypothesis, 172
Consumption function, 175
Marginal propensity to consume, 176

Marginal propensity to save, 177
Life-cycle hypothesis, 178
Permanent income hypothesis, 178
Real exchange rate, 196
Currency depreciation, 200

REVIEW QUESTIONS

1. Distinguish between the money wage, the net money wage, and the net real wage. What happens to the real wage if the price level rises and everything else remains unchanged? What happens to the real wage if the money wage and the price level rise by the same proportion?

2. Distinguish between the substitution effect of an increase in the net real wage and the income effect. Are these effects positive or negative?

3. Indicate whether the following question is true or false and explain why: "An increase in the net real wage unambiguously increases the probability that an individual not participating in the labor market will choose to work, but it has an ambiguous effect on the number of hours that an individual already in the labor market chooses to work."

4. Suppose that we have the following consumption function: $C^d = 100 + .75 \cdot YD$.

    a.   What is the marginal propensity to consume?

    b.   What is the marginal propensity to save?

    c.   If real disposable income is initially $1000, what are desired consumption and saving equal to?

    d.   If real GNP rises by $100, what happens to real consumption demand and saving?

    e.   If net real taxes are raised by $10, what happens to real consumption demand and saving?

5. What is the key notion behind both the life-cycle hypothesis and the permanent income hypothesis? How do these hypotheses differ from the consumption function suggested by Keynes?

6. What do we mean by a household's permanent income?

    a.   An assistant professor named Jerry, with a great gift for telling jokes but not much ability for playing tennis, receives tenure at a university whose major claim to fame is that it has a very large smokestack with lights on top. Along with the tenure goes an increase in salary. Jerry had initially thought that there wasn't the proverbial snowball's chance in heck that he would get tenure. Does Jerry's permanent income rise or fall?

    b.   Another assistant professor, who shall remain nameless, does not get tenure at this same university with a large smokestack and returns to a lower income as a part-time tennis pro. This individual had anticipated correctly that there wasn't the proverbial snowball's chance in heck that he would get tenure and the associated high university pay. What happens to his permanent income?

7. In the year following 1982, the stocks on the New York Stock Exchange increased by more than 50 percent in value.

    a.   What effect should this have had on aggregate consumption demand?

    b.   Consider two individuals who own exactly the same stock portfolios. One individual is aged 60 while the other is 35. Whose permanent income rises by the larger amount? Whose consumption demand would we predict would rise the most?

8. In the early years of the Reagan administration, some significant tax cuts were enacted by Congress. These tax cuts were discussed far in advance of when they were enacted. Compare the implications that the simple consumption function of Equation 6.3 and the permanent income hypothesis have concerning the time pattern of consumption demand.

9. Suppose that households in Fredonia initially have real money holdings in the amount of $200. If their desired end of period real money holdings are $250, what is their desired accumulation of real money balances? If total desired saving in Fredonia is $240, how many real financial assets do Fredonia households want to purchase?

10. What effect does an increase in real GNP have on households' real money demand? Why?

11. Suppose that the increased use of computers reduces the cost of converting financial assets into money balances. What happens to the real demand for money? Why?

12. Why does an increase in real GNP have an ambiguous effect on households' real financial asset demand?

13. If the interest rate is 8 percent and the expected inflation rate is 3 percent, what is the expected real interest rate? If the expected rate of inflation rises, other things being equal, what happens to the expected real rate of interest? Why? What is the resulting effect on households' desired saving in the form of real financial assets?

14. Being the modern economy that it is, Fredonia has its own currency, the Fredonian peso.

   a. Suppose that it takes fifty cents to buy one Fredonian peso in the foreign exchange market. What is the price of a dollar in terms of Fredonian pesos?

   b. The peace-loving people of Fredonia know a good profit opportunity when they see one and so get into cocoa production in a big way. Suppose that the price of a kilo of cocoa in Fredonia is 200 pesos. What is the dollar price of Fredonian cocoa?

   c. If the price of U.S. goods is $4, what is the relative price of Fredonian cocoa in terms of U.S. goods?

   d. If the price of a dollar in terms of Fredonian pesos falls, what happens to the relative price of Fredonian cocoa?

15. Explain how you would compare the rate of return on a Japanese bond with a U.S. bond. How does this expected rate of return vary with the expected rate of appreciation of the dollar in the foreign exchange market?

16. "An increase in the price of a dollar in terms of foreign currency reduces the relative price of foreign goods, thereby leading to an increase in import demand and an increase in the supply of dollars in the foreign exchange market." Is this statement sometimes true, always true, or never true? Why?

17. A country that has a 200-year-old leader with a very long white beard and whose women hide behind veils buys $42 million dollars worth of defensive military hardware from U.S. arms manufacturers. What effect does this have on the demand for dollars in the foreign exchange market? Why?

18. Suppose that there is an increase in the rate at which the dollar is expected to appreciate in the foreign exchange market.

    a. If other things are held constant, what happens to foreigners' demand for U.S. financial assets? Why?

    b. What happens to the demand for dollars in the foreign exchange market? Why?

19. Starting with a simple proportional tax rate t, show graphically (using indifference curves and budget lines) the situation in which the imposition of a higher tax rate for wage income above a certain level (i.e., going to a progressive tax rate system) will lead to a reduction in the optimal supply of labor.

20. With respect to the choice of consumption across two periods, show graphically the situation in which an individual chooses to be neither a borrower nor a lender. Ignore tax considerations.

    a. Now show graphically the effect of a tax (equal to proportional rate θ) on interest earnings. Would this lead the individual who before had been neither a borrower nor a lender to alter his consumption plans? If so, how?

    b. Show graphically the effect of interest expenses that are tax deductible (i.e., let there now be tax savings proportional to interest expenses). Would this lead the individual who before had been neither a borrower nor a lender to alter his consumption plans? If so, how?

21. In the February 1, 1988 issue of the *Wall Street Journal,* the following information on the prime rates of interest in various countries was reported: U.S. (8.74%); West Germany (6.25%); and Canada (9.75%). At that time, the current exchange rates for the dollar were

    1 dollar = 1.275 Canadian dollars

    1 dollar = 1.68 marks

    At that time, the exchange rates expected approximately one year later (as suggested by the prices quoted in futures markets for currency) were

    1 dollar = 1.293 Canadian dollars

    1 dollar = 1.64 marks

    Calculate the return to a U.S. lender from lending in foreign markets (Canada and West Germany) and compare these returns to the return to lending in the U.S. Are they as different as one might think by looking solely at the rates of interest in the various countries?

Household Labor Supply and Saving: Further Analysis

In this appendix, we analyze household labor supply and saving decisions in more detail. In order to do this, we develop what is known as indifference curve analysis. We begin by reconsidering the labor supply decision.

Labor Supply

Consider a household deciding how many hours to work in the current period. By working fewer hours, the household earns less labor income but is able to enjoy more leisure. In deciding how many hours to work the household must compare its own valuation of leisure with that of the market. We can analyze this decision with the help of *indifference* curves and the *budget line.*

The Budget Line. The budget line indicates the different leisure-income combinations that are available to the household. For every hour that it works, the household receives $(1 - t)W$ dollars, where W is the money wage rate and t is the rate at which labor income is taxed. Thus if the household works h hours, it receives net after-tax labor income of $(1 - t)Wh$ dollars. To obtain real nonlabor income, we must, of course, divide this amount by the price level, P. That is, if the household works h hours, its after-tax real labor income is $(1 - t)(W/P)h$, the net (after-tax) real wage rate multiplied by the number of hours worked. In addition to its labor income, the household probably receives some nonlabor income, which may include such things as interest and dividend payments and government transfer payments. Denoting real nonlabor income as v, the household's total real (disposable) income (YD) is given by

$$YD = v + (1 - t)(W/P)h. \qquad \textbf{(A6.1)}$$

This equation indicates the relationship between the household's real income and the number of hours that it works. Naturally, since the total number of hours in a period is fixed, there is an implied relationship between the household's real income and the leisure that it enjoys. For our purposes, it is useful to rewrite Equation A6.1 in order to make explicit this relationship between real income and leisure.

Let T be the total number of hours in a period and let L be the number of leisure hours the household enjoys. Since an hour can be devoted to either leisure or working, the household's leisure hours and its working hours must sum to T, or $L + h = T$. Equivalently, the number of hours

Figure A6.1   The Income-leisure Budget Line

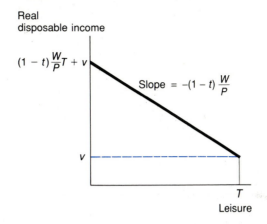

The budget line shows that as an individual reduces leisure and works more, income increases.

the household works is equal to the difference between the number of hours in the time period and number of leisure hours:

$$h = T - L \tag{A6.2}$$

Substituting Equation (A6.2) into Equation (A6.1), we obtain

$$YD = v + (1 - t)(W/P)(T - L) \tag{A6.3}$$

Equation (A6.3) indicates the various income-leisure combinations available to the household. Figure A6.1 summarizes these combinations graphically.

In Figure A6.1, note that leisure hours are graphed on the horizontal axis and total real income on the vertical axis. If the household does not work at all, then L is equal to T and, as Equation A6.3 indicates, the household income is v. Furthermore, for every hour of leisure that the household gives up, its real income goes up by $(1 - t)W/P$. Hence, the household leisure-earnings constraint takes the form of a line with a slope equal to $-(1 - t)W/P$. The budget line's vertical intercept is $(1 - t)(W/P)T + v$, the amount of real income the household would earn in the unlikely event that it chose to enjoy no leisure at all. Note that the number of hours the household works can be seen on the diagram by moving from right to left along the horizontal axis since an increase in the hours worked reduces leisure.

Indifference Curves. While the budget line summarizes the various income-leisure possibilities open to the household, the household's preferences are summarized by its indifference curves. As its name indicates, an indifference curve indicates the various income-leisure combinations about which the household is indifferent. Expressed differently, all income-leisure combinations on an indifference curve yield the same level of satisfaction or utility to the household. Several representative indifference curves are depicted in Figure A6.2.[42]

Naturally, the household places a positive value on both leisure and real income. For a given real income, the household's level of satisfaction or utility increases as its leisure time increases. Similarly, for a given level of leisure, the household's utility increases as real income increases because additional income raises the amount of consumption goods that can be purchased.[43] Thus as we move up and to the right in the indifference curve diagram, we attain indifference curves corresponding to higher levels of utility.

The slope of an indifference curve indicates the decrease in the household's real income that must accompany a one-hour increase in leisure so as to leave the household's utility or level of satisfaction unchanged. Since the household values both real income and leisure, an indifference curve's slope is always negative. The absolute value of the indifference curve's slope is called the marginal rate of substitution of real income for leisure ($MRS_{YD\ for\ L}$). In other words, the household's marginal rate of substitution of real income for leisure is the maximum amount of real income the household is willing to give up for one additional hour of leisure. Note that the household's indifference curves are drawn convex to the origin, indicating that the household's marginal rate of substitution of real income for leisure falls as the household moves from left to right along an indifference curve. In other words, as the household's leisure increases and its real income falls, the value of additional leisure diminishes, and the household is willing to give up less real income to get an additional hour of leisure.

The Optimal Choice of Leisure and Real Income

The household's labor supply problem involves choosing the optimal number of hours to work. The solution to this problem is illustrated in Figure A6.3. The household's feasible combinations of real income and leisure depend on its nonlabor income and after-tax real wage. As we have seen, the budget line summarizes the household's allowable choices. The household's problem is to choose the point on the budget line that yields the greatest level of

---

[42] It is not practical to graph all of the household's indifference curves because every income-leisure combination is associated with some level of household satisfaction and thus is on a separate indifference curve.

[43] It is not necessary for all of this consumption to occur today. By putting some of its current income into savings, the household can raise its future consumption. Later in this appendix, we return to the household's saving decision. For the time being, we need not concern ourselves with the household's decision regarding the allocation of real income between current and future consumption.

Figure A6.2   Indifference Curves for Income and Leisure

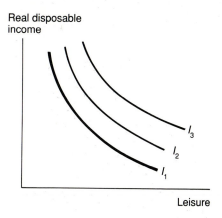

An indifference curve shows the combinations of leisure and income that keep the utility level constant for a worker. Higher indifference curves (moving toward the northeast) correspond to higher levels of utility.

utility. Expressed differently, the household will choose the income-leisure combination that occurs on the highest possible indifference curve, while staying on the budget line.

As Figure 6A.3 indicates, point A represents the household's optimal income-leisure combination given the budget line as drawn. The household's maximum utility is obtained when it chooses L_0 hours leisure, works $h_0 (= T - L_0)$ hours, and obtains a real disposable income of YD_0. Examining the optimal point more closely, we see that it has the following property: The indifference curve through A is just tangent to the budget line. Since the slope of the budget line is $-(1 - t)W/P$ and the slope of the indifference curve is $MRS_{YD \text{ for } L}$, the optimal income-leisure combination occurs when the marginal rate of substitution of real income for leisure just equals the real wage. In other words, at the optimal or "utility-maximizing" point, the household's valuation of leisure (as indicated by $MRS_{YD \text{ for } L}$, the amount of real income that the household is willing to give up to get an additional hour of leisure) just equals the market's valuation of leisure (as indicated by $(1 - t)W/P$, the amount of real income that the household must give up to obtain an additional hour of leisure).

To gain better insight into the optimality condition

$$MRS_{YD \text{ for } L} = (1 - t)(W/P)$$

note that if this condition does not hold, then the household can always make a change in order to increase its utility. For example, if $MRS_{YD \text{ for } L}$ is greater than $(1 - t)(W/P)$, as at point B, then the household's valuation of an hour of leisure exceeds the market's, which means that the household

Figure A6.3   The Choice Between Leisure and Real Income

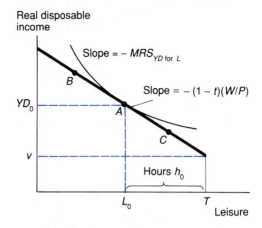

Point A represents the optimal combination of leisure (L_0) and income (YD_0). It is the point of tangency between an indifference curve and the budget line.

can raise its utility by choosing more leisure and less real income. On the other hand, if $MRS_{YD \text{ for } L}$ is less than $(1 - t)(W/P)$, as at point C, then the household can do better by choosing less leisure and more real income.

The Effect of Changes in Nonlabor Income and the Real Wage

The household's labor supply decision is affected by changes in both nonlabor income and the after-tax real wage. Figure A6.4 illustrates the effect of an increase in nonlabor income. An increase in real non-labor income from v to v' causes a parallel outward shift in the budget line. The household's optimal income-leisure combination changes from (L_0, YD_0) to (L_1, YD_1). In this case, YD and L both increase and the number of hours worked decreases. If an increase in income causes desired leisure to rise, as it does in the current case, then leisure is said to be a normal good. The empirical evidence indicates that leisure is in fact a normal good for most people.

Now consider the effect of a change in the after-tax real wage. For example, suppose that either the money wage (W) rises, the tax rate (t) falls, or the price level (P) falls. Any one of these three changes would mean a higher net real wage. Figure A6.5 depicts the resulting effect on the household's labor supply decision. As the figure indicates, an increase in the net real wage means a steeper budget line. As a consequence, the household's optimal income-leisure combination changes from L_0 and YD_0 (point A) to L_2 and YD_2 (point C).

An increase in the net real wage has two conceptually distinct effects on the household's labor supply decision: An income effect and a substitution

Figure A6.4   The Effect of a Change in Nonlabor Income on the Income-leisure Choice

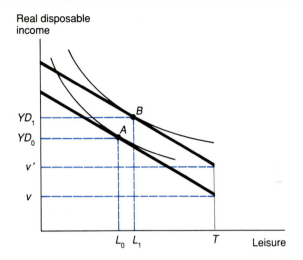

An increase in non-labor income results in a parallel shift up in the budget line. If leisure is a normal good, individuals will choose greater leisure ($L_1 > L_0$) and thus less work.

effect. The income effect refers to the fact that an increase in the net real wage makes the household better off because it leads to an increase in the household's feasible consumption set. As Figure A6.5 makes clear, the higher net real wage means that the household, if it so desires, can increase both its leisure and its total real income. Thus the household is able to reach a higher indifference curve which has associated with it a higher utility level. The substitution effect refers to the fact that the increase in the after-tax real wage makes an hour of leisure relatively more expensive in terms of the real income that must be forgone.

To isolate the substitution effect and income effect of the change in the net real wage, suppose that after the net real wage increases, there is a temporary reduction of just enough of the household's nonlabor income so that it is just able to attain its original indifference curve. As Figure A6.5 indicates, the household's choice of leisure and income will then be L_1 and YD_1 (point B). Thus if we hold the household's utility level constant, the increase in the net real wage leads unambiguously to a lower level of leisure: Since an hour of leisure is relatively more expensive, the household substitutes away from leisure, choosing to work more hours. The movement from point A to point B constitutes the pure substitution effect of the higher net real wage.

Now suppose that the household is given back the nonlabor income that was temporarily taken away. This causes an outward shift in the budget

Figure A6.5   The Effect of Change in After-tax Real Wage on the Income-leisure Choice

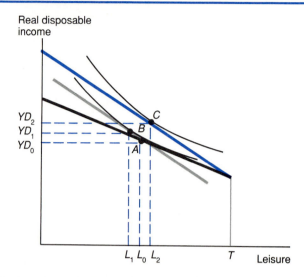

An increase in the net real wage has both an income and a substitution effect. The substitution effect (point A to point B) would result in a fall in leisure and an increase in labor supply. However, the income effect (point B to point C) goes in the opposite direction. The graph shows the case where the income effect outweighs the substitution effect.

line and the household's new choice of leisure and real income will be L_2 and YD_2 (point C). The movement from B to C constitutes the income effect of the change in the net real wage. In the present case, the income effect on the choice of leisure is positive, reflecting the fact that leisure is a normal good.

Note that the substitution and income effects on leisure work in opposite directions. The substitution effect of the higher real wage causes leisure to fall and hours worked to rise, while the income effect causes leisure to rise and hours worked to fall. The net effect on leisure and hours worked depends on which effect dominates. If the substitution effect dominates, then a higher net real wage results in a decrease in desired leisure and an increase in desired working hours. If the income effect dominates, the opposite is true and the household's labor supply curve is backward-bending.

The Participation Decision

Thus far we have assumed that the household chooses to work a positive number of hours. However, this need not always be the case. To see this, consider Figure A6.6. The household attains the highest feasible indifference

Figure A6.6   The Participation Decision

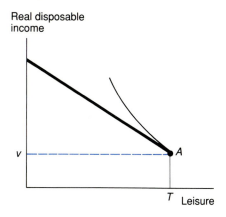

In a "corner" solution, the household's preferences are such that all leisure and no work is chosen.

curve at point *A*, where it devotes all of its hours to leisure and does not work at all. Since the household chooses the maximum amount of leisure possible, we say that it is at a "corner solution."

To gain better insight into the nature of the corner solution, note that at point *A* the corresponding indifference curve is more steeply sloped than the budget line. Thus even when all hours are devoted to leisure and none to work, the household's marginal rate of substitution of real income for leisure still exceeds the net real wage rate. In other words, the household's valuation of leisure exceeds the market's valuation of leisure. As a result, it does not find it worthwhile to participate in the labor market.

The greater the net real wage, the greater is the probability that a given household will choose to participate in the labor market. A higher real wage rotates the budget line outward. Since the household is not working, an increase in the net real wage does not make the household better off and thus has no income effect. There is only a substitution effect. Thus if the real wage rises sufficiently, the individual can be induced to enter the labor market.

Consumption and Saving Decisions

Indifference curve–budget line analysis can also be applied to an examination of household saving behavior. Recall that the household budget constraint tells us that a household's saving and consumption spending must add up to its real disposable income:

$$C^d + S = YD \qquad\qquad \textbf{(A6.4)}$$

For a given level of disposable income, Equation A6.4 indicates the relationship between a household's current consumption spending and its disposable income. Since current saving can be turned into future consumption, there is an implied relationship between current and future consumption spending. In order to apply indifference curve–budget line analysis, it is helpful to rewrite Equation A6.4 so as to make explicit this relationship between real consumption today and real consumption in the future. For simplicity, we consider the case of a two-year time horizon involving the current period (year 0) and the next period one year later (year 1).

As we noted in the text, a household's consumption in year 1 is equal to its labor earnings in year 1 minus taxes plus the expected real income derived from saving. That is, letting YD_1^e denote the household's disposable labor income in the second period and letting R denote the expected real interest rate, the household's consumption spending in period 1 (C_1^d) is given by[44]

$$C_1^d = YD_1^e + S(1 + R) \qquad \textbf{(A6.5)}$$

From Equation A6.4, we know that $S = YD - C^d$. Substituting this result into Equation A6.5 gives us

$$C_1^d = YD_1^e + (YD - C^d)(1 + R) \qquad \textbf{(A6.6)}$$

Equation A6.6 is simply another way of writing the household budget constraint. It relates the household's consumption spending in year 1 to its disposable labor income in year 1 and to its disposable income and consumption in year 0. Specifically, Equation A6.6 indicates that the household's consumption spending in year 1 can exceed its disposable income in that year if the household saved in the prior period by not consuming all the income it received. Similarly, the household can increase its consumption spending above its disposable income in year 0 by borrowing. In this case, the household pays back with interest in year 1 the amount it borrowed in year 0. Its consumption is thus less than its disposable labor income in year 1.

Equation A6.6 indicates the various combinations of consumption over the two periods available to the household. These combinations are summarized by the budget line depicted in Figure A6.7. When interpreting this budget line, note that consumption in year 0 is graphed on the horizontal axis and consumption in year 1 on the vertical axis. If the household's consumption in year 0 just equals its disposable income in year 1, then it does not borrow or save, and consumption in year 1 is equal to disposable labor income in year 1. If the household reduces consumption in year 0, then it can increase its consumption in year 1. If consumption in year 0 falls by one dollar, saving rises by one dollar. Since the real return on saving is the expected real interest rate (R), consumption in year 1 rises by the amount $(1 + R)$.

---

[44] Recall that the term disposable labor income (YD_1^e) refers to expected income earned from labor services minus total expected taxes. Also note that unlike the case in the text, for simplicity we are assuming that the household has not accumulated financial assets prior to year 0.

Figure A6.7   **Current versus Future Consumption Decision**

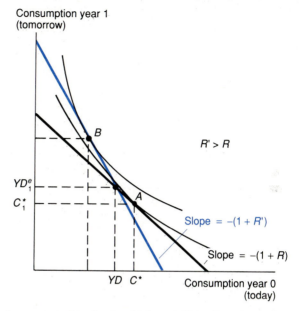

An increase in the expected real rate of interest (from R to R') is shown to lend to a reduction in consumption today in favor of increased consumption in the future.

Similarly, if in year 0 the household consumes a dollar more than it earns, its consumption in year 1 falls by $1 + R$. Thus we see that the slope of the household's budget line is $-(1 + R)$.

Just as we used indifference curves when we discussed a household's preferences over leisure and income, we can use them here to represent its preferences over consumption in years 0 and 1. Each indifference curve in Figure A6.7 indicates the various consumption combinations that will provide the household with a specified level of utility. Note that the slope of an indifference curve is negative because the household places a positive value on consumption in both year 0 and year 1. The absolute value of the slope is called the household's marginal rate of substitution of consumption in year 1 for consumption in year 0. The convex indifference curves indicate that the household's value of consumption in year 0 falls as the household moves from left to right along an indifference curve.

The household chooses consumption across time periods so as to maximize its utility. Inspecting Figure A6.7, we see that the utility-maximizing consumption point occurs at point A with consumption spending in year 0 equal to C^* and consumption in year 1 equal to C_1^*. At point A, the associated indifference curve is just tangent to the budget line. Utility maximization thus requires that a household's marginal rate of substitution of consumption in year 1 for consumption in year 0 should be equal to 1 plus the expected real interest rate.

Now consider the effect of a change in the interest rate on the household's desired pattern of consumption spending. Figure A6.7 shows the effect of an increase in the expected real interest rate from R to R' by a rotation to the new dashed budget line. Note that the budget line becomes steeper as the cost of consumption in year 0 in terms of foregone consumption in year 1 is now higher. Although the new budget line becomes steeper, it does have one point in common with the initial budget line. From Equation A6.6, we see that one option open to the household, no matter what the interest rate, is to neither borrow nor save—that is, to choose $C^d = YD$ and $C_1^d = YD_1^e$. Thus this consumption point is on both the original budget line and the new budget line corresponding to the higher interest rate.

As Figure A6.7 indicates, the higher expected real interest rate causes the household to choose a new time pattern of consumption. In the present case, the optimal combination changes from point A to point B. Consumption in year 0 falls and consumption in year 1 rises. Note that the effect of a change in the real interest rate on household consumption choices, like the effect of change in the real wage on household labor supply, can be divided into two effects—an income effect and a substitution effect.

The substitution effect of an increase in the expected real interest rate results in a shift away from consumption in year 0 toward consumption in year 1, as consumption in year 0 is now relatively cheaper. The income effect depends critically on whether the household is saving or borrowing. If the household saves in year 0, then it is clearly better off as a result of the higher expected real interest rate. As Figure A6.7 indicates, the household can increase its choice of consumption in both periods. Thus there is a positive income effect on consumption spending in at least one, and possibly both, years. In contrast, if the household is a borrower and has negative saving, then it is made worse off by an increase in the real interest rate. As Figure A6.7 indicates, if the household is a borrower, the increase in the real interest rate reduces its set of consumption choices. Thus there is a negative income effect on consumption spending in at least one, and possibly both, periods.

Part Three

Determining Equilibrium in the Economy

Chapter 7

Equilibrium in the Economy: Aggregate Supply and Demand

ONE of the puzzling features of the macroeconomy are the wide fluctuations in prices, real GNP, employment, interest rates, and foreign exchange rates. We have already noted that the U.S. economy experienced 13.5 percent inflation in 1980 but that this dropped off to 3.1 percent by 1983. Unemployment was 10.8 percent in late 1982 and down to around 5.5 percent by mid-1988. Perhaps the sharpest variation came in interest rates; the prime rate charged by banks, which peaked at 21.5 percent in January of 1981, plummeted to half of that in the ensuing two years. What causes these fluctuations?

Often they are caused by changes in the behavior of some of the agents in the economy that affect output demand. For instance, firms' investment demand can rise with an increase in anticipated future prices. Households' consumption demand can fall with a downward reevaluation of anticipated future income, perhaps as a result of future plant closings.[1] The government can raise taxes or lower its spending, the Fed can increase the money supply, or foreigners can suddenly find the United States an attractive haven for their savings. Fluctuations in the macroeconomy may also have as their

---

[1] For example, in early November 1986, General Motors announced plans to close six plants over the following three years, eliminating 29,000 UAW jobs. It is likely that those workers who were permanently laid off lowered current consumption in anticipation of lower (nonunion) future wage income. In addition, anyone depending on the spending of these 29,000 workers would also anticipate a reduction in future income and adjust current consumption accordingly.

source supply-side changes, such as a wave of technological innovations, extensive crop failures, or even an oil embargo, that alter the productive capabilities of the economy. Economists refer to these various sources of economy-wide fluctuations as macroeconomic shocks.

To fully understand the effects of the various macroeconomic shocks, we must determine simultaneously what happens in each of the four markets in the economy: labor, output, financial, and foreign exchange. Thus a crucial feature of macroeconomic analysis is its focus on the interrelationships between the economy's various markets, interrelationships clearly delineated by the aggregate budget constraint. Economists sometimes refer to this approach of macroeconomics as indicative of a **general equilibrium analysis.** By this they mean that in analyzing the effects of macroeconomic shocks, we cannot look at individual markets in isolation.

General equilibrium analysis: An examination of simultaneous equilibrium in all the markets in an economy.

As an example of the general equilibrium character of macroeconomics, consider the effects of a higher interest rate in the financial market stemming, say, from the fall in depository institutions' supply of loanable funds that accompanies a decrease in the money supply. A higher interest rate causes firms and households to decrease their demand for goods and services in the output market since it raises the cost of borrowing and increases the return to saving. If prices fall in response to the reduced demand for output, the resulting change in the real wage will alter the demand for and the supply of workers in the labor market. At the same time, a lower price level changes the relative price of foreign goods, leading to changes in the demand for and supply of dollars in the foreign exchange market.[2] This example illustrates how a change in one market—the financial market—can lead to changes in each of the other three markets in the economy. In attempting to understand the entire impact of a macroeconomic shock, we face the sometimes difficult task of tracing this shock through all of the markets in the economy.

Fortunately, by using the graphical tools of *aggregate demand* and *aggregate supply* curves, we can simplify our general equilibrium analysis of macroeconomic shocks. This chapter shows how we can condense the events in the various markets into aggregate demand and supply curves. The first section of the chapter shows how the aggregate supply curve summarizes activity in the labor market. As subsequent chapters will make clear, the aggregate supply curve plays a critical role in determining how the economy adjusts to macroeconomic shocks. When faced with a demand shock, the economy can adjust either through changing output or changing prices. In this chapter, our analysis of the aggregate supply curve assumes flexible prices and fully informed economic agents. These assumptions are similar to those found in the *classical* macroeconomic model, which has existed since the seventeenth century. For this reason, the aggregate supply curve developed in this chapter is often called the neoclassical aggregate supply curve. In

---

[2] We may also note that the lower output prices feed back into the financial market, since a lower price level changes the real supply of money and thus the real supply of loanable funds.

later chapters, we explore how an economy with inflexible prices and imperfectly informed agents adjusts to a macroeconomic shock through changes in output.

Following the development of the neoclassical aggregate supply curve, we turn to the aggregate demand curve. For a closed economy without international trade, we show how the aggregate demand curve summarizes events in the financial and output markets. We then show how in an open economy with trade, the aggregate demand curve summarizes events in the foreign exchange market as well as in the financial and output markets.

7.1 THE LABOR MARKET AND THE AGGREGATE SUPPLY CURVE

Just as an individual firm's level of output depends on its inputs, the aggregate production function indicates that for all firms in the economy, the total production of output is related to the quantities of the inputs they employ.[3] Of particular importance to the production process are the total amount of labor services employed and the size of the economy's capital stock (plant, machinery, etc.). If our concern is with output produced during the current period, then we can take the capital stock as essentially fixed and thus view changes in real output as reflecting changes only in the employment of labor.

Because macroeconomics views the employment of labor as the key determinant of current output, our analysis of production in the economy naturally focuses on the labor market. In fact, as we will see, the analysis of the labor market provides the underpinning for the aggregate supply curve. We begin our analysis of the labor market within the context of the neoclassical model. Although the neoclassical macroeconomic model has as its roots discussions that began over 350 years ago, we will see in the next two chapters that current analyses of monetary policy, government deficits, supply-side policies, and oil supply disruptions rely on the same basic ideas.[4]

The Neoclassical Model: The Assumptions of Full Information and Flexible Prices

The neoclassical model has two key assumptions. The first is that all *prices adjust to maintain equilibrium continuously in all markets*. The money wage

---

[3] Chapter 5 discussed the aggregate production function in more detail.

[4] The neoclassical macroeconomic model is a descendant of classical economic theory. Its roots thus lie in the work of Sir William Petty in the 1600s. In *Das Kapital* (vol. 1, 1867, p. 85), Karl Marx stated that "by classical Political Economy, I understand that economy which, since the time of W. Petty, has investigated the real relations of production in bourgeois society." As Marx suggested, early classical economists focused on the determinants of the economy's productive capacity. The neoclassical macroeconomic model shares this focus on the productive capacity of the economy as the determinant of total output.

rate adjusts to continuously maintain equality between the demand for and supply of labor. The price of output adjusts to maintain equality between the demand for and supply of output. The price of financial assets (and thus the interest rate) adjusts to maintain equality between the demand for and supply of financial assets and, in an open economy, foreign exchange rates adjust to equate supply and demand in the foreign exchange markets.[5]

The second key assumption of the neoclassical model is that *agents are perfectly informed about these prices.* For example, when making their labor supply decisions, it is assumed that households know not only the nominal wage that they are paid but also the prices they will have to pay to purchase output. Thus they are correctly informed about their compensation in real terms.

A model that assumes flexible prices and fully informed agents is appropriate for a long-run analysis of the economy's performance. Given sufficient time, we would expect prices in the various markets to adjust to eliminate any possible excess demands or supplies in the economy. We would also expect agents to learn the levels of all prices. Over shorter time periods, however, these assumptions are less realistic. In later chapters, therefore, we look at how the neoclassical model can be modified to explain the workings of the economy in the short run in the face of incomplete information. When analyzing the short-run behavior of the economy, we will have to alter the assumptions of perfect price flexibility and perfect information. Even in this context, however, the neoclassical model is still useful since it provides a benchmark against which we can compare the predictions of other, short-run macroeconomic models.

Labor Market Equilibrium

As a first step toward deriving the aggregate supply curve given the neoclassical model's assumptions of perfect price flexibility and perfect information on prices, let's examine the nature of the labor market, which is represented graphically in Figure 7.1. Note that in this figure, the real wage rate is on the vertical axis and the aggregate employment level is on the horizontal axis. The real wage is the money wage (W) divided by the price level (P); the real wage indicates the payment in terms of goods and services made to workers.

As mentioned in Chapter 5, the demand for labor is inversely related to the real wage rate. For instance, consider a fall in the money wage from W_0 to W_1 in Figure 7.1. At the existing price level P_0, the real wage falls from W_0/P_0 to W_1/P_0. With the fall in the real wage, firms' optimal level of employment rises from N_0 to N_1. The decrease in the real wage reduces the real cost to firms of hiring additional labor and leads firms to raise the

---

[5] Recall from Chapter 3 that the price of financial assets is inversely related to the interest rate. It makes no difference whether we talk about the price of financial assets or the interest rate—changes in one imply changes in the other in the opposite direction.

Figure 7.1 Equilibrium in the Labor Market

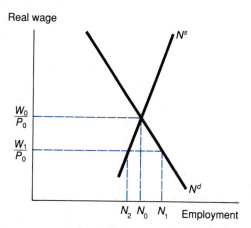

Equilibrium in the labor market occurs at the real wage W_0/P_0, where the demand for labor equals the supply of labor. The resulting equilibrium employment is N_0.

quantity of labor demanded. Thus the labor curve N^d slopes downward. Note that an important feature of this curve is the underlying assumption that each firm finds ready buyers for its output at the prevailing price level.[6]

In contrast to the labor demand curve, the labor supply curve N^s in Figure 7.1 is upward-sloping. This indicates that a decrease in the real wage induces a lower aggregate quantity of labor supplied. For instance, a decrease in the real wage from W_0/P_0 to W_1/P_0 reduces the quantity of labor supplied from N_0 to N_2. The lower real wage rate results in reduced participation in the labor market as the real return to entering the labor force falls. The lower real wage might also induce some to work fewer hours.

In the neoclassical model, the money wage is assumed to adjust freely to equate the demand for labor with the supply of labor. As Figure 7.1 illustrates, for a given price (P_0) there is a unique money wage rate (W_0) and an associated real wage (W_0/P_0), which is consistent with equilibrium in the labor market. The corresponding equilibrium employment level is N_0.

The Effect of a Change in the Price Level on the Labor Market

In interpreting Figure 7.1, it is important to remember that we have taken the price of output as given and we have assumed that the money wage changes to attain a real wage that equates the quantity of labor demanded and the quantity of labor supplied. However, money wages are not the only component of the real wage subject to frequent fluctuations; the price level

---

[6] This is sometimes referred to as the assumption of "price taking" in the output market.

also changes. A critical aspect of the neoclassical model is the impact on the labor market of a change in the price level; as we see below, changes in output prices have no effect on real variables such as employment and production. To understand this point, let's consider how a price level change affects the labor market.

Figure 7.2 illustrates the effect of an increase in the price level on the labor market. In this figure, the labor market is initially in equilibrium at the real wage W_0/P_0 and employment level N_0. Now suppose that the price level rises from P_0 to P_1. At the original money wage (W_0), the higher price level means a fall in the real wage to W_0/P_1. At this lower real wage, firms seek to increase hiring, and the quantity of labor demanded rises from N_0 to N_1. Households also recognize the increase in the level of output prices and the consequent fall in the real wage, so the quantity of labor supplied falls from N_0 to N_2. Thus at the initial money wage rate (W_0), there exists an *excess demand* for labor.

This situation of excess demand will not persist since firms competing for the scarce labor input will bid up the money wage. In fact, as Figure 7.2 indicates, the money wage will rise until equilibrium is restored at the original employment level (N_0) and at the real wage (W_1/P_1) equal to the original real wage (W_0/P_0). In order for the change in price level to leave the real wage unaffected, the money wage must rise by exactly the same proportion as the increase in the price of output. For example, if the price level rises by 10 percent, the equilibrium money wage will rise by 10 percent as well.

The finding that an increase in the price level results in a higher equilibrium money wage is commonly borne out by what we observe in the real world. In fact, labor agreements often make this relationship between the price level and the money wage explicit. In particular, labor contracts often contain cost of living allowance (COLA) clauses that adjust money wages automatically to reflect increases in prices, as measured by the consumer price index. We also find that workers not covered by COLA clauses usually receive larger raises in their money wages in years when there is higher inflation.

The Aggregate Supply Curve

Aggregate supply curve: A supply curve that depicts combinations of price levels and real GNP that reflect the underlying relationship between employment and the price level determined by the labor and other input markets.

Our analysis of the labor market provides us with a framework for deriving the relationship between the price level and real GNP. This relationship is summarized by the **aggregate supply curve.** The aggregate supply curve depicts the combinations of price levels and real GNP that reflect the underlying relationship between employment and the price level as determined in the labor market and other input markets.

As we have seen, changes in prices lead to equiproportionate changes in money wages and no change in the equilibrium level of employment. Thus in the neoclassical model, the employment level in the labor market is independent of changes in the price level. With a given capital stock, the level of real GNP is determined by the employment level. Since a change

Figure 7.2   The Effect of an Increase in the Level of Output Prices on the Labor Market

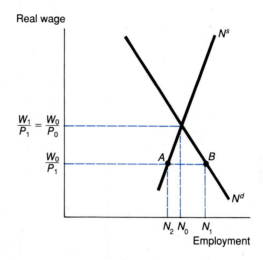

An increase in the level of output prices from P_0 to P_1 leads to a decrease in the real wage and consequent increase in the quantity of labor demanded and decrease in the quantity of labor supplied. The resulting excess demand for labor (equal to AB) causes the money wage to be bid up. At the new equilibrium, the money wage is higher but there is no change in either employment or the real wage.

in the price level leaves employment unaffected, it now leaves real GNP unchanged as well. Thus if we plot real GNP on the horizontal axis and the level of prices on the vertical axis, the aggregate supply curve is vertical, which reflects the fact that real GNP is independent of changes in the price level. If the level of output prices rises, then firms bid up the money wage rate. The real wage does not change, nor do employment and output. Similarly, a fall in the level of output prices leads to lower money wages but does not cause a change in the real wage, employment, or output.

The exact position of the aggregate supply curve can be determined by using the aggregate production function. The aggregate production function relates the economy-wide level of capital and employment to aggregate output as measured by real gross national product (Y). We denote this aggregate production function by $Y = f(N,K)$, where N equals total employment and K equals the economy's stock of capital. With equilibrium employment (N_0) and fixed capital stock ($\overline{K}$), the corresponding level of production in the economy is given by $Y_0 = f(N_0, \overline{K})$. Figure 7.3 depicts the vertical aggregate supply curve (AS) at this level of real GNP (Y_0).

An important implication of the vertical aggregate supply curve is that a country cannot increase the production of real goods and services merely by raising the price level. This makes sense intuitively. If raising the price

Figure 7.3   The Aggregate Supply Curve: The Neoclassical Model

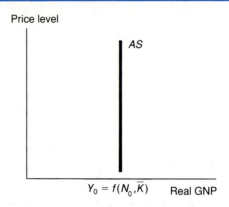

With flexible money wages and complete information, changes in the price level do not alter equilibrium employment. Since output is determined by the level of employment, output is also unaffected by changes in the price level, and the resulting aggregate supply curve (AS) is vertical.

level could cause a sustained increase in the production of real goods and services, then all the poor countries of the world would be able to escape their poverty simply by engaging in policies that generate rising prices.

There are, however, factors other than price changes that can lead to increases or decreases in aggregate supply. Three obvious examples that would lead to an increase in real GNP are: an increase in population, which increases labor supply and thus employment; a rise in the capital stock; and improvements in technology. Chapter 9 considers in detail these and a number of other macroeconomic supply factors that affect the growth of real GNP, such as oil supply shocks and tax changes that affect labor supply or the demand for labor.

Key Assumptions of the Neoclassical Model

At this point, it might be useful to review the role played by the two key assumptions of the neoclassical model, namely price flexibility and complete information on prices. In most cases, and this one is no exception, one can gain an understanding of the role of a particular assumption by exploring how the analysis would proceed if the assumption were not made. Consider first the implications of dropping the neoclassical model's assumption that prices are perfectly flexible.

Suppose that the demand for output decreases and firms cannot sell all they desire at prevailing prices. With flexible prices, output prices will fall, and, as we will see in the discussion of the aggregate demand curve that follows, the falling price level will restore demand to its previous level.

However, if output prices are inflexible and do not adjust downward in response to a reduced demand for output, firms will respond to the fall in demand by reducing production. With production curtailed in the face of falling sales, firms will demand less labor and employment will fall. Furthermore, firms' labor demand will no longer depend upon the real wage but will be determined by what can be sold in the output market.

In short, if output prices are inflexible, then the overall level of demand for goods and services is paramount in determining the level of employment. This leads to the important conclusion that the management of demand by government can play a role in affecting output and employment. Chapters 10 and 11 provide a more complete analysis of the effects of inflexible or "sticky" prices. As we will see, this is the crucial feature of what is called the macroeconomic model with predetermined prices, or the non-market-clearing model.

A second modification of the neoclassical model, discussed in Chapter 12, is to assume that output prices are flexible but money wages are not. If wages are "sticky" relative to output prices, then changes in the price level will alter the real wage. For instance, in the late 1970s high inflation rates led workers and employers in certain industries to bargain for long-term contracts that specified substantial future growth in money wages. The high expected inflation did not materialize in the early 1980s. The lower actual rate of inflation, with no change in the rate of increase in wages, meant a rise in the real wage. The resulting fall in the quantity of labor demanded led to lower employment and output. Thus we see that when wages are fixed, a reduction in output prices below that anticipated when labor contracts were signed can lead to a fall in output and employment. With inflexible money wages, the aggregate supply curve will be upward-sloping when plotted against the level of output prices.

Let's consider one more modification of the neoclassical model, a modification that will also be discussed in Chapter 12. Suppose that workers have incomplete information on output prices and the real wage. A firm determines its relevant real wage by dividing the money wage it pays its workers by the price it anticipates for the particular product its workers produce. In contrast, workers must anticipate prices for a variety of different goods to be purchased in order to determine their relevant real wage. As a result, firms may more accurately anticipate changes in prices and thus real wages than workers.

Now suppose that there is an increase in output prices. Given our current assumption of incomplete information, this will not only lead to an increase in the demand for labor and to higher wages, as firms anticipate the fall in real wages, but may also lead to an increase in the quantity of labor supplied. The reason for this is that workers, who have not anticipated the rise in output prices, will perceive the higher money wages as implying a rise in the real wage and will increase the quantity of labor supplied accordingly. As a result, equilibrium employment will rise with an increase in output prices. Once again, the aggregate supply curve will be upward-sloping when plotted against the level of output prices. If workers had complete information concerning the rise in output prices, they would seek a higher money wage to compensate for the rise in prices. As a consequence, the real wage would not have fallen and equilibrium employment would remain unchanged (as we saw in our discussion of Figure 7.2).

To the Point

THE LABOR MARKET AND AGGREGATE SUPPLY

- The neoclassical assumption of flexible prices results in a labor market in which equilibrium employment and the money wage are determined by the intersection of the labor demand and supply curves.

- The neoclassical assumption of fully informed agents means that an increase in output prices is recognized by both buyers and sellers in the labor market. As a consequence, assuming flexible wages, a rise in the price level leads to an equiproportionate change in the money wage; the real wage and level of employment remain unchanged.

- The aggregate supply curve depicts the combinations of price levels and real GNP that reflect the underlying relationship between employment and the price level determined in the labor markets and other input markets. Since a change in the price level does not change the level of employment in the neoclassical model, a change in the price level does not change real GNP; the aggregate supply curve is vertical.

7.2   THE AGGREGATE DEMAND CURVE FOR THE CLOSED ECONOMY

To analyze macroeconomic shocks in an economy without a foreign sector, we must simultaneously analyze the effects of the shocks on the labor, output, and financial markets, as well as the money "market." As we have seen, the aggregate supply curve summarizes events in the labor market. The aggregate supply curve indicates all price-output combinations consistent with the equilibrium level of employment.

Aggregate demand curve: A demand curve that depicts all combinations of output and price levels associated with equilibrium in the output, financial, and money markets.

The **aggregate demand curve** also summarizes events, but in the other three markets. Specifically, the aggregate demand curve depicts combinations of output and levels of output prices associated with equilibrium in the output, financial, and money markets. Equilibrium in the output market means that the output produced equals output demand. (In a closed economy, output demand is the sum of consumption demand, gross investment demand, and government demand.) Equilibrium in the financial market means that the demand for loanable funds equals the supply of loanable funds. Equilibrium in the money market means the real demand for money equals the real supply of money. Figure 7.4 illustrates the aggregate demand curve.

Figure 7.4   **The Aggregate Demand Curve**

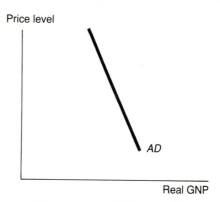

The aggregate demand curve slopes downward, indicating that a fall in the level of output prices implies a rise in the level of real GNP. Each point on the aggregate demand curve indicates a combination of real GNP and a price level that represents equilibrium in the output, financial, and money markets.

It's important to realize that when we use the phrase "equilibrium in the output market," we are abstracting from supply-side considerations. At each price level, the aggregate demand curve indicates the output that, if produced, would equal output demand. Production of output equal to that demanded would occur if firms sought simply to produce to meet market demand and if workers were readily available for employment—which means that firms could hire whatever quantity of workers necessary to achieve production equal to what was demanded. In this context, the term "equilibrium in the output market" does not imply equality between output demand and the output that our analysis of the labor market suggests would be supplied. Such a level or levels of "output supply" are shown graphically by the aggregate supply curve. Later in this chapter, we will combine the aggregate demand and supply curves. The intersection of these two curves will identify the unique level of output at which a) output produced equals output demand (i.e., we are on the aggregate demand curve) and b) output produced equals what would be supplied from our analysis of the labor market (i.e., we are on the aggregate supply curve).

The downward slope of the aggregate demand curve indicates that higher price levels require lower levels of output to maintain equilibrium in the output, financial, and money markets. However, this downward slope is deceptively simple, for although the aggregate demand curve may look like the standard demand curve in microeconomics with which you are accustomed, it is really quite different. A standard demand curve depicts how the quantity of a particular good demanded varies with a change in the price of that good. Along a standard demand curve, the fall in a good's price relative to the prices of other goods leads consumers to substitute more of that good for other goods.

Along the aggregate demand curve, however, we must consider how a change in the price level in general affects the aggregate demand for real goods and services in the economy. The aggregate demand curve differs from the demand curve of microeconomics in that it takes into account the interplay between markets, a situation that is for the most part ignored in microeconomic analysis. The key to analyzing the effect of a change in the level of prices on the economy is to look at what is happening simultaneously in the financial, output, and money markets. We begin our discussion of the reason for the downward-sloping aggregate demand curve by examining the nature of equilibrium in the financial market.

Equilibrium in the Financial Market

Equilibrium in the financial market occurs at the interest rate at which the real demand for new financial assets by households and depository institutions equals the real supply of new financial assets by firms and the government.[7] As first mentioned in Chapters 5 and 6, a graphical representation of the financial market is easier to work with if the financial market is presented in terms of the demand for and supply of loanable funds rather than in terms of the supply of and demand for financial assets. In terms of loanable funds then, equilibrium occurs in the financial market at the interest rate at which the supply of loanable funds by households and depository institutions equals the demand for loanable funds by firms and government.

Figure 7.5 depicts equilibrium in the financial market. In the figure, the interest rate appears on the vertical axis and the real amount of loanable funds appears on the horizontal axis. The equilibrium interest rate is r_0. At this interest rate, the quantity of loanable funds demanded just equals the quantity supplied.

The real demand for loanable funds is the sum of the borrowing by firms and the government. As discussed in Chapter 5, firms' investment decisions depend inversely on the interest rate. A rise in the interest rate leads firms to curtail their purchases of capital goods since borrowing is more costly. Because a rise in the interest rate reduces investment demand, we know from the firm financing constraint that a rise in the interest rate also reduces firms' demand for loanable funds. The demand for loanable funds curve also incorporates government's demand for loanable funds, which reflects the government deficit. We typically view the government deficit as unresponsive to changes in the interest rate.[8] Rather, the deficit is the result of exogenous

---

[7] Remember that we are considering a closed economy. In an open economy, demanders of financial assets (suppliers of loanable funds) would include foreigners.

[8] In practice, a rise in the interest rate will over time lead to an increase in government interest payments, which are part of government transfer payments. This rise in transfer payments will lead to a fall in net real taxes and an increased government deficit if there is no change in total tax revenues. In such a case, we will assume that total tax revenues change in order to maintain a constant level of net real taxes and thus a constant government deficit.

Figure 7.5   Equilibrium in the Financial Market

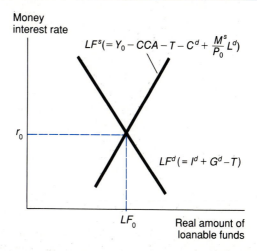

Given a price level (P_0), real GNP (Y_0), and an interest rate that adjusts quickly to clear the financial market, the quantity of loanable funds demanded by firms and government will equal the quantity supplied by households and depository institutions at the interest rate r_0. At that interest rate, the financial market is in equilibrium. From the financing constraints, the supply of loanable funds equals real disposable income (Y_0-CCA-T) minus consumption demand (C^d) plus the difference between the real supply of money (M^s/P_0) and real money demand (L^d). The real demand for loanable funds equals net investment demand (I^d) plus the government deficit (G^d-T).

policy decisions concerning spending and taxation. Thus although the demand for loanable funds curve LF^d includes both the demand by firms and government, the negative slope of the demand for loanable funds curve solely reflects changes in firm's borrowing in response to changes in the interest rate.

The real supply of loanable funds is the sum of the lending by households and depository institutions. As discussed in Chapter 6, household saving in the form of financial assets is directly related to the interest rate, as a rise in the interest rate induces households to reduce consumption and to economize on their real holdings of money. Both actions, according to the household budget constraint, imply a rise in the household supply of loanable funds (demand for financial assets). The banking system's supply of loanable funds is independent of the interest rate.[9] Consequently, the total *real supply of loanable funds is directly related to the interest rate*. The upward-sloping supply of loanable funds curve (LF^s) in Figure 7.5 reflects this direct relationship between the supply of loanable funds and the interest rate.

---

[9] In Chapter 16, we consider the possibility of the money supply, and thus depository institutions' supply of loanable funds, being affected by changes in the interest rate. (See, in particular, Review Question 14 in that chapter.)

Decisions Underlying the Supply of and Demand for Loanable Funds

To get a better feel for the factors that influence the demand for and supply of loanable funds in the financial market, let's use the financing constraints confronting each of the market participants to make explicit the decisions that underlie the demand for and supply of loanable funds. Consider first the demand for loanable funds. From the firm financing constraint, firms' demand for loanable funds (their supply of financial assets A_f^s) equals net investment demand I^d. From the government financing constraint, the government's demand for loanable funds (its supply of financial assets A_g^s) equals its demand for goods and services (G^d) minus net taxes (T). Thus as indicated in Figure 7.5, the total demand for loanable funds is given by

$$LF^d \quad\equiv\quad A_f^s + A_g^s \quad=\quad I^d + (G^d - T)$$

Demand for   Supply of   Net investment demand
loanable funds   financial assets   plus government deficit
by firms and government   **(7.1)**

According to this equation, the demand for loanable funds equals net investment demand plus the government deficit.

The total supply of loanable funds is the sum of loanable funds supplied by households and by depository institutions. From the household budget constraint, households' supply of loanable funds (their demand for financial assets, A_h^d) equals their real disposable income (YD) minus consumption demand (C^d) and saving in the form of real additions to money holdings ($L^d - \overline{M}/P$). From the depository institution financing constraint, banks supply of loanable funds (their demand for financial assets A_b^d) equals the real change in the supply of money $[(M^s/P) - \overline{M}/P]$. Thus the total supply of loanable funds is given by

$$LF^s \quad\equiv\quad A_h^d + A_b^d \quad= YD - C^d - (L^d - \overline{M}/P) + (M^s/P) - \overline{M}/P$$
$$= YD - C^d + M^s/P - L^d$$

(7.2)

Supply of   Demand for   Saving plus difference
loanable funds   financial assets   between real supply and
by households   demand for money
and "banks"

According to this equation, the supply of loanable funds equals households' planned saving ($YD - C^d$) plus the difference between the real supply and real demand for money.

Equation 7.2 makes an important point. Since a change in the level of prices affects the real supply of money (M^s/P), it also alters the real supply of loanable funds. We shall find out shortly that the role that prices play in affecting the real supply of loanable funds and thus the interest rate has important implications for the slope of the aggregate demand curve. Before exploring this further, however, let's look at equilibrium in terms of the demand for and supply of money.

Equilibrium in the Money "Market"

Even though the interest rate is determined in the financial market, it affects demands in the output and money markets. In this section, we consider how interest rate changes affect the money market. Figure 7.6 depicts two curves, a demand for money curve (L^d) and a supply of money curve (M^s/P_0) plotted against the interest rate. The money supply curve is vertical, which indicates that the real money supply is assumed to be invariant to changes in the interest rate. Changes in the nominal money supply (M^s) are, like government spending and taxation, considered to be exogenous, reflecting the policy decisions of the Federal Reserve.

In contrast, money demand is responsive to changes in the interest rate, reflecting the fact that individuals desire to economize on their real money holdings at higher interest rates. By holding money, households can reduce the costs involved in making transactions. Yet when households hold wealth in the form of money, they give up the opportunity to put it into financial assets that offer higher interest earnings.[10] The higher the interest rate, the greater is the cost to holding money, and consequently the smaller is the quantity of real money balances demanded. This inverse relationship between the interest rate and the real quantity of money demanded is depicted in Figure 7.6 by the downward-sloping money demand curve (L^d).

Real money demand is also directly related to real GNP. Money is a medium of exchange and people hold money for use in transactions. The higher the level of real GNP, the greater the amount of transactions that households engage in and thus the greater the amount of real money balances that households desire to hold. The money demand curve in Figure 7.6 is thus drawn for a particular level of real GNP (Y_0). An increase in real GNP will shift the money demand curve to the right.

Given real GNP (Y_0) and the price level (P_0), Figure 7.6 indicates that there is a unique interest rate (r_0) at which the quantity of real money balances demanded equals the quantity supplied. Suppose that the interest rate that establishes equilibrium in the financial market is this same r_0. The existence of equilibrium in the financial and money markets implies then from the aggregate budget constraint that the output market is also in equilibrium at the combination of interest rate r_0, price level P_0 and real GNP Y_0. In other words, the price-output combination (P_0, Y_0) defines one point

---

[10] Remember that, unlike financial assets, coins, currency, and checking accounts pay no interest. Although other forms of money, such as checkable deposits at depository institutions, pay some interest, this interest rate on monetary assets is typically less than that available on financial assets and only partially adjusts in response to changes in the market interest rate on financial assets.

Figure 7.6   Equilibrium in the Money "Market"

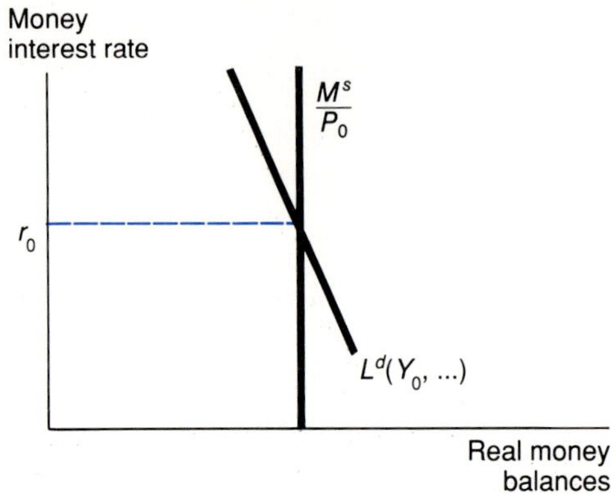

Given the real GNP (Y_0) and the price level (P_0), the figure indicates that there is a unique interest rate (r_0) at which the quantity of real money balances demanded equals the quantity supplied.

on the aggregate demand curve since that price-output combination is consistent with equilibrium in all three markets. This is true of other points on the aggregate demand curve as well.

We will now see how changes in the price level require changes in real output and the interest rate in order to maintain equilibrium in the output, financial, and money markets. In the process, we will demonstrate the rationale for the downward-sloping aggregate demand curve.

The Effect of Price Changes on Equilibrium in the Output, Financial, and Money Markets

To verify the inverse relationship between the price level and real GNP depicted by the aggregate demand curve that was illustrated in Figure 7.4, we simply need to establish that a fall in the price level requires increased output to restore equilibrium in the output, financial, and money markets. We will start with a combination of a price level P_0 and real GNP Y_0 that is a point on the aggregate demand curve. We denote this price–real GNP combination as point E in Figure 7.7.

Since the initial price level P_0 and real output Y_0 combination is a point on the aggregate demand curve, we know that at these levels of prices and output, the output, money, and financial markets are in equilibrium. Figure 7.8 depicts this initial equilibrium in the financial market (part a) and money market (part b) at the interest rate r_0. Now suppose that the price level falls from P_0 to P_1. According to Figure 7.7, a rise in real GNP from Y_0 to Y_1 would be required to restore equilibrium in the output, financial and money

Figure 7.7 A Movement Down the Aggregate Demand Curve

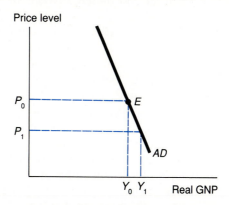

A fall in price level from P_0 to P_1 leads to a lower interest rate and excess demand in the output market at the original output level Y_0. Real GNP must increase from Y_0 to Y_1 to restore equilibrium in the output, financial, and money markets. This change in real GNP is represented by a movement down the aggregate demand curve.

Figure 7.8 The Impact of a Decrease in the Price Level on the Financial and Money Markets

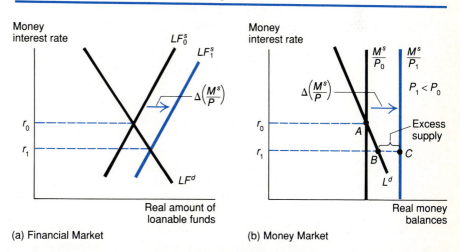

(a) Financial Market   (b) Money Market

With a decrease in the price level, the real supply of money increases. This leads to an equivalent increase in the real supply of loanable funds from LF_0^s to LF_1^s. The interest rate associated with equilibrium in the financial market thus falls from r_0 to r_1, as shown in part (a). At the new, lower interest rate, there is an excess supply of money as indicated by the gap between B and C in part (b). Corresponding to this excess supply of money is an excess demand for output as the lower interest rate stimulates investment and consumption demand.

markets. To see why this is the case, let us first consider the effect on the financial and money markets of a fall in the price level with no change in real GNP.

For a given nominal money supply (M^s), a fall in the price level from P_0 to P_1 means an increase in the real supply of money from M^s/P_0 to M^s/P_1. This is shown in Figure 7.8(b) by a shift to the right in the money supply curve. Note that the change in the price level does not affect the demand for *real* money balances. As discussed in Chapter 6, a change in the price level leads to an equiproportionate change in the demand for nominal money balances, leaving the real demand for money balances unaffected.

As the depository institution financing constraint makes clear, coincident with the higher real supply of money is an equivalent increase in the real supply of loanable funds by depository institutions. The intuition behind this result is clear: A fall in the price level means that a given nominal supply of loanable funds by banks can be used by borrowers to buy more goods and services.[11] This increase is the real supply of loanable funds is depicted as a shift to the right in the supply of loanable funds curve, from LF_0^s to LF_1^s in Figure 7.8(a).

The increase in the supply of loanable funds causes a fall in the interest rate from r_0 to r_1.[12] Although the financial market is in equilibrium at the new, lower interest rate r_1, Figure 7.8(b) indicates there is now an excess supply of money. Even though the lower interest rate raises the quantity of real money balances demanded from point A to B, the increase in the real supply of money is greater. To see why there is an excess supply of money equal to the gap B and C, consider what is happening in the output market.

The fall in the interest rate leads to an increase in output demand as desired investment spending by firms and desired consumption spending by households both increase. Given no change in output, this rise in output demand means that there is now excess demand in the output market. From the aggregate budget constraint introduced in Chapter 4, we know that the excess demands in the output, financial, and money markets must sum to zero. At the lower interest rate r_1 in Figure 7.8, the financial market is in equilibrium, which means excess demand is zero in the financial market. Since there remains only the money "market," there must exist an excess supply of money exactly equal to the excess demand for output. In essence, there are money balances in the economy that individuals desire to spend, not hold.

What we have just shown is that starting with an equilibrium in the output, financial, and money markets (point E in Figure 7.7), a lower price

---

[11] Recall that depository institutions' *nominal* supply of loanable funds, like the nominal money supply, is independent of the price level. As we saw in Chapter 5, depository institutions' nominal supply of loanable funds, like the nominal money supply, is determined primarily by the amount of reserves in the banking system (something which is largely at the discretion of the Fed).

[12] For expository ease, we assume in our discussion that the interest rate adjusts in order to continuously equate demand and supply in the financial market.

level with no change in real output will lead to excess demand in the output market. It is important to realize that the lower price level need not directly affect any of the components of real output demand. Rather, the link between lower output prices and the real sector of the economy is through changes in credit conditions in the financial market.[13]

The excess demand in the output market can be eliminated by a rise in real GNP, as production rises to meet demand.[14] Equivalently, we can say that a higher output eliminates the excess supply of money since the rise in real GNP increases households' desired real money holdings. Figure 7.7 indicates that if the price level falls from P_0 to P_1, equilibrium in the output and money markets can be restored if real GNP rises from Y_0 to Y_1. The new price-output combination (P_1, Y_1) is on the aggregate demand curve and thus it is associated with simultaneous equilibrium in the output, financial, and money markets. With the new equilibrium price-output combination, there is a new, lower interest rate that stimulates output demand to equal the new, higher level of production.

To the Point

THE AGGREGATE DEMAND CURVE

- The aggregate demand curve is not like the simple demand curve of microeconomics. Points along the aggregate demand curve represent price level and real GNP combinations that are consistent with equilibrium in the output, money, and financial markets simultaneously.

- A decrease in the price level increases the real supply of money, shifts the supply of loanable funds curve to the right, and decreases the interest rate. The lower interest rate increases investment and consumption demand which results in excess demand in the output market. Corresponding to this is an excess supply of money. To restore equilibrium, output must rise.

---

[13] Although a fall in the price level increases households' real money holdings, it leaves household wealth essentially unchanged. It may surprise you that a lower price level can have little impact on household wealth in the aggregate. It is true that households' dollar claims on the banking sector—their money holdings—(including both the Fed and private depository institutions) do increase in real value. This apparent rise in household wealth in the form of money holdings (households' assets; depository institutions' liabilities) is offset by the coincident rise in real holdings of bonds by depository institutions (households' liabilities; depository institutions' assets). Remember that the bonds held by banks rise in real value to reflect the fact that lower prices raise real interest and principal payments; these higher real payments represent real claims on households either directly (when households borrow from the banking sector) or indirectly (when firms or the government borrow from the banking sector, in which case households ultimately pay for the increase in the real value of the banking sector's interest and principal receipts through lower real dividends or higher real taxes). The discussion above highlights a property of an economy in which money is "inside money."

[14] Note that an increase in real GNP eliminates the excess demand in the output market even though increased output means an equivalent increase in household income and thus an increase in consumption demand. Since the increase in income funds increases in both consumption and saving, consumption demand alone rises by less that output. Thus a rising output level serves to reduce excess demand in the output market.

- The inverse relationship between the price level and real GNP consistent with equilibrium in the output, financial, and money markets is summarized by the aggregate demand curve.

7.3   THE AGGREGATE DEMAND CURVE FOR THE OPEN ECONOMY

When we open the economy to foreign trade, the aggregate demand curve now depicts price-output combinations consistent with equilibrium not only in the output, financial, and money markets but also in the foreign exchange market. To show how the foreign sector and the accompanying foreign exchange market affect our analysis, we now consider how a change in the level of prices affects the various markets of the open economy.

The Effect of Price Changes on the Financial Market in an Open Economy

In a closed economy, the total supply of loanable funds equals the sum of lending by households and depository institutions. In the open economy, we must allow for the fact that some U.S. citizens may choose to purchase foreign financial assets, thereby diverting loanable funds into foreign markets. At the same time that U.S. dollars are going abroad, foreigners are purchasing U.S. financial assets and thus supplying loanable funds in the United States. Our discussion in Chapter 3 of the influx of foreign capital into the United States in the 1980s is a recent, vivid example of this latter phenomenon.

To account for the new flows in an open economy, we subtract lending abroad by households (U.S. households' demand for foreign financial assets AF_h^d) from the total supply of loanable funds and add foreign lending in the U.S. financial market (foreigners' demand for U.S. financial assets A_{for}^d). Thus the total supply of loanable funds in the U.S financial market for an open economy is given by

$$LF^s \equiv A_h^d - AF_h^d + A_b^d + A_{for}^d$$

Supply of loanable funds   Demand for financial assets by households (net of demand for foreign assets), "banks," and foreigners   **(7.3)**

Using Equation 7.2, we can rewrite this expression for the total supply of loanable funds in an open economy as

$$LF^s = YD - C^d + M^s/P - L^d + (A_{for}^d - AF_h^d)$$

Supply of loanable funds   Saving plus difference between real supply and demand for money plus net U.S. capital inflows   **(7.4)**

where the new term $(A_{for}^d - AF_h^d)$ denotes the net capital inflow into the United States.

Equation 7.4 summarizes the decisions that underlie the supply of funds in the financial market in the open economy. Equation 7.1 summarizes the decisions underlying the demand for funds. Table 7.1 illustrates the actual financial flows reflecting these demands and supplies in the U.S. economy. In the table, we assume money demand equals money supply, so that households' supply of loanable funds can be represented by their saving.[15]

Household saving and net capital inflows constitute the sources of supply of loanable funds in the U.S. financial market. These funds are used by firms to finance investment spending and by government to finance deficit spending. As Table 7.1 indicates, each year the supply of funds just equals the demand. Upon examining the financial flows, a couple of interesting features of the data stand out. We see that in recent years, the government has been a relatively large demander of loanable funds. Furthermore, an increasing amount of the supply of loanable funds to the U.S. financial markets has come from foreigners. We will say more about these observations later.

Even though we have opened the financial sector to account for international capital flows, price changes still play an important role in influencing the availability of loanable funds in the United States. Let us reconsider the impact that a change in the price level has on financial markets in an open economy.

As we now know, a fall in the price level causes an increase in the real supply of money and, according to Equation 7.4, an equivalent increase in the real supply of loanable funds in the financial market. Figure 7.9(b) depicts the increase in the money supply in the money market by the shift to the right in the real supply of money from M^s/P_0 to M^s/P_1. The corresponding increase in the supply of loanable funds in the financial market is depicted in Figure 7.9(a) by the shift to the right in the loanable funds curve from LF_0^s to LF_1^s. At the original interest r_0, there is now an excess supply of loanable funds in the financial market equal to the increase in the real supply of money. As Figure 7.9 illustrates, the equilibrium interest rate, which is determined in the financial market, therefore falls from r_0 to r_1.

Figure 7.9 shows that the fall in the interest rate from r_0 to r_1 eliminates the excess supply of loanable funds (part a) in part by reducing the quantity of loanable funds supplied by households (the movement from B to C) and in part by increasing the quantity of loanable funds demanded by firms (the movement from A to C). The more responsive the quantity of loanable funds supplied to changes in the interest rate (i.e., the "flatter" the loanable funds supply curve), the smaller is the reduction in the interest rate that is required to eliminate an initial excess supply in the financial market. As we discuss below, the quantity of loanable funds supplied is, in fact, more responsive to changes in the interest rate in an open economy than it is in a closed economy.

---

[15] As we shall see in the next section, prices typically adjust over time so as to achieve equilibrium in the various markets in the economy, including the money market. From Equation 7.2, we see that when money demand equals money supply (i.e., $M^s/P = L^d$), the supply of loanable funds reduces to household saving plus the net capital inflow into the United States.

Table 7.1   **The Demand for and Supply of Loanable Funds in the U.S. Financial Market (billions of 1982 dollars)**

Year	Demand for Loanable Funds			Supply of Loanable Funds		
	Net Investment	Government Deficit	Total Demand	Household Saving	Net Capital Inflow	Total Supply
1970	151.7	25.2	176.9	147.0	30.0	177.0
1971	179.8	43.9	223.7	183.9	39.7	223.6
1972	212.0	7.3	219.3	169.8	49.4	219.2
1973	257.2	−16.0	241.2	209.6	31.5	241.1
1974	205.3	8.0	213.3	214.0	−0.8	213.2
1975	96.3	109.4	205.7	224.6	−18.9	205.7
1976	156.2	60.9	217.1	206.1	11.0	217.1
1977	211.7	28.4	240.1	204.5	35.5	240.0
1978	253.2	0.6	253.8	227.0	26.8	253.8
1979	233.9	−14.6	219.3	223.0	−3.6	219.4
1980	153.2	40.3	193.5	250.4	−56.9	193.5
1981	175.8	31.6	207.4	256.8	−49.3	207.5
1982	64.1	110.8	174.9	201.2	−26.3	174.9
1983	109.6	123.8	233.4	213.5	20.0	233.5
1984	251.2	97.5	348.7	264.7	84.0	348.7
1985	209.8	119.5	329.3	221.2	108.3	329.5
1986	212.0	129.5	341.5	195.8	145.8	341.6
1987	226.7	91.2	317.9	183.6	134.3	317.9

Source: Economic Report of the President (1988). Due to rounding errors, total demand for loanable funds sometimes differs slightly from total supply.

We have already noted that in a closed economy a fall in the interest rate causes U.S. households to reduce the amount of loanable funds they supply in the U.S. financial market, as they 1) increase planned consumption and 2) increase their desired holdings of money balances. As Equation 7.4 highlighted, a fall in the interest rate in an open economy has these same two effects plus two others that affect net capital inflows, $A_{for}^d - AF_h^d$. First, the fall in the interest rate causes U.S. households to substitute purchases of foreign financial assets for U.S. financial assets (AF_h^d rises). Second, the fall in the interest rate discourages foreigners from purchasing U.S financial assets (A_{for}^d falls). Since the amount of loanable funds supplied is more responsive to a change in the interest rate, the supply of loanable funds curve is "flatter" in an open economy.

In order to compare the effects that a change in the price level has on the equilibrium interest rate in an open and a closed economy, Figure 7.9(a) uses lighter lines to denote the supply of loanable funds curves for the closed economy both before and after the fall in the price level. Note that the supply curves for the open economy are less steep than those for the closed economy, reflecting the fact that in the open economy the supply of loanable funds includes net capital inflows that are responsive to interest rate changes. Thus

Figure 7.9   The Impact of a Decrease in the Price Level on the Financial and Money Markets

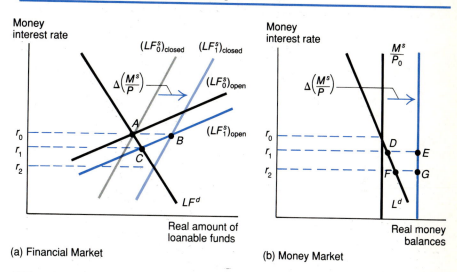

(a) Financial Market

(b) Money Market

With a decrease in the price level, there is an increase in the real supply of loanable funds in the open economy from LF_0^s to LF_1^s and the real supply of money from M^s/P_0 to M^s/P_1. The interest rate associated with equilibrium in the financial market thus falls from r_0 to r_1, as shown in part (a). At the new, lower interest rate, there is an excess supply of money as indicated by the gap DE in part (b). In an open economy, the fall in the interest rate from r_0 to r_1 restores equilibrium in the financial market. In a closed economy, the supply of loanable funds curves (the lighter lines) are steeper, indicating that the quantity of loanable funds supplied is less responsive to the interest rate. Thus the fall in the interest rate required to restore equilibrium is greater (from r_0 to r_2) in the closed economy than in the open economy. Note that the money market graph indicates that the excess supply of money in an open economy, DE in part (b), is greater than the excess supply in the closed economy, FG in part (b), since the interest rate falls by less in the open economy.

---

as Figure 7.9 indicates, while the interest rate would fall from r_0 to r_2 in a closed economy, it would fall by the lesser amount of r_0 to r_1 in an open economy.

   With less of a fall in the interest rate required to restore equilibrium in the financial market in an open economy, the result is that a fall in the price level leads to smaller initial increases in investment and consumption demand in the open economy. At first glance, then, it appears as though adding a foreign sector means that output demand responds less to a price change. However, as Figure 7.9(b) indicates, the excess supply of money is greater in an open economy since the interest rate does not fall by as much. Assuming equilibrium in the foreign exchange market, the aggregate budget constraint for the open economy (Equation 4.21) indicates that this greater excess supply of money implies a greater initial excess demand for output in the open economy than in the closed economy.

Since consumption and investment demand rise by less in response to the falling interest rate in the open economy, how can there be a greater excess demand for output in the open economy? The fact that the economy is open to trade should be your clue. Changes in the foreign exchange rates required to maintain equilibrium in the foreign exchange markets lead to a rise in net exports that stimulates output demand. To understand why this is the case, let's see what is happening in the foreign exchange market and how that affects net export demand.

Exchange Rate Determination and the Foreign Exchange Market

A foreign exchange rate is nothing more than the price of one currency in terms of another. As with many prices, the interaction of supply and demand determines exchange rates. To see how foreign exchange rates are determined, we will look at an example of trade between Japan and the United States. Associated with this trade is the exchange of yen for dollars by Japanese buying U.S. exports. There is also an exchange of dollars for yen by U.S. importers of Japanese goods. Figure 7.10 depicts the interaction between the demanders and suppliers of dollars in the foreign exchange market. The equilibrium exchange rate is E_0 yen for one dollar.

As we discussed in Chapter 6, a depreciation of the dollar raises the quantity of dollars demanded in the foreign exchange market since it reduces the cost of U.S. goods to foreigners. Thus the demand for dollars curve in Figure 7.10 slopes downward. The supply of dollars curve slopes upward in Figure 7.10, indicating that a depreciation of the dollar reduces the quantity of dollars supplied in the foreign exchange market. As we saw in Chapter 6, a fall in the foreign currency price of a dollar means a higher dollar price of foreign currency. The implied rise in the cost of foreign goods to U.S. importers leads to a fall in U.S. imports and thus a reduction in the quantity of dollars supplied.[16]

Armed with this information, we are ready to examine the impact that a fall in the price level has on the foreign exchange market in the open economy. In the previous section, we saw that a fall in the price level leads to a lower interest rate in the financial market. We now demonstrate how this lower return on U.S. financial assets leads to a depreciation of the dollar in the foreign exchange market.

In response to a decrease in the U.S. interest rate, U.S. households shift some of their lending from the domestic financial market to foreign financial markets. The increased purchase of foreign financial assets (the rise in lending in foreign financial markets) requires that U.S. households convert more dollars into foreign currency. Thus a lower return on U.S. financial assets

---

[16] Recall from Chapter 6 that this assumes the price elasticity of demand for foreign goods is elastic (greater than one), so that the percent fall in the quantity of foreign goods demanded exceeds the percent increase in their dollar price.

Figure 7.10   Equilibrium in the Foreign Exchange Market

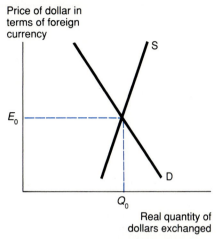

At a price of one dollar equal to E_0 yen, the foreign exchange market is in equilibrium (the demand for dollars equals the supply of dollars).

causes U.S. households to increase their supply of dollars in the foreign exchange market. Figure 7.11 depicts this increase in U.S. capital outflows, and the accompanying increase in the supply of dollars in the foreign exchange market, by the shift to the right in the supply of dollars curve from S_0 to S_1.

Similarly, the fall in U.S. interest rates leads foreigners to reduce their purchases of U.S. financial assets and thus to reduce their demand for dollars in the foreign exchange market. Figure 7.11 depicts this decreased capital inflow to the U.S., and thus reduced demand for dollars in the foreign exchange market, by the shift to the left in the demand for dollars curve from D_0 to D_1.

As Figure 7.11 indicates, the lower U.S. interest rate and resulting fall in net U.S capital inflows causes the dollar to depreciate from E_0 to E_1. The decrease in the price of the dollar has two important effects. First, foreigners are encouraged to purchase more U.S. goods and U.S. exports increase, which is shown by the downward movement along the new demand for dollars curve (D_1). Second, since a depreciation of the dollar means a higher price of foreign currency in terms of dollars, U.S. imports decrease, as indicated by the movement down the new supply of dollars curve (S_1).

Thus the change in international capital flows induced by a lower U.S. interest rate, which causes a depreciation of the dollar, leads to an increase in net export demand (U.S. exports minus U.S. imports). This means that in an open economy, a fall in the interest rate leads to increases not only in investment and in consumption demand but also in a new component of output demand—net export demand.

Figure 7.11   The Effect of a Decrease in the U.S. Interest Rate on the Foreign Exchange Market

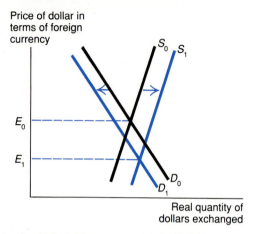

With a decrease in the U.S. interest rate, the demand for dollars falls from D_0 to D_1 and the supply of dollars rises from S_0 to S_1. These changes reflect the increase in U.S. households' purchases of foreign financial assets and the reduction in foreigners' purchases of U.S. financial assets.

The Effect of Price Changes on Equilibrium in the Output, Financial, Money, and Foreign Exchange Markets

Having seen how a reduction in the price level affects the interest rate, net capital inflows, and net exports, we are now ready to examine the nature of the aggregate demand curve in an open economy. Remember, the aggregate demand curve indicates price-output combinations consistent with equilibrium in the output, financial, money, and, for the open economy, foreign exchange markets.

As discussed previously, a fall in the price level leads to a smaller fall in the interest rate at the original output level and thus a smaller increase in investment and consumption demand in an open economy since the supply of loanable funds curve is flatter, as was illustrated in Figure 7.9(a). In an open economy, however, there is an additional effect in the output market associated with the fall in the interest rate. By reducing net capital inflows, the lower interest rate leads to a depreciation of the dollar and an increase in net export demand (see Figure 7.11).

The excess demand in the output market at the original level of output due to the fall in the price level is *greater* in an open than in a closed economy because the fall in the price level leads to an increase not only in consumption and investment demand but also in net export demand. One way to see this is to examine what is happening in the money market. We know from the aggregate budget constraint that the excess demand in the output market corresponds to an excess supply in the money market, assuming

Figure 7.12   Aggregate Demand Curves for Open and Closed Economies

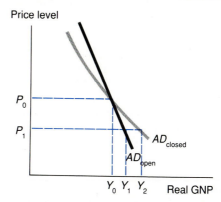

A reduction in the price level from P_0 to P_1 increases the real money supply, which leads to an excess demand for output at the original output Y_0. For the closed economy, simultaneous equilibrium is restored in the output, financial, and money markets by a rise in output from Y_0 to Y_1. For the open economy, the rise in output to restore simultaneous equilibrium in the output, financial, money, and foreign exchange markets is greater, as output must increase from Y_0 to Y_2. That is, the aggregate demand curve for an open economy (AD_{open}) is flatter than the aggregate demand curve for a closed economy (AD_{closed}).

that the interest rate adjusts to clear the financial market. Figure 7.9(b) confirms that a fall in the price level causes a greater initial excess supply of money (and excess demand for output) in an open economy; a greater increase in output is thus required to restore equilibrium in the money and output markets.

In an open economy, the interest rate is, in a sense, doing less "work" to eliminate the excess supply of money caused by the fall in the price level, so that a greater increase in income is required to restore equilibrium. The fact that a given decrease in the price level leads to a greater increase in equilibrium output in an open economy means that the open economy's aggregate demand curve is "flatter" than its closed economy counterpart. In Figure 7.12, this flatter aggregate demand curve for the open economy is denoted by AD_{open}, while AD_{closed} denotes the aggregate demand curve for a closed economy.[17]

---

[17] It should be pointed out that the adjustment in income to restore equilibrium in the output (and money) market is not affected by the introduction a foreign sector. It is true that with an open economy, an increase in income implies increased purchases of foreign goods (U.S. imports). This increase in imports means an increase in the supply of dollars in the foreign exchange market, however, which causes the price of the dollar to fall (a reduction that is in addition to that caused by the fall in the interest rate). This depreciation of the dollar increases U.S. exports and reduces U.S. imports. In fact, the rise in net export demand due to this depreciation of the dollar will exactly offset the initial fall in net export demand that resulted from the rise in income. Thus given flexible exchange rates, a change in income alone does not alter *net* export demand.

To summarize, a fall in the price level in an open economy requires a greater increase in output than in a closed economy to restore equilibrium in the output, financial, money, and foreign exchange markets. At the new equilibrium, the interest rate that clears the financial market is lower, although the interest rate does not fall by as much as it does in the closed economy. The lower interest rate reduces capital inflows and increases capital outflows, resulting in a depreciation or fall in the price of a dollar to maintain equilibrium in the foreign exchange market. This depreciation induced by a lower interest rate causes net export demand to increase. The dollar also depreciates with the rise in output that stimulates imports, but this output adjustment leaves net export demand unaffected.

7.4   EQUILIBRIUM: THE AGGREGATE DEMAND AND SUPPLY CURVES

Having explored the aggregate supply and aggregate demand curves separately, we can now combine the two curves to determine the levels of prices and real GNP associated with simultaneous equilibrium in all the various markets in the economy. The aggregate supply curve depicts combinations of the price level and output that are consistent with equilibrium in the labor market. The aggregate demand curve shows the combinations of the price level and output that are consistent with equilibrium in the output, financial, and money markets; in an open economy, the foreign exchange market is added to this list. The intersection of the aggregate demand and aggregate supply curves thus shows the price-output combination at which all markets in the economy are simultaneously in equilibrium.

Figure 7.13 depicts both the aggregate supply and demand curves in the same diagram. The two curves have one price-output combination in common, (P_0, Y^*). Only with a price level P_0 and an output level Y^* can equilibrium exist in every market in the economy simultaneously. Furthermore, associated with this equilibrium price-output combination are an equilibrium interest rate, money wage, and, in an open economy, foreign exchange rate.

Figure 7.13 highlights an important feature of the neoclassical model, namely that the level of real GNP is determined solely by the position of the aggregate supply curve. Factors that shift only the aggregate demand curve—for example, changes in the money supply, changes in government spending and taxation, and autonomous changes in investment—will lead to changes in the equilibrium price level but not in real GNP.

Full employment: A level of employment that occurs at the equilibrium level of output predicted by the neoclassical model. Only frictional unemployment exists.

Associated with the equilibrium level of real GNP determined by the neoclassical aggregate supply curve is a level of employment that we refer to as **full employment.** Thus we call the level of real GNP (Y^*) in Figure 7.13 the full employment level of real GNP. As we discuss below, there is a corresponding level of unemployment that is commonly denoted as the *natural rate of unemployment.*

Figure 7.13   The Aggregate Supply and Demand Curves

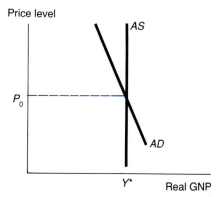

The aggregate supply curve *AS* depicts combinations of the price level and output at which equilibrium exists in the labor market. The aggregate demand curve *AD* shows combinations of the price level and output that are consistent with equilibrium in the output, financial, money, and, in an open economy, foreign exchange markets. The intersection of the two curves at price level P_0 and real GNP Y^* indicates the unique price-output combination that is consistent with simultaneous equilibrium in all markets in the economy.

7.5   THE NATURAL RATE OF UNEMPLOYMENT

We have seen how the level of prices, interest rates, output, and employment are determined in the neoclassical model. Conspicuously absent from the discussion has been any mention of unemployment. Recall that a key feature of the neoclassical model is the assumption that prices adjust to continuously maintain equilibrium in the various markets. It might seem, therefore, that the existence of unemployment, which suggests that there is an excess supply of labor, is inconsistent with the assumptions of the neoclassical model. If the labor market is in equilibrium, how can there be any unemployment?

To answer this question requires recognition of two facts. First, the labor market is in a constant state of flux. Not only do individuals enter and leave the labor force continuously, but labor demand varies across firms as they experience variations in the relative demand for their output. This instability of jobs—in an average year one in every nine jobs disappears and one in every eight is newly created—has been estimated to account for roughly one quarter of the average unemployment rate.[18] Second, information about jobs is costly. It takes time for new workers entering the labor force, and for workers who have been laid off or quit previous jobs, to discover which employers have vacancies and how wages vary across employers.

---

[18] Jonathan S. Leonard, "In the Wrong Place at the Wrong Time: The Extent of Frictional and Structural Unemployment," National Bureau of Economic Research Working Paper No. 1979 (July 1986).

Frictional unemployment: Unemployment associated with the typical flow of new entrants into the labor market and quits, as well as permanent layoffs reflecting a change in the composition of output produced by the economy.

Natural rate of unemployment: The rate of unemployment associated with the neoclassical model. It consists solely of frictional unemployment.

When we take into account the continuous flows to unemployment together with workers' imperfect information about job vacancies, we see that unemployment is no longer inconsistent with the neoclassical model. At any single moment, there exist new entrants into the labor market who are spending time searching for acceptable jobs. There also exist laid-off workers who are either searching for alternative jobs or awaiting recall. And there are workers who quit their jobs and are searching for other jobs. This kind of unemployment is generally referred to as **frictional unemployment.**

Sometimes part of frictional unemployment, called *structural unemployment*, is caused by a change in the composition of aggregate output across firms. For example, the replacement of steel with plastic in automobiles led to a shift in employment from steel factories to firms making plastic. During this transition, some steel workers experienced structural unemployment.

To summarize, when the labor market is in equilibrium, there exists a positive unemployment rate because workers continuously move into and out of the labor force and between jobs. To signify that this unemployment rate is "natural," or consistent with equilibrium in the labor market, it is generally called the **natural rate of unemployment.**[19] The corresponding level of employment is then often referred to as the *full employment* level.

Like equilibrium output and employment in the neoclassical model, "supply factors" are important in determining the natural rate of unemployment. Among these is the demographic composition of the labor force. For example, in the past 20 years, young workers and female workers have come to make up an increasing proportion of the labor force. Young workers tend to change jobs more frequently than older workers, as they search for a job that is to their liking. Both young workers and female workers tend to enter and leave the labor force more frequently than older male workers, as they combine periods of employment with periods of school and home activity. As a result, the natural unemployment rate rose in the 1970s and early 1980s. According to the September 11, 1984 *Wall Street Journal*, "Until the late 1950s, most government agencies and economists put the [natural jobless rate] at about 4 percent. But as the baby-boom generation and more women entered the labor market, the figure began to creep up. The Congressional Budget Office, for instance, puts the natural unemployment rate at 6 percent."

Unemployment insurance also affects the natural unemployment rate. Such insurance compensates workers who have lost their jobs and are "looking for work."[20] Unemployment compensation reduces the cost to a worker of

[19] Unemployment may also result if prices in the economy do not adjust quickly enough to ensure that all markets (particularly, the labor market) are continuously in equilibrium. Unemployment associated with labor market disequilibrium is sometimes referred to as "involuntary" unemployment. We analyze such unemployment in subsequent chapters.

[20] For the most part, state governments set eligibility rules and benefit levels. Generally, an unemployed worker must have been employed for some minimum period of time in order to qualify for unemployment compensation. In addition, the length of time (generally less than one year) over which benefits will be paid out is limited.

being unemployed and thus increases the average length of time before unemployed workers accept alternative employment. As a consequence, it raises the natural unemployment rate. Minimum wage legislation also raises the natural rate of unemployment, since a minimum wage tends to reduce employment and raise unemployment among low-productivity workers.

In recent years a large body of literature has analyzed labor markets and the sources of unemployment. This literature on search and labor contracts is important enough that we devote all of Chapter 15 to it. Among other things, we will discover that an understanding of the natural rate of unemployment is important in determining the effects of government policies aimed at the unemployed.

SUMMARY

An analysis of an economy can be quite complex since we must look simultaneously at the activity in a number of markets. Our task is simplified, however, by our ability to collapse the activity in these markets into two curves: the aggregate supply curve and the aggregate demand curve. The intersection of the aggregate demand and aggregate supply curves depicts the price level and output associated with simultaneous equilibrium in the various markets in an economy—the labor, financial, output, and money markets in the closed economy, and the labor, financial, output, money, and foreign exchange markets in the open economy.

The aggregate supply curve depicts combinations of output and price levels that reflect the underlying level of employment determined in the labor market. In the neoclassical macroeconomic model, the aggregate supply curve is vertical. This reflects the fact that a change in the price level ultimately leads to an equiproportionate change in equilibrium money wages. The result is that there is no change in either the real wage or the equilibrium level of employment. Since employment is not affected by changes in the price level, neither is real GNP. As we have seen, crucial to the above analysis are the two key assumptions of the neoclassical model: flexible prices and fully informed economic agents.

The aggregate demand curve depicts all combinations of output and levels of output prices associated with equilibrium in the output, financial, and money markets. The aggregate demand curve shows that there is an inverse relationship between the price level and demand for real GNP. A lower price level increases the real supply of money. In the financial market, this appears as an increase in the supply of loanable funds and results in a lower interest rate. In a closed economy, the lower interest rate increases consumption and investment demand and output must rise to restore equilibrium in the output market. In an open economy, the lower interest rate also increases net capital inflows, leading to a depreciation of the dollar and a rise in net export demand.

At any moment, there will always be some new entrants into the labor market who are spending time searching for an acceptable job. There will also be some laid-off workers who are either searching for an alternative job or awaiting recall. And there will be workers who have quit their job as a result of dissatisfaction and are searching for another job. The resulting unemployment, generally referred to as frictional unemployment, comprises the natural rate of unemployment in the neoclassical model. The corresponding level of employment is the full employment level.

LOOKING AHEAD

This chapter presented a view of the economy from the perspective of neoclassical macroeconomic analysis. The useful tools of aggregate supply and demand were introduced as an aid in determining such variables as the equilibrium price level, output, interest rate, and employment level. In the next two chapters, we look at factors that, by altering the position of either the aggregate supply or demand curve, affect equilibrium output, employment, interest rates, and prices. Among the topics we consider are the effects of monetary and fiscal policy changes, "supply-side" economics, and the macroeconomic effects of oil embargoes.

SUMMARY OF KEY EQUATIONS

demand for loanable funds

$$
\begin{aligned}
LF^d &\equiv A_f^s + A_g^s \\
&= I^d + (G^d - T)
\end{aligned}
\tag{7.1}
$$

supply of loanable funds (closed economy)

$$
\begin{aligned}
LF^s &\equiv A_h^d + A_b^d \\
&= YD - C^d + M^s/P - L^d
\end{aligned}
\tag{7.2}
$$

supply of loanable funds (open economy)

$$
\begin{aligned}
LF^s &\equiv A_h^d + A_b^d - AF_h^d + A_{for}^d \\
&= YD - C^d + M^s/P - L^d + (A_{for}^d - AF_h^d)
\end{aligned}
\tag{7.3}
$$

KEY TERMS

REVIEW QUESTIONS

1. What are the two key assumptions of the neoclassical model? Are these assumptions more appropriate for a long-run or short-run analysis of the economy's performance? Why?

2. What information is summarized in the aggregate supply curve? Is this curve a supply curve in the ordinary sense? Why or why not?

3. Why is the neoclassical aggregate supply curve vertical? What does this curve tell us?

4. Starting from a position of labor market equilibrium, illustrate the effect of a reduction in the price level. What happens to the money wage, real wage, and employment? Now suppose that firms are aware that output prices are lower in general, but workers are not aware of this. Show the effect of reduction in the price level on the labor market. (Hint: to do this, graph labor demand and supply against the money wage.) What happens to the money wage, the real wage, and the employment level? What does the aggregate supply curve look like in this case?

5. What information is summarized by the aggregate demand curve?

   (a) How does this curve differ from the ordinary demand curve of microeconomics?

   (b) A student at a university whose major claim to fame is a large smokestack with lights on top and a mascot who walks around with a big hammer gave the following answer in response to a test question: "The aggregate demand curve slopes downward because a reduction in price causes demand to increase." Did the student score well on this question? Why or why not?

6. Explain why the demand for loanable funds curve is downward-sloping and the supply of loanable funds curve is upward-sloping.

7. Why would a rise in the level of output prices, other things being held constant, not directly affect households' real income? Would it affect their money income?

8. Suppose that the price level rises.

   (a) What happens to the real supply of money, the demand for real money balances, the supply of nominal money balances, and the demand for nominal money balances?

   (b) What happens to the real demand for and supply of loanable funds? Explain why this happens. Illustrate the resulting effect on equilibrium in the financial market.

   (c) What happens to the interest rate that clears the financial market?

   (d) What effect does the change in the interest rate have on output demand? Will the output market be characterized by excess demand or supply? What about the money market?

(e) To restore equilibrium in all markets, must real GNP rise or fall?

9. Summarize the explanation for the downward-sloping aggregate demand curve.

10. What effect does an increase in U.S. interest rates have on the demand for and supply of dollars in the foreign exchange market? Why does this happen?

(a) Illustrate the effect on the equilibrium price of the dollar in the foreign exchange market.

(b) What happens to U.S. households' import demand and export demand by foreigners?

11. Discuss the additional considerations that have to be taken into account when we derive the aggregate demand curve for the open, as opposed to the closed, economy.

12. What do we mean by the natural rate of unemployment?

13. What effect would a reduction in unemployment compensation have on the natural rate of unemployment? Why?

14. Do you think that unemployment can be productive in any way? Are there cases where the occurrence of unemployment today can result in future output gains to the economy? (For example, think about possible gains to "search" unemployment).

An Algebraic Derivation of the Equilibrium Output, Price Level, Interest Rate, Employment, and Money Wage

In this chapter, we have seen how the aggregate demand curve summarizes simultaneous equilibria in the output, financial, and money markets. At each price level (P), the curve indicates the level of output (Y) and implicitly the interest rate (r), associated with equilibrium in these three markets. We have also seen how a graphical analysis of the labor market can be used to derive, for a given price level P, the levels of the money wage W and employment N consistent with equilibrium in the labor market. By changing the level of prices, this labor market analysis, combined with the aggregate production function that relates employment to real GNP, can be used to trace out points on the aggregate supply curve.

Finally, we have seen how we can combine the aggregate demand and supply curves to depict graphically the price level and real GNP consistent with equilibrium in the labor, output, money, and financial markets. We also know that an equilibrium interest rate, money wage, and level of employment are also implied at the point these two curves intersect, although they are not shown on the aggregate demand and aggregate supply diagram.

In this appendix, we will retrace the steps taken to derive the equilibrium price level (P^*), real GNP (Y^*), employment (N^*), interest rate (r^*), and money wage (W^*), by using algebraic rather than graphical analysis. We start by introducing linear approximations for the key behavioral relations underlying the various markets. Specifically, for the labor market, we have

$$N^d = f - g \cdot (W/P) \tag{A7.1}$$

and

$$N^s = h + j \cdot (W/P) \tag{A7.2}$$

These two linear equations indicate that firms' labor demand (N^d) is inversely related to the real wage, and households' labor supply (N^s) is directly related to the real wage.

The aggregate budget constraint allows us to focus on just two of the other three markets in the economy. Let's consider the output and money markets. For the output market, the key underlying behavioral relations are

$$C^d = a + b \cdot (Y - CCA - T) - c \cdot r \tag{A7.3}$$

$$I^d = d - e \cdot r \tag{A7.4}$$

Equation A7.3 indicates that households' consumption demand (C^d) is directly related to real disposable income and inversely related to the interest rate, while Equation A7.4 indicates that firms' investment demand (I^d) is inversely related to the interest rate.

For the money market, the key underlying behavioral relation is

$$L^d = l \cdot Y - m \cdot r \qquad \text{(A7.5)}$$

Equation A7.5 indicates that households' money demand is directly related to real income and inversely related to the interest rate.

The equilibrium money wage equates the demand for labor (N^d) with the supply of labor (N^s). That is, the equilibrium wage W^* satisfies

$$N^d = N^s \qquad \text{(A7.6)}$$

Substituting Equations A7.1 and A7.2 into A7.6, the equilibrium money wage satisfies

$$f - g \cdot (W^*/P) = h + j \cdot (W^*/P) \qquad \text{(A7.7)}$$

Solving Equation A7.7 for the equilibrium money wage W^*, we obtain

$$W^* = [(f - h)/(g + j)] \cdot P \qquad \text{(A7.8)}$$

Note that, as we discussed in the text, Equation A7.8 indicates that the equilibrium money wage is proportionate to the price level. Thus changes in the price level do not lead to changes in the equilibrium real wage.

We can now obtain the equilibrium employment level N^* by substituting Equation A7.8 into either Equation A7.1 or A7.2. Doing so, we obtain

$$N^* = [1/(j + g)] \cdot [jf + gh] \qquad \text{(A7.9)}$$

Equation A7.9 tells us that the equilibrium level of employment does *not* depend on the level of prices.

We can substitute Equation A7.8 into the aggregate production function $Y = f(N, \overline{K})$ to obtain the equilibrium real GNP Y^* for given a fixed capital stock $\overline{K}$. Doing so, we obtain:

$$Y^* = f(N^*, \overline{K}) = f\{[1/(j + g)] \cdot [jf + gh], \overline{K}\} \qquad \text{(A7.10)}$$

As Equation A7.10 indicates, since equilibrium employment is independent of the price level, so too is equilibrium real GNP. Graphing Equation A7.10 against the price level thus gives us a *vertical* aggregate supply curve at the level of real GNP equal to Y^*.

To derive an expression for the aggregate demand curve, let's solve for the relationship between the price and real GNP consistent with equilibrium in the output and money markets. By virtue of the aggregate budget constraint (Equation 4.18), equilibrium in these two markets implies equilibrium in the financial market. In a closed economy, the conditions for equilibrium in these output and money markets are

$$C^d + I^d + CCA + G^d = Y \qquad \text{(A7.11)}$$

and

$$L^d = M^s/P \qquad \text{(A7.12)}$$

Substituting the expressions from consumption demand (Equation A7.3), investment demand (Equation A7.4), and money demand (Equation A7.5) into the equilibrium conditions (Equation A7.11 and A7.12), we obtain

$$a + b \cdot (Y - CCA - T) - c \cdot r + d - e \cdot r + CCA + G^d = Y \qquad \text{(A7.13)}$$

and

$$l \cdot Y - m \cdot r = M^s/P \qquad \text{(A7.14)}$$

Solving Equation A7.13 for output Y, we obtain

$$Y = CCA + [1/(1 - b)] \cdot [a' - c' \cdot r] \qquad \text{(A7.15)}$$

where $a' = a + d + G^d$ and $c' = c + e$. Changes in the variable a' indicate changes in the autonomous component of consumption (the term a in Equation A7.3), autonomous investment demand (d in Equation A7.3), and government purchases of goods and services (G^d). By autonomous, we mean that part of households' and firms' output demand that is independent of the variables to be determined by the analysis, particularly income and the interest rate. The variable c' indicates the combined response of consumption demand (c in Equation A7.3) and investment demand (e in Equation A7.4) to a one-unit change in the interest rate.

Solving the money market equilibrium condition (Equation A7.14) for the interest rate r yields

$$r = (1/m)(l \cdot Y - M^s/P) \qquad \text{(A7.16)}$$

Substituting this expression into the equilibrium condition for the output market (Equation A7.15), we obtain

$$Y = CCA + [1/(1 - b)] \cdot [a' - (c' \cdot l/m) \cdot Y + (c'/m)(M^s/P)] \qquad \text{(A7.17)}$$

Solving for Y, we have

$$Y = [1/(1 - b + c' \cdot l/m)] \cdot [(1 - b) \cdot CCA + a' + (c'/m)(M^s/P)] \qquad \text{(A7.18)}$$

Note that we obtained Equation A7.18 by combining the equilibrium conditions for the output and money markets. In so doing, we were able to solve for output Y in terms of the price level P and a host of parameters. For any price level P, Equation A7.18 tells us the output level that is consistent with simultaneous equilibrium in the output and money markets, and thus, by the aggregate budget constraint, the financial market. Thus Equation A7.18 is precisely the equation for the aggregate demand curve. According to this equation, a rise in the price level P, by reducing the real money supply, M^s/P, leads to a fall in the level of output Y associated with simultaneous equilibrium in the output, financial, and money markets. In other words, the aggregate demand curve *slopes downward*.

Combining the expressions for the aggregate supply curve (Equation A7.10) and the aggregate demand curve (Equation A7.18), we can solve for the equilibrium levels of prices and output. Since aggregate supply is independent of the price level in the neoclassical model, Equation A7.10 is sufficient to define the equilibrium level of output Y^*. To obtain an expression for the equilibrium level of prices P^*, substitute Equation A7.10 into Equation A7.18 to obtain

$$f\{[1/(j + g)] \cdot [jf + gh], \overline{K}\}$$
$$= [1/(1 - b + c' \cdot l/m)] \cdot [(1 - b) \cdot CCA + a' + (c'/m)(M^s/P)] \quad \text{(A7.19)}$$

Solving for the equilibrium price level, we have

$$P^* = \left[M^s \cdot (c'/m)\right] \cdot \left[1/\{(1 - b + c' \cdot l/m) \cdot f([1/(j + g)] \right.$$
$$\left. \cdot [jg + gh], \overline{K}) - (1 - b)CCA - a'\}\right] \quad \text{(A7.20)}$$

Equations A7.8, A7.9, A7.10, and A7.20 are expressions for the equilibrium money wage, employment, real GNP and price level, respectively. We can obtain an expression for the equilibrium interest rate by substituting the expressions for the equilibrium levels of output Y^* and prices P^* into Equation A7.16. As the equations indicate, and as we will see in the following chapters, changes in such variables as the money supply (M^s), government spending (G^d), autonomous investment (the parameter d in the investment demand function), labor supply (the parameter h in the labor supply function), and the capital stock ($\overline{K}$) will affect the equilibrium levels of prices, output, employment, wages, and the interest rate. From the behavioral equations (A7.3 and A7.4), we can then infer the effects of such macroeconomic shocks on households' consumption spending and firms' investment purchases.

Chapter 8

Policy Changes and the Neoclassical Model

After cutting tax rates in the early 1980s, the Reagan administration responded to congressional pressure for tax increases by proposing various excise taxes. One of these proposed taxes was a nickel-per-gallon tax on gasoline. The revenue from the tax was to be targeted toward rebuilding the nation's failing transportation infrastructure. Not only was the program supposed to improve the nation's roads, but it was supposed to create 300,000 jobs as well. Chrysler Corporation president Lee Iacocca, who has long called for higher gasoline taxes, extended this line of thought by saying that if five cents per gallon would generate 300,000 jobs, why not make it 25 cents per gallon tax and create 1.5 million jobs? For that matter, why not make it a $2 tax per gallon and eliminate unemployment in America?

As the gasoline tax question makes clear, a widely held view exists both in and out of government that government fiscal policy can play a role in the overall management of the economy. One purpose of this chapter is to explore the impact of fiscal policy on the economy; in the process we will discover that, at least in the context of the neoclassical macroeconomic model, government spending increases will not increase aggregate employment.

Many individuals also believe that monetary policy plays a role in managing the levels of employment and real GNP, as the reaction of Congress and the stock market to the Fed's reports of changes in the rate of growth in the money supply indicate. A second purpose of this chapter is to examine the impact of monetary policy in the context of the neoclassical model.

Up until the last half century, the roles that government fiscal and monetary policies played in affecting the macroeconomy were minimized.

The view that government should not intervene in economic affairs was summarized by the eighteenth-century economist Adam Smith's defense of "laissez-faire" economics.[1] Laissez-faire is a French term meaning "allow (them) to do." Views changed, however, after the worldwide depression of the late 1920s and early 1930s, when real GNP fell drastically and unemployment levels reached staggering heights. In 1936, John Maynard Keynes provided the theoretical basis for government intervention in his *General Theory*, and the "New Deal" policies of Franklin D. Roosevelt were the first attempts to apply these ideas to the real world. Government intervention to stabilize the economy reached its zenith in the early 1960s when government "fine tuning" of the economy was a "fait accompli."[2]

With the onslaught of simultaneous high employment and high inflation in the early 1970s, the ability of government to influence the economy through monetary and fiscal policy became a hotly debated topic in economics and public policy. This debate fostered new macroeconomic analysis that attempted to develop an "equilibrium theory of business cycles."[3] The neoclassical model presented in Chapter 7 captures the flavor of the new equilibrium business cycle analysis. The vertical aggregate supply curve, which is the key element of the neoclassical model, implies that factors that affect aggregate supply are the sources of fluctuations in the rate of growth of real GNP and employment.

In this chapter, we show that a vertical aggregate supply curve means that monetary and fiscal policies that affect aggregate demand leave current output unchanged. Macroeconomic demand shocks fostered by changes in monetary policy do lead to inflation, however, and changes in fiscal policy do lead to changes in the way that output is divided among consumption, investment, and government spending. This division of output has potentially important effects. For example, changes in investment alter the size of the economy's future capital stock and thus its future productive capacity.

In the next chapter, we offer some explanations suggested by the neoclassical model for the changes in output and employment known as "business cycles."[4] Macroeconomic shocks that affect the position of the vertical aggregate supply curve and alter the full employment level of output are explanations

---

[1] Adam Smith, *An Inquiry into the Nature and Causes of the Wealth of Nations,* 1776.

[2] Another French term, meaning a thing done and not worth opposing (an accomplished fact).

[3] See Victor Zarnowitz, "Recent Work on Business Cycles in Historical Perspective: A Review of Theories and Evidence," *Journal of Economic Literature* 23 (June, 1985): 552. According to Zarnowitz, the objective of the new macroeconomic analysis is to develop "a general business cycle theory in strict adherence to the basic principles of the analysis of economic equilibrium: consistent pursuit of self-interest by individuals and continuous clearing of all markets by relative prices."

[4] J. Huston McCulloch ("The Monte Carlo Cycle in Business Activity," *Economic Inquiry* (September, 1975): 303–321) has shown that once an expansion or contraction in an economy has exceeded its minimum historical duration, the probability of its being reversed in a given month is independent of its age. Thus although suggestive, our use of the term "business cycle" is somewhat loose since output fluctuations do not show the periodicity typically associated with a "cycle."

of business cycles in the neoclassical model. Sources of these supply shocks include changes in marginal tax rates, unemployment insurance benefits, technology, and the supply of oil.

Most economists seriously doubt that the neoclassical model provides a comprehensive framework for explaining short-term fluctuations in output.[5] In later chapters, we consider in some detail modifications of the neoclassical model that introduce sluggish adjustment of prices in the short run. These chapters introduce the potential for demand shocks to affect current output, as well as a potential role for government fiscal and monetary policy to stabilize the economy at full employment.

8.1 MACROECONOMIC ANALYSIS: AN OVERVIEW

The macroeconomic analysis of aggregate demand and supply developed in Chapter 7 allows us to depict graphically the equilibrium values of real GNP and the price level for a particular period. A graphical analysis of the financial market, which underlies the aggregate demand curve, illustrates that the equilibrium interest rate is the one that equates the quantity of loanable funds demanded to the quantity supplied. The graphical analysis of the labor market, which underlies the aggregate supply curve, illustrates the accompanying equilibrium levels of money wage and employment as those that equate the quantity of labor demanded to the quantity supplied.

Having characterized equilibrium in the economy, the next step is to explore how a change in a particular variable—such as the money supply, government spending, taxes, or the supply of oil—alters the equilibrium values of prices, wages, employment, real GNP, and the interest rate. This is the task of this and future chapters. We keep the analysis manageable by usually examining how a change in only one of these exogenous variables alters the equilibrium values of prices and the other endogenous variables. **Exogenous variables** are variables such as government spending and the money supply that are not determined by the analysis. Exogenous variables are taken as given. **Endogenous variables** are variables such as prices, real GNP, and the interest rate that are to be determined by the analysis.

In macroeconomic analysis, we look at the effect on the economy of what is known as a **macroeconomic shock,** which can be defined as a change in an exogenous variable. These changes can come either from the private sector or the public sector. Some examples of private sector shocks are a reduction in firms' investment plans or an increase in households' consumption expenditures. Public sector macroeconomic shocks include unexpectedly large deficits or a change in the pattern of monetary growth. The crucial facet of a shock is that it alters the equilibrium state of the economy.

Exogenous variables: Variables such as government spending and the money supply that are not determined by the analysis. Exogenous variables are taken as given.

Endogenous variables: Variables such as prices, real GNP, and the interest rate, that are to be determined by the analysis.

Macroeconomic shock: A change in an exogenous variable.

---

[5] Some of these criticisms of existing equilibrium theories of business cycles are discussed by Zarnowitz (see footnote 3).

Our task throughout much of the book will be to compare the new equilibrium values of prices, real GNP, and other endogenous variables with the values these variables would have taken in the absence of the shock. For instance, in the next section when we consider the effect of a change in the money supply, we identify this monetary shock as the difference between M_0^s, what the money supply would be without the shock, and M_1^s, what the money supply is with the shock. Our analysis will determine the difference between the levels of such equilibrium variables as prices and real GNP with and without the shock. For example, we will compare the price level P_0 that would exist without a monetary shock with the price level P_1 that would exist with the shock.

Interpreting Changes in Levels in Terms of Rates of Change

It is important to realize that although our analysis is couched in terms of levels, the predictions concerning how shocks can alter levels of various variables imply predictions concerning the rate of change in these variables. For instance, let's say that the price level in the previous period was $\overline{P}$. In the absence of the monetary shock, the current price level would have been P_0 and the rate of change in the price level would then have been $(P_0 - \overline{P})/\overline{P}$. With the monetary shock, the new equilibrium price level is P_1 and the rate of change in the price level would be $(P_1 - \overline{P})/\overline{P}$. If our analysis predicts that P_1 is greater than P_0, then we can interpret the macroeconomic shock of a higher money supply as both increasing the price *level* from what it would have been and increasing the *rate of change* in prices (the rate of inflation) from what it would have been. For example, suppose that the price level in the preceding period ($\overline{P}$) was 100, the price level in the current period in the absence of the shock (P_0) would have been 110 and with the shock the price level (P_1) is 120. Then the monetary shock raises the current price level from 110 to 120 and increases the rate of inflation from 10 percent to 20 percent.

The above discussion makes an important point. When the macroeconomic analysis in this book predicts a change in the current *levels* of variables such as prices and real GNP, this is the same as predicting a change in the rate of inflation and the growth rate of real GNP. Similarly, an increase in an exogenous variable such as the money supply (from M_0^s to M_1^s) can be interpreted as an increase in the growth in the money supply from its level in the previous period ($\overline{M}$)—from $(M_0^s - \overline{M})/\overline{M}$ to $(M_1^s - \overline{M})/\overline{M}$.

Analyzing Changes in Aggregate Demand in Two Steps

Analyzing how the economy adjusts to a change in an exogenous variable can be quite complex. There are three markets behind the aggregate demand curve—the output, financial, and money markets. And there are the labor and other input markets behind the aggregate supply curve. The starting point will always be an initial situation of equilibrium in the various markets.

Graphically, we start at the point of intersection of the aggregate demand and aggregate supply curves. This is the easy part.

Analysis in macroeconomics often involves examining macroeconomic shocks that affect aggregate demand. Examples of such shocks are changes in the money supply, government spending, planned investment, or consumption. As we will see, changes such as these lead to shifts in the aggregate demand curve. In order to explain how the economy reaches a new equilibrium, we will break down our analysis of the adjustment process into two steps:

1. An examination of the initial effects of the macroeconomic shock on the financial, money, and output markets at the original levels of output and prices.

2. An examination of the adjustment in output and/or the price level that restores equilibrium in all of the various markets in the economy.

In step one, we utilize the graphs of the financial and money markets to determine what would happen if prices and output did not change. As we will see, the analysis in step one is critical to understanding the process by which the economy adjusts. It will provide us with the rationale for any shift in the aggregate demand curve. However, an important limitation of the analysis in step one is that it does not actually depict the adjustments required to reach the economy's new equilibrium.

In step two, we utilize the aggregate demand and aggregate supply curves to determine how prices and/or output adjust to restore equilibrium in the economy. With the vertical aggregate supply curve of the neoclassical model, the adjustment to a change in aggregate demand takes the form of price adjustments alone. However, in later chapters we will introduce conditions under which output adjustments play a critical role in restoring equilibrium. At that time, we will rely not only on aggregate demand and supply analysis but also on what are know as ''IS'' and ''LM'' curves to illustrate the change in real GNP required to restore equilibrium in the economy.

Our two-step procedure to describe the economy's adjustment to a macroeconomic demand shock in essence means assuming that the interest rate adjusts very rapidly (nearly instantaneously) in response to disequilibrium in the financial market, while the price level and output adjust more slowly. This adjustment procedure, one that macroeconomists have frequently adopted, follows in the time honored tradition of the noted classical economist Swedish economist K. Wicksell, among others.[6] Yet the fact that we break the analysis down into these two steps should not be taken to mean that there is an invariant chronology in the adjustment process. The steps used to describe the adjustment process between two equilibriums may not actually occur in the particular order we present. Nevertheless, altering the precise sequence

---

[6] Wicksell. *Interest and Prices,* translation by R. F. Kahn (London, 1936). For a further discussion of the contributions of Wicksell, see Chapter XV, ''A Critique of Classical and Keynesian Interest Theory,'' in Patinkin, *Money, Interest, and Prices* (Harper and Row, 1965).

of events will not affect the final outcome. It will, however, obscure the intuition of why the adjustments are occurring.

8.2   MONETARY POLICY IN A CLOSED ECONOMY

We saw in Chapter 5 that the central bank, which in the United States is the Federal Reserve System, determines the level of the money supply and thus monetary policy. The Fed alters the money supply predominantly by changing the monetary base. It does this through the open-market sale or purchase of government securities. Changes in the monetary base lead to multiple changes in the money supply through the deposit creation process. In this section, we analyze the effects of a change in the nominal money supply on real GNP, employment, money wages, the price level, and the interest rate in the context of the neoclassical model.

The Impact of an Increase in Monetary Growth If Prices and Output Do Not Change

Suppose that the monetary authorities picked a higher level for the money supply in the current period. We will let M_1^s denote this new, higher money supply and M_0^s denote what the money supply would have been otherwise. Remember that this change can be interpreted not only as an increase in the money supply level but also as an increase in the rate of growth of the money supply. We begin our analysis by determining the effects of a higher money supply on the output and financial markets at the initial price level and real GNP. This is what we referred to above as the first step in analyzing the effect of a change in aggregate demand.

From the depository institution financing constraint, we know that an increase in the money supply means an equal increase in the supply of loans that depository institutions make. Figure 8.1(a) shows the increase in the real supply of loanable funds that accompanies an increase in the real money supply as a shift to the right in the supply of loanable funds curve from LF_0^s to LF_1^s.

As a result of the increase in the real supply of loanable funds, the interest rate falls from r_0 to r_1 in order to maintain equilibrium in the financial market. The reduction in the interest rate induces firms to increase the quantity of loanable funds demanded to finance increased investment, as Figure 8.1(a) shows by the movement from A to C along the demand for loanable funds curve LF^d.

At the same time, the fall in the interest rate causes households to reduce the quantity of loanable funds supplied, as Figure 8.1(a) shows by the movement from point B to C along the new loanable funds curve LF_1^s. Households reduce the quantity of loanable funds supplied in response to the lower interest rate in part to increase their consumption demand. The

Figure 8.1 The Effect of an Increase in the Money Supply on the Financial and Money Markets

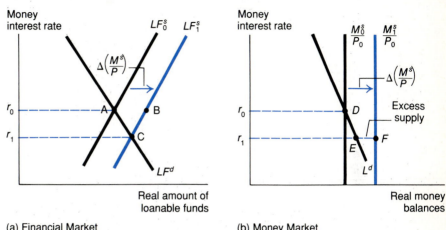

(a) Financial Market   (b) Money Market

An increase in the money supply from M_0^s to M_1^s not only increases the real supply of money as in part (b) but means an equivalent increase in the real supply of loanable funds from LF_0^s to LF_1^s, as in part (a). The interest rate that clears the financial market is bid down from r_0 to r_1. At this lower interest rate and original price level P_0 and output Y_0, there is an excess supply of money, shown by the gap EF in part (b).

reduction in the quantity of loanable funds supplied by households also reflects an increase in the quantity of real money balances demanded. This increase is shown in Figure 8.1(b) by the movement down the money demand curve from point D to point E.

While the new lower interest rate r_1 clears the financial market, there is an excess demand in the output market as the lower interest rate stimulates firms' investment and households' consumption demand. The aggregate budget constraint states that the sum of excess demands in the output, financial, and money markets must equal zero. With the financial market in equilibrium, the excess demand for output must be mirrored by an excess supply of money. This excess supply of money is shown by the gap EF in Figure 8.1(b).

The above outcome has a straightforward interpretation. With the increase in the money supply, individuals' actual holdings of real money balances now exceed their desired holdings. This is the excess supply of money. They would like to exchange their excess money holdings for additional output. This explains the excess demand for output.

The Effect on Equilibrium Prices and Output: An Analysis Using Aggregate Demand And Supply Curves

The intersection of the aggregate demand curve AD_0 and the aggregate supply curve AS in Figure 8.2 shows the equilibrium price and output combination,

Figure 8.2   The Effect of an Increase in the Money Supply on Output and Prices

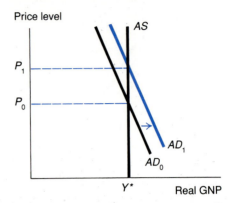

An increase in the money supply shifts the aggregate demand curve up and to the right from AD_0 to AD_1; the equilibrium price level rises from P_0 to P_1, with no change in real output.

P_0 and Y^*, that existed prior to the monetary shock. With an increase in the money supply, we have demonstrated that there will be excess demand in the output market at the original price level and real GNP. This means that this initial combination of output and prices no longer identifies a point on the aggregate demand curve. (Recall that the aggregate demand curve represents combinations of output and price levels associated with *simultaneous* equilibrium in the output, financial, and money markets.) Further, the excess demand in the output market at the original output and price level means the new aggregate demand curve AD_1 lies to the right and above the original aggregate demand curve AD_0.

Given excess demand in the output market at the original output and price level, either an increase in output or a rise in prices will restore equilibrium in the output market. In the neoclassical model with flexible prices and complete information, the response to excess demand in the output market consists of an increase only in the level of prices. Buyers competing for the scarce output bid up prices. The increase in the price level reduces the real money supply and thus the real supply of loanable funds. As a result, the interest rate rises, leading to a fall in the quantity of firms' investment demand and households' consumption demand.[7] This process of rising prices, falling real supply of loanable funds, rising interest rate, and decreasing consumption and investment continues until the excess demand for output is eliminated.

---

[7] Unless otherwise noted, the expected rate of future inflation is constant in our analysis. Thus changes in the nominal interest rate imply equivalent changes in the expected real rate of interest (the nominal interest rate minus the expected rate of inflation).

As Figure 8.2 indicates, equilibrium is restored in the output market at the higher price level P_1 but the same real GNP Y^*.

In the labor market, the higher price level leads to an equiproportionate increase in the money wage with no change in either the real wage or the level of employment. The fact that neither employment nor real GNP is changed is summarized by the vertical aggregate supply curve in Figure 8.2.

In the financial market, as we saw in Figure 8.1(a), the increase in the nominal money supply shifted the supply of loanable funds to the right, which resulted in a lower interest rate. The reduction in the interest rate is only transitory, however. As output prices rise in response to the excess demand in the output market, the real money supply and the real supply of loanable funds return to their initial levels. In Figure 8.1, this adjustment involves a shift to the left in the supply of loanable funds curve back to its original position and equivalent shift to the left in the real supply of money.

In short, the neoclassical model predicts that changes in the nominal money supply result only in changes in money prices. No *real* variables are affected. An increase in the nominal money supply does not affect the real stock of money, the real interest rate, real consumption, real investment spending, the real wage, employment, or output. The fact that a change in the money supply has no long-run effect on any real variables when prices fully adjust is referred to as the **neutrality of money.**

Neutrality of money: In the neoclassical model, the fact that a change in the money supply has no long-run effect on any real variables.

The proposition that a change in the money supply can be neutral is practically as old as the economics profession itself. A description of the process by which the economy reacts to a change in the money supply is found in the writings of the classical economists, as evidenced by the following quote from David Ricardo in a work published in 1810:

> Increases in currency issued would be sent into every market, and would everywhere raise the prices of commodities, till they were absorbed in the general circulation. It is only during the interval of the issue, and their effect on prices, that we should be sensible of an abundance of money; interest would, during that interval, be under its natural level; but as soon as the additional sum of notes or currency became absorbed in the general circulation, the rate of interest would be as high, and new loans would be demanded with as much eagerness as before the additional issue.''[8]

8.3   THE EXCHANGE EQUATION: INFLATION AS A MONETARY PHENOMENON

The analysis we just completed contains an important lesson: Changes in the money supply can be a significant cause of changes in the price level.

---

[8] David Ricardo, *The High Price of Bullion* (1810).

The neoclassical model predicts that, if everything else is held constant, an increase in the money supply results in an equiproportionate increase in the price level. For instance, a 20 percent increase in the money supply will lead to a 20 percent increase in prices.

Figure 8.3 provides a striking illustration of the relationship between changes in the money supply and changes in the general price level. For the period 1963 to 1987, the inflation rate, as measured by semiannual changes in the GNP deflator, appears as the black line in Figure 8.3. The semiannual rate of growth of M1 lagged two years appears as the colored line in the figure. Lagged money growth is used instead of current money growth because changes in the money supply tend to affect inflation not immediately, but often with a lag of one to two years. This reflects the fact that the flexible price assumption of the neoclassical model is more likely to be met over a longer time period.

Figure 8.3 illustrates the generally close relationship between money supply growth and the inflation rate. As the figure indicates, changes in the money supply are generally mirrored by subsequent changes in the price level. Furthermore, the increasing inflation from the mid 1960s to 1980 is associated with a rising rate of growth in the money supply during this period.

Although Figure 8.3 illustrates the close relationship between changes in the price level and changes in the money supply, it also indicates that this relationship is not perfect. For one thing, as noted above, changes in the money supply often translate into price level changes only after some time lag. Furthermore, the inflation rate does not perfectly follow the same path as changes in the money supply. In fact, upon examining Figure 8.3, one cannot help but be struck by the divergence between the inflation rate and money supply growth that has occurred in the 1980s. While money supply growth has been quite rapid during this period, inflation has been relatively low. Obviously, then, other things besides changes in the money supply can have effects on the general price level. As we see below, the exchange equation provides a useful way of summarizing the effects of the money supply and these other factors on the price level.

Deriving the Exchange Equation

Exchange equation: An equation derived from equilibrium in the money market, expressed as $M^s \cdot V = P \cdot Y$.

Our preceding analysis focused on the effects of an increase in the money supply on the output and financial markets. If we focus instead on the money market and the demand for and supply of money, we obtain what is known as the **exchange equation.** The exchange equation is an alternative way of showing the relationship between changes in the money supply and changes in the price level. It provides the framework for what is often referred to as the quantity theory of money. Early expositions of the quantity theory of money are most often associated with Irving Fisher, the author of *The Purchasing Power of Money*, which was published in 1911.

Figure 8.3   Money Supply Growth and Inflation

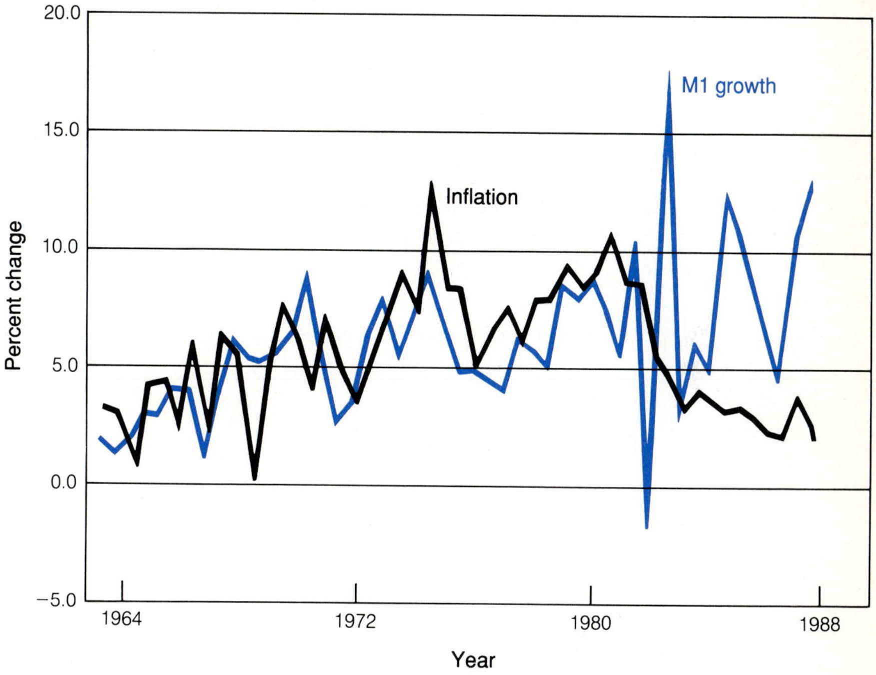

Source: The Economic Report of the President (1988) and various Federal Reserve publications.

The exchange equation has a simple form, namely,

$$M^s \cdot V = P \cdot Y \tag{8.1}$$

On the right side of the equation, $P \cdot Y$ represents the dollar value of GNP, which equals real output Y multiplied by price level P. On the left side of the equation, M^s represents the total supply of money in the economy and V represents the **velocity of money.** The velocity of money has a straightforward interpretation. Dividing Equation 8.1 by M^s, we see that the velocity of money is simply the ratio of nominal GNP to the money supply—i.e., $V = P \cdot Y/M^s$. Velocity may thus be interpreted as the average number of times the money supply turns over per year in transactions involving the purchase of final output. If the money supply is $400 billion and nominal gross national product is $2,400 billion, then the velocity of money is six. In general, the greater the nominal GNP for a given money supply, the higher the velocity, which indicates that money is turning over more rapidly in the economy.

The exchange equation is simply a statement of the equality between the quantity of money demanded and supplied that must hold when the

Velocity of money (V):
The average number of times the money supply turns over per year in transactions involving the purchase of final output.

economy is in equilibrium. To see this, recall that household real demand for money balances L^d is directly related to the real value of output Y. We may express this relationship by the linear equation

$$L^d = k \cdot Y, k > 0, \tag{8.2}$$

where k is the ratio of desired real money balances to output. Note that the parameter k itself depends on other variables, such as the money interest rate.

To derive the exchange equation, we consider the equality between the quantity of real money balances supplied and the quantity demanded:

$$M^s/P = L^d \tag{8.3}$$

Substituting the expression for the demand for money (Equation 8.2) into Equation 8.3, the money "market" equilibrium condition, we obtain the equation:

$$M^s/P = k \cdot Y \tag{8.4}$$

Multiplying each side of Equation 8.4 by the price level P and dividing each side by k (households' desired ratio of real money balances to real output), we can rewrite Equation 8.4 to obtain the following form of the exchange equation:

$$M^s \cdot (1/k) = P \cdot Y \tag{8.5}$$

Note that the term $(1/k)$ is simply the ratio of equilibrium nominal GNP to the money supply. Replacing $1/k$ by velocity V, Equation 8.5 becomes

$$M^s \cdot V = P \cdot Y \tag{8.6}$$

The inverse relationship between k and V indicates that a fall in money demand at any given level of real output means a higher velocity.

Interpreting the Exchange Equation

The exchange equation is useful because it summarizes in a very simple way the relationship between money and economic activity. The link we have just discussed is that a change in the money supply results in an equiproportionate change in prices, an idea that is known as the **quantity theory of money.** The early quantity theorists stressed that the velocity of money was stable and changed only slowly and very predictably. The number of times a dollar turned over in a given year was dependent upon such things as habits of payments and technology, and these were not factors given to rapid and unpredictable changes.

If velocity is fixed, then the exchange equation indicates that a change in the money supply results in an equiproportionate change in nominal GNP $(P \cdot Y)$. Of course, without additional assumptions, one cannot say whether an increase in nominal GNP means an increase in prices, real GNP, or both. However, since the early quantity theorists had their roots in the classical

Quantity theory of money: A theory that assumes that velocity is stable, so that changes in money supply will result in equiproportionate changes in nominal GNP.

model (just as modern monetarists have their roots in the neoclassical model), they took real output to be determined solely by supply factors. With real GNP given, a change in the money supply thus translates into an equiproportionate change in the price level.

Our analysis in Section 8.2 provides the formal justification for the conclusions reached by quantity theorists concerning the effects of a change in the money supply. According to the neoclassical model, real GNP is determined solely by the position of the vertical aggregate supply curve and thus not affected by changes in the money supply. Furthermore, the equilibrating adjustments occurring in the economy after an initial monetary disturbance mean that the equilibrium values of all other real variables, including the interest rate, are also not affected by a money supply change. All that is affected are money prices, which rise by exactly the same proportion as the money supply.

Since an increase in the money supply leads to an equiproportionate change in the price level with no change in output, it follows from the exchange equation that velocity must be unchanged. This makes intuitive sense. With no change in the interest rate, households maintain the same ratio of real money demand to output (k in Equation 8.3). Equilibrium in the money market thus means that the ratio of the real money supply to output, which is the reciprocal of velocity, is invariant as well.

Factors Affecting Velocity

The exchange equation is useful not only for interpreting the effects of money supply changes but also for determining the impact that nonmonetary shocks have on the economy. For example, later in this chapter we explore the effects of government fiscal policy within the context of the neoclassical model, and in Chapter 11 we will explore the effects of fiscal policy within the context of the predetermined price model. According to both models, a fiscal policy change such as an increase in government deficit spending causes nominal GNP to rise. In the neoclassical model, the increase in nominal GNP takes the form solely of higher output prices as the expansionary fiscal policy only succeeds in bidding up the price level. In contrast, in the predetermined price model the increase in nominal GNP takes the form solely of an increase in output. In this context, fiscal policy changes emerge as a potentially powerful tool for raising real GNP.

Whether or not a fiscal policy change raises output or prices, it affects nominal GNP by raising the velocity of money. To see this, note from the exchange equation that if the money supply is unchanged and nominal GNP is higher, then velocity must be higher. Behind this increase in velocity is a higher interest rate, which induces individuals to economize on their money holdings. To see why, we need only re-examine the equilibrium in the money market that underlies the exchange equation. Figure 8.4 indicates that with real output Y_0 and price level P_0, the quantity of money demanded equals the quantity supplied at the interest rate r_0.

Figure 8.4   **The Effect of an Increase in Output on the Money Market**

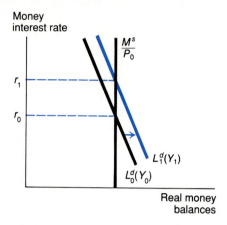

With an increase in output, household demand for money increases from L_0^d to L_1^d. The interest rate that would equate the quantity of money demanded and supplied rises from r_0 to r_1.

Suppose that there is an increase in government deficit spending and that the result is an increase in real GNP with no change in prices. This in fact will be the prediction of the predetermined price macroeconomic model discussed in Chapter 10 and 11. If real GNP increases from Y_0 to Y_1, money demand will increase at each interest rate, as households seek to increase their real money holdings to facilitate making increased transactions. This is shown in Figure 8.4 by the shift to the right in the money demand curve from L_0^d to L_1^d.

As Figure 8.4 illustrates, given the increase in money demand, equality between the quantity of money demanded and supplied is restored at the higher interest rate r_1. The rise in the interest rate leads individuals to economize on their money balances, so that even though income is higher, individuals desire to hold the same amount of real money balances. The fact that the increase in the interest rate increases the desired ratio of nominal output $(P \cdot Y)$ to money holdings (M^s) means that velocity (V) is higher.

If, as the neoclassical model predicts, an increase in government deficit spending only succeeds in driving up output prices, the same outcome occurs: the rise in velocity implied by the exchange equation reflects a higher interest rate. In this case, however, the rise in the interest rate that maintains equilibrium in the money market is in response to a fall in the real supply of money. Figure 8.5 shows the impact of an increase in the price level from P_0 to P_1 by the shift to the left in the real supply of money curve from M^s/P_0 to M^s/P_1. The interest rate must rise from r_0 to r_1 if the equality between the quantity of money demanded and supplied is to be restored.

Figure 8.5   The Effect of an Increase in the Price Level on the Money Market

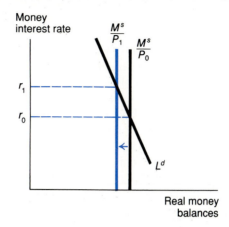

With an increase in the price level from P_0 to P_1, the real supply of money falls from M^s/P_0 to M^s/P_1. The interest rate that equates the quantity of money demanded and supplied rises from r_0 to r_1.

In summary, whether or not an increase in government spending causes a higher nominal output because it increases either the price level or real GNP, the increase in velocity implied by the exchange equation is induced by a higher interest rate. Fiscal policy changes, however, are not the only shocks that affect the velocity of money. For example, the neoclassical model predicts that an exogenous increase in investment demand, like an increase in government spending, causes the price level and the interest rate to rise but leaves real GNP unaffected. Since P is higher while M^s and Y are unchanged, the exchange equation tells us that velocity increases. This simply reflects the fact that the higher interest rate causes individuals to economize on their money balances, so that money turns over more rapidly in the economy.

An exogenous change in real money demand is a final example of a shock that causes velocity to change. Suppose that households desired real money balances increase and household financial asset demand (real supply of loanable funds) falls. The fall in the supply of loanable funds will lead to a higher interest rate that reduces investment and consumption spending. At the original level of prices and output, the resulting excess supply in the output market will simply lead, according to the neoclassical model, to a bidding down of prices with no change in real GNP. The outcome—a lower nominal GNP—reflects a lower velocity of money. The intuition behind the change in velocity is straightforward. Since desired real money demand has exogenously increased, households must be holding more real balances at the new equilibrium. The fact that they are holding more real money balances means that money must on average be turning over less rapidly—that is, velocity must be lower.

Economists are divided as to whether or not exogenous shocks originating in the private sector are important empirically in causing velocity to vary over time. In fact, the stability of velocity is a focal point in the debate between those who believe that the government should actively attempt to stabilize the economy through appropriate adjustments in fiscal and monetary policy and those who believe in nonintervention. If velocity is relatively stable in the absence of shocks initiated by the government, then the case for active discretionary policy by the government is weakened since nominal GNP will be fairly stable without government intervention.

We will return to the issues raised here in subsequent discussions throughout the book. At this juncture, let us improve our understanding of the exchange equation by showing how we can use it to interpret the behavior of money, output, and prices over time.

The Evidence on Monetary Changes and Prices

Our discussion above has been in terms of changes in the levels of the money supply and prices. However, the exchange equation ($MV = PY$) can be reinterpreted in terms of rates of change in the different variables:

$$\%\Delta M^s \quad + \quad \%\Delta V \quad \approx \quad \%\Delta P \quad + \quad \%\Delta Y \qquad \textbf{(8.7)}$$

| Percent change in money supply | Percent change in velocity | Percent change price level | Percent change in real GNP |

Using Equation 8.7, we can interpret the behavior of money, output, and prices over time. Table 8.1 presents data on changes in the money supply and the price level, as well as data on the other components of the exchange equation, for three ten-year periods (1955 to 1964, 1964 to 1973, and 1973 to 1982) as well as the recent six-year period of 1982 to 1987. We use averages over extended time periods since the assumptions of the neoclassical model are more likely to be met over a longer time period.

For each ten-year period preceding the 1982 to 1987 period, the money supply grew at an increasing rate. In the 1973 to 1982 period, the rate of growth of the money supply (6.8 percent annual rate) was more than three times that for the 1955 to 1964 period (2.1 percent annual rate). Accordingly, the rate of growth of prices was also higher in each succeeding ten-year period, as the rate of inflation rose from an annual rate of 2 percent during the 1955 to 1964 period to a 4.2 percent and then to a 7.8 percent annual rate during the 1964 to 1973 and 1973 to 1982 periods, respectively. However, note that the rates of increase in the price level do not equal the rates of increase in the money supply.

The neoclassical model predicts that increases in the money supply lead to equiproportionate increases in prices, *other things being equal.* However,

THE MATHEMATICAL RELATION BETWEEN VARIABLES AND THEIR GROWTH RATES

If we let the variable z denote the product of the variables a and b, (that is, $z = a \cdot b$), then the following relationship holds as an approximation:

$$\text{Percent change} = \text{Percent change} + \text{Percent change}$$
$$\text{in } z \qquad\qquad \text{in } a \qquad\qquad \text{in } b$$

For example, suppose that a is 100 and b is 50, which means that z equals 5000. If a increase by 2 percent, to 102, and b increases by 4 percent, to 52, then z, which increases from 5000 to 5304 (102 multiplied by 52), has increased by approximately 6 percent (actually, 6.08 percent).

For our exchange equation, we can say that $M^s \cdot V = P \cdot Y$. The above discussion suggests the following approximations:

$$\text{Percent change} = \text{Percent change} + \text{Percent change}$$
$$\text{in } M^s \cdot V \qquad\qquad \text{in } M^s \qquad\qquad \text{in } V$$

and

$$\text{Percent change} = \text{Percent change} + \text{Percent change}$$
$$\text{in } P \cdot Y \qquad\qquad \text{in } P \qquad\qquad \text{in } Y$$

For example, if velocity does not change (change in V is 0 percent) and the money supply rises by 5 percent, then the percent change in $M^s \cdot V$ is the sum of these two changes, or 5 percent. Since the exchange equation indicates that $M^s \cdot V$ equals $P \cdot Y$, this means that nominal output $P \cdot Y$ grows by 5 percent as well. If real output Y grows by 3 percent, then we know from the above that the change in price level P equals approximately 2 percent, since the sum of percent change in P and the percent change in Y equals approximately 5 percent.

as we can see from Table 8.1, other things have not been equal over the time period covered. For example, until 1982, velocity exhibited a steady upward trend. In part, this rising velocity reflected an upward trend in interest rates over the past 30 some years, as well as technological innovations (such as automated tellers), both of which tended to reduce households' real money demand. The dynamic exchange equation (Equation 8.7) highlights the fact that an increasing velocity of money accentuates a rising money supply's effect on inflation.

Real output has also risen during each of the time periods due to an expanding labor force and increases in labor productivity. The exchange equation indicates that a rising real output offsets a higher money supply's effect on prices. For example, notice that in the 1982 to 1987 period, even though the money supply grew at a faster pace than during the preceding

Table 8.1   The Exchange Equation and Changes in Money, Output, and Prices

Components of the Exchange Equation*	Annual Percent Change			
	(1955–1964)	(1964–1973)	(1973–1982)	(1982–1987)
M^s (money supply—M1)	2.1	5.7	6.8	9.4
V (velocity)	3.1	2.3	2.5	−2.0
$M{\cdot}V$	5.2	8.1	9.5	7.2
P (GNP deflator)	2.0	4.2	7.8	3.3
Y (real GNP)	3.3	3.7	1.6	3.8
$P{\cdot}Y$ (nominal GNP)	5.2	8.1	9.5	7.2

Source: Economic Report of the President (1988).
*Note that the sum of percent changes in two numbers (e.g., for P and Y or for M and V) only approximates the percent change of the product of these two numbers (e.g., for $P{\cdot}Y$ or $M^s{\cdot}V$).

ten-year period, the rate of inflation was less than it was in the preceding period. This was due in part to the greater growth in real GNP during the 1982 to 1987 period and in part to the reduction in velocity growth during the 1982 to 1987 period. Some of the reasons for the lower growth in real GNP in the mid 1970s compared to the 1980s are explored in the next chapter. In a subsequent chapter, we will look at explanations for the fall in velocity in the 1980s.

To the Point

MONEY SUPPLY CHANGES IN THE NEOCLASSICAL MODEL

- Our analysis of macroeconomic shocks compares the resulting equilibrium interest rate, prices, and output with what they would have been in the current period had there not been a macroeconomic shock. Thus the impact of the shock is measured by the deviation from what would have existed.

- In the neoclassical model, the impact of a monetary shock is a change in prices alone. An x percent increase in the money supply will lead to an x percent increase in output prices and wages from what they otherwise would have been. No real variables are affected by a change in the money supply. The absence of any long-run impacts on any real variables is referred to as the neutrality of money.

- The exchange equation ($M^s \cdot V = P \cdot Y$) helps us to interpret the impact of a monetary shock on the economy. Since a monetary change leaves equilibrium velocity V and real output Y unchanged in the neoclassical model, the direct and proportionate causality from money changes to price changes is apparent from the exchange equation.

8.4 CHANGES IN EXPECTED INFLATION: RATIONAL EXPECTATIONS

Up to this point, we have assumed that changes in current monetary policy do not directly alter individual expectations of *future* inflation. Under this assumption, we have seen that a money supply change does not affect the money interest rate r. In this respect, our analysis thus far does not explain the experience of the 1970s, when an accelerating rate of growth of the money supply led not only to higher inflation rates but also to higher money interest rates. As we will see, the higher interest rates were the result of an increase in individuals' inflationary expectations. Before discussing the effects of inflationary expectations on the economy, however, we first need to gain an understanding of how inflationary expectations are formed.

If individuals recognize what we have just learned—that changes in the money supply lead to changes in prices—then "rational" individuals forming their expectations of future inflation rates will take into account their beliefs about the course of future monetary policy. They base these beliefs on current monetary policy, on past monetary policies, on the Fed's announced intentions about future policy, and on any other relevant information that is available to them. These expectations about the future course of prices are said to be "rational expectations" in that they are formed by using all available information, including individual best guesses about the values of the key exogenous variables and their understanding of how these variables have an impact on the economy.[9]

Suppose that some event causes individuals to anticipate a higher inflation rate in the future. For example, if individuals anticipate a higher monetary growth in the future, expected inflation will rise. As we see below, the increase in expected inflation will cause an increase in the equilibrium money interest rate which, in fact, explains a substantial part of the fluctuations in interest rates in the 1970s. In order to see how a change in expected inflation affects the economy, we first analyze the immediate effect that the higher expected future inflation has on the financial market. After this, we analyze the resulting impact on current prices in the output market.

The Impact of Higher Expected Inflation on the Financial Market

Since the expected real rate of interest is nothing more than the money interest rate r minus the expected future inflation rate π^e, a rise in the

---

[9] The term "rational expectations" is derived from John F. Muth's pathbreaking article "Rational Expectations and the Theory of Price Movements," *Econometrica* (July 1961). Muth noted that expectations are not formed in a vacuum but rather in light of an understanding of how the economy works. As he stated, "I should like to suggest that expectations, since they are informed predictions of future events, are essentially the same as the predictions of the relevant economic theory. . . . We call such expectations 'rational' " (p. 316).

expected rate of inflation reduces the expected real rate of interest for any given money interest rate. Recall from Chapter 3 that the expected real rate of interest determines the anticipated real cost to borrowing and the anticipated real return to lending. Thus the reduction in the expected real rate of interest due to the rise in expected inflation will induce firms (as borrowers) to increase investment and induce households (as lenders) to reduce saving in favor of higher consumption.[10]

As Figure 8.6(a) indicates, at the initial nominal interest rate r_0 an increase in the expected rate of inflation raises the demand for loanable funds from LF_0^d to LF_1^d, as firms react to a lower expected real interest rate by increasing their investment demand and thus their demand for loanable funds. At the same time, at the initial nominal interest rate r_0, the higher expected inflation rate reduces the supply of loanable funds from LF_0^s to LF_1^s, as households react to a lower expected real interest rate by reducing their saving.

The rightward shift in the demand for loanable funds curve from LF_0^d to LF_1^d and the leftward shift in the supply of loanable funds curve from LF_0^s to LF_1^s causes the equilibrium interest rate to increase from r_0 to r_1. Although the financial market is in equilibrium at the new higher interest rate, there is now excess demand in the output market at the original price level and output.

To see this, let's look at what happens to the quantity of money demanded and supplied. With the rise in the interest rate, there is a reduction in the quantity of money demanded, as illustrated by Figure 8.6(b). What has happened is that, with a higher money interest rate, households shift part of their portfolio out of money into stocks and bonds. Remember, when households hold money, they forgo holding stocks and bonds that pay the interest rate r. With an increase in the money interest rate, it becomes more costly to hold money, so households cut back on their money holdings. Thus at the higher interest rate r_1 in Figure 8.6, the quantity of money demanded is lower and there is an excess supply of money.

From our knowledge of the aggregate budget constraint and given equilibrium in the financial market, this excess supply of money implies an excess demand for output at the original price level and real GNP. The excess demand in the output market reflects a higher level of firms' investment demand and households' consumption demand induced by a lower expected real rate of interest. Thus we know that the rise in the money interest rate from r_0 to r_1 is less than the increase in the expected rate of inflation, so that the expected real rate of interest is lower. This excess demand in the output market cannot persist for long, as either output or prices must adjust to eliminate the excess demand.

---

[10] Chapters 5 and 6 provide a more in-depth look of the impact of changes in the expected real rate of interest on the investment behavior of firms (Chapter 5) and on the saving behavior of households (Chapter 6).

Figure 8.6   The Effect of an Increase in the Expected Rate of Inflation on the Financial and Money Markets

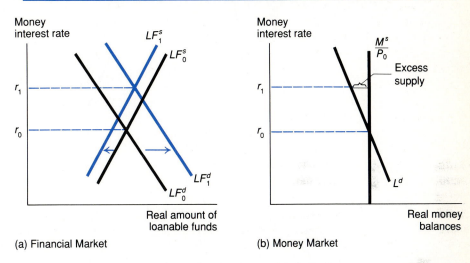

(a) Financial Market   (b) Money Market

The impact on the financial market of an increase in the expected rate of inflation is an increase in investment spending and reduced saving at any nominal interest rate. These changes are illustrated by the shift to the right in the demand for loanable funds curve from LF_0^d to LF_1^d and the shift to the left in the supply of loanable funds curve from LF_0^s to LF_1^s in the financial market. The nominal interest rate rises, the quantity of money demanded falls, and there is excess supply in the money market at the original levels of output and prices.

The Effect on Equilibrium Prices and Output

The fact that an increase in either output or prices is required to eliminate the excess demand for output is represented by a shift in the aggregate demand curve up and to the right, as illustrated in Figure 8.7. As the aggregate demand curve shifts from AD_0 to AD_1, the equilibrium price level rises from P_0 to P_1. The higher price level restores equilibrium by reducing the real money supply and the corresponding real supply of loanable funds. The fall in the supply of loanable funds leads to a further increase in the interest rate, which causes the quantity of investment and consumption spending to fall back to their original levels, thereby eliminating the excess demand in the output market.

Comparing the new equilibrium with the one that would have existed without the increase in the expected rate of inflation, we see that both the price level and the nominal interest rate are higher. Two factors cause the nominal interest rate to rise. First, there is the initial increase in firms' demand for loanable funds and the decrease in households' supply of loanable funds directly attributable to the increase in expected future inflation; second, there is the reduction in the real supply of loanable funds (and the real money

Figure 8.7   **The Effect of an Increase in Expected Inflation on Output and Prices**

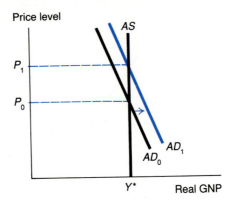

An increase in expected inflation leads to excess demand in the output market at the original output level Y^* and price level P_0. As a consequence, the aggregate demand curve shifts to the right and the new equilibrium price level rises to P_1.

supply), which accompanies the rise in the price level to restore equilibrium in the output market.

As our aggregate demand-supply analysis indicates, output remains unchanged at the new equilibrium. Since we know real government spending remains unchanged, real investment and consumption spending must also remain unchanged. But real investment and consumption spending stay constant only if the expected real interest rate does not change. Since the expected real interest rate equals the difference between the money interest rate r and the expected rate of inflation, the money interest rate must increase by an amount *precisely equal to* the increase in the expected inflation rate.

The above relationship between expected future inflation and money interest rates is known as the **Fisher effect,** named after Irving Fisher.[11] Robert Barsky characterizes Fisher's well-known hypothesis: "That nominal interest rates rise point-for-point with expected inflation, leaving the real rate unaffected, (is) one of the cornerstones of neoclassical monetary theory."[12] The evidence for the post–World War II era strongly supports the predicted high correlation between short-term money interest rates and proxies for expected inflation.[13]

Fisher effect: A theory stating that the money interest rate must increase by an amount equal to the increase in the expected inflation rate.

[11] Irving Fisher, *The Theory of Interest* (New York: Macmillan 1930).

[12] Robert B. Barsky, "The Fisher Hypothesis and the Forecastability and Persistence of Inflation", *Journal of Monetary Economics* (January 1987): 3–24.

[13] With taxes collected as a fraction of nominal rather than real income, the Fisher effect is slightly modified. From the lenders point of view, the after-tax real rate of interest would then remain constant only if a one-unit increase in expected inflation was accompanied by an increase in the nominal interest rate equal to $1/(1 - t)$, where t is the marginal tax rate. This "Darby

Besides the effect of an increase in expected inflation on money interest rates, we can also see from the exchange equation that the increase in expected future inflation leads to a higher velocity of money. We have seen how an increase in expected future inflation causes the price level to rise. Because real GNP and the current money supply do not change, it follows from the exchange equation ($M^sV = PY$) that velocity must rise as well. We can state this change in velocity in terms of the underlying change in money demand: The higher velocity reflects the higher money interest rate that leads households to economize on their money holdings.

Our results concerning the predictions of the neoclassical model of the effects of money supply changes can be summarized as follows. First, a higher rate of growth in the money supply leads to an equivalent increase in the rate of change in prices with no change in real GNP. Second, if the higher inflation is anticipated, the higher inflationary expectations will be incorporated into higher money interest rates, with expected real rates being unaffected. The higher money interest rates will induce lower real money demand and cause velocity to rise as individuals economize on their money holdings. A recent empirical study by John Geweke analyzes U.S. data for the past century and concludes that the evidence supports these predictions.[14]

Case Study

INFLATION AND INTEREST RATE MOVEMENTS

It is important to realize from the above discussion that money interest rates change with *expected* future inflation, not *actual* current inflation. Some economists have suggested that the Fisher hypothesis did not hold in the pre–World War II era—Fisher's own time—since money interest rates responded little to changes in actual inflation.[15] As Barsky argues, however, the evidence

effect'' suggests that the money interest rate will tend to rise by more than the increase in expected inflation. See Michael Darby, ''The Financial and Tax Effects of Monetary Policy on Interest Rates,'' *Economic Inquiry* (June 1975): 266–276.

[14] John Geweke, ''The Superneutrality of Money in the United States: An Interpretation of the Evidence,'' *Econometrica* 51 (January 1986): 1–21. Money is said to be ''neutral'' if changes in the money supply affect only nominal but not real variables in the economy. Money would be ''superneutral'' if variations in the entire path of money (and hence in future rates of monetary growth) do not affect real variables. Geweke finds that over the long run money is superneutral with respect to real GNP and the real rate return but not with respect to velocity. See also Victor Zarnowitz and Louis A. Lambros, ''Consensus and Uncertainty in Economic Prediction,'' *Journal of Political Economy* (June 1987): 591–621. The authors find evidence that expectations of high inflation are often associated with greater uncertainty about inflation and that a rise in inflation uncertainty can have adverse affects on real GNP growth. We discuss this possibility in Chapter 13.

[15] Lawrence Summers, ''The Nonadjustment of Nominal Interest Rates: A Study of the Fisher Effect'', in *Macroeconomic Prices and Quantities: Essays In Memory of Arthur Okun*, ed. James Tobin (Washington, D.C.: Brookings Institution, 1983).

from this period does not really contradict Fisher's hypothesis because changes in actual inflation during this period showed little tendency to persist. Thus changes in actual inflation did not cause individuals to alter their expectations of future inflation. With expected inflation not changing much, it is not surprising that money interest rates were largely uncorrelated with changes in actual inflation during this period. Similarly, expected and actual inflation also differed in the 1980s. During the early and mid-1980s, there was a dramatic drop in actual inflation rates from the double-digit levels of the late 1970s and early 1980s to below 4 percent by 1983. Yet individuals did not immediately lower their expectations of future inflation.

At other times, actual inflation has coincided with what individuals expected. The simultaneous occurrence of high money interest rates and high inflation that we observed in the 1970s came about largely because expected inflation was also high during that period. Figure 8.8 illustrates the fluctuations in short-term interest rates and the actual inflation rate over this period. It has been estimated that from 1961 to 1979 the bulk of changes in nominal interest rates can be attributed to variations in the expected rate of inflation.[16] Figure 8.8 highlights this general relationship for most of this period. If one assumes that the realized inflation rate reflected the inflation rate that had been expected, then the actual and the expected real rate of interest were, by and large, constant prior to 1973.

Beginning in 1973, however, increases in the actual rate of inflation tended to precede increases in nominal interest rates, and decreases in the actual inflation rate tended to precede decreases in the nominal interest rate. In retrospect, it appears that during this period expected inflation differed from the inflation that actually materialized. In the mid and late 1970s, individuals apparently did not fully anticipate the acceleration in inflation that occurred. As a consequence, nominal interest rates, which reflect expected, not actual inflation, did not rise with the increase in the rate of inflation that occurred during this period. The outcome was that actual real interest rates were negative for most of the 1970s. Following 1979, individuals adjusted their expectation of inflation upward and forecast high future inflation rates. These expectations of high inflation contributed to the high nominal interest rates of the early 1980s. When the high rates of inflation failed to fully materialize during this period, the result was a high real rate of interest.

It is unlikely, however, that the high real interest rate of the early 1980s was due solely to individuals overestimating inflation during this period. Instead, it is likely that during this period the expected real rate of interest tended to be above that of earlier periods. As we will see in the next section, one explanation of high real interest rates in the context of the neoclassical model is increased government spending. Other sources of high real rates

---

[16] Carl E. Walsh, "The Three Questions Concerning Nominal and Real Interest Rates," *Economic Review* (Federal Reserve Bank of San Francisco, no. 4, Fall 1987): 5–21.

Figure 8.8 Actual Inflation and Interest Rates

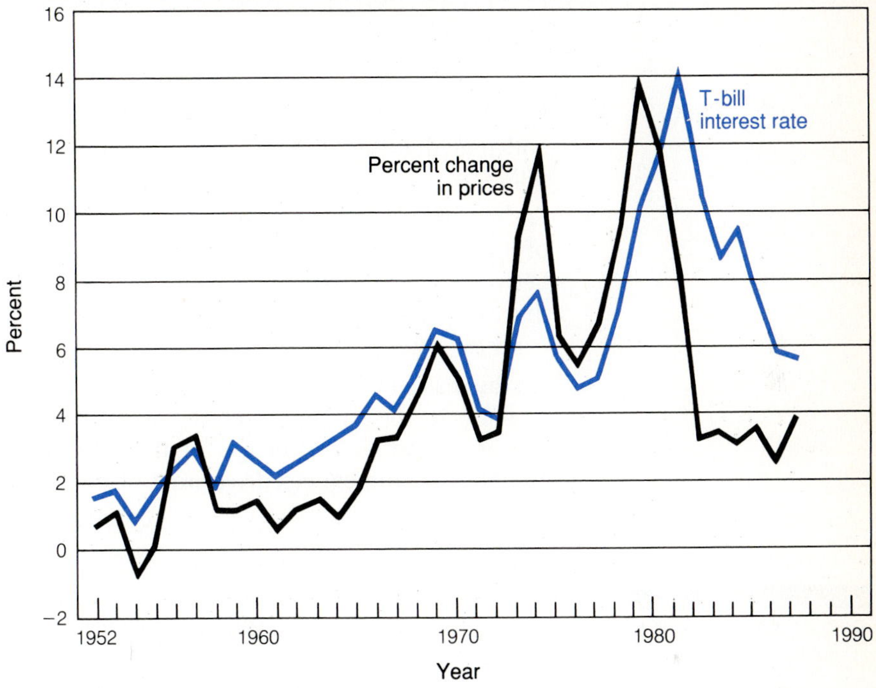

Source: Economic Report of the President (1988).

of interest discussed in the next chapter are supply-side disturbances such as oil supply shocks. In later chapters, we examine how both fiscal and monetary policy actions can lead to high real rates of interest in the context of the macroeconomic model with predetermined prices.

At this point, let's see how our analysis can help explain the changes in the term structure of interest rates discussed in Chapter 3. Recall that the term structure of interest rates describes differences in interest rates across various bonds due solely to differences in maturity. While interest rates on bonds with long maturities are typically higher than short-term rates, during the early 1980s the short-term interest rate on treasury bills rose above the long-term rate on treasury bonds. Our analysis suggests that one reason for this was that individuals in the early 1980s anticipated high inflation in the immediate future but not over the long run. By the mid-1980s, the term structure of interest rates realigned itself, reflecting the fact that short-term inflationary expectations had fallen.

To the Point

MONETARY POLICY AND INFLATIONARY EXPECTATIONS

- A change in the current money supply alters the current rate of inflation. If individuals form expectations of future inflation "rationally," then anticipated future money supply changes will affect expected future inflation.

- For a given nominal interest rate, a change in the expected future rate of inflation affects both households' division of real disposable income between consumption and saving and firms' investment because it alters the expected real rate of interest (the money interest rate minus the expected rate of inflation).

- An increase in the expected rate of inflation will result in a similar increase in the money interest rate, while a decrease in the expected rate will lead to a decrease in the money interest rate. At the new equilibrium, the expected real rate of interest will be the same.

8.5 MONETARY POLICY IN AN OPEN ECONOMY

We are now ready to reconsider the effects of monetary changes in the context of an open economy. To do this, we introduce exports, imports, and international capital flows into our analysis. Introducing a foreign sector does not alter the results of the neoclassical model. A change in the money supply still leads to equiproportionate changes in the money prices of output and the money wages paid labor, with no effect on any real variables. As we see below, however, a change in the money supply does alter foreign exchange rates.

Domestic Price Changes and Exchange Rates

Let's return to our simple two-country example first discussed in Chapter 7, where the United States exports computers to Japan and imports cars from Japan. Now consider the effect of a 10-percent increase in the U.S. money supply. Our analysis of the closed economy predicts that an increase in the money supply leads to an equiproportionate increase in U.S. prices with no change in U.S. real GNP or interest rates. This 10-percent increase in the general price level serves to re-establish equilibrium in the economy.

As our discussion below will demonstrate, in an open economy there is a corresponding adjustment in foreign exchange rates, so that the 10-percent increase in prices also serves to re-establish equilibrium in the open economy. To see this, suppose that after the increase in the money supply the prices of all U.S. goods, including computers, go up by 10 percent.

Figure 8.9   The Effect of U.S. Inflation on the Foreign Exchange Market

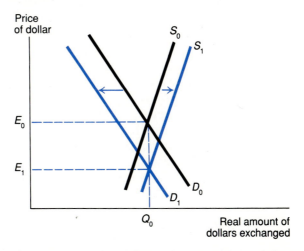

A higher level of prices in the United States decreases the real demand for dollars from D_0 to D_1 and increases the real supply of dollars from S_0 to S_1. As a consequence, the price of the dollar falls from E_0 to E_1.

At the initial exchange rate for the dollar, the rise in the dollar price of U.S. goods means an increase in the yen price of U.S. goods. Thus assuming that the prices of Japanese goods do not change, at the initial exchange rate Japanese consumers will find that the price of U.S. goods have risen *relative* to Japanese goods. The rise in the relative cost of U.S. goods will reduce Japanese purchases of computers and other U.S. goods. The effect on the foreign exchange market of the reduction in the real demand for dollars that will accompany this fall in Japanese purchases of U.S. goods is depicted in Figure 8.9 by the leftward shift in the real demand for dollars curve in the foreign exchange market, from D_0 to D_1.

As this figure indicates, the higher prices of U.S. goods also lead to an increase in the real supply of dollars from S_0 to S_1. At the initial exchange rate, the higher dollar prices of U.S. goods will result in a fall in the *relative* price of Japanese goods to U.S buyers. This will increase the real supply of dollars in the foreign exchange market, as U.S. consumers will buy more Japanese goods.

The decrease in the demand for dollars and the increase in the supply of dollars cause a depreciation of the dollar, as Figure 8.9 depicts by the fall in the equilibrium exchange rate from E_0 to E_1. This depreciation of the dollar means an increase, or appreciation, in the price of the yen. In fact, with 10 percent inflation in the United States, everything that has a dollar price goes up by 10 percent, including the price of yen. This 10 percent appreciation of the yen serves to re-establish equilibrium in the foreign exchange market. Japanese goods with unchanged yen prices now have dollar prices that are 10 percent higher. Since U.S. goods have prices that are 10 percent higher as well, relative prices remain unchanged. Thus since *relative prices are unchanged,* U.S. consumers will purchase at the new equilibrium exchange rate E_1 the same amount of Japanese goods as before—which means that their real supply of dollars in the foreign exchange market is unchanged. Similarly, Japanese consumers purchase the same quantity of U.S. goods and demand the same quantity of real dollars as initially. Even though U.S. goods have a higher dollar price at the new equilibrium, they have the same yen price since the price of a dollar has depreciated.

Flexible exchange rates are common today. For most of this century, however, exchange rates have not been flexible but have instead been fixed by government agreement. Chapter 17 reviews the history of international financial arrangements and also examines the implications of change in the money supply in the context of fixed exchange rates.

Purchasing Power Parity

We can summarize our previous discussion in one statement. In considering two countries, assuming that other things are held constant, *the country with the lower inflation rate tends to have an exchange rate that is appreciating at a rate approximately equal to the difference in inflation rates between the two countries.* In the preceding example, the rate of inflation in Japan was zero, while the United States had an inflation rate of 10 percent. Thus the yen appreciated (its price in terms of U.S. dollars rose) by the difference between the two inflation rates, or by 10 percent. This appreciation of the yen keeps the relative prices of goods constant between the two countries. We can gain a better understanding of the relationship between differences in inflation rates between countries and changes in the exchange rate by looking at the expression for the relative price of foreign goods to domestic buyers.

Let P denote the dollar price of a typical U.S. good and let P_f denote the price of a typical foreign good in terms of the foreign currency, say yen. To calculate the price of the U.S. good relative to the foreign good, we must express both in terms of the same currency. Since E denotes the number of yen per dollar, then $P \cdot E$ represents the foreign currency price of the U.S. good. For example, if the price of a U.S. good (P) is \$4 and the number of yen per dollar (E) is 100, then the yen price of the U.S. good ($P \cdot E$) is 4 dollars multiplied by 100 yen per dollar, or 400 yen.

To calculate the relative price of the U.S. good in terms of the foreign good, we simply divide the yen price of the U.S. good ($P \cdot E$) by the yen price of the foreign good (P_f):

$$\text{Relative price of the U.S. good} = \frac{P \cdot E}{P_f} \tag{8.8}$$

For instance, in our above example the yen price of the U.S. good ($P \cdot E$) is 400 yen. If the yen price of the foreign good (P_f) is 200 yen, then the relative price of the U.S. good in terms of the foreign good is 400/200, or 2. That is, by purchasing one unit of the U.S. good, the buyer has forgone purchasing two units of the foreign good. As we saw in Chapter 6, we can call this relative price of U.S. goods the "real exchange rate for U.S. goods."

If relative prices are to stay constant, then we can see from Equation 8.8 that the percent changes in the yen prices of U.S. and foreign goods must be the same. From our understanding of the mathematical relation between variables and their growth rates, we can express this as

$$\%\Delta P \quad + \quad \%\Delta E \quad \approx \quad \%\Delta P_f \tag{8.9}$$

| Percent change in U.S. prices | Percent change in the dollar exchange rate | Percent change in foreign prices |

Rearranging the above equation, we obtain

$$\%\Delta E \approx \%\Delta P_f - \%\Delta P \tag{8.10}$$

which demonstrates that if relative prices are to remain unchanged, the rate of appreciation of the dollar ($\%\Delta E$) must equal the difference between the rate of inflation in the foreign country ($\%\Delta P_f$) and in the U.S. rate of inflation ($\%\Delta P$).

Table 8.2 presents some evidence on the predicted relationship between the difference in inflation rates between two countries and the change in their exchange rate. To highlight this relationship, the table considers countries that have had a high rate of inflation compared to the United States in the recent past. As the table indicates, the pattern of inflation differences and exchange rate changes is as expected. For instance, during the 1967 to 1985 period the annual average rate of inflation in Israel of 64.8 percent exceeded the 6.5 percent average annual rate of inflation in the United States by 58.3 percent. This difference was associated with an approximately equal annual rate of appreciation of the dollar (58.8 percent appreciation of the dollar).

Purchasing power parity: A condition indicating that with flexible exchange rates, foreign exchange rates vary in order to maintain constant relative prices.

This pattern of changes in foreign exchange rates is sometimes referred to as the **purchasing power parity** (PPP) theory. The condition of purchasing power parity implies that the purchasing power of each country's currency remains the same even though inflation rates differ across countries. Purchasing power parity exists for monetary shocks in the neoclassical model since such shocks lead to changes not only in domestic prices but also in foreign exchange rates. As a result, *relative prices* remain constant.[17]

---

[17] Other evidence during periods of flexible exchange rates supports the purchasing power parity argument; For example, see Nurhan Davutyan and John Pippenger, "Purchasing Power Parity Did Not Collapse During the 1970s," *American Economic Review* (December 1985): 1151–1158. Mark Rush and Steven Husted, "Purchasing Power Parity in the Long Run," *Canadian Journal of Economics* (February 1985) find that at least for U.S. data, purchasing power parity holds; they find mixed results for other countries. Hali J. Edison, "Purchasing Power Parity in the Long Run: A Test of the Dollar/Pound Exchange Rate (1890–1978)," *Journal of Money, Credit, and Banking* (August, 1987): 376–387, finds support for purchasing power parity in the long run between the United States and Britain.

Table 8.2   Differential Inflation Rates and Exchange Rate Changes

Country	Annual Rate of Inflation (1967–1985)	Annual U.S. Inflation Rate (1967–1985)	Difference from Annual U.S. Inflation Rate	Rate of Appreciation in U.S. Dollar Against Foreign Currency
South Korea	13.13	6.51	6.62	6.97
Colombia	19.09	6.51	12.58	13.55
Indonesia	19.23	6.51	12.72	11.80
Iceland	34.04	6.51	27.53	28.71
Zaire	38.18	6.51	31.67	32.07
Peru	43.00	6.51	36.50	38.04
Uruguay	56.53	6.51	50.02	45.66
Brazil	57.46	6.51	50.95	52.02
Israel	64.79	6.51	58.28	58.77

Source: Data are from International Monetary Fund, *International Financial Statistics* (various issues).

It is important to note that purchasing power parity is a long-run relationship. Short-run movements in exchange rates often occur independently of inflation differentials across countries. In addition, even in the long-run, real exchange rates can and do vary as a result of long term structural changes such as differences between countries in the rate of growth of real GNP. Other shocks that can affect the relative prices of goods traded between countries are oil embargoes, droughts, technological changes, and changes in tax policies.

To the Point

MONEY SUPPLY CHANGES IN AN OPEN ECONOMY

- In an open economy, changes in the money supply still lead to equiproportionate changes in prices and no change in any real variables. Money supply changes do, however, lead to changes in foreign exchange rates. Comparing two countries, the country with the lower rate of inflation will have its exchange rate appreciating at a rate equal to the difference in inflation rates.

- Purchasing power parity summarizes the impact of money supply changes and the resulting change in prices on exchange rates. The condition of purchasing power parity means that exchange rates change in order to maintain constant relative prices between two countries.

8.6 FISCAL POLICY IN A CLOSED ECONOMY

As we have seen, in the context of the neoclassical model, monetary policy does not affect any real variables, although changes in the money supply play an important role in explaining inflation and changes in exchange rates. Furthermore, if future changes in the money supply are anticipated, they can affect the current money interest rate by altering expectations of future inflation. We now turn our attention to an analysis of the other half of the government policy dyad—fiscal policy.

The government's fiscal policy includes decisions on such issues as spending on output, net taxes, and borrowing. As we saw in Chapter 4, fiscal policy decisions are constrained by the government financing constraint, which indicates that government purchases of goods and services (G^d) must equal the sum of net real taxes (T) and the government's real financial asset supply (A_g^s). The government financing constraint makes clear that a change in one of the government fiscal policy variables, such as spending, must be accompanied by a change in at least one of the other two fiscal policy variables, either taxes or borrowing.

To simplify our analysis, we will consider only cases where no more than two of the three fiscal policy variables change at one time. This means that three fiscal policy possibilities exist:

1. A change in government spending accompanied by an equivalent change in the government deficit.

2. A change in government spending accompanied by an equal change in taxes.

3. A change in taxes accompanied by an exactly offsetting change in government borrowing, so that government spending remains unchanged.

In the context of the neoclassical model, the following sections examine two types of fiscal policy changes that result in an increase in the government deficit: an increase in deficit spending (rise in government spending with taxes constant) and a substitution of government borrowing for taxes (a cut in taxes with no change in government spending). A more extensive discussion of fiscal policy changes and their potential effects on output and employment awaits our introduction of the short-run macroeconomic models in later chapters.

The Impact of a Change in Government Spending if Prices and Output Do Not Change

We know from the government financing constraint ($G^d = T + A_g^s$) that an increase in real government spending must be financed by an increase in government borrowing (A_g^s) or net taxes (T). Let's assume that the gov-

Figure 8.10   The Effect of an Increase in Government Deficit
               Spending

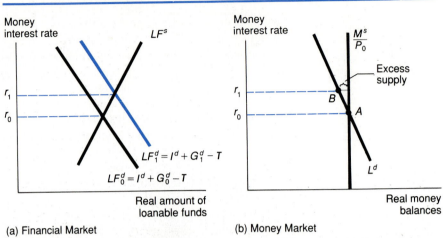

Money
interest rate LF^s

Money
interest rate $\dfrac{M^s}{P_0}$

Excess
supply

r_1

r_0

$LF_1^d = I^d + G_1^d - T$

$LF_0^d = I^d + G_0^d - T$

r_1 B

r_0 A

L^d

Real amount of
loanable funds

Real money
balances

(a) Financial Market   (b) Money Market

An increase in government deficit spending causes a shift to the right in the demand
for loanable funds curve from LF_0^d to LF_1^d in the financial market in part (a). This
results in an increase in the equilibrium interest rate from r_0 to r_1. As indicated by
the graph of the money market in part (b), the higher interest rate leads to an excess
supply of money at the original price level and output. From the aggregate budget
constraint, this implies an excess demand for output at the original price levels and
real GNP.

ernment finances its increased spending entirely by borrowing. Exactly this
type of fiscal action occurred during the early years of the Vietnam War.
Primed by the large spending increases of the federal government on defense
and on President Lyndon Johnson's Great Society programs, total real government purchases of goods and services rose from 19.6 percent of real GNP
in 1965 to 22 percent in 1967. At the same time, the government deficit
rose from close to zero in 1965 to over $14 billion in 1967, which was then
the largest deficit in the post–World War II era.

    We begin our analysis of an increase in deficit spending by considering
the impact that deficit financing has on the financial market. Figure 8.10(a)
illustrates the impact on the financial market of a borrowing-financed increase
in real government spending. Prior to the fiscal policy change, the equilibrium
interest rate equals r_0. Suppose that the government increases its real spending
on final output from G_0^d to G_1^d and finances this increase in spending by an
equal increase in its supply of financial assets (demand for loanable funds).
Then, as indicated by the figure, the demand for loanable funds curve shifts
to the right from LF_0^d to LF_1^d. In order to restore equilibrium in the financial
market, the interest rate must rise from r_0 to r_1.

    The increase in government demand has the direct effect of increasing
demand in the output market. As Figure 8.10(a) shows, however, because

the increase in government deficit spending means a rise in the demand for loanable funds, it leads to a rise in the interest rate. The increase in the interest rate from r_0 to r_1 reduces investment and consumption demand because both are inversely related to the interest rate. But this fall in investment and consumption demand only partially offsets the rise in government demand. Thus at the new, higher interest rate r_1 and original levels of output and prices, there is now excess demand in the output market. This outcome of excess demand in the output market can be confirmed by examining the money market.

Recall that an increase in the interest rate reduces the quantity of real money balances demanded, as households substitute financial assets for money holdings. This is shown in Figure 8.10(b) by the movement up the money demand curve from point A to B. At interest rate r_1, there is thus an excess supply of money at the original levels of prices and real GNP. From the aggregate budget constraint we know that, since at interest rate r_1 there is equilibrium in the financial market, this excess supply of money implies an excess demand for output.

The Effect on Equilibrium Prices and Output

As we have just seen, a borrowing-financed increase in government spending creates excess demand in the output market at the original levels of prices and real GNP. Figure 8.11 illustrates the resulting impact on the economy in terms of aggregate demand and supply curves. The creation of an excess demand in the output market at the original output Y^* and level of prices P_0 means the aggregate demand curve has shifted to the right from AD_0 to AD_1.

As Figure 8.11 indicates, a rightward shift in the aggregate demand curve causes the equilibrium level of prices to rise from P_0 to P_1, with no change in real GNP. The initial excess demand for output caused by the deficit-financed increase in government spending leads to the bidding up of output prices as buyers compete for the relatively scarce output. The increase in output prices, in turn, reduces the real money supply and thus the real supply of loanable funds. The reduction in the supply of loanable funds causes the interest rate to rise above r_1 in Figure 8.10. This leads to a further reduction in investment and consumption demand. Prices continue to rise until the excess demand for output is eliminated by the fall in investment and consumption.[18]

The 1965 to 1967 episode of increased government spending on the Vietnam conflict financed by increased government borrowing provides support for the above analysis. Government purchases of goods and services as a

---

[18] In the money market, excess supply is eliminated by a rising price level because this reduces the real supply of money.

Figure 8.11   **The Effect of an Increase in Government Deficit Spending on Output and Prices**

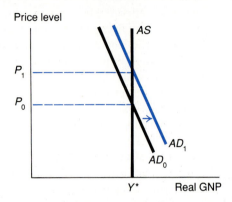

An increase in government spending on output leads to excess demand in the output market at the original price level P_0 and output Y^*, and thus causes a shift to the right in the aggregate demand curve from AD_0 to AD_1. In the neoclassical model, this results in a rise in the equilibrium price level to P_1. A new, higher equilibrium interest rate accompanies the new equilibrium price level.

percent of real GNP rose by 2.1 percentage points. At the same time, interest rates on high-grade corporate bonds rose from 4.49 percent to 5.13 percent. This resulted in a fall in gross investment from 17.6 percent of real GNP to 16.5 percent of real GNP, a 1.1 percentage point decrease. Consumption fell from 59.2 percent to 58.9 percent of real GNP, a .3 percentage point decrease. Note that the fall in consumption and investment as a percentage of real GNP (1.4 percentage points) is not as large as the increase in government spending as a percentage of real GNP. As we will see in our discussion of the impact of fiscal policy in an open economy, what we have neglected is the fall in net exports caused by the fiscal policy expansion.

To summarize, a borrowing-financed increase in government spending causes both the price level and the interest rate to increase but leaves the real GNP unchanged. This has important implications for the long-run impact of fiscal policy on the economy. Remember that we are assuming that the increase in government spending does not affect supply factors. As a consequence, a change in government spending will also not affect output in the neoclassical model since only supply factors determine output. Furthermore, since the real GNP remains unchanged, the fact that the government purchases more output means that the private sector must be purchasing less output. Expressed differently, increased government spending results in a **crowding out** of private spending. This reduction in private spending is in response to the higher interest rate.

Crowding out: A situation where increases in one component of spending, such as government spending, crowds out other components of spending, such as investment and consumption spending, in the output market.

Deficit Spending, Crowding Out, and the Future Capital Stock

Whenever the government engages in large amounts of spending, someone usually speaks out on how government deficits crowd out spending by the private sector. For example, in 1975 and 1976 the Ford administration proposed consecutive deficits on the order of $75 billion. William Simon, the Secretary of the Treasury at the time, opposed the large deficits and lamented that the federal government would be "raiding private capital markets for $150 billion over the next two years." Although Simon's choice of phraseology was somewhat pejorative (he later resigned, mainly as a result of the controversy), his statement reflected the concern that government deficits compete with and crowd out private investment as well as consumption. The neoclassical model reinforces this concern by predicting that such deficit spending raises interest rates and reduces real investment spending by firms and consumption spending on durable goods by households.

A fall in investment spending has important potential effects on the future productive capacity of the economy, since a lower rate of investment results in a smaller stock of capital *in the future*. Thus the neoclassical model predicts that deficit spending today will lower output in the future. At least one factor may mitigate this effect, however. Government purchases can, in fact, augment the economy's capital stock. Some examples of potentially beneficial government expenditures include the construction of roads and dams, spending on government supported research and development, and education.

The Impact of a Substitution of Borrowing for Taxes if Prices and Output Do Not Change

The government deficit has grown substantially in recent years, not only because government spending has increased but also because government has substituted borrowing for taxes. For example, governments at all levels (federal, state, and local) financed 96.1 percent of their total expenditures through tax receipts in 1980. By 1986, this percentage had plummeted to 90 percent. This implies that the proportion of government expenditure financed through borrowing increased by 6.1 percentage points, from 3.9 percent to 10 percent. The bulk of this increase in deficit financing can be attributed to a cut in taxes. Let's look at the effect of a substitution of borrowing for taxes, beginning with its impact on the financial and money markets.

Figure 8.12(a) illustrates the effect on the financial market of a substitution of borrowing for taxation. The rise in government borrowing causes an increase in the demand for loanable funds from LF_0^d to LF_1^d. At the same time, the fall in taxes increases real *disposable* income, which leads to an increase in saving. Figure 8.12(a) shows the increase in saving as a shift to the right in the supply of loanable funds curve from LF_0^s to LF_1^s. On net,

Figure 8.12   The Effect of a Decrease in Taxes with No Change in Government Spending

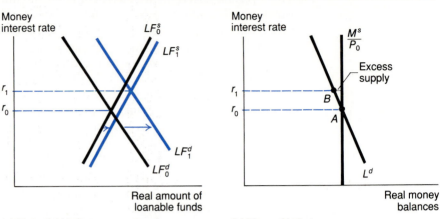

(a) Financial Market   (b) Money Market

A tax cut results in an increase in household disposable income. Part of the increase in disposable income goes to increased saving in the form of the supply of loanable funds. This is shown in part (a) by the shift to the right in the supply of loanable funds curve from LF_0^s to LF_1^s. At the same time, a tax cut with no change in government spending implies from the government financing constraint an increase in government borrowing. This is shown in part (a) by the shift to the right in the demand for loanable funds curve, from LF_0^d to LF_1^d, equal to the fall in taxes. As a consequence, the interest rate that clears the financial market rises from r_0 to r_1. At the higher interest rate, as part (b) indicates, there is excess supply in the money market at the original output and price level.

the equilibrium interest rate rises from r_0 to r_1 because, as we discuss below, the increase in the demand for loanable funds by government exceeds the increase in the supply of loanable funds by households.

There is a reason why the increase in the household supply of loanable funds depicted in Figure 8.12(a) does not completely offset the increase in government demand for loanable funds. Although household real disposable income rises by the amount of the fall in taxes, part of the increased disposable income goes toward increased consumption. Letting *MPC* denote the marginal propensity to consume, the increase in consumption demand resulting from the fall in taxes ($\Delta T < 0$) is given by $\Delta C^d = MPC \cdot \Delta T$. Even though we assume that the entire increase in saving due to the fall in taxes takes the form of an increase in the household supply of loanable funds—an amount equal to $-(1 - MPC) \cdot \Delta T$—this increase falls short of the increase in government borrowing, which equals $-\Delta T$.

At the new, higher equilibrium interest rate, excess demand exists in the output market. The rise in consumption demand due to the increase in disposable income more than offsets the fall in investment and consumption demand due to the increase in the interest rate from r_0 to r_1. This outcome of excess demand in the output market is indicated by the situation with respect to the money market.

Recall that an increase in the interest rate reduces the quantity of real money balances demanded, as households substitute financial assets for money holdings. This is shown in Figure 8.12(b) by the movement up the money demand curve, from point A to B. At the higher interest rate r_1, there is thus an excess supply of money. From the aggregate budget constraint we know that since at interest rate r_1 there is equilibrium in the financial market, the excess supply of money implies an excess demand for output.

The Effect on Equilibrium Prices and Output

As we have just seen, the replacement of taxes with government borrowing initially causes excess demand in the output market. Figure 8.13 depicts how replacing taxes with government borrowing affects equilibrium output and the price level. As you now know, the creation of excess demand in the output market at the original output Y^* and price level P_0 means the aggregate demand curve shifts to the right from AD_0 to AD_1. As a consequence, the equilibrium level of output prices rises from P_0 to P_1.

At the new equilibrium depicted in Figure 8.13, the price level has risen but real output has not changed. Although this figure does not explicitly show it, the interest rate has increased as well. Two reasons exist for the higher interest rate. First, the increased borrowing by the government has the direct effect of increasing the interest rate, as Figure 8.12(a) indicated. Second, the higher equilibrium price level reduces the real supply of loanable funds, which causes the interest rate to rise.

Although the substitution of government borrowing for taxes has not affected the production of output, the composition of output demand has changed.[19] We know that the higher interest rate causes firms' investment spending to fall. Since government spending has been constant, consumption spending must be higher. The increase in household real disposable income that accompanies the tax cut leads to a rise in household consumption spending that more than offsets the negative effect on consumption of the higher interest rate.

To summarize, the way in which the government finances its expenditures has real effects on the composition of output demand. Increased government borrowing causes a shift away from firm investment spending to household consumption spending. Over time, the lower investment results in a reduced capital stock, which lowers the future productive capacity of the economy.

---

[19] Note that we are assuming the tax cut does not alter incentives to supply labor or accumulate capital. In the next chapter, we consider specific changes in tax rates that have supply-side effects and thus can affect output in the neoclassical model.

Figure 8.13   The Effect on Output and the Price Level of Replacing Taxes with Borrowing

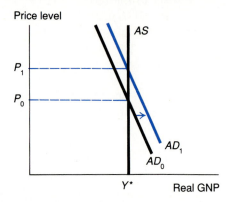

A cut in taxes, with no change in government spending, leads to excess demand in the output market at the initial price level and output. The result is a rightward shift in the aggregate demand curve from AD_0 to AD_1 and an increase in the equilibrium price level from P_0 to P_1.

Government Debt as Taxation—Ricardian Equivalence

According to our preceding analysis, if the government changes the way it finances its purchases from tax financing to deficit financing, it leads to a rise in the interest rate and thus has real effects on the economy. Yet in both cases, the output available for private use is the same. Should not the two forms of financing thus be equivalent?

Some economists argue that they should, in which case a change in the method of financing government spending will not alter the interest rate and will have no real effects on the economy. These economists believe that households take into account the fact that when the government borrows today, it means that the government must raise taxes in the future in order to make interest payments on the newly issued government bonds. The life-cycle and permanent income hypotheses, introduced in Chapter 6, suggest that this increase in future taxes will, at least to some extent, be taken into account when households make their current consumption decision.[20]

If households fully take into account the future increase in taxes required to pay off the newly issued government bonds, then a tax cut and offsetting increase in government borrowing, while leading to a rise in household *current* disposable income, will not lead to any increase in current consumption.

---

[20] The degree to which individuals take into account changes in future taxes largely reflects the length of their time horizon, as can be seen from our analysis of the intertemporal household budget constraint in Chapter 6.

Figure 8.14 **The Effect of a Deficit-financed Tax Cut Under Ricardian Equivalence**

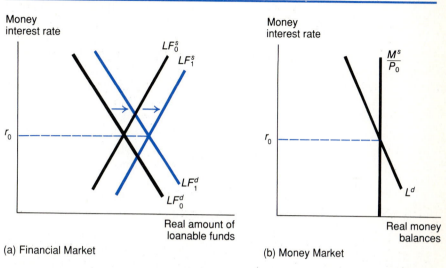

(a) Financial Market   (b) Money Market

A tax cut with no change in government spending requires an increase in government borrowing equal to the fall in taxes. This is shown by a shift to the right in the demand for loanable funds curve from LF_0^d to LF_1^d. Under Ricardian equivalence, households allocate the entire increase in current disposable income that accompanies a tax cut toward saving in the form of the supply of loanable funds. Thus as shown in part (a), the shift to the right in the supply of loanable funds curve, from LF_0^s to LF_1^s, equals the shift to the right in the demand for loanable funds curve. As a consequence, the interest rate that clears the financial market is unchanged at r_0. At the same interest rate, as part (b) indicates, there is equilibrium in the money market.

The entire increase in disposable income will go toward saving.[21] Figure 8.14 shows the resulting effect of a deficit increasing tax cut on the financial and money markets.

Figure 8.14(a) indicates that if households fully incorporate the implications of government debt on future taxes, then a tax cut accompanied by an increase in government borrowing leaves the equilibrium interest rate r_0 unchanged. As before, the increase in the demand for loanable funds by the government, which equals the tax cut, shifts the demand for loanable funds curve to the right from LF_0^d to LF_1^d. However, this shift is now exactly offset by the shift to the right in the supply of loanable funds curve, from LF_0^s to LF_1^s, as household saving increases by the amount of the tax cut. As a consequence, the equilibrium interest rate r_0 remains unchanged.

---

[21] A formal statement of this argument is presented by Robert J. Barro, "Are Government Bonds Net Wealth?" *Journal of Political Economy* (November/December 1974): 1095–1119.

As Figure 8.14(b) indicates, the fact that the interest rate is not affected by the tax cut means that equilibrium in the money market is maintained at the original price level and output. Thus as we know from the aggregate budget constraint, there is equilibrium in the output market at the original price level and output. In other words, changing the method of financing a given level of government spending from taxes to borrowing now has no real effects.

Several recent studies by economist Paul Evans of the effects of large U.S. deficits provides some support for the proposition that debt financing and taxation are equivalent.[22] Evans finds that U.S. interest rates have not been significantly higher in years in which the deficit has exceeded 10 percent of national income.[23] In line with our preceding discussion, Evans suggests that changes in the deficit "have been offset by essentially equal changes in private saving, thereby removing the need for interest rates to change."[24] Similarly, economist Charles Plosser finds "little evidence that the way in which the government finances its expenditures is systematically related to movements in rates of return."[25]

Ricardian equivalence theorem: A theory stating the possibility that deficit financing is equivalent to taxation. Named after the noted early nineteenth century economist David Ricardo.

The possibility that deficit financing is equivalent to taxation is referred to as the **Ricardian equivalence theorem,** named after the noted early nineteenth-century economist David Ricardo. In considering whether a war should be funded through borrowing or taxation, Ricardo noted that in theory "there is no real difference in either of the modes." Ricardo did conclude, however, that while these two methods of financing government spending are theoretically equivalent, taxpayers do not view them as equivalent.[26] As Ricardo notes, "We are too apt to think that the war is burdensome only in proportion to what we are at the moment called to pay for it in taxes, without reflecting on the probable duration of such taxes. It would be difficult to convince a man ... that a perpetual payment of 50£ per annum was equally burdensome with a single tax of 1000£."

---

[22] Paul Evans, "Do Large Deficits Produce High Interest Rates?" *American Economic Review* (March 1985): 68–87. Evans comes to a similar conclusion in "Interest Rates and Expected Future Budget Deficits in the United States," *Journal of Political Economy* 95, no. 1 (1987): 34–58.

[23] Evans' paper focuses on deficits in war years since most large deficits have occurred during times of war. As Evans notes, it is possible that interest rates were stable in the face of these large deficits because patriotism encouraged people to purchase savings bonds, thereby shifting the supply of loanable funds curve to the right. For example, the bond rallies during World War II urged people to "take stock in America." This is sometimes referred to as the "Andrews Sisters Effect."

[24] As support for this claim, Evans refers to a study by Roger C. Kormendi, "Government Debt, Government Spending, and Private Sector Behavior," *American Economic Review* (December 1983): 994–1110.

[25] Charles Plosser, "Government Financing Decisions and Asset Returns," *Journal of Monetary Economics* (May 1982): 325–352.

[26] See Piero Sraffa, ed., *The Works and Correspondence of David Ricardo* (New York: Cambridge University Press, 1951). A lucid account of Ricardo's views on this subject is provided by Gerald P. O'Driscoll, Jr., "The Ricardian Nonequivalence Theorem," *Journal of Political Economy* (February 1977): 207–210.

We should make some of the assumptions in Ricardo's quote explicit. Ricardo assumed that the government borrowed by issuing a perpetuity at the then prevailing interest rate of 5 percent. Thus in order to borrow 1000£, the government would have to pay 50£ a year in perpetuity. Future tax liabilities would thus rise by 50£ per year. The present value of these future tax liabilities is 1000£. Consequently, whether the government finances by taxing or borrowing, the present cost to the taxpayer is equivalent. Ricardo doubted, however, whether individuals would really see these two burdens as equivalent. We thus have the irony that the idea is referred to as Ricardian equivalence even though Ricardo himself did not believe its empirical validity.

Strict equivalence between debt and taxes requires that households correctly foresee the implications of current debt issues on future tax liabilities and also that they care about them. (They might not care if they and their heirs do not live long enough to incur all future tax liabilities.) Martin Feldstein, former Chairman of the Council of Economic Advisers, agrees with Ricardo that taxpayers do not adjust their consumption behavior to account for the present value of their future tax liabilities. According to Feldstein, "each of the basic implications of the . . . equivalence hypothesis is contradicted by the data."[27] Others also view the weight of evidence as against the Ricardian equivalence propositions.[28]

The debate has found its way into the political arena, as unprecedented deficits occurred after the Reagan tax cuts of the early 1980s. Congress debated the efficacy of raising taxes to offset these deficits and, perhaps without realizing it, some of the participants in the debate applied the Ricardian equivalence theorem. They argued that the method used by the government to raise revenue does not really matter; the total level of government spending is the key. In this regard, it should be pointed out that, although the evidence on the equivalence between government borrowing and taxes is mixed, there is little doubt that "the capital market is not indifferent with respect to the level of government expenditures as higher interest rates are associated with increases in government purchases."[29]

---

[27] Martin Feldstein, "Government Deficits and Aggregate Demand," *Journal of Monetary Economics* (January, 1982): 1–20.

[28] For instance, B. Douglas Bernheim argues that "the existing body of theory and evidence establishes a significant likelihood that deficits have large effects on current consumption, and there is good reason to believe that this would drive up interest rates." B. Douglas Bernheim, "Ricardian Equivalence: An Evaluation of Theory and Evidence," NBER Working Paper No. 2330 (July 1987). Others, however, do not agree with his interpretation of the evidence.

[29] Charles Plosser, "Government Financing Decisions and Asset Returns," *Journal of Monetary Economics* (May 1982). See also Robert Barro, "Government Spending, Interest Rates, Prices, and Budget Deficits," NBER Working Paper No. 2005 (1986). For the almost 200 year period between 1701 and 1981, Barro found that the ten episodes of substantial budget deficits in the United Kingdom, almost always associated with increased government spending to finance wars, generally led to higher long-term interest rates.

To the Point

FISCAL POLICY CHANGES IN THE NEOCLASSICAL MODEL

- Government fiscal policy takes the form of changes in government spending, borrowing, and taxation. For example, an increase in government spending requires an equal increase in either taxes or borrowing. A cut in taxes with no change in government spending requires an equal increase in government borrowing.

- In the neoclassical model, a change in government fiscal policy has no effect on real GNP. It does, however, lead to a change in prices and the interest rates. The change in the interest rate induces a change in the composition of output demand. For instance, a rise in government spending leads to a higher interest rate that induces an offsetting fall in investment and consumption demand. A tax cut that stimulates consumption demand is offset by a higher interest rate that results in a lower level of investment demand.

- Under a condition known as Ricardian equivalence, a cut in taxes and resulting increase in government borrowing leads individuals to increase their saving by the entire amount of the tax cut. In this case, taxes and borrowing are equivalent forms of financing government spending, and a substitution of one for the other does not affect the interest rate or prices.

8.7   FISCAL POLICY IN AN OPEN ECONOMY

Our preceding analysis shows that an increase in the deficit due to an increase in government spending leads to both a higher interest rate and a higher price level in a closed economy. In the absence of Ricardian equivalence, a deficit-increasing cut in taxes has a similar impact in a closed economy. An increase in the deficit, either due to higher government spending or a tax cut, leads to increases in prices and the interest rate in an open economy as well, although the extent of the increases in the interest rate and the price level is less. Furthermore, analysis of a fiscal policy change in an open economy allows us to examine its effects on foreign exchange rates, exports, and imports. To understand the new features of a fiscal policy change in an open economy, we will start by looking at the effect of an increase in government deficit spending on the various markets in the open economy if the price level and output do not change.

The Impact of Increased Government Deficit Spending if Prices and Output Do Not Change

A higher interest rate in U.S. financial markets makes U.S. financial assets such as treasury bills and U.S. corporate bonds more attractive to hold in comparison to foreign assets. As a consequence, a rise in the interest rate increases foreigners' purchases of U.S. financial assets and leads U.S. households to substitute domestic for foreign financial assets. Thus as we saw in Chapter 7, the quantity of loanable funds supplied in the U.S. financial market is more responsive to interest rate changes in an open economy—which means that the supply of loanable funds curve is flatter. A flatter curve means that the increase in the demand for loanable funds that accompanies a rise in government deficit spending requires less of an increase in the interest rate to restore equilibrium in the financial market. In the money market, because there is less of a rise in the interest rate, there is a smaller excess supply of money at the original price level in an open economy. Thus in an open economy, an increase in government deficit spending leads to a smaller excess demand for output at the original price level and output. We can see why this is the case by examining the effect on the foreign exchange market of the rise in the interest rate.

With a higher domestic interest rate induced by the fiscal policy change, the real demand for dollars in the foreign exchange market increases, since foreigners wish to purchase more U.S. financial assets (U.S. capital inflows rise). Likewise, the real supply of dollars decreases, since individuals in the United States seek to purchase fewer foreign securities (U.S. capital outflows fall). Figure 8.15 illustrates these effects of a higher interest rate on the foreign exchange market for the dollar.

As this figure indicates, a higher U.S. interest rate causes an appreciation of the dollar.[30] This increase in the price of the dollar has two important effects. First, it discourages foreign purchases of U.S. goods, as the upward movement from point A to point B along the new real demand for dollars curve D_1 shows. Thus the level of U.S. exports falls. Second, since an appreciating dollar implies a falling price of foreign currencies in terms of dollars, the level of U.S. imports increases. The movement from point C to point B along the new real supply of dollars curve S_1 illustrates this.

To summarize, the rise in government deficit spending, because it alters the interest rate, is accompanied in an open economy by changes in international capital flows that lead to an appreciation of the dollar and thus a fall in U.S. net export demand (U.S. exports fall and U.S. imports rise). This series of events has been cited by some analysts as reasonably approximating

---

[30] As drawn, Figure 8.15 indicates that the real quantity of dollars exchanged in the foreign exchange market falls. Although this is not necessarily the case, note that it is immaterial for our analysis whether the equilibrium quantity of dollars exchanged rises or falls.

Figure 8.15   **The Effect of an Increase in the U.S. Interest Rate on the Foreign Exchange Market**

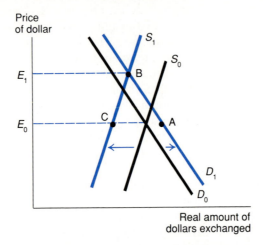

With higher domestic interest rates, the real demand for dollars in the foreign exchange markets increases from D_0 to D_1, since foreigners purchase more U.S. financial assets. Likewise, the real supply of dollars falls from S_0 to S_1, since individuals in the United States purchase fewer foreign securities. The equilibrium price of a dollar (in terms of foreign currency) rises from E_0 to E_1 as a result.

what occurred in the United States from 1981 to 1985. Note in our analysis that the increase in government demand is now partly offset by the fact that the accompanying increase in the interest rate causes not only a fall in investment and consumption demand, as occurred in a closed economy, but also a fall in net export demand. This is the reason why, in an open economy, an increase in government deficit spending leads to less of an excess demand in the output market at the original price level and output.

The Effect on Equilibrium Prices and Output

As we have seen, the fact that an increase in government deficit spending leads to an excess demand in the output market at the original price level and output means that the aggregate demand curve shifts to the right. The result in the neoclassical model, similar to that shown for the closed economy in Figure 8.11, is a rise in the equilibrium price level, but no change in real GNP. As indicated above, the initial excess demand is less in an open economy, so that the shift to the right in the aggregate demand curve induced by an increase in government deficit spending is less than it would be in a closed economy. Therefore the rise in the price level is less in an open economy than it is in a closed economy. In addition, the rise in the price level is less because, as we saw in Chapter 7, the aggregate demand curve is flatter in an open economy: Recall that in an open economy, output demand, which now includes net export demand, is more responsive to a rising price level.

At the economy's new equilibrium, the interest rate is higher, reflecting not only the increase in government demand for loanable funds but also the fall in the real supply of loanable funds due to the rise in the price level. In the previous section, we saw the impact of a rise in the interest rate on the foreign exchange market: an increase in U.S. capital inflows and a decrease in U.S. capital outflows that leads to an appreciation of the dollar and resulting fall in net export demand. The early 1980s provides an example of the above effect, as the rise in U.S. interest rates, attributed partly to higher government deficits, led to an appreciation of the dollar. This, in turn, was largely responsible for the reduction in exports from 12.8 percent of GNP in 1980 to 9.2 percent of GNP in 1985.

Table 8.3 sheds further insight into our experience of the 1980s. It shows the values as a percentage of GNP of the government budget deficit, household saving, firm net investment, and the net capital inflow for the period 1979 to 1987. The columns showing the government budget deficit and net investment are sources of demand for loanable funds in the financial market. In recent years, U.S. capital inflows have exceeded capital outflows, as foreigners have dramatically increased their lending in the U.S. financial markets. Thus net capital inflows appears as one source of supply of loanable funds in recent years. Table 8.3 indicates that household saving is the other source of supply of loanable funds.

Household saving is directly a source of loanable fund supply for that part of saving that goes toward the acquiring of additional financial assets. The other part of household saving that goes toward the accumulation of real money balances is indirectly a source of supply of loanable funds. To see why, first remember that when the economy is in equilibrium, money demand equals money supply. Second, recall from the depository institutions financing constraint that an increase in the real supply of money balances is matched by an equivalent supply of loanable funds from depository institutions.

In 1979, federal, state, and local governments combined were actually running a budget surplus. In 1980, this turned into a deficit. In 1983, the deficit became quite large, reaching 3.9 percent of GNP, and it has been large ever since. As the table indicates, there has been a corresponding increase in net capital inflows. Interestingly, net capital inflows did not become terribly large until 1984. The economy was in a severe recession up until 1982 and, as a consequence, investment was quite low during the early 1980s. It did not fully recover until 1984, well after the start of the economic upturn. During the course of the expansion, household saving fell as a percent of GNP and the government budget deficit remained high. Thus the domestic demand for loanable funds exceeded the supply from domestic

Table 8.3   **Demand for and Supply of Loanable Funds as a Percent of GNP**

| | Demand for Loanable Funds | | Supply of Loanable Funds | |
Year	Government Budget Deficit	Firm Net Investment	Household Saving	Net Capital Inflow
1979	−0.47	7.33	6.98	−0.11
1980	1.26	4.81	7.86	−1.79
1981	0.99	5.41	7.90	−1.52
1982	3.41	2.02	6.36	−0.83
1983	3.91	3.34	6.51	0.61
1984	2.97	7.17	7.56	2.40
1985	3.41	5.82	6.13	3.00
1986	3.59	5.71	5.27	3.93
1987	2.46	5.94	4.81	3.52

Source: Economic Report of the President (1988).

sources. The shortfall was made up by foreign lending, as reflected by the fact that between 1984 and 1987 the net capital inflow ranged from 2.4 to 3.93 percent of GNP.

SUMMARY

The assumptions of flexible prices and fully informed agents—critical elements of neoclassical macroeconomic analysis—lead to a vertical aggregate supply curve. In such a context, changes in monetary and fiscal policies that affect aggregate demand leave current output unchanged. However, the neoclassical model does predict changes in other macroeconomic variables as a result of monetary and fiscal policy changes.

The impact on the economy of a money supply change in the neoclassical model is limited to price changes. After all adjustments have occurred, output prices and wages are higher at the new equilibrium, but the level of employment, output, and the interest rate remain unchanged. In short, the neoclassical model predicts that changes in the nominal money supply result only in changes in money prices and that no *real* variables are affected. The idea that a change in the money supply has no long-run affect on any real variables is referred to as the neutrality of money. This point is highlighted by the exchange equation ($M^s \cdot V = P \cdot Y$).

Although changes in the current money supply leave the interest rate unchanged, anticipated changes in the future money supply can alter the money interest rate. If individuals have "rational expectations" about future inflation, then an anticipated increase in the rate of changes in the money supply will cause them to revise their expectation of future inflation upward. The higher expected inflation will cause an increase in the money interest rate, however, so that the expected real rate of interest remains unchanged.

In the neoclassical model, a change in the money supply has the same outcome in an open economy as in a closed economy: No real variables are affected. The change in the money supply does alter foreign exchange rates, however, since it affects output prices. As summarized by the doctrine of purchasing power parity, the country with the lower rate of inflation will tend to have an exchange rate that is appreciating at a rate approximately equal to the difference in inflation rates between the two countries.

The government's fiscal policy involves decisions concerning spending on output, net taxes, and borrowing. Our discussion considered two possible fiscal policy changes: An increase in government deficit spending and a substitution of government borrowing for taxes. An increase in government deficit spending causes a higher interest rate and thus crowds out private investment and consumption spending. A fall in investment spending has important potential effects on the future productive capacity of the economy since a lower rate of investment implies a smaller future stock of capital.

The substitution of borrowing for taxes has the similar effect of raising the interest rate and crowding out firms' investment spending, although in this case investment is crowded out by increased household consumption. The rise in consumption spending reflects the fact that a tax cut raises households' disposable income. A different result emerges if households fully take into account the future taxes required to make interest payments on the bonds issued today to finance government expenditures. In this case, taxation and borrowing are equivalent ways by which the government can finance expenditures and a substitution of gevernment borrowing for taxes has no real effects on the economy. This possibility is referred to as the Ricardian equivalence theroem.

In an open economy, fiscal policy changes that alter the interest rate lead to changes in international capital flows, exchange rates, and net exports. For instance, a fiscal policy change that causes the interest rate to rise will increase U.S. capital inflows (demand for dollars in the foreign exchange market) and reduce U.S. capital outflows (supply of dollars in the foreign exchange market), which will thus lead to an appreciation of the dollar and a consequent fall in U.S. exports and an increase in U.S. imports.

LOOKING AHEAD

In this chapter, we have examined the effects of changes in various demand factors that affect the position of the aggregate demand curve in the context of the neoclassical model. Although the neoclassical model predicts that such changes will alter the equilibrium price level and interest rate, the model does not predict any change in employment or output since the aggregate supply curve is vertical. In the neoclassical model, it is only changes in supply factors that cause changes in output and employment. In the next chapter, we examine the effect of various supply factors on the growth of an economy.

In subsequent chapters, we show how modifications of the neoclassical model can lead to the prediction that monetary policy and fiscal policy have significant effects on output and employment in the short run. Specifically, we show that if prices are not perfectly flexible, or if workers are not perfectly informed concerning the general level of prices, then increases in government spending and expansionary monetary policy can lead to increases in both employment and output.

SUMMARY OF KEY EQUATIONS

Exchange equation

$$M^s \cdot V = P \cdot Y \tag{8.1}$$

Dynamics of the exchange equation

$$\%\Delta M^s + \%\Delta V \approx \%\Delta P + \%\Delta Y \tag{8.7}$$

Purchasing power parity equation

$$\%\Delta E \approx \%\Delta P_f - \%\Delta P \tag{8.10}$$

KEY TERMS

Exogenous variables, 267
Endogenous variables, 267
Macroeconomic shock, 267
Neutrality of money, 273
Exchange equation, 274
Velocity of money, 275

Quantity theory of money, 276
Fisher effect, 286
Purchasing power parity, 293
Crowding out, 298
Ricardian equivalence theorem, 304

REVIEW QUESTIONS

1. According to the neoclassical model, what is the long-run effect of an increase in the money supply on the levels of real GNP and output prices? Briefly trace out the process by which the economy adjusts to an increase in the money supply.

2. A November 26, 1984 *Wall Street Journal* article reported as follows: "The latest Fed figures showed that the basic money supply, known as

M1, declined by $1.3 billion in the week ending November 12. The Fed estimated M1 averaged a seasonally adjusted $545.5 billion in the latest week, down from $546.7 billion the previous week. That left M1 only $1.1 billion above the lower end of the Fed's target range, which calls for 4 percent to 8 percent growth this year."

a. If the money supply is reduced, what do we know about depository institutions' financial asset demand? Draw a diagram that will illustrate the effect on equilibrium in the financial market. What happens to the interest rate? Why?

b. What happens to investment and consumption demand? Why?

c. Is there now an excess demand for or supply of output? What does this imply about the money market? Why?

d. According to neoclassical analysis, what will happen to the price level over time? Why?

e. What effect does the change in the price level have on real money supply? On financial asset demand? Show this effect on the diagram you made for your answer to (a). What will now happen to the interest rate? To investment demand? To consumption demand?

f. Illustrate the effect that the change in the price level has on equilibrium in the labor market.

g. Use aggregate demand-supply analysis to illustrate the effect that the change in the money supply has on the economy's equilibrium price and output levels.

h. How do the new equilibrium values of the following variables compare with their values before the change in the money supply: nominal money supply, real money supply, real GNP, price levels, and real investment demand.

3. Explain what we mean when we talk about the "neutrality of money."

4. How does one obtain the exchange equation?

a. Use the exchange equation to explain the effect of a change in the money supply.

b. How does a change in the interest rate affect the velocity of money?

c. Use the exchange equation to explain the effects of a borrowing-financed increase in real government spending.

d. Use the exchange equation to explain the effects of a reduction in expected inflation.

5. An April 24, 1985 *Wall Street Journal* article reported as follows: "Preston Martin, vice chairman of the Federal Reserve Board, said rapid growth in the money supply may be necessary this year to prevent unemployment from rising. . . . Although Mr. Martin often advocates a looser monetary stance than his colleagues on the Fed's policy-setting committee, sluggish

economic growth in the face of rapid money growth may have convinced Fed Chairman Paul Volcker and other Fed members to share that view. . . . The reports caused interest rates to *rise* in the credit markets.''

a. According to the neoclassical model, what effect does an increase in the rate of growth in the nominal money supply have on the inflation rate?

b. The *Wall Street Journal* reported on March 13, 1985: ''By inflationary expectations, economists mean the tendency of consumers and businesses to anticipate future speedups in price increases.'' Assume ''businesses and consumers'' anticipate a higher rate of increase in the money supply and understand the implications of your analysis in (a). Discuss and depict graphically the immediate impact on the financial market. What happens to the interest rate? Why?

c. What happens to the demand for real money balances? Can the output market be in equilibrium at the initial price and output levels? What will happen as a result?

d. According to the neoclassical model, what effect does an increase in the expected rate of increase in the money supply have on the following: current price level, current real GNP, real investment demand, the nominal interest rate, the real expected interest rate, and the real money supply?

6. Suppose that the prices of U.S. goods fall by 5 percent. What happens to the demand for and supply of dollars in the foreign exchange market?

a. Illustrate the effect on the price of the dollar in the foreign exchange market. Does the price of the dollar rise or fall? By how much?

b. What happens to the dollar prices of foreign goods?

c. Indicate what we mean by ''purchasing power parity.''

7. The *Wall Street Journal* reported on April 5, 1985: '' 'The budget agreement was 'a pleasant surprise,' said David M. Jones, senior vice president and economist at Aubrey G. Lanston & Co. But he warned against being too optimistic about the prospects for congressional passage of the package. 'There's a long road to go,' he said. 'There's still a major question whether the rank-and-file Republicans will go along with the Senate leadership on the deep surgery on proposed spending.' ''

a. Suppose that the government does indeed perform ''deep surgery'' on its real spending on output. What is the direct effect on output demand in the economy? If the government does not change real net taxes, what happens to its real supply of financial assets? Why?

b. Show the immediate effect that the government's new policy has on the financial and money markets. What happens to the interest rate? What effect does the change in the interest rate have on output and money demand?

    c.   Given the new government policy, will there be an excess demand for or supply of output at the economy's original levels of real GNP and output prices? What does the neoclassical model predict will happen to the price level and to real GNP? What will be the resulting effect on the financial market, and consumption and investment demand?

    d.   Use aggregate demand-supply analysis to show the effect of the reduction in government spending on the economy's equilibrium price and output levels.

    e.   Indicate how the equilibrium values of the following variables are affected by the reduction in government spending: the interest rate, real consumption demand, real investment demand, and firms' real financial asset supply.

8. What do we mean by the crowding-out effect?

    a.   If the government increases its spending on real output by, say, $70 billion, what must happen to real investment and consumption spending after prices in the economy have adjusted to their new equilibrium values?

    b.   What are the two ways that the government can finance its increase in spending? What effect is the method of financing likely to have in your answer to (a)?

9. Suppose that household desired saving increases.

    a.   In light of the household intertemporal budget constraint, what does the increase in desired saving mean with respect to households' preferences for present versus future consumption? What does this suggest with respect to how resources in the economy should be allocated?

    b.   Suppose that household saving takes the form of an increased demand for financial assets. Show the immediate effect in the financial market. What happens to the interest rate?

    c.   The early classical economists assumed that money demand was independent of the interest rate. Assuming that this is the case, are the output market and the money market in equilibrium at the economy's original price and output levels? Why or why not?

    d.   Use aggregate demand-supply analysis to show the effect of the increase in saving on the economy's equilibrium price and output levels.

    e.   Indicate how the new equilibrium values of the following variables compare with their initial levels before the increase in saving: real consumption spending, real investment spending, the price level, and the real money supply?

    f.   Now assume, as we have done in the text, that money demand is inversely related to the interest rate. How is your answer in (c) affected? Why?

g. To restore equilibrium in the output market, what must happen to the price of output? What effect does this change in output price have on the financial market?

h. Show the effect of the increase in saving on the economy's equilibrium price and output levels by using aggregate demand-supply analysis. Indicate how the new equilibrium values of the following variables compare with their initial levels before the increase in saving: real consumption spending, real investment spending, the price level, the real money supply.

10. Suppose that the government increases the transfer payments that it pays to a selected subgroup of the population. It can pay for this in one of two ways: either tax the rest of the population or borrow.

a. Suppose that the government finances the increased transfer payments by taxing the remainder of the population. (For example, increased social security payments to current recipients are frequently paid for by raising taxes on the current contributors to the fund). What is the net effect of the government's policy on real net taxes?

b. What happens to the desired consumption spending and the financial asset demand of the households who receive the increased transfer payments? What happens to the desired consumption spending and the financial asset demand of the households who have to pay higher taxes. If all households have the same marginal propensity to consume out of real disposable income, what is the effect of the policy change on the total consumption demand and financial asset demand of all households? What happens to the equilibrium interest rate, the equilibrium price level, the real output level, and real investment spending in the economy.

c. Now suppose that the government finances the increased transfer payments by borrowing. What effect does this policy have on financial asset demand and financial asset supply? Why? Indicate the immediate effect on equilibrium in the financial market. What happens to the interest rate required to maintain equilibrium in the financial market at the economy's original price and output levels?

d. Is there excess demand or supply in the output market. Why? What will happen to the price level? How will this restore equilibrium in the output market?

e. Indicate how the equilibrium values of the following variables have been affected by the policy change: the interest rate, the price level, real investment demand, real consumption demand, and real government spending. Compare your answer with that in (b).

f. Consider the simultaneous increase in social security payments to current recipients and social security taxes to current contributors alluded to in (a). What does the life-cycle hypothesis suggest about the marginal propensities to consume of older and younger individuals? How does this affect your answer to (b).

11. What is meant by the Ricardian equivalence theorem? What is the reasoning behind this proposition?

12. If households fully incorporate the implications of current government borrowing for their future taxes, how will your answers to Question 10 (c), (d), and (e) be affected?

13. Consider the cut in real government spending that you analyzed in Question 7. Now suppose that we have an open economy.

   a. What effect does the change in the interest rate referred to in Question 7(b) have on the demand for and supply of dollars in the foreign exchange market. Illustrate the effect on foreign exchange market equilibrium. Does the equilibrium price of dollars rise or fall?

   b. What will happen to net export demand for U.S. goods?

   c. How is your answer to Question 7(c) affected if we have an open instead of a closed economy?

14. How does your answer to Question 8(a) change if we have an open rather than a closed economy?

15. In the April 29, 1985 issue of *Time*, Alice Rivlin, director of economic studies at the Brookings Institution was quoted as follows: "The single greatest threat to the economic recovery is a precipitous fall in the dollar. Such a decline would mean that foreigners were pulling vast sums of cash out of the United States. Since money from abroad has helped to finance the huge deficit, the outflow of funds would drive up interest rates. . . . [The effects would be felt] by nations that have been fueling their economies by exports to the U.S."

   a. Suppose that for some unspecified reason there is an "outflow of funds" as "foreigners [pull] vast sums of cash out of the U.S." Illustrate the resulting effect on the foreign exchange market. What happens to the demand for foreign output by U.S. households and the demand for U.S. output by foreigners? Why?

   b. Illustrate the effect on the U.S. financial market if "foreigners [pull] vast sums of cash out of the U.S." What happens to the interest rate? What effect does this have on consumption and investment demand. At this changed interest rate, what do we know about the money market? Why? What does this tell us about the output market?

   c. According to the neoclassical model, what will happen to the U.S. price level?

   d. How do the new equilibrium values of the following variables compare with what they were initially: real consumption spending, real investment spending, real net export demand, and the interest rate?

16. Assume that the money supply grows by 10 percent and velocity grows at 3 percent. What is the change in nominal GNP according to the exchange equation? If real GNP grows by 2 percent, what is the predicted rate of inflation? What rate of change in velocity will result in the same predicted rate of inflation even though the money supply is now growing at a 20 percent rate?

17. In the February 24, 1988 issue of the *Wall Street Journal,* it is reported that comments by Alan Greenspan, the current chairman of the Federal Reserve Board, have "intensified speculation that inflation will remain subdued and prompted some investment managers to predict even further declines in _____ (interest rates, bond prices) over the next few months. . . . Prices of some actively traded 30-year treasury bonds wound up the day with _____ (gains, losses) of about three quarters of a point, or about $7.50 for each $1000 face amount." Let's consider the macroeconomic implications of "intensified speculation that inflation will remain subdued." In other words, let's consider what is implied by a situation in which, as one financial consultant stated, the "concerns of rising inflation have been put to bed."

    a. Identify the exogenous variable that the above quote suggests has changed. Depict graphically the initial impact (at the original level of output prices and real GNP) of such a change in this exogenous variable on the financial and money markets. Label the axis.

    b. According to (a) at the original levels of output prices and real GNP, what is the situation in the output and money markets. Depict the implication of this in terms of aggregate demand-supply analysis. Assume the neoclassical model. Label the axis.

    c. Compare the new equilibrium situation with what would have existed had there not been a change in the exogenous variable identified in (a). In particular, indicate what has happened to each of the following variables (increased, decreased, no change, or ambiguous):

Price level	Real GNP
Money interest rate	Expected real interest rate
Money wage	Real wage
Investment demand	Consumption
Velocity	Real money supply

    d. Briefly identify the Fisher effect. Is your analysis consistent with this effect?

18. In the February 22, 1988 issue of the *Wall Street Journal,* it is stated that "to expand exports far beyond the current modest increases, the country must invest heavily in the requisite plant and equipment. A surge in such investment implies at least a temporary rise in saving—a reduction in consumer spending. Mr. Hale [chief economist at Kemper Financial Services, Inc.] adds; 'Since merely eliminating the trade deficit would

push the U.S. capacity utilization rate close to 95 percent compared to previous non-inflationary thresholds of 85 percent, it may be difficult to generate an actual trade surplus for debt servicing without reducing the standards of the American people.' In other words, consumer spending will have to decline. Lower consumer spending . . . by reducing demand and making companies hesitate to raise prices, . . . would take some of the steam out of inflationary pressure." Let's see if this train of thought (higher investment leads to lower consumption that reduces inflationary pressures) makes sense.

a. Suppose that there is a change in government policies that heightens the incentives of firms to invest in capital goods. Depict graphically the initial impact of the resulting rise in autonomous investment demand on the financial and money markets. Assume a *closed* economy. Label the axis.

b. According to (a), at the original price level and real GNP, is the output market in equilibrium? Is consumption demand higher or lower? Is investment demand higher or lower? Is the sum of consumption and investment demand higher or lower?

c. Using the aggregate demand-supply analysis of the neoclassical model, depict the effect of the autonomous increase in investment spending. Label the axis.

d. Compare the new equilibrium situation with what would have existed had there not been the change in the exogenous variable identified in (a). What does the model predict will happen to each of the following:

Price level	Real GNP
Money interest rate	Expected real interest rate
Money wage	Real wage
Velocity	Real money demand
Household saving	Consumption
Investment	Consumption plus investment

19. In a February 25, 1988 *Wall Street Journal* article, Fed Chairman Alan Greenspan suggests that progress on narrowing the federal government budget deficit could help persuade foreign investors to continue to hold U.S. securities: "What we have seen in the past is that the willingness on the part of foreigners to hold dollars is very closely related to their sense of soundness of our economic policies." Indicate the effect on the foreign exchange market for the dollar if foreigners suddenly lose faith in the soundness of the U.S. economy and thus seek to reduce their purchases of U.S. (dollar denominated) financial assets. Label the axis. Explain what is implied by the following terms: relative prices of foreign goods, U.S. exports, U.S. imports, and the U.S. balance of trade.

20. According to the February 12, 1988 *Wall Street Journal*, "Mr. Greenspan called for congressional action to lower the federal budget deficit, arguing, among other points, that reducing the gap could stimulate the economy over the long term by bringing down rates. He said the existence of the large deficit keeps interest rates high, hurting capital investment and housing."

   a. Let's suppose that a lower federal budget deficit is achieved by a reduction in military spending. Assume no change in net real taxes. Depict graphically the initial impact on the financial and money market of such a change in government spending. Identify whether there now exists an excess demand for or supply of money and excess demand for or supply of output at the original levels of prices and real GNP.

   b. In an open economy, depict graphically the initial impact on the foreign exchange market for the dollar of the above reduction in government spending. What is the initial impact of such a change on exports and imports?

   c. Depict graphically the effect of the reduction in government deficit spending in terms of aggregate demand-supply analysis.

   d. For an open economy, identify the effect of the fall in government deficit spending on the following:

Price level	Real GNP
Money interest rate	Expected real interest rate
Consumption	Investment
Exports	Imports
Relative price of foreign goods	

21. According to the February 22, 1988 *Wall Street Journal*, the price of the dollar in terms of West German marks is anticipated to depreciate over the next six months from 1.708 marks to 1.679 marks, a 1.7 percent fall. Equivalently, the West German mark is anticipated to appreciate in terms of the U.S. dollar from .5855 to .5956 over this same period, a 1.7 percent rise. Assuming such changes solely reflect anticipated differences across the two countries in monetary policy (that is, purchasing power parity is anticipated to hold), what is the implied difference between the anticipated inflation in the United States and expected inflation in West Germany over the next six months? If inflation over the next six months is anticipated to be 3 percent in the United States, what is it anticipated to be in West Germany?

22. According to a recent *Wall Street Journal*, W. Lee Hoskins, president of the Federal Reserve Bank of Cleveland, stated in a speech to the Conference Board that the Fed's role is "to maintain price stability over the long run."

a. Write down the exchange equation. Define any symbols.

b. As suggested by the exchange equation, if real GNP is rising by 3 percent per year and there is no anticipated change in the ratio of real GNP to real money demand, then what is the appropriate monetary policy to achieve price stability?

23. In an April 22, 1988 *Wall Street Journal* article, it was reported that the Vice Chairman of the Fed, Manuel Johnson, looks to financial markets in shaping his views of appropriate Fed monetary policy: "He especially monitors the 'yield curve'—the spread between long-term and short-term interest rates. Rising long-term rates, many economists believe, signal financial-market expectations that inflation is building. A falling dollar or rising commodity prices, he says, send similar signals."

a. Identify the exogenous variable that the above quote suggests has changed when it refers to "financial-market expectations that inflation is building." Depict graphically the initial impact (at the original level of output prices and real GNP) of such a change in this exogenous variable on the financial and money markets. Label the axes.

b. According to (a), at the original levels of output prices and real GNP, what is the situation in the output and money markets. Depict the implication of this situation in terms of aggregate demand and supply analysis. Assume the neoclassical model. Label the axes.

c. Compare the new equilibrium situation with what would have existed had there not been a change in the exogenous variable identified in (a). In particular, what has happened to each of the following variables (increased, decreased, no change, or ambiguous):

Level of prices

Real GNP

Money interest rate

Expected real interest rate

Money wage

Real wage

Investment demand

Consumption

Velocity

Real money supply

d. Assume "financial-market expectations" are "rational" expectations formed in light of the predictions of the neoclassical model. In this case, what announced change in the future rate of growth of the money supply, if believed, would reduce such "financial-market expectations": an increase, a decrease, no change, either an increase or decrease?

24. According to a recent *Wall Street Journal* article (April 11, 1988), "Conspicuous consumption is out and saving is in, according to Edward Yardeni, director of economics and fixed-income research at Prudential-Bache Securities, Inc. Mr. Yardeni believes that the personal savings rate will rise 10% over the next five years, largely because of the decline of the Yuppie and the rise of the 'couch potato.'"

a. Depict graphically the initial effect on the financial and money markets of the saving increase brought on by the "decline of the Yuppie and the rise of the "couch potato." Assume no change in real money demand. Label the axes.

b. According to (a), at the original levels of output prices and real GNP, what is the situation in the output and money markets. Depict the implication of this situation in terms of aggregate demand and supply analysis. Assume the neoclassical model. Label the axes.

c. Compare the new equilibrium situation with what would have existed had there not been a change in the exogenous variables identified in (a). In particular, what has happened to each of the following variables (increased, decreased, no change, or ambiguous):

Level of prices   Real GNP

Money interest rate   Expected real interest rate

Money wage   Real wage

Investment demand   Consumption

Velocity   Real money supply

Chapter 9

Supply Shocks

In Chapter 8, we examined changes in factors that affect aggregate demand and discovered that macroeconomic demand shocks leave current output unchanged in the neoclassical model. Prices and interest rates can be affected, however, as well as the way in which output is divided among households, firms, and the government. In this chapter, we turn our attention to another type of macroeconomic shock—changes in factors affecting aggregate supply. Just as government policies can affect aggregate demand, they can also affect aggregate supply. In fact, supply-side economics has been perhaps the most controversial economic policy issue of the 1980s. Although the term supply-side economics is relatively new, the ideas behind it have their roots in the neoclassical model.

Supply-side economics emphasizes that after-tax wages and the after-tax return to investment are the important forces behind the incentives to work, save, and invest. Accordingly, tax rates play an important role in analyzing factor supply, and reducing tax rates is the linchpin of any government supply-side policy. The supply-side view of the economy can be juxtaposed against the view that aggregate demand is the key determinant of the overall level of output, employment, and prices in the economy.

Although many people associate the idea of cuts in tax rates with the Reagan administration's Economic Recovery Tax Act (ERTA) of 1981 and the Tax Reform Act of 1986, it was Congressman Jack Kemp who was one of the early well-known supply-side politicians. In 1977, Kemp proposed the then revolutionary, across-the-board tax cuts in the Kemp-Roth Bill. The bill never made it to the floor of Congress for a vote, but it set the stage for future efforts at cutting taxes.

To equate supply-side analysis with tax cutting is somewhat of an over-simplification. Yet, as our analysis in the first two sections of this chapter will show, government taxes and subsidies can play potentially important roles in determining the overall level of output in the economy. The first section of this chapter examines government policy actions, such as changes in marginal tax rates and unemployment insurance programs, that supply-side economics suggests affect the labor market and ultimately alter unemployment, employment, and real GNP. The second section of the chapter looks at government policy actions, such as special tax treatments for capital purchases, that seek to alter firms' investment. Changes in investment have important supply-side effects, since investment determines the growth in the capital stock and thus the long-run productive capacity of the economy.

The final section of the chapter examines some non-tax, supply-side disturbances that cause business fluctuations, such as the reversals of growth in real GNP that occurred during the 1970s. A key type of supply shock that we will look at is disruptions of the supply of oil, such as those that occurred in 1973 and 1979. Our analysis also applies to the converse of oil disruptions—oil gluts—such as occurred in the mid-1980s. Analyses that rely on macroeconomic supply shocks to explain fluctuations in the economy have been termed "real business cycle theories." Later chapters examine the role played by macroeconomic demand shocks in explaining business fluctuations.

9.1   POLICY CHANGES THAT CAN AFFECT THE LABOR INPUT

The neoclassical model emphasizes that output responds to changes in the supply of inputs. Decisions that affect employment determine current output, while decisions that affect the size of the capital stock determine the rate of growth in output in the future. Such decisions include those on labor force participation, hours worked, households' saving, and firms' investment. In this section, we examine how government policy actions affect labor supply decisions.

Changes in Marginal Tax Rates and the Labor Market

The rate at which government taxes labor income influences employment and thus real GNP. When we examined labor supply in Chapter 6, we noted that the supply of labor by households depends on the real wage net of taxes. Many legislators have embraced this idea, as was evidenced by the overwhelming support in 1986 for a radical reduction in marginal tax rates.[1] Let's analyze the effects of a reduction in the marginal tax rate levied on

---

[1] These changes were part of the historic 1986 overhaul of the tax code that has been called the Tax Reform Act.

wage income. In order to focus on the supply-side effects of a reduction in the tax rate on wages, we assume that the government increases other taxes to keep total taxes unchanged.[2] This combination of a change in tax rates with no expected change in total tax revenues was a key element of the 1986 tax legislation, which both lowered tax rates and claimed revenue neutrality.[3]

Figure 9.1 illustrates how a reduction in the tax rate on worker's wage income affects the labor market. Since a reduction in the tax rate increases workers' after-tax wage income, workers are willing to supply more labor at any real wage. Thus the labor supply curve shifts to the right from N_0^s to N_1^s. Equivalently, the labor supply curve shifts downward by the amount of the tax cut (from point A to point C), indicating that the same amount of labor will be supplied at a lower real wage but at the identical after-tax wage income.

As shown in Figure 9.1, the increase in the supply of labor that results from the cut in tax rates causes a fall in the equilibrium real wage from $(W/P)_0$ to $(W/P)_1$ and a rise in employment from N_0 to N_1. Although the cut in the tax rate causes a fall in the equilibrium wage, the real wage *net* of taxes actually rises. The reason we know this is quite simple. The increase in equilibrium employment means that households are willing to supply more labor at the new equilibrium real wage. To be induced to increase the quantity of labor services supplied, households must receive a greater payoff to working in the form of increased after-tax wages.[4]

A higher level of equilibrium employment means not only that households are willing to supply more labor at the new equilibrium real wage but that firms are willing to hire more labor. Although the tax cut raises the real wage *net* of taxes received by households, it reduces the real wage paid by firms, which thus means that firms find it profitable to increase employment. To see this, let's look at a numerical example. Suppose that the wage is $10 and the tax rate on wage income is 40 percent. Thus while it costs employers $10 to hire one hour of labor, employees' wages net of taxes are $6 per hour. If the tax rate on wage income is cut to 20 percent, and the wage falls, say, to $9, then firms and employees both gain. Employers obviously pay less, while the employee's after-tax income rises to $7.20 (80 percent of gross wage income).

In essence, a lower tax rate reduces the tax on the exchange of labor services and thus can lead to an increase in the amount of labor services exchanged. Buyers buy more labor and sellers sell more labor since each receives, either directly through the fall in taxes or indirectly through the

---

[2] Hence, the aggregate demand curve does not shift in the analysis below.

[3] In the 1986 tax bill, revenue neutrality was sought by reducing certain exemptions and deductions and increasing taxes on business earnings. These changes have potential effects on firms' investment decisions, as we see in the next section.

[4] Recall that the supply curve for labor slopes up for precisely this reason: The quantity of labor supplied increases only if additional compensation is forthcoming.

Figure 9.1   The Effect of a Reduction in Marginal Tax Rates on the Labor Market

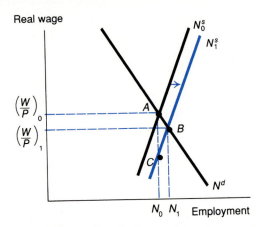

With a reduction in the tax rate on labor income, at a given real wage, the real after-tax wage rises. This induces an increase in labor supply at each real wage, as shown by a shift to the right in the labor supply curve from N_0^s to N_1^s. Equivalently, the labor supply curve shifts down. At each level of labor supply, the vertical difference between the two labor supply curves (for instance, the difference between points A and C) indicates the reduction in the real wage that leaves after-tax real wages unaffected given the cut in the tax rate. As a consequence of the increase in labor supply, the equilibrium real wage falls from $(W/P)_0$ to $(W/P)_1$ and employment rises from N_0 to N_1.

fall in real wages, part of the gains to the further exchange of labor services that arise with the lower taxes.[5]

Our analysis indicates that a tax cut can raise real GNP since it increases the equilibrium level of employment in the economy. Similarly, the analysis predicts that a rise in tax rates will lead to a fall in real GNP. A recent study of the Swedish economy by economist Charles E. Stuart supports this analysis, at least for large changes in tax rates: "Effective marginal tax rates on labor income for the 'representative' Swede have increased from roughly 50 percent in 1959 to 80 percent today (1979). . . . The estimated long-run effects are sufficient to explain up to 75 percent of the recent decline in the measured growth rate of the Swedish GNP. . . . During the period 1969–1977, (when

---

[5] A fall in the payroll tax on employers has a similar effect to that of a fall in the tax rate on labor income. Such a reduction leads to an increase in the demand for labor and an increase in employment and wages. Although the real wage rises, the real wage inclusive of payroll taxes falls. (If the real wage inclusive of payroll taxes does not fall, then firms will not be willing to hire more labor.) Naturally, the higher real wage induces an increase in the quantity of labor that households supply. As we have seen before, it often makes little difference whether taxes are levied on firms or directly on households.

the marginal tax rate rose from 65.6 percent to close to 80 percent) the ratio of hours worked divided by the population of working age fell roughly 7 percent."[6]

Changes in Tax Rates and the Aggregate Supply Curve

A decrease in the tax rate increases employment and, for any given capital stock, an increase in employment increases the productive capacity of the economy. As Figure 9.2 indicates, the reduction in the tax rate on wage income, since it is predicted to increase the equilibrium level of employment, causes a shift to the right in the aggregate supply curve, from AS_0 to AS_1, as output increases from Y_0 to Y_1. This shift to the right in the aggregate supply curve means not only to an increase in real GNP but also to a decrease in the level of prices from P_0 to P_1.

To understand why an increase in equilibrium employment and the supply of output causes a decrease in the equilibrium price level, consider the effect of the higher output on demand and supply in the output market. With the increased output comes an equal increase in household disposable income, which causes consumption spending to increase. Given a marginal propensity to consume that is less than one, however, the *increase in consumption demand is less than the increase in disposable income and output*. The remainder of the increase in disposable income goes toward increased household saving. Since output demand rises by less than output, excess supply exists in the output market at the original level of prices. It is this excess supply of output that is the impetus for the fall in output prices.

The rise in real GNP leads not only to a lower price level but also to a reduced interest rate. As Figure 9.2 indicates, the new equilibrium is reached by simply moving down the aggregate demand curve. The reason for the fall in the interest rate is that the fall in the price level increases the real money supply, and hence the real supply of loanable funds. This chain of events is the same one discussed in Chapter 7 to explain the downward slope of the aggregate demand curve. In the output market, the fall in the interest rate induces an increase in investment and consumption demand, which eliminates the excess supply of output.

To summarize, a reduction in the tax rate on wage income can lead to an increase in employment, output, and the net real wage while it decreases the price level, the real wage rate, and the interest rate. Note that the fall in the real wage is due entirely to the increase in labor supply induced by the lower tax rate, as was illustrated in Figure 9.1. The fall in price level has no effect on the real wage because changes in the price level simply lead to equiproportional changes in the money wage. As we saw in Chapter 7, the fact that changes in the price level do not affect the real wage explains why the aggregate supply curve is vertical.

---

[6] Charles E. Stuart, "Swedish Tax Rates, Labor Supply, and Tax Revenues," *Journal of Political Economy* (October 1981) p. 1020–1038.

Figure 9.2   The Effect of a Reduction in Marginal Tax Rates on Output and Prices

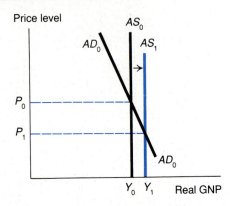

With a reduction in tax rates and consequent increase in equilibrium employment, the supply of output rises from Y_0 to Y_1. The shift to the right in the aggregate supply curve from AS_0 to AS_1 shows this increase in supply, which causes a fall in the level of prices from P_0 to P_1.

Supply-Side Economics: Some Important Qualifications

Supply-side economics: The argument that a reduction in taxes raises the rewards to work, and can thus lead to increased employment, increased real output, lower inflation, and lower interest rates.

The argument that a reduction in tax rates raises the rewards to work and can thus lead to increased employment, increased real output, lower inflation, and lower interest rates is part of what has become known as "**supply-side economics.**" In addition to all these predicted benefits, supply-side economics also argues that lower tax rates will reduce the natural rate of unemployment since higher net real wages raise the costs to remaining unemployed. There should thus be little surprise that supply-side advocates tout lower taxes as the panacea for an economy's ills since most people embrace the goals of higher employment, an increased growth rate in real GNP, lower inflation, lower interest rates, and lower unemployment. We should, however, bear three important considerations in mind when we assess the overall benefits of a reduction in tax rates.

First, we conducted our preceding analysis in the context of the neoclassical model. The long-run assumptions of perfect price flexibility and perfect information on the part of market participants may not be appropriate, however. For example, if in the short run prices are rigid, as is often the case, then demand-side, not supply-side, considerations determine employment and output. As we will see in later chapters, when inflexible prices result in deficient demand, a change in tax policy that leads only to an increase in the supply of labor affects neither employment nor output since the demand for the additional output is not forthcoming.

Second, although the neoclassical model predicts that a reduction in the tax rate leads to an increase in employment and output and a decrease in the interest rate and prices, it cannot accurately predict the magnitude of these effects. Much of the controversy over the effects of supply-side economics concerns the *magnitude* of the predicted effects, not their direction. As we saw in Chapter 6, the evidence indicates that labor supply is not that responsive to changes in the after-tax real wage. Even the admitted supply-sider Martin Feldstein states that "although we would expect some increase in work effort from the reduction in the highest marginal tax rates, past evidence all points to relatively small changes." [7]

Third, the example of a change in tax rates that we examined was engineered so that it did not alter total taxes. In reality, tax rate reductions can result in lower total tax revenues. This affects government spending and/or borrowing, which alters the macroeconomic effects of the tax rate change. It also puts pressure on the government to reduce spending on some government programs that many consider important. In fact, much of the clamor over the 1981 Reagan tax legislation that reduced tax rates came from individuals who saw it as an indirect way of reducing tax revenues, which put the squeeze on various government programs.

The relationship between tax rates and tax revenues has received much attention in the recent literature on the Laffer curve. We explore the historical roots of the Laffer curve in the next section, as well as how cuts in tax rates have affected government tax revenues in recent experience.

Tax Rate Changes and Tax Revenues: The Laffer Curve

"If a tax is gradually increased from zero up to the point where it becomes prohibitive, its yield is at first nil, then increases by small stages until it reaches a maximum, after which it gradually declines until it becomes zero again." This quote embodies the concept known as the **Laffer curve.** The words are not those of modern-day economist Arthur Laffer, however, but of the nineteenth-century French economist, Jules Dupuit.[8] Yet the concept is attributed to Laffer because of press reports in 1974 that he drew a graphical interpretation of the Dupuit relationship on a napkin in a Washington restaurant. Figure 9.3 depicts this relationship, with tax rates on the horizontal axis and tax revenues on the vertical axis.

Laffer curve: A curve depicting the relationship between the income tax rate and total tax revenues.

The revenue that the government generates from any of its taxes equals the tax base multiplied by the tax rate. For example, the revenue collected from a sales tax equals the sales tax rate multiplied by the dollar value of retail sales; the revenue that a property tax generates equals the property tax rate multiplied by the assessed value of the property. The most important source of tax revenues—the income tax—has as its base the level of income

---

[7] Martin Feldstein, "Supply-side Economics: Old Truths and New Claims," *American Economic Review* (May 1986) p. 29.

[8] Jules Dupuit, "On the Measurement of the Utility of Public Works," in *Readings in Welfare Economics*, eds. Kenneth Arrow and Tibor Scitovsky, translated from "De la Mesure de l'Utilité des Travaux Publics," *Annales des Ponts et Chaussées*, 2d series, vol. 8, 1844.

Figure 9.3   The Laffer Curve

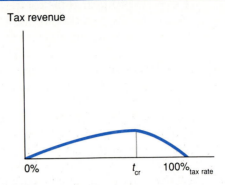

The Laffer Curve depicts the relationship between the income tax rate and total tax revenues. Above the critical tax rate t_{cr}, increases in the tax rate reduce total tax revenues, due to the negative effects on taxable income.

in the economy. As we have seen, a change in tax rates can lead to a change in the level of income in the opposite direction. This raises an interesting question. Will a reduction in tax rates stimulate a large enough increase in income to result in an increase in total tax revenues? The Laffer/Dupuit curve indicates that below some critical tax rate, denoted in Figure 9.3 by t_{cr}, tax increases raise total tax revenues. Above that tax rate, however, increases in tax rates lower total tax revenues.

In 1921, the marginal income tax rate was 73 percent for those in the top income bracket. By 1926, the tax rate on income over $100,000 was reduced to 25 percent. As economist Yale Brozen reports, "A remarkable thing happened. Despite a nearly two-thirds reduction in [the] tax rate on the top bracket group, they paid 86 percent more taxes in 1926 than they paid in 1921. . . . With this steep reduction in top bracket rates, incentives for earning taxable income in this bracket increased greatly."[9]

As reported in *The Wall Street Journal* (December 31, 1987), Lawrence Lindsey, professor of economics at Harvard and former senior staff economist for tax policy at the Council of Economic Advisers, has found a similar pattern for those in the highest tax brackets after the tax cut of 1981. More specifically, Lindsey estimates that by 1985 revenue collected from taxpayers with incomes over $200,000 was 25% above what it would have been at the top pre-1981 tax rate of 70%.

We must make two clarifications on this point. The first concerns whether

[9] Yale Brozen, "Government and Income Redistribution: Its Effects on the Private Market," in *Economic Growth and Income Redistribution: Are They Compatible Goals?* ed. Gerald Lynch, (Muncie, Indiana) 1982. Of course, part of the increase in taxes was due to the 37 percent increase in nominal GNP during this period. Nevertheless, note that the percent increase in taxes far outstripped the change in nominal GNP.

current average U.S. tax rates are above or below the critical level indicated by the Laffer curve illustrated in Figure 9.3. In the United States, recent reductions in the *overall* schedule of tax rates have not led to increased total tax revenues. For instance, one study found that in response to the cut in tax rates in 1981, the increase in taxable income in 1982 offset only one third of the effect on federal receipts of the cut in tax rates.[10] Brozen's contrary result largely reflects the high marginal tax rates faced by people in the top brackets.

The second clarification on the relationship between tax rates and total tax revenues is to point out that the increase in taxable income that results from a fall in tax rates reflects not only a potential increase in labor supply but also a reduction in tax avoidance. As we noted in Chapter 2, a large underground economy exists in the United States in which transactions involve mainly currency in order to avoid detection by the tax authorities. Economist Vito Tanzi notes that the presence of an underground economy constitutes a significant source of the demand for currency. Consistent with the hypothesis that tax evasion increases with the tax rate, Tanzi finds that an increase in the tax rate (and thus tax avoidance in the underground economy) leads to a rise in the demand for currency.[11] It has also been shown that tax avoidance is greatest for individuals in the highest tax brackets, with avoidance falling as tax rates fall.[12]

Another legal means of tax avoidance that is affected by changes in tax rates comes when firms pay out compensation in the form of untaxable fringe benefits, such as pensions and group insurance. When the government reduces tax rates, it reduces the gains to receiving payments in the form of nontaxed fringe benefits. Other things being equal, it is estimated that the lower tax rates of the 1981 tax act increased federal government revenues by as much as 4 percent by leading to a substitution of cash income for fringe benefits which thus expanded the federal and payroll tax bases.[13]

Some Effects of Changes in Government Transfer Programs

In addition to tax rates affecting labor supply and thus real GNP, government programs involving transfer payments can have an impact on labor supply. For example, according to a study by labor economist Donald Parsons, "the rate of non-participation in market work among prime-aged males in the United States [rose] persistently during the postwar period. The rate among

---

[10] Lawrence Lindsey, "Taxpayer Behavior in the Distribution of the 1982 Tax Cut," NBER Working Paper No. 1760 (1985).

[11] Vito Tanzi, "The Underground Economy in the United States: Estimates and Implications," *Banca Nazionale del Lavoro Quarterly Review* (December 1980).

[12] Charles Clotfelter, "Tax Evasion and Tax Rates: An Analysis of Individual Returns," *The Review of Economics and Statistics* (August 1983).

[13] James E. Long and Frank A. Scott, Jr., "The Impact of the 1981 Tax Act on Fringe Benefits and Federal Tax Revenues," *National Tax Journal* (1984).

Figure 9.4   **The Effect of an Increase in Disability Pensions on the Labor Market**

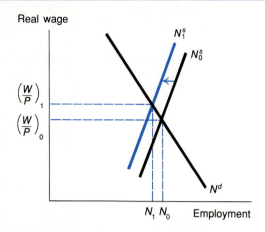

An increase in disability pensions, which increases the gains to not participating in the labor force, results in a shift to the left in the labor supply curve from N_0^s to N_1^s. This results in an increase on the wage from $(W/P)_0$ to $(W/P)_1$ and a fall in employment from N_0 to N_1.

males ages 45–54, for example, [rose] from 4.2 percent to 8.4 percent from 1948 to 1976, with similar trends among other age groups. . . . labor force withdrawals [have] been induced by the rapid expansion of welfare alternatives to work, principally the Social Security disability program.'' [14]

Parsons' study indicates that a change in one type of government transfer payment—social security disability pensions—can adversely affect the supply of labor. Although you might think that the supply of "disabled" people is fixed, this study shows that it is not.[15] Parsons found that a 10 percent increase in disability pensions raises the nonparticipation rate by 6 percent, if other things remain unchanged. In terms of the labor market, an increase in disability pensions causes a shift to the left in the labor supply curve, from N_0^s to N_1^s in Figure 9.4.

Figure 9.4 illustrates that the decrease in labor force participation caused by an increase in disability pensions results in an increase in the equilibrium real wage from $(W/P)_0$ to $(W/P)_1$ and a decrease in the equilibrium level of employment from N_0 to N_1. With the reduction in the equilibrium employment level comes a reduction in the level of output supplied by firms. As a con-

---

[14] Donald Parsons, "The Decline in Male Labor Force Participation," *Journal of Political Economy* (February 1980) p. 117. Data on labor force participation rates through 1986 indicate that this trend has not been reversed in recent years for males.

[15] To qualify for a disability pension, a worker must have been unable to work for at least five months and the disability must be expected to last 12 months or more.

Figure 9.5 **The Effect of an Increase in Disability Pensions on Output and Prices**

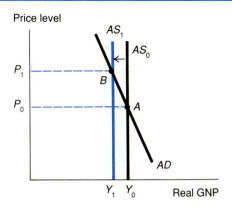

A rise in disability pensions results in a fall in labor force supply and employment, which means a reduction in aggregate supply from AS_0 to AS_1. Real GNP falls from Y_0 to Y_1 and the price level rises from P_0 to P_1.

sequence, the aggregate supply curve, which is illustrated in Figure 9.5, shifts to the left from AS_0 to AS_1. Note that in this analysis the increase in transfer payments (specifically, disability pension payments) is assumed to be accompanied by an increase in government tax revenues, which means that the level of net taxes is unchanged and thus the aggregate demand curve does not shift.

Equilibrium real GNP falls from Y_0 to Y_1, and the equilibrium level of prices rises from P_0 to P_1. The increase in the price level, in turn, has the effect of reducing the real money supply and thus reducing the real supply of loanable funds from what they otherwise would have been. This leads to a higher interest rate than would have otherwise existed. The rise in the interest rate reflects the fact that we reach the new equilibrium by moving up the aggregate demand curve AD from point A to point B. These macroeconomic consequences follow from the fact that increased generosity of disability payments raises the attractiveness of alternatives to work and thus reduces the supply of labor.

Unemployment insurance benefits are another type of government transfer payment that can affect labor supply and thus the aggregate supply curve. An increase in real unemployment compensation reduces the cost to a worker of being unemployed.[16] This results in an increase in the average length of time that laid-off workers spend unemployed before accepting alternative

---

[16] An increase in unemployment compensation that affects the aggregate labor supply may take any combination of the following: (1) an increase in the amount of benefits paid each week; (2) an increase in the number of weeks that unemployed workers are eligible to receive benefits; or (3) an increase in the number of individuals who qualify for unemployment compensation.

employment. Both a higher natural unemployment rate and a lower equilibrium level of employment result.[17] Several studies have found that states providing more generous benefits have higher unemployment rates, other things equal.[18]

To summarize, an increase in real unemployment compensation leads to a reduction in employment and output, and to an increase in unemployment, inflation, and the interest rate. Although unattractive, these effects are offset by the fact that unemployment insurance allows workers displaced from their jobs to spend additional time finding suitable employment. With more time to find a job, these displaced workers will be able to find jobs for which they are better suited and which pay higher wages. This improved matching of workers to jobs results in increased output, partially offsetting the lower output due to the reduced employment level.[19] In addition, in the context of macroeconomic models whose intent it is to describe the short-run behavior of the economy (a subject to be developed in later chapters), the unemployment insurance program and similar transfer programs can reduce the magnitude of recessions. These programs help stabilize the economy in the short run by reducing the fall in household disposable income and thus the fall in household consumption, given a fall in real GNP.

The Accumulation of Human Capital

We have focused on the response of labor supply to government policies concerning tax rates and transfer payments, but other factors must be considered. "Possibly more important sources of long-run variations in the supply of labor services, especially for prime age males, are differences in formal education and on-the-job training in the choice of occupation, and in the intensity of effort with which a particular occupation is pursued."[20]

---

[17] Evidence that higher unemployment insurance benefits lead to lower search efforts by workers and thus reduced likelihood of becoming employed is contained in two articles by John M. Barron and Wesley Mellow: "Search Effort in the Labor Market," *Journal of Human Resources* (Summer 1979) p. 389–404 and "Changes in the Labor Force Status Among the Unemployed," *Journal of Human Resources* (Summer 1981) p. 427–441.

[18] See, for instance, Martin Feldstein, "Unemployment Compensation: Adverse Incentives and Distribution Anomalies," *National Tax Journal* (June 1974) p. 231–244. As Feldstein points out in another paper, "The Effect of Unemployment Insurance on Temporary Layoff Unemployment," *American Economic Review* (December 1978) p. 834–847. Existing unemployment programs not only affect the duration of unemployment but also have an important effect on the frequency of unemployment spells. Unemployment insurance payments are funded by taxes on employers, but these taxes often do not change with changes in the unemployment insurance that their workers collect. This means that when firms lay off their workers, other firms subsidize the unemployment compensation benefits they receive. Thus the program has encouraged firms to organize production in ways that increase their use of layoffs.

[19] See Ronald Ehrenberg and Ronald Oaxaca, "Unemployment Insurance, Duration of Unemployment, and Subsequent Wage Gain," *American Economic Review* (December 1976) p. 754–766. The authors find some support for the idea that an increase in unemployment benefits induces additional productive job search.

[20] Martin Feldstein, *Capital Taxation* (Cambridge, Mass.: Harvard University Press, 1983), p. 377.

Human capital: Investments in schooling, on-the-job training, medical care, and job search that influence future monetary and psychic income by increasing the resources in people.

Formal education and training resemble capital in that their accumulation today increases the output of workers in future periods. Given this similarity, economists view formal education and training as the acquisition of **human capital.** Gary Becker, a potential future Nobel Prize winner for his research on human capital, defines investments in human capital as "activities that influence future monetary and psychic income by increasing the resources in people. . . . The many forms of such investments include schooling, on-the-job training, medical care, migration, and search for information about prices and incomes."[21]

Government spending and taxation policies recognize the critical role that human capital accumulation plays in economic growth. For example, extensive subsidies to formal education exist—from state-supported kindergartens to state universities. Federal and state scholarship and loan programs also invest in formal education. The Comprehensive Employment and Training Act (CETA) of 1975 supported on-the-job training for disadvantaged youth.[22] The government has also subsidized the acquisition of human capital by making expenditures for job relocation and the search for improved employment opportunities tax deductible.

At the same time, certain government policies restrain the accumulation of human capital. These policies include a progressive income tax system that increases the proportion of income taxed as income rises and thus reduces the incentive to acquire additional human capital either through schooling or on-the-job training. Minimum wage legislation has also reduced the investment in human capital.[23] Employers often have their employees pay for their on-the-job training, in a sense, by offering them a low starting wage. By putting a lower bound or minimum on the starting wage, minimum wage laws restrict the extent to which employees can pay for their on-the-job training through a lower wage. Minimum wage laws thus have a negative effect on the amount of on-the-job training opportunities available to employees. Economist Masanori Hashimoto finds that the increases in both the nominal minimum wage rate and the coverage (of workers) introduced by the 1967 amendments to the Fair Labor Standards Act "reduced the value of training per hour by somewhere between . . . 2.7 and 15 percent from what it would have been in the absence of changes in the law."[24]

---

[21] Gary S. Becker, *Human Capital,* 2nd ed. (National Bureau of Economic Research, 1975), p. 1.

[22] CETA was eliminated in the Reagan budget cuts of the early 1980s.

[23] For example, see Finis Welch, *Minimum Wages: Issues and Evidence* (Washington, D.C.: American Enterprise Institute for Public Policy Research, 1978).

[24] Masanori Hashimoto, "Minimum Wage Effects on Training on the Job," *American Economic Review* (December 1982): 1070–1087.

To the Point

SUPPLY-SIDE POLICIES AND THE LABOR INPUT

- In the neoclassical model—which was shown to have a vertical aggregate supply curve—changes in aggregate demand have no influence on the level of output. Only factors that alter the supply side of the economy change the level of real GNP.

- Factors that affect the input of labor will alter aggregate supply in the economy. These factors include changes in marginal tax rates, disability insurance, unemployment compensation, and policies that affect the investment in human capital. For example, unemployment compensation raises the reward to not working, which thus lowers the supply of labor and ultimately decreases aggregate output.

- An important aspect of tax rate changes is the impact on total tax revenues. The Laffer curve suggests that at some point tax rates can get so high and offer such a disincentive to work that increases in tax rates will actually decrease tax revenues. Regardless of the impact of tax rates on tax revenues and thus aggregate demand, changes in tax rates can alter aggregate supply in the economy by changing individuals incentives to work.

9.2   POLICY CHANGES THAT CAN ALTER THE CAPITAL INPUT

In recent years, the United States has experienced productivity growth that is considered low when compared with past U.S. history and with the growth rates of other countries. This has spurred much interest in the relationship between tax incentives, capital formation, and economic growth.[25] Although models of economic growth consider myriad factors that contribute to productivity growth, two of the most significant are the accumulation of physical capital and improvements in technology.

In examining the factors that lead to high growth rates of capital formation, it is important to recognize the role of incentives. Entrepreneurs who invest must be able to reap the return to their risk-taking or the incentive to engage in capital formation will be low. Historian William McNeill provides us with an interesting example of the historical importance of an environment that is conducive to capital accumulation.

McNeill observes that the advent of extended market exchange in China around the tenth century A.D. had a stunning impact on the Chinese economy: "The effect was to increase the country's wealth spectacularly. . . . China's cities grew to a size that dazzled and amazed such sophisticated world

---

[25] Capital formation is simply additions to the economy's capital stock.

travelers as Marco Polo and the Moslem, Ibn Battuta.''[26] However, the attitude of the Chinese toward the accumulation of wealth subsequently stifled investment, and China's relative superiority in commerce had evaporated by the fifteenth century.

The Chinese, who were primarily Confucians, believed that a man who got rich from trade did so by cheating others. Confucius had classed merchants with soldiers as ''human parasites, because they bought cheap and sold dear without adding anything to the value of the goods they dealt in. Good government therefore required that no one could get conspicuously rich from trade.'' This made private accumulation of capital risky in imperial China, setting a ceiling on technical advance. China therefore saw ''little private development of mining and shipbuilding, the two forms of economic activity that most conspicuously required relatively large capital investment. Not by accident, it was in these domains that the skilled and commercially sophisticated Chinese fell behind the comparatively unskilled Europeans by about 1450. It is no exaggeration to suggest that the course of modern history turned on this reversal of the earlier relationship between the Far Eastern and Far Western segments of the Old World.''

Although not as dramatic as the reversal McNeill notes, the trend in capital accumulation and productivity growth seems to be swinging back toward a favorable position for the Eastern nations. The rapid growth of productivity in Japan in the post–World War II era and the recent rise in the Pacific Rim of newly industrialized countries (NICs) such as South Korea, Taiwan, and Malaysia have led to a reexamination of the U.S. policies toward saving and investment. In the following sections, we examine the macro-economic implications of the 1981 tax changes that were intended to spur capital accumulation and growth in the United States. We also examine the implications of the Tax Reform Act of 1986 tax bill that reversed some of the incentives for investment.

Investment Tax Incentives: An Examination of the 1981 Tax Bill

In order to sustain long-term growth, average productivity or output per worker must increase. In this way, there is more of ''the pie'' to divide up among the population. As we now know, investments in human capital, such as formal schooling and on-the-job training, lead to productivity increases. Also crucial to the growth of productivity are investments in the amount of physical capital workers have to work with.

The rate of productivity growth in the United States declined in the 1970s and early 1980s. Between 1949 and 1968, output per hour grew at an average annual rate of 3.3 percent. In the ensuing five years (1968–1973), productivity increased by only 1.8 percent per year. Starting with

---

[26] William McNeill, ''Command Vs. Market Across the Centuries,'' in *Economic Growth and Income Redistribution: Are They Compatible Goals,* ed. Gerald Lynch (Muncie, Indiana: 1982) p. 16.

the recession year of 1974, productivity growth in the United States nosedived. Over the next 14 years (1973–1987), the rate of growth in productivity fell to an average annual rate of 1 percent.

This decline in productivity growth spawned a number of research efforts attempting to identify its causes.[27] Economist Edward Denison, who has conducted lengthy studies of the causes and consequences of economic growth, came to the following conclusion however: "None [of seventeen alleged causes of the productivity slowdown] could be shown to account for much of the drop in the growth rate . . . so I describe its cause as a mystery. That mystery remains."[28]

Politicians and other economists are not so circumspect. Government officials believe the paucity of investment in productivity-improving capital has been a major cause of the slowdown. The 1981 *Economic Report of the President*, authored under the Carter administration, identifies "one of the causes of the decline in productivity growth has been the decline in the growth of the capital stock relative to the labor force."[29] One reason for this fall in investment was a sharp rise in effective tax rates on capital income during the late 1960s and 1970s caused by the interaction of inflation with tax rules that were not indexed to price changes.[30] It has been estimated that without this increase in effective taxes on investment, the average investment-GNP ratio would have been 24 percent higher over the 1965 to 1977 period.[31]

In response to the lower investment and coinciding reduced growth in productivity of the late 1960s and 1970s, Congress enacted the Economic Recovery Tax Act of 1981.[32] The act sought to increase productivity by

---

[27] For instance see John Kendrick, "International Comparisons of Recent Productivity Trends", in *Essays in Contemporary Economic Problems: Demand, Productivity and Population*, ed. William Fellner 1981; Martin Baily, "Productivity and the Services of Capital and Labor," *Brookings Papers on Economic Activity*, 1981; and Michael Bruno, "World Shocks, Macroeconomic Response, and the Productivity Puzzle," NBER Working Paper No. 942R (July, 1982).

[28] Edward Denison, "The Interruption of Productivity Growth in the United States," *Economic Journal* (March, 1983).

[29] *Economic Report of the President* (1981), p. 70.

[30] A discussion of the somewhat complex interaction between inflation and tax rules that lead to this increase in the user cost of capital is contained in a series of papers by Martin Feldstein. "Inflation, Tax Rules, and Capital Formation," NBER monograph (Chicago: University of Chicago Press, 1983). This work extends upon his earlier paper "Inflation, Tax Rules, and Investment: Some Econometric Evidence," *Econometrica* 50 (1982): 825–862.

[31] Martin Feldstein, "Tax Rates and Business Investment: Reply," *Journal of Public Economics* 32 (1987) 389–396.

[32] The Economic Recovery Tax Act of 1981 called for a phased-in liberalization of depreciation allowances and tax rates, and an increase in the investment tax credit stretched over several years. Some of these provisions never took effect because of modifications to the law made in the Tax Equity and Fiscal Responsibility Act of 1982. In future references, we will refer to the combined effects of both of these pieces of legislation as the Economic Recovery Tax Act of 1981.

increasing investment in physical capital. One way in which the 1981 tax act attempted to increase investment was by influencing household saving. The act lowered marginal tax rates and deferred taxation on income put into Individual Retirement Accounts (IRAs). By increasing the after-tax return to saving, the government hoped that household saving in the form of the supply of loanable funds would increase. This would lower the interest rate, leading to increases in firms' investment levels.

In the years immediately following the 1981 Tax Act, it became conventional wisdom that 1) the majority of IRA contributions were made by the wealthy and 2) IRAs resulted in little increase in total household saving, as individuals simply switched from other financial asset saving to IRA accounts. Recent evidence, however, suggests these views are incorrect. In the first three years following the introduction of IRA accounts, 90 percent of the contributions to such accounts were made by individuals earning less than $50,000 per year and 70 percent of contributions were by families earning less than this amount. Further, the evidence suggests that "the vast majority of IRA saving represented new saving, not accompanied by a reduction in other financial asset saving."[33]

The 1981 tax act also attempted to directly encourage firms' investment by lowering the after-tax cost of capital and thus increasing the return to investment in capital. One change was the Accelerated Cost Recovery System (ACRS), or accelerated depreciation allowance, which allowed a more generous treatment of the way in which capital can be depreciated for tax purposes. Firms reduce their taxable profits by deducting allowed depreciation of their capital stock. Before the passage of the 1981 act, a firm could "write off" a machine over an average period of approximately nine years. The act lowered the average period over which the equipment could be written off to five years. Your understanding of present value from Chapter 5 should convince you that the accelerated depreciation allowance made the purchase of a machine less costly today, since the savings in the form of lower taxes come at an earlier date. Thus this allowance increased the present value of the net gains to capital purchases.

The investment tax credit was first introduced by the Kennedy administration in 1962. This credit enabled firms to reduce their tax payments by a fraction of their capital equipment purchases. A second change in the 1981 tax act was to increase the investment tax credit. In the next section, we examine how an accelerated depreciation allowance and an increased investment tax credit affect firms' incentive to invest. We then analyze the macroeconomic effects of such a change in investment incentives. As we will see, these changes in the tax treatment of capital expenditures contributed to the high real interest rates of the early and mid-1980s.

---

[33] Steven Venti and David Wise, "Have IRAs Increased U.S. Saving?: Evidence from Consumer Expenditure Surveys," NBER Working Paper No. 2217, January 1987, p. 38.

The Effects on Aggregate Demand and the Composition of Output Demand

Recall from Chapter 5 that firms' investment decisions involve comparing the return to purchasing an additional unit of capital with the cost. The real return to using a piece of capital for one period is the increase in output attributable to the increased capital input. This increment in output that stems from using an additional unit of capital is called the marginal product of capital (*MPK*).

The real cost to using a piece of capital for one period is not as simplistic as it might first appear. If someone pays $100,000 for a piece of capital equipment, this is not the cost to using the capital. The per-unit cost of using the capital for one period is the expected real interest rate (the money interest rate (r) minus the expected rate of inflation π^e) plus the rate of capital depreciation (d). The expected real rate of interest indicates what the buyer of an additional unit of capital must pay in real terms to borrow the money to purchase the equipment for use during the period. The rate of depreciation is the cost to the buyer of using the machine for the period in terms of its loss in value due to use. These two taken together make up the real user cost of capital, which is denoted by $r - \pi^e + d$.

To maximize profits, firms purchase capital up to point where the return during the next period from an extra unit of capital investment (the marginal product of capital) just equals the cost (the real user cost of capital). That is, capital is purchased up to the point where

$$MPK \quad = \quad r - \pi^e \quad + \quad d$$

| Marginal product of capital | Expected real interest rate | Rate of capital depreciation | **(9.1)** |

In order to incorporate tax incentives into the investment decision, we must modify Equation 9.1. As mentioned above, there have been a variety of tax laws, such as the accelerated depreciation allowance and investment tax credits, that reduce the real user cost of capital. For example, the accelerated depreciation allowance raises the present value of future tax savings from purchasing capital, while investment tax credits reduce the tax liability of firms by an amount equal to a percentage of the value of capital purchases. We wish to capture the effect on the capital purchase decision of such laws in a general way. To do so, we will let ϕ denote the proportion of real capital purchases that such laws allow firms to recoup in the next period. These tax savings are the result of either a reduction in taxable income in the case of the accelerated depreciation allowance or a reduction in taxes in the case of the investment tax credit.

Rewriting Equation 9.1 to incorporate tax considerations, we have capital being purchased up to the point where

$$MPK \quad = \quad r - \pi^e \quad + \quad d \quad - \quad \phi$$

| Marginal product of capital | Expected real interest rate | Rate of capital depreciation | Rate of tax saving on capital purchases | **(9.2)** |

An increase in ϕ in Equation 9.2 is consistent with the introduction of an accelerated depreciation allowance or the introduction of an investment tax credit. In either case, the expected real user cost of capital is reduced, and thus firms will increase investment. The 1981 tax bill, which dramatically increased the pace at which investment could be depreciated for tax purposes, is a good example of an increase in ϕ and consequent reduction in the expected real user cost of capital. Olivier Blanchard and Lawrence Summers cite these increased tax savings from investment as one reason why investment spending was stronger than otherwise would have been the case in 1983 and 1984.[34]

We can use aggregate demand-supply analysis to investigate the effects of this rise in investment demand on the economy.[35] As before, we start by considering the impact on the economy at the original level of prices and real GNP. This in turn will enable us to determine the effect on the aggregate demand curve.

Autonomous spending change: A change in a variable such as investment or consumption demand that is not induced by a change in variables to be determined by the analysis, such as the current interest rate or income.

Figure 9.6 depicts the impact of the rise in firms' autonomous investment demand on the financial market and the money market. A change in **autonomous** investment demand means a change in investment demand that is independent of changes in the current interest rate or income level. From the firm financing constraint, we know that a rise in investment demand causes an equal increase in the demand for loanable funds, as firms borrow to finance their capital purchases. This is shown in Figure 9.6(a) by a shift to the right in the demand for loanable funds from LF_0^d to LF_1^d. The equilibrium interest rate thus rises from r_0 to r_1.

The rise in the interest rate from r_0 to r_1 reduces the quantity of investment from what it would have been had the interest rate not changed. This is shown by the movement up the new demand for loanable funds curve LF_1^d in Figure 9.6(a) from point A to point B. At the same time, part of the increase in the quantity of loanable funds supplied shown by the movement from point C to point B reflects a fall in household consumption demand and an offsetting rise in saving. However, the rise in autonomous investment demand due to the more favorable tax treatment of capital purchases more

---

[34] Olivier Blanchard and Lawrence Summers, "Perspectives on High World Real Interest Rates," *Brookings Papers on Economic Activity,* 1984, pp. 273–334.

[35] In the analysis that follows, we presume that the favorable tax treatment on capital purchases is accompanied by no change in the total net taxes levied by the government on businesses and households.

Figure 9.6   The Effect of an Increase in Autonomous Investment on the Financial Market and Money Market

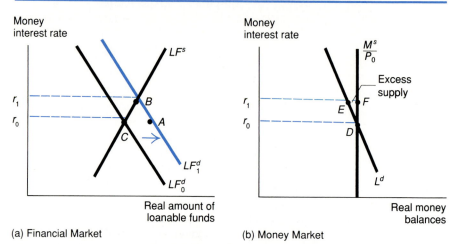

(a) Financial Market   (b) Money Market

With an increase in investment, firms' demand for loanable funds increases. This increase in the demand for loanable funds is shown by the shift in the demand for loanable funds curve from LF_0^d to LF_1^d. The equilibrium interest rate rises from r_0 to r_1. In the money market, the higher interest rate reduces the quantity of money demanded and thus leads to an excess supply of money at the original level of output and prices.

than offsets the reduction in investment and consumption demand due to a rise in the interest rate from r_0 to r_1 depicted in Figure 9.6(a). Thus at the original levels of output and prices, there is excess demand in the output market.

To confirm that there is excess demand in the output market, recall from the aggregate budget constraint that if there is excess demand for output then there must be an excess supply of money if there is equilibrium in the financial market. The reason for the excess supply of money is that the higher interest rate decreases the quantity of money demanded. This fall in the quantity of money demanded is reflected in Figure 9.6(b) by the movement up the money demand curve from point D to point E as the interest rate rises from r_0 to r_1. Thus as Figure 9.6(b) illustrates, at the original price level and output there is excess supply in the money market denoted by EF.

Since excess demand exists in the output market at the original price-output combination (P_0, Y_0), this point does not lie on the aggregate demand curve. To restore equilibrium in the output market, the price level and/or output must rise. Thus the aggregate demand curve shifts upward and to the right. Figure 9.7 depicts this shift to the right in the aggregate demand curve from AD_0 to AD_1.

According to Figure 9.7, the aggregate supply curve and the new aggregate

Figure 9.7 **The Effect of an Increase in Investment on Output and Prices**

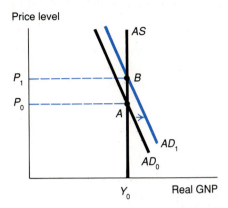

An increase in investment demand leads to excess demand in the output market at the original price-output combination (P_0, Y_0). Thus the aggregate demand curve shifts up from AD_0 to AD_1, and the equilibrium price level rises from P_0 to P_1.

demand curve intersect at the higher price level P_1. The shift in the aggregate demand curve causes an upward movement along the vertical aggregate supply curve AS from point A to point B. Output prices rise but real GNP does not change. Note that the increase in investment will lead to a higher capital stock in the future. The next section examines the effect *over time* of a change in investment. For the moment, however, we consider a time frame over which the capital stock is essentially unchanged.

At the new equilibrium price level and output, the money interest rate is higher for two reasons. First, as was indicated by Figure 9.6(a), the increase in autonomous investment demand leads to a rise in the interest rate from r_0 to r_1 at the original price level. Second, the rise in prices that re-establishes equilibrium in the economy reduces the real stock of money and thus the real supply of loanable funds. This fall in the real supply of loanable funds pushes the interest rate even higher than the interest rate r_1 in Figure 9.6(a). The rise in the interest rate above r_1 serves to curtail investment and consumption demand, eliminating the excess demand in the output market.

Although the higher interest rate reduces firms' desired investment, this fall does *not* completely offset the original increase in investment caused by the change in tax incentives. To see this, note that at the new, higher equilibrium interest rate, consumption demand is lower. Since government spending and output remain unchanged, investment demand must on net be higher. The funds for this higher investment are provided by households who increase saving in response to the higher interest rate.

It is important to realize that since individuals' anticipations of future inflation are held constant in the above analysis, a predicted higher nominal interest rate means a higher expected real rate of interest. In Chapter 3, we noted that real interest rates were unusually high in the mid 1980s. Our analysis in Chapter 8 pointed out that large government deficits were one possible cause of these higher interest rates. The analysis in this section indicates that an increase in investment demand due to changes in the tax treatment of capital expenditures could have been a second factor contributing to the high real interest rates of the mid-1980s.[36]

Some economists have argued that tax changes and technology shocks that alter the returns to capital expenditures are important factors leading to changes in investment demand over time.[37] Our analysis here indicates that such shocks cause investment and the expected real rate of interest to move together. Note that this does not refute the prediction that, *other things being equal,* an increase in interest rates will reduce investment demand. However, it does help us understand why the predicted inverse relationship between investment and the real rate of interest is one that has been difficult to establish empirically.

So far our analysis has been carried out in the context of a closed economy. In an open economy, an exogenous increase in investment demand leads to an even larger net increase in investment since there is less of an increase in the interest rate. The interest rate rises by less in the open economy because the supply of loanable funds is more responsive to interest rate changes in an open economy, as the potential sources of loanable funds are now expanded to include foreign lenders and U.S. households who redirect their savings from foreign to domestic financial markets. The larger net increase in investment reflects the fact that in an open economy both consumption and net export demand fall with the rise in the interest rate. Net export demand falls since a rising interest rate leads to increased capital inflows, an appreciation of the dollar, and thus a rise in U.S. imports and fall in U.S. exports.

The 1981 tax law introduced other provisions that also had the intent of raising investment by directly increasing households' incentives for saving. By introducing such tax-free forms of saving as IRAs, the government attempted to increase household saving in the form of financial assets. To the extent that these incentives lead to an increase in saving, the result will be a shift the supply of loanable funds curve to the right, reducing the interest rate and consequently enhancing the anticipated rise in investment, as investment is substituted for consumption.

---

[36] It has been suggested by some economists that restrictive monetary policy is a third factor behind the high real interest rates during this period. In this regard we may note that our analysis in Chapter 8 demonstrated that in the neoclassical model, a reduced rate of growth in the money supply would not be predicted to alter *real* interest rates. However, as we observed earlier, the neoclassical model is more appropriate in the long run than the short run. As we will see in subsequent chapters (10 through 12), when prices are not perfectly flexible, monetary policy changes have effects on various real variables including real interest rates.

[37] See, for example, Matthew D. Shapiro, "Investment, Output, and the Cost of Capital," *Brookings Papers on Economic Activity,* 1986, pp. 111–164.

The Effects Over Time on the Capital Stock and Aggregate Supply

The decline in the long-run rate of economic growth in the 1970s generated interest in the long-run, supply-side effects of government policies and influenced the changes in tax policy initiated in 1981 that were intended to spur investment spending. As the 1982 *Economic Report of the President* noted: "[A] key element that distinguishes current policies from those of the past is that they are fundamentally long term in nature. Economic growth is a long-run process that is determined by technological change and the supply and allocation of such productive factors as raw materials, labor, and capital. . . . The government has some direct influence on factor inputs, but its main influence is through the indirect and long-term incentives it provides."[38]

Our previous analysis showed that in the neoclassical model, a change in incentives that leads to a higher rate of investment has the effect of altering the disposition of spending but not of total output. We know from Chapter 2, however, that an increase in net investment today means a higher capital stock in the future. One estimate suggests that the tax law enacted in 1981 and its modifications in 1982 resulted in a long-run increase in the capital stock of about 5 percent, with half of this response occurring within five years.[39]

From our discussion of the aggregate production function in Chapter 5, we know that a higher capital stock in the future will increase future output at any level of employment. In terms of our aggregate demand-supply analysis, the future aggregate supply curve shifts to the right from AS_0 to AS_1, as depicted in Figure 9.8.

As we saw in our analysis of a reduction in tax rates on wage income, the resulting increase in aggregate supply leads to a higher equilibrium output level and lower equilibrium price level. A similar outcome holds with respect to a change in the tax law that increases the incentive for investment, although the effect on aggregate supply is now in the future. The resulting higher investment today raises the economy's future capital stock; thus the future level of real GNP will be higher and the future price level will be lower than either would have been otherwise.

Investment Tax Incentives That Alter Tax Revenues: The Conflicting Influences

Critical to the tax act of 1981 was the altering of tax incentives for business investment and household saving that would lead to an increase in investment. We have considered the immediate effects of a change in investment on the composition of output demand, and the effects over time on the productive capacity of the economy. What we have not discussed is the potential effect

---

[38] *Economic Report of the President* (1982), p. 109.

[39] See Shapiro, Footnote 37.

Figure 9.8   The Effect of a Higher Capital Stock on Output and Prices

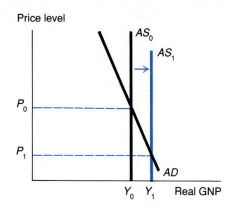

With increased tax incentives for investment, current investment rises. This will lead to a higher future capital stock and thus a shift to the right in the future aggregate supply curve from AS_0 to AS_1. With the higher capital stock, the future level of real GNP rises from Y_0 to Y_1, and the price level in the future will be reduced from what it would have been, as shown by the fall from P_0 to P_1.

of the change in tax rates on tax revenues, and the fiscal policy changes that this implies. Yet the 1981 tax rate cuts did indeed lead to a substantial increase in the deficit, which we know can affect investment. Let's review the effects of a deficit-increasing tax cut, which we first discussed in Chapter 8.

Because a deficit-increasing tax cut raises household disposable income, it will lead to an increase in consumption demand. At the same time, the increase in government borrowing means a higher demand for loanable funds and consequently an increase in the interest rate.[40] The higher interest rate decreases consumption and investment spending, but this is more than offset by the increase in consumption due to the higher disposable income. Thus at the original level of prices and output, excess demand exists in the output market. In order to restore equilibrium in the neoclassical model, the price level rises. This higher price level provides a second impetus toward a higher interest rate since a higher price level reduces the real supply of loanable funds. At the new equilibrium, the fiscal policy effects of a tax cut alone would result in reduced investment.

If a cut in tax rates that is intended to stimulate investment also reduces tax revenues, then our discussion above indicates that the fiscal policy effects

---

[40] This analysis assumes that Ricardian equivalence (the equivalence of taxes and government borrowing in raising revenues) does not hold. Otherwise, the increase in the household supply of loanable funds from the tax savings would equal the increase in the government demand for loanable funds.

of this tax cut can inhibit investment. The net impact on investment of such tax changes then becomes an empirical issue—one that depends on the sensitivity of investment to tax incentives and to changes in the interest rate induced by the accompanying fiscal policy change of increased government borrowing replacing reduced tax revenues.

Investment Tax Incentives and the 1986 Tax Bill

The Accelerated Cost Recovery System (ACRS) we discussed earlier is indicative of the intent of the 1981 tax bill to encourage investment in plant and equipment. Many observers saw the 1981 tax changes as the final blow to an effective tax on business, as the ample write-offs that the 1981 bill provided for capital intensive companies enabled many of them to escape federal income taxes altogether. Although real GNP in the economy grew steadily in the four years following the last half of 1982, many were dissatisfied with what they considered the "fairness" of the tax code under the 1981 provisions. A survey in the August 18, 1986 *Wall Street Journal* showed that many Americans thought the tax code was riddled with provisions that allowed individuals and corporations to escape high marginal tax rates.

A key feature of the 1986 bill was its aim at shifting a larger portion of the tax burden back onto corporations.[41] The new bill was anticipated to increase corporate taxes by roughly $120 billion over the first five years after its enactment. These higher taxes on firms, as well as the elimination or reduction of an array of tax breaks to individuals, allowed the 1986 tax bill to dramatically cut individual tax rates, so that by 1988 the highest rate fell by approximately one half, from 50 percent to 28 percent.

To increase the tax take from corporations, the 1986 bill reduced the extent of deductions firms could take in computing their taxable earnings. For instance, in the early 1960s the Kennedy administration introduced investment tax credits that allowed companies purchasing new equipment to take a tax credit of from 6 percent to 10 percent of the cost within one year. This lowered the after-tax cost of capital equipment. Under the 1986 code, this provision was completely done away with.

The 1986 tax bill also reduced depreciation allowances. The new depreciation scheme slowed down the depreciation allowed for tax purposes on plant and equipment somewhat, as well as drastically cutting the write-offs for real estate. Most types of manufacturing equipment, which formerly could be written off over five years, now had to be depreciated for tax purposes over seven years, which meant that a smaller fraction of the capital purchase could be taken as an expense each year. The 1986 tax bill also ruled that residential real estate was to be written off in a straight-line fashion over 27 years, as opposed to 19 years under the former tax legislation.

The analysis in this section suggests that the 1986 tax changes, in particular

---

[41] Recall that in the final analysis, corporations do not pay taxes, only individuals do, either in the form of higher prices or in reduced dividend payments.

the elimination of the investment tax credit and the reduction in allowed depreciation deductions, will reduce investment by increasing the expected real rental cost of capital inclusive of tax effects. Some observers predict that the implied lower future capital stock will hasten the transition of the American economy from smokestacks to services since manufacturing industries are the ones that previously benefited the most from investment tax incentives. However, since the changes in the tax law were numerous, it is still too early to determine what all the effects of the 1986 tax bill will be.

To the Point

SUPPLY-SIDE POLICIES AND THE CAPITAL INPUT

- Policies that alter investment lead to change over time in the capital stock and thus can have an impact on the future aggregate supply. In recent years, the U.S. economy has experienced a decline in productivity due in part to a lack of investment in capital. Politicians have sought policies that would enhance investment in capital.

- The 1981 tax bill reduced the expected real rental cost of capital. A fall in the expected real rental cost of capital leads to an increase in investment and thus an increase in firms' borrowing to finance capital purchases.

- Changes in the tax laws have also attempted to stimulate household saving and thus the supply of loanable funds in order to indirectly increase investment. With an increase in the supply of loanable funds, the interest rate falls, and that induces increased investment.

- The 1986 tax bill did away with many of the provisions of the 1981 bill to stimulate investment. Instead, the emphasis in the 1986 bill was on cutting marginal tax rates on income to individuals.

Cross-Country Productivity Comparisons for the 1960s and 1970s

The concern over how taxes affect investment stems from the general concern in the United States today about the amount of investment and the long-run implications for growth and productivity. In particular, there is a great deal of interest in how the United States stacks up against its trading partners in the area of growth and productivity. In this section, we compare the experience of the U.S. in the 1960s and 1970s with that of other countries.

Comedian Sam Levenson told a story about what his father expected to find when he came to America as an immigrant from Russia and what he actually discovered. His father heard on the boat on the way to America that the streets were paved with gold. On arriving he discovered three things: The streets were not paved with gold, many of the streets were not paved at all, and he was expected to pay for the paving of the streets through his taxes. Despite similarly rude awakenings, immigrants came into this country in the early 1900s seeking a better life. Despite the disappointments of the

Great Depression, a large number of them found the good life they sought as U.S. industrial growth became the envy of the world. As we have seen, however, in the mid-1960s the healthy economic growth that the United States had been experiencing for most of the century seemed to fade. It is difficult to pin down a single year as a turning point, but 1966 has often been mentioned. From 1947 to 1966 real GNP grew at an annual average rate of 3.84 percent. From 1967 to 1985 the annual growth rate dipped to 2.5 percent. To put those figures in a slightly different perspective, if there is a growth rate of 3.84 percent each year, the real amount of goods and services available doubles every 19 years. A growth rate of 2.5 percent means a doubling of real GNP every 28 years.

In contrast to the U.S. experience, during the 1960s and 1970s many other industrial countries achieved significantly higher growth rates in real GNP. Behind these differences is the fact that the growth of productivity—output per work hour—in this country has lagged behind that of other countries. This is clearly shown in Figure 9.9. While the United States sat firmly in the rear with an average growth in productivity of approximately 2 percent average growth in productivity from 1965 to 1979, Japan went to the head of the class with an annual growth rate of approximately 8 percent during this period.

Figure 9.9 demonstrates a direct relationship between the level of investment as a percent of GNP and the rate of productivity growth. Countries with higher productivity growth tend to devote a greater share of their output to investment. We have suggested one reason for low investment in the United States in the late 1960s and 1970s—the discouraging effect on firms' investment decisions of increases in the effective tax on capital purchases. Yet in comparing investment patterns in various countries, two other sources for the relatively low investment rate and accompanying low productivity growth in the United States during this period are also suggested.

Some observers think slowdowns in investment and productivity growth in the United States are inevitable since productivity growth naturally declines as the capital stock grows. Countries such as West Germany and Japan that had a great deal of their capital destroyed in World War II were naturally going to have higher rates of growth initially as they went from having very little capital to a larger stock of all-new capital. According to this explanation, the remarkable gains in productivity experienced by Japan and West Germany in the 1960s and 1970s will cease when the capital stock in these countries reaches the level in the United States.

Other observers look at differences in the incentives to save as an explanation for the low investment and productivity growth in the United States. Remember that firms' investment is financed by borrowing. The ease with which they can borrow is influenced by the extent of household saving. Let's look at possible reasons for differences in saving and thus investment by comparing the two extremes in Figure 9.9: Japan and West Germany with the highest levels of investment and the United States with the lowest level of investment as a percentage of GNP.

Figure 9.9   **Productivity Growth versus Investment by Country:
1965–1979**

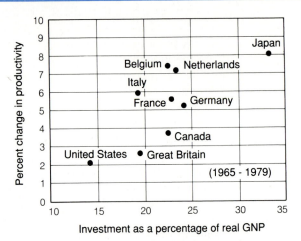

Source: Michael K. Evans, "An Econometric Model Incorporating the Supply-Side Effects of Economic Policy," *The Supply-Side Effects of Economic Policy* (St. Louis Federal Reserve, 1980), p. 51.

One standard explanation, of course, is that the Japanese (substitute Germans) were naturally more frugal than Americans and that is why they saved more. That may be the case, but frugality is not easily measurable. There are some distinctions that are measurable and of more interest to economists: differences in government tax and income supplement programs.

Martin Feldstein, former chairman of the Council of Economic Advisers, believes that the social security system has been a strong deterrent to private personal savings in this country. For the majority of Americans, he argues, the most important form of household wealth is the anticipated social security retirement benefits. As these benefits have increased, he argues, employees have reduced their private savings almost dollar for dollar. Sweden, a country with a liberal retirement program, also has a low saving rate. Japan, in contrast, has had a modest social security and government-sponsored pension plan and high saving. These casual observations would suggest a link between government sponsored security and the individual's demand for privately provided security.

Yet there are countries—for example, Germany—with well-funded and generous social security programs that still have had higher saving rates than the United States. When one looks for differences there, they can usually be found in the way the income tax system has treated saving. In the United States, labor earnings that are saved are typically taxed twice, once when earned and again when they earn interest. A dollar spent, therefore, is worth more than a dollar saved in a system that rewards spending and penalizes saving. In contrast, tax laws in foreign countries have been more lenient in allowing income from saving, as well as income that is saved, to be exempt from taxation.

In West Germany, a certain level of interest income—it varies each year—has been exempt from taxation. In addition, life insurance premiums (a form of saving) have been deductible from taxable income within certain limits. Finally, deposits in special savings accounts that are frozen for six or seven years can earn, on top of interest, a hefty tax-free bonus plus extra bonuses for each dependent. Similarly, through a variety of schemes the Japanese government has exempted from taxation virtually all interest income earned by average Japanese citizens. A Japanese can theoretically shelter up to $62,000 (in 1980 dollars) in savings from taxes or interest income. A number of studies suggest that tax incentives such as those available to Germans and Japanese could affect the extent of saving in the United States. For instance, Stanford economist Michael Boskin has estimated that a 10 percent increase in the rate of return on saving would bring forth a 4 percent rise in saving.

Not all attention is focused on capital stock formation in discussions of productivity growth, however. MIT economist Lester Thurow, who is widely cited on this topic, has stated there was no major cause; the slowdown was more like "death from a thousand cuts." Nonetheless he laid much blame at the feet of management. Writing in his weekly column in *Newsweek,* Thurow said, "The key to productivity improvement lies not on the factory floor, but in the office."[42] A few months later he reiterated that a "well-motivated work force interested in raising productivity is ultimately a management responsibility."[43] Since 1982 U.S. productivity growth has been positive, but it still has not caught up with Japanese rates of growth. However, as we discuss in the following case study, the performance of the U.S. economy in the 1980s has improved as compared to the experience of European countries.

Case Study

SUPPLY-SIDE ECONOMICS AND THE EUROPEAN EXPERIENCE DURING THE 1980S

The above discussion indicates that in the late 1960s and 1970s average productivity growth was higher in Europe than in the U.S. Although true, this statement hides an important recent trend: the performance of European economies has been deteriorating relative to that of the U.S. economy. For example, as Table 9.1 shows, while the growth rate of Gross Domestic

[42] *Newsweek,* 24 August 1981.

[43] *Newsweek,* 7 December 1981.

Table 9.1   Comparison of Economic Performance in the European Community, U.S., and Japan, 1960–1985

	Average Real Gross Domestic Product (GDP) Growth Rate Per Capita			
	1960–1973	*1973–1980*	*1980–1985*	*1960–1985*
European Community	3.81	1.95	1.05	2.73
U.S.	2.76	1.14	1.53	2.07
Japan	8.59	2.77	3.22	5.84

	Unemployment Rate			
	1960	*1973*	*1980*	*1985*
European Community	2.5	2.5	5.8	11.1
U.S.	5.5	4.9	7.1	7.1
Japan	1.7	1.3	2.0	2.7

	General Government Expenditure as a Fraction of Gross Domestic Product (GDP)			
	1960	*1973*	*1980*	*1985*
European Community	32.1	39.8	47.4	51.5
U.S.	26.8	30.7	33.1	35.5
Japan	18.2	22.1	32.4	n.a.

	Estimate of the Wedge Between Gross Wages and Wages Net of Direct Taxes and Social Security Contributions as a Percentage of the Net Wage			
	1960	*1973*	*1980*	*1985*
Germany	42.5%	59.3%	66.1%	69.9%
France	39.8	51.2	69.5	74.5
U.K.	23.1	32.0	34.9	39.4
Italy	32.9	37.5	49.0	47.1
Netherlands	43.4	74.1	81.8	103.2
Sweden	32.0	55.3	79.7	78.1
U.S.	29.2	35.7	39.1	36.9
Japan	18.3	26.3	33.6	37.8

Source: Giuseppe Tullio, "Long Run Implications of the Increase in Taxation and Public Debt For Employment and Economic Growth in Europe," *European Economic Review*, 1987.

Product (GDP) per capita in Europe exceeded that in the United States from 1960 to 1985, in the latter part of this period per capita GDP was growing more quickly in the U.S. than in Europe. Similarly, while the unemployment rate in Europe was about half that in the U.S. in the 1960s, by the 1980s the European unemployment rate had risen significantly above the U.S. unemployment rate.

In a recent paper, Giuseppe Tullio attributes much of the apparent decline in European economic performance to adverse supply effects stemming from the policies of European governments. Tullio notes that total spending by

European governments has increased dramatically over time and now exceeds 50 percent of their GDP (Gross Domestic Product). The increased spending has been financed in part by borrowing, which as we saw earlier, tends to push up interest rates and reduce capital formation.

The higher government spending has also been financed in large part through higher taxes on employers and workers, thus increasing the difference between gross wages and net after tax wages, or the "tax wedge."[44] From our analysis in the preceding sections, we know that increases in taxes on the exchange of labor services can be expected to reduce after-tax wages, employment, and output. Tullio argues that because of their considerable monopoly power in Europe, unions have been able to limit the fall in after-tax wages, thereby imposing much of the burden of the higher taxes on employers. As a consequence, the increased taxes appear to have led to an unusually large reduction in employment and a sizable increase in unemployment.

To understand this argument, note first that assessing taxes on employers causes the demand for labor to fall and second, that the resulting effect on employment will be larger if for some reason the wage is prevented from falling to its new equilibrium level. The resulting excess supply of labor will translate into an increase in measured unemployment.[45] Olivier Blanchard and Lawrence Summers have also argued that the wage setting process in Europe has been a big factor behind the current high unemployment rates. They argue that unions may "bargain only on behalf of their incumbent members."[46] Thus, instead of accepting lower wages that would have the effect of increasing employment, unions have instead tried to keep the wages of their currently employed members as high as possible.[47]

While the preceding discussion has emphasized supply factors and the wage setting process, we should not ignore the role played by demand factors in Europe's declining economic performance. In fact, Tullio is in agreement with others that "some of the existing high unemployment might very well

---

[44] It makes sense to include indirect taxes such as sales and value-added taxes as part of the tax wedge since such taxes reduce the purchasing power of workers' wage payments. Upon including indirect taxes, the wedge becomes significantly larger (see Tullio).

[45] Tullio also mentions another reason for the rise in unemployment—namely, the growth in unemployment benefits, which reduces the incentive to find new employment. In fact, "if the workers can supply their services in the hidden economy, as they do in many countries, they can end up better financially by remaining registered as unemployed." (Tullio, p. 759).

[46] Olivier Blanchard and Lawrence Summers, "Beyond the Natural Rate Hypothesis," *American Economic Review,* (May 1988) pp. 182–88. Blanchard and Summers also point out that "the same phenomenon is also at work in non-union settings; in such settings, unemployed workers will be disenfranchised if currently employed workers have a significant amount of job specific capital or if they can credibly threaten to withhold cooperation from workers hired at low wages." ("Fiscal Increasing Returns, Real Wages, and European Unemployment," *European Economic Review,* March 1987, p. 555).

[47] In Blanchard and Summers' analysis, there is no set natural unemployment rate. Instead, as they note in their paper, "Hysteresis in Unemployment" (*European Economic Review,* March 1987), "the actual level of unemployment appears to be the equilibrium level." According to their model, if a demand or supply shock alters the existing unemployment rate, then unions will set wages in the future so as to maintain the new unemploymet rate.

be due to insufficient aggregate demand'' (p. 770). As we have seen, in the neoclassical model prices continually adjust to maintain equilibrium in all markets. As a consequence, all unemployment is ''frictional'' in nature; unemployment is always at the natural rate.

When we study the short-run (Keynesian) models in subsequent chapters, we will see that reductions in output demand can lead to increases in unemployment above the natural rate if prices do not adjust sufficiently quickly. In the case of Europe, Robert Coen and Bert Hickman estimate that much of the current unemployment is due to deficiencies in demand rather than to increases in the natural unemployment rate and that, as a consequence, ''there is substantial room for demand expansion to reduce unemployment'' (p. 193).[48]

9.3   REAL THEORIES OF BUSINESS FLUCTUATIONS

Demand shock: Changes in variables such as autonomous investment or consumption demand, as well as misguided monetary and fiscal policies that affect aggregate demand.

Supply shock: Changes in variables such as oil supply, weather, technology, strikes, or government policies that affect aggregate supply.

Beginning with the Great Depression of the 1930s, economic downturns were thought to be caused primarily by macroeconomic **demand shocks.** In particular, fluctuations in autonomous investment and consumption demand, as well as misguided monetary and fiscal policies, were thought to be the key determinants of fluctuations in the growth of real GNP. Recent views now include **supply shocks** as important causes of fluctuations in real GNP.[49] Supply shocks not directly related to government policy changes include changes in agricultural conditions, technological innovations, strikes, oil supply disruptions, and changes in the composition of output demand, but not total output demand, that require the reallocation of labor across firms. Recent business cycle theories emphasize that these ''real'' shocks change the economy's productivity and wealth. These shocks set in motion economy-wide adjustments in wages, prices, and interest rates, as well as in output, consumption, investment, and employment, that ultimately restore equilibrium in the various markets in the economy.

As with so many current topics in economics, the idea that supply shocks lead to changes in real GNP is not new. In the late nineteenth century and early twentieth century, two classical economists, W.S. Jevons and H.S. Jevons, proposed ''harvest theories'' as the primary determinants of the business cycle.[50] They went a step further and tried to predict harvests by

---

[48] Robert M. Coen and Bert G. Hickman, ''Is European Unemployment Classical or Keynesian?'', *American Economic Review*, May 1988, pp. 188–193.

[49] An example of research suggesting an important role for supply shocks in explaining business fluctuations is the recent study by Matthew Shapiro and Mark Watson, *Sources of Business Cycle Fluctuations*, Working Paper, April 1988. While they find aggregate demand shocks are the main determinant of prices, inflation, and interest rates, aggregate demand changes account for only ''between twenty and thirty percent of the variation in output at business cycle horizons.'' (p. 34).

[50] H.S. Jevons, *The Causes of Unemployment: The Sun's Heat and Trade Activity* (London: 1910). For a further discussion of harvest theories of the business cycle, see Gottfried Haberler, *Prosperity and Depression* 1963).

analyzing "sun spots." Although sun-spot theory suffered a great deal of ridicule in the ensuing years, economists now recognize that supply-side factors play an important role in business fluctuations. We begin with a discussion of what constitutes a business cycle, and then proceed to a discussion of business cycles that are caused by supply-side factors.

The Business Cycle

Alternating periods of contractions and expansions in economy-wide real output form what is termed a **business cycle.** In the vernacular, business cycles are recessions and expansions. Changes in the production of *real* goods and services determine the business cycle, and business cycles are measured with respect to the total output produced in an economy. A rise or drop in real activity in only one sector of the economy does not constitute a business cycle.

We must also point out that while people often talk of a business "cycle," few economists believe that fluctuations in output follow any true cyclical pattern, with a certain fixed and predictable periodicity. Even though it has been cited that the average expansion in the post–World War II era has been 15 quarters, and the average contraction in the same period has been 3.6 quarters, this does not imply cycles. Any set of n numbers when added up and divided by n will yield an average, though that average may be a very poor predictor of the future. Remember, if you put your head in a freezer and your feet in an oven, "on average" you will experience a comfortable temperature.

Fluctuations in real output related to supply shocks are known as **real business cycles.** Oil supply shocks are an important source. As reported by economist James Hamilton, "All but one of the U.S. recessions since World War II have been preceded, typically with a lag of around three fourths of a year, by a dramatic increase in the price of crude petroleum." [51] In the next several sections, we explore the impact of an oil supply shock by using the aggregate demand-supply analysis of the neoclassical model.

The Effects of an Oil Supply Shock

Up until now, we have focused on supply disturbances that originate in the labor market or in disturbances that affect the capital stock. We now examine

> **Business cycle:** Alternating periods of contractions and expansions in economy-wide real output.

> **Real business cycle:** Fluctuations in real output related to supply shocks such as oil disruptions.

---

[51] James Hamilton, "Oil and the Macroeconomy," *Journal of Political Economy* (April, 1983): 228. Hamilton went on to state that "This does not mean that oil shocks caused these recessions. However . . . over the period 1948–1972 this correlation is statistically significant and nonspurious, supporting the proposition that oil shocks were a contributing factor in at least some of the U.S. recessions prior to 1972. By extension, energy price increases may account for much of post-OPEC macroeconomic performance."

disturbances originating in other input markets. In Chapter 5, we simplified the aggregate production function by ignoring variable inputs other than labor. Clearly, however, other inputs are important determinants of output. One of these is the oil input, or more generally, the "energy" input. Since 1950, disruptions have occurred periodically in the supply of oil. These included the Iranian nationalization of 1951 and 1952, the Suez crisis of 1956 and 1957, and the 1970 rupture of the Trans-Arabian pipeline. The most severe oil supply disruptions occurred later: In 1973 and 1974, the Organization of Petroleum Exporting Countries (OPEC) embargoed oil to certain Western countries, causing the real price of oil to the United States to more than triple; in 1979 during the Iranian revolution and in 1980 at the onset of the Iran-Iraq war, the real price of oil (the money price of oil divided by the general price level) increased by over 150 percent. More recently, we have experienced an oil supply shock in the opposite direction, with the collapse in 1985 and 1986 of OPEC's collusive agreement to limit supplies.

The Effect on the Energy and Labor Input Markets. According to supply and demand analysis, a reduction in the supply of energy causes the *real* price of energy to *increase* which, in turn, induces firms to use less energy. Figure 9.10(a) indicates this effect of a fall in the supply of energy on the energy input market. The energy supply curve shifts to the left from e_0^s to e_1^s, leading to a rise in the real price of energy from $(P^e/P)_0$ to $(P^e/P)_1$ and a reduction in energy usage from e_0 to e_1.

In addition to the direct effect on the energy input market, an oil supply disruption will alter firms' demand for labor. Given that energy and labor are *complements*, the increase in the real price of energy reduces the demand for labor.[52] One reason for a complementarity between labor and energy is that increased energy costs make it less profitable to use older, less energy-efficient machinery, so that some of that machinery is retired from usage. Workers are less productive since they have less capital to work with.

Figure 9.10(b) indicates the effect on the labor market of the increase in the real price of energy, given that labor and energy are complements. Firms' labor demand falls, as shown by the shift to the left in the labor demand curve from N_0^d to N_1^d, which leads to a fall in the level of employment from N_0 to N_1 and a fall in the real wage from $(W/P)_0$ to $(W/P)_1$.

The Effect on Equilibrium Prices and Output. Both the reduced use of energy and the decrease in the employment of labor that result from an oil supply disruption lead to a decrease in total output.[53] In the context of

---

[52] If energy and labor are *substitutes* in production, then the reduction in firms' energy use will lead to an increase in their labor demand.

[53] If the labor and energy inputs are substitutes rather than complements, then equilibrium employment will rise rather than fall. Nevertheless, it can be shown that total output will still fall.

Figure 9.10   The Effect of an Oil Supply Disruption on the Energy and Labor Input Markets

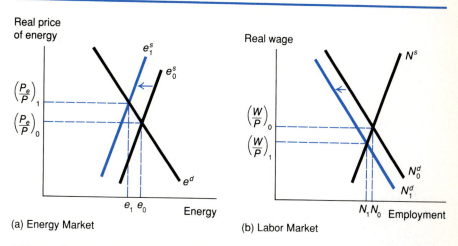

(a) Energy Market   (b) Labor Market

With an oil supply disruption, there is a fall in the supply of energy, as indicated in part (a) by the shift to the left in the energy supply curve from e_0^s to e_1^s. The result is a fall in energy usage from e_0 to e_1 and a rise in the real price of energy from $(P_e/P)_0$ to $(P_e/P)_1$. Given that labor and energy are complements in the production process, the rise in the relative price of energy will reduce the demand for labor, as shown in part (b) by the shift to the left in the labor demand curve from N_0^d to N_1^d. Consequently, employment falls from N_0 to N_1 and the real wage falls from $(W/P)_0$ to $(W/P)_1$.

aggregate demand-supply analysis, the aggregate supply curve shifts to the left from AS_0 to AS_1 in Figure 9.11.

With a lower output level, excess demand exists in the output market at the original price level. The price level is therefore bid up, as we move up the aggregate demand curve in Figure 9.11 from point A to point B. The higher price level reduces the real supply of loanable funds, leading to a higher equilibrium interest rate. The higher interest rate reduces investment and consumption demand, which eliminates the excess demand in the output market.

To summarize, the neoclassical model predicts that a reduction in the supply of energy results in a reduced rate of growth in real GNP, a higher real price of energy, a lower real wage, reduced employment, a higher price level, and a higher interest rate.[54] The effects of the 1973 to 1974 OPEC embargo mirror these results. The energy component of the CPI rose 16.8 percent from December 1972 to December 1973, and another 21.6 percent from December 1973 to December 1974, while prices overall rose 4.7 percent

---

[54] The procyclical movement in the real wage predicted by this real business cycle theory distinguishes it from other business cycle theories that rely on demand-side disturbances, as we will see in Chapter 11.

Figure 9.11   The Effect of a Reduced Supply of Energy on Output and Price Level

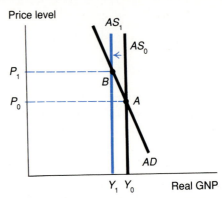

A reduced supply of energy leads to a fall in the energy input. At the same time, a reduced supply of energy leads to a rise in the relative price of energy, which reduces labor demand. The fall in labor demand leads to a lower equilibrium real wage and a fall in the equilibrium level of employment. The lower levels of both the energy and labor inputs reduce real output, as shown by the shift in the aggregate supply curve from AS_0 to AS_1. Real GNP falls from Y_0 to Y_1 and the price level rises from P_0 to P_1.

from December 1972 to December 1973, and 11.3 percent from December 1973 to December 1974. Thus real energy prices rose, and the underlying energy supply disruption led to higher output prices. At the same time, both the average real wage and the size of the labor force fell relative to trend, and the economy experienced a recession that began in November 1973 and continued until March 1975. Interest rates rose as well, with three-month treasury securities increasing from about 4 percent in 1972 to close to 8 percent in 1974.

Other Potential Sources of Supply Shocks

In the previous section, we analyzed the effects of a particular "supply shock," namely, a reduction in the supply of oil. There are a variety of other sources of real business cycles with similar effects. All of these supply shocks affect the macroeconomy through shifts in the aggregate supply curve. We will review four additional possible sources of the real business cycles.

We begin with an influential study of business cycles by Finn Kydland and Edward Prescott.[55] They note that random changes in technology that

[55] See Finn E. Kydland and Edward C. Prescott, "Time to Build and Aggregate Fluctuations," *Econometrica* (November 1982) p. 1345–1370.

affect the productive capacity of the economy can lead, under certain circumstances, to the patterns of fluctuations in output and employment that we observe. Kydland and Prescott have expanded upon the work of the late business-cycle theorist, Joseph Schumpeter, who related changes in the business cycle primarily to a process of innovation. As noted by Zarnowitz, "Schumpeter (1939) saw economic growth itself as a cyclical process reflecting technological progress and spurts of innovation—opening up and temporary exhaustion of opportunities for new profitable investment."[56] Kydland and Prescott carry Schumpeter further by noting that the lag involved in the time to build capital equipment means that any perturbation in production will be carried on beyond the time period coincident with the shock.

A second possible source of supply shocks is suggested from an analysis of the experience during the Great Depression of the 1930s. A study by Ben Bernanke suggests that at least part of the dramatic fall in real GNP that characterized the Great Depression of the 1930s can be traced to the failure of banks.[57] As we saw in Chapter 5, private depository institutions act as financial intermediaries when they accept deposits from lenders and use the funds raised from these deposits to make loans to borrowers. The widespread failure of banks during the depression resulted in a rise in the real costs of "intermediation" between borrowers and lenders inhibiting borrowing and lending. As noted by Robert Barro, "it is not difficult to see why a sudden decline in the quantity of financial intermediation would have adverse real consequences for the economy. In fact, a cutback in financial intermediation is not so different from a negative shock to production functions, which is the type of disturbance that appears in real theories of business cycles."[58]

A third source of supply shock is suggested by David Lilien. In our discussion of the vertical aggregate supply curve, we noted that associated with the equilibrium level of output is a certain natural rate of unemployment. Changes in the natural rate of employment will cause changes in aggregate supply. Lilien argues that shifts in household preferences may lead to changes in the structure of demand in the economy, as demand for some products rises while the demand for others falls. This reallocation of demand across sectors of the economy, sometimes referred to as sectoral shifts in demand, occurs even though the economy-wide demand for total output remains unchanged. As Lilien states, "Shifts in employment demand between sectors of the economy necessitate continuous labor reallocation. Since it takes time for workers to find new jobs, some unemployment is unavoidable. . . . Most

---

[56] Victor Zarnowitz, p. 533.

[57] See Ben S. Bernanke, "Nonmonetary Effects of the Financial Crisis in the Propagation of the Great Depression," *American Economic Review* (June 1983) pp. 257–77.

[58] Robert Barro, "Rational Expectations and Macroeconomics in 1984," *American Economic Review* (May 1984) pp. 179–183.

of the unemployment fluctuations of the seventies ... were induced by unusual structural shifts in the U.S. economy." [59]

Lilien's view of the importance of sectoral shifts in employment demand in explaining fluctuations in aggregate unemployment is supported by a study of the Canadian experience for the 1957 to 1983 period.[60] As Lucie Samson points out, "since moving from one sector to another is a time-consuming process, real shocks that necessitate a reallocation of labor from declining sectors to growing sectors will result in an increase in the unemployment rate."

Lilien's findings are challenged by Abraham and Katz, who argue that the conclusions Lilien draws from his observation of the data are incorrect. Specifically, for the post–World War II period, the data are on the whole not supportive of sectoral shifts.[61] If Lilien's hypothesis that higher unemployment rates reflect unusual structural shifts is correct, then periods of higher unemployment will also be characterized by higher vacancy rates, reflecting the increased mismatching of workers and jobs. However, Abraham and Katz observe the contrary—that the unemployment rate is inversely related to the job vacancy rate. In a second study, it is argued that the Lilien reallocative shocks have been a major source of cyclical variation in unemployment only during the oil shocks of the 1950s and 1970s.[62]

A fourth source of supply shocks is one we have already noted—changes in harvests reflecting random changes in weather. Two final supply shocks can come from quotas that restrict international trade or labor disruptions. For example, the September 11, 1984 *Wall Street Journal* reported that "in 1970 Leonard Woodcock had just taken over the UAW, and the strike that ensued was horrendous, lasting 67 days. The economy had seemed to be pulling out of a mild recession in the third quarter, but it quickly suffered a relapse."

Naturally, for a strike to be a significant supply shock to the economy, the industry-wide disruption has to be large enough to affect the entire economy. There are few unions that have such power, although the United Auto Workers union might qualify, as would the coal miners in Britain as evidenced by their effect on the British economy through a long strike in 1984. As reported in the November 11, 1984 *Wall Street Journal*, "in Britain,

---

[59] David Lilien, "Sectoral Shifts and Cyclical Unemployment," *Journal of Political Economy* (August 1984) p. 777. Other papers that develop the theoretical propositions relating sectoral reallocation to unemployment variations include Robert E. Lucas and Edward C. Prescott, "Equilibrium Search and Unemployment," *Journal of Economic Theory,* (February 1974): 188–209) and Richard Rogerson "An Equilibrium Model of Sectoral Reallocation," *Journal of Political Economy* (1987): 824–834.

[60] Lucie Samson, "A Study of the Impact of Sectoral Shifts on Aggregate Unemployment in Canada," *Canadian Journal of Economics* (1985): 518–530.

[61] Katharine Abraham and Lawrence Katz, "Cyclical Unemployment: Sectoral Shifts or Aggregate Disturbance?" *Journal of Political Economy* (June 1986)

[62] Prakash Loungani, "Oil Price Shocks and the Dispersion Hypothesis," *The Review of Economics and Statistics* (August 1986): 536–539.

. . . growth of total output also has been limited by the miners' strike. . . . The forecast for growth in the current fiscal year is 2.5 percent down from an earlier projection of 3.5 percent."

Robert Barro has noted that "after mentioning the oil crises and harvest failures, one is often asked to name the third example of an important real shock."[63] This section has looked at potential sources of real business cycles other than oil crises and harvest failures. All of these can have important and significant impacts on the economy and can result in significant changes in output, employment, and prices.

SUMMARY

Although it is a simplification to merely associate supply-side economics with tax cuts, government taxes and subsidies do play an important role in determining the overall level of output in the economy. For instance, a reduction in marginal tax rates or in government transfer payments such as disability pensions and unemployment insurance raise individuals' incentives to work and can thus reduce unemployment and increase the level of employment and real GNP. With an increase in real GNP, the price level and the interest rate fall. Similarly, changes in tax laws that affect firms' purchases of capital (for example, the accelerated depreciation allowance) or households' decisions to save (for example, IRAs), can alter real GNP in the future by affecting the current level of investment.

A supply-side analysis of tax rate changes assumes such changes are revenue neutral, which means that total tax revenues are assumed to be unaffected by changes in tax rates. One might expect, however, that a lower tax rate will reduce tax revenues and thus affect government borrowing or spending. The Laffer curve indicates that, although likely, this need not occur. In particular, the Laffer curve suggests that reduction in marginal tax rates when they are above some critical level, by encouraging output, can result in higher total tax revenues.

The neoclassical model is useful not only in understanding the analysis behind the policy prescriptions of supply-side economics but also in explaining fluctuations in real GNP that emanate from supply factors. Among the possible macroeconomic supply shocks are changes in agricultural conditions, technological innovations, changes in households' preferences that lead to fluctuations in product demand for different goods, strikes, and oil supply shocks. Real business cycle theories emphasize these "real" shocks that change the economy's productive capacity and wealth.

The experience of the 1970s and 1980s focused attention on one type of macroeconomic supply shock, the oil supply shock. A reduction in the

---

[63] Robert Barro, "Rational Expectations and Macroeconomics in 1984," *American Economic Review* (May, 1984): 180.

supply of energy causes the *relative* price of energy to *increase* and this, in turn, induces firms to use less energy. At the same time labor demand falls, and thus equilibrium employment is reduced. The combination of reduced energy usage and employment leads to a fall in real GNP. Accompanying the fall in real GNP is a higher price level and interest rate.

LOOKING AHEAD

In this chapter, we have examined various factors that affect the supply side of the neoclassical model. We have seen that changes in supply factors affect the position of the aggregate supply curve, thereby altering equilibrium output, employment, prices, and interest rates. In the next chapter, we modify the neoclassical model to incorporate inflexible, or "sticky" prices. In the new, non-market-clearing macroeconomic model, we discover that demand-side shocks can play an important role in causing business cycles as well. In subsequent chapters, we introduce other modifications of the neoclassical model to help explain the behavior of the economy in response to macroeconomic shocks. We should bear in mind, however, that the neoclassical model remains a useful tool not only to explain the eventual effect of macroeconomic shock when all prices fully adjust but also to serve as a benchmark against which to compare the predictions of the other macroeconomic models.

KEY TERMS

Supply-side economics, 328

Human capital, 335

Demand shock, 354

Business cycle, 355

Laffer curve, 329

Autonomous spending, 341

Supply shock, 354

Real business cycles, 355

REVIEW QUESTIONS

1. In the text, we analyzed the effect of a reduction in the rate at which the labor income of workers is taxed by the government. Not all taxes on the exchanges of labor services are assessed on workers. Some are assessed by firms. Examples include social security taxes (half of which workers pay directly, the other half of which employers pay), required payments by employers to a workers' compensation fund (which is used

for job-related injuries), and required payments by employers into an unemployment insurance fund.

a. Let T_p denote the dollar amount of payroll taxes that employers must pay per unit of labor hired. Let P denote the price of output, let MPN denote the marginal product of labor, and let W denote the wage rate. What condition must be satisfied if employers are to hire labor so as to maximize profit?

b. Suppose that the government reduces the effective payroll tax per unit of labor from \$2 to \$1. What happens to the demand for labor by employers?

c. Illustrate the resulting effect on equilibrium in the labor market. Does the wage rate rise or fall? By more or less than the one dollar reduction in the payroll tax? Why? What happens to the equilibrium employment level?

d. What happens to production in the economy? What happens to the aggregate supply curve? Why?

e. Suppose that the government increases other taxes in order to keep total taxes on households and firms unaltered. Use aggregate demand-supply analysis to show the effect of the change in the government's tax policy on the economy's equilibrium price and output levels.

f. Why does the price of output rise or fall?

2. What do we mean by supply-side economics? What types of disagreements exist between those who advocate supply-side type policies and those who do not?

3. What does the Laffer curve tell us? What shape does this curve have? Give the reasons for this shape.

4. Minimum wage legislation was first enacted in 1938 as one of the provisions of the Fair Labor Standards Act. This legislation forces employers in covered sectors to pay their workers some specified minimum amount, which in 1988, was \$3.35. The United States is not the only country with minimum wage laws. For example, the April 7, 1986 *Wall Street Journal* reported that "Argentina's government . . . increased the minimum wage in a bid to pump up its economy." (Interestingly, another article on the same page noted that according to Princeton political economist Atul Kohli, "While military juntas and dictators worry about economic performance, democracies are more likely to face demands for economic equity.")

a. Starting from an initial labor market equilibrium without a minimum wage, show the effect of imposing a minimum wage. Does employment rise or fall? Why? What happens to total output?

b. Is there excess demand or supply at the new output level? What will happen to the price level? How will this restore equilibrium in the output market?

    c. Use aggregate demand-supply analysis to show the effect that the minimum wage has on the economy's equilibrium output and price levels.

    d. In much of the analysis in this book, we do not worry about the fact that workers are heterogeneous with respect to their productivities and preferences. However, such factors may be important to note here. For example, suppose that there are two types of workers: older workers who tend to be more productive and more stable, and younger workers, who tend to be less productive and less stable. Do you think that imposing the minimum wage might have different effects in the two different labor markets? Could the more productive workers possibly be made better off by the legislation?

5. The accelerated depreciation allowances in the 1981 tax act lowered the average period during which firms could depreciate their plant and equipment for tax purposes from about nine years to five years.

    a. Explain why accelerated depreciation lowered the effective purchase price of capital equipment.

    b. What is the resulting effect on the real rental cost of capital?

    c. What will happen to the economy's equilibrium levels of price and real GNP in the current period (which is sufficiently short in duration that the capital stock can be taken as fixed)? Why? What happens to real consumption spending?

    d. What effect will the current change in tax laws have on output in the future? Why?

    e. What will happen to the aggregate supply curve in the future? What will happen to the equilibrium price level in the future? Why?

    f. Assuming that capital and labor are complements, show the effect of the current change in tax laws on labor market equilibrium in the future.

6. Discuss the key provisions of the (so-called) 1986 tax reform act with respect to the taxation of individuals and corporations. Contrary to what some of its proponents claim, why is it unclear whether the 1986 act will have a positive or negative effect on aggregate supply?

7. The Economic Recovery Tax Act of 1981 provided tax advantages to saving—for example, income put into the Individual Retirement Accounts (IRAs) and Supplementary Retirement Accounts (SRAs) was not taxed until the time it was actually withdrawn. The 1986 tax act has reduced these tax advantages. For example, it has restricted the use of IRAs and it has imposed penalties for the early withdrawal of funds from SRAs.

    a. What is the predicted effect of these 1986 changes on desired saving?

    b. What is the resulting effect on the economy's equilibrium output level, price level, and interest rate? Why?

    c. What happens to investment spending and the future capital stock?

8. Unemployment compensation is one of the government transfer programs that affects labor supply and thus aggregate supply. This program provides cash payments to individuals who work for a specified period of time and lose their jobs.

   a. What effect does an increase in unemployment compensation have on the supply of labor? Why?

   b. Besides its effect on the willingness of unemployed persons to accept employment, the unemployment compensation program affects the employment level in another way. Consider two firms. Suppose that Firm A has a policy of laying off workers frequently over time, while firm B seldom lays off workers. Which firm will have to pay a higher wage to its workers? Why?

   c. How does the existence of unemployment compensation affect the wage differential between the two firms? Why?

   d. The unemployment compensation program is funded by assessing taxes on firms. Suppose that all firms pay the same tax. Is there any sense in which some firms are subsidizing other firms?

   e. Does the unemployment compensation program have an effect on the mix of jobs (stable versus unstable) in the economy? Why? Does it encourage any given firm to choose more layoffs on average than it otherwise would?

   f. How does your answer to (e) change if the firms with histories of more layoffs have to make greater contributions to the unemployment insurance fund. (such an unemployment insurance system is said to be experience-rated. In Chapter 15, we will see that the unemployment insurance system in the United States is only imperfectly experience-rated).

9. According to the November 13, 1984 *Wall Street Journal*, "The French economy took a nose dive after the Socialist government was elected in 1981. Mr. Mitterrand's government shortened the workweek, raised the minimum wage and increased various social benefits, whereupon unemployment actually increased."

   a. Illustrate the effect that an increase in social benefits such as unemployment insurance has on labor market equilibrium. Does employment rise or fall?

   b. What happens to the aggregate supply curve?

   c. According to the neoclassical model, what happens to real GNP, the price level, and interest rates?

10. In the early and mid-1980s, the collapse of OPEC and the discovery of large oil deposits have resulted in an increase in the world supply of oil.

   a. Show the effect on the oil market. What happens to the relative price of oil?

    b.   What happens to the usage of the energy input by U.S. firms?

    c.   If energy and labor are complements in production, show the effect on the labor market. What happens to employment? What happens to the real wage?

    d.   What happens to total output?

    e.   At the original price level, is there an excess demand or supply in the output market? Why?

    f.   What will happen to the price level? How will this restore equilibrium in the output market?

    g.   A *Wall Street Journal* article noted that "helping to spark yesterday's bond rally was a large drop in oil prices." Is this consistent with your answer to (f)?

    h.   Use aggregate demand-supply analysis to show the effect that the increase in energy supply has on real GNP and output prices in the U.S.

11. In a 1979 *Wall Street Journal* article, Harold B. Erlich, chairman of Bernstein-Macaulay Inc. declared that "the main propellants of the most recent burst of inflation have been the vast increases in the costs of energy, housing, and services." From the point of view of the U.S. economy, what would cause an increase in the real price of energy? Will this increase in the real price of energy lead to an increase in the price level? If so, why? Does it seem more appropriate to call the increase in the price of energy a cause of inflation or a symptom?

12. In the 1980s, economists have paid increased attention to real business cycle theories.

    a.   What do we mean by a real business cycle theory?

    b.   Give several examples of supply shocks not directly related to government policy changes. Discuss the types of economy-wide adjustments in wages, prices, output, and interest rates that these shocks may set in motion.

13. According to the November 1984 *Wall Street Journal*, "In Britain, . . . the eight month coal miners' strike also has affected budget planning, since it has been costly for the government to maintain electricity supplies. . . . Growth in total output also has been limited by the miners' strike, according to the chancellor's [Nigel Lawson] statement. The forecast for growth in the current year is 2.5 percent, down from an earlier projection of 3.5 percent."

    a.   Show graphically the effect of the British coal miners' strike on the British labor market.

    b.   Use aggregate demand-supply analysis to show the effect on the equilibrium level of British output prices and real GNP. What happens to the equilibrium interest rate? Why?

14. It is sometimes said that, for many in the labor force, income effects dominate substitution effects with respect to changes in real after-tax wages. Under such circumstances, an aggregation of labor supply decisions across individuals in the economy could result in a downward sloping economy-wide labor supply curve. Assume, however, that this labor supply curve is "steeper" than the labor demand curve, so that a real wage below the equilibrium real wage would lead to an excess demand for labor. Conversely, a real wage above the equilibrium real wage would lead to an excess supply of labor.

   a. Taking the view of the neoclassical model, indicate the effect on the labor market of an increase in the marginal tax rate on wage income from t_0 to t_1. Indicate on the graph the real wage that would have resulted in no change labor supply (i.e., the real wage associated with moving vertically to the new labor supply curve). Express this real wage in terms of the two tax rates, t_0 and t_1, and the original real wage, $(W/P)_0$.

   b. Using aggregate demand and supply curves, show the predicted effect on real GNP and the price level of the higher marginal tax rate. What are the implied effects on the nominal interest rate, the expected real rate of interest, the real wage, and the real wage after taxes?

Chapter 10

Macroeconomic Analysis with Predetermined Prices

THE neoclassical model assumes that prices adjust quickly to unanticipated changes in demands and supplies in order to maintain equilibrium in the various markets in the economy. Consequently, changes in aggregate demand cause changes in wages and prices but not in employment or output. But what happens if prices are set at levels inconsistent with equilibrium in the various markets and do not adjust quickly? Then an excess demand for, or supply of, output will lead to a change in real GNP rather than a change in the price level.[1]

John Maynard Keynes made precisely this point in his seminal work, *The General Theory*, in which he argued that adjustments to macroeconomic demand shocks may take the form of changes in output rather than prices. In fact, Don Patinkin has argued that the idea of quantity equilibration was the central analytical innovation of Keynes's book.[2] Keynes was responding to the Great Depression of the 1930s, when a reduction in output demand led not only to lower prices but also to a substantial fall in output and a dramatic rise in unemployment.

---

[1] See Robert J. Gordon, "Price Inertia and Policy Ineffectiveness in the United States, 1890–1980," *Journal of Political Economy* (December 1982) p. 1087–1117. The author finds that "short-run inertia in price setting" was an important feature of the United States economy over the 90-year period from 1890 to 1980.

[2] Don Patinkin, *Keynes' Monetary Thought* (Durham, North Carolina: Duke University Press, 1976).

In this chapter, we modify the neoclassical model by introducing inflexible prices. The model that emerges can be termed the non-market-clearing model, for prevailing prices do not clear the output and labor markets. Non-market-clearing prices result in production below what firms would like to supply and employment below what households would like to supply. Firms' production is limited by the demand for output, so that output is demand-determined. Similarly, households' employment is limited by firms' demand for labor.

With inflexible prices, changes from the supply side are no longer the sole cause of recessions and high unemployment. Exogenous changes in investment demand or consumption demand can now affect real GNP and employment. Just as importantly, fiscal and monetary policy changes can affect real GNP through their impact on aggregate demand. Later chapters explore this potential new role that monetary and fiscal policy changes can play in stabilizing the economy at full employment.

Because fixed, or predetermined, prices can have such important consequences, the next section discusses why prices may be inflexible or "sticky." We then analyze the adjustment of output and employment to a demand-side disturbance when prices are inflexible.[3] Our analysis highlights a key feature of the Keynesian model, namely, that the effects of initial output demand disturbances are amplified by the dependence of consumption spending on income. We focus initially on how the simple "multiplier" summarizes this feature of the analysis by examining the output market in isolation. We then introduce the graphical framework of the *IS-LM* curves to explore more fully the output-interest rate adjustments characteristic of an economy with inflexible prices.

The *IS-LM* model developed in this chapter captures some aspects of short-run behavior that the neoclassical model omits. We should point out, however, that assumptions that result in either a pure price adjustment or a pure output adjustment in response to a demand shock are both simplifying ones. As economist Axel Leijonhufvud notes, "At one extreme of a spectrum of possibilities are the traditional full employment models where the brunt of adjustments is borne by prices; at the other extreme are the 'pure Keynesian' models where prices are essentially given and income moves. . . . The choice is no doubt mainly a question of the 'Long View and the Short.' "[4] In this chapter, we take the extreme view of fixed prices and fluctuating output—the "pure Keynesian" model—as opposed to the neoclassical "full employment"

---

[3] See Robert Clower, "The Keynesian Counterrevolution: A Theoretical Appraisal" in *The Theory of Interest Rates*, eds. F. Hahn and F. Brechling, (London: MacMillan, 1965); Don Patinkin, *Money, Interest, and Prices* (New York: Harper and Row, 1965); and Robert Barro and Herschel Grossman, *Money, Employment and Inflation* (New York: Cambridge University Press, 1976). These works provide formal statements of the non-market-clearing model as a characterization of an economy with sticky prices.

[4] Axel Leijonhufvud, *On Keynesian Economics and the Economics of Keynes* (London: Oxford University Press, 1968), pp. 58–59.

model of the previous three chapters. In the final section of the chapter, we show how to combine the analyses of the pure Keynesian model and the neoclassical model to trace out the dynamic adjustment of the economy to a demand shock.

10.1   INERTIA IN PRICE CHANGES

Our discussion of the neoclassical model presumed that prices are such that quantity supplied exactly equals the quantity demanded in every market. Consequently, buyers and sellers are able to buy and sell all they want at prevailing prices. The typical reason given for why such market-clearing prices occur is that prices adjust quickly in order to maintain equilibrium in all markets. For example, a fall in output demand is assumed to be met by an immediate downward adjustment in all nominal prices, so that no change in relative prices, employment, or output need occur. This neoclassical outcome to a demand shock is summarized by the vertical aggregate supply curve.

But quick price adjustment is not necessary for the market-clearing outcome of the neoclassical model. For example, suppose that market participants correctly anticipated current demand and supply when setting prices in some prior period. Then, unless there is an unanticipated change in demand or supply, these preset prices will be such that all markets will be in equilibrium. Relative prices, employment, and output will all be consistent with full employment.[5] Thus the neoclassical outcome emerges even with sticky prices if individuals correctly foresee future market conditions when prices are set.[6]

Yet often buyers and sellers do not fully anticipate the various factors affecting future demand and supply, and thus they err in setting prices. Expressed differently, prices based on incomplete or "imperfect" information on future demand and supply conditions may not be market-clearing. Furthermore, prices do not appear to be as quick to adjust as the neoclassical model assumes. The predetermined price model captures this notion of inflexible prices by the extreme assumption that current prices are fixed and completely invariant with respect to current macroeconomic shocks.[7]

---

[5] See Armen Alchian, "Information Costs, Pricing, and Resource Unemployment," in *Microeconomic Foundations of Employment and Inflation Theory*, ed. Edmund Phelps, 1970. The author notes that in the context of specific markets, if demand "shifted *predictably*, prices would vary—as they do for afternoon and evening restaurant and theater, for example."

[6] This condition is sometimes referred to as one of "perfect foresight."

[7] See James Potera, Julio Rotemberg, and Lawrence Summers "A Tax-Based Test for Nominal Rigidities," *American Economic Review* (September, 1986) pp. 659–675. The authors support the contention that in the short run prices and wages do not respond to macroeconomic shocks as completely as the neoclassical model predicts. In their words, "we find it impossible to

If market participants anticipate no demand and supply changes when prices are set, then the assumption of inflexible prices means that prices will not be changing over time. This, in fact, typified the noninflationary period in the U.S. from 1957 to 1966, when, according to economist Dennis Carlton, "the degree of price rigidity in many industries [was] significant. It [was] not unusual in some industries for prices to individual buyers to remain unchanged for years."[8]

It is important to realize, however, that the assumption of "sticky" prices in the current period is entirely consistent with the observation of rising (or falling) prices over time. Remember that the critical aspect of the predetermined price model is that agents set prices before demands and supplies are fully revealed to them. These predetermined prices may well be set above the prices that existed in prior periods, in which case there is inflation. The assumption that current prices do not respond to unanticipated changes in demand simply means that the rate of inflation is not affected by current macroeconomic shocks. As we will see, however, other macroeconomic variables—for example, real GNP and the interest rate—do change in response to macroeconomic demand shocks.

Imperfect Information and Sticky Prices

The story often told to explain the quick adjustment of prices assumed by the neoclassical model is commonly attributed to Leon Walras. It was in 1874 that Walras described the process by which prices adjust to excess demand or supply as a groping, or *"tatonnement"* process, with a fictitious auctioneer calling out different prices for the various markets and no exchange occurring until equilibrium prices are reached.[9] In reality, of course, there is no auctioneer. In fact, some think that Walras would have been the first to question such a description of the economy as realistically capturing the true dynamic process by which the economy reaches the equilibrium described by supply and demand curves.[10]

How then do the numerous sellers and buyers in the various markets in the economy collectively reach a new set of equilibrium prices when there

---

convincingly account for the empirical regularities in the data without assuming some sort of price rigidity." (p. 674)

[8] Dennis W. Carlton, "The Rigidities of Prices," *American Economic Review* (September 1986) pp. 637–658.

[9] Walras' description of *tatonnement* can be found in his seminal work *Eléments d'économie politique pure* (the definitive 1926 Paris edition) as translated and edited by W. Jaffé under the title *Elements of Pure Economics* (London, 1954). A brief description of the theory is contained in Don Patinkin, *Money, Interest, and Prices* (New York: Harper and Row, 1965), p. 531.

[10] See Donald A. Walker, "Walras' Theories of *Tatonnement*," *Journal of Political Economy* (August 1987): 758–774. The author points out that Walras promoted a "disequilibrium-production model of *tatonnement*" as more representative of Walras' thought than the *tatonnement* model with an "auctioneer."

are unanticipated changes in demands and supplies. One view is that sellers respond to unanticipated excess demands and supplies through a trial and error sequence of price changes, a time-consuming process during which exchanges occur at prices other than market-clearing prices. As economist Axel Leijonhufvud notes, "If prices are not perfectly flexible—that is, if they do not adjust instantly and fully 'before any trade takes place'—transactions will be concluded at disequilibrium prices."[11]

How long will this trial and error process of groping to a new set of equilibrium prices take? We can only be reasonably sure that prices will ultimately adjust "in the long run." One simple reason why prices may not adjust quickly to an unanticipated change in demand and supply is that there are costs to changing prices. Consider the following example.[12] Suppose that you are the president of a company that produces office furniture and sells it to various retail outlets and corporations. You produce a certain number of chairs and desks this month, post a price for each item, and *anticipate* selling all that you produce. However, you lack perfect information as to the actual sales that will materialize at the posted prices. If sales differ from what you initially expected, what will you do?

If your response to unexpected demand fluctuations is to change prices, you will impose explicit costs on yourself, as well as implicit costs on your customers. The explicit costs that you bear are sometimes referred to as the "menu" costs of price changes. This term derives from the costs borne by a restaurant of printing a new menu every time it changes its prices.[13] Even if these menu costs are small, you still may not change your prices often because price fluctuations impose costs on your customers, which may reduce their long-term loyalty to your product.[14] When your customers make their purchasing plans, they want to know what prices they will confront. If in months of unexpectedly high demand, you raise prices, your customers may have to make costly revisions in their plans, either forgoing the purchase of

---

[11] Leijonhufvud (p. 54), see Footnote 4.

[12] The discussion to follow does not offer a complete, rigorous explanation as to why prices are sticky. Such a comprehensive explanation does not exist at the present time. Rather, in providing a rationale for the macroeconomic model with predetermined prices, one must currently, "in the ancient and honorable tradition of Keynesians past, . . . take it for granted that there are disadvantages from too-frequent or too-precipitate revisions of price lists and wage schedules." Edmund S. Phelps and John B. Taylor, "Stabilizing Powers of Monetary Policy Under Rational Expectations," *Journal of Political Economy* (February 1977): 166.

[13] See Michael Parkin, "The Output-Inflation Trade-Off When Prices are Costly to Change," *Journal of Political Economy* (February 1986) pp. 200–204. The author examines the implications of "a technologically given cost of changing prices—what has been called a menu cost." Parkin suggests that for "plausible conditions, small menu costs will generate price change frequencies similar to those observed in actual economies."

[14] See Arthur Okun, "Inflation: Its Mechanics and Welfare Costs," *Brookings Papers on Economic Activity*, vol. 2, 1975) and Julio Rotemberg, "Sticky Prices in the United States," *Journal of Political Economy* (December 1982). The authors explore the issue of price inflexibility further. Rotemberg, for example, "presents a theory that justifies price stickiness, namely, that firms, fearing to upset their customers, attribute a cost to price changes." p. 1187.

the furniture until later or incurring search costs to locate other furniture vendors with lower prices.[15]

Customers may prefer a competing furniture vendor down the street who follows an alternative policy of offering a stable price. Just as price fluctuations carry some cost, however, price stability too is costly. During times of high demand, some customers may find no furniture to buy, as the stable price results in excess demand. During times of low demand, furniture will go unsold. Customers want a vendor who not only offers stable prices, but who also has furniture available when they want it. Thus stores hold inventories so that they can avoid the embarrassment of not meeting customer demand. In summary, in order to foster long-term customer relationships, firms find it advantageous to remove some of the risk of unexpected price changes. This requires that they not only limit the number of times they change their prices but also that they hold inventories in order to be able to meet any unexpectedly high demands.

The above discussion suggests some lags in price adjustments to changes in market conditions at the level of the individual firm. What is critical to macroeconomic analysis is the cumulative effect that these lags in price adjustment have on the responsiveness of the aggregate price level. As Olivier Blanchard notes, "slow adjustment of the price level comes from cumulation of small lags at the individual level. While individual price setters adjust their prices to wages and other input prices quickly, interactions between price decisions lead to a cumulation of those small lags and to slow aggregate price adjustment."[16]

Sticky Wages and Prices as Fixed Mark-ups

Input markets constitute one set of markets in which attempts to maintain constant prices, and thus avoid price uncertainty, appear to be particularly strong. For instance, we often observe that when firms subcontract the production of certain inputs to other producers, they agree on specific fixed prices for these inputs in future periods. More important is the often-made observation that the money wage paid labor is sticky. For example, we often see unions and employers entering into long-term contracts that specify fixed future money wages.

Although input prices often seem to have an element of fixity, the critical assumption of the predetermined price model is fixed *output* prices, not fixed wages. Fixed wages can translate directly into fixed output prices, however, if output prices depend solely on costs factors. Economist Martin Weitzman, among others, has argued that just such a situation approximates the state

---

[15] If you lower prices in months of unexpectedly low demand, then this implies that you raise them when demand returns to normal.

[16] Olivier Jean Blanchard, "Aggregate and Individual Price Adjustment," *Brookings Papers on Economic Activity*, vol. 1, 1987, p. 58.

of the economy in the short run. In particular, Weitzman asserts that it is often the case that (a) money wages are fixed or predetermined at a level such that an excess supply of labor exists and (b) for the relevant range of output, the marginal product of labor is approximately constant.[17] Under these conditions, the cost of producing an additional unit of output (the marginal cost of production) does not increase as output rises. Since a constant marginal cost of production implies a horizontal supply curve for output, the entire adjustment to any change in the demand is in output.

In Weitzman's "Keynesian model," output prices are fixed since money wages are fixed and prices are essentially fixed markups over costs (that is, prices depend solely on cost factors such as wages). In this important way, Weitzman's model captures the essence of the macroeconomic model with predetermined prices, for in the model demand shocks lead to output, not price changes. Weitzman's view of the determination of output prices is atypical from the usual supply and demand view of the output market, however, and this leads to a different characterization of the long-run response to a demand shock. For instance, consider a fall in aggregate demand.

As we discuss in the concluding section of this chapter, the usual view is that output prices ultimately fall in response to contractionary demand shock, as firms react to the fact that sales fall short of what was anticipated at the posted prices. Naturally, the fact that prices do not immediately fall captures the assumption that it take time for firms to recognize the change in the market-clearing level of prices. With this sluggish adjustment in prices, the brunt of the economy's response to the fall in aggregate demand thus takes the form of reduced output.

In contrast to this usual view, even over time a fall in aggregate demand would not directly induce a reduction in output prices according to Weitzman's model. In this model, prices equal fixed markups over wages, and firms simply lower sales with the fall in demand. Over time, the impetus for falling output prices comes from the fact that the fall in aggregate demand reduces output and employment, leading to excess supply in the labor market. The resulting reduction in wages over time is what leads to falling prices, since prices are directly tied to wages and other production costs.[18]

---

[17] See Martin L. Weitzman, "The Simple Macroeconomics of Profit Sharing," *American Economic Review* (December 1985) pp. 937–953. In developing a markup model of price setting behavior, Weitzman also assumes that prices are set by individual firms rather than by the interaction of market demand and supply. Thus his result requires the additional assumption that the downward-sloping demand curve facing each firm has a constant elasticity of demand. Given fixed wages that lead, along with an invariant marginal product of labor, to a constant marginal cost of production, the constant price elasticity of demand means that each firm will find it optimal to set prices as a fixed markup over the wage.

[18] This analysis is similar to the coming analysis in Chapter 12, where we generate an upward-sloping aggregate supply curve by assuming a fixed money wage. The difference between the two analyses is that in Chapter 12 prices as well as output respond to changes in output demand.

10.2   AGGREGATE DEMAND AND SUPPLY WITH NON-MARKET-CLEARING PRICES

Our preceding discussion suggests that in modeling the economy, we can presume that prices are set at some predetermined level for a certain period of time. Prices will be set at levels that individuals expect to be market-clearing. If these prices turn out to be non-market-clearing, output can fall below its full employment level.

The Great Depression is the classic example of non-market-clearing prices. Unemployment rose to nearly 25 percent during the depths of the Depression and real GNP fell by one third between 1929 and 1933. Although prices fell during the period, they did not fall fast enough or far enough to restore equilibrium in the output and labor markets. In the next section, we look at what it means to be at **non-market-clearing prices** in terms of the aggregate demand/aggregate supply analysis.

Non-market-clearing prices: In the predetermined price model, the setting of output prices at a level such that firms cannot sell all they desire at existing prices.

On the Aggregate Demand Curve/Off the Neoclassical Aggregate Supply Curve

In the non-market-clearing model, prices are fixed at a predetermined level above what would exist in the neoclassical model. As Figure 10.1 illustrates, at the price level P_0 above the neoclassical price level P_n, it is not possible to be on both the aggregate demand and aggregate supply curves. As Keynes stated, in such a situation output is "demand determined." Firms will produce exactly what is demanded and vary output in response to changes in aggregate demand. In terms of Figure 10.1, output at the price P_0 thus equals Y_0. An important outcome of the price level being too high is that Y_0 falls below the full employment level of output Y^*.

The situation in Figure 10.1, in which output is determined by demand conditions, contrasts with the neoclassical model. In the neoclassical model, output is determined by supply conditions and prices adjust to ensure that firms can sell all they would like to produce. In the predetermined price model, firms cannot sell all they produce at existing prices and they face what may be called a binding "sales constraint" in the output market.[19] The

---

[19] This critical aspect of short-run adjustments to macroeconomic shocks is supported by a recent study by Mark Bils, "The Cyclical Behavior of Marginal Cost and Price," *American Economic Review* (December 1987): p. 838–855. Bils argues that the evidence supports "theories that explain low production in a recession by the inability of firms to sell their output." (p. 838) As we will see, this view contrasts with that taken by the models to be developed in Chapter 12. Such models rely on wage stickiness and resulting cost changes to explain cyclical fluctuations in output and employment rather than "imperfections in the goods market" (Bils, p. 854) and the resulting sales constraint.

Figure 10.1   **Aggregate Demand at Predetermined Prices**

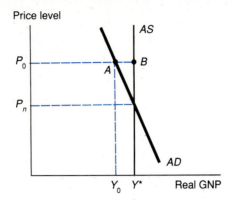

At the predetermined price level P_0, aggregate demand (point A) is less than aggregate supply (point B). In such a situation, output is determined by aggregate demand and thus equals Y_0.

fact that production is demand-determined has important implications for the behavior of firms in the labor market.

Labor Demand When Firms Face a Sales Constraint

When firms cannot sell all they desire at the prevailing price level, the quantity of labor demanded by firms is determined by the amount of output that they can sell, not by the real wage. Even if wages are reduced, firms will not increase the quantity of labor demanded since they will not be able to sell the additional output produced. This means that the demand for labor curve is now vertical, with its position determined by the amount of output that firms can sell. Figure 10.2 shows this curve.

At real wage levels above $(W/P)^*$ the desired level of production is sufficiently low that firms are able to sell all that they would like to produce. In other words, above $(W/P)^*$ the real wage is sufficiently high that the constraint on sales is not binding and thus the standard downward-sloping neoclassical demand for labor curve represents the labor demand of firms.

At real wage levels below $(W/P)^*$ in Figure 10.2, firms face a sales constraint in the output market. The level of employment N_0 is just sufficient to produce the restricted level of output demanded in the output market. At a real wage such as $(W/P)_0$, firms will not hire more than N_0 workers, since they are not able to sell the additional output that those workers will produce.[20] If the demand for output increases, the vertical section of the

---

[20] In the literature, this new labor demand curve is referred to as the "effective" demand curve for labor. Effective labor demand, unlike the "notional" demand curve of the neoclassical

Figure 10.2 **The Effect on the Labor Market of a Sales Constraint in the Output Market**

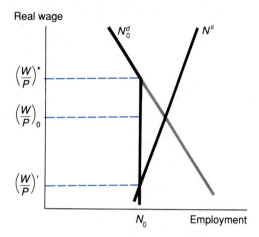

If there is a limit on sales in the output market, the demand for labor curve is given by the solid line N_0^d. The result of a sales constraint is a vertical labor demand curve for real wages below $(W/P)^*$, indicating that labor demand is insensitive to changes in the wage rate. (The grey line indicates the contrasting labor demand curve in the neoclassical model.)

labor demand curve will shift to the right and employment will rise. If the demand for output decreases, the labor demand curve will shift to the left and employment will fall.

Figure 10.2 illustrates several important features of the labor market that emerge when output prices are inflexible. First, an excess supply of labor exists if the real wage is fixed at any level above $(W/P)'$. Second, if we introduce flexible money wages and the real wage falls to $(W/P)'$, the excess supply of labor will be eliminated entirely by a fall in the quantity of labor supplied (as shown by a movement down the labor supply curve).[21] But, the quantity of labor demanded and employment will not increase at all, since it is the lack of adjustment in output prices, not money wages, that is the source of the lower output and employment that accompanies a decrease in output demand. Naturally, if one assumes prices are fixed markups over wages, then the failure of wages to fall could be cited as the reason for no adjustment in output prices.

model, depends on the amount of output that firms can sell rather than on the real wage. See Robert J. Barro and Herschel I. Grossman, *Money, Employment, and Inflation* (Cambridge University Press, 1976) and Edmond Malinvaud, *The Theory of Unemployment Reconsidered* (Oxford, England: Blackwell, 1977).

[21] This statement assumes that the level of output prices is held constant.

Involuntary Unemployment: The Rationing of Jobs

Recall that unemployment arises in the neoclassical model because workers continuously move into and out of the labor force and between various jobs, and because locating an acceptable job usually takes time. This unemployment, discussed in Chapter 7, occurs even though the labor market is in equilibrium. We usually refer to it as frictional and structural unemployment and it determines the natural rate of unemployment. Unemployment arising in the non-market-clearing model differs fundamentally, because it results from a macroeconomic shock that leads to excess supply in the labor market. This type of extra unemployment is often referred to as **involuntary unemployment.**

> **Involuntary unemployment:** A type of unemployment that occurs in the predetermined price model when workers cannot find employment at prevailing wages.

Workers who are involuntarily unemployed would like to be employed at the prevailing wage rate, but jobs are simply not available. Layoffs occur, hiring ceases, and lines form at factories and workplaces throughout the economy; the involuntarily unemployed wait with many others for job vacancies to appear, rather than engage in productive search for the best use of their labor services. It is a deficiency in output demand that causes involuntary unemployment. Further, while a reduction in the wage can eliminate the involuntary nature of this unemployment, without any change in output prices it will not increase the level of employment. Employment is determined by what can be sold, not by the real wage, and therefore the problem is not that the real wage is "too high."

Firms would be willing to hire more workers if they could pay the newly hired workers by simply returning to them part of their physical product. But an individual producer, such as a steel firm, "cannot pay a newly hired worker by handing over to him his physical product (nor will the worker try to feed his family on a ton-and-a-half of cold-rolled sheet a week)."[22] Workers demand money payments for their productive services, which means that firms must be able to sell what the workers produce. But—and this is the critical aspect of the non-market-clearing model—output prices for the current period have been preset at a level "too high" in light of the actual output demand. Furthermore, costly adjustment precludes prices from adjusting downward in the short run.

To the Point

STICKY PRICES AND THE OUTPUT AND LABOR MARKETS

- Prices do not appear to be nearly as quick to adjust as the neoclassical model assumes; they are often said to be sticky in the short run.
- If prices are fixed at too high a level, then output is determined by the aggregate demand curve and falls below the full employment level of output. Output is constrained by the amount that firms can sell.

---

[22] Leijonhufvud (p. 190), see Footnote 4.

- In the labor market, employment responds not to wage changes but to changes in the demand for output. It is the demand for output that determines the effective demand for labor.

10.3 THE OUTPUT MARKET WITH FIXED PRICES: A SIMPLIFIED ANALYSIS

As we have seen, when output prices are predetermined at too high a level, changes in aggregate demand lead to changes in output. These output adjustments serve to restore equilibrium in the output, financial, and money markets, but not at the full employment level of real GNP. This contrasts sharply with the neoclassical model, where output is determined solely by the position of the aggregate supply curve and shifts in the aggregate demand curve cause prices, but not real GNP, to change. To understand the nature of the output adjustments that occur in response to demand shifts in the predetermined price model, we start by focusing on the output market. Later, we broaden our discussion to include the money and financial markets.

Equilibrium in the Output Market

Equilibrium in the output market means that demand equals production. Since output demand in a closed economy is simply the sum of consumption demand plus gross investment demand plus government demand, we can express this equilibrium condition as

$$\underset{\substack{\text{Consumption} \\ \text{demand}}}{C^d} + \underset{\substack{\text{Gross investment} \\ \text{demand}}}{I^d + CCA} + \underset{\substack{\text{Government} \\ \text{demand}}}{G^d} = \underset{\text{Output}}{Y} \qquad \textbf{(10.1)}$$

Note that this equation differs from that of an open economy in that it neglects the net exports component of output demand.

Equation 10.1 suggests that an increase in, say, real government spending (G^d) would lead to an equal increase in equilibrium output (Y). However, this is *not* the case since an increase in output typically leads to a rise in consumption demand and consequent further increases in output. The result is that a given change in autonomous spending can lead to a larger change in output demand and output.

To take account of the fact that consumption demand can change with changes in income, we need to modify Equation 10.1 to explicitly introduce the relationship between income and consumption demand. In Chapter 6, we introduced the following linear consumption function to express the relationship between income and consumption demand:

$$C^d = a + b \cdot (Y - CCA - T), \qquad \textbf{(10.2)}$$

where a and b are positive parameters. Equation 10.2 simply indicates that household consumption demand (C^d) depends directly on real disposable income ($Y - CCA - T$). In Chapter 6, we saw that consumption demand depended not only on directly disposable income but also on such factors as the interest rate (inversely) and anticipated future disposable income (directly). The impact on consumption demand of changes in such factors can be captured by changes in the intercept term a in Equation 10.2.

Marginal propensity to consume (MPC): The ratio of the increase in households' real consumption demand to the increase in their real disposable income.

Recall from our discussion in Chapter 6 that the parameter b is referred to as the **marginal propensity to consume,** for it tells us the change in consumption demand resulting from a one-unit change in real disposable income. For instance, if b is .8 and real disposable income rises by $10, then consumption demand will rise by $8. The marginal propensity to consume is positive but less than one, because an increase in real disposable income causes consumption spending to rise but by an amount smaller than the total increase in income.[23] This reflects the fact that households generally respond to an increase in real disposable income by increasing not only consumption spending but also saving.

When we substitute this expression for the consumption function (Equation 10.2) into the output market equilibrium expression (Equation 10.1), we have

$$\underset{\text{Consumption demand}}{a + b\cdot(Y - CCA - T)} + \underset{\text{Gross investment demand}}{I^d + CCA} + \underset{\text{Government demand}}{G^d} = \underset{\text{Output}}{Y} \qquad \textbf{(10.3)}$$

Keynesian cross diagram: An illustration of equilibrium in the output market in terms of firms producing an amount equal to output demand.

We can illustrate this equilibrium condition for the output market graphically with the **Keynesian cross diagram.** Figure 10.3 depicts this diagram, which involves two solid curves that form a "cross."

In the Keynesian cross diagram, the curve labeled Y^d plots the relationship between output demand and output as indicated by the left side of Equation 10.3. This curve is upward-sloping because each $1 increase in output (and thus income) raises consumption demand by some positive amount. In fact, the slope of the output demand curve is simply the marginal propensity to consume since the marginal propensity to consume tells us the increase in consumption demand stemming from a $1 increase in real income. Formally, the output demand curve is a straight line with an intercept equal to ($a - b\cdot T + I^d + G^d + (1 - b)\cdot CCA$) and a slope equal to b, the marginal propensity to consume.[24]

The second solid curve in the Keynesian cross diagram depicted is a 45-degree line. Each point along the 45-degree line is equidistant from the two

---

[23] According to Keynes, "The fundamental psychological law, upon which we are entitled to depend with great confidence both *a priori* from our knowledge of human nature and from the detailed facts of experience, is that men are disposed, as a rule and on the average, to increase their consumption as their income increases, but not by as much as the increase in their income" (*General Theory,* p. 96)

[24] The intercept is the point where the curve intercepts the vertical axis (i.e., the value of output demand when income Y equals zero). The slope measures the change in output demand given a one-unit increase in disposable income.

Figure 10.3 The Keynesian Cross Diagram and Equilibrium Output

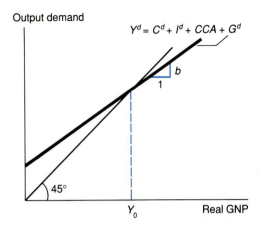

The Keynesian cross diagram consists of two curves. One, which is always at a 45-degree angle, denotes points of equality between output produced, or real GNP, plotted on the horizontal axis, and output demand, plotted on the vertical axis. The other curve indicates the level of output demand at various levels of income. The slope of the output demand curve equals the marginal propensity to consume. Equilibrium output Y_0 is where the two curves intersect, since at that point output equals output demand.

axes. Thus at each point on this line, output demand (plotted on the vertical axis) equals real output (plotted on the horizontal axis). At points above the 45-degree line, output demand exceeds actual output, while at points below the line, output demand is less than output produced. In Figure 10.3, the equilibrium output level is Y_0; at that point the output demand curve Y^d intersects or "crosses" the 45-degree line so that demand equals output.

In the above discussion, we have simplified the analysis by assuming that only consumption demand depends on changes in income. In so doing, we have ignored a number of factors that affect the responsiveness of output demand to changes in output such as the links between changes in income and taxes and changes in income and investment demand.

In the case of taxes, an increase in income typically leads to a rise in net taxes since many taxes, such as state and federal personal income taxes, are tied to income. As you will see in working through Review Question 8 at the end of this chapter, if we let net taxes vary directly with income, the slope of the output demand curve in Figure 10.3 become flatter. A given increase in income results in less of an increase in disposable income if taxes rise with the increase in income, and thus results in less of an increase in consumption demand. Chapter 14 discusses further the implications of the link between net taxes and income. Later in this chapter we will look at the implications of a link between income changes and investment demand.

Changes in Output to Restore Equilibrium in the Output Market

Figure 10.3 indicates that equilibrium output is dependent on such factors as taxes, government spending, consumption demand, and investment demand. Changes in any of these variables shift the output demand curve and would thus mean a change in equilibrium output. Furthermore, as we show in this section, such a change can lead to multiple changes in equilibrium output. To illustrate this point, we consider below a change in autonomous investment spending. In general, as we have said before, changes in *autonomous spending* are changes in spending unrelated to changes in variables such as income and the interest rate. Expressed differently, changes in autonomous spending are output demand changes that are spontaneous and often unexplainable.

Our analysis will focus on a change in investment, in part because Keynes stressed the important role played by changes in autonomous investment demand in initiating recessions and, in the extreme, depressions.[25] For example, in a famous line from the *General Theory*, Keynes espoused the notion that the "animal spirits" of entrepreneurs are an important source of fluctuation in autonomous investment in the economy: "In estimating the prospects of investment, we must have regard, therefore, to the nerves and hysteria and even the digressions and reactions to the weather of those upon whose spontaneous activity it largely depends."[26] Keynes' point is that a key determinant of investment, the expected future return to capital purchases, is inherently subjective in nature. The resulting uncertainty about the profitability of investment leads to the possibility of wide swings in investment demand and thus can result in investment being "the component of aggregate demand at the source of unemployment problems."[27]

In the years that followed the Depression, there was widespread acceptance of the importance of fluctuations in autonomous spending, particularly investment spending, in causing the business cycle. This was underscored in the 1950s by the then best-selling principles of economics textbook in the country, written by Nobel prize winner Paul Samuelson, which boldly asserted that "all modern economists are agreed that the important factor in causing employment and income to fluctuate is investment."[28] To the extent that investment demand does fluctuate autonomously and unpredictably, then

---

[25] Indicative of this view of the Depression is the following quote: "the Depression was generated by a fall in autonomous spending. At a given level of income, desired investment and consumption fell. . . . The Depression was severe because the fall in autonomous spending was large and sustained." Peter Temin, *Did Monetary Forces Cause the Great Depression* (New York: Norton) 1976, p. 9.

[26] John Maynard Keynes, *The General Theory*, p. 162.

[27] Peter Howitt, "The Keynesian Recovery," *Canadian Journal of Economics* (November 1986) p. 626–641.

[28] Paul Samuelson, *Economics*, 3rd ed. (New York: McGraw-Hill, 1955).

instability in investment can in fact be an important source of instability in the economy. Let's trace through the impact that an unanticipated autonomous fall in investment has on real GNP when prices are predetermined.

Suppose that output demand is initially given by Y_0^d in Figure 10.4 such that equilibrium output is Y_0. A change in output demand appears as a vertical shift in the output demand curve. For example, if investment demand falls from I_0^d to I_1^d, the output demand curve shifts down from Y_0^d to the color line Y_1^d. As Figure 10.4 indicates, this causes equilibrium output to fall from Y_0 to Y_1. Let's analyze this output adjustment process in more detail.

With the fall in autonomous investment demand, firms will initially find that they are producing more than they can sell. This excess supply in the output market will likely show up as **unintended inventory accumulation** by firms.[29] If firms respond to the unintended inventory accumulation by reducing their rate of production by the same amount as the fall in output demand, this decrease in production will *not* restore equilibrium in the output market.[30]

Recall that changes in the level of output imply equivalent changes in income. Not only will the fall in employment that accompanies the fall in output reduce wage earnings, but other forms of household income, such as dividend earnings, will also decrease. As Equation 10.2 indicated, the reduction in household income causes consumption spending and output demand to fall. Consequently, excess supply will again exist in the output market and firms will again have to curtail production. An example should make this clearer.

Suppose that output demand initially falls by $10. Given the fixed price level, specified quantities of real output correspond to fixed dollar amounts. We can thus use dollar amounts to represent specified real amounts. Firms will respond to the resultant excess supply in the output market by reducing their production of output by $10. This means that households' real disposable income also falls by $10.[31] Since every $1 fall in disposable income causes households to reduce their spending by the marginal propensity to consume (b), the $10 reduction in disposable income will cause consumption demand

Unintended inventory accumulation: A situation that firms experience when output demand falls short of planned production. In contrast, if output planned demand exceeds planned production, firms experience unintended inventory depletion.

---

[29] Since inventories are part of investment, the condition of excess supply in the output market can be characterized as one in which actual or realized investment is greater than desired investment. In contrast, if output demand increases, then there will be an excess *demand* for output market and firms will experience unintended inventory *depletion*. This condition of excess demand in the output market can be characterized as one in which realized investment is less than desired investment.

[30] Remember that we have ruled out the possibility of prices adjusting in the current period.

[31] Recall that we are implicitly assuming that the net taxes households pay are independent of income. If these taxes are positively related to the level of income (for instance, because of the existence of income taxes), then households real disposable income will fall by an amount less than $10.

Figure 10.4   The Keynesian Cross Diagram and a Fall in Investment Demand

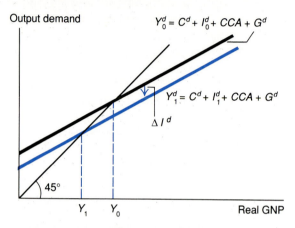

Initial equilibrium output is Y_0. The fall in investment demand from I_0^d to I_1^d is equal to the shift down in the output demand curve from Y_0^d to Y_1^d. Note that the fall in equilibrium output from Y_0 to Y_1 is an amount greater than the initial fall in investment demand.

to fall by $b \cdot \$10$. If the marginal propensity to consume equals .8, then the reduction in consumption demand will equal $.8 \cdot \$10$ or $\$8$.[32]

Firms now face disappointing news. They initially reduced their production of output by $10 in response to the drop in investment demand. However, this causes another $8 reduction in output demand, as households cut their consumption demand due to the reduction in their income. Firms now must reduce their output by an additional $8, which leads to a repetition of the process. Income falls by $8 and consumption demand falls by the change in income multiplied by .8 (the marginal propensity to consume), or $6.40. Firms again cannot sell all they produce and again cut back on production. Note, however, that the reductions in output and output demand become successively smaller. The initial fall in output demand is $10, the second reduction is $8, the third $6.40, and so on. Eventually, the reductions in the demand for output become negligible and equilibrium is restored in the output market, with output again equal to output demand.

The important point to note from our analysis is that the reduction in the equilibrium output level equals a *multiple* of the initial change in autonomous spending. We call the ratio of the change in equilibrium income to the initial change in output demand the **multiplier.** The multiplier tells

Multiplier: In the context of the predetermined price model, the ratio of the change in equilibrium output to an initial change in autonomous spending.

---

[32] The household budget constraint tells us that desired saving must fall by $2. If this reduction in saving consists partly of a reduction in financial asset demand (instead of entirely a reduction in the demand for real money balances), then the interest rate will be affected. This, in turn, will affect investment demand. We will disregard this effect until a later section.

us the change in equilibrium output caused by each $1 change in autonomous spending. In the next section, we determine the actual size of the simple multiplier. The simple multiplier is the multiplier that exists if the interest rate is unaffected by the change in autonomous spending and if taxes and investment demand are independent of income changes.[33]

The Simple Multiplier Calculation

We have just seen that an initial change in autonomous spending leads to a magnified change in equilibrium income. From Equation 10.3, we can determine the value of the multiplier. To do so, we simply solve this equation for the equilibrium level of output Y.[34] Doing so, we obtain the following expression for the equilibrium output Y:

$$Y = (1/(1 - b)) \cdot (a - b \cdot T + I^d + G^d) + CCA \qquad (10.4)$$

This equation summarizes the relationship between the equilibrium output level and autonomous spending. It tells us that increases (decreases) in autonomous consumption spending (a), net investment demand (I^d), and government demand (G^d) lead to increases (decreases) in equilibrium income. It also indicates how much equilibrium output will change for each dollar change in autonomous spending. Specifically, we see that for each $1 change in autonomous spending equilibrium output changes by $1/(1 - b)$, where b denotes the marginal propensity to consume for our linear consumption function (Equation 10.2). Thus, in general, the simple multiplier equals one divided by one minus the marginal propensity to consume:[35]

$$\text{Simple multiplier} = 1/(1 - \text{MPC}) \qquad (10.5)$$

Since the marginal propensity to consume (MPC) is smaller than one, the multiplier must be greater than one, which is consistent with our discussion above. In fact, with the .8 marginal propensity to consume in our preceding example, the multiplier will equal $1/(1 - .8)$ or 5. This means that for every $1 reduction in autonomous spending equilibrium output falls by $5, so that the initial $10 reduction in output demand will lead to a $50 reduction in equilibrium output.

In the *General Theory*, Keynes noted that "if the marginal propensity to consume is not far short of unity, small fluctuations in investment will lead to wide fluctuations in employment. . . . If, on the other hand, the marginal propensity to consume is not much above zero, small fluctuations in investment will lead to correspondingly small fluctuations in employment."[36] This statement

---

[33] Later in this chapter we modify our multiplier analysis to incorporate such effects.

[34] Specifically, subtract $b \cdot Y$ from both sides, then divide both sides of Equation 10.3 by $(1 - b)$.

[35] Remember that this expression for the multiplier is for the special case when interest rate effects are not considered and changes in income affect neither investment demand nor taxes.

[36] Keynes (p. 118).

is easy to interpret in light of our formula for the multiplier. If the marginal propensity to consume is large, then we see from Equation 10.5 that the multiplier will also be large, so that a small change in investment or other autonomous spending component will lead to a relatively large change in equilibrium output and hence employment. More generally, the greater the marginal propensity to consume, the larger the multiplier.

Finally, let us relate our discussion of the multiplier back to Figure 10.4, which indicated the change in equilibrium output caused by an initial change in output demand. Recall that the initial fall in output demand is represented by downward shift in the output demand curve from Y_0^d to Y_1^d. As the figure indicated, the resulting fall in the equilibrium output from Y_0 to Y_1 exceeds the initial reduction in output demand (which simply equals the vertical distance between Y_0^d and Y_1^d). This reflects the fact that the multiplier is greater than one.

To the Point

OUTPUT ADJUSTMENT: THE MULTIPLIER PROCESS

- Equilibrium in the output market can be depicted graphically by the Keynesian cross diagram. The intersection of the output demand curve and the 45-degree line determines the level of output equal to that demanded.

- Even though firms react to a reduction in demand by reducing output, this reduction in output does not immediately restore equilibrium in the output market. The reduction in output and the consequent fall in employment leads to further reductions in output demand.

- The concept that an initial reduction in output demand leads to multiple rounds of falling output is termed the multiplier effect. The numerical value of the simple multiplier is the ratio of the reduction in equilibrium output to the initial reduction in output demand.

- The value of the multiplier depends on the value of the marginal propensity to consume. The simple multiplier equals $1/(1 - MPC)$.

10.4   THE OUTPUT AND MONEY MARKETS WITH FIXED PRICES: *IS-LM* ANALYSIS

Earlier in this chapter, we noted that the distinguishing feature of the non-market-clearing model is that output is determined solely by the position of the aggregate demand curve. In Chapter 7, we saw that points on the aggregate demand curve represent output-price combinations consistent with equilibrium in the output, financial, and money markets. Yet so far our description of the output adjustments that occur in response to demand shifts in the predetermined price model have focused exclusively on the output market. We have done this to highlight the essentials of the multiplier process without having to take account of the feedback effects between the output, financial, and money markets. However, it is now time to broaden our discussion to encompass the latter two markets.

In order to analyze the interaction between the output, financial, and money markets, we develop what are commonly referred to as *IS* and *LM* curves. For a given level of output prices, the *IS* curve depicts combinations of interest rates and output that clear the output market, while the *LM* curve shows combinations of interest rates and output that clear the money market. The intersection of the *IS* and *LM* curves determines the interest rate and output level associated with simultaneous equilibrium in the output and money markets at a given level of output prices. From the aggregate budget constraint for a closed economy, we then know that the financial market is in equilibrium as well. We begin our discussion with the output market and the derivation of the *IS* curve.

Equilibrium in the Output Market and the *IS* Curve

The output market is in equilibrium when the demand for output equals the amount of output firms produced. Recall that the total demand for output in a closed economy equals the sum of household consumption demand (C^d) firm gross investment demand ($I^d + CCA$) and government demand (G^d). Reproducing Equation 10.1, we may thus write the output market equilibrium condition as

$$C^d + I^d + CCA + G^d = Y \qquad (10.6)$$

The *IS* curve summarizes the relationship between the interest rate r and level of output Y consistent with equilibrium in the output market. The name for the *IS* curve comes from the fact that if the government has a balanced budget ($G^d = T$) and we ignore net exports, then the equilibrium condition in the output market can be restated in terms of an equality between investment demand (I) and planned saving (S). To see this, substitute taxes T for G^d in the output market equilibrium condition (Equation 10.6) and rearrange terms to obtain

$$\underset{\substack{\text{Investment} \\ \text{demand}}}{I^d} = \underset{\text{Saving}}{Y - CCA - T - C^d}$$

The left side of this equation is investment demand, while the right side is household planned saving.

Let's suppose that the output market is initially in equilibrium, with the amount of output that the market participants demand equal to the amount produced. As we have previously discussed, investment and consumption demand are inversely related to the interest rate, due to the fact that a higher interest rate causes firms to curtail capital purchases and households to reduce expenditures on consumption durables. If the interest rate falls, the quantity of investment and consumption demand will increase and excess demand will exist in the output market at the initial level of output. As Figure 10.5 indicates, in terms of the Keynesian cross diagram, this rise in investment and consumption demand at the original level of output is shown by an upward shift in the output demand curve from Y_0^d to Y_1^d. The result is an increase in the market clearing level of real GNP from Y_0 to Y_1.

The inverse relationship between the interest rate and real GNP associated with equilibrium in the output market derived in Figure 10.5 is summarized by the **IS curve** drawn in Figure 10.6. The *IS* curve depicts all output-interest rate combinations consistent with equilibrium in the output market. For example, since the points (Y_0, r_0) and (Y_1, r_1) both appear on this curve, they represent output-interest rate combinations consistent with output market equilibrium. Since a reduction in the interest rate increases the level of output consistent with output market equilibrium, the *IS* curve has a negative slope.

IS **curve:** A curve depicting all output-interest rate combinations consistent with equilibrium in the output market.

Equilibrium in the Money Market and the *LM* Curve

The money market is in equilibrium when the demand for real money balances equals the supply. Recalling that the real demand for money is denoted by L^d and real money supply by M^s/P, we can express equilibrium in the money market as

$$
\underset{\substack{\text{Real demand for} \\ \text{money balances}}}{L^d} \quad = \quad \underset{\substack{\text{Real supply of} \\ \text{money balances}}}{M^s/P} \tag{10.7}
$$

The *LM* curve summarizes the relationship between the interest rate r and level of output Y consistent with equilibrium in the money market, as defined by the above equation. The source of the name for the *LM* curve comes from the fact that the equilibrium condition in the money market can be stated in terms of an equality between the desired holdings of money or liquid assets (L) and the money supply (M).

As we have discussed, an increase in the interest rate makes financial assets more attractive to households and money less attractive, thereby inducing households to reduce their holdings of real money balances. Consequently, as Figure 10.7 depicts, the demand for money curve L_0^d at income level Y_0 is downward-sloping with regard to the interest rate.

As we indicated when we discussed equilibrium in the financial market, the nominal money supply (M^s) is determined by the monetary authorities and is taken to be independent of the interest rate. Since the real money supply is simply the nominal money supply divided by the fixed price level

Figure 10.5 The Keynesian Cross Diagram and a Rise in Investment and Consumption Demand

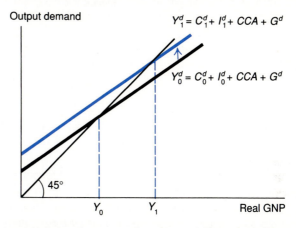

Output demand

$$Y_1^d = C_1^d + I_1^d + CCA + G^d$$

$$Y_0^d = C_0^d + I_0^d + CCA + G^d$$

45°

Y_0 Y_1 Real GNP

With a rise in investment and consumption demand, the output demand curve shifts from Y_0^d to Y_1^d. Note that the rise in equilibrium output from Y_0 to Y_1 is greater than the initial rise in output demand.

Figure 10.6 The *IS* Curve

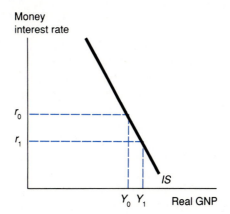

Money interest rate

r_0

r_1

IS

Y_0 Y_1 Real GNP

The *IS* curve has a negative slope because a reduction in the interest rate increases investment demand and thus the level of output consistent with output market equilibrium.

Figure 10.7   The Money Market

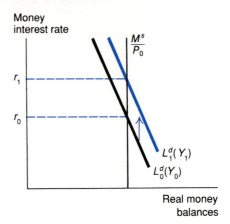

The money market is in equilibrium when the real demand for money equals the supply. With an increase in output from Y_0 to Y_1, the real money demand curve shifts to the right from L_0^d to L_1^d. The interest rate must rise from r_0 to r_1 to re-equate money demand and supply.

(P_0), it too is independent of the interest rate. The real money supply is thus represented in Figure 10.7 by the vertical line M^s/P_0. This vertical curve does not mean, of course, that the money supply never changes, only that it does not respond to changes in the interest rate.

As Figure 10.7 indicates, if the level of output equals Y_0, the quantity of money demanded equals the quantity supplied at the interest rate r_0. If output rises to Y_1, however, the demand for money will increase from L_0^d to L_1^d as individuals desire to hold increased money balances to facilitate the implied increase in transactions. The result will be an excess demand for money at the original interest rate r_0. The interest rate will have to rise from r_0 to r_1 to re-equate the quantity of money demanded with the quantity supplied. The higher interest rate restores equilibrium in the money market by reducing the quantity of money demanded as individuals economize on their money holdings.

To summarize, a higher level of income Y requires a higher interest rate r to maintain equality between quantity of money demanded and supplied. This direct relationship is represented by the **LM curve.** The *LM* curve depicts all output-interest rate combinations consistent with equilibrium in the money market. For example, since the points (Y_0, r_0) and (Y_1, r_1) appear on the *LM* curve in Figure 10.8, both points represent output-interest rate combinations consistent with equilibrium in the money market. The *LM* curve has a positive slope since the interest rate required to maintain equality between the quantity of money demanded and supplied is positively related to the level of output.

LM **curve:** A curve depicting all output-interest rate combinations consistent with equilibrium in the money market.

Figure 10.8   The *LM* Curve

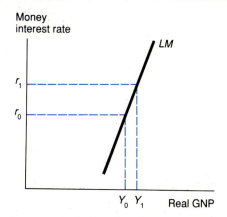

The *LM* curve has a positive slope since the interest rate required to clear the money market is positively related to the level of output.[37]

Simultaneous Equilibrium in the Output, Financial, and Money Markets

The *IS* and *LM* curves indicate, respectively, the output-interest rate combinations consistent with equilibrium in the output and money markets. In order to analyze the two markets simultaneously, we graph both the *IS* and *LM* curves in Figure 10.9. As the figure indicates, there exists a unique output-interest rate combination consistent with equilibrium in both the output and money markets. Only at output Y_0 and interest rate r_0 (point *A* in Figure 10.9) are the output market and the money market both in equilibrium. From the aggregate budget constraint for the closed economy, we know that the financial market must also be in equilibrium at this interest rate and output level.

To the Point

IS-LM ANALYSIS

- The *IS* curve depicts output-interest rate combinations consistent with equilibrium in the output market. The *LM* curve depicts output-interest rate combinations consistent with equilibrium in the money market. The *IS* curve slopes downward, while the *LM* curve slopes upward.

- The intersection of the *IS* and *LM* curves establishes the output-interest rate combination consistent with simultaneous equilibrium in the output

---

[37] An algebraic derivation of the *IS* and *LM* curves is contained in the appendix to this chapter.

Figure 10.9   Equilibrium in the Output and Money Markets

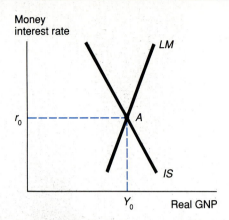

The intersection of the *IS* and *LM* curves indicates the output-interest rate combination (Y_0 and r_0) consistent with equilibrium in both the output and money markets.

and money markets. From the aggregate budget constraint, this combination is also consistent with equilibrium in the financial market.

10.5   MULTIPLIER ANALYSIS WITH INTEREST RATE EFFECTS: *IS-LM* ANALYSIS

In Section 10.3, we ignored the interest rate effects of a fall in autonomous investment demand so that we could focus on the essentials of the multiplier process. Using the *IS-LM* analysis developed in the previous section, we may now remedy this deficiency. This more complete description of the multiplier process is important, for the income adjustments it captures occur not only for changes in autonomous investment but also for changes in fiscal policy variables such as government spending and taxes. As we will see, taking into account interest rate effects tends to reduce the size of the multiplier.

Figure 10.10 uses *IS-LM* curves to determine the changes in equilibrium output and the interest rate resulting from a decrease in autonomous investment spending. The original equilibrium interest rate and output levels are r_0 and Y_0, respectively. With the fall in autonomous investment demand, the *IS* curve shifts to the left from IS_0 to IS_1. Since neither real money demand nor money supply changes at the original interest rate and level of real GNP, the quantity of money demanded still equals the quantity of money supplied at the original interest rate and level of real GNP. In other words, the *LM* curve does not shift.

Figure 10.10   **The Effect of a Fall in Autonomous Investment
Using *IS-LM* Analysis**

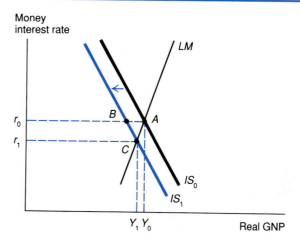

With a fall in autonomous investment, excess supply exists in the output market at the original level of output Y_0 and interest rate r_0. A lower interest rate induces increased investment and consumption demand, and it can restore equilibrium in the output market. Thus a fall in autonomous investment shifts the *IS* curve down from IS_0 to IS_1. With predetermined prices, equilibrium output falls from Y_0 to Y_1 and the interest rate falls from r_0 to r_1.

The extent of the shift to the left of the *IS* curve in Figure 10.10 is given by the simple multiplier, for this leftward shift indicates the change in output required to restore equilibrium in the output market if there is no change in the interest rate. More exactly, assuming taxes and investment demand are unaffected by income changes, the shift to the left of the *IS* curve equals the fall in autonomous investment demand multiplied by $1/(1 - MPC)$.

As Figure 10.10 shows, with a fall in autonomous investment demand the new *IS* curve and the *LM* curve now intersect at the equilibrium output-interest rate combination (Y_1, r_1). This new combination is consistent with equilibrium in the output, financial, and money markets after the fall in autonomous investment spending. At the predetermined price level P_0, output must drop from Y_0 to Y_1 and the interest rate must fall from r_0 to r_1 if equilibrium is to be restored in the output, money, and financial markets.

Note that the fall in real GNP shown in Figure 10.10 (Y_0 to Y_1) is less than the shift to the left in the *IS* curve (from point *A* to point *B*). The reason real GNP falls by less than what would be predicted by simple multiplier analysis is that with the drop in autonomous investment demand, the interest rate falls and that leads to a partially offsetting increase in investment and consumption demand. In other words, at point *C* the quantity of investment and consumption demand are greater than they would have been had the interest rate remained at r_0 (point B).

10.6   OTHER MODIFICATIONS TO THE MULTIPLIER ANALYSIS

In the preceding section, we modified our simple multiplier analysis to take into account interest rate effects occurring in the financial market and feeding back into the output market. In this section, we consider two additional modifications of the simple multiplier analysis.

The Life-cycle and Permanent Income Hypotheses: A Rationale for a Reduced Multiplier

When we discussed household consumption behavior in Chapter 6, we stated that consumption demand need not depend solely on current real disposable income. According to both the life-cycle hypothesis and the permanent income hypothesis, hereafter collectively referred to as the permanent income hypothesis, consumption depends upon an average of current and anticipated future disposable income. This means that a temporary or transitory increase in disposable income will have little effect on current consumption, since the responding fall in consumption will be spread out over an individual's time horizon. In contrast, changes in disposable income that are expected to be long-term will have substantial effects on consumption.

The permanent income hypothesis suggests that the multiplier may be smaller than our analysis above indicates. Suppose that a macroeconomic shock leads to lower output demand; with prices predetermined, the response is a fall in output. As output and income fall, consumption demand also falls, which leads to further reductions in output demand and output. As we have seen, the marginal propensity to consume is a key determinant of the magnitude of the total reduction in output. The larger the marginal propensity to consume, the greater the total reduction in output given an initial fall in output demand.

The permanent income hypothesis states that the magnitude of the marginal propensity to consume depends on how households view the change in current income. If households view a fall in current disposable income as temporary, then the fall in consumption demand will not be great. Consequently, there is a smaller marginal propensity to consume and thus a smaller multiplier. Thus if households believe that an autonomous fall in investment demand will lead to lower output only in the near future, output will be less affected than if they view the fall in income to be long-term.

Investment Demand and Output Changes: A Rationale for an Increased Multiplier

If we assume that predetermined prices do not fully adjust in the near future to a demand shock, then changes in current output can affect investment demand. Given an unexpected reduction in demand, firms face a sales constraint in current output markets. If firms expect the sales constraint to continue in the near future, then the anticipation of lower future demand will lower their desired capital stock. Similarly, an increase in anticipated future demand will raise the desired capital stock.[38]

If firms then use current sales to form expectations of future demand, this will have the effect of linking current sales to the desired capital stock in the future. In particular, let K^* denote the desired capital stock at the end of the current period and let us assume for the sake of simplicity that the relationship between K^* and current output Y (a proxy for expected future demand) is linear. Then we have

$$K^* = \alpha \cdot Y, \tag{10.8}$$

where α is a positive constant indicating the desired relationship between the capital stock and sales, other things being held constant. Let's assume that firms' investment in the prior period led to the attainment of a capital stock $\overline{K}$ equal to the desired stock as determined by last period's sales $\overline{Y}$, which gives us

$$\overline{K} = \alpha \cdot \overline{Y} \tag{10.9}$$

During the current period, $d \cdot \overline{K}$ of the capital inherited from the prior period is used up in the production process, where d is the rate of depreciation of the capital stock.[39] Thus if the desired capital stock K^* is to be attained at the end of the current period, firms must have gross investment equal to the difference $K^* - \overline{K}$ plus the depreciation $d \cdot \overline{K}$. That is, to attain the desired stock of capital, not only must firms make up the difference between where they were at the start of the period and where they want to be, but they must also replace the capital that is worn out during the current period.

Net investment demand I^d, which reflects the desired change in the capital stock, is equal to gross investment $(K^* - \overline{K} + d \cdot \overline{K})$ minus the depreciation $(d \cdot \overline{K})$ or simply

$$I^d = K^* - \overline{K} \tag{10.10}$$

---

[38] John Barron, Dan Black, and Mark Loewenstein, "Note on Adjustment Costs and Aggregate Demand Theory," *Economica* (August 1983) p. 361–364. The authors examine the effect of a sales constraint on optimal investment.

[39] This depreciation is what we have previously denoted the capital consumption allowance (*CCA*).

Substituting into Equation 10.10 Equations 10.8 and 10.9 for K^* and $\overline{K}$, we obtain the following expression for investment demand:[40]

$$I^d = \alpha \cdot Y - \alpha \cdot \overline{Y} = \alpha \cdot \Delta Y \tag{10.11}$$

Accelerator model: A model that predicts that the level of net investment demand depends directly on changes in output.

According to Equation 10.11, investment demand is directly related to the change in output from last period. Since firms' desired capital stock depends on the level of output Y, and since investment demand is the desired change in the capital stock, investment depends on the *change in output* ΔY. This relationship is frequently referred to as the **accelerator model.** When growth of output increases at a faster rate, or accelerates, investment demand rises. This means that investment will tend to rise during economic recoveries, when real GNP grows more rapidly, and to fall in downturns, when output is growing slowly or is falling. In fact, the fall in investment during recessions is generally greater than the fall in real GNP so that investment falls as a proportion of real GNP.

What does an investment demand that depends on the change in output imply about the multiplier? When output falls, not only does consumption demand fall but now investment demand falls as well. Thus an initial excess demand or supply in the output market results in a larger change in equilibrium output. The dependence of investment on output changes makes the multiplier larger. A larger multiplier means that minor instability in autonomous consumption or investment spending will cause larger fluctuations in output.

To the Point

THE LIFE-CYCLE MODEL, THE ACCELERATOR MODEL, AND MULTIPLIER ANALYSIS

- The value of the multiplier depends directly on the value of the marginal propensity to consume. If individuals perceive a fall in income to be temporary, then the life-cycle and permanent income hypotheses suggest that they will not alter their current consumption significantly. This lower marginal propensity to consume means a smaller multiplier.

- If investment depends on changes in output as well as interest rates, then any initial change in demand will have a larger effect on equilibrium output; that is, the multiplier will be larger. The relationship between investment demand and changes in output is represented by the accelerator model.

---

[40] Since our focus here is on how changes in real GNP can alter investment demand, we assume that the ratio of the desired capital stock to the level of anticipated income, denoted by α, is the same across time. In fact, changes in such factors as the expected real user cost of capital will affect α, so that Equation 10.11 will have other terms in it that reflect the impact on investment demand of different α's across periods.

10.7   THE EFFECTS OF A DEMAND SHOCK IN AN OPEN ECONOMY

When we analyze the effect of a demand shock in an open economy, we must consider how a change in income and the interest rate affects foreign exchange rates, exports, and imports. We start by examining the effect of an income change in an open economy.

The Multiplier in an Open Economy

As we saw in our preceding analysis of the multiplier, a change in autonomous spending causes a magnified change in equilibrium output. Interestingly, although changes in income affect imports, foreign exchange rates, and exports, introducing international trade may not significantly affect our previous multiplier analysis. Let's see why.

Recall that in the simple multiplier analysis, an initial decrease in income causes consumption demand to fall, which in turn causes further reductions in output and income. In an open economy, the fall in income leads households to reduce both their purchases of domestically produced output and their purchases of foreign goods. While falling income lowers one component of output demand—consumption demand—it appears to raise a second component of output demand—net export demand (exports minus imports)—by reducing imports. Thus one might think that the introduction of foreign trade means a smaller multiplier. Sometimes things are not as they appear, however, Net export demand, in fact, can remain *unaffected* by changes in income when exchange rates are flexible.

As we have just seen, if other things are held constant, a fall in income causes a decrease in U.S. imports. Among the things held constant is the foreign exchange rate. But the decrease in imports decreases the real supply of dollars in the foreign exchange market. Figure 10.11 depicts this decrease in the supply of dollars in the foreign exchange markets as the shift to the left in the real supply of dollars curve from S_0 to S_1. The resulting excess demand for dollars will lead to an increase, or appreciation, of the dollar from E_0 to E_1.

The appreciation of the dollar causes U.S. exports to decrease and U.S. imports to increase. Thus net export demand decreases. In fact, assuming no change in international capital flows, this fall in net export demand due to the appreciation of the dollar must exactly offset the initial rise in net export demand due to the fall in income. At the new equilibrium, net export demand is thus unchanged, with there being an equal fall in the quantity of real dollars demanded (reflecting the decrease in U.S. exports) and supplied (reflecting the decrease in U.S. imports).

In summary, given flexible exchange rates our simple multiplier analysis remains unaffected by the introduction of international trade. Although a

Figure 10.11   The Effect of a Decrease in U.S. Income on the Foreign Exchange Market

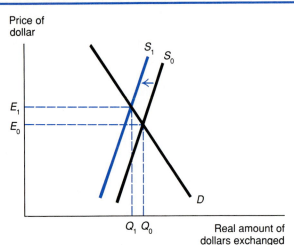

A decrease in income causes U.S. imports to fall, which reduces the real supply of dollars in the foreign exchange markets from S_0 to S_1. The exchange rate (the price of a dollar in terms of foreign currency) rises from E_0 to E_1.

fall in real GNP causes imports to fall, the resulting appreciation of the dollar leads to offsetting decreases in exports and increases in imports. The end result is that the fall in output does *not* change net exports, as both exports and imports fall by the same amount.

IS-LM Analysis in an Open Economy

We saw in our discussion of the aggregate demand curve in Chapter 7 that opening an economy to foreign trade results in a flatter aggregate demand curve. The key element behind the flatter open economy aggregate demand curve is that output demand is more sensitive to interest rate changes in the open economy. The reason for this is that an' open economy includes an additional component of output demand that is sensitive to interest rate changes—net export demand. The equilibrium condition for the output market in an open economy is

$$
\underset{\substack{\text{Consumption} \\ \text{demand}}}{C^d} + \underset{\substack{\text{Gross investment} \\ \text{demand}}}{I^d + CCA} + \underset{\substack{\text{Government} \\ \text{demand}}}{G^d} + \underset{\substack{\text{Net export} \\ \text{demand}}}{X^d - Z^d} = \underset{\text{Output}}{Y} \qquad \textbf{(10.12)}
$$

Like consumption and investment demand, net export demand responds inversely to interest rate changes. The reasoning for this is as follows: A rise in the U.S. interest rate induces an increase in net capital inflows into the

Figure 10.12   The Effect of a Decrease in U.S. Interest Rates on the Foreign Exchange Market

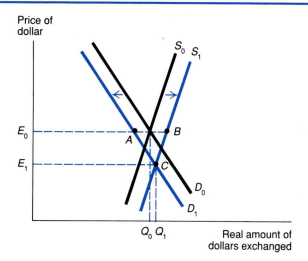

A lower U.S. interest rate decreases capital inflows and increases capital outflows, as indicated by the fall in the demand for dollars in the foreign exchange market from D_0 to D_1 and the rise in the supply of dollars from S_0 to S_1. As a consequence, the foreign exchange rate is bid down from E_0 to E_1. This depreciation of the dollar leads to an increase in net export demand, as U.S. exports rise and U.S. imports fall.

United States, which results in an appreciation of the dollar. Because a higher value of the dollar limits exports and encourages imports, it reduces net export demand. Conversely, a fall in the U.S. interest rate leads to reduced net capital inflows into the United States. The accompanying fall in the demand for the dollar and increase in supply of dollars associated with this change in international capital flows leads to a depreciation of the dollar and thus an increase in net export demand. Below we formally develop this link between changes in interest rates and net export demand, and we see that this means the *IS* curve is flatter in an open economy.

Consider the effect of a fall in the U.S. interest rate. Lower domestic interest rates cause the demand for dollars in the foreign exchange markets to decrease, since foreigners wish to purchase fewer U.S. financial assets (i.e., U.S. capital inflows fall). Likewise, the supply of dollars in the foreign exchange market rises, since individuals in the U.S. purchase more foreign securities (i.e., U.S. capital outflows rise). Figure 10.12 illustrates these effects of a lower U.S. interest rate on the foreign exchange market.

As this figure indicates, a lower U.S. interest rate results in a depreciation of the dollar. That is, the price of a dollar in terms of other currencies falls. This decrease in the price of the dollar has two important effects. First, it encourages foreign purchases of U.S. goods, as shown by the downward movement from point A to point C along the new demand for dollars curve D_1. Thus U.S. exports rise. Second, since a depreciation of the dollar means higher prices of foreign currencies in terms of dollars, U.S. imports fall. The movement from point B to point C along the new supply of dollars curve S_1 shows this. Thus the change in international capital flows caused by the lower interest rate leads to an increase in net export demand (as U.S. exports rise and U.S. imports fall). Since net export demand is one of the components of aggregate output demand, the rise in net export demand causes the reduction in output due to the initial fall in autonomous spending to be smaller.

IS-LM analysis can be used to summarize the effect of changes in autonomous spending on output. Note that in an open economy three components of output demand—not two—are inversely related to the interest rates. Not only do investment and consumption rise with a fall in the interest rate as in a closed economy, but now net exports rise as well. The reason, as we saw above, was that a lower interest rate increases net capital outflows, which causes the dollar to depreciate and thus leads to increased U.S. exports and decreased U.S. imports.

With output demand more sensitive to interest rate changes in an open economy, any change in the interest rate will cause a larger change in output demand than in the closed economy. This larger impact on output demand of an interest rate change in the open economy means that for any change in the interest rate, a greater change in output is required to restore equilibrium in the output market. That is, the *IS* curve is flatter for the open economy. For this reason, Figure 10.13 shows the *IS* curves in the open economy before and after a fall in autonomous investment spending (IS_0^{open} and IS_1^{open}, respectively) as flatter than the corresponding *IS* curves in the closed economy (IS_0^{closed} and IS_1^{closed}, respectively).

Remember that open and closed economies do not differ in the multiplier process that restores equilibrium in the output market after an initial demand disturbance, since changes in income do not affect net export demand. Thus a fall in autonomous investment spending requires the same multiple reduction in output to restore equilibrium in the output market at the original interest rate. Figure 10.13 shows this by the fact that the fall in autonomous investment spending causes the *IS* curve to shift to the left by the same amount (from point A to point B) in the open or closed economy. For the open economy, the shift in the *IS* curve is from IS_0^{open} to IS_1^{open}, while for the closed economy the shift is from IS_0^{closed} to IS_1^{closed}.

Figure 10.13 illustrates two important points. First, as we have already discussed, the adjustment process that restores equilibrium in the money and output markets involves changes in both income and the interest rate. Second, the changes in income and the interest rate required to restore equilibrium differ between an open and closed economy. In an open economy, since the *IS* curve is flatter, a reduction in autonomous spending leads to a smaller reduction in equilibrium real GNP (compare Y_0 to Y_1 for the open economy with Y_0 to Y_2 for the closed economy). A reduction in autonomous

Figure 10.13   Using *IS-LM* Analysis to Determine the Effect of a Decrease in Autonomous Spending: A Comparison of Open Versus Closed Economy

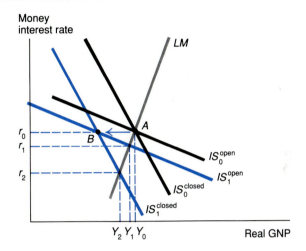

A fall in autonomous spending shifts the *IS* curves horizontally to the left by the same amount (from point *A* to point *B*) for both the open economy and the closed economy. In the case of an open economy, this is represented by the shift to the left from IS_0^{open} to IS_1^{open}. For the closed economy, the shift in the *IS* curve is from IS_0^{closed} to IS_1^{closed}. Since the *IS* curve is flatter in an open economy, the fall in autonomous spending leads not only to less of a fall in the interest rate (the fall from r_0 to r_1 is less than the fall from r_0 to r_2) but also to less of a reduction in real GNP (the fall from Y_0 to Y_1 is less than the fall from Y_0 to Y_2).

spending also leads to less of a fall in the interest rate in an open economy (compare r_0 to r_1 for the open economy with r_0 to r_2 for the closed economy).

The intuition for these different results in an open versus a closed economy is as follows. The fall in autonomous spending means a decrease in the demand for loanable funds in the financial market. In an open economy, the fall in the interest rate to maintain equilibrium in the financial market need not be as great as in a closed economy since the supply of loanable funds, which now includes changes in U.S. net capital inflows, is more responsive to interest rate changes in an open economy.

Even though there is less of a fall in the interest rate in an open economy, the fall in the interest rate has a greater impact on output demand, for in the open economy there is a new component of output demand—net export demand—that increases with a fall in the interest rate. With the fall in the interest rate doing more of the "work" to restore equilibrium in the output market by raising output demand, less of a fall in output is required to restore equilibrium in the output market.

10.8   THE LONG-RUN EFFECT OF DEMAND SHOCKS

In the non-market-clearing model that we have been studying in this chapter, unanticipated demand shocks cause the prices that are predetermined to differ from (long-run) equilibrium prices. Such demand shocks can come from changes in autonomous spending by firms (investment demand) and households (consumption demand) as well as from changes in government fiscal or monetary policies. In an open economy, demand shocks can also include an exogenous change in international capital flows that leads to a change in net export demand. Because adjusting prices quickly is costly, the short-run result of such demand "surprises" is to change equilibrium output, as firms alter production rates and employment. Given predetermined prices, the horizontal shift in the aggregate demand curve shows the effect of a demand shock on output.

Although prices may be sticky in the short run, we expect them to ultimately adjust to a demand shock as firms respond to existing market conditions. The price adjustment we have in mind can be simply stated, although in practice there remains much about price adjustment that is still not fully understood. If output at the predetermined price level falls below the full-employment level of output, prices will adjust downward over time. The sales constraint that firms face means that at the current prices they would like to produce more than can be sold. This desire to sell more provides the impetus for firms to revise prices downward. Similarly, a demand shock that leads to a demand for output greater than the full employment level of output will lead to price increases over time. At existing prices, firms are reaching the limits of their productive capacity, and thus they have the incentive to adjust prices upward over time to improve profitability.

The above discussion suggests that the analysis with predetermined prices is best used to indicate the effect of demand shocks in the short run, when prices do not fully adjust. In the long run, when prices can be viewed as completely flexible, the neoclassical model often better predicts the effects of demand shocks.[41]

Price Adjustment: Aggregate Demand-Supply Analysis

We can use the aggregate demand and supply curves of the neoclassical model to illustrate how the economy adjusts, both in the short run and in the long run, to a fall in autonomous spending. Let's start at point A in Figure 10.14. The price level is P_0 and there exists a planned production rate Y^* consistent with equilibrium in all markets, including the labor market. In other words, we begin at the intersection of the aggregate demand curve and the neoclassical aggregate supply curve, with resources fully employed. A fall in output demand will lead to a shift to the left in the aggregate demand curve from AD_0 to AD_1. With prices not adjusting, the rate of production in the short run falls from Y^* to Y_1.

At the predetermined price level P_0 and the new, lower output Y_1, firms are producing less output than they would like, given existing wages and prices. The accompanying excess supply of labor means workers are not selling as much labor as they would like at existing wages. This leads to a bidding down of prices and wages over time, which causes us to move down the aggregate demand curve from point B to point C. In the long run, the price level falls to P_1 and the rate of production returns to the full employment level of the neoclassical model, Y^*. In the next section, we use *IS-LM* analysis to illustrate how a price reduction can lead the economy back to full employment.

Price Changes in Terms of *IS-LM* Analysis

As we have seen, the crucial feature of the analysis illustrated by Figure 10.14 is that prices are fixed for a period of time at a level too high to sustain full employment. At the price level P_0 and at the new, lower aggregate demand AD_1, output falls below the full employment level Y^*. The *IS-LM* analysis provides us with a graphical means for illustrating how a fall in the price level will restore the economy to full employment. In the process, we can formally demonstrate the inverse relationship between the price level and real GNP that is summarized by the aggregate demand curve.

---

[41] An extreme adverse demand shock, such as the one experienced during the Great Depression of the 1930s, is a case in which downward price adjustments, by leading to defaults on loan agreements and the collapse of the banking system, added an element of instability into the adjustment process.

Figure 10.14   The Long-run Effect of a Decrease in Autonomous Spending: The Adjustment in Prices

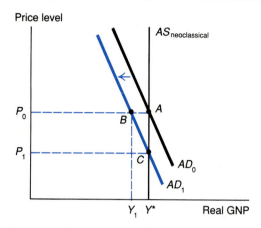

A fall in autonomous spending shifts the aggregate demand curve to the left from AD_0 to AD_1. With the price level predetermined at P_0, output falls from Y^* to Y_1. Since output falls short of what firms would like to produce given existing wages and prices, prices adjust downward over time. In the long run, the price level falls to P_1 and the rate of production returns to that level associated with the neoclassical model.

Recall that for any price level, the aggregate demand curve indicates the corresponding output level consistent with equilibrium in the output, financial, and money markets. In Figure 10.15, we start on the aggregate demand curve AD at point B in part (b). Given price level P_0 and aggregate demand AD, output is Y_1. Figure 10.15(a) indicates this same equilibrium in the output and money markets in terms of the IS-LM analysis at interest rate r_0 and output Y_1. As indicated above, the fact that output is below the full employment level of output puts downward pressure on prices. According to Figure 10.15(b), the price level must fall to P_1 to restore the economy to full employment.

For a given nominal money supply, the fall in the price level from P_0 to P_1 increases the real supply of money. In terms of IS-LM analysis, the result is a shift to the right and down in the LM curve in Figure 10.15(b) from $LM(M^s/P_0)$ to $LM(M^s/P_1)$. The reason for the shift is as follows. At the original interest rate r_0 and output Y_1, the increase in the real supply of money means an excess supply in the money market. A higher real output will restore equilibrium in the money market by raising households' real money demand to equal to the new higher real supply of money. Thus the new LM curve lies to the right of the original LM curve. Alternatively, we can say that at each level of output, a lower interest rate will restore equilibrium in the money market by raising households' desired real money holdings. Thus the new LM curve lies below the original LM curve.

Figure 10.15 Using *IS-LM* Analysis to Derive the Aggregate Demand Curve

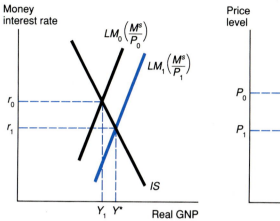

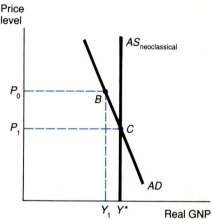

(a) *IS – LM* Analysis

(b) Aggregate Demand and Supply With a Predetermined Price Level in the Short Run

When the price level is P_0, the output and money markets are in equilibrium at the interest rate r_0 and output level Y_1. A reduction in the price level to P_1 increases the real money supply, causing the *LM* curve to shift to the right from $LM(M^s/P_0)$ to $LM(M^s/P_1)$ in part (a). At the lower price level, the output and money markets are in equilibrium at the interest rate r_1 and output level Y^*. The aggregate demand curve in part (b) summarizes this inverse relationship between the price level and equilibrium output.

As Figure 10.15(a) indicates, the lower price level P_1 and resulting shift to the right and down in the *LM* curve means that the new output-interest rate combination (r_1, Y^*) is now consistent with simultaneous equilibrium in the output and money markets. This new equilibrium combination of a lower price level and higher output is depicted on the aggregate demand curve drawn in Figure 10.15(b) by point C. The above discussion illustrates two things: First, the *IS-LM* analysis shows the fall in the interest rate that occurs as we move down the aggregate demand curve. Second, the juxtaposition of the *IS-LM* analysis against the aggregate demand curve illustrates how a fall in the price level leads to a higher real GNP to maintain simultaneous equilibrium in the output, money, and financial markets.

SUMMARY

The neoclassical model assumes that prices adjust quickly to eliminate excess demands and supplies. Consequently, markets remain in equilibrium and changes in aggregate demand cause changes in wages and prices, not employment and output. Yet, if prices do not quickly adjust, then the excess demand or supply in the output market caused by demand shocks leads to output changes. The sources of recessions and high unemployment are no longer limited to changes in supply conditions, but now include fluctuations in demand.

With inflexible prices, firms faced with a demand shock can no longer sell all they desire at the prevailing price level; the result of non-market-clearing prices is that firms face a sales constraint in the output market. This sales constraint affects labor demand, as firms' demand for labor now depends solely on what can be sold, and not on the real wage.

In the neoclassical model, unemployment was only structural and frictional. With predetermined prices, there now exists "involuntary" unemployment in the non-market-clearing model. Workers would like to be employed at the prevailing wage rate, but jobs simply do not exist. The "involuntary" unemployment can be eliminated by a fall in the wage rate, but only because the fall in the wage will lead some individuals to withdraw from the labor market. The fall in the wage rate will by itself not increase the level of employment. Employment is demand determined, and aggregate demand will be directly stimulated only by a fall in output prices, not wages.

In the predetermined price model, firms respond to a reduction in the demand for output by reducing output and employment. This has further repercussions as the fall in income leads to a reduction in consumption spending. The ultimate change in equilibrium income that results from an initial change in output demand is determined by the multiplier. In the absence of interest rate and other considerations, the simple multiplier for a change in output demand equals one divided by one minus the marginal propensity to consume $(1/1 - MPC)$. More generally, the *IS-LM* analysis can be used to determine the effect of changes in exogenous variables such as autonomous investment or the money supply on both equilibrium output and the interest rate.

In an open economy, a demand shock affects not only employment, real GNP, and the interest rate, but also foreign exchange rates, exports, and imports. A fall in income reduces imports, which means a fall in the supply of dollars in the foreign exchange markets and thus an appreciation of the dollar. When we take into account this accompanying appreciation of the dollar, we see that a fall in income does not change *net* export demand, as both imports and exports fall by the same amount. However, changes in international capital flows in response to changes in the interest rate do lead to changes in net export demand by altering exchange rates. As a consequence, output demand is more sensitive to interest rate changes in an open economy.

In terms of the *IS-LM* analysis, in an open economy the *IS* curve is flatter. One outcome is that a change in autonomous spending that shifts the *IS* curve leads to a smaller change in both the interest rate and output in the open as opposed to the closed economy. In contrast, changes in the money supply that shift the *LM* curve will have a greater effect on real GNP in an open economy.

The analysis in this chapter can be viewed as indicating the effect of demand shocks on the economy in the short run, when prices do not fully adjust. In the long-run, the effects of demand shocks tend to be as predicted by the neoclassical model.

LOOKING AHEAD

The neoclassical macroeconomic model does not explain how factors that affect output demand can lead to changes in output. In this chapter, by modifying the neoclassical model to incorporate predetermined output prices, we have taken an important step in improving our understanding of how the economy works. As we have seen, inflexible prices imply that unanticipated demand shocks lead to changes in equilibrium real GNP.

Neoclassical analysis offers insights into how changes in demand and supply ultimately affect the economy, since, given sufficient time, prices ultimately adjust to excess demand or supply. In the short run, however, the lack of flexibility in prices means, as the model with predetermined prices shows, that income can fall below its full employment level. Policymakers, concerned for their unemployed constituents, may not want to wait for prices to ultimately adjust "in the long run." As we see in the next chapter, viewing these two models in this way introduces a potential role for fiscal and monetary policy changes as tools to affect employment and output in the short run.

SUMMARY OF KEY EQUATIONS

Output market equilibrium (closed economy) $\qquad C^d + I^d + CCA + G^d = Y$ (10.6)

Money market equilibrium $\qquad L^d = M^s/P$ (10.7)

Accelerator model of investment demand function $\qquad I^d = K^* - \overline{K} = \alpha \cdot \Delta Y$ (10.11)

Output market equilibrium (open economy) $\qquad C^d + I^d + CCA + G^d + X^d - Z^d = Y$ (10.12)

Key Terms

Non-market-clearing prices, 375   Multiplier, 384
Involuntary unemployment, 378   *IS* curve, 388
Marginal propensity to consume, 380   *LM* curve, 390
Keynesian cross diagram, 380   Accelerator model, 396
Unintended inventory accumulation,
   383

REVIEW QUESTIONS

1. What is the key feature distinguishing "Keynesian" macroeconomic analysis from neoclassical analysis?

2. What are some of the reasons for prices that are "sticky," that is, prices that do not adjust instantaneously to market-clearing levels?

3. Is the Keynesian model more appropriate for an analysis of short-run or long-run behavior? Why?

4. Suppose that household real consumption demand falls by $100.

   (a) What must happen to desired saving by households? Why?

   (b) Suppose that the change in household saving takes the form of a change in the desired accumulation of real money balances. What is the immediate effect on the interest rate?

   (c) At the economy's initial price and output level, is there excess demand or supply in the output market? Of how much? If the price of output is fixed in the current period, what will happen to output? Why?

   (d) Suppose that instead of taking the form of a desired increase in real money balances, the change in saving takes the form of a change in the desired accumulation of financial assets. Show the resulting effect in the financial market. What happens to the interest rate?

   (e) At the economy's initial price and output level, is there excess demand or supply in the output market? Why? How does this compare with the excess supply or demand in (c)? If the price of output is fixed in the current period, what will happen to output?

   (f) Compare your answer to that in Review Question 9 in Chapter 8. Why are firms not (entirely) reallocating resources in accord with consumers' wishes? What price signal is missing (at least in part)?

5. Illustrate the effect that the fall in consumption demand in the preceding question has on the labor market.

   (a) What happens to employment? What name do we give to the type of unemployment created? Why?

(b) Might we expect further changes in output and employment? Why or why not? If there are further changes in output, can we tell unambiguously what will be the effect of such changes on the equilibrium interest rate in the financial market? Why or why not?

(c) Suppose that the marginal propensity to consume is .75. Ignoring possible interest rate effects in the financial market, by how much will output fall in total?

6. What do we mean when we refer to the demand for labor being constrained by firms' sales in the output market? Can this ever occur in the neoclassical model? Why or why not?

7. What does the multiplier tell us? Ignoring interest rate effects in the financial market, is the multiplier bigger or smaller than 1? Why? If the marginal propensity to consume is b, what is the multiplier equal to?

8. In deriving the multiplier, we assumed implicitly that changes in real income did not affect household real net taxes. In reality, this is not true. Not only do increases in income result in higher income taxes, but they also result in lower transfer payments as payments such as unemployment compensation and welfare payments tend to fall automatically. Let t denote the increase in net real taxes associated with a 1-unit increase in real income.

(a) If output in the economy rises by 1 unit, how much does real disposable income rise by?

(b) In the absence of interest rate effects in the financial market, what will the multiplier be equal to?

9. An article in the November 11, 1984 *Wall Street Journal* reported that "inventories expanded rapidly during the July-September quarter, as companies were caught off guard by the slowdown in consumer spending growth. Many companies now are trying to work off these inventories. As a result, analysts said, economic growth may be as slow or slower than third-quarter growth."

(a) Discuss the preceding quote in light of our discussion in the text of changes in autonomous spending and intended or unintended inventory accumulation or decumulation.

(b) According to the Keynesian model, what effect should the change in autonomous spending referred to in the above quote have on real GNP?

10. Suppose that autonomous spending falls, resulting in excess supply in the output market.

(a) What happens to the aggregate demand curve? Why?

(b) Assuming that output prices are fixed or "predetermined" in the current period, use aggregate demand-supply analysis to show what happens to the level of real GNP.

(c) What effect does the reduction in autonomous spending have on the *IS* curve? Why?

(d) Use *IS-LM* analysis to show the effect of the change in autonomous spending on the equilibrium interest rate and output level. Relate this figure to that in (b).

(e) What has happened to nominal GNP? From your knowledge of the exchange equation, what has happened to velocity. Relate this change in velocity to your answer in (d).

11. Suppose that household demand for real money balances increases.

(a) If total saving does not change, what will happen to households' desired real accumulation of financial assets? Why?

(b) Show the resulting effect in the financial market. What will happen to the interest rate?

(c) What effect does the change in the interest rate have on investment and consumption demand. According to the Keynesian model, what will happen to output? Why?

(d) Show the effect that the increase in the demand for money has on the *LM* curve. (Remember that this curve indicates all output-interest rate combinations consistent with "money market" equilibrium. At any output level, what happens to the interest rate required to equate money demand to money supply?)

(e) Given that the current price of output is fixed, use *IS-LM* analysis to show the effect of the increase in money demand on real GNP and the interest rate.

(f) What has happened to the velocity of money? Why? Interpret this effect.

12. The following was reported in a *Wall Street Journal* article on August 18, 1984: "The drop in sales provided a boost to the credit market where many traders believe a slowing economy would relieve upward pressure on short-term interest rates." Use *IS-LM* analysis to determine whether or not a reduction in autonomous spending does in fact lead to lower interest rates.

13. The following was reported in a *Wall Street Journal* article on August 15, 1984: "The American Bankers Association said demand for credit has been growing 'at a perhaps unsustainable pace' this year. Strong credit demands from business, consumers, and government have held interest rates high and are likely to push them higher next year, the association said in a report released yesterday."

(a) Illustrate the effect on the financial market of an increase in credit demand by business.

(b) If firms' credit demand rises, what do we know about their demand in the output market? Why?

(c) If the economy is initially experiencing unemployment, use *IS-LM* analysis to show the resulting effect on the interest rate on real GNP.

14. Suppose that real GNP rises.

   (a) What effect does such an increase have on import demand by households?

   (b) Show the resulting effect in the foreign exchange market.

   (c) What effect does the change in the price of dollar have on import demand by U.S. households and export demand by foreigners.

   (d) What is the net effect of the increase in real GNP and the change in the foreign exchange rate on net export demand? Why?

15. Explain why an increase in the interest rate can be expected to lead to a reduction in net export demand.

   (a) Based on your answer, it follows that the responsiveness of total output demand to a change in the interest rate is _____ (greater, less) in an open economy as compared to a closed economy. What does this imply about the *IS* curve?

   (b) Explain why a change in autonomous spending will result in a change in real GNP that is smaller in the open economy than in the closed economy.

16. Suppose that household consumption demand falls. Use aggregate demand-supply analysis to show the effect on the economy's real GNP if output prices are fixed in the short run.

   (a) Given sufficient time, what should we expect to happen to output prices if the economy is operating at a less than full-employment output level? Why?

   (b) Will this have the effect of stimulating output demand? If so, how?

   (c) Indicate the effect on real GNP of the adjustment in the price level.

17. What information is summarized by the *IS* curve? What slope does this curve have? Why? What information is summarized by the *LM* curve? What slope does this curve have? Why?

18. At the point of intersection of the *IS* and *LM* curves, what do we know about the financial market? Why?

19. Use *IS-LM* curves to demonstrate that an increase in the price level leads to an increase in the interest rate and reduction in the real output level consistent with equilibrium in the output, money, and financial markets.

20. An article in the February 22, 1988 *Wall Street Journal* reported that "economists are weighing U.S. inventories to gauge whether the pileup could pinch the economy into a recession. . . . much of the [increased] output from U.S. factories lately seems to go either on the ship or on the shelf. Economists such as Mr. Roach (senior economist at Morgan Stanley & Co.) fear that if export demand slows, the buildup of goods

could pinch output and turn a mere slowdown into a full-blown recession this year."

(a) Using a simple linear consumption function, derive (do *not* merely state) an expression for the simple multiplier in the context of the closed economy, predetermined price model. Assume taxes and investment demand are independent of income. Identify the role of the marginal propensity to consume.

(b) Let's say that firms face the situation of reduced output demand (say, an initial fall in autonomous spending equal to $10) and resulting unintended inventory accumulation suggested by the above quote. If the *MPC* is .75, what would be the equilibrium change in output according to your analysis in (a)? Using *IS-LM* graphical analysis, compare this change to the actual change that occurs when we consider more fully the implications of an initial fall in output demand. Label the axes.

(c) Compare the new equilibrium situation with what would have existed had there not been the change in autonomous spending identified in (b). What is predicted with respect to the price level, real GNP, money interest rate, expected real interest rate, velocity, real money demand, household saving, consumption, investment, and consumption plus investment?

(d) If taxes are directly related to income, then is the multiplier smaller than, larger than, or the same as the simple multiplier derived in (a)?

(e) If investment demand is directly related to income, then is the multiplier smaller than, larger than, or the same as the simple multiplier derived in part (a)?

21. The following was reported in a *Wall Street Journal* article of April 15, 1988: "For the present, at least, Japan doesn't seem to be suffering. Some jobs were lost when plants moved abroad, but the consumer has taken up the slack by beginning, for the first time since World War II, to live a little." Let's see if the two changes suggested by this quote offset one another in terms of their impact on Japanese output demand.

(a) Depict graphically the initial effect on the Japanese financial and money markets of the change in autonomous consumption demand in Japan suggested by the above quote. Assume no change in real money demand.

(b) According to (a), does this increase in autonomous consumption demand alone lead to an excess demand or supply in the output market at the original level of output and prices due to its effect on output demand?

(c) Now depict graphically the initial effect of the increase in Japanese lending abroad (suggested by their purchase of foreign financial assets) on the Japanese financial and money markets. (Think of these foreign financial assets as stock issued by foreign firms who then contract for the construction of the car plants as part of their capital investment.) Assume no change in either Japanese real money demand or consumption demand.

(d) According to (c), does the interest rate rise, fall, or not change to clear the financial market? Does this imply a rise, fall, or no change in consumption and investment demand in Japan? Yet your analysis implies excess demand in the output market. Let's see why.

(e) Depict graphically the effect of the increase in Japanese lending abroad on the foreign exchange market for the *yen*. According to your analysis will the increased foreign lending by the Japanese lead to an appreciation, a depreciation, or no change in the price of the yen? As a consequence, would you expect Japanese exports to rise, fall, or not change, and Japanese imports to rise, fall, or not change? What is implied in terms of Japanese net export demand?

(f) Summarizing the analysis in (c) through (e), what is the initial impact of the increased Japanese lending abroad on investment demand, consumption demand, and net export demand? Is the net result an increase, a decrease, or no change in output demand?

(g) Combining the analysis of (b) and (f) suggests that if there is both an increase in autonomous consumption demand and an increase in Japanese lending abroad, the initial impact would be for:

Japanese investment demand to _____ , and

increase, decrease, either increase or decrease

Japanese output demand to _____ .

increase, decrease, either increase or decrease

22. It is often the case that if there are forecasts of high inflation over the coming year, union and nonunion workers alike are granted substantial increases in their wages, as firms anticipate demand being sufficiently strong so that they can find ready buyers at correspondingly higher prices for their output. Once these higher output prices are set by firms, however, assume that demand turns out to be less than anticipated.

(a) Depict graphically the impact of this on the labor market. Show what happens to employment and the shape of the labor demand curve when output prices are set "too high" so that firms face a sales constraint in the output market.

(b) If workers recant and "give back" part of their raises, show the effect, if any, of this change alone on the labor market and employment.

(c) With give-backs, what is implied in terms of the division of firm revenues between wages and other forms of compensation, such as dividends to shareholders? Assuming shareholders as a group have a lower marginal propensity to consume than workers, what is the implied effect of give-backs on output demand, and thus labor demand and employment?

23. Let's say that all money is held as checkable deposits that pay an interest rate r_m. Further, let us assume that unregulated competition among depository institutions results in the interest rate on checkable deposits being adjusted to always be x percent points below the interest rate on financial assets.

   (a) At the initial levels of output and prices, depict the impact on the financial and money markets under such circumstances if there is an increase in autonomous investment demand. Is there an excess demand or supply in the money market? (Be careful in drawing the money demand curve to incorporate the nature of money demand when the interest rate differential between money and financial asset holdings remains constant in light of changes in the interest rate on financial assets.)

   (b) Depict the effect of the increase in autonomous investment demand cited in (a) in terms of *IS-LM* analysis. At existing prices, what is the effect on the equilibrium output and interest rate?

   (c) According to your analysis, is velocity affected by changes in autonomous spending such as the one considered?

An Algebraic Derivation of *IS-LM* Analysis

In this chapter, we have seen how the *IS* and *LM* curves summarize simultaneous equilibria in the output and money markets in the economy in terms of the equilibrium levels of real GNP and the interest rate. In a closed economy, equilibria in these two markets implies equilibrium in a third market, the financial market. This follows from the aggregate budget constraint, which shows why we can omit explicit consideration of one market in the economy. Recall that the aggregate budget constraint for the closed economy indicates that the excess demands in the output, financial, and money markets must sum to zero.

In an open economy, equilibria in the output and money markets no longer imply equilibrium in the financial market since another market has been added—the foreign exchange market. In this case, the *IS* and *LM* curves are constructed under the implicit assumption that the foreign exchange rate adjusts to maintain equilibrium in the foreign exchange market. One result is that the interest rate and real GNP at which the *IS* and *LM* curves intersect is one at which there is equilibrium in the financial market. A second result is a flatter *IS* curve since a lower interest rate now increases not only investment and consumption demand but also net export demand, as a lower interest rate reduces net international capital inflows and thus leads to a depreciation of the dollar.

The purpose of this appendix is to retrace the analysis behind the *IS-LM* curves in both a closed and an open economy, but to do so using algebraic rather than graphical analysis. We start with a closed economy. For the output market, linear approximations for the key behavioral relations are

$$C^d = a + b \cdot (Y - CCA - T) - c \cdot r \quad \text{and} \tag{A10.1}$$

$$I^d = d - e \cdot r \tag{A10.2}$$

Equation A10.1 indicates that households' consumption demand C^d is directly related to real disposable income and inversely related to the interest rate, while Equation A10.2 indicates that firms' investment demand I^d is inversely related to the interest rate. Note that while we assumed in the text that changes in the interest rate affected consumption demand by altering the intercept term in Equation 10.2, we now explicitly identify the effect of interest rate changes on consumption demand in Equation A10.1.

For the money market, the key underlying behavioral relation in linear form is

$$L^d = k \cdot Y - m \cdot r \tag{A10.3}$$

This equation indicates that households money demand is directly related to real income and inversely related to the interest rate.

In a closed economy, the conditions for equilibrium in the output and money markets are

$$C^d + I^d + CCA + G^d = Y \qquad \text{and} \qquad \text{(A10.4)}$$

$$L^d = M^s/P \qquad \text{(A10.5)}$$

Substituting the expressions from consumption demand (Equation A10.1), investment demand (Equation A10.2), and money demand (Equation A10.3) into the equilibrium conditions (A10.4) and (A10.5), we obtain

$$a + b \cdot (Y - CCA - T) - c \cdot r + d - e \cdot r + CCA + G^d = Y \quad \text{(A10.6)}$$

$$\text{and} \qquad k \cdot Y - m \cdot r = M^s/P \qquad \text{(A10.7)}$$

Solving the output market equilibrium condition (Equation A10.6) for output Y, we obtain

$$Y = CCA + [1/(1 - b)] \cdot [J - H \cdot r], \qquad \text{(A10.8)}$$

where $J = a + d + G^d - bT$ and $H = c + e$. Equation A10.8 is the equation for the *IS* curve. As the equation indicates, an increase in the interest rate r requires a lower Y to maintain equilibrium in the output market. Thus the *IS* curve is downward-sloping.

Solving the money market equilibrium condition (Equation A10.7) for the interest rate r yields

$$r = (1/m)(k \cdot Y - M^s/P) \qquad \text{(A10.9)}$$

Equation A10.9 is the equation for the *LM* curve. As this equation indicates, an increase in real GNP requires a higher interest rate to maintain equilibrium in the money market. Thus the *LM* curve is upward-sloping.

Substituting the *LM* "curve" expression for the interest rate (Equation A10.9) into the *IS* "curve" expression for the equilibrium output (Equation A10.8), we obtain an expression for the equilibrium output that corresponds to the intersection of the *IS* and *LM* curves. This equilibrium output Y^* is given by

$$Y^* = CCA + [1/(1 - b)] \cdot [J - (H \cdot k/m) \cdot Y^* + (H/m)(M^s/P)] \quad \text{(A10.10)}$$

Solving for Y^*, we have

$$Y^* = \{1/[1 - b + (H \cdot k/m)]\} \cdot [(1 - b) \cdot CCA + J + (H/m)(M^s/P)] \quad \text{(A10.11)}$$

This equation is the algebraic equivalent to an *IS-LM* graphical analysis that determines the equilibrium level of real GNP. We see that a one-unit increase in government spending (an element of J) leads to an increase in real GNP equal to $1/[1 - b + (H \cdot k/m)]$ or, multiplying through by m/m, an increase in real GNP equal to $m/(m - mb + H \cdot k)$.

As we will see in the next chapter, the impact of a fiscal policy change on equilibrium output depends in part on the shape of the *LM* curve. If the

LM curve is vertical, this means that money demand is completely insensitive to interest rate changes, or $m = 0$. In this case, the expression $m/(m - mb + H \cdot k)$ equals zero, and changes in government spending leave output unaffected. As money demand becomes increasingly sensitive to interest rate changes (m increases), the expression $1/(1 - b + (H \cdot k/m))$ rises and the impact of a change in government spending on real GNP increases. In other words, the flatter the *LM* curve, the greater the impact of fiscal policy changes on real GNP.

The shape of the *IS* curve also affects the extent to which fiscal policy changes impact real GNP, as we will see in the next chapter. The less sensitive investment and consumption demand are to interest rate changes (the smaller are c and e), the greater the impact of fiscal policy changes on real GNP. In the extreme, if output demand is completely insensitive to interest rate changes ($H \equiv c + e = 0$), the *IS* curve is vertical and a one-unit change in government spending results in the simple multiplier of $1/(1 - b)$ change in real GNP.

In contrast, monetary policy is completely ineffective if the *IS* curve is vertical. To see this, note from Equation A10.11 that a one-unit increase in the real money supply (M^s/P) leads to an increase in real GNP equal to $(H/m)/[1 - b + (H \cdot k/m)] = H/[m \cdot (1 - b) + H \cdot k]$. If output demand is completely insensitive to interest rate changes ($H \equiv c + e = 0$ and the *IS* curve is vertical), then the expression $H/[m \cdot (1 - b) + H \cdot k]$ equals zero, and real GNP is unaffected by money supply changes.

In an open economy, we can summarize the underlying assumption of exchange rate adjustments that clear the foreign exchange markets by expressing net export demand ($X^d - Z^d$) as inversely related to the interest rate. To see why this is the case, note that equilibrium in the foreign exchange market implies that the demand for dollars equals the supply of dollars. Behind the demand for dollars are real exports (X^d) and foreign demand for domestic financial assets (A^d_{for}). Behind the supply of dollars are real imports (Z^d) and domestic households demand for foreign financial assets AF^d_h. Thus equilibrium in the foreign exchange market means that

$$X^d + A^d_{for} = Z^d + AF^d_h \qquad \textbf{(A10.12)}$$

Rewriting this equation, we have

$$\underset{\text{Net export demand}}{X^d - Z^d} = \underset{\text{Net capital outflows}}{AF^d_h - A^d_{for}} \qquad \textbf{(A10.13)}$$

According to Equation A10.13, equilibrium in the foreign exchange market implies that net export demand equals net capital outflows. Thus since an increase in the interest rate reduces net capital outflows, it will reduce net exports. This relationship is given in linear form by

$$X^d - Z^d = w - x \cdot r \qquad \textbf{(A10.14)}$$

This equation reflects the idea that with a rise in the interest rate, net capital outflows fall as domestic financial assets become attractive. The accompanying increase in the demand for dollars and fall in supply of dollars leads to an appreciation of the dollar. A higher price of the dollar discourages exports and encourages imports (since it implies a lower dollar price for foreign currencies), thus leading to a fall in net export demand that exactly offsets the real decrease net capital outflow. According to Equation A10.14, changes in income are not included as a factor altering net export demand since it is assumed that income changes do not affect net capital outflows. With income changes, exchange rate adjustments lead to changes in exports and imports that exactly offset any initial change in imports induced by a change in household income.

Substituting Equation A10.14 into the output equilibrium condition (Equation A10.6) that is now expanded to include net export demand, we obtain

$$a + b \cdot (Y\text{-}CAA\text{-}T) - c \cdot r + d - e \cdot r + CCA + G^d + w - x \cdot r = Y \qquad \textbf{(A10.15)}$$

Solving for Y, we have

$$Y = CCA + [1/(1 - b)] \cdot [J_f - H_f \cdot r] \qquad \textbf{(A10.16)}$$

where $J_f = a + d + G^d - bT + w$ and $H_f = c + e + x$. We can now proceed as before and combine Equation A10.16 (the *IS* "curve" equation for an open economy) and Equation A10.9 (the *LM* "curve" equation) to obtain an expression for equilibrium real GNP in an open economy.

Two items should strike you in comparing the equation for the *IS* curve in an open economy (Equation A10.16) with that in a closed economy (Equation A10.8). First, H_f in Equation A10.16 is greater than H in Equation A10.8, indicating that for the open economy *IS* curve a given change in the interest rate requires a large change in output to maintain equilibrium in the output market. In other words, the *IS* curve is flatter for an open economy. Second, note that we now have an exogenous change in net export demand, as represented by changes in w in the term J_f, as a potential source for a shift in the *IS* curve and thus a change in real GNP. Remember from Equation A10.13 that such an exogenous change in net exports at a given level of U.S. interest rates is accompanied by an equivalent change in net capital outflows.

Chapter 11

Policy Changes and the Predetermined Price Model

THERE is some controversy about the government's ability to manage output demand in order to counteract economy-wide fluctuations in real GNP. One extreme is the view offered by the neoclassical model, which is that monetary changes affect only money prices; they have no *real* effects. Further, although fiscal policy changes can have real effects in the neoclassical model, these effects are limited to changes in how output is used—whether for household consumption, firm investment, or the government.[1] Fiscal policy changes, like monetary policy changes, do not alter either total employment or output, according to the neoclassical model.

One feature of the neoclassical model that troubles many economists is its failure to account for the fact that changes in the money supply, as well as fiscal policy changes, do appear to affect real GNP. For example, evidence indicates that reductions in the growth rate of the money supply are associated with temporary drops in the growth of real GNP and increased unemployment. The neoclassical model, however, fails to provide a causal link between monetary shocks and fluctuations in output and employment.[2]

---

[1] Even here, the Ricardian equivalence doctrine raises questions as to whether changes in government taxation and borrowing have any real effects in the absence of a change in government spending.

[2] This point is made by Olivier Blanchard in his survey of research on this topic ("Why Does Money Affect Output? A Survey," NBER Working Paper No. 2285, June 1987). Some economists have suggested that the neoclassical model may still be appropriate, arguing that the causality

The analysis of the last chapter offers one explanation of how insufficient demand can lead to recessions. With inflexible prices in the short run, the neoclassical model's tenet that reductions in demand shocks do not affect output and employment no longer holds. A sudden reduction in the money supply, a fall in autonomous investment, a reduction in government spending, or a fall in consumption purchases can now lead to a reduction in real GNP below the full employment level.

Conversely, an economy experiencing high unemployment and real GNP below the full employment level due to a price level set too high can be aided by a rise in the money supply or an expansionary fiscal policy action, since both can lead to an increase in real GNP and employment. It is important to recognize, however, that these corrective effects of monetary and fiscal policy changes may depend on whether such policy changes were anticipated at the time prices were set. Not all monetary or fiscal policy changes need affect real GNP and employment even in the short run. We start this chapter with a discussion of the potential distinction between policy changes that do affect real GNP and employment versus those that do not. This distinction, suggested by the rational expectations hypothesis, involves contrasting "unanticipated" with "anticipated" policy changes.[3]

11.1   PREDETERMINED PRICES AND RATIONAL EXPECTATIONS

In the predetermined price macroeconomic model, although prices are assumed to be fixed, they are not fixed forever. At various times, contracts for labor and raw materials are negotiated and prices adjusted. Taking the neoclassical view of price determination, one can assume that prices are set to reflect anticipated market-clearing levels. Then even though prices are fixed in the current period, prices are fixed at levels such that markets will clear as long as individuals correctly anticipate demands and supplies in the various markets. This view has potentially important policy implications when coupled with the assumption of "rational expectations."

---

runs not from money supply changes to real output but from real output changes to the money supply. For example, see Robert G. King and Charles I. Plosser "Money, Credit, and Prices in a Real Business Cycle," *American Economic Review*, (June 1984) pp. 363–380. King and Plosser suggest that the correlation between the money supply and real GNP reflects to a large extent the fact that fluctuations in real variables—supply-side factors—induce changes in monetary aggregates. They explain the correlation between real GNP and the money supply by noting that increases in output cause households to demand more money; this causes interest rates to rise, which induces private depository institutions to supply more money. In Chapter 16 we look at the implications of an "endogenous money supply," that is a money supply that is affected by changes in the interest rate.

[3] The discussion reviews some of the points made at the outset of Chapter 10.

To understand these policy implications, assume that when individuals set prices they use all available information in forming expectations of future demands and supplies, including how anticipated monetary and fiscal policy changes affect future demands, supplies, and thus equilibrium prices. In this case, they are said to have **rational expectations**. As noted by Steven Sheffrin, rational expectations "will diverge from actual values only because of some unpredictable uncertainty in the system. If there were no unpredictable uncertainty, expectations of variables would coincide with the actual values— there would be **perfect foresight**."[4]

Rational expectations: Expectations formed by using all available information, including how anticipated monetary and fiscal policy changes affect future demands, supplies, and thus equilibrium prices.

Perfect foresight: The situation in which individual expectations turn out to be correct.

Let's assume economic agents (firms and households) formed such rational expectations of future demands and supplies and fixed prices for future periods equal to anticipated market-clearing levels. For example, let's say individuals setting prices for next year anticipate that the money supply will increase by 10 percent in the next year. Then if wages and prices are set based on anticipated market-clearing levels, they will be set 10 percent higher for the next year, other things being equal.

Note the implication. Although prices will be "fixed," they will be fixed so as to completely adjust for the effect of the anticipated policy-driven demand shock. The outcome is that policy-driven demand shocks that were anticipated when prices were set alter neither employment nor output. In our example, the 10 percent increase in the money supply will then lead only to higher prices, not to any change in real GNP or employment.[5]

The above discussion suggests that if one accepts rational expectations *and* price setting to clear markets, then the analysis in this chapter should be viewed as presenting the short-run effects on output and employment of policy changes that were *unanticipated at the time prices were set.*[6] This does not mean, however, that these short-lived effects are unimportant. A worker

---

[4] Steven M. Sheffrin, *Rational Expectations* (Cambridge: Cambridge University Press, 1983), p. 9.

[5] This "neutrality of money" proposition has been popularized by such economists as Robert Lucas, Thomas Sargent, and Neil Wallace. See Robert E. Lucas, Jr., "Expectations and the Neutrality of Money," *Journal of Economic Theory* (April 1972) pp. 103–124, and Thomas Sargent and Neil Wallace, " 'Rational' Expectations, the Optimal Monetary Instrument, and the Optimal Money Supply Rule," *Journal of Political Economy,* (April 1975) pp. 241–254.

[6] The evidence concerning this proposition is mixed. Mark Rush, "Unexpected Money and Unemployment" *Journal of Money, Credit, and Banking* 18 (August 1986): 259–274, and Robert Barro, "Unanticipated Money Growth and Unemployment in the United States," *American Economic Review* 67 (March 1977): 101–115, find some support for the proposition that while unanticipated monetary shocks can have real effects, expected changes are neutral. Similarly, Ali Darrat, "Unanticipated Inflation and Real Output: The Canadian Experience," *Canadian Journal of Economics* (February 1985): 146–155, finds for Canada that during the period 1960 to 1982 "anticipated short-run monetary policies cannot influence real economic activity." There are a number of important criticisms of this view. See, for example, David Small, "Unanticipated Money Growth and Unemployment in the United States: Comment," *American Economic Review* (December 1979): 996–1003, Edmund Sheehey, "The Neutrality of Money in the Short Run: Some Tests," *Journal of Money, Credit, and Banking* (May 1984): 237–241, and F. S. Mishkin, "Does Anticipated Aggregate Demand Policy Matter," *American Economic Review* (September 1982): 788–802.

laid off from a job or a recent graduate who cannot find employment will take little solace in the fact that prices will adjust to clear the market in a few years. And there does exist the possibility that until prices adjust, monetary or fiscal policy changes could increase real output and employment.[7]

11.2   MACROECONOMIC DEMAND SHOCKS: MONETARY POLICY ACTIONS

In the neoclassical model, a change in the money supply has only a transitory effect on the interest rate. Output prices adjust quickly to the resultant excess demand or supply in the output market, and the interest rate returns to its original level. The change in the money supply affects neither output nor employment but leads solely to changes in prices. In the model with predetermined prices, however, a change in the money supply has very different effects.

To analyze the effects of a change in the money supply when prices are predetermined, consider a reduction in the nominal stock of money in the current period. (Naturally, this implies a lower growth rate in the money supply.) We first examine how this change in the money supply affects the output and financial markets at the original price and output levels. This initial impact mirrors that of the neoclassical model. The difference between the neoclassical model and the non-market-clearing model is in the way the economy adjusts to the excess supply or demand that is created in the output market at the original levels of prices and real GNP.

The Impact of a Reduction in Monetary Growth If Prices and Output Do Not Change

There have been numerous instances when a reduction in the rate of growth in the money supply has been pointed to as the culprit causing an economic downturn. An often cited example is the Fed's reduction in the rate of growth of the money supply in the early 1980s as they attemped to squeeze double-digit inflation out of the economy. It is generally accepted that this tight monetary policy was one of the major causes of the 10.8 percent unemployment the economy experienced in 1982. Figure 11.1 illustrates how a reduction in the money supply from M_0^s to M_1^s will affect the financial and money markets at the original level of prices P_0 and output Y_0. At existing prices,

---

[7] This point—that fixed prices impart a potential stabilizing role for policy changes—is made in numerous papers: see, for example, Stanley Fischer, "Long-Term Contracts, Rational Expectations, and the Optimal Money Supply Rule," *Journal of Political Economy* (February 1977): 191–206, and Edmund S. Phelps and John B. Taylor, "Stabilizing Powers of Monetary Policy Under Rational Expectations," *Journal of Political Economy* (February 1977): 163–190.

Figure 11.1 **The Impact of a Decrease in the Money Supply on the Financial and Money Markets**

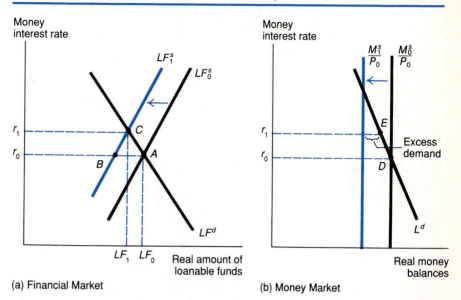

(a) Financial Market

(b) Money Market

At the given price level P_0, a fall in the nominal money supply from M_0^s to M_1^s implies a fall in the real money supply from M_0^s/P_0 to M_1^s/P_0 and thus an equivalent fall in the real supply of loanable funds. As shown in part (a), the equilibrium interest rate rises from r_0 to r_1. Since the rise in the interest rate reduces the quantity of investment and consumption demand, there is excess supply in the output market at the original level of output. From the aggregate budget constraint, this implies an excess demand in the money market, as part (b) indicates.

the reduction in the nominal money supply implies a reduction in the real money supply from M_0^s/P_0 to M_1^s/P_0 and thus the real supply of loanable funds falls by an equivalent amount.

The reduction in the real supply of loanable funds causes the interest rate required to maintain equilibrium in the financial market to rise from r_0 to r_1, as Figure 11.1(a) indicates. This higher interest rate causes the quantity of investment and consumption demand to fall. The fall in investment is reflected by the upward movement along the demand for loanable funds curve from point A to point C, as the fall in investment means an equivalent fall in the quantity of loanable funds demanded by firms. The fall in consumption and increase in saving partly explains the movement up the new supply of loanable funds curve from point B to point C. The increase in the interest rate from r_0 to r_1 also increases the quantity of loanable funds households supply because it reduces their desired holdings of money, as indicated in Figure 11.1(b) by the movement up the real money demand curve from point D to point E.

At the initial levels of output and prices but the higher interest rate r_1, the lower investment and consumption spending means that there is excess supply in the output market. From the aggregate budget constraint for a closed economy, we know that this means there is excess demand in the money market. Figure 11.1(b) shows the fall in the real money supply from M_0^s/P_0 to M_1^s/P_0 and resulting excess demand in the money market.

The Effect on Equilibrum Output and the Interest Rate

The excess supply in the output market (and excess demand in the money market) means that the combination of initial output Y_0 and level of prices P_0 no longer identifies a point on the original aggregate demand curve; the aggregate demand curve shifts to the left from AD_0 to AD_1, as shown in Figure 11.2(b). With predetermined prices, firms respond to initial excess supply in the output market by reducing production. This fall in output, since it implies an equivalent fall in income, leads to a fall in consumption demand and thus further reductions in output—this is the multiplier analysis that was discussed in Chapter 10. Eventually, equilibrium in the output market is restored at the lower level of income Y_1.

We can use *IS-LM* analysis to determine the horizontal shift in the aggregate demand curve and the corresponding fall in equilibrium output caused by the fall in the money supply. At the same time *IS-LM* analysis provides us with the impact of the monetary change on the interest rate. Figure 11.2(a) indicates that a decrease in the real supply of money shifts the *LM* curve to the left and up from LM_0 to LM_1. As can be seen in Figure 11.1(b), with a fall in the real supply of money, a higher interest rate will restore equilibrium in the money market at the original output level. This explains the upward shift in the *LM* curve.[8]

With a lower real money supply, equilibrium in the money and output market is restored at the higher interest rate r_2 and lower real output Y_1, as Figure 11.2(a) shows. The fall in real output from Y_0 to Y_1 occurs at the predetermined price level P_0. Thus the output-price level combination (Y_1, P_0) is a point on the new aggregate demand curve AD_1 in Figure 11.2(b).

The Responsiveness of Output to Money Supply Changes: An Analysis Using *IS-LM* Curves

We now know that given predetermined prices, changes in the money supply can affect real GNP and thus employment in the economy. It is important to recognize further that changes in the money supply can have quantitatively

---

[8] We introduced the *IS* and *LM* curves in Chapter 10. If you are having trouble understanding why the *LM* curve shifts, you may want to review our earlier discussion.

Figure 11.2   The Effect of a Money Supply Decrease on Output and Interest Rate

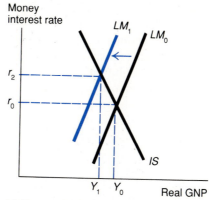

(a) *IS – LM* Analysis

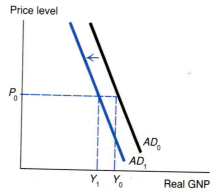

(b) Aggregate Demand with Predetermined
Price Level

A fall in the money supply leads to an excess supply in the output market at the original output and price level. Consequently, as depicted in part (b), there is a shift to the left in the aggregate demand curve from AD_0 to AD_1. At the predetermined price level P_0, the fall in output from Y_0 to Y_1 restores equilibrium in the economy. Part (a) indicates the effect of the fall in the money supply by using *IS-LM* analysis. A lower money supply shifts the *LM* curve to the left. Equilibrium in the economy is restored with a rise in the interest rate from r_0 to r_2 and a fall in output from Y_0 to Y_1. As the two graphs indicate, the fall in equilibrium output shown by *IS-LM* analysis defines the shift to the left in the aggregate demand curve.

different effects on the economy depending on the responsiveness of households' consumption and firms' investment spending to interest rate changes. *IS-LM* analysis allows us to make clear the conditions that determine whether a monetary shock will significantly affect real GNP.

Remember that the interest rate links the financial and output markets in the economy. A change in the money supply, by changing the interest rate, causes real consumption and investment demand to change. Thus it should not be surprising that the magnitude of the impact of a money supply change on output depends upon the responsiveness of consumption and investment demand to changes in the interest rate. The more responsive are consumption and investment demand to a change in the interest rate, the greater is the impact of a given change in the money supply on real GNP.

In terms of *IS-LM* analysis, as consumption and investment demand become more responsive to a change in the interest rate, the *IS* curve becomes flatter. This is because a fall in the interest rate will require a greater increase in output to restore equilibrium in the output market. Figure 11.3 depicts *IS* curves with different slopes, reflecting two different views of the economy. In Figure 11.3(a), the *IS* curve is flatter, which characterizes the situation in which consumption and investment demand are relatively responsive to interest rate changes. The steeper *IS* curve in Figure 11.3(b) reflects the view that consumption and investment demand are relatively unresponsive to interest rate changes.

In Chapter 10, we demonstrated that if the nominal money supply remains unchanged, a rise in the price level causes a fall in the real supply of money, and thus a shift to the left in the *LM* curve. With a constant price level, a fall in the nominal money supply has the exact same effect. It causes the real money supply to fall and the *LM* curve to shift to the left from LM_0 to LM_1 in Figure 11.3. It is important to note that this shift to the left is identical in both parts (a) and (b) of Figure 11.3.[9]

In Figure 11.3(a), which has the flatter *IS* curve, the change in the money supply causes a relatively large change in output from Y_0 to Y_1. In Figure 11.3(b), which has the steeply sloped *IS* curve, the change in the money supply and resulting shift in the *LM* curve affects real GNP less in this case, as can be seen by the smaller fall in real GNP from Y_0' to Y_1'. In contrast, the change in the interest rate is greater in the case of a steeper *IS* curve, as you can see by comparing the change from r_0 to r_1 in part (a) with the change from r_0' to r_1' in part (b).

The above analysis illustrates the general proposition that the more responsive the demand for consumption and investment with respect to the rate of interest (the "flatter" the *IS* curve), the larger is the effect of a change in the money supply on real GNP, and the smaller is the effect of a change in the money supply on the interest rate. Remember that the link between

---

[9] This happens because at the original interest rate r_0, the fall in the money supply requires the same reduction in income to re-equate money demand and supply.

**Figure 11.3   The Responsiveness of Output to a Fall in the
Money Supply: The Effect of a Flatter *IS* Curve**

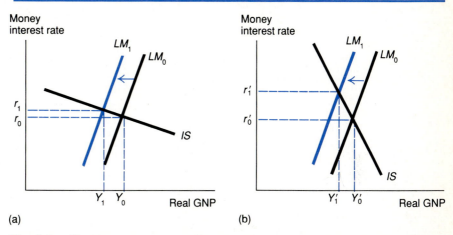

(a)   (b)

The flatter *IS* curve in part (a) (which indicates that investment and consumption
demand are quite sensitive to changes in the interest rate) leads to a larger drop
in output in response to a fall in the money supply. The steeply sloped *IS* curve in
part (b) (which indicates that investment and consumption demand are insensitive
to changes in the interest rate) means a less dramatic fall in output in response to
the same fall in the money supply, even though the fall in the money supply and
consequent shift to the left in the *LM* curve are identical in both cases.

money supply changes and output demand is through the effect of money
supply changes on the interest rate; this link is strengthened if components
of output demand are more sensitive to interest rate changes. It follows that
those who are sympathetic with the view that consumption and investment
demand are relatively responsive to interest rate changes believe that monetary
changes are an important source of changes in real GNP.

The responsiveness of money demand to interest rate changes is a second
factor that affects how large an impact a money supply change will have
on real GNP. When money demand is very sensitive to a change in the
interest rate, the *LM* curve is quite flat. In this situation, an increase in the
interest rate causes a large reduction in money demand, so that a large
increase in output is required to get money demand back in line with the
unchanged money supply.

A comparison of part (a) and part (b) in Figure 11.4 shows how a
money supply reduction has different effects depending on the degree of
responsiveness of money demand to changes in the interest rate. In Figure
11.4 (a), the *LM* curve is relatively steep, indicating that money demand is
insensitive to changes in the interest rate. In this case, a fall in the real
supply of money and resulting shift to the left in the *LM* curve from LM_0

Figure 11.4   The Responsiveness of Output to a Fall in the Money Supply: The Effect of a Steeper *LM* Curve

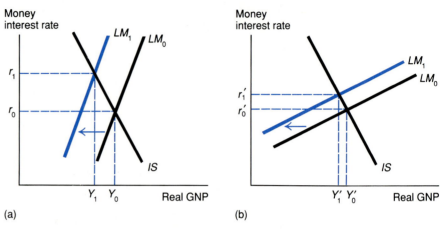

(a)   (b)

The steep *LM* curve in part (a) (which indicates a money demand that is relatively insensitive to changes in the interest rate) leads to a large rise in the interest rate and a large drop in output in response to a fall in the money supply. The flatter *LM* curve in part (b) (which indicates a money demand that is relatively sensitive to changes in the interest rate) leads to a small increase in the interest rate and a small drop in output in response to a change in the money supply.

to LM_1 causes a relatively large increase in the interest rate from r_0 to r_1, and consequently a relatively large drop in real GNP from Y_0 to Y_1.

In contrast, the *LM* curve in Figure 11.4 (b) is relatively flat, indicating money demand is very responsive to interest rate changes. As a consequence, a fall in the real supply of money and resulting shift to the left in the *LM* curve from LM_0 to LM_1 causes a relatively small increase in the interest rate from r_0' to r_1' and, consequently, a relatively small drop in real GNP from Y_0' to Y_1'. A small rise in the interest rate is sufficient to reduce the quantity of money demanded to equal the new, lower real money supply. Since the interest rate rises less with a "flatter" *LM* curve, the drop in output demand, and thus in output, is less. Note that in both parts of Figure 11.4 the *horizontal* leftward shifts in the *LM* curves are identical.

We can draw an important conclusion from the above analysis. If money demand is insensitive to changes in the interest rate (the *LM* curve is steep), then changes in the money supply have a relatively large impact on real GNP and the interest rate. In contrast, Keynes termed the **liquidity trap** as a hypothetical situation in which money demand is extremely sensitive to a change in the interest rate, implying a nearly flat *LM* curve. In this context, there is little role for money supply changes to influence real GNP

Liquidity trap: According to Keynes, a hypothetical situation in which the response of money demand to a change in the interest rate is extremely high, implying a nearly flat *LM* curve.

since a given horizontal shift in the *LM* curve will have little effect on real GNP. This theory has led some economists to conclude over the years that Keynes completely opposed monetary policy since he felt there would be little effect from it. Although the concept of the liquidity trap is associated with Keynes, Keynes actually felt that the liquidity trap was an unusual occurrence and not likely to be found in the normal workings of the economy.

11.3   A MONETARY SHOCK IN AN OPEN ECONOMY

When we analyze a monetary policy change in the open economy, we find that the qualitative effects on real GNP, employment, and the interest rate remain the same. The magnitude of the change in these variables is, however, affected. We can also now predict how a money supply change will affect foreign exchange rates, exports, imports, and international capital flows when prices are inflexible.

To analyze the effects of opening an economy to exchange with other countries, we return to *IS-LM* analysis. As we discussed in Chapter 10, the *IS* curve is flatter in an open economy for the following reason. An increase in the interest rate raises net international capital inflows (capital inflows increase and capital outflows decrease), which leads to an appreciation of the dollar. This rise in the price of a dollar results in lower exports and increased imports. Thus in an open economy, a rise in the interest rate causes not only a fall in investment and consumption demand but also a fall in net export demand.

Since the *IS* curve is flatter in an open economy, a contractionary monetary policy that shifts the *LM* curve to the left causes the interest rate to increase less but output to fall more than in a closed economy, as was illustrated by Figure 11.3. The intuition behind this result should be clear. Monetary policy affects the output market through its impact on the financial market and the equilibrium interest rate. Since in the open economy output demand is more sensitive to interest rate changes, monetary shocks that affect the interest rate have a greater impact on real GNP.

In summary, a money supply reduction has *quantitatively* different effects in an open economy than in a closed economy. The interest rate increases less but real GNP and employment fall by more. In addition, the increased interest rate raises net international capital inflows, which implies an appreciation of the dollar, a fall in exports, and an increase in imports. The fall in income also contributes to the dollar's appreciation since it reduces imports and thus the supply of dollars in the foreign exchange market. As we have seen, the change in income by itself leaves net export demand unchanged, since it reduces imports and exports by the same amount.

11.4   THE LONG-RUN EFFECT OF A CHANGE IN THE MONEY SUPPLY

The previous two sections demonstrate that while a change in the money supply affects output and employment in the short run, in the long run output and employment will return to their natural rates.[10] We can best summarize the short-run and long-run effects of a fall in the money supply on output by using aggregate demand-supply analysis.

Suppose that output is originally at the full employment level Y_0 and prices are set at the predetermined level P_0. As Figure 11.5 shows, a reduction in the money supply causes the aggregate demand curve to shift to the left from AD_0 to AD_1. At the predetermined price level P_0 and original output Y^*, excess supply exists in the output market; firms find that they can no longer sell all they produce. Consequently, equilibrium output falls, as the movement from point A to point B illustrates.

At the predetermined price level P_0, firms initially adjust to the fall in demand by reducing output to Y_1. However, this new level of production is below what firms would like to sell at the existing wages and prices and this leads to a bidding down of prices over time. In the long run, according to the neoclassical model, the price level falls to P_1 and the rate of production returns to the full employment level Y^*, indicated by point C in Figure 11.5.

How long will it take for the long-run adjustment in prices to work its way through the economy? The time involved may be considerable. Milton Friedman has suggested the following: "Because prices are sticky, faster or slower monetary growth initially affects output and employment. But these effects wear off. After about two years, the main effect is on inflation. . . . For example, the quantity of money (as measured by M1—currency plus checking deposits) grew at successive annual rates of 3.1, 5.0, 6.2 and 7.3 percent from 1960 to 1965, 1965 to 1970, 1970 to 1975, and 1975 to 1979. In corresponding periods (two years later), inflation, as measured by the consumer price index, was 2.0, 4.6, 7.7 and 10.7 percent. From 1979 to 1981, monetary growth slowed to 6.7 percent—and inflation fell from 1981 to 1982."[11]

Friedman's quote raises two issues. The first issue is the idea that a monetary change can temporarily affect real GNP and employment. Our analysis of a contractionary monetary change fits Friedman's description of

---

[10] Some recent research has questioned the idea that the economy, left to itself, will always eventually return to its natural level of unemployment. For example, it has been suggested that the prolonged period of high unemployment in Europe in the 1980s, as well as the experience of the pre–World War II U.S. and U.K. depressions, are examples of unemployment not returning to a fixed equilibrium value. In other words, in some circumstances, there may be "hysteresis," where the steady state of the economy depends on its path. See Olivier Blanchard and Lawrence Summers, "Hysteresis and European Unemployment," NBER Macroeconomics Annual, 1986: pp. 15–89.

[11] Milton Friedman, *Newsweek,* 12 July 1982.

Figure 11.5   The Long-run Impact of a Reduction in the Money Supply

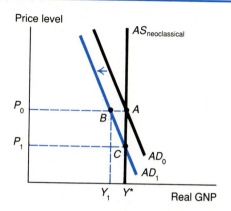

A reduction in the money supply causes the aggregate demand curve to shift to the left from AD_0 to AD_1. Initially, this leads to a reduction in equilibrium output from Y^* to Y_1 at the predetermined price level P_0. Eventually, prices fall to P_1 and output adjusts back to its full employment level. The new long-run equilibrium is at price level P_1 and output Y^*.

the actual impact of monetary changes on the economy. A slower growth in the money supply reduces real GNP in the short run, as real GNP falls below its full employment level. But ultimately prices adjust and the economy returns to full employment. The only lasting effect of the slower rate of growth in the money supply is a lower rate of inflation.

But, what of the situation in which the economy starts at the full employment level of output and the money supply rises. Can an increase in the money supply temporarily raise real GNP above the full employment level? Yes. Chapter 12 will discuss the reasons for such a temporary increase in an aggregate output above its natural level. In the long run, however, output will return to the full employment level and the monetary increase will translate into higher prices, as predicted by the neoclassical model.

The second issue raised by the Friedman quote is the idea that an increase in the money supply must ultimately lead to higher inflation. In fact, there are certain instances in which increases in the money supply need not imply greater inflation. In particular, let's make our starting point an economy at less than full employment. In this case, an expansion in the money supply could simply restore full employment in the economy without increasing prices.

You should be able to analyze the effect of such an increase in the money supply on the economy by using *IS-LM* curves. The analysis will be similar to a fall in the money supply except that the direction of changes in such variables as output and the interest rate will be the opposite. Graphically, the *LM* curve will now shift to the right. As noted above, an important aspect of analyzing an increase in the money supply in terms of *IS-LM* analysis is the presumption that initially output is below its full employment level, so that firms respond to increases in demand by expanding production. The potential role of monetary policy in moving the economy to full employment is discussed in some detail in Chapter 13.

To the Point

MONETARY CHANGES WITH PREDETERMINED PRICES

- Many prices are inflexible in the short run. If prices are set too high, the result is that firms face a sales constraint in the output market. In such a setting, a change in the money supply affects real output, employment, and the interest rate.

- A change in the money supply has a greater effect on real GNP if money demand is relatively unresponsive to interest rate changes (relatively steep *LM* curve) or if consumption and investment are relatively responsive to a change in the interest rate (relatively flat *IS* curve).

- In an open economy, a change in the money supply has a greater impact on real GNP as the accompanying change in the interest rate alters international capital flows, which leads to changes in the exchange rate that affect net export demand. For instance, a money supply reduction leads to a higher interest rate that increases capital inflows (and thus the demand for dollars in the foreign exchange market) and reduces capital outflows (and thus the supply of dollars). The resulting appreciation of the dollar reduces exports and increases imports.

- In the long run, prices tend to fully adjust to a change in the money supply. As the neoclassical model predicts, with flexible prices, money supply changes do not affect real GNP in the long run.

11.5   MACROECONOMIC DEMAND SHOCKS: A FISCAL POLICY ACTION

As we discussed in previous chapters, the government's fiscal policy decisions deal with the levels of spending (G^d), borrowing (A_g^s), and taxes (T). In making its decisions, the government is constrained by the fact that spending must be financed either from taxes or from the sale of financial assets, that is, $G^d = T + A_g^s$. We saw in Chapter 8 that fiscal policy changes, like monetary policy changes, alter the position of the aggregate demand curve. In the neoclassical model, these fiscal policy changes alter both the equilibrium price level and the interest rate but not real GNP. Since changes in the interest rate affect investment and consumption demand, fiscal policy changes will also affect the composition of output demand. For example, since an increase in government spending does not alter equilibrium output in the neoclassical model, it must crowd out an equal amount of investment and consumption spending. Similarly, a reduction in taxes that the government offsets by an increase in borrowing increases consumption spending at the expense of investment spending.[12]

In contrast to the neoclassical model, fiscal policy changes do alter real GNP as well as interest rates in the predetermined price model. We will begin our analysis with an example of a "pure" fiscal policy action, one that is not accompanied by a change in the money supply. Recent evidence suggests that money supply changes are, in fact, often not linked to fiscal policy changes. For instance, for ten industrialized countries over the post–World War II period it has been found that, "the central bank can conduct independent monetary policy over long periods, notwithstanding government deficits."[13] Later in the chapter we will analyze a fiscal policy change that is accommodated by a change in the money supply. As we will see, accommodating monetary policy involves a money supply change that reduces or eliminates the impact on the interest rate of a fiscal policy change.

The Impact of a Bond-Financed Increase in Government Spending If Prices and Output Do Not Change

Suppose that the government increases its real spending on output and finances this increased spending by selling government bonds. Suppose also that the Fed does not adopt an accommodating monetary policy, so that the money supply does not change. Exactly this situation occurred in the United States during the military buildup for the Vietnam War. Led by increases in defense spending, real government spending increased by 16.6 percent from late 1965 through 1967. During the same period, the real money supply grew by only 1.68 percent, or about one tenth of the increase in government spending. The government financed the defense buildup mainly by borrowing. In 1965, the federal government ran a surplus of one-half billion dollars. (Honest, you can look it up!) By 1967 the federal government's budget had slipped into a $13.2 billion deficit.

This borrowing-financed increase in government defense spending caused the demand for loanable funds in the financial market to increase. Figure 11.6 illustrates how a borrowing-financed increase in government spending

---

[12] This is not the case, however, if one assumes Ricardian equivalence, in which case households view taxes and debt as equivalent means of financing government purchases.

[13] Aris A. Protopapadakis and Jeremy J. Siegel, "Is Money Growth Related to Government Deficits? Evidence from Ten Industrialized Economies," Working Paper No. 86-11, Federal Reserve Bank of Philadelphia (May 1986).

Figure 11.6   The Effect of an Increase in Government Deficit Spending

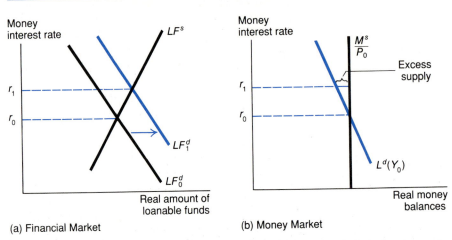

(a) Financial Market   (b) Money Market

An increase in government deficit spending causes a shift to the right in the demand for loanable funds curve from LF_0^d to LF_1^d in the financial market, as shown in part (a). This results in an increase in the equilibrium interest rate from r_0 to r_1. As indicated by the graph of the money market in part (b), the higher interest rate leads to an excess supply of money at the original price level and output. From the aggregate budget constraint, this implies an excess demand for output.

affects the financial and money markets at the initial levels of output (Y_0) and the predetermined price level (P_0). The initial effect of the fiscal policy change is an increase in the equilibrium interest rate in the financial market from r_0 to r_1, as the increase in government spending leads to an increase in the demand for loanable funds from LF_0^d to LF_1^d in part (a).

As we discussed in Chapter 8 when we looked at the effects of borrowing-financed increases in government spending in the neoclassical model, the higher interest rate crowds out consumption and investment spending, but not enough to offset the rise in government spending. At the predetermined price level and original output level, excess demand exists in the output market and thus, as the aggregate budget constraint dictates, excess supply exists in the money market. As Figure 11.6(b) illustrates, it is the rise in the interest rate from r_0 to r_1 that reduces the quantity of money demanded and thus leads to excess supply in the money market.

The Effect of Deficit Spending on Equilibrium Output and the Interest Rate

At the original price level P_0 and output Y_0, excess demand in the output market means a shift to the right in the aggregate demand curve, as Figure 11.7(b) illustrates. Firms are not producing enough to meet demand at prevailing prices and so they increase production. Increased production means higher income for households, which causes consumption demand to rise and leads to further increases in output.

In Chapter 10 we traced through an initial decrease in output demand and demonstrated how that resulted in larger decrease in output. The same process is at work here except that we are looking at an initial increase in output demand that leads to a multiple increase in output. Once the multiplier process has worked its way through the economy, equilibrium is restored in the economy at the new, higher output Y_1.

In our discussion of the impact of a change in monetary policy, we used *IS-LM* analysis to indicate the effect of a monetary shock on the interest rate and output level. Similarly, we can use *IS-LM* analysis to determine the rise in equilibrium output and the change in the interest rate that an increase in government deficit spending causes.

Recall that the *IS* curve depicts combinations of income and interest rates associated with equilibrium in the output market. With an increase in government demand, either the interest rate or output must rise to restore equilibrium in the output market. A higher interest rate restores equilibrium by reducing investment and consumption demand, while a higher output eliminates the gap between demand and production. Figure 11.7(a) depicts the effect of increased government spending as a shift to the right in the *IS* curve from IS_0 to IS_1.

The increase in government spending does not affect the *LM* curve since neither the increase in spending nor the increase in the government's demand for loanable funds directly alters money demand or money supply at the original interest rate r_0 and output Y_0. The *IS* and *LM* curves now intersect at the higher output level Y_1 and the higher interest rate r_2 in Figure 11.7(a). A rise in government spending causes an increase in real GNP at existing output prices from Y_0 to Y_1, although the increase comes at the expense of a higher interest rate, which stifles investment.[14]

The previously mentioned 1965 to 1967 episode of increased government deficit spending to finance the Vietnam War supports the prediction of the model, as interest rates rose. During that time period the prime rate rose from 4.54 percent to 5.61 percent, a 23.5 percent increase. Given the relatively low and constant rate of inflation during this time period, this represented primarily a rise in the real rate of interest. If this inflationary experience led individuals to expect continued low future inflation, then the expected real rate of interest was higher as well.

---

[14] Remember that, unless otherwise stated, the analysis assumes a constant expected future rate of inflation. That is, the future expected rate of inflation is an exogenous variable. Thus our prediction of a higher nominal or money interest rate implies a higher expected real rate of interest (the nominal interest rate minus the expected rate of inflation). Also note that, as we discussed in Chapter 10, the increase in income could cause an offsetting increase in investment demand.

Figure 11.7   The Effect of an Increase in Government Deficit Spending on Equilibrium Output and the Interest Rate

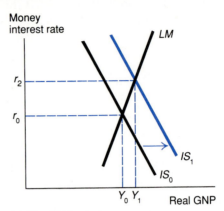

(a) *IS − LM* Analysis

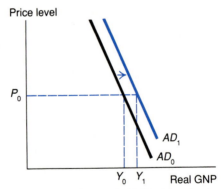

(b) Aggregate Demand with Predetermined Price Level

A rise in government spending leads to an excess demand in the output market at the original output and price level. Consequently, as depicted in part (b), there is a shift to the right in the aggregate demand curve from AD_0 to AD_1. At the predetermined price level P_0, the rise in output from Y_0 to Y_1 restores equilibrium in the economy. Part (a) indicates the effect of the increased government spending by using *IS-LM* analysis. A higher level of government spending shifts the *IS* curve to the right. Equilibrium in the economy is restored with a rise in the interest rate from r_0 to r_2 and a rise in output from Y_0 to Y_1. As the two graphs indicate, the increase in equilibrium output shown by the *IS-LM* analysis defines the shift to the right in the aggregate demand curve.

The Role of the Multiplier in *IS-LM* Analysis of a Fiscal Policy Change

We will now incorporate the multiplier into our *IS-LM* analysis in order to identify explicitly its role in determining the magnitude of the change in real GNP in response to an expansionary fiscal policy.[15] In fact, the size of the multiplier affects the magnitude of the horizontal shift in the *IS* curve.

In Chapter 10, we demonstrated that if the interest rate does not change, then an initial change in output demand causes a change in equilibrium output equal to the simple multiplier multiplied by this initial change in output demand. The simple multiplier—one that ignores not only interest rate effects but also the impact of changes in income on taxes and investment—equals one divided by one minus the marginal propensity to consume. For example, if the marginal propensity to consume equals .75, the simple multiplier equals four—$1/(1 - .75)$—and a $5 change in output demand will require a $20 increase in output to restore equilibrium in the output market. This change in output is shown graphically in Figure 11.8 by the horizontal shift in the *IS* curve. Specifically, at a *given interest rate*, the *IS* curve shifts to the right by $1/(1 - MPC)$ multiplied by the increase in government spending ΔG^d.

As Figure 11.8 illustrates, the change in equilibrium output that results from a rise in government spending is less than the rightward shift in the *IS* curve. As we have discussed previously, the reason is that the accompanying rise in the interest rate reduces investment and consumption demand.

Case Study

THE CANADIAN AND U.S. EXPERIENCES IN THE EARLY 1980s

In the early 1980s, the United States and Canada almost simultaneously experienced their most severe post–World War II recessions, with the recession in Canada starting just one quarter before it did in the United States. More interesting than the timing of the start, however, is that the recession was more severe in Canada and lasted for a longer period of time. During the same time, money growth and government spending rose more rapidly in the United States than in Canada, and wages and prices appeared to be more flexible in the United States. Both of these sets of conditions help explain why the recession was shorter and less severe in the United States than in Canada.

---

[15] The term expansionary refers to fiscal (or monetary) policy changes that lead to increased output. In the neoclassical model, such fiscal policy changes might be better described as "inflationary," since they lead to an increase in the price level.

Figure 11.8   The Multiplier and the Shift in the *IS* Curve

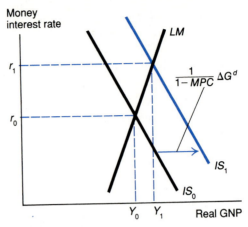

An increase in government spending, denoted by ΔG^d, shifts the *IS* curve to the right by the simple multiplier $1/(1 - MPC)$ multiplied by the change in government spending. Equilibrium in the economy is restored with a rise in the interest rate from r_0 to r_1 and a rise in output from Y_0 to Y_1.

In late 1981, when the economic downturns started in both countries, conditions differed in the two economies. The United States had gone through four relatively prosperous years and unemployment was around the 6-percent mark. Canada entered the recession in the third quarter of 1981 having just gone through a two-year "growth recession," during which there was zero growth in GNP. From the start of the recession to the trough, real GNP fell by 2.8 percent in the United States but by 6.6 percent in Canada. As one might expect, the increase in unemployment was more severe in Canada, rising by 5.7 percentage points to a peak of 12.8 percent. In the United States, the unemployment rate rose by 3.2 percentage points from the start of the recession to the trough.

Residential construction was particularly hard-hit in Canada, falling by 24 percent from peak to trough as opposed to a 5 percent fall in the United States. The one area where the Canadian economy outperformed the United States economy during this time period was in export growth. Growth of exports in Canada was five times higher than in the United States. To a large extent, this difference can be explained by the 70 percent appreciation in the value of the United States dollar in international markets during this period.

How can we explain these different patterns in the two countries? Can the differences be attributed to the monetary and fiscal actions taken by the countries? For one thing, government spending grew more in the United

States than in Canada. In the United States, federal government spending spurted by 11.7 percent and total government spending (state, local, and federal) grew by 4.6 percent. In Canada, government spending rose by 2.9 percent. In conjunction with the rise in United States government spending was a cut in taxes in the United States, which contributed to a 2.2 percent increase in consumer spending in the United States while consumer spending in Canada was falling by 2.7 percent. Finally, the Economic Recovery Tax Act (ERTA) passed in the United States in 1981 had the impact of stimulating investment, although the recovery had already started in the United States by the time the full impact was felt. Nonetheless, real net investment in the United States more than doubled from 1983 to 1984. It is clear that there was a much stronger fiscal stimulus in the United States than in Canada, which certainly played some role in starting the recovery.

Changes in the money supply in the United States were also more expansive than they were in Canada. Although the fact that the money supply declined shortly after Paul Volcker became chairman of the Fed in 1979 received much publicity at the time, the decline was really very short-lived. From the third quarter of 1979 until mid-1980, the money supply growth in the United States was either flat or negative. However, from the third quarter of 1979 until the third quarter of 1982 there was an overall 6 percent rate of growth in the money supply. By way of contrast, starting in the fourth quarter of 1980, one quarter after the downturn had started, until the third quarter of 1982, the money supply in Canada actually fell by 1.3 percent. The money supply started fairly sharp upward trends in both countries at that time, but the prolonged decline in the money supply in Canada already had already taken a major toll on the economy.

Both theory and evidence suggest that greater wage and price flexibility reduces the real output response to any aggregate demand shocks. An inspection of the data of the two countries during the recessions shows that a sharp drop in wages in the United States occurred two quarters before it did in Canada.[16] Considering that the recession started a quarter earlier in Canada, there was really a three-quarter lag. The lag between the changes in the two price deflators was about four quarters and, once again, prices adjusted in the United States more quickly than they did in Canada. There is no evidence to suggest why prices and wages adjusted in this way, but certainly the more rapid adjustment in the United States contributed to the more rapid recovery.

What are the lessons to be drawn from comparing the two recessions? First, the greater monetary and fiscal stimulus in the United States appears to have played a role in the more rapid recovery in that economy. Second, the flexibility of wages and prices also seems to have contributed to the United States having a shorter downturn. There are also interesting parallels.

---

[16] T. A. Wilson, ''Lessons of the Recessions,'' *Canadian Journal of Economics* (November, 1985): 693–722.

In particular, for both the United States and Canada, the time it took for prices to adjust enough to counteract a demand shock was less than three years.

FISCAL POLICY CHANGES WITH PREDETERMINED PRICES

- A pure fiscal policy action is not accompanied by a change in the money supply. By analyzing pure fiscal policy actions, the impact of the fiscal policy change alone can be isolated.

- A deficit-financed increase in government spending shifts the *IS* curve to the right. The amount of the shift is equal to the initial net increase in output demand multiplied by the multiplier $1/(1 - MPC)$. The greater the marginal propensity to consume, the larger the change in equilibrium GNP for any initial change in output demand.

- In the predetermined price model, an increase in government deficit spending raises not only output and employment but also the interest rate. The increase in the interest rate reduces private investment.

11.6   AN ANALYSIS OF OTHER FISCAL POLICY ACTIONS

Fiscal policy actions are not limited to deficit-financed increases in government spending. In this section, we will analyze the effects of the other two types of expansionary fiscal policy actions. First, we will examine the effects of a reduction in net taxes with no change in government spending. This reduction in the net taxes can come from either reduced government tax collections or increased transfer payments. Second, we will examine the effects of an increase in government spending accompanied by an equal rise in taxes.

The Impact of a Deficit-Increasing Tax Cut

As usual, we begin by looking at the impact of each fiscal policy change at the original levels of output and prices. Since the process by which output adjusts is similar for each of the three types of fiscal policy changes, the fiscal action that generates the largest initial excess demand in the output market is the one that ultimately has the largest impact on real GNP.

The early 1980s offer a prime example of a deficit-increasing tax reduction. Although the Reagan administration's tax cuts were not supposed to cause increased deficits, the government deficit certainly did increase during this

Figure 11.9   Federal Government Deficits as a Percentage of Total Federal Government Outlays

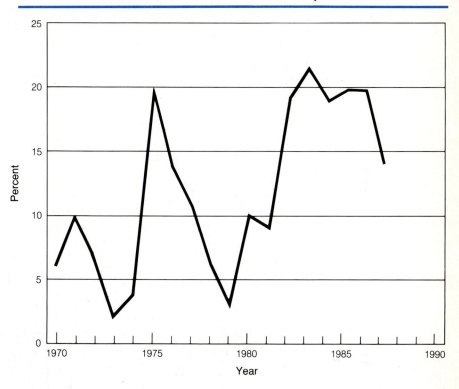

Source: *Economic Report to the President* (various issues).

tax-cutting period. Figure 11.9 shows government deficits as a percentage of government spending from 1970 to 1987. In 1979, the federal government deficit equaled 3.1 percent of total federal government expenditures. By 1983, that had risen to over 20 percent, due in large part to a cut in taxes. Let's focus on the demand-side effects that these tax cuts had. (For an analysis of the potential supply-side effects of the tax cuts, see Chapter 9.)

Figure 11.10 illustrates how a decrease in taxes ($\Delta T < 0$) and an associated increase in government borrowing affects the financial and money markets at the original levels of output and prices. Reduced taxes cause households' real disposable income to increase by $-\Delta T$, which increases desired saving by the increase in real disposable income multiplied by the marginal propensity to save, or $MPS \cdot (-\Delta T)$. Since the marginal propensity to save equals one minus the marginal propensity to consume, another way of expressing the increase in saving induced by the tax cut is that it equals $(1 - MPC) \cdot$

$(-\Delta T)$. The increase in saving shifts the supply of loanable funds curve to the right from LF_0^s to LF_1^s in Figure 11.10(a).[17] Simultaneously, the cut in taxes with no change in government spending leads to an increased government sale of bonds equal to $-\Delta T$. Figure 11.10(a) depicts this by the shift to the right in the demand for loanable funds curve from LF_0^d to LF_1^d.

While the goverment's demand for loanable funds increases by an amount equal to the tax cut, the increase in household saving is but a fraction of the tax cut because the marginal propensity to save is less than one. Thus in Figure 11.10(a), the demand for loanable funds curve shifts further to the right than the supply of loanable funds curve, which causes the equilibrium interest rate to rise from r_0 to r_1. In the money market, there is an excess supply at the higher interest rate, as illustrated by Figure 11.10(b).

Because disposable income increases by an amount equal to the reduction in taxes, household consumption demand increases by an amount equal to the tax cut multiplied by the marginal propensity to consume

$$\Delta C^d = MPC \cdot (-\Delta T)$$

This generates the excess demand in the output market implied by the excess supply of money. The excess demand in the output market falls short of the tax cut for two reasons. First, given a marginal propensity to consume less than one, a \$1 reduction in taxes causes less than a \$1 increase in consumption demand. Second, since the interest rate increases, as we have just seen, consumption and investment demand decrease, which partially offsets the rise in consumption demand caused by the reduction in taxes.

Figure 11.11 illustrates the adjustment in output and the interest rate to restore equilibrium in the output, financial, and money markets. Since at the initial interest rate r_0, consumption demand rises by $MPC \cdot (-\Delta T)$, the IS curve shifts to the right, from IS_0 to IS_1, by this initial change in output demand multiplied by the simple multiplier, or $[1/(1 - MPC)] \cdot [MPC \cdot (-\Delta T)]$. Consequently, the equilibrium interest rate rises from r_0 to r_2 and equilibrium output rises from Y_0 to Y_1.

The Impact of a Tax-Financed Increase in Government Spending

The final type of expansionary fiscal policy action is a tax-financed increase in real government spending ($\Delta G^d = \Delta T > 0$). Figure 11.12 illustrates the impact on the financial and money markets of a tax-financed increase in real government spending at the original level of real GNP and prices. The decreased disposable income that results from the increased taxes causes

---

[17] For simplicity, we assume that tax changes do not affect households' desired real money holdings. Thus the increase in saving resulting from a reduction in taxes consists exclusively of an increase in households' desired purchases of financial assets.

Figure 11.10   The Effect of a Deficit-Increasing Tax Cut on the Financial and Money Markets

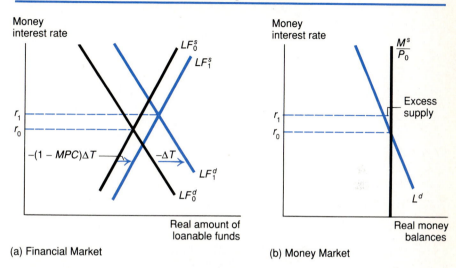

(a) Financial Market   (b) Money Market

A cut in taxes ($\Delta T < 0$) financed by increased government borrowing increases the demand for loanable funds from LF_0^d to LF_1^d in the financial market. At the same time, lower taxes increase real disposable income, causing household saving to rise, as shown by the shift to the right in the supply of loanable funds curve from LF_0^s to LF_1^s. The result is a bidding up of the interest rate from r_0 to r_1. In the money market, the increase in the interest rate reduces the quantity of money demanded, resulting in an excess supply in the money market.

households to reduce not only their consumption spending but also their saving. As Figure 11.12(a) illustrates, this shifts the supply of loanable funds curve to the left from LF_0^s to LF_1^s, which causes the interest rate to increase from r_0 to r_1. This increased interest rate reduces investment and consumption demand. In addition, higher taxes have reduced consumption demand. Nevertheless, the accompanying increase in government spending results in an excess demand in the output market at the original level of output, which corresponds to the excess supply in the money market shown in Figure 11.12(b).

At existing prices, output must rise in order to restore equilibrium in the output, financial, and money markets. In terms of *IS-LM* analysis the *IS* curve will shift to the right. The increase in government spending causes output demand to increase by the amount ΔG^d, while the increase in taxes causes consumption spending to fall by the amount $MPC \cdot \Delta T$. Thus at the original interest rate and output, the net increase in output demand is the amount $(1 - MPC)\Delta G^d$. Consequently, as shown in Figure 11.13, the *IS* curve shifts to the right by the amount $[1/(1 - MPC)] \cdot (1 - MPC)\Delta G^d$, which simply equals ΔG^d.

Figure 11.11   The Effect of a Deficit-increasing Tax Cut on Equilibrium Output and the Interest Rate

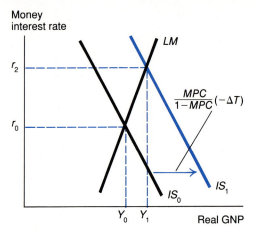

A cut in taxes ($\Delta T < 0$) shifts the *IS* curve to the right by the amount $[MPC/(1 - MPC)] \cdot [-\Delta T]$. Equilibrium in the economy is restored with a rise in the interest rate from r_0 to r_2 and a rise in real GNP from Y_0 to Y_1.

Figure 11.12   The Effect on the Financial and Money Markets of a Tax-financed Increase in Government Spending

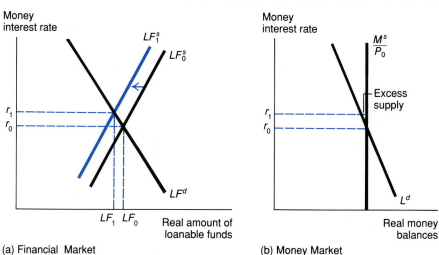

(a) Financial Market   (b) Money Market

A tax-financed increase in government spending causes disposable income and thus household saving to fall. The resultant leftward shift in the supply of loanable funds curve from LF_0^s to LF_1^s in the financial market causes the interest rate to rise from r_0 to r_1. The rise in the interest rate, by reducing the quantity of money demanded, leads to an excess supply in the money market, as shown in part (b).

Figure 11.13   **The Effect of a Tax-Financed Increase in Government Spending on Equilibrium Output and the Interest Rate**

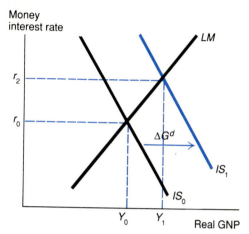

An increase in government spending financed by higher taxes ($\Delta G^d = \Delta T > 0$) shifts the *IS* curve to the right by the amount $[1/(1 - MPC)] \cdot [(1 - MPC)\Delta G^d = \Delta G^d]$. Equilibrium in the economy is restored with a rise in the interest rate from r_0 to r_2 and a rise in real GNP from Y_0 to Y_1.

A Comparison of Fiscal Policy Actions

We have considered three fiscal policy actions: a deficit-financed increase in government spending, a deficit-financed decrease in taxes, and a tax-financed increase in government spending. All three expansionary fiscal policy actions lead to a shift to the right in the *IS* curve. Even if government spending and/or borrowing increase by the same amount in all three cases, however, the three expansionary fiscal policy changes do not all have the same effect on equilibrium output.

The borrowing-financed increase in government spending ($\Delta G^d > 0$) shifts the *IS* curve to the right by the amount $\Delta G^d/(1 - MPC)$. To be concrete, if the increase in government spending is $10 and the marginal propensity to consume is .75, then the *IS* curve will shift to the right by $40.[18]

For a deficit-increasing tax cut ($\Delta T < 0$), the *IS* curve will shift to the right by the amount $-[MPC/(1 - MPC)] \cdot \Delta T$. In our numerical example, a $10 tax cut with a marginal propensity to consume of .75 means the *IS* curve shifts to the right by $30. As we just saw in the preceding section, a tax-financed increase in government spending ($\Delta G^d = \Delta T > 0$) shifts the

---

[18] Note that this $40 amount is measured in "real" or "constant dollars."

IS curve to the right by the amount ΔG^d. In our numerical example, a \$10 increase in government spending financed by increased taxes shifts the *IS* curve to the right by \$10.

There are two interesting implications of the above analysis. First, of the three fiscal policy actions, an increase in government deficit spending leads to the greatest shift to the right in the *IS* curve and thus to the greatest increase in equilibrium income. Second, the relative magnitude of the shift in the *IS* curve for the other two fiscal policy actions depends on the size of the marginal propensity to consume. If the marginal propensity to consume is greater than .5, the *IS* curve will shift further to the right with a deficit-increasing tax cut than with a tax-financed increase in government spending of the same magnitude. If the marginal propensity to consume is less than .5, then the tax financed increase in government spending has the greater impact.

Let's return to our numerical example where the marginal propensity to consume is .75. For a deficit-increasing tax cut of \$10, there is a \$30 shift to the right in the *IS* curve, as opposed to a \$10 shift to the right in the *IS* curve for a tax-financed increase in government spending. If the marginal propensity to consume is less than .5—let's say it is .2—then the situation is reversed. Now a deficit-increasing tax cut of \$10 shifts the *IS* curve to the right by \$2.50 ($-[MPC/(1 - MPC)] \cdot \Delta T$), which is less than the \$10 shift to the right in the *IS* curve for a \$10 tax-financed increase in government spending. The marginal propensity to consume assumes importance whenever tax changes are considered, because it determines by how much the change in taxes directly affects output demand due to altered consumption spending by households.

Temporary Versus Permanent Tax Changes: The Different Effects

When we introduced household consumption behavior in Chapter 6, we discussed the possibility that consumption demand depends on future as well as current income, as the life-cycle and permanent income hypotheses state. According to both hypotheses, consumption depends upon an average of current and future disposable income. This average has been termed households' *permanent income*. A temporary increase in disposable income affects consumption little, since it affects households' permanent income little. It follows that a tax change that households consider to be temporary will not significantly affect consumption demand. In contrast, if households expect a change in taxes to persist for an extended time, it will have a significant effect on consumption demand.

Two temporary tax changes passed within the last 20 years highlight the practical consequences of this discussion. The first involved government spending on the Vietnam War and the Great Society programs of President Johnson, which increased output demand and strained the productive capacity of the economy. In mid-1968, Congress passed a "temporary tax surcharge" of 10 percent intended to restrain demand. A tax surcharge is a tax on taxes. For example, if an individual has been paying $1000 in taxes, the temporary tax surcharge adds an additional $100 to that individual's tax bill. The permanent income hypothesis predicts that this *temporary* decrease in after-tax income will affect consumption little. In reality, the increase in taxes resulting from the 1968 surcharge was met almost completely by a reduction in household saving, and consumption demand hardly fell.

The tax rebate plan of 1975 under the Ford administration serves as a second example of a temporary tax change. Again, since this temporary tax change had little effect on permanent income, it led primarily to an increase in saving and only a small increase in consumption demand. These and other episodes have led economist Alan Blinder to conclude that temporary tax changes have only from 20 to 60 percent of the impact on expenditures of tax changes that are viewed as permanent.[19] Therefore tax changes that are viewed as temporary are likely to be less effective fiscal policy tools than tax changes that are viewed as permanent.

Crowding Out: Factors Affecting Its Importance

By now, it is clear that an expansionary fiscal policy action such as an increase in government spending causes the interest rate to rise. The higher interest rate reduces consumption and investment spending, but not enough to fully offset the increase in government spending. When increased government spending causes spending in the private sector to fall, the fiscal policy action is said to have "crowded out" private spending. To analyze the extent of crowding out, we must look at two factors. The first is the responsiveness of money demand to interest rate changes, for this affects how much the interest rate rises due to the expansionary fiscal policy action. The second is the interest elasticity of investment and consumption demand—that is, how responsive investment and consumption demand are to changes in the interest rate. The more responsive investment and consumption demand are to changes in the interest rate, the more crowding out will occur for a given rise in the interest rate.

Figure 11.14 illustrates how we can use *IS-LM* analysis to show that the magnitude of the crowding out depends on the responsiveness of money demand to a change in the interest rate. If money demand is insensitive to interest rate changes, then the *LM* curve is steep, indicating that a given increase in income requires a large increase in the interest rate to maintain equilibrium in the money market. Figure 11.14(a) depicts a steep *LM* curve. In the extreme case in which money demand does not respond at all to changes in the interest rate, the *LM* curve will be vertical.

---

[19] Alan Blinder, "Temporary Tax Changes and Consumer Spending," *Journal of Political Economy* (February, 1981) pp. 26–53.

Figure 11.14   The Responsiveness of Output to an Increase in Government Spending: The Effect of the Slope of the *LM* Curve

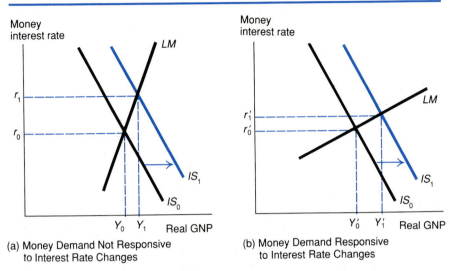

(a) Money Demand Not Responsive
to Interest Rate Changes

(b) Money Demand Responsive
to Interest Rate Changes

The steep *LM* curve in part (a), which indicates that money demand is less sensitive to changes in the interest rate, leads to a large increase in the interest rate and a small increase in output in response to a rise in government spending. Part (b) shows a flatter *LM* curve, which indicates that money demand is more sensitive to changes in the interest rate. In this case, an increase in government spending leads to less of an increase in the interest rate and a greater increase in output. Crowding out is less in this case.

If money demand is sensitive to interest rate changes, the *LM* curve is flatter. This is because a given increase in the interest rate leads to a large fall in the quantity of money demanded, which means that it takes large increases in income to restore equilibrium in the money market. Figure 11.14(b) depicts this flatter *LM* curve.

As you know by now, an expansionary fiscal policy action such as an increase in government spending shifts the *IS* curve to the right. This effect is depicted in Figure 11.14 by the shift in the *IS* curve from IS_0 to IS_1. Comparing both parts of this figure, it is clear that a steeper *LM* curve results in a greater rise in the equilibrium interest rate, as is illustrated by r_0 and r_1 in part (a) and r_0' and r_1' in part (b). It also results in less of an increase in equilibrium output, as is illustrated by Y_0 and Y_1 in part (a) and Y_0' and Y_1' in part (b).

In the extreme case of money demand being completely insensitive to change in the interest rate, the *LM* curve will be vertical and crowding out will be one-for-one, as each $1 increase in government spending leads exactly to a $1 fall in private spending. This extreme assumption has sometimes been attributed to the "classical model," although it is *not* assumed by its modern-day descendant, the neoclassical model. The implications of this extreme assumption can perhaps be more clearly seen by looking at what occurs in the financial and money markets.

Figure 11.15(b) shows the vertical money demand curve that would result if money demand were completely insensitive to changes in the interest rate. Prior to an increase in government deficit spending the financial and money markets are in equilibrium at interest rate r_0. By virtue of the aggregate budget constraint, the output market is also in equilibrium. Equilibrium in the money market is shown in Figure 11.15(b) by a vertical money demand curve that lies on top of the real money supply curve. Note that changes in the interest rate do not lead to an excess demand for or supply of money. This makes intuitive sense because money demand is independent of the interest rate.

Now consider a $10 increase in government deficit spending (that is, $\Delta G^d = \Delta A_g^s = \$10$). In Figure 11.15(a), the increased government borrowing appears as a shift to the right in the demand for loanable funds curve from LF_0^d to LF_1^d by $10. The interest rate rises from r_0 to r_1 to restore equilibrium in the financial market. Since the rise in the interest rate does not affect the quantity of real money demanded, equilibrium still exists in the money market at the higher interest rate and original level of output. From the aggregate budget constraint, we know that if the money market is in equilibrium then the output market is also in equilibrium at the higher interest rate r_1 and original output level Y_0.

In Figure 11.15(a), the complete crowding out that accompanies an increase in government deficit spending is reflected in the adjustment in both the quantity of loanable funds demanded and the quantity supplied to restore equilibrium in the financial market. The rise in the interest rate from r_0 to r_1 reduces the quantity of loanable funds demanded by firms, and hence their investment demand, as shown by the movement up the new demand for loanable funds curve from points A to point C. Suppose that this fall in investment is $7. Since the government's demand for loanable funds increased by $10, this means that the quantity of loanable funds supplied by households must rise by $3 to restore equilibrium in the financial market. This is shown by the movement up the supply of loanable funds curve from point B to point C. The key assumption embodied in the vertical money demand curve is that none of these additional loanable funds supplied by households come from a reduction in desired money holdings. They thus reflect entirely a $3 decrease in consumption demand.

Since the $10 increase in government deficit spending causes a fall in investment and consumption spending exactly equal to the rise in government spending (in our example, a $7 fall in investment and a $3 fall in consumption), output demand is unchanged. Thus if money demand does not respond to changes in the interest rate, there is complete crowding out, as each $1 rise in government spending causes a $1 fall in private spending.

We can also analyze crowding out by using the exchange equation introduced in Chapter 8. According to the exchange equation ($M^s \cdot V = P$

Figure 11.15   The Effect on the Financial and Money Markets of Increased Government Spending if Money Demand is Completely Insensitive to Interest Rate Changes

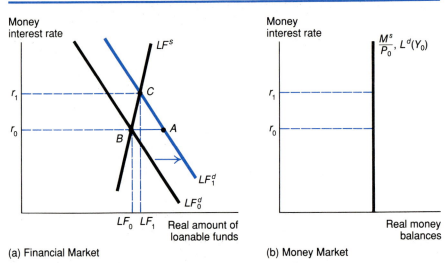

(a) Financial Market   (b) Money Market

An increase in government deficit spending results in a shift to the right in the demand for loanable funds curve, from LF_0^d to LF_1^d, in the financial market, which causes the interest rate to rise from r_0 to r_1. However, since the rise in the interest rate is assumed not to affect real money demand, at the new higher interest rate equilibrium still exists in the money market at the original level of output. Thus the rise in government spending is exactly offset by a fall in investment demand (reflected by the movement from point A to point C along the new demand for loanable funds curve) and consumption demand (reflected by the movement from point B to point C on the supply of loanable funds curve).

$\cdot Y$), given a fixed money supply M^s, fiscal policy only changes nominal income ($P \cdot Y$) to the extent that it affects equilibrium velocity V. Recall from Chapter 8 that an increase in the interest rate causes velocity to rise because such an increase causes real money demand to fall. Thus if money demand is insensitive to changes in interest rates, so too is velocity. In the extreme case where money demand is completely insensitive to changes in the interest rate, velocity is completely unresponsive to interest rate changes. In this case, a pure fiscal action, even though it alters the interest rate, can have no impact on output since velocity is unchanged.

In the 1970s during a notable exchange between James Tobin and Milton Friedman—two Nobel prize winners—Tobin claimed that monetarists such as Friedman view crowding out as complete because they believe the *LM* curve is completely vertical. Friedman responded that he thought the *LM* curve was steep, not completely vertical, but that the shape of the *IS* curve was also important.[20] Although our previous discussion focused on the shape of the *LM* curve, as the Tobin-Friedman debate highlights, our analysis of crowding out should also consider the shape of the *IS* curve.

The more responsive investment and consumption demand are to a change in the interest rate, the flatter is the *IS* curve. As Figure 11.16(a) shows, an increase in government spending shifts the *IS* curve to the right from IS_0 to IS_1. With a fairly flat *IS* curve, however, output changes little. Figure 11.16(b) shows an identical shift to the right in an *IS* curve when investment and consumption demand are not responsive to changes in the interest rate. The *IS* curve is fairly steep, and government spending increases cause less crowding out of private spending. Consequently, although the interest rate changes more, so too does output.

When consumption and investment demand are not very responsive to changes in the interest rate (a steep *IS* curve), the rise in the interest rate induced by expansionary fiscal policy has little impact on investment and consumption demand. In this instance, crowding out is less severe, and fiscal policy changes have a great impact on real GNP.

Crowding Out and the Role of an Accommodating Monetary Policy

Given that an increase in government spending can raise interest rates and result in a fall in private spending, let's now look at how an expansionary monetary policy, by reducing interest rates, can eliminate the crowding out effect. Figure 11.17 illustrates how expansionary fiscal policy (which shifts the *IS* curve to the right from IS_0 to IS_1) can be accommodated by an increase in the money supply (which shifts the *LM* curve to the right from LM_0 to LM_1) so as to eliminate the rise in the interest rate that would accompany the fiscal policy change alone.

In Figure 11.17, we have assumed that the monetary increase is sufficient to maintain a constant interest rate r_0. This figure makes it clear that output increases by a greater amount than it would have if the money supply had not changed. Expansionary fiscal policy now does not increase the interest rate and thus choke off private investment and consumption spending. This explains why advocates of expansionary fiscal policy changes often urge the Federal Reserve to pursue simultaneous increases in the money supply. In contrast, those who oppose accommodating monetary policy in the face of a fiscal policy expansion are concerned that the combined monetary/fiscal stimulus may overheat the economy, setting off a round of inflation. In the early 1980s, as large government deficits coincided with high interest rates,

---

[20] See James Tobin, "Friedman's Theoretical Framework," *Journal of Political Economy* (September/October 1972) p. 852–863, and Milton Friedman, "Comments on the Critics," *Journal of Political Economy* (September/October 1972) p. 906–950.

Figure 11.16   The Responsiveness of Output to an Increase in Government Spending: The Effect of the Slope of the *IS* Curve

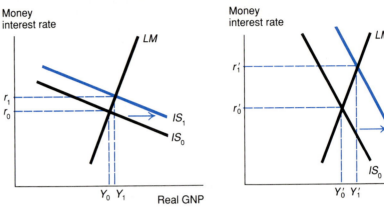

(a) Consumption and Investment
    Responsive to Interest Rate Changes

(b) Consumption and Investment Not
    Responsive to Interest Rate Changes

The flatter *IS* curve in part (a) (which indicates that investment and consumption demand are sensitive to changes in the interest rate) leads to a small increase in output (Y_0 to Y_1) and the interest rate (r_0 to r_1) in response to a rise in government spending that shifts the *IS* curve to the right from IS_0 to IS_1. The steep *IS* curve in part (b) (which indicates that investment and consumption demand are less sensitive to changes in the interest rate) leads to a large increase in output (Y_0' to Y_1') and the interest rate (r_0' to r_1') in response to a rise in government spending.

many called for expansionary monetary policy. Paul Volcker, the chairman of the Federal Reserve at that time, declined to accommodate the deficits with easy money, expressing the concern of rekindling the fires of inflation of the late 1970s and early 1980s.

To the Point

COMPARING FISCAL POLICY EFFECTS

- The extent to which fiscal policy changes shift the *IS* curve is one determinant of the effect of fiscal policy changes on real GNP. A deficit-financed increase in government spending has the greatest impact on the economy, for it leads to the largest shift to the right in the *IS* curve.

- The stimulative effect of a deficit-increasing tax cut versus a tax-financed increase in government spending depends on the value of the marginal propensity to consume. If the marginal propensity to consume (*MPC*) is greater than one half, a deficit-increasing tax cut shifts the *IS* curve to

Figure 11.17 **An Increase in Government Spending with an Accommodating Monetary Policy Change**

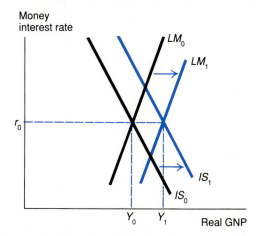

An increase in government spending shifts the *IS* curve to the right from IS_0 to IS_1. An accommodating monetary policy that maintains a constant interest rate increases the money supply, shifting the *LM* curve to the right from LM_0 to LM_1. As a consequence, the crowding out of a fiscal policy change is eliminated, and the increase in real GNP (from Y_0 to Y_1) is greater than it would have been if the money supply had not changed.

the right by the greater amount. The more permanent that a tax change is, the greater will be the change in consumption caused by a change in current disposable income—that is, the greater will be the *MPC*.

- The effect of an expansionary fiscal policy change on real GNP is tempered by the fact that it raises the interest rate. The amount of private spending crowded out increases as money demand becomes less responsive to interest rate changes and as output demand becomes more responsive to interest rate changes. Crowding out is lessened if expansionary fiscal policy is accompanied by an increase in the money supply.

11.7 DISCRETIONARY FISCAL POLICY VERSUS AUTOMATIC STABILIZERS

Discretionary fiscal policy: Changes in fiscal policy initiated at the discretion of government policymakers.

Up until this point we have viewed fiscal policy changes in government purchases and taxes as something that occurs at the discretion of policymakers. Such policy changes constitute what is known as **discretionary fiscal policy**. Often, however, changes in government purchases and taxes occur without any active decision by government officials. For instance, when income increases, so do net taxes. This happens because some taxes, such as income taxes, are computed as a fraction of income. Increased income also raises net taxes because of the resulting fall in transfer payments such as unemployment compensation and welfare payments. (Net taxes are total government tax revenues minus transfer payments. Thus a fall in transfer payments means an increase in net taxes.)

The size of the multiplier decreases when net taxes are directly related to income. A rise in income now causes a smaller change in real disposable income, since net taxes rise too. Consequently, consumption demand changes less with a given change in income.[21] The smaller multiplier means that shocks to the economy that generate excess demands or supplies in the output market result in smaller changes in equilibrium output. Chapter 14, which examines fiscal policy in more detail, formally develops the multiplier when taxes depend on income. As we will see, when net taxes depend directly on income, this is an **automatic stabilizer**—an automatic fiscal policy change that reduces fluctuations in real GNP ("stabilizes the economy") for given changes in autonomous spending. Many economists consider automatic stabilizers to be the first line of defense against fluctuations in demand.

Automatic stabilizer:
An automatic fiscal policy change that partially counters the impact on the economy of changes in autonomous spending.

11.8   THE LONG-RUN EFFECT OF A FISCAL POLICY CHANGE

If prices are predetermined, changes in output demand affect production in the economy. If the economy is initially at full employment, the effect of a change in demand on output is temporary, as price adjustments eventually tend to move the economy back to full employment. If the economy is at less than full employment, expansionary fiscal policy and monetary policy have the potential of speeding the economy's adjustment to full employment by directly increasing demand, as our discussion of the Canadian and U.S. experience of the early 1980s demonstrated. Such policy actions can replace price adjustments as the means by which the economy returns to its natural level of employment and output. In the case of fiscal policy changes, however, there are implications for resource use in the long run. These implications were discussed in our analysis of the neoclassical model in Chapter 8.

Recall from Chapter 8 that in the neoclassical model a fiscal policy change does not affect output, but it does affect the disposition of output. If government increases its real spending, for example, it crowds out an equal amount of

---

[21] For simplicity, we are ignoring how the change in net taxes affects the government budget constraint and thus the government's real demand for loanable funds.

private consumption and investment spending in the long run. The length of the time period before complete crowding out occurs is an open question. In a 1973 study, Gary Fromm and Lawrence Klein simulated government expenditure and tax multipliers for a number of econometric models. They found that "most of the models . . . show . . . multipliers reaching a peak in two or three years and then declining thereafter in fluctuating paths. At the end of five to ten years some of the models show that continued sustained fiscal stimulus has ever increasing *perverse* impacts."[22]

Perverse impacts mean that some long-run multipliers can be negative. In other words, expansionary fiscal policy may reduce output in the long run. This finding is consistent with the predictions of the neoclassical model. Since an expansionary fiscal policy crowds out net investment spending, it may reduce the future capital stock and hence the future productive capacity of the economy.

11.9   A FISCAL POLICY SHOCK IN AN OPEN ECONOMY

The more responsive output demand is to interest rate changes, the smaller is the net effect that an expansionary increase in government deficit spending has on output demand and thus output. As Figure 11.17 illustrated, the more responsive is output demand to changes in the interest rate, the flatter is the *IS* curve, which means that expansionary fiscal policy has little effect in raising output and employment. Considering an open economy means adding net exports as a component of output demand. Since net exports are sensitive to interest rate changes, the *IS* curve is flatter in the open economy than in the closed economy. Thus fiscal policy affects both the interest rate and the level of real GNP less in an open economy. Let's explore why this is so.

In an open economy, the higher interest rate that results from an expansionary fiscal policy causes net international capital inflows to increase—that is, capital inflows rise and capital outflows fall. The resulting increase in the demand for dollars and decrease in the supply of dollars in the foreign exchange market cause the dollar to appreciate. This appreciation of the dollar stimulates imports and reduces exports, which means a fall in net export demand. Thus in the open economy, the increase in the interest rate caused by expansionary fiscal policy leads to a greater offsetting fall in output

---

[22] Gary Fromm and Lawrence Klein, "A Comparison of Eleven Econometric Models of the United States," *The American Economic Review* (May, 1973): 385–393.

demand, so that the net impact on output demand is less. As discussed in Chapter 8, the experience of the mid-1980s demonstrates these effects. Increased deficits and higher interest rates led to a 40 percent appreciation in the price of the dollar, which resulted in a substantial balance of trade deficit, as U.S. imports rose and U.S. exports fell.

The higher income that accompanies expansionary fiscal policy also stimulates imports. Remember from Chapters 7 and 10, however, that the change in income *by itself* does not affect net export demand.[23] The higher imports lead to an increase in the supply of dollars, which by itself would cause the dollar to depreciate. This stimulates exports and reduces imports, so as to leave net exports unchanged. Note that the effect of the higher income on the exchange rate offsets to some extent the effect of the higher interest rate on the exchange rate.

SUMMARY

The neoclassical model's prediction that money is neutral is not consistent with the fact that changes in the money supply appear to affect real economic variables, at least in the short run. The existence of inflexible or sticky prices in the short run, as is assumed by the predetermined price model, does offer an explanation as to why an output adjustment can occur in response to macroeconomic demand shocks, such as a change in the money supply.

In a model with predetermined prices, a reduction in the nominal money supply leads to an increase in the interest rate and consequent reduction in investment and consumption demand. Firms respond to the decrease in demand by reducing output. This begins the multiplier process, which finally ends with the economy back in equilibrium with a decrease in output equal to some multiple of the initial excess supply. In an open economy, the interest rate rises by a smaller amount since capital inflows are responsive to interest rate changes. However, real GNP falls by more since net exports as well as investment and consumption spending respond to the higher interest rate.

The size of the impact of a change in the money supply on output depends on (a) the responsiveness of consumption and investment demand to a change in the interest rate and (b) the responsiveness of money demand to interest rate changes. The more responsive are investment and consumption demand to a change in the interest rate, the larger is the effect of an increase in the money supply and consequent fall in the interest rate on output. In contrast, if money demand is very responsive to a change in the interest

---

[23] When we say "by itself," one item in particular that we are holding constant is international capital flows.

rate, then a change in the money supply will have a small effect on equilibrium output. Naturally, in the long run, when all prices are flexible, output and employment tend to return to their full employment levels, and money supply changes have no real effects.

We know that fiscal policy changes, like monetary policy changes, can alter the position of the aggregate demand curve. In the model with predetermined prices, fiscal policy changes lead to changes in both output and interest rates. Several factors determine the extent to which a fiscal policy change affects equilibrium output. The first is whether the change in fiscal policy is permanent or temporary. If a change—say a tax change—is not perceived as permanent, it will not have much of a stimulative effect on the economy. The second factor is the degree to which private spending is crowded out. Because expansionary fiscal policy raises the interest rate, it can reduce investment and consumption spending, as well as net export demand in an open economy.

If the powers that are changing fiscal policy can convince the monetary authorities to accommodate the change in fiscal policy by increasing the money supply, there will be less of a rise in the interest rate and thus less crowding out. Not all fiscal actions require congressional action. Certain types of fiscal policy changes occur automatically as the economy changes; these are referred to as automatic stabilizers. Finally, as with monetary policy actions, changes in fiscal policy affect output in the short run. Once there is a full adjustment in prices, the economy tends to return to the natural level of output and employment.

LOOKING AHEAD

The neoclassical macroeconomic model does not explain how demand-side factors can lead to changes in output. In this chapter, taking the view of the predetermined price model, we have made an important step in improving our understanding of the potential short-run effects of fiscal and monetary policy changes on output. It is apparent that modifying the neoclassical model to incorporate inflexible prices in the short run leads to quite different policy implications.

Chapter 12 will offer two alternative modifications of the neoclassical model in which demand shocks can lead to changes in *both* output and the price level. The models developed in that chapter are used to analyze the potential for a trade-off between higher inflation and higher unemployment. As with the predetermined price model, common elements of these models include some degree of inflexibility in prices, in particular input prices, and the existence of incomplete information.

KEY TERMS

Rational expectation, 421   Discretionary fiscal policy, 453
Perfect foresight, 421   Automatic stabilizer, 454
Liquidity trap, 428

REVIEW QUESTIONS

1. Explain what is meant when we say that individuals have "rational expectations." Do you think it is sensible to assume such expectations on the part of individuals? Why or why not?

2. Suppose that in the past you have observed that a certain political party has a preference for large levels of government spending. Suppose that someone from this party is elected president. If you now expect that government spending will be increased, do your expectations conform to what we have termed "rational expectations"?

3. "In the model with predetermined prices, unanticipated changes in output demand affect real GNP, but anticipated changes do not." Explain this statement. What does your answer suggest about the effects of fiscal and monetary policy changes?

4. Suppose that the Federal Reserve purchases government securities on the open market. Suppose further that these purchases were not anticipated by agents when setting their prices at the beginning of the period.

   (a) What effect will the Fed's open-market purchases have on the amount of money supplied by depository institutions?

   (b) Show the initial effect of this policy on the financial market. What happens to the interest rate? Is there now an excess demand or supply in the output market?

   (c) What will happen to output? Can you tell what effect this, in turn, will have on the interest rate.

   (d) Use *IS-LM* analysis to determine the effect of the Fed's action on the interest rate and level of real GNP in the economy.

   (e) If money demand is less sensitive to the interest rate, will the *LM* curve be flatter or steeper? Will real GNP increase by a greater or smaller amount?

   (f) If money demand is less sensitive to the interest rate, will the demand by households for financial assets be more or less sensitive, other things (particularly, desired saving by households) being the same. Will the initial impact of the Fed's policy change on the interest rate in the financial market, which was presented in (b), be greater or smaller? Does this help you interpret your result in (e)?

5. If investment demand is more responsive to the interest rate, will the *IS* curve be flatter or steeper? Use *IS-LM* analysis to determine whether the change in real GNP caused by an increase in the money supply will be bigger or smaller. Does this result make intuitive sense? Will an increase in the money supply have a bigger impact on real GNP in an open economy or a closed economy? Why?

6. On November 26, 1984, the *Wall Street Journal* reported that "the latest Fed figures showed that the basic money supply, known as M1, declined by $1.3 billion in the week ending November 12. The Fed estimated M1 averaged a seasonally adjusted $545.5 billion in the latest week, down from $546.7 billion the previous week. That left M1 only $1.1 billion above the lower end of the Fed's target range, which calls for 4 percent to 8 percent growth this year. . . . The Federal Reserve must ease its grip further in order to keep the economy from falling into a recession, bankers and analysts say."

   (a) If the rate of growth of M1 from the beginning to the end of the period is lower than anticipated, what does this imply about the money supply at the end of the period? What does this imply about depository institutions' demand for financial assets?

   (b) Discuss the resulting effects of the Fed's restrictive monetary policy on real GNP and interest rates in the context of the model with predetermined prices.

7. Suppose that the government unexpectedly increases its real spending and finances this by borrowing.

   (a) Show the immediate effect (at the initial price and output level) that this policy has on the financial market. Does the interest rate rise or fall?

   (b) The increase in government spending has a direct effect on output demand, while the increase in the interest rate has an indirect effect on output demand. Is the net effect on output demand positive or negative? According to the model with predetermined prices, what will happen to output demand?

   (c) Use *IS-LM* analysis to show the effect of the change in fiscal policy on the equilibrium interest rate and real GNP.

   (d) What has happened to the velocity of money? Interpret this result with respect to your answer to (c).

8. Consider the increase in real government spending analyzed in Question 7.

   (a) If investment demand is more responsive to the interest rate, will the change in real GNP be greater or smaller? [Hint: Refer to your answer to Question 5.]

   (b) Interpret your result in (a) with respect to the crowding out effect.

   (c) If money demand is less responsive to the interest rate, will the change in real GNP be greater or smaller? [Hint: Refer to your answer to Question 4(e).]

(d) Interpret your result in (c). [Hint: Refer to your answer to Question 4(f).]

(e) If money demand is completely independent of the interest rate, what does the *LM* curve look like? What effect does the increase in government spending have on real GNP? What effect does the increase in real government spending have on velocity in this case? What is true concerning the crowding out effect?

9. In the early 1980s, the Reagan administration enacted a deficit-increasing reduction in taxes.

(a) Suppose that net taxes are reduced by $100 and the marginal propensity to consume is .75. What effect does the reduction in taxes have on consumption demand?

(b) What effect does the reduction in taxes have on desired saving? What effect does it have on the demand for financial assets by households? What happens to the supply of financial assets by the government? Why?

(c) At the original price and output levels, illustrate the effect of the reduction in net taxes on the financial market. Does the interest rate rise or fall? At the original price and output levels, will there be excess supply or demand in the output market? What will happen to output? Why?

(d) In the model with predetermined prices, which type of expansionary fiscal policy will have a bigger impact on real GNP: a borrowing-financed increase in real government spending or a borrowing-financed reduction in real net taxes? Give the reason for your answer.

10. Why will the effect of a change in net taxes likely depend on whether or not individuals think the change is permanent or temporary?

11. The February 10, 1986 *Wall Street Journal* reported that "pending the outcome of an appeal to the Supreme Court, Gramm-Rudman remains in effect. . . . As enacted in December, Gramm-Rudman envisions a balanced budget by 1991 and orders automatic spending cuts if Congress and the president fail to agree on how to meet prescribed deficit targets. . . . If sharp cuts in government spending are going to occur this fall, many economists believe that the Fed must decide to act soon to offset the economic drag caused by tighter budgets."

(a) Illustrate the effect on the financial market of a deficit-reducing cut in government spending.

(b) Is there excess supply or demand in the output demand?

(c) Use *IS-LM* analysis to show the effect of the spending cut on real output and the interest rate.

(d) Indicate the effect that the reduction in government spending has on the following variables: real GNP, employment, unemployment, consumption spending, investment spending, interest rates and the velocity of money.

(e) According to the above quote, the Fed might "decide to act soon to offset the economic drag caused by tighter budgets." To do this will the Fed have to increase or reduce the money supply? Use *IS-LM* analysis to show how, through the appropriate monetary policy, the Fed can offset the effect of the reduced government spending on output.

12. On November 11, 1984, the *Wall Street Journal* reported that "Britain's chancellor of the exchequer, Nigel Lawson, foreshadowed the equivalent of a $1.9 billion in tax cuts next spring, while reaffirming government plans to keep a rein on spending."

(a) Discuss the immediate effects (at the original price and output levels) that the policy change has on the financial market and the output market. (Be sure to mention both direct and indirect effects on output demand.) How do these effects depend on the size of the marginal propensity to consume?

(b) Use aggregate demand-supply analysis to show the effect of the policy change on Britain's real GNP.

(c) What will happen to the price of output over time? Indicate the resulting effect in your diagram to (b). Describe the process by which the economy adjusts to long-run equilibrium.

(d) How do the new long-run equilibrium values of real consumption spending, real investment spending, and real government spending compare with their initial levels?

13. What do we mean by "automatic stabilizers"? Give several examples.

14. Some researchers have found that expenditure and tax multipliers seem to reach a peak in two or three years and then decline. At the end of five years, some multipliers even turn out to be negative. How can you explain these results?

15. According to a recent *Wall Street Journal* article (April 22, 1988), "In January, signs of a weakening economy prompted Chairman [of the Federal Reserve] Greenspan and Vice Chairman Johnson to push through a slight easing of policy, allowing interest rates to _____(fall, rise). [Federal Reserve] Governor Angell, worried by the strong commodity prices, was reluctant to go along."

(a) Assume that Greenspan and Johnson ascribe to the short-run view of the economy suggested by the predetermined price model. Depict graphically the effect of the implied policy change using *IS-LM* analysis. Label your axes.

(b) Compare the new equilibrium situation with what would have existed had there not been the change in the exogenous variable identified in (a). What is predicted with respect to the price level, real GNP, money interest rate, expected real interest rate, velocity, real money demand, household saving, consumption, investment, and consumption plus investment?

Chapter 12

When Input Prices Do Not Fully Adjust: Price-Responsive Aggregate Supply

Up to this point, when we have analyzed macroeconomic shocks we have focused on how responsive prices are to demand changes. At one extreme is the non-market-clearing model, which assumes that prices are predetermined or fixed for the current period and adjust slowly in subsequent periods. At the other extreme is the neoclassical model, which presumes that prices adjust quickly to demand shocks. At first glance, these two views appear to conflict. But they are in fact potentially complementary views of the economy. If output prices are inflexible in the short run, then the non-market-clearing model is appropriate. The neoclassical model, in contrast, considers the long-run outcome of demand shocks when prices fully adjust.

Some economists have criticized the non-market-clearing model as not being completely satisfactory at characterizing the short run. They argue that prices are more flexible than the model suggests. If this is true, then there must be some other explanation for the demand induced, short-run output fluctuations that we observe in the economy. Two modifications of the neoclassical model offer such explanations.

The first modification assumes that while output prices change freely in response to excess demand or supply in the output market, input prices do not. Rather, input prices, such as the money wage, are assumed to be inflexible in the short run. This results in an aggregate supply curve that slopes upward. Thus shifts in the aggregate demand curve lead to adjustments in both output and prices. We examine this modification in the first part of the chapter.

The second modification drops the neoclassical model's assumption that all participants in the economy are completely aware of all changes in prices and/or wages. In particular, sellers of inputs, such as the suppliers of labor, may not be fully aware of changes in output prices. In the second section of this chapter, we see that if workers and other sellers of inputs have incomplete price information, then once again the aggregate supply curve slopes upward and demand shocks lead to changes in both output and prices in the short run.

Several common themes run through both modifications of the neoclassical model. First, as we discuss in the third section of the chapter, both modifications rely on economic agents making errors in their forecast of what output prices will be. With forecasting errors, demand shocks alter relative prices and thus the incentives for production. Both modifications also focus on the short run; in the long run, both modifications revert to the neoclassical model. Finally, both predict an inverse relationship between inflation and unemployment in the short run. This relationship is commonly referred to as the Phillips curve. We present an explanation of the Phillips curve at the end of the chapter and re-examine the potential roles of monetary and fiscal policy as stabilization tools in the context of the Phillips curve.

12.1 THE MODEL WITH INFLEXIBLE INPUT PRICES

In the neoclassical model, output prices adjust to clear the output market. Unlike the non-market-clearing model, firms do not face sales constraints in the output market. Rather, when demand falls, prices fall enough to maintain equilibrium in the output market.

From our discussion in Chapter 10, we know why prices may be inflexible, at least in the short run. While we focused on output prices, some economists argue that the *key* inflexibility lies not in output prices but in input prices. That is, while output prices adjust fairly quickly to demand or supply shocks, input prices are rigid. Below we examine how inflexible input prices affect the labor market and the aggregate supply curve. Keep in mind that there are a number of different inputs in the production process of any firm, and hence a number of different input prices. To keep things simple, we will focus on the labor input, and its price, the money wage.[1] It is primarily

---

[1] Instead of assuming that the wages of all workers are fixed at a point in time, we can assume that workers at the various firms in the economy agree to contracts that come up for renewal at different points in time. An important paper by John Taylor shows that the effects of staggered

through variations in this input that aggregate demand fluctuations lead to changes in production.

The Labor Market and the Aggregate Supply Curve

In light of the discussion above, let's suppose that output prices respond to demand shocks but that money wages are inflexible. Then demand shocks will cause output prices to change relative to wages. For instance, with a fixed money wage, a rise in the price level reduces the real wage while a fall in output prices raises the real wage. Such changes in the relative price of the labor input cause changes in labor demand and thus in employment and output. Since this inflexibility of wages alters the way the economy responds to demand shocks, let's examine why the money wage may be inflexible or "sticky."

Contractual Rigidities and Fixed Money Wages. It is costly to firms when workers quit. Firms invest in their workers by offering substantial amounts of on-the-job training, which often involves learning skills unique to each firm. As a result, firms usually suffer a loss when replacing current workers, because new workers are not as productive.

Not only is it costly to train new workers but it is also costly to hire them. When filling a job vacancy, firms must locate and interview job candidates. Both activities entail some cost and require time. In addition, during the time that a key position is vacant, other workers will generally be less productive.

To minimize hiring and training costs, firms seek long-term relationships with their employees. Firms promote such relationships by offering higher wages to their experienced workers. Long-time employees become attached or "loyal" to their employers since the wages they receive are greater than those that other firms would offer them. In essence, employers are sharing the returns to their investments in hiring and training with their workers in order to reduce quits.[2]

This long-term attachment of workers to particular firms also stems from the high costs to workers of finding alternative employment, as obtaining such employment means that workers must generally interview various employers, visit employment agencies, and spend valuable time simply waiting for decisions on job applications to be made.

---

labor contracts on the aggregate supply curve are like those of fixed wages. John Taylor, "Aggregate Dynamics and Staggered Contracts," *Journal of Political Economy* (February 1980): 1–23.

[2] For further discussions of the long-term relationships between firms and workers in general, and more specifically, of firms' hiring, employment, and wage decisions in the presence of hiring and training costs, see the appendix to Chapter 5 and Section 15.4 in Chapter 15.

Given long-term employment contracts between firms and their workers, wages are typically specified for extended periods of time. These long-term wage agreements are sometimes explicit, as with many labor union contracts.[3] In other cases, only an implicit understanding exists on the wages that a firm will pay its employees over some extended period of time. If these contracts or understandings specify wages in money terms, and if modifying these agreements is costly, then there exists an inherent inflexibility in money wages, which is referred to as **sticky wages**. In the extreme, current money wages could be considered fixed.

Sticky wages: Money wages that do not quickly adjust to changes in labor demand or supply.

As a general rule, labor agreements are specified in money terms. However, there is some evidence that when changes in output prices become substantial and erratic, employment agreements are more likely to be made explicitly in real terms. An example of this is the extensive introduction of cost of living adjustments (COLAs) as part of union wage contracts in the United States during the 1960s and 1970s.

COLAs adjust money wages automatically to changes in prices, typically using changes in the consumer price index to measure price changes. COLA coverage rose from about 25 percent of workers under major collective bargaining agreements in 1967 to its peak of over 60 percent in 1977. It has remained fairly stable since then. However, the percentage of all workers that have contracts with cost of living adjustments is much smaller than this, as less than 20 percent of the total labor force was covered by collective bargaining agreements in 1987. Furthermore, not all COLA clauses offer 100 percent protection against general price increases, as wages may rise by only some percentage of the increase of the CPI. Considering these qualifications, for the time being we simplify by assuming that all labor agreements are specified in money terms.

The Effects of Changes in Output Prices on the Labor Market. As we suggested above, change in prices that result from demand shocks have important effects on the labor market when money wages are inflexible. Let's examine these more closely. Suppose that the labor market initially is in equilibrium at employment level N_0 and real wage W_0/P_0. Now consider a contractionary demand shock that leads to a fall in the price level from the initial price level P_0 to P_1. What happens if the money wage remains fixed at W_0?

Figure 12.1 shows that the new, lower price level raises the real wage from W_0/P_0 to W_0/P_1. The increase in the real wage leads to an increase in the quantity of labor supplied and a decrease in the quantity of labor demanded. Thus as Figure 12.1 indicates, there is a surplus in the labor market at the new higher real wage.

---

[3] The typical union contract runs for three years. Often, however, there are provisions that permit parts of the agreement to be renegotiated at specific times during the three-year contract period.

Figure 12.1   The Effect of a Fall in Output Prices on the Labor Market: A Fixed Money Wage

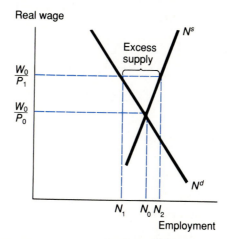

A fall in output prices raises the real wage from W_0/P_0 to W_0/P_1. This rise in the real wage reduces the quantity of labor demanded from N_0 to N_1 and increases the quantity of labor supplied from N_0 to N_2 (the movement up the labor supply curve). At the fixed money wage W_0, demand-determined employment falls from N_0 to N_1 and excess supply exists in the labor market.

If the money wage falls so as to clear the labor market, then the real wage will not change and employment will remain unchanged. But we are assuming a resistance to reductions in wages due to the presence of long-term employment agreements. Thus at the existing fixed money wage, employment falls to N_1. Excess supply exists in the labor market and employment is determined by labor demand alone.

The early 1980s offer some support for this view of the labor market. High inflation in 1979 and 1980 led many workers to negotiate long-term agreements that specified rising money wages to offset anticipated high rates of inflation. However, the Federal Reserve pursued an unexpectedly restrictive monetary policy that abruptly slowed the rate of inflation from 13 percent in 1980 to 3.5 percent in 1982. With the previously negotiated high money wages, some workers had higher real wages, but there were fewer jobs. Unemployment rose from 7.2 percent in 1980 to 10.8 percent in 1982.

The Shape of the Aggregate Supply Curve. Figure 12.2 depicts the aggregate supply curve when money wages are fixed. This curve slopes upward: A lower price level is associated with a lower level of real GNP. Why is this so? Remember that the aggregate supply curve summarizes behavior in the labor market. As we have just discussed, a fixed money wage means that employment is determined by labor demand. An unanticipated

Figure 12.2   **The Aggregate Supply Curve Given Fixed Money Wages**

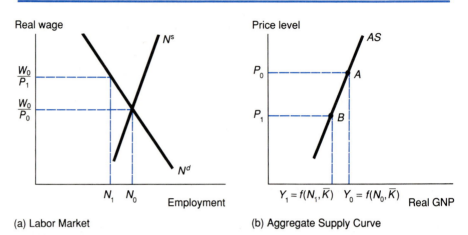

(a) Labor Market   (b) Aggregate Supply Curve

With a fixed money wage in the labor market (part a), a decrease in the price level from P_0 to P_1 reduces employment from N_0 to N_1. With the fall in employment, real output falls from Y_0 to Y_1, as shown by the movement down the aggregate supply curve from point A to point B. This direct relationship between the price level and real GNP is summarized in part b by the upward-sloping aggregate supply curve AS.

decrease in prices, by raising the real wage, leads to a lower quantity of labor demanded and thus decreased employment and output. Conversely, an unanticipated increase in prices will lower the real wage, increase the quantity of labor demanded, and thus lead to increased employment and output.[4]

Figure 12.2 shows initial equilibrium in the labor market at the real wage W_0/P_0 and employment N_0. Associated with this level of employment is real output Y_0. The price-output combination (P_0, Y_0) is point A on the aggregate supply curve in Figure 12.2(b). We have just demonstrated that with a fixed money wage, a decrease in the price level from P_0 to P_1 reduces employment from N_0 to N_1. Associated with this decrease in employment is a decrease in output from Y_0 to Y_1, as shown by the movement down the aggregate supply curve from point A to point B.

We should make two points concerning our analysis. First, we have focused on the labor input and fixed money wages. Yet, an upward-sloping aggregate supply curve results if the prices of any of a variety of inputs are fixed, not just the labor input. Second, while we have assumed a fixed money wage, all that is necessary for an upward-sloping aggregate supply

---

[4] This analysis presumes employers can satisfy any increase in the quantity of labor demanded from the available labor supply.

curve is that the money wage be less flexible than output prices. The key element behind the upward-sloping aggregate supply curve is that a change in output prices alters the relative prices of some input or inputs. It is the changes in relative input prices that lead to the positive relationship between output prices and production that the upward-sloping aggregate supply curve summarizes. An example will illustrate this point.

Suppose that you own a firm producing one-piece bathing suits. You read an article in the *Wall Street Journal* in which the experts predict that output demand in general will be strong next year. (Your belief that the demand for your product will be high is further bolstered by a psychic's prediction in the *National Enquirer* that the weather next year will be scorching and by an article in *Cosmopolitan* that one-piece suits will be in.) In anticipation of a high price for one-piece bathing suits, you contract with your cloth and labor suppliers for high fixed nominal payments. But the experts turn out to be wrong. The high output demand and output prices that they predicted do not materialize. With the low price you are able to obtain for your product, you go to your suppliers and workers and plead for reductions in the prices you must pay them. But they ask that you live up to your contract, whereupon you curtail production, and lay off workers. Other firms, faced with the same problem, behave similarly. The lower price level has lead to a reduction in output.

In summary, an inflexibility in the adjustment of input prices results in a direct relationship between changes in the price level and changes in employment and real GNP. Having derived and interpreted the aggregate supply curve given inflexible input prices, let's re-examine the effects of shifts in the aggregate demand curve.

The Response of Price and Output to a Demand Shock

Although the effect of a macroeconomic demand shock on the aggregate demand curve is the same in the model with fixed money wages as in our earlier analyses, the new equilibrium that emerges after the demand shock is not. Since the aggregate supply curve now slopes upward, a shift in the aggregate demand curve affects *both* prices and output. We now describe the process by which the economy adjusts to a macroeconomic demand shock when some input prices, specifically money wages, are inflexible. For variety, we take a change in autonomous consumption as our macroeconomic shock.

The Impact of a Fall in Autonomous Consumption. Many economists believe that a fall in autonomous consumption demand was an important factor contributing to the Great Depression. From the household budget constraint, we know that a fall in autonomous consumption implies an equivalent increase in saving. This increase in saving can take the form of either increased desired money holdings or increased desired holdings of financial assets.

Let's suppose that the rise in saving consists entirely of an increase in money demand. This, in fact, happened during the Depression, as consumers cut consumption demand and increased their saving by stuffing money in their mattresses. As a result of the concerns raised by the collapse of the stock market at the start of the Great Depression, households' increase in saving did not take the form of additional purchases of stocks and bonds.[5]

Figure 12.3 illustrates the impact on the financial and money markets of the fall in consumption and increase in money demand at the initial levels of prices and real GNP. As part (a) indicates, there is no impact on the financial market. This reflects the fact that the increase in saving consists entirely of an increase in money demand, so that the supply of loanable funds is unaffected. However, in the money market the increase in the demand for money balances from L_0^d to L_1^d leads to an excess demand for money, as show in part (b).

Since the financial market is in equilibrium, we know from the aggregate budget constraint that the excess demand for money implies an excess supply of output at the original level of prices and output. This excess supply of output should be expected since it simply reflects the fall in household consumption demand.

The Effect on Real GNP and Prices. The creation of an excess supply in the output market at the original output and level of prices means that the aggregate demand curve shifts down and to the left. In the neoclassical model, this shift in the aggregate demand curve causes a movement down the vertical aggregate supply curve. Only prices and wages fall; real GNP remains the same. In contrast, in the non-market-clearing model with pre-determined prices the shift in the aggregate demand curve causes only a fall in real GNP. What happens, however, if output prices can vary but input prices are fixed?

Figure 12.4 shows the effect of the reduction in aggregate demand on real GNP and the price level when money wages are rigid. In this case, since the aggregate supply curve is upward-sloping, the shift to the left in the aggregate demand curve from AD_0 to AD_1 results in both a lower price level and a lower output level. The reduction in aggregate demand causes the price level to fall from P_0 to P_1 and real GNP to fall from Y_0 to Y_1.

The movement down the aggregate supply curve to the lower equilibrium levels of prices and real GNP depicted in Figure 12.4 can be described as follows. The excess supply in the output market causes producers to lower prices. With inflexible wages and other input prices, this fall in output prices raises the relative prices of inputs. Firms now find it less profitable to produce.

---

[5] Alexander J. Field, "Asset Exchanges and the Transaction Demand for Money: 1919–1929," *American Economic Review*, vol. 74 (March 1984): 43–59.

Figure 12.3   **The Effect of a Shift from Consumption Demand
to Money Demand on the Financial and
Money Markets**

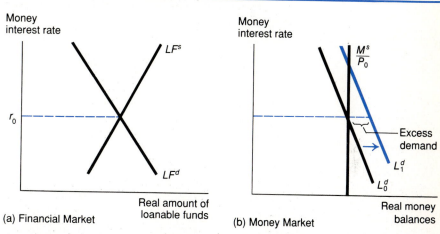

(a) Financial Market

(b) Money Market

A reduction in autonomous consumption has no impact on the financial market (part
a) if the increase in saving consists entirely of an increase in desired money holdings.
The increase in money demand from L_0^d to L_1^d (part b) leads to an excess demand
for money at the original price level and output.

Figure 12.4   **The Effect of a Fall in Aggregate Demand on Output
and Prices**

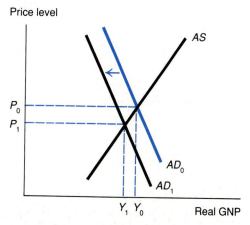

A fall in autonomous consumption demand leads to an excess supply exist in the
output market at the original price level P_0 and real GNP, Y_0. The aggregate demand
curve thus shifts to the left from AD_0 to AD_1. Employment and output fall, and the
new equilibrium is at the lower price level P_1 and real GNP Y_1. As the economy
moves down the aggregate supply curve, the combination of falling output prices
and inflexible wages leads to a rise in the relative price of labor, and thus a reduction
in the quantity of labor demanded, employment, and thus real GNP.

In the labor market, the fall in the quantity of labor demand and resulting excess supply of labor that accompany the higher real wage does not lead to a reduction in money wages since employees have previously entered into long-term agreements that specify given money payments. Thus employment and real GNP fall.

The Long-Run View: A Vertical Aggregate Supply Curve

Even though fixed money wages are critical to the preceding analysis, we know that money wages are not fixed forever. Over time, labor agreements are renegotiated, and money wages change to once again equate the demand for and supply of labor. In the long run, therefore, the economy behaves as neoclassical analysis predicts; money wages and output prices adjust to restore equilibrium to the various markets in the economy.

Thus although in the *short run* the aggregate supply curve slopes upward due to inflexible wages, in the *long run* the aggregate supply curve is vertical at the full employment level of real GNP. Figure 12.5 depicts the short-run upward-sloping aggregate supply curve and the long-run (neoclassical) aggregate supply curves in order to show the short-run and long-run responses to a reduction in aggregate demand.

Figure 12.5 assumes that prior to the fall in aggregate demand, the economy is at full employment at real GNP Y^* and price level P_0. After the fall in aggregate demand, the economy reaches a new, *temporary* equilibrium at the lower output Y_1 and output prices P_1 shown by point B. Real GNP is below its full employment level and unemployment is above the natural rate. In the labor market, the money wage has not yet adjusted to the fall in quantity of labor demanded caused by the lower output prices.

Over time, the pressure of excess supply in the labor market causes workers to renegotiate money wages downward. Even union contracts that typically run for three years often allow for some of their provisions to be renegotiated during the three-year contract period. Examples include the United Auto Workers (UAW) and the United Rubber Workers (URW) who renegotiated contracts in 1982 to provide for wage givebacks. The extensive unemployment that union members had experienced provided the impetus for these contract revisions.

The fall in nominal wages relative to prices causes the real wage to fall, which leads to an increase in the amount of labor that firms demand, and thus increased employment and output and lower unemployment. The expanding output lowers output prices since a marginal propensity to consume of less than one means that output demand increases by a smaller amount than output. These changes appear in Figure 12.5 as a downward movement along the new aggregate demand curve AD_1 from point B to point C. This can be viewed as a shifting to the right of the short run aggregate supply curve.

The adjustment process ends when the money wage falls just sufficiently to eliminate excess supply in the labor market, restoring employment to the

Figure 12.5   **The Effect of a Decrease in Aggregate Demand on Output and Prices: The Short Run versus the Long Run**

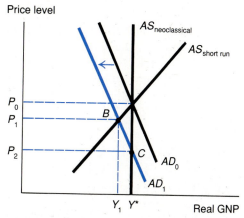

In the short run, a fall in aggregate demand from AD_0 to AD_1 leads both to a fall in price level from P_0 to P_1 and a fall in real GNP from Y^* to Y_1. Over time, as input prices ultimately adjust downward, the price level falls to P_2 and real GNP returns to its full employment level, Y^*.

full employment level. At this time, the money wage stops falling (relative to output prices) and employment and output stop rising. We are now at the intersection of the new aggregate demand curve AD_1 and the long-run (neoclassical) aggregate supply curve in Figure 12.5. Output returns to its original level Y^*, while the new, long-run equilibrium price level is P_2. Although the new money wage is lower, the real wage exactly matches the one that existed before the fall in aggregate demand.[6]

To the Point

MACROECONOMIC ANALYSIS WITH INFLEXIBLE WAGES

- Because it is costly for workers to quit and look for new employment, and because it is also costly for employers to search for new employees, workers and employers often enter long-term employment agreements and specify money wages for an extended period of time.

- If there is a fall in output prices below that expected and if money wages

---

[6] We can draw an important conclusion from the analysis in this section: When output prices fall below individuals' prior expectations, unemployment temporarily rises. This relationship between prices and unemployment is illustrated by what has become known as the Phillips curve. We investigate the Phillips curve later in the chapter.

are inflexible, the real wage rises, employment falls, and unemployment rises. There is excess supply in the labor market. With the fall in employment, real GNP falls. Thus prices and output move together. This is shown by a upward-sloping aggregate supply curve.

- Over time, the excess supply in the labor market will lead to a downward adjustment in money wages. In the long run, money wages are flexible and the aggregate supply curve is vertical at the full employment level of real GNP. That is, in the long run we return to the neoclassical aggregate supply curve.

12.2   THE MODEL WITH INCOMPLETE INFORMATION ON THE PART OF SELLERS OF INPUTS

An alternative modification of the neoclassical model that also arrives at an upward-sloping aggregate supply curve is one that introduces incomplete information on the part of some market participants. Even though both input and output prices are assumed flexible in this modified model, macroeconomic demand shocks still lead to simultaneous changes in real GNP and prices, as incomplete information leads some individuals to mistakenly view changes in *money* prices as reflecting changes in *relative* prices.

The Labor Market and the Aggregate Supply Curve

The introduction of sticky wages represents one departure from the neoclassical model. A second departure is to maintain flexible wages but to assume that workers do not fully anticipate changes in output prices. Let's consider the justification for this assumption.

Incomplete Information on the Part of Workers. In order to determine the real wage relevant for its labor demand decision, a firm must only know the money wage and the output price of the *particular* product that it produces. If the firm produces cars and if the firm does not face a sales constraint, then its labor demand depends on the money wage and the money price of cars. If the firm produces toilet paper, its labor demand depends on the money wage and the money price of toilet paper. In both cases, in order to know how many workers to hire, the firm needs to know only the money wage and the price of the good that it produces. These two prices completely determine the real wage that is *relevant* for the firm. Even for firms that produce a number of different products, the manager in charge of each division typically has good information about the particular prices that are relevant—indeed, that is an important part of the manager's job.

Sellers of inputs, however, typically require more information to make their supply decisions and often have less time to acquire this information. For example, workers attempting to determine the real wage appropriate for their labor supply decisions must know not only the money wage but also the prices of all of the different goods they plan to purchase over the period.[7] The money prices of cars, toilet paper, snack foods, chewing tobacco, and a host of other commodities enter into the determination of the worker's real wage. Thus in order to determine their *relevant* real wage, workers require information on the general level of output prices.

Since the information on prices required by a firm to ascertain the relevant real wage for its employment decision is less than the information required by workers to ascertain the relevant real wage for their employment decisions, workers are more likely than firms to possess **incomplete information** on prices. Note that this simply means that there is an asymmetry in the information requirements of firms and workers. It does not suggest that firms are more informed than workers about general economic conditions, only that they require less information to make their relevant decisions.

Incomplete information: Information that is not complete regarding actual changes in prices.

The Effects of Changes in Output Prices on the Labor Market. In our previous analysis of the labor market, we plotted labor supply and demand against the real wage. To analyze the effects of incomplete price information on the part of workers, however, we must work with the money wage instead of the real wage. The reason for this is that there is no longer a unique relationship between the real wage and the quantity of labor supplied. That is, while either a rise in the money wage or a fall in output prices implies a higher real wage, the response in the quantity of labor supplied can differ depending on what led to the higher real wage. If the rise in the real wage is due to higher money wage, then, as expected, there will be an increase in the quantity of labor supply. In contrast, a rise in the real wage due to a fall in the price level can leave labor supply unchanged if the price change is not anticipated by workers.

In light of the above discussion, our graphical analysis of the labor market will plot the money wage rather than the real wage on the vertical axis. Since an increase in the money wage means an equivalent increase in the real wage, the labor demand curve still slopes downward and the labor supply curve still slopes upward. For a change in the price level, however, the graphical analysis is different. Since an increase (decrease) in the price level reduces (raises) the real wage for a given money wage, the effect is represented by a leftward (rightward) shift of the labor demand curve. And if workers anticipate the increase (decrease) in the price level, there will be

---

[7] As we discussed in Chapter 7, the information problem is made particularly difficult because firms and workers must agree on a labor contract at the beginning of the production period while output prices are not realized until the end of the period.

a rightward (leftward) shift in the labor supply curve. Of course, if workers do not anticipate the change in the price level, then they will not realize the change in the real wage and the labor supply curve will not shift.

Figure 12.6 depicts equilibrium in the labor market at the money wage W_0 and employment N_0. Consider now the impact of lower output prices that are anticipated by firms but not by workers. With lower prices, each firm knows that at the existing money wage, real wages have risen. In Figure 12.6, the shift to the left in the labor demand curve from N_0^d to N_1^d reflects the decrease in labor demand in response to the rise in real wages.

As a result of their more extensive information requirements, workers may not immediately realize the extent of the decrease in output prices and the consequent rise in their real wage. We can simplify our analysis by assuming that workers anticipate none of the decrease in the level of output prices—that is, they believe that output prices will remain the same. Since at a given money wage workers do not perceive any change in the real wage, the labor supply curve does not shift in Figure 12.6.

According to Figure 12.6, when firms but not workers anticipate the decrease in output prices, the equilibrium money wage falls, as does equilibrium employment (as is shown by the new equilibrium money wage W_1 and the new equilibrium employment level N_1). The real wage increases since the fall in the money wage does not fully offset the decrease in output prices.[8] The higher real wage explains why firms' labor demand is lower.

But why is the quantity of labor supplied lower despite the higher real wage? Workers have observed a fall in money wages and, coupled with their misperception that output prices are unchanged, they believe real wages are lower. Workers incorrectly view the fall in the money wage as representing a fall in the real wage. This is the important effect of incomplete information.

The converse occurs if output prices increase. The real wage will fall and labor demand will increase. The increase in the demand for labor will lead to a bidding up of the money wage, but not by an amount sufficient to leave the real wage unchanged. In fact, at the new equilibrium money wage the real wage will be lower, which explains why firms hire more labor at the new equilibrium. Workers supply more labor since they believe the higher money wage implies a higher real wage. Workers' incomplete information on the rise in output prices is critical if the real wage is to fall and if employment is to increase. This point was noted some time ago by the classical economist Arthur C. Pigou, who stated the following:

> If a workman realizes that the raising of prices through inflation is going to hit him he will normally ask for an increase in money wages corresponding to the rise in prices, and you only will get your decrease in

---

[8] If workers were fully aware of the reduction in output prices, then their labor supply curve shifts to the right and the nominal wage falls sufficiently so that at the new equilibrium, the real wage and employment will be unchanged.

Figure 12.6   **The Effect of a Decrease in Output Prices on the Labor Market When Workers Have Increased Information**

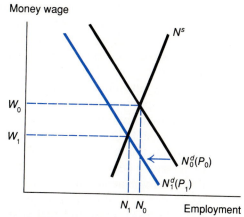

A fall in output prices shifts the demand for labor curve to the left from N_0^d to N_1^d as firms recognize the resulting increase in the real wage. If workers do not anticipate the lower output prices, the labor supply curve does not shift. Thus the equilibrium money wage and employment fall.

real wages if, when you bring about those price rises by inflation and all the rest of it, you somehow prevent the workman from asking for a corresponding rise in his money wage."[9]

The Shape of the Aggregate Supply Curve. Earlier we saw that the introduction of rigid wages generates an upward-sloping aggregate supply curve. The existence of incomplete information can also explain an aggregate supply curve that slopes upward, as a rise in output prices increases employment and thus output, while a fall in output prices reduces employment and output. The aggregate supply curve slopes upward because individuals are mistaken in their view of how relative prices have changed. For instance, labor suppliers mistakenly view a rise in money wages as implying higher real wages, not fully taking into account the coincident rise in prices. As a consequence, higher money wages induced by higher prices result in increased employment and output—thus the upwardly sloping aggregate supply curve. Let's now see how the economy adjusts to a demand shock when workers have incomplete information on prices.

---

[9] Arthur C. Pigou, as cited in Stephen Nickell, "A Historical Perspective on Unemployment: A Review Article," *Journal of Political Economy* (1987): 858.

The Response of Price and Output to a Demand Shock

Although we have already discussed how the economy adjusts to a macroeconomic demand shock when the aggregate supply curve slopes upward, we go through it again here for one major reason. The nature of the adjustment is somewhat different when it is incomplete information on the part of workers that causes the aggregate supply curve to slope upward.

Suppose that the economy is in equilibrium at some output, interest rate, and level of prices. Suppose, too, that workers are initially fully informed about output prices. Given flexible output prices and wages, equilibrium is at full employment. Now suppose that the Fed decreases the money supply. We know from our previous analysis that this causes the aggregate demand curve to shift to the left, as there is now an excess supply in the output market at the original price level P_0 and level of real GNP Y_0. Given the fall in aggregate demand, a reduction in either the price level or real GNP could restore simultaneous equilibrium to the output, financial, and money markets. As Figure 12.7 illustrates, with an upward-sloping aggregate supply curve, both the price level and real GNP fall to restore equilibrium at output Y_1 and price level P_1.

Figure 12.8 shows the effect that this reduction in output prices has on the labor market. Falling output prices raise the real wage and thus reduce the demand for labor. The fall in labor demand lowers the equilibrium money wage from W_0 to W_1. Workers observe the fall in money wages but do not anticipate the accompanying fall in output prices. As a result, they believe that the real wage has fallen, and reduce the quantity of labor supplied, as shown by the movement down the labor supply curve from point A to point B. At the new lower money wage that clears the labor market, employment is thus lower. Although suppliers of labor believe the opposite, the new real wage is higher.

We started our analysis with the economy at full employment. Reducing the money supply has led to a new level of real GNP below the full employment level and to unemployment above the natural rate. In contrast, if aggregate demand increases real GNP and prices will rise. Starting again from the full employment level of output, equilibrium output will rise above the full employment level and unemployment will fall below the natural rate. The question we now turn to is whether either of these situations persist over time.

The Long-Run View: A Vertical Aggregate Supply Curve

Our analysis assumes that workers mistake changes in money wages for changes in real wages. It is unlikely, however, that workers will continue to make such mistakes over an extended period of time. This suggests that the effects of a demand shock on output will be short-lived. Figure 12.9

Figure 12.7   **The Effect of a Decrease in Aggregate Demand
on Output and Prices**

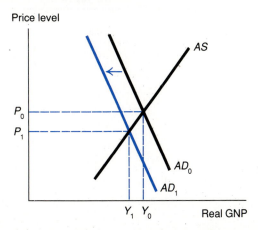

A fall in aggregate demand, as shown by the shift to the left in the aggregate demand curve from AD_0 to AD_1, results in both a fall in real GNP from Y_0 to Y_1 and a fall in the level of prices from P_0 to P_1.

Figure 12.8   **The Effect of a Decrease in Aggregate Demand on
the Labor Market When Workers Have Incomplete
Information on Prices**

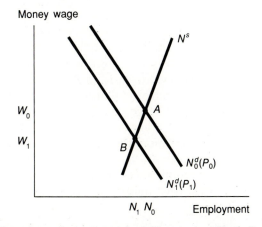

With a fall in output prices, the demand for labor curve shifts to the left from N_0^d to N_1^d as firms recognize the resulting increase in the real wage. If workers do not perceive the lower output prices, the labor supply curve does not shift. Thus the equilibrium money wage falls from W_0 to W_1 and employment falls from N_0 to N_1. The equilibrium real wage rises, although workers believe that the opposite is true.

Figure 12.9   The Effect of a Decrease in Aggregate Demand on Output and Prices: The Short Run versus the Long Run

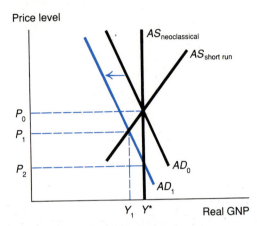

In the short run, a fall in aggregate demand from AD_0 to AD_1 results in a movement down the short-run aggregate supply curve, leading to both lower prices (the level of output prices falls from P_0 to P_1) and reduced output (real GNP falls from Y^* to Y_1). Over time, workers correctly perceive the lower output prices, labor supply rises, and the money wage is bid down. This causes firms to increase employment and output. Ultimately, output returns to its full employment level Y^* and the price level falls to P_2.

compares the short-run and long-run effects of a decrease in aggregate demand. In the short run, when incomplete information causes the aggregate supply curve to slope upward, a fall in aggregate demand causes both a fall in the price level from P_0 to P_1 and a fall in real GNP from Y^* to Y_1.[10] Over time, workers realize that output prices are below what they anticipated, and that the real wage has therefore risen. As a result, they will supply more labor at any money wage and labor supply will increase. This increase in labor supply causes the wage rate to fall, inducing firms to increase their employment and expand production. Since workers eventually perceive the actual level of output prices, the long-run (neoclassical) aggregate supply curve is vertical; real GNP returns to its full employment level Y^* and the price level falls to P_2.

---

[10] We can draw an important conclusion from the analysis in this section: When output prices fall below individuals' initial expectations, unemployment temporarily rises. This relationship between prices and unemployment is illustrated by what has become known as the "Phillips curve," to be discussed later in the chapter.

To the Point

MACROECONOMIC ANALYSIS WITH IMPERFECT INFORMATION

- If workers are not fully aware of a change in prices, then they can mistake a change in the money wage as indicating a change in the real wage. An unanticipated rise in the price level that leads to an increase in labor demand and consequent higher money wage will then induce a rise in both the quantity of labor supplied and employment. An unanticipated lower price level will result in a fall in the quantity of labor supplied, as workers mistake the accompanying lower money wage as implying a lower real wage.

- Incomplete information concerning price changes on the part of workers results in an upward-sloping aggregate supply curve in the short run, meaning that a macroeconomic demand shock affects both prices and real GNP.

- Over time, workers become aware of the actual level of output prices. In the long run, this leads to an adjustment in the supply of labor, money wages, and the price level such that the economy returns to the full employment level of GNP. In the long run, the aggregate supply curve is vertical at the full employment level of real GNP.

12.3 COMMON ELEMENTS OF THE TWO MODIFICATIONS OF THE NEOCLASSICAL MODEL

We have examined two alternative modifications of the neoclassical model that allow for simultaneous changes in both real GNP and prices in response to a macroeconomic demand shock. The first modification introduced rigidities with respect to input prices such as money wages. The second modification assumed that workers have incomplete information on output prices and thus mistake changes in money wages for changes in real wages.

In these two modifications, macroeconomic demand shocks lead to changes in output for somewhat different reasons. In both models, a reduction in output demand causes output prices to fall. When there are fixed money wages, this reduction in output prices results in a higher real wage, a fall in labor demand, and excess supply in the labor market. When workers have incomplete information on output prices, however, the reduction in output prices leads to a fall in employment because workers mistake the consequent fall in the nominal wage as a fall in the real wage and thus supply less labor. In contrast to the sticky wage model, the market clears in the case of incomplete information, albeit at a reduced employment level.

Despite their differences, the two modifications of the neoclassical model do have several important common elements. First, both predict that a macroeconomic demand shock *ultimately* affects only the level of prices. In other words, in both modifications the aggregate supply curve slopes upward only in the short run. In the long run, the aggregate supply curve is the vertical one of neoclassical analysis.

Two other elements that the models have in common may not be so apparent. First, both models share an element of wage inflexibility. Whether wages are fixed or workers' information on prices is incomplete, nominal wages are less flexible than output prices in the short run. Thus although only the first modification of the neoclassical model explicitly assumes that nominal wages are inflexible, they turn out to be "sticky" in the second modification as well.[11]

Also common to the two models is the existence of incomplete information. The second modification of the neoclassical model explicitly assumes that workers have incomplete information on output prices. To see the role that incomplete information plays in the model that assumes sticky wages, note that in this model, the fixed money wage turns out to be inconsistent with equilibrium in the labor market given a macroeconomic shock. This means that at the time the wage agreements were made, workers and firms had incomplete information on the appropriate money wage. In this sense, both analyses assume either explicitly or implicitly that errors occur in forecasting the level of output prices in the current period.

12.4   A TEMPORARY TRADE-OFF BETWEEN UNEMPLOYMENT AND INFLATION

Phillips curve: A curve depicting the relationship between inflation and unemployment.

We may interpret the predictions derived from an upward-sloping aggregate supply curve as supportive of a *short-run* relationship between inflation and unemployment. This relationship is referred to as the **Phillips curve**, named after A. W. Phillips, who noted the empirical relationship between wage inflation and unemployment for the British economy for the 100 years up to 1957.[12] Later depictions of the Phillips curve replaced the rate of change in wages with the inflation rate. Figure 12.10 depicts a Phillips curve.

Let's see how the modifications of the neoclassical model introduced in this chapter can explain the short-run inverse relationship between the inflation

[11] See Mark Gertler, "Imperfect Information and Wage Inertia in the Business Cycle," *Journal of Political Economy* (October 1982). The author makes this point when he notes that "temporary wage inflexibility" can arise in a model with incomplete information in which "agents cannot disentangle permanent versus transitory movements in key state variables." (p. 967)

[12] See A. W. Phillips, "The Relation Between Unemployment and the Rate of Change of Money Wage Rates in the U.K., 1861–1957," *Economica* (November 1958): 283–299.

Figure 12.10   A Short-run Phillips Curve

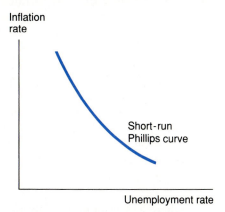

A short-run Phillips curve plots the potential trade-off between unemployment and inflation. The lower the unemployment rate, the greater the inflation rate.

rate (π) and the unemployment rate (U) indicated by the Phillips curve. Remember that the rate of inflation is simply the rate of change in price level. In other words, letting P denote the current price level and letting $\overline{P}$ denote the price level in the previous period, the actual rate of inflation is defined as $\pi = (P - \overline{P})/\overline{P}$. As we have seen, an upward sloping aggregate supply curve means that an increase in aggregate demand results not only in a higher price level P, and thus a higher inflation rate π, but also a rise in real GNP and thus a lower level of unemployment. Conversely, a decrease in aggregate demand leads to a lower price level and thus reduced inflation, at the same time that real GNP falls and thus unemployment rises.

If we consider more closely our analysis of what underlies an upward sloping aggregate supply curve, we can relate the short-run Phillips curve relationship to differences between the rate of change in the price level that individuals had expected for the current period (π_c^e) and the actual inflation rate (π).[13] Consider, for instance, an increase in aggregate demand that leads to a higher current price level, P, and thus a greater rate of inflation, π. If this higher price level had not been anticipated, actual inflation will exceed what had been expected for the current period ($\pi > \pi_c^e$). The result is that wages will not fully reflect the higher prices, the real wage will fall, employment will rise, and real GNP will be above its fully-employment level. Expressed

---

[13] Note that you should be careful to recognize the distinction between π_c^e, the inflation rate that had been expected for the current period, and π^e, the inflation rate expected in the future. As we have seen, it is expected future inflation (π^e) that enters into the determination of the expected real rate of interest ($r - \pi^e$) and affects households' decisions to consume rather than save and firms' decisions to invest in capital goods.

differently, if actual inflation exceeds expected inflation, then unemployment will fall below the natural rate ($U < U_n$).

In contrast, a decrease in aggregate demand that leads to an actual rate of inflation less than what had been expected ($\pi < \pi_c^e$) means that money wages will overstate the rise in prices, with the result that there will be an increase in the real wage. Employment will fall, real GNP will be below the full-employment level, and the level of unemployment will rise above the natural rate.

We can summarize the relationship between the actual rate of inflation (π), the rate of inflation that had been expected for the current period (π_c^e), the unemployment rate (U), and the natural rate of unemployment (U_n) by the following equation:

$$\pi = \lambda(U_n - U) + \pi_c^e, \tag{12.1}$$

where λ is a positive constant. According to this equation, an increase in aggregate demand that reduces the unemployment rate below the natural rate implies an increase in the actual rate of inflation above that expected (that is, if $U < U_n$, then $\pi > \pi_c^e$). Similarly, a decrease in aggregate demand that increases the unemployment rate above the natural rate implies a reduction in the actual inflation below that expected (that is, if $U > U_n$, then $\pi < \pi_c^e$). Thus for any expected inflation rate, the unemployment rate and inflation are inversely related.

The Long-Run Phillips Curve

The idea of a trade-off between unemployment and inflation was generally accepted in the 1960s both by economists and politicians. When Richard M. Nixon was elected to his first term as president in 1968, inflation had reached an unacceptably high rate of 4.2 percent. Nixon indicated that inflation was the primary problem in the economy and that his administration was going to lower inflation, even if this resulted in a higher rate of un-employment. Nixon was thinking in terms of a Phillips curve like that depicted in Figure 12.7.

Economists accepted the idea of a trade-off between inflation and un-employment because plotting unemployment against inflation in the 1950s and 1960s yielded a "well-behaved" Phillips curve.[14] In 1968 in an address to the American Economics Association, however, Milton Friedman stated that there "is always a temporary trade-off between inflation and unem-ployment; there is no permanent trade-off. The temporary trade-off comes not from inflation, per se, but from unanticipated inflation . . ."[15]

---

[14] The case study at the end of this section explores the actual inflation-unemployment "trade-off" that has existed since the 1960s.

[15] Milton Friedman, "The Role of Monetary Policy," *American Economic Review* (March 1968): Vol. 58, p. 11.

It is now widely accepted that greater inflation only generates lower unemployment in the short run. The short-run Phillips curve holds only as long as individuals err in their forecasts of inflation. These mistakes will not persist over time, however. For example, assume that unemployment is initially at the natural rate. Now suppose that the Fed engages in expansionary monetary policy. In the short-run, an increased rate of monetary growth causes unemployment to fall below the natural rate. Figure 12.11 shows this as the movements from point A to point B on the short-run Phillips curve. The expansionary monetary policy causes the actual inflation rate to exceed the expected inflation rate. Workers failing to fully anticipate higher output prices mistake higher money wages for higher real wages and supply more labor. This causes the real wage to fall, which in turn causes firms to expand employment and output above the full-employment level. Corresponding to the increase in employment is a fall in unemployment below the natural rate. As Figure 12.11 indicates, unemployment falls from U_n to U_1, while the inflation rate rises from π_0 to π_1.

This is, however, a short-run phenomenon. Over time, individuals will see that they underestimated inflation and revise their expectation of inflation upward.[16] Since their corresponding expectation of the real wage falls, they supply less labor. As we saw from our earlier analysis, this in turn causes output and employment to fall and unemployment to rise. In terms of Equation 12.1, an increase in expected inflation causes the Phillips curve to shift upward: Any unemployment rate is associated with a higher inflation rate or, equivalently, any inflation rate implies a higher unemployment rate.

As long as workers find that they are underestimating inflation, they will keep revising their expectations of inflation upward. This in turn means that the Phillips curve will keep shifting upward. Only when workers are correct in their estimation of the inflation rate and the corresponding level of output prices will they quit revising their expectation of inflation upward. Thus the economy does not reach long-run equilibrium until the inflation expected for the current period (π_c^e) has been brought into equality with actual inflation (π). In other words, the long-run equilibrium condition is given by the condition $\pi = \pi_c^e$.

From Equation 12.1, we see that if $\pi = \pi_c^e$, then unemployment must be at the natural rate. When individual expectations of the inflation rate and current output prices are correct, individual beliefs about the real wage will also be correct. As a consequence, employment will be at the full employment level and unemployment will be at the natural rate. In other words, as Figure 12.11 shows, the long-run Phillips curve will be vertical; there is no long-run trade-off between inflation and unemployment.

---

[16] This assumes that individuals adjust their inflationary expectations upward if actual inflation exceeds expected inflation, and they reduce their expectation of inflation if actual inflation is less than expected inflation. This method of changing expectations is called adaptive expectations.

Figure 12.11   **Short-run and Long-run Phillips Curves**

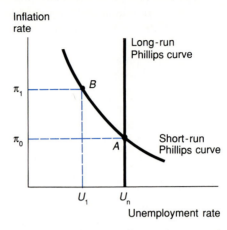

In the short run, an increase in the rate of monetary growth results in an upward movement from point *A* to point *B* along the short-run Phillips curve, as unemployment falls and inflation rises. Over time, expected inflation increases and the short-run Phillips curve shifts upward. At the new long-run equilibrium, unemployment returns to the natural unemployment rate, but inflation is higher. Thus the long-run Phillips curve is vertical at the natural rate U_n. In the long run, unemployment below the natural rate cannot be bought with high inflation.

Our analysis has an important policy implication. Lowering unemployment below the natural rate requires that current inflation be raised above anticipated inflation. However, when current inflation exceeds what had been anticipated, individuals will revise their inflationary expectations upward. Thus maintaining the same low unemployment rate in the next period requires an even higher inflation rate. Efforts to maintain unemployment below the natural rate will only succeed in generating accelerating inflation in the long run.[17]

The discussion in this section reconfirms a result we obtained earlier when we analyzed the predictions of the neoclassical model. In the long-run, an increase in the rate of monetary growth tends to have no effect on the unemployment rate. An increase in the rate of monetary growth is simply matched by an increase in the long-run inflation rate.[18] Thus as the vertical Phillips curve indicates, in the long run changes in the inflation rate are not associated with changes in the unemployment rate. Naturally, this result is

---

[17] In addition, it has been argued that the potential trade-off of the short-run Phillips curve "tends to fade away the more frequently it is used, or abused." See Robert E. Lucas, Jr., "Some International Evidence on Output-Inflation Tradeoffs," *American Economic Review* vol. 63 (June 1973): 334.

[18] In the next chapter, we will see that higher inflation may have negative effects on the economy's potential real GNP. For the time being, we are abstracting from the possibility.

weakened to the extent that short-run adjustments have long-run consequences. For example, if a monetary expansion affects investment in the short-run, it can lead to higher capital stock in the long-run. This can alter labor demand and the natural rate of unemployment. Such possibilities are not addressed by the simplified long-run analysis of the neoclassical model.

Although our analysis has focused on an expansionary monetary policy, we can tell a similar story regarding contractionary policy. A reduction in monetary growth will initially cause expected inflation to exceed actual inflation. In terms of the Phillips curve diagram, this will appear as a downward movement along the initial short-run Phillips curve. Over time, we would expect that households will reduce their expectations of inflation and the Phillips curve will shift downward. Eventually, long-run equilibrium will be restored at the natural unemployment rate and a lower inflation rate.

In the case study that follows, we look at some actual experiences of the 1970s and 1980s in terms of the shifting short-run Phillips curve.

Case Study

THE SHIFTING SHORT-RUN PHILLIPS CURVE

In the 1960s and early 1970s, many economists urged the fiscal and monetary authorities to follow the dictates of the short-run Phillips curve and trade off higher inflation for lower unemployment. Evidence that the government pursued such a policy is provided by Figure 12.12, which charts the inflation and unemployment rates experienced by the economy from 1961 to 1969. As the data in the figure indicate, the unemployment rate fell during this period from 6.7 percent in 1961 to 3.5 percent in 1969, while the inflation rate (measured by the CPI) rose from under 1.0 percent in 1961 to over 6 percent in 1969. The most striking feature in Figure 12.12 is that the inflation rate-unemployment combinations appear to lie on a "well-behaved," negatively sloped Phillips curve.

Although high inflation rates may be able to lower the unemployment rate temporarily, they cannot maintain the unemployment rate permanently below the natural rate. In order to lower unemployment below the natural rate, policymakers must raise the inflation rate above that which is expected. But over time, individuals will revise their estimates of inflation upward and the Phillips curve will shift up. Further efforts by policymakers to keep unemployment below the natural rate will only accelerate inflation. This appears to be exactly what happened at various times in the 1970s. Comparing Figure 12.12 with Figure 12.13, we see that the inflation-unemployment trade-off apparently worsened during the 1970s.

Upward shifts in the short-run Phillips curve are caused not only by increases in individual expectations of inflation. Supply shocks of the sort

Figure 12.12   Inflation and Unemployment Rate Combinations from 1961 to 1969

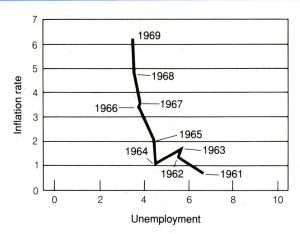

Inflation figures indicate percent change in CPI during each year (January to January). Unemployment figures are average unemployment rate over each year.

Source: Various issues of *Economic Report of the President.*

described in Chapter 9 can also cause the Phillips curve to shift. The U.S. economy was hit by two adverse oil supply shocks in the 1970s. The first occurred between 1973 and 1974 as a consequence of the OPEC oil embargo. As we noted in Chapter 9, the energy component of the CPI rose by about 38.4 percent from December 1972 to December 1974, while overall prices rose by 16 percent. This translates into a 22.4 percent increase in the real price of oil. Another large increase in the real price of energy occurred between 1979 and 1980 when OPEC again raised oil prices. As we discussed in Chapter 9, such adverse supply shocks can cause employment to fall, unemployment to rise, real GNP growth to fall, and prices to increase. In terms of our present discussion, the short-run Phillips curve shifts up and to the right.

As the data in Figure 12.13 indicate, the inflation rate accelerated during the 1970s, rising from under 4 percent in 1971 to close to 14 percent in 1979 and 12 percent in 1980. As indicated above, the high inflation of the 1970s was due not only to large increases in the money supply but also to adverse oil supply shocks. Nevertheless, the experience still provides a prime example of the error of believing that a long-run trade-off exists between inflation and unemployment. The expansionary policies of the 1970s, together with the adverse supply shocks, led to some of the highest inflation rates of this century. Yet where were the benefits? Unlike the 1960s, the high inflation in the 1970s was accompanied by high, not low, unemployment. For example, in the high inflation year of 1980 the unemployment rate averaged over 7 percent. Our experience in the 1970s introduced and pop-

Figure 12.13 Inflation and Unemployment Rate Combinations from 1970 to 1987

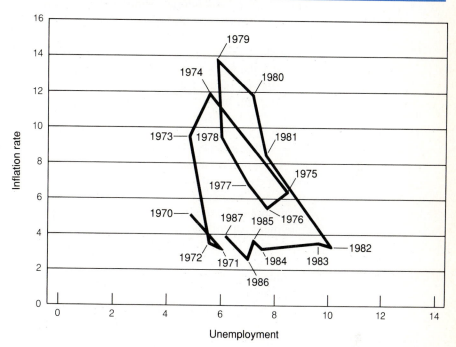

Inflation figures indicate percent change in CPI over each year (January to January). Unemployment figures are average unemployment rate over each year. *Source:* Various issues of *Economic Report of the President.*

ularized the concept of "stagflation"—a term used to describe the simultaneous occurrence of high inflation with high unemployment and low real GNP growth.

In the late 1970s and early 1980s, the Federal Reserve tightened its monetary policy. As Figure 12.13 indicates, inflation accordingly fell from 12 percent in 1980 to under 4 percent in 1982. As the theory predicts, the lower monetary growth and consequent reduction in inflation led to a recession and an increase in unemployment. The recession was fairly deep, with the unemployment rate reaching a yearly average of 10 percent in 1982. Our analysis tells us, however, that a reduction in monetary growth and inflation will only lead to a temporary recession. Individuals will eventually revise their inflationary expectations and the short-run Phillips curve will shift downward. In point of fact, the economy began recovering in 1983. By 1984, the unemployment rate had fallen back to below 8 percent, although the economy did not return to its 1979 unemployment level of around 6 percent until late 1987.

There is some debate, however, concerning the extent to which the economy's own self-corrective forces were responsible for the fall in unemployment, as additional factors have been given some credit for the recovery. One factor is the fact that OPEC's ability to maintain high oil prices weakened considerably in the 1980s, as the demand for oil fell and the supply rose. With the sharp drop in the price of oil in early 1986, the real price of oil reached its 1973 level. This beneficial oil supply shock had the effect of lowering the short-run Phillips curve, thereby leading to a fall in both unemployment and inflation. In addition, some have argued that the tax cuts enacted in 1981 stimulated output supply and demand, with unemployment falling as a consequence. Finally, accommodating monetary policy has been suggested as another key factor aiding the economy's return to full employment.

In summary, although the analysis is complicated by supply-side shocks, our experience of the 1960s and 1970s illustrates the limitations of expansionary fiscal and monetary policy. Buoyed by their initial success in the 1960s, many policymakers thought that they could permanently trade off unemployment for inflation, a belief that found its way into many of the leading economics texts of the day. As events in the 1970s demonstrated, however, the trade-off could at best only be temporary, as inflationary expectations would eventually adjust to higher inflation rates. As we noted in Chapter 1, this sequence of events has played a very important role in shaping current macroeconomic thought, leading to a movement away from the simpler "Keynesian" models of earlier years and toward the "new classical macroeconomics." Macroeconomists are now nearly unanimously agreed that expansionary fiscal and monetary policies are limited in their ability to affect unemployment and output over the longer run. As we see below, when we discuss the "new classical" hypothesis of economist Robert Lucas, there are some today who question whether such policies can systematically affect unemployment in the short-run.

To the Point

THE PHILLIPS CURVE

- An upward-sloping aggregate supply curve means that macroeconomic demand shocks lead to changes in the current level of prices and real output in the same direction. Since a rise in the current level of prices implies a higher rate of inflation and an increase in employment implies a fall in unemployment, a short-run upward-sloping aggregate supply curve indicates a temporary trade-off between inflation and unemployment, which is known as the Phillips curve.

- In order for there to be a trade-off between inflation and unemployment, workers must either be uninformed about real wages or have sticky money wage contracts. Since neither of these conditions persist in the long run, the long-run aggregate supply curve is vertical at the full employment level of real GNP and the long-run Phillips curve is vertical at the natural unemployment rate.

- Since lower unemployment can be bought with high inflation in the short run, there is a tendency to use inflation as a policy tool to deal with unemployment. The ultimate result of such a policy is no change in the natural rate of unemployment but higher inflation.

12.5   RATIONAL EXPECTATIONS AND INFLATION UNCERTAINTY

Recall from Chapters 9 and 10 that changes in autonomous investment and consumption are often cited as sources of demand instability in the economy. The idea that instability exists in the private sector, together with the analysis in this chapter of a short-run upward-sloping aggregate supply curve, suggest that nongovernmental demand shocks can lead to changes in output. Under these circumstances, discretionary monetary and fiscal policy changes may have a stabilizing influence on the economy. However, successful government macroeconomic stabilization policy depends crucially on several factors.

First, the "short-run" must not be too short if discretionary monetary and fiscal policy is to play a significant role in stabilizing the economy. The output effects of macroeconomic shocks depend on the length of time before sellers of inputs fully recognize changes in output prices and input prices are renegotiated. Many argue that the short run has substantial length, being measured in terms of years. Keynes made a famous statement that revealed how distant is the long run: "In the long run, we are all dead." Others believe that the short-run is not so great. One reason for the lack of consensus is that it is rare to observe over an extended period of time only one macroeconomic shock in isolation. This makes it difficult to determine the economy's exact reactions over time to a macroeconomic shock.

A second factor affecting the discretionary policy's ability to stabilize the economy has to do in part with how individuals in the economy formulate their expectations. This is especially the case for the macroeconomic models considered in this chapter since they retain the neoclassical perspective of prices adjusting to clear the output markets.

Rational Expectations, the New Classical Macroeconomics, and Policy Ineffectiveness

Expectations play an important role in the two modifications of the neoclassical model. In the modification of the neoclassical model with fixed wages, the level at which negotiators fix money wages depends on the expectation of future prices. The higher the expected level of output prices, the higher the level of wages set in labor agreements between workers and firms. If price expectations turn out to be incorrect, then as we have seen output will differ from the full employment level. For instance, a shock that causes actual output prices to fall below those expected means that the money wage will have been fixed at a level that is too high for full employment. Consequently, employment and output fall below the full employment level.

In the model with incomplete information, suppliers of labor anticipate a certain level of prices. The higher are workers' expectations of output prices, the lower is their labor supply at a given money wage. If these expectations are incorrect, then output will vary from the full employment level. For example, a shock that causes actual output prices to fall below those expected means lower employment and output, as firms respond to the lower prices by reducing wages and workers mistake lower money wages for lower real wages.

According to either modification of the neoclassical analysis, appropriate fiscal and monetary policy can stabilize output and employment. They do so by changing output demand, and thus equilibrium output prices, so that they match expected output prices. For instance, let output fall below the full employment level, reflecting the situation of prices falling short of the expected level. In such a case, expansionary fiscal and monetary policy, by raising output prices, can raise real GNP and restore full employment.

But what if expansionary monetary and fiscal policies are anticipated at the time wages are negotiated and set, and their effect on prices is reflected in individuals' price expectations? Then these policies will not raise the level of prices *relative to what is expected.* Thus *anticipated* monetary and fiscal policies cannot affect output. Only *unanticipated* policy changes affect output. This rather discouraging view of monetary and fiscal policy is known as the *new classical economics.* In recent years, it has been the focus of widespread attention among macroeconomists.

The new classical hypothesis rests on two assumptions. First, deviations in output from the full employment level are caused by deviations in the price level from what is expected. Second, individual expectations of prices are ''rational'' in that individuals make use of all available information to form expectations of prices.[19] The information that is available includes both past policy prescriptions and current policy pronouncements. Given these two hypotheses, the role for discretionary fiscal and monetary policy to affect real GNP and employment is substantially reduced.

---

[19] The basic notion of rational expectations was first introduced by John Muth, ''Rational Expectations and the Theory of Price Movements,'' *Econometrica* (July 1961): 315–35. The important implications of the concept for macroeconomics were pointed out by Robert Lucas in ''Some International Evidence on Output-Inflation Trade-offs,'' *The American Economic Review* vol. 63 (June 1973): 326–364. For further discussion of the applications of rational expectations to economics, see Robert Lucas, ''Understanding Business Cycles'' in *Carnegie-Rochester Conference Series on Public Policy.*

The view that monetary policy in particular is an ineffective policy tool is often referred to as the policy ineffectiveness proposition. It has also been called the Lucas-Sargent proposition, since these two economists are the leading proponents of the idea of policy ineffectiveness. Bennett McCallum summarizes this idea as follows: "If aggregate-supply fluctuations are initiated by informational errors and if economic agents' expectations are formed rationally, then countercyclical monetary policy will be entirely ineffective."[20]

To gain better insight into the policy ineffectiveness proposition, recall our discussion in the preceding section of the short-run and long-run trade-off between inflation and unemployment. We showed that a negatively sloped Phillips curve means that in the short run government policymakers can trade off inflation for unemployment. By raising inflation relative to what is expected, expansionary monetary and fiscal policy can cause the economy to move upward along the short-run Phillips curve, thereby trading off lower unemployment for higher inflation. Over time, however, individuals will revise their expectations of inflation upward, which causes the short-run Phillips curve to shift up. In fact, in the long run the expected inflation rate will just equal the actual inflation rate. As Equation 12.1 indicated, this means that the Phillips curve is vertical in the long run. Government policymakers cannot trade off inflation for unemployment in the long run.

If expectations are rational, then individuals' expectations will incorporate their beliefs about future monetary and fiscal policy. For instance, if individuals anticipate a more expansionary monetary policy and take the view of the neoclassical model that such a change will lead to higher prices, then they will expect a higher rate of inflation. As a consequence, the more expansionary monetary policy, since it was anticipated, leaves unchanged actual inflation relative to what is expected. As Equation 12.1 indicated, such *anticipated* policy changes are therefore powerless to affect unemployment. Thus the idea of rational expectations in this context suggests that not only can policymakers not trade off inflation for unemployment in the long run, but they may also not be able to do so in the short run.

In the next two chapters, we discuss the policy implications of rational expectations in more detail when we examine optimal monetary and fiscal policy and the arguments for rules versus discretion. In anticipation of this discussion, we conclude this chapter by saying a few words concerning the effects of government policy on the economic environment in general and inflation uncertainty in particular. We will show how this leads to the possibility of a long-run *inverse* relationship between inflation and real GNP.

---

[20] Bennet T. McCallum, "Price-Level Stickiness and the Feasibility of Monetary Stabilization Policy with Rational Expectations," *Journal of Political Economy* (June 1977): 627. An alternative to rational expectations is "adaptive expectations," in which individuals' expectations of, say, future inflation equal last period expected inflation with some adjustment or "adaptation" in light of any difference between what was expected in the prior period compared to the actual inflation that occurred.

The Effect of Inflation Uncertainty on Employment

In his Nobel lecture, Milton Friedman raised the possibility that the long-run Phillips curve may be sloped positively.[21] Friedman argued that greater inflation uncertainty on the part of individuals in the economy usually goes hand in hand with higher inflation. The result is a reduction in the efficiency of the price system, a fall in employment and a lower real GNP. Friedman went on to note, however, that over time institutions were likely to adapt so as to reduce the losses associated with the higher inflation uncertainty.

In a recent paper, A. Steven Holland attempts to test the Friedman hypothesis.[22] More specifically, Holland estimates the "impact of inflation uncertainty on employment, while also considering the second-round effects of labor market adjustments designed to reduce the risk associated with inflation uncertainty." In terms of our discussion earlier in this chapter, increased uncertainty about inflation means that workers will be less certain about how much output they will be able to purchase with their nominal wage earnings. For workers who dislike such risk, the gain to working will be lower. Thus the labor supply curve will shift to the left and as a consequence both employment and real GNP will fall. However, this is not the end of the story as additional adjustments will occur over time.

Workers facing increased uncertainty as to the purchasing power of their nominal wage earnings will be more likely to find it worthwhile to incur the costs associated with wage indexation so as to insulate their wages from the effects of unexpected inflation. Thus over the longer run, increased inflation uncertainty should lead to increased indexation of wages, which in turn will mitigate the effects of inflation uncertainty on employment. Holland's empirical results provide support for these predicted effects.

Looking at data from 1961 to 1983, Holland estimates inflation uncertainty on the basis of the errors made by individuals in estimating inflation. Holland finds that inflation uncertainty was about twice as high toward the end of the period as at the beginning of the period, something which should not be very surprising in light of our previous description of events during this period. As expected, Holland finds that the increase in inflation uncertainty led to an increase in the proportion of workers who are covered by cost of living clauses in their contracts. Holland also finds that increased uncertainty with respect to inflation leads to a significant reduction in employment. However, the negative impact on employment is highest in the first few years of the increased inflation uncertainty. Over time, the increased indexation of wage contracts "offsets a large part, but not all, of the effect of a permanent change in inflation uncertainty on the level of employment."

---

[21] Milton Friedman, "Nobel Lecture: Inflation and Unemployment," *Journal of Political Economy* 85, (June 1977): 451–72.

[22] A. Steven Holland, "Wage Indexation and the Effect of Inflation Uncertainty on Employment: An Empirical Analysis," *American Economic Review* vol. 76 (March 1986): 235–243.

The discussion in this section contains an important lesson. Employment and real GNP are affected not only by the difference between actual inflation and expected inflation but also by the general level of inflation uncertainty. This in turn is influenced by the fiscal and monetary policy actions taken by the government since the more unpredictable are these policy actions, the less predictable is inflation. More generally, the basic decision rules that guide government policy actions have important effects on the economic environment in which market participants must operate and, as a consequence, can have a crucial impact on a nation's economic well-being. As we will see in the next chapter, this observation plays a significant role in much of the debate concerning the optimal form of government policy in general and the appropriate conduct of monetary policy in particular.

SUMMARY

We have analyzed two modifications of the neoclassical model in which price and output adjust simultaneously to macroeconomic demand shocks. One modification assumes fixed input prices, such as wages, while the second assumes incomplete information on changes in the price level by sellers of inputs, in particular, workers.

With fixed money wages, a fall in the level of output prices reduces labor demand at existing money wages because it means a higher real wage. With no downward adjustment in wages, employment falls. Similarly, a rise in the level of output prices implies a lower real wage, which increases labor demand and employment.

When information is incomplete, a change in output prices also leads to changes in employment. For example, if a fall in output prices is not anticipated by workers, then the money wage will fall less than output prices, so that the real wage will rise and labor demand and employment will be lower. Even though the real wage rises, the quantity of labor supplied by workers falls. Workers believe incorrectly that the real wage is lower, mistaking a fall in the money wage for a fall in the real wage. Similarly, an increase in output prices increases labor demand, which causes the money wage to rise. If workers do not anticipate the rise in output prices, the real wage falls and employment rises. Workers now mistakenly believe that a higher money wage means a higher real wage.

Both modifications of the neoclassical model generate an aggregate supply curve that slopes upward. As a result, changes in aggregate demand lead to changes in both the level of prices and real GNP. Associated with the change in real GNP is a change in employment caused by a change in real wages. This contrasts with the neoclassical analysis, where flexible prices and complete information mean that macroeconomic shocks do not alter real input prices.

Besides having in common changes in relative prices underlying movements along an upward-sloping aggregate supply curve, the two modifications of the neoclassical model have other things in common: wage inflexibility and incomplete information are important in both theories. In the model with fixed money wages, it is assumed explicitly that wages are fixed. In the model with incomplete information, wage inflexibility appears in the sense that nominal wages vary less than prices in the short run, so that price change lead to changes in the real wage. The model with incomplete information explicitly assumes that workers' information on the price level is incomplete. In the model with fixed wages, this assumption is implicit. Given a macroeconomic shock, the fixed money wage turns out to be inconsistent with equilibrium in the labor market. At the time wage agreements were made, workers and firms therefore must have had incomplete information on prices and thus the appropriate money wage.

Both modifications of the neoclassical model predict that in the long run, macroeconomic demand shocks affect only prices, not real GNP. That is, the assumptions of fixed wages and incomplete information on prices are appropriate only in the short run. Fixed wages are renegotiated over time, and workers gain information on price changes. Since money wages adjust and workers learn about prices in the long run, the effects of a demand shock on output will be short-lived.

The two modifications of the neoclassical model both predict a short-run inverse relationship between inflation and unemployment, which is known as the Phillips curve. This relationship is summarized by Equation 12.1:

$$\pi = \lambda(U_n - U) + \pi_c^e.$$

According to this equation, the actual rate of inflation (π) can be expressed as equal to the sum of the expected rate of inflation for the current period (π_c^e) and a term that depends positively on the difference between the natural rate of unemployment (U_n) and the actual rate of unemployment (U). This tells us that if the actual rate of inflation exceeds the expected rate of inflation, then unemployment will be below the natural rate. The explanation for this result is straightforward. If the actual inflation rate exceeds the expected inflation rate, then individuals must be underestimating the price level. Money wages are set "too low," unemployment falls below the natural rate, and real GNP rises above the full employment level. In contrast, if the actual rate of inflation falls short of the expected rate, the implied "too high" money wages lead to an unemployment rate above the natural rate of unemployment and a level of real GNP below the full employment level.

In the long run, actual inflation equals expected inflation. This implies that the long-run Phillips curve is vertical at the natural rate of unemployment. Such a curve has important policy implications since it means that discretionary fiscal and monetary policies can at best achieve only a temporary reduction in the unemployment rate below the natural rate. Rational expectations on the part of individuals reduce still further the ability of government policymakers to affect unemployment in the context of the modified neoclassical models. Given rational expectations, only *unanticipated* monetary and fiscal policy changes can reduce the rate of unemployment below the natural rate, even in the short run.

LOOKING AHEAD

We have now analyzed several different models explaining how an economy responds to various macroeconomic shocks. In the chapters to follow, we expand upon this discussion and highlight some of the controversies that surround macroeconomic analysis—such as the optimal fiscal and monetary policy. In addition, since the labor and money markets have been shown to be critical markets in macroeconomic analysis, we provide a more detailed analysis of them. Finally, we examine some issues that have to do with an open economy.

We begin our expanded discussion in the next chapter by looking at various proposals for what monetary policy should be. In so doing, we will draw on the analysis of this and earlier chapters.

SUMMARY OF KEY EQUATIONS

Phillips Curve

$$\pi = \lambda(U_n - U) + \pi_c^e \qquad (12.1)$$

KEY TERMS

Sticky wages, 466

Incomplete information, 475

Phillips curve, 482

REVIEW QUESTIONS

1. Explain why a fall in output prices leads to lower employment and higher unemployment if money wages are fixed.
2. Why is it plausible to believe that firms have better information than do workers on output prices and the real wage?
3. Explain why the aggregate supply curve is upward-sloping in the model where workers have incomplete information on output prices.

4. Suppose that the price level rises and that firms are aware of the increase in the price level, but workers are not.

   (a) What happens to the demand curve for labor? What happens to the supply curve for labor? Why?

   (b) Show the resulting effect on labor market equilibrium. What happens to employment? What happens to the nominal wage?

   (c) What happens to the real wage? Do workers supply more or less labor now than they did initially? Why? Do firms demand more or less labor now than they did initially? Why?

   (d) What should happen to workers' expectations of output prices over time? Show the resulting effect in your diagram to (b).

5. Would the two modifications of the neoclassical model analyzed in this chapter predict that real wages move procyclically or countercyclically? How does this compare with the model with predetermined output prices and with the neoclassical model?

6. Suppose that the nominal wage is fixed at a level so high that there is excess supply in the labor market.

   (a) Illustrate this situation in the labor market.

   (b) Is real GNP at the full employment level? Why or why not?

   (c) Now suppose that the Fed pursues an expansionary monetary policy. Show the initial impact of this policy in the financial and money markets. At the original output and price levels, what happens to the interest rate? Is there excess demand or supply in the output market? Why?

   (d) What happens to the aggregate demand curve? Why? Show the resulting effect on real GNP and the level of output prices. Are output prices higher or lower? What causes this?

   (e) Show the resulting effect on the labor market in your diagram to (b). What happens to the real wage? To employment? Why? Does this explain what happens to real GNP in your answer to (d)?

   (f) Was the Fed able to increase employment with its expansionary monetary policy? Why? How does this result compare with that in the neoclassical model?

7. A March 26, 1979 *Wall Street Journal* article stated that "the President is already taking steps to revise and strengthen his flagging anti-inflation program; . . . that program now has been battered by news that the consumer price index rose in February at an annual rate of 14.4 percent . . . He may . . . be forced to back . . . a politically unpopular rise in interest rates in the hope of slowing the economy and curbing inflation." Later the same article reported that "the feeling is growing among his economic advisors that President Carter will soon have to sit down with Chairman G. William Miller of the Federal Reserve Board and urge the

central bank to tighten credit further in an attempt to slow growth and restrain inflation.''

(a) Show the real impact of a fall in the money supply on the financial and money markets. What happens to the interest rate? At the initial output and price levels is there excess demand or supply in the output market?

(b) What happens to the aggregate demand curve? Show the resulting effect on real GNP and prices in the model with incomplete information on output prices on the part of workers.

(c) Show what happens in the labor market.

(d) What has happened to the following: real GNP, employment, unemployment rate, interest rate, price level, and real wage. How do workers' expectations of the real wage compare with what the real wage actually is? Why?

(e) What will happen over time to workers' expectations of the price level? Show the resulting effect in your diagram to (c). What happens to employment and output?

(f) Show what now happens in your diagram to (b). Does the price level rise or fall? Explain why.

(g) When will the adjustment process eventually stop? Why?

8. What elements do the two modifications of the neoclassical model have in common? How do the two models differ?

9. What effect does a change in workers' expectation of the price level have on the aggregate supply curve in the neoclassical model? Why?

10. What does the Phillips curve tell us?

(a) What is the equation for the short-run Phillips curve?

(b) Suppose that the actual inflation rate exceeds the expected inflation rate. What does the equation for the Phillips curve tell us about how the unemployment rate compares with the natural rate? Interpret this result.

11. Consider the fall in the money supply analyzed in Question 7.

(a) What effect does the contractionary monetary policy have on the inflation rate? Why? What happens to the inflation rate relative to expected inflation? Why? Show the movement on the short-run Phillips curve that is caused by restrictive monetary policy.

(b) What will happen to the short-run Phillips curve over time?

(c) What will eventually happen to the unemployment rate?

12. Explain why the long-run Phillips curve is vertical.

13. Why can discretionary monetary and fiscal policy trade off inflation for unemployment in the short run but not in the long run?

14. How and why does the attempt to lower the rate of unemployment by deliberately causing inflation depend on the ability to fool people?

15. What do we mean when we say that individuals' expectations of output prices are "rational"? What is the chief tenet of the "policy ineffectiveness proposition"? What is the reasoning that leads to this proposition?

16. Suppose that the chairman of the Federal Reserve Board has a policy of announcing his intentions with respect to changes in the money supply and that he wants monetary policy to have an impact on *real* GNP over the next few years. According to the rational expectations hypothesis, should the chairman tell the truth about money suppy changes or should he lie?

17. Suppose that Congress wants to affect the level of employment in the economy. According to the rational expectations hypothesis, should they open up fiscal policy negotiations to the press or not?

18. In 1972 during President Nixon's reelection campaign, there was an acceleration in the growth rate of the money supply.

    (a) What effect should this increase in the rate of monetary growth have had on the rate of inflation?

    (b) According to the modified neoclassical model with incomplete information on output prices, what is the slope of the short-run Phillips curve? Why? What should have consequently happened to unemployment in 1972?

    (c) What should happen to expected inflation in the future? What effect will this have on the short-run Phillips curve? On the aggregate supply curve?

    (d) What should happen to inflation and unemployment in the years after 1972?

    (e) Are the data in Figure 12.13 consistent with your answers to this question?

    (f) Why on earth did Nixon and Rosemary Woods erase only 18 minutes of the "smoking gun" tape?

19. We often tend to observe significant increases in monetary growth during presidential election years.

    (a) Does this observation make sense in light of our discussion of short-run and long-run Phillips curves? Why or why not?

    (b) Some economists have talked about a "political business cycle." In light of your answer to (a), indicate what the political business cycle might look like. (Note that the pattern of unemployment and inflation in the years of the Carter presidency do not seem to fit the pattern of the political business cycle. One can think of two possible explanations for this. First, other factors, such as an oil supply shock came into play. Second, Carter and the Fed simply messed up on their timing.)

(c) According to the rational expectations hypothesis, should individuals make use of all available information when forming their price expectations?

(d) What happens if individuals in the private sector take into account the incentives facing politicians who are up for re-election?

20. According to a recent *Wall Street Journal* (April 25, 1988):

"Presidential candidates do fulfill their campaign promises—at least the big macroeconomic ones—according to a report from Paine Webber Inc. For instance: President Eisenhower fought inflation as he promised, even at the expense of economic growth. And President Carter focused on higher employment, paying the price of higher inflation. Considering the current candidate pledges, the report figures that a President Dukakis, for example, would favor the Democratic theme of cutting the budget deficit through lower defense spending and higher taxes, possibly including a gasoline tax or value-added tax."

(a) Depict graphically the impact on the financial and money markets of higher taxes (with no change in government spending).

(b) Taking the view of the macroeconomic model in which money wages are fixed but output prices are variable, depict the effect of the above fiscal policy change on the economy in terms of aggregate demand and supply curves. Would Dukakis be behaving more like Eisenhower or Carter (see quote)?

(c) Compare the new equilibrium situation with what would have existed had there not been a change in the exogenous variables identified in (a). In particular, what has happened to the level of prices, real GNP, the money interest rate, the expected real interest rate, the money wage—real wage, investment demand, consumption, velocity, and the real money supply?

(d) Write down the equation for the Phillips curve and indicate how the above fiscal policy affects the various terms in the equation. Assume the initial starting point was one at which the unemployment rate equaled the natural rate of unemployment.

(e) Depict graphically the effect of such a fiscal policy change on the labor market (recall the assumption of a fixed money wage). As in (d), assume prior to the shock that the economy was at full employment.

Part Four

Special Topics: Issues in Monetary and Fiscal Policy

Chapter 13

Optimal Monetary Policy: Rules Versus Discretion

Discretionary monetary policy: A monetary policy that involves changes in the money supply made purely at the discretion of the Fed.

IN our discussion of monetary policy, we have examined the potential effects on the economy of a change in the money supply under a variety of circumstances: when prices are completely flexible, when prices are predetermined, and when incomplete information introduces inflexibility in certain input prices, particularly wages. We now turn our attention to another important consideration. What type of monetary policy should the Fed pursue? One option is for the Fed to tailor money supply growth to the situation at hand, with no precommitment about exactly how it will proceed. This type of monetary policy is termed **discretionary monetary policy**, since money supply changes are made purely at the discretion of the Fed depending on its current reading of the economy. With a discretionary policy, the Fed changes the money supply each period in an attempt to achieve such goals as full employment, price stability, low and stable interest rates, a trade balance or surplus, and stable exchange rates. Advocates of such an activist monetary policy argue that it allows the Fed to offset disturbances in the private sector, thereby lessening the volatility in real GNP and inflation.

Another type of monetary policy bases current money supply changes on previously established rules. Milton Friedman has proposed a rule of this type that would increase the money supply at a constant rate each year, perhaps 3 percent.[1] Such a rule would not take current events into account;

---

[1] Friedman's view concerning a monetary rule was first spelled out in Milton Friedman, *A Program for Monetary Stability* (New York: Fordham University Press, 1959).

Monetarist: A proponent of the belief that the Fed should base current money supply changes on previously stated rules.

it purposefully blindfolds the policymakers as well as tying their hands. Those who argue for such rules are often called **monetarists**. They recognize the potential problems of a policy that blinds and disables the Fed, but fear that the alternative of discretionary policy is more dangerous since it gives the Fed total freedom to choose the path it wants the money supply to take.

Between the extremes of a purely discretionary monetary policy and one specifying a constant growth rate in the money supply is a monetary policy with *reactive rules*. Reactive rules remove the blindfold of the fixed monetary growth rule but leave the Fed's hands tied. A reactive rule specifies *in advance* how the growth of the money supply will change based on new information on the state of the economy. One such rule is that the growth in the monetary base, and thus the money supply, should automatically adjust whenever the growth of nominal GNP deviates from its trend.[2] An alternative reactive rule is that the Fed commit itself to holding the CPI to a preannounced target and adjust the monetary base, and thus the money supply, accordingly.[3] In fact, Wayne Angell, a 1986 appointee to the Board of Governors of the Federal Reserve, has argued for a monetary policy that will stabilize a price index constructed from a basket of basic commodities (perhaps including gold).

What arguments exist in favor of discretionary monetary policy rather than monetary rules? If one does favor rules, does a preferred set of rules exist and how are these rules to be implemented? The answers to these questions depend to a large extent on one's view of the economy. In the first part of this chapter, our perspective is the short-run view of the economy embodied in the macroeconomic model with predetermined prices. Recall from our analysis in Chapters 10 and 11 that in the macroeconomic model with predetermined prices, production and employment are determined by the level of output demand. We then take the neoclassical model's long-run view of the economy. As we saw in Chapters 7 and 8, only prices are affected by demand management in the neoclassical model. Thus we focus in this part of the chapter on the objective of low stable inflation and whether a simple monetary rule achieves that objective. We also consider various reactive rules and point out some potential difficulties involved in implementing policy rules. Finally, we reexamine the arguments for and against rules in the context of the modified neoclassical model with incomplete information.

---

[2] See Bennett T. McCallum, "On Consequences and Criticisms of Monetary Targeting," *Journal of Money, Credit, and Banking* (November 1985), pp. 570–597.

[3] See Robert E. Hall, "Explorations in the Gold Standard and Related Policies for Stabilizing the Dollar," in *Inflation: Causes and Effects*, ed. Robert Hall, (Chicago: University of Chicago Press, 1982). Hall's suggestion echoes Henry Simons's proposal in 1936 for "a monetary rule of maintaining the constancy of some price index." Henry C. Simons, "Rules Versus Authorities in Monetary Policy," *The Journal of Political Economy* (February 1936), pp. 1–30.

13.1 OPTIMAL MONETARY POLICY IN THE SHORT RUN

The macroeconomic model with predetermined prices predicts that unanticipated decreases in aggregate demand impose significant income losses on the participants in an economy, as real GNP temporarily falls and unemployment rises. It is this short-run model of the economy that provides the strongest case for discretionary monetary policy.

Supporters of discretionary policy stress that instability in the purchasing behavior of firms, households, and foreigners is an important source of fluctuations in output. Aggregate demand can fluctuate because of changes in investment spending, consumption spending, and net export demand. As indicated by the macroeconomic model with predetermined prices, this can lead to fluctuations in real GNP and employment. This introduces a potential role for the Fed to counteract the adverse effects of changes in private purchasing behavior through appropriate changes in the money supply. Monetary policy can thus "cure" output fluctuations.

Monetarists counter this argument for discretionary monetary policy by raising the possibility that many output fluctuations result from misguided monetary policy decisions. In other words, inappropriate changes in the growth rate of the money supply are an important "cause" of fluctuations in real GNP. Economists holding the view that demand-induced output fluctuations largely reflect an erratic monetary policy argue that the Fed should minimize its meddling in the economy.

Both views of monetary policy—that it is an important cause of output fluctuations and that it can be used as a cure to output fluctuations—have a number of supporters. In this section, we will explore both views since no clear consensus exists. We start by examining the view that discretionary monetary policy "cures" output fluctuations, a view that supports discretionary monetary policy. We then consider the view that discretionary monetary policy "causes" output fluctuations, a view that supports the arguments for monetary rules.

The Private Sector as an Important Source of Output Fluctuations

Those economists who argue for the use of discretionary monetary (and also fiscal) policy draw many of their conclusions from an analysis based on the macroeconomic model with predetermined prices. This model incorporates the view of Keynes, presented in the *General Theory,* that aggregate demand is an important determinant of employment and output. These nonmonetarists are therefore sometimes called Keynesians or neo-Keynesians.

We can understand the nonmonetarist view most easily if we recall the condition for equilibrium in the output market. In an open economy, the output market is in equilibrium when the demand for output equals output production Y, or

$$C^d + I^d + CCA + G^d + (X^d - Z^d) = Y, \tag{13.1}$$

where C^d is consumption demand, $I^d + CCA$ is gross investment demand, G^d is government demand, and $X^d - Z^d$ is net export demand (exports X^d minus imports Z^d). Upon substituting the linear consumption function $C^d = a + b \cdot (Y - CCA - T)$ into the above equilibrium condition and solving for equilibrium output Y, we obtain the following expression for equilibrium output:

$$Y = [1/(1 - b)] \cdot (a - b \cdot T + I^d + G^d + X^d - Z^d) + CCA \tag{13.2}$$

where the constant b denotes the marginal propensity to consume and changes in a reflect changes in autonomous consumption demand. Equation 13.2 indicates that equilibrium output depends on factors such as investment (I^d), consumption spending (the consumption function intercept a), export demand (X^d), import demand (Z^d), and fiscal policy variables (net taxes T and government spending G^d).

Nonmonetarists use Equation 13.2 to highlight changes in autonomous private expenditures as sources of instability in an economy. They attribute these changes to several factors:

1. Shifts in households' attitudes toward consumption and saving that affect consumption demand.

2. Changes in household desired holdings of money that spill over into changes in consumption and investment demand.

3. Changes in firms' expectations of the future profitability of investment that alter investment demand.

The resulting impact on output of fairly small changes in autonomous spending can be considerable in light of the multiplier process as well as the accelerator hypothesis discussed in Chapter 10.

Equation 13.2 can also be used to highlight the fact that increases in government spending or tax cuts have the potential to offset these demand-side shocks from the private sector. In addition, discretionary monetary policy changes can be used to counter downturns in the economy since increases in the money supply lead to reductions in the interest rate which, in turn, stimulates consumption and investment demand.

Discretionary Monetary Policy to Offset Private Sector Demand Shocks

Nonmonetarists cite the Great Depression of the 1930s as providing important evidence of the effects nonmonetary shocks can have on the economy. The following quote summarizes this view quite well:

Figure 13.1   The Effect of a Fall in Autonomous Spending
and a Money Supply Increase on Full Employment

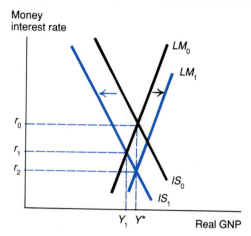

A fall in autonomous spending causes the *IS* curve to shift to the left from IS_0 to IS_1. If output prices do not adjust, real GNP falls to Y_1 and unemployment rises above the natural rate. An appropriate increase in the money supply will shift the *LM* curve from LM_0 to LM_1, thus restoring equilibrium at the full employment level of output Y^*.

The Depression was generated by a fall in autonomous spending. At a given level of income, desired investment and consumption fell . . . The Depression was severe because the fall in autonomous spending was large and sustained.[4]

We can use the *IS-LM* analysis developed in Chapters 10 and 11 to represent this Keynesian view of the Depression. Recall that for a given price level, the *IS* curve summarizes output-interest rate combinations consistent with equilibrium in the output market and the *LM* curve summarizes output-interest rate combinations consistent with equilibrium in the money market. The intersection of the two curves determines the economy's equilibrium interest rate and output level.

Suppose that the economy is initially in equilibrium at the full employment output level Y^*, but that for some reason autonomous spending falls. As Figure 13.1 indicates, this causes the *IS* curve to shift to the left from IS_0 to IS_1 and, at the predetermined price level, equilibrium real GNP falls to Y_1. Corresponding to the fall in real GNP is a fall in employment and an increase in unemployment.

_____

[4] Peter Temin, *Did Monetary Forces Cause the Great Depression?* (New York: W. W. Norton, 1976), p. 9.

We know from our discussion earlier in this book that prices will eventually adjust to restore equilibrium at full employment real GNP. Nonmonetarists argue that this adjustment process can take a long time. In particular, non-monetarists cite the Depression, with its protracted period of high unemployment from 1933 to 1940, as one of many instances when prices were slow to adjust to restore output to its full employment level. During the Depression, the official unemployment rate reached its peak of 25 percent in 1933 and remained over 14 percent until the outbreak of World War II. The existence of such a lengthy adjustment process increases the importance of the government engaging in an activist policy in order to avoid long periods of high unemployment and low or negative growth in real GNP.

The fiscal policy side of government can offset the initial fall in autonomous spending by increasing government spending or by instituting a tax cut. As we saw in Chapter 11, this would have the effect of shifting the *IS* curve back to the right. For a sufficiently large increase in government demand or a sufficiently large tax cut, equilibrium can be restored at full employment output Y^* even without any adjustment in the price level.

As Figure 13.1 indicates, discretionary monetary policy can also be used to bring the economy back to full employment equilibrium. An increase in the money supply will cause the *LM* curve to shift to the right. Equilibrium interest rates fall, which stimulates private spending. A sufficiently large increase in the money supply will restore equilibrium at full employment output Y^* at the economy's initial price level. As this analysis demonstrates, the Fed's ability to implement money supply increases at its discretion when private spending drops can be viewed as a critical tool to minimizing the losses of high unemployment and reduced output.

The Monetarist's Counter: Monetary Policy as the Cause of Output Fluctuations

Monetary rule: A monetary policy that commits the Fed to a fixed rate of growth in the money supply.

Unlike nonmonetarists, monetarists do not believe that it is advisable to allow the Fed to engage in discretionary monetary policy. Instead, monetarists argue for a **monetary rule** that fixes the rate of growth of the money supply. The reason for this is twofold. First, in the context of the short-run predetermined price model, monetarists think that an active discretionary monetary policy is the cause of more output fluctuations than it cures. Second, in the context of the long run, monetarists are concerned that discretionary monetary policy leads to high and variable inflation rates. We start in this section by developing the monetarists' reasons for questioning the advantage of discretionary monetary policy in the short run. These reasons are best understood in the context of the exchange equation.

Recall from Chapter 8 that the exchange equation is obtained by equating the demand for money to the supply and takes the form

$$M^s \cdot V = P \cdot Y, \tag{13.3}$$

where M^s denotes the money supply, V the velocity of money, P the level of output prices, and Y real GNP. Looking at this equation, if prices are fixed in the short run, then there are two types of shocks that can affect real GNP—changes in the money supply and changes in velocity.

Changes in velocity can be attributed to changes in such factors as changes in autonomous private expenditures. For example, consider the reduction in autonomous spending portrayed in Figure 13.1 by the shift to the left in the IS curve. We saw that this fall in output demand causes real GNP to fall if the money supply is held constant. Equation 13.3 tells us that under this circumstance, the fall in real GNP must be accompanied by a fall in velocity.

In light of the fact that *nonmonetary* demand disturbances in the economy show up as changes in velocity in the exchange equation, we have another way of stating the disagreement between monetarists and nonmonetarists in terms of the volatility of velocity: Nonmonetarists believe that velocity is volatile and that it reflects significant and relatively frequent changes in autonomous spending. It follows that money supply changes can be used to offset these velocity changes. For instance, if velocity falls, Equation 13.3 suggests that an increase in the money supply (M^s) can negate the effect of the lower velocity on GNP ($P \cdot Y$).

Figure 13.2 presents evidence on the past behavior of velocity. As the figure indicates, velocity has been far from constant over time. For example, in 1982 velocity increased by 6.1 percent over the previous year, while in 1983 velocity fell by 2.1 percent. This appears to be consistent with the position of the nonmonetarists. However, monetarists counter that past fluctuations in velocity sometimes have as their root cause erratic behavior on the part of the monetary authority rather than an inherent instability in the private sector.

An example offered by monetarists of how government discretionary policy can lie behind much of the fluctuation in velocity is the following. Let's say that individuals, in light of past changes in government monetary policies, alter their anticipation of the future policies of the Fed. In particular, let's say that individuals now expect the Fed to expand the money supply less rapidly in the future. We know from our analysis in Chapter 8 that over the long run reduced monetary growth leads to lower inflation. Let's assume that individuals understand this link between monetary growth and inflation that is predicted by the neoclassical model. In this case, the anticipation of a lower monetary growth will lead individuals to expect a lower rate of inflation in the future. As we saw in Chapter 8, a decrease in expected future inflation results in lower nominal interest rates, and thus a fall in velocity as individuals are williing to hold more money relative to nominal GNP. [Recall from the exchange equation that velocity (V) equals nominal GNP ($P \cdot Y$) divided by the money supply (M).]

The example above illustrates how a fall in velocity can be traced back to an anticipated change in monetary policy. In fact, William Poole suggests

Figure 13.2   The Velocity of Money

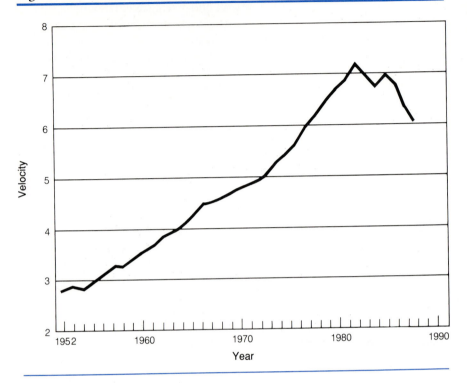

Source: Business Conditions Digest, various issues.

that the above scenario helps explain the drop in velocity in the early 1980s. As he puts it, "without question, inflationary expectations did decline, and the Federal Reserves's willingness to maintain a restrictive policy long into the 1981–1982 cyclical contraction must have had something to do with the decline."[5] The resulting major decline in interest rates that accompanied lower inflationary expectations is viewed by Poole as one of the factors explaining the decrease in velocity.

Even though there appears to be validity to the assertion that some changes in velocity have as their source changes in the behavior of monetary (and also fiscal) authorities, nonmonetarists argue that the fluctuations in velocity are too great to be due entirely to changes in government policies. Furthermore, no matter what their source, it seems as though the occurrence of changes in velocity means that there is a potential role for offsetting changes in the money supply. After all, doesn't the exchange equation indicate that the monetary authority can prevent a change in velocity from affecting

---

[5] William Poole, "Monetary Policy Lessons of Recent Inflation and Disinflation," NBER Working Paper, No. 2300, June 1987, p. 24.

GNP simply by adjusting the money supply so as to prevent the shock? In fact, the large decline in velocity in the 1980s, although possibly induced by an anticipated change in future monetary policy, would have almost certainly caused immediate severe economic problems had the Federal Reserve not accommodated the decline by money supply increases.

Monetarists respond that even though an omniscient monetary authority can enact discretionary changes in the money supply to negate demand disturbances, in practice this does not occur often. Successful discretionary stabilization policy means that policymakers have to enact policy changes that affect the economy at the appropriate times. This requires, for example, that they be able to predict the lag that will occur before a change in the money supply actually affects output demand. They also have to predict how responsive output demand will be to changes in the money supply. And finally, they have to be able to successfully diagnose the economy's current and future economic ills and needs.

The more successful policymakers are at doing these things, the more successful will discretionary policy be. Conversely, the less successful they are at doing these things, the less successful will discretionary policy be. Monetarists believe that given our current knowledge and limitations, discretionary policy changes often do more harm than good. Long and variable lags in the effect of money supply changes on the economy rule out effective countercyclical monetary policy. In fact, monetarists see a very real danger that faulty discretionary monetary policy can result in destabilization. Thus they support a simple monetary rule specifying a constant growth rate in the money supply. It is interesting to note that monetarists, just like non-monetarists, refer to the experience of the Depression as providing support for their viewpoint.

Case Study

MONETARY POLICY IN THE GREAT DEPRESSION

Monetarists cite the Great Depression, which witnessed a dramatic fall in the nominal money supply, as a particularly graphic example of the dangers in not following a simple monetary rule of constant growth in the money supply. Milton Friedman and Anna Schwartz summarize the monetarists' view of the Depression: "A 'normal' short-lived recession was converted into a major continued downswing in income and prices by the collapse of the banking system." The collapse of the banking system was important because it caused the money supply to fall dramatically. According to Friedman and Schwartz, it was this fall in the money supply that led to the sharp reduction in real GNP and employment; the Depression is thus "tragic testimony to the importance of monetary forces.''[6] Let's investigate this argument more closely.

As we discussed in Chapter 5, with a fractional reserve banking system the monetary base supports a money supply much larger than the base. The money multiplier summarizes the relationship between the money supply and the monetary base. The early years of the Depression were characterized by a series of banking panics. Although banking panics had occurred before the Depression, Friedman and Schwartz point out that misguided actions by the Fed made the banking panics of the Depression much more severe.[7] It was through their effect on the money multiplier that the banking panics caused the money supply to fall.

A banking panic occurs when individuals perceive that banks are in a precarious financial situation. Remember from the discussion of the depository institutions' balance sheet in Chapters 3 and 4 that deposits are the primary liabilities of banks and loans are their primary assets. Fearing that many outstanding bank loans would be defaulted on, with the result that banks' assets would be insufficient to meet their deposit liabilities, individuals rushed to their banks in droves, like herds of drought-stricken cattle to a watering hole, in an attempt to liquidate their liabilities. Under such an onslaught, even solvent banks failed since under a fractional reserve banking system only a fraction of bank deposits are held as reserves readily available to meet depositors' demands.[8]

As individuals lined up at banks to convert their deposits to currency during the ensuing banking panic, the composition of the monetary base changed to less reserves and more currency in the hands of the nonbank public. As our discussion of the money multiplier in Chapter 5 indicated, when the public increases its holdings of currency, reserves are removed from the banking system and the money multiplier falls.[9] Furthermore, the loss of public confidence led banks to increase their desired reserve-to-deposit ratios in anticipation of potential runs. This also reduced the money multiplier.

In light of the banking panics and reduced money multiplier, what should the Fed have done during the Depression? According to many monetarists, the Fed should have pursued a policy of a constant rate of growth in the money supply.[10] In order to achieve such a goal, the Fed would have had

---

[6] Milton Friedman and Anna Schwartz, *A Monetary History of the United States* (Princeton: Princeton University Press, 1963), p. 300.

[7] We discuss this point in more detail in Chapter 16.

[8] With the inception of federally backed insurance on bank deposits, such as that provided by the Federal Deposit Insurance Corporation (FDIC) established in 1933, loss of deposits no longer accompanies most bank failures.

[9] Chapter 16 discusses in more detail the relationship between the currency-to-deposit ratio and the money mutiplier.

[10] Given the variety of different measures of the money supply, some monetarists argue that the Fed's policy should be to attain a constant rate of growth in the monetary base instead. However, it should be noted that important changes in the money supply can occur due to shifts from deposits to currency (e.g., the experience of the Depression) even if the monetary base is unchanged.

Figure 13.3 **The Effect on Real GNP of the Sharp Reduction in the Money Supply that Occurred During the Depression**

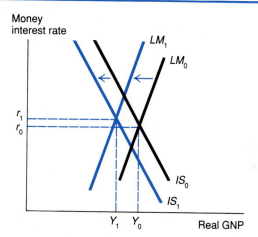

A fall in autonomous spending causes the *IS* curve to shift to the left from IS_0 to IS_1. In addition, a sharp reduction in the money supply causes an upward shift in the *LM* curve from LM_0 to LM_1. The result is a greater fall in real GNP and employment.

to offset the falling money multiplier by increasing the monetary base. But the Fed did not do this, and thus there was a fall in the money supply. In fact, the money supply fell at an average annual rate of 10 percent from 1929 to 1933. Monetarists assert that this dramatic fall in the money supply is the key reason for the dramatic fall in real output and prices that characterized the Depression. Between 1929 and 1933, real GNP fell by approximately 36 percent and, due to substantial deflation, nominal GNP fell by 56 percent. Even in ensuing years, the Fed did not realize the error of its ways. Between 1936 and 1938, the Fed doubled reserve requirements, thereby stalling the economy's recovery following the sharp contraction of the early 1930s.

In Figure 13.3, we use *IS-LM* analysis to illustrate the monetarist argument about the causes of the Depression. As in Figure 13.1, the fall in autonomous spending occurring in the early years of the Depression is represented by a leftward shift in the *IS* curve from IS_0 to IS_1. This in itself would have caused real GNP to fall given fixed prices in the short run. However, in addition, the sharp reduction in the money supply caused a large upward shift in the *LM* curve from LM_0 to LM_1. This accentuated the reduction in real GNP and employment, converting a recession into a depression.

The Monetarist Prescription of a Monetary Rule

Our discussion in the preceding section indicates that rather than mitigating the Great Depression, the Fed's behavior served to exacerbate it. In Chapter

1, we referred to Santayana's famous aphorism that those who cannot remember the past are condemned to repeat it. What policy lesson can we draw from the debacle of the 1930s?

Two different policy conclusions are possible.[11] The first is the more optimistic one and the one that the nonmonetarist is more likely to make: Having pursued the wrong discretionary policy in the past, we can follow improved discretionary policy in the future. As our understanding of the macroeconomy and the effects of policy changes has improved, we have progressed to the point where we can follow successful stabilization policy. Even though we may make some policy mistakes, as a general rule, we can improve macroeconomic stability.

The alternative conclusion, the one that the monetarist is likely to make, is a more pessimistic one: The Depression is but one example of the problems that misguided discretionary policy can create. Given the current state of our knowledge, we are better off not attempting discretionary policy changes. Monetarists do not believe that our macroeconomic knowledge is sufficient to pursue a success stabilization policy through discretionary policy changes. Instead, monetarists believe that the Fed should follow a simple monetary rule. The one that is typically advocated is to maintain a constant growth rate in the money supply. Such a monetary rule would eliminate the alleged ill-timed monetary policy changes that monetarists believe lead to output fluctuations in the short run. To summarize, perhaps the most important difference between nonmonetarists and monetarists is that the former believe that we have the wherewithal to pursue a successful stabilization policy and the latter do not.

Discretionary Monetary Policy to Counter the Real Effects of Cost-Push Inflation

As we have seen, nonmonetarists contend that autonomous spending shifts are important sources of output fluctuations and that under these circumstances the Fed can and should use discretionary monetary policy to stabilize the economy at a full employment level of output. In addition, as we discuss below, nonmonetarists see discretionary monetary policy as a way to offset price shocks that otherwise would lead to lower output and employment.

Two prime examples of price shocks to nonmonetarists are increases in the price level in response to increases in wages or increases in the price of oil. These are sometimes termed cases of **cost-push inflation**. In these instances, nonmonetarists argue that the Fed should be free to accommodate

Cost-push inflation: Inflation that is induced by increases in wages or increases in the price of oil.

---

[11] Although there are disagreements about what the Depression tells us concerning the advisability of discretionary money policy, there are other lessons about which there is unanimous agreement. As we noted earlier, the FDIC was initiated following the Depression. This has all but eliminated the occurrence of widespread banking panics so that another collapse of the banking system is highly improbable. Further, even without the safeguard provided by the FDIC, few economist predict that the Fed would countenance another such collapse of the banking system.

the price increase, for without an increase in the money supply, a higher price level means a lower real stock of money, and a consequent contraction in economic activity. Figure 13.4 illustrates these points.

In Figure 13.4(b), an increase in the price level from P_0 to P_1, with no change in the money supply, leads to a fall in real GNP from Y^* to Y_1, as the economy moves upward along the aggregate demand curve AD_0 from point A to point B. Recall that the reason for a movement up the aggregate demand curve is that a higher price level reduces the real supply of money. In terms of IS-LM analysis, the rise in the price level shifts the LM curve to the left, as shown in Figure 13.4(a). If the money supply is now increased from M_0^s to M_1^s so that the real money supply is the same as before the price increase, the aggregate demand curve shifts to the right from AD_0 to AD_1. At the new higher price level, the level of real GNP is maintained at Y^*. In terms of IS-LM analysis, this compensatory increase in the money supply returns the LM curve to its original position.

This analysis suggests an increase in money supply is the appropriate monetary policy given a one-time increase in the price level. Nonmonetarists do not, however, believe that the Fed's accommodation to price increases should be automatic. As James Tobin notes, "A one-shot price increase can be accommodated; a stubborn attempt to raise nominal wages and prices to sustain infeasible real wages and markups cannot be." According to the nonmonetarists, the Fed should be able to accommodate unanticipated price shocks, and "this is one substantial reason for the Fed's reluctance to tie its own hands as much as "rules" advocates . . . wish."[12] This discussion offers an additional argument for why nonmonetarists believe that there is a value to discretionary monetary policy.

The Monetarist's Counter: Inflation as a Monetary Phenomenon

In circumstances of cost-push inflation, what policies have been suggested to limit inflation in the long run? Some economists suggest that a mandated limit on wages and prices is a potentially effective way of reducing cost-push inflation. We will discuss the widespread use of price controls in the appendix to Chapter 14. It is sufficient now simply to point out that while price controls may reduce the measured rate of inflation, there are often costs. For instance, price controls tend to restrict changes in relative prices, which distorts the role of relative prices in allocating resources.

From the point of view of monetarists, there is an even more telling point to be made concerning cost-push inflation. Monetarists will simply ask why prices have risen in the first place. Monetarists look at changes in prices as the outcome of an equilibrating process that, in the long run, maintains the economy at a full employment level of real GNP. Thus what

---

[12] James Tobin, "Comment by Tobin on Consequences and Criticisms of Monetary Targeting," *Journal of Money, Credit, and Banking* (November 1985): pp. 605–608.

Figure 13.4   Cost-Push Inflation and an Accommodating Increase in the Money Supply

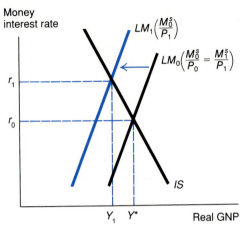

(a) *IS–LM* Analysis

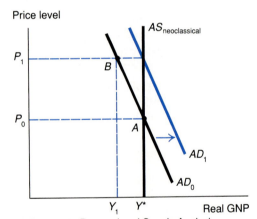

(b) Aggregate Demand and Supply Analysis

An increase in the price level from P_0 to P_1 leads to a fall in real GNP from Y^* to Y_1. The increase in the price level reduces the real money supply, which shifts the *LM* curve to the left from LM_0 to LM_1. In part (b), this is shown by the economy moving up the aggregate demand curve from point *A* to point *B*. A compensatory increase in the money supply to restore the real money supply to its original level shifts the aggregate demand curve to the right from AD_0 to AD_1, and real GNP remains at its original level Y^*. In terms of *IS-LM* analysis (part a), the compensatory increase in the money supply restores the *LM* curve to its original position.

nonmonetarists call cost-push inflation, monetarists link to underlying market factors. To monetarists, one obvious candidate for these underlying market factors would be too rapid a rate of growth in the money supply.

The above discussion highlights an important difference in the non-monetarist and monetarist view of how the economy operates. Monetarists believe that if the economy is left alone, prices adjust to restore the economy to full employment. The "too high" price level of the predetermined price model is something not expected to persist. Many monetarists would even contend that our experience of the Depression does not contradict this hypothesis. They note that the official unemployment statistics classified as unemployed the millions of employees on the payrolls of government emergency relief projects such as the Works Progress Administration and the Civilian Conservation Corps. If these individuals were classified as employed, as monetarists claim they should have been, then the unemployment rate would have fallen significantly during the Depression. In fact, had the Fed not intervened and doubled reserve requirements between August 1936 and May 1937, the natural unemployment rate (about 5 percent at that time) would likely have been reached by 1938.[13]

The belief by monetarists regarding the tendency for prices to adjust to changes in output demand leads them to stress another perceived advantage that a constant growth rate monetary rule would have: the establishment of a stable price level. In the next section, we examine this contention more closely. To do so, we couch our discussion not in terms of the predetermined price model but rather in terms of the neoclassical model. For as we have seen, it is the neoclassical model that provides the framework for analyzing the long-run behavior of the price level.

To the Point

MONETARY POLICY IN THE CONTEXT OF THE PREDETERMINED PRICE MODEL

- There are two opposing views of the effectiveness of monetary policy as a countercyclical tool. Monetarists believe that the best monetary policy is a monetary rule of a constant money growth. Nonmonetarists (or neo-Keynesians) believe that an activist monetary policy can be an effective tool in combating fluctuations in the economy.

- Monetarists believe that many past business fluctuations have as their source ill-conceived monetary policy. Nonmonetarists believe that aggregate demand fluctuates autonomously and unpredictably, so that discretionary monetary policy can add to the stability of the economy. Furthermore,

---

[13] Michael Darby, "Three-and-a-Half Million U.S. Employees Have Been Mislaid: Or an Explanation of Unemployment," *Journal of Political Economy* 1976): vol. 84, February 1976, pp. 1–16.

nonmonetarists cite the Depression as evidence of the inability of the economy to correct itself.

- In the macroeconomic model with predetermined prices, nonmonetarists believe that cost pressures may sometimes result in prices set too high to achieve full employment. According to nonmonetarists, these "price shocks," like changes in autonomous demand shocks, should be offset by countercyclical monetary policy. In contrast, monetarists view the expansion of the money supply as a key contributor to inflation.

13.2   OPTIMAL MONETARY POLICY IN THE LONG RUN

Recall from our discussion earlier in this book that the neoclassical model can be viewed as describing the long-run performance of the economy. In the long run, real GNP is determined by factors that underlie the aggregate supply curve; changes in aggregate demand cause prices to adjust in order to maintain equilibrium at full employment. In this section, we analyze optimal monetary policy from this long-run perspective.

In taking a long-run view of the economy, our concern is with how various monetary policies affect the inflation rate. Like the general public, most economists are in agreement that we should strive to maintain a low, predictable rate of inflation; some economists have even suggested that a negative inflation rate is desirable. We begin this section by exploring the advantages that price stability offers. We then look at what type of monetary policy we should conduct in order to achieve the goal of price stability.

The Goal of a Noninflationary Economy

One may wonder why a monetary policy with a goal of price stability or even prices falling at a constant rate would be optimal. The answer is not immediately obvious in the context of the neoclassical model since money supply changes are predicted to affect only money prices. Real variables that influence society's well-being, such as the levels of employment and real GNP, are unaffected by money supply changes. Why then should we be concerned if monetary policy causes money prices to rise by 10, 50, 100, or 1000 percent per year? Why should we be concerned if our monetary policy is responsible for an inflation rate of 5 percent last year, 15 percent this year, and who knows what next year?

The general public's dislike of inflation often appears to stem from reasons that have little to do with identifiable economic costs. When talking about the effects of inflation, individuals often do not recognize it as a general rise in prices and wages that is reflected not only in the prices that they must pay but also in the prices that they receive for their productive services. Not realizing that their own money incomes are rising because of inflation, individuals often mistakenly think that their real income would be higher if inflation were lower. Clearly, however, this reasoning is invalid, for if inflation were lower, not only would the prices that individuals pay to buy things rise at a slower rate, but so also would the money income that they earn. If we want to discover the economic costs of inflation, we have to look deeper.

In Chapters 3 and 4, we discussed the importance of money in the modern economy. In serving as a medium of exchange and a unit of account, money plays a crucial role in lowering transactions costs. However, the anticipation by individuals of a high and an erratic inflation rate in the future severely curtails money's usefulness. As we discuss below, a high and uncertain expected inflation rate implies a low, erratic real return to holding money, which limits its use as a medium of exchange. Furthermore, erratic inflation by itself limits the use of money as a unit of account in long-term contracts. With erratic inflation, individuals will be less willing to engage in long-term contracts that specify future money payments because of the great uncertainty that will exist concerning the real value of these payments.

A Computation of the Real Return to Holding Money

In Chapter 8, we saw that the neoclassical model predicts that an increase in the expected future inflation rate not only causes the nominal interest rate on financial assets to increase but also results in an increase in the current equilibrium price level. The higher price level means that individuals' real money holdings are reduced. Thus other things being constant, an increase in expected inflation will lower individuals' real money holdings. To understand the intuition behind this result, let's look more closely at the effect that higher inflation has on the cost of holding money balances.

The real return on money depends on its precise form. The real return on currency, or any other money component that earns no interest, is simply the negative of the rate of inflation. For example, if the rate of inflation is 6 percent, the real return on currency and other non–interest-bearing forms of money is minus 6 percent. Obviously, the higher the inflation rate, the lower is the real return on non–interest-bearing money. Interest-bearing checkable accounts are also a form of money. The expected real return on money offering the nominal interest rate r_m, is the nominal interest rate on money holdings minus the inflation rate π, or $r_m - \pi$. Since the nominal return on interest-bearing money is relatively inflexible, an increase in the expected rate of inflation reduces the real rate of return on this form of money as well as on non–interest-bearing forms of money.

To see why the real return on currency is $-\pi$ (and $r_m - \pi$ on interest-bearing money), consider the following example. Let's say that today's price of pencils, the only good in our economy, is P dollars. Then \$1 in money holdings is equal in value to $1/P$ pencils. If P is 10 cents, then \$1 in money holdings will equal 10 pencils in real terms. Letting π denote the rate of change in the price of pencils over the coming year, the price of pencils next year will be $P(1 + \pi)$, and we can purchase $1/P(1 + \pi)$ pencils next year with our initial money holdings of one dollar. For instance, if the inflation rate is .10, or 10 percent, then next year the price of pencils will be 11 cents [$10(1 + .10)$], and the initial \$1 money holdings will purchase approximately nine pencils. Computing the real rate of return to holding money, or the rate of change in the purchasing power of money, we have the following:

$$\frac{\text{Real return}}{\text{to money}} = \frac{1/[P(1 + \pi)] - 1/P}{1/P} = \frac{-\pi}{1 + \pi} \approx -\pi \qquad \textbf{(13.4)}$$

This equation shows that we can approximate the real return on non–interest-earning money holdings as the negative of the inflation rate. In the numerical example, the inflation rate of .10 (or 10 percent) for pencils implies a real rate of return for money of approximately $-.10$ (or minus 10 percent).[14] Simply expressed, currency loses purchasing power at the same rate as the price level increases.

Equation 13.4 suggests that individuals who expect a high inflation rate anticipate a substantial *negative* real return to holding money. If individuals have the alternative of holding assets such as property, inventories of goods, etc., then the negative return on money holdings will induce them to shift out of money into holdings of other real assets. Or as some economists say, inflation leads to a flight from money.[15] The outcome is that money is exploited less fully as a medium of exchange. With fewer money holdings, there are higher transaction costs of arranging exchanges.[16]

The attractiveness of holding money balances depends not only on the rate at which prices are expected to increase but also on the predictability

---

[14] The exact real return according to Equation 13.3 is $-\pi/(1 + \pi)$ or $-.10/1.1 = -.091$ (or a negative 9.1 percent).

[15] In the exchange equation, the fall in desired holdings of money appears as an increase in the velocity of money. The relationship between expected inflation and money demand is explored more fully in Chapter 16, where we carry out a more detailed analysis of the factors affecting the demand for money.

[16] Some have argued that the optimal inflation rate is actually negative since this would make the real return on money holdings positive, thus enhancing the desirability of holding money. After all, money costs practically nothing to create. Thus we should encourage individuals to hold money since this reduces transaction costs. Milton Friedman was the first to present this argument in his essay, "The Optimum Quantity of Money," which can be found in Milton Friedman, *The Optimum Quantity of Money and Other Essays* (Chicago: Aldine, 1969). More recently, Robert Lucas, "Principles of Fiscal and Monetary Policy," *Journal of Monetary Economics* (January 1986): 120, reiterates Friedman's claim that "a monetary policy that withdraws currency from circulation in a lump-sum fashion so as to induce a predictable deflation . . . is economically efficient." We shoud note, however, that tax considerations may well serve to qualify this argument. As we discuss in Chapter 14, a positive inflation rate implicitly provides revenue to the government in the form of an inflation tax on government debt. It may be desirable to utilize this inflation tax since other forms of taxation are also costly.

of inflation. Most individuals prefer a certain return to a risky return. Thus a monetary policy that leads to predictable as well as low future inflation rates increases the attractiveness of holding money, which in turn enhances money's use as a medium of exchange.[17]

The Costs of Contracting with Variable Inflation

Besides encouraging individuals to hold money balances, predictable inflation provides another economic benefit—a benefit that in fact is likely to be far more important and one that economists have recently started to pay more attention to. The use of long-term contracts is prevalent in our economy and does much to facilitate exchange. Predictable inflation makes it less costly for individuals to use long-term contracts that express future payments in money terms, which on simplicity grounds alone constitutes a preferred way of expressing such commitments. Examples of such long-term contracts are employment contracts between companies and unions that specify money wage payments over a period of several years and loan contracts between lenders and borrowers that specify the payment of interest and principal over the future.

When future inflation is known, so too will be the real value of the future money payments specified in long-term contracts. Conversely, when it is difficult to predict future inflation rates, it will also be difficult to predict the real value of specified future money payments. Since unpredictable inflation increases the risk associated with long-term contracts that specify payments in money terms, increased variability in the inflation rate should decrease the use of such contracts. Individuals will to some extent lean toward contracts that do not use money as a unit of account. However, since it is costly to enter into agreements where money is not used as the unit of account, fewer long-term contracts will occur in total.

The reduced use of long-term contracts can be expected to have important real economic effects. Since such contracts are important in facilitating trade, there should be an adverse effect on real GNP. In terms of the neoclassical model, a more unpredictable inflation rate causes the aggregate supply curve to shift to the left, resulting in a lower output level.

To summarize our above argument, an increase in the variability of inflation has an important economic cost because it is predicted to have a negative, albeit indirect, impact on real GNP.[18] Recent empirical work has found evidence of this effect. For instance, Victor Zarnowitz and Louis Lambros

---

[17] There is some evidence that the level of expected inflation and its predictability are related. See for example, Victor Zarnowitz and Louis A. Lambros, ''Consensus and Uncertainty in Economic Prediction,'' *Journal of Political Economy* (June 1987): 616. The authors find evidence that expectations of higher inflation generate greater uncertainty about inflation.

[18] Our earlier argument concerning the effects of high expected inflation could also be stated in terms of the effect on real GNP. To say that increased holdings of real money balances reduce transaction costs is essentially equivalent to saying that they enter into the economy's aggregate production function. Thus a reduction in real money balances causes overall production to fall.

find that "the idea of inflation uncertainty as a short-term depressant of real activity receives substantial support."[19] However, the impact of higher inflation uncertainty on the economy's performance becomes less severe over time as institutions adjust and individuals learn to adapt in order to lessen their risk.[20]

We can see most clearly the costs to an economy of a monetary policy that leads to high and variable inflation rates by looking at the extreme case of hyperinflation. Bolivia provides a recent example. Bolivia's money supply grew 6151 percent from 1984 to 1985, and its consumer price index rose 8170 percent. The social consequences are illustrated vividly by the following newspaper account:

> The inflation was threatening the very fabric of society. The banking system practically collapsed as black market speculators took over its role. Prices changed by the minute, and people literally carried money around in suitcases. Currency, which was printed abroad, was the third largest import in 1984. The two-inch stack of money needed to buy a chocolate bar far outweighed the candy. Strikes were everyday occurrences. . . . In one typical week, workers in 34 factories took 180 executives hostage in disputes. . . . Companies weren't investing.[21]

Bolivia's situation illustrates the serious consequences to a modern, monetary economy of the extreme price instability that characterizes hyperinflations.[22] Since it requires substantial resources simply to make exchanges and to negotiate agreements involving money payments, much trading reverts to barter. Barter is costly, as you would realize if at the end of the summer you tried to use a tennis racket as payment for a celebration at the local nightspot. You would have to search far and wide to find an entertainment spot that would offer pizza and beer for a used tennis racket. A pure barter economy would require such search costs for all exchanges. With money as the medium of exchange, however, you could simply sell the racket for money and then use that money to buy pizza and beer.

Naturally, Bolivia's situation is extreme. Fluctuating inflation in the, say, 10 to 15 percent range would not have nearly as dire consequences. Still, as discussed above, the available evidence supports the general proposition that there are economic costs associated with high and unpredictable inflation.

---

[19] Victor Zarnowitz and Louis A. Lambros, "Consensus and Uncertainty in Economic Prediction," *Journal of Political Economy* (June 1987): 616. Vol. 95. See also John Makin, "Anticipated Money, Inflation Uncertainty, and Real Economic Activity," *Review of Economics and Statistics* (February 1982): 126–135.

[20] Recall our discussion in Chapter 12 of the increased wage indexation that followed the higher inflation uncertainty of the 1960s and 1970s.

[21] *The Wall Street Journal*, 13 August 1986 p. 1.

[22] Note that in Bolivia the rise in the price level exceeded the rise in its money supply, indicating a fall in real money holdings. This is consistent with our analysis in Chapter 8 of the effects of an increase in expected inflation. For, as noted above, this analysis predicts a jump in the price level and a resultant reduction in real money holdings.

The question that arises, therefore, is what type of monetary policy is most conducive to achieving a stable price level?

The Case for a Simple Money Supply Rule to Achieve Price Stability

The above discussion indicates that in the long-run context of the neoclassical model, optimal monetary policy should have as its goal low, predictable inflation. In light of past discussions, you should be able to anticipate the monetarist policy prescription for achieving this role: Adopt a monetary rule that would commit the Fed to a fixed rate of growth in the money supply. As Milton Friedman explains it:

1. The target should be growth in some monetary aggregate.
2. Monetary authorities should adopt long-run targets for monetary growth that are consistent with no inflation.
3. Monetary authorities should avoid fine tuning.[23]

Using the exchange equation (Equation 13.3), it is easy to ascertain the conditions under which such a rule will bring about price stability: If real GNP and velocity both grow at a steady rate, then an announced monetary policy that sets the growth rate in the money supply at a low, fixed level assures both a low and a predictable inflation rate. As we saw in our earlier discussion, monetarists believe that as a general rule these conditions do tend to hold (or at least that they would hold in the absence of the Fed pursuing discretionary monetary policies). For as we have seen, monetarists downplay the role of private demand disturbances in causing changes in velocity. And they believe that prices adjust reasonably quickly to demand shocks. As the neoclassical model indicates, this means that real GNP is determined primarily by supply factors. Consequently, steady growth in the labor force and the capital stock will translate into steady growth in real GNP, and changes in the rate of growth of the money supply translate into equivalent changes in the inflation rate.

Obstacles to a Simple Money Supply Rule: Sources of Changes in Velocity

Although under ideal conditions a monetary rule will stabilize the price level, things are not always so simple. From the exchange equation ($M^s V = PY$), we see that a simple monetary rule of allowing the money supply (M^s) to grow at a low, constant rate will not result in a low, steady rate of increase in the price level (P) if real GNP (Y) and/or velocity (V) do not grow at a constant rate over time. In point of fact, neither real GNP nor velocity grows

---

[23] Milton Friedman, "Monetary Policy," *Journal of Money, Credit, and Banking* (February 1982): 101.

at a constant rate over time. In Chapter 9, we saw how supply shocks can lead to changes in real GNP in the neoclassical model. These supply-side shocks may be disruptions in the oil supply, harvest failures, or changes in tax policies that alter the incentives to work and invest.

Earlier in this chapter we discussed one potential source of changes in velocity—a change in autonomous investment or consumption demand. In Chapter 8, we saw that changes in government deficit spending and in expected inflation also cause velocity to change. Behind all these changes in velocity is a change in the interest rate that alters money demand. For example, as we saw in Figure 13.2, velocity fell during the 1982 to 1986 period. A major reason for this was the fall in inflationary expectations that led to a lower money interest rate. As a consequence, individuals were willing to hold larger money balances, so that the ratio of nominal GNP to money holdings (velocity) fell.

However, velocity can also change because of an exogenous change in desired money holdings. For instance, consider the impact of the introduction of new banking technology such as automated tellers and various nationwide credit cards. The result was a decline in money demand and thus rising velocity during the 1970s since such innovations reduced the amount of money people had to keep on hand for purposes of exchange. Individuals conserved on their money holdings and diverted their wealth from monetary assets to alternative assets such as bonds and stocks.

Figure 13.5 illustrates the initial impact on the financial and money markets of an exogenous fall in money demand at the original levels of real GNP and prices. In Figure 13.5(b), the fall in real money demand shifts the real money demand curve to the left from L_0^d to L_1^d. Assuming no change in consumption demand, the fall in money demand means an offsetting rise in the household demand for financial assets as shown in Figure 13.5(a) by the shift to the right in the supply of loanable funds curve from LF_0^s to LF_1^s. The interest rate that clears the financial market falls from r_0 to r_1.

As indicated in the figure, at the new, lower interest rate that clears the financial market, there is excess supply in the money market at the original levels of real GNP and prices. From the aggregate budget constraint, this implies an excess demand for output, as the fall in the interest rate has stimulated investment and consumption demand. Excess demand in the output market at the original levels of output and prices means that the aggregate demand curve has shifted to the right, as shown in Figure 13.6. In the neoclassical model, this causes the equilibrium price level to rise from P_0 to P_1.

This increase in the price level reduces the real money supply and thus the real supply of loanable funds. The reduction in the real supply of loanable funds causes the interest rate to rise. In fact, at the new equilibrium level of prices, the interest rate is the same as before the fall in the money demand. With the interest rate equal to its original level, output demand again matches the (unchanged) production of real GNP Y^*.

Figure 13.5   The Initial Impact of a Decrease in Money Demand

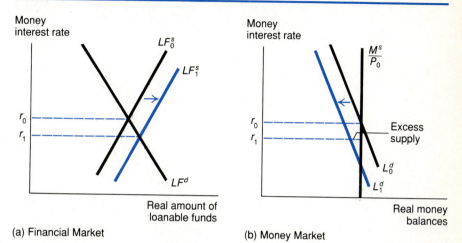

(a) Financial Market

(b) Money Market

A decrease in money demand causes a shift to the left in the money demand curve from L_0^d to L_1^d in the money market, as illustrated in part (b). With wealth being diverted from monetary assets to financial assets, the fall in the demand for money is accompanied by an increase in demand for financial assets, as shown in part (a) by the shift to the right in the supply of loanable funds curve from LF_0^s to LF_1^s. This results in a decrease in the equilibrium interest rate from r_0 to r_1. As indicated by the graph of the money market, at the lower interest rate there is an excess supply of money at the original price level and output. From the aggregate budget constraint, this implies an excess demand for output.

Figure 13.6   The Effect of a Decrease in Money Demand on Real GNP and Prices

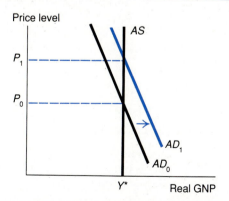

A fall in money demand leads to excess demand in the output market at the initial levels of prices and output. The result is a shift to the right in the aggregate demand curve from AD_0 to AD_1 and an increase in the equilibrium price level from P_0 to P_1.

In terms of the exchange equation, the fall in money demand is equivalent to a rise in velocity. In fact, from Equation 13.3 we know that in the neoclassical model the money supply and real GNP are unaffected by the change in money demand, so that the percent increase in velocity exactly equals the percent increase in prices.

Revisions of the regulatory and tax environment are other sources of changes in money demand and thus velocity. The Monetary Control Act of 1980 made checkable deposits more widely available at financial institutions such as credit unions and mutual savings banks, which meant that checkable accounts that pay interest became more widespread.

The above changes made holding money more attractive, which, in conjunction with falling interest rates, helps explain the fall in velocity during the 1980 to 1986 period. During this period velocity fell at an annual average rate of approximately 1 percent, marking a reversal of the steady growth in velocity that had occurred from the end of World War II until that time period. The reduction in marginal tax rates on income initiated by the tax simplification act of 1986 should partially offset the reductions in velocity that occurred during the 1980 to 1986 period. Since lower marginal taxes tend to reduce tax avoidance, holding currency in order to hide taxable income should decrease. This fall in the demand for money (specifically, in the demand for currency) would mean an increase in velocity, other things being equal.

Fluctuations in velocity, whether instigated by changes in autonomous spending (households, firms, or government) or by autonomous changes in money demand, mean that a simple money supply rule will not succeed in achieving a steady inflation rate. Of course, whether or not we should still choose to follow such a fixed money supply rule depends on the available alternatives. One alternative we have discussed in an earlier section is allowing the Fed to engage in pure discretionary policy. In the next section, we discuss a second alternative that has received attention in recent years, namely reactive rules. As we will see, reactive rules are a compromise between a simple monetary rule and pure discretion.

To the Point

MONETARY POLICY IN THE CONTEXT OF THE NEOCLASSICAL MODEL

- A noninflationary economy enhances the use of money as a medium of exchange. Predictable inflation also increases the use of long-term contracts that express future payments in money terms.

- According to the neoclassical model, monetary changes lead to price increases. Excessive monetary growth thus means inflation.

- In order to achieve a zero inflation rate, the money supply would have to grow at a rate equal to the difference between the rate of growth of real GNP and the rate of growth of velocity. Monetarists advocate a monetary rule that increases the rate of growth of the money supply at a constant rate each year.

- If supply shocks that affect real GNP and fluctuations in velocity are significant, a simple money supply rule will not achieve a low, predictable rate of inflation.

13.3 MOVING TOWARD DISCRETION: REACTIVE RULES

The conflict between a monetary rule and a variable velocity was noted by Henry Simons as far back as 1936 when he wrote that "the obvious weakness of a fixed quantity [of money] as a sole rule of monetary policy, lies in the danger of sharp changes on the velocity side, for no monetary system can function effectively or survive politically in the face of extreme alterations of hoarding and dishoarding."[24]

Should we modify the simple money supply rule in the face of fluctuations in velocity? If so, how? Some monetarists respond that we should limit the length of time that we follow a particular growth rate in the money supply. Milton Friedman has suggested a target path for the growth in the money supply of several years, at which time we could use updated information on velocity changes to commit to new, noninflationary rates of increase in the money supply. Alternatively, William Poole, a member of the President's Council of Economic Advisers from 1982 to 1985, has suggested that monetary rules should be adopted but that the rule should be "subject to change at any time upon presentation of a convincing case with supporting evidence."[25]

A possible alternative to the monetarist simple money supply rule is to adopt a rule that automatically offsets fluctuations in velocity.[26] For example, it has been suggested that the growth rate of the money supply be targeted on the growth rate of nominal GNP. Let's look at the implications of such a **reactive rule**—a monetary policy that specifies in advance how the money supply will be adjusted in the face of new information.

Reactive rule: A rule that specifies in advance how government policies will change based on new information on the state of the economy.

Substituting a GNP Target for a Money Supply Target

Replacing a fixed money supply rule with a reactive monetary rule that targets nominal GNP ($P \cdot Y$) means that fluctuations in velocity (V) will be automatically offset by changes in the money supply. For example, if an

---

[24] Henry C. Simons, "Rules Versus Authorities in Monetary Policy," *Journal of Political Economy* (February 1936): 5.

[25] William Poole, "Comment: On Consequences and Criticisms of Monetary Targeting," *Journal of Money, Credit, and Banking* (November 1985) Vol. 17: 602–604.

[26] This approach is outlined by Bennett McCallum, "On Consequences and Criticisms of Monetary Targeting," *Journal of Money, Credit, and Banking* (November 1985) Vol. 17: 570–597.

increase in velocity puts upward pressure on nominal GNP, it will automatically be offset by a reduction in the money supply. Fluctuations in velocity will no longer cause changes in the level of prices.

In terms of our aggregate demand and supply curves, exogenous changes in aggregate demand will automatically be offset by changes in the money supply. For instance, consider either an increase in autonomous investment or a fall in money demand, both of which shift the aggregate demand curve to the right from AD_0 to AD_1 as shown in Figure 13.7. This increase in aggregate demand will not cause prices (and thus nominal GNP) to rise if it is accompanied by an offsetting reduction in the money supply, which would shift the aggregate demand curve back to its original position (AD_0).

The proposal for a reactive rule that targets nominal GNP ($P \cdot Y$) has the attractive feature of inducing a monetary response to changes in either prices (P) or real GNP (Y). Consider the position of those who argue for the Fed to engage in countercyclical monetary policy to offset short-run fluctuations in real GNP. A rule that targets a level of nominal GNP would call for an increase in the money supply when velocity falls, thereby preventing a reduction in nominal, and thus real, GNP in the short run. And consider the rule's ability to eliminate price volatility. A rule that targets nominal GNP would call for a decrease in the money supply when velocity increases, so that the rise in velocity need not imply higher prices in the long run.[27]

There are, however, several potential problems with a reactive monetary rule that targets nominal GNP. The first concerns the target; if the key objective of monetary policy is price stability, a nominal GNP target will not be successful given supply shocks. The next section examines this problem and suggests an alternative reactive rule. We then discuss a second, more serious problem with reactive rules in general that arises when implementation of such rules is attempted.

Supply Shocks and Targeting Prices

As we saw in Chapter 9, the full employment level of real GNP can fluctuate from its trend rate of growth due to supply-side shocks such as oil supply disruptions, changes in tax rates that alter incentives to work and save, demographic changes that alter the composition and size of the labor force, and surges of technological innovations. Supply-side shocks present a potentially serious problem with a monetary rule that targets nominal GNP. With any of these supply-side shocks, the inflation rate will vary despite a reactive

---

[27] As Barro notes, "In effect, the proposal to stabilize nominal GNP is an attempt to unite the principal warring factions in macroeconomics. The new classicists are supposed to be happy because monetary policy is governed by a rule, and that rule does not entail stabilization of some nominal magnitude. . . . Keynesians are supposed to be happy with the scheme because it allows for an active response of money to recessions and booms." Robert J. Barro, "Recent Developments in the Theory of Rules Versus Discretion," *Economic Journal* (Supplement, 1986): 23–37.

Figure 13.7   Monetary Changes That Offset Demand-side Shocks

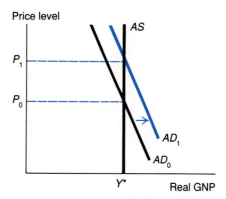

An increase in autonomous investment or a fall in money demand increases aggregate demand, as shown by the shift in the aggregate demand curve from AD_0 to AD_1. The higher price level that results can be offset, however, if the money supply is decreased sufficiently to reduce aggregate demand back to AD_0.

rule targeting nominal GNP. In fact, a rule that maintains a constant nominal GNP will mean that a 1 percent fall in real GNP will be accompanied by a 1 percent increase in prices.

In terms of our aggregate demand and aggregate supply curve analysis, achieving stable prices in light of supply-side fluctuations in the growth of real GNP requires changes in the money supply that shift the aggregate demand curve in the same direction as the aggregate supply curve. For instance, in Figure 13.8 the increase in prices that would accompany a fall in aggregate supply from AS_0 to AS_1 can be eliminated if the money supply falls sufficiently to reduce aggregate demand from AD_0 to AD_1.[28]

Our analysis suggests that the optimal monetary policy for achieving a low, stable inflation rate would target the price index, not nominal GNP. After all, if the goal is stable prices, why not make that the target as well? Following this rule, the growth rate in the money supply will be reduced when policy makers anticipate inflation and increased when they anticipate deflation. With such a *reactive* monetary policy rule, a stable price level could in principle be achieved as the effect on prices both only changes in aggregate demand but also changes in aggregate supply could be offset by changes in the money supply.[29] It should be noted that since a substantial portion of

[28] A good, though dated, example of a reduction in aggregate supply is the outbreak of the plague that reduced the labor force in Europe in the fourteenth century, when 25 percent of the population succumbed to the bubonic plague spread by vermin of the non–two-legged variety.

[29] Although we do not discuss them, reactive rules based on variables other than nominal GNP or prices have also been proposed. One rule suggests that the money supply be changed each

Figure 13.8   **Monetary Changes That Offset Supply-side Shocks**

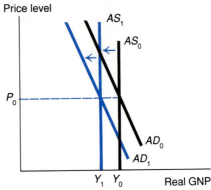

The effect on price level of a decrease in aggregate supply from AS_0 to AS_1 can be offset by a decrease in aggregate demand from AD_0 to AD_1 brought about by a decrease in the money supply.

fluctuations in nominal interest rates reflects fluctuations in expected inflation, a credible commitment to a stable price level will also eliminate this source of interest rate fluctuations.

Reactive rules such as the one outlined above are appealing, at least if we accept the neoclassical world of flexible prices. Monetarists point out potential drawbacks to a reactive monetary rule that targets either nominal GNP or a price index, however. These drawbacks arise in specifying exactly how to implement such targeting.

13.4   POTENTIAL PROBLEMS IN IMPLEMENTING RULES

In our discussion of discretionary monetary policy in the context of the predetermined price model, we indicated that one of the difficulties in implementing discretionary monetary policy is predicting the impact of monetary changes on the economy. As we discuss in the first part of this section, the presence of long and variable lags between changes in the money supply

period in response to differences between the current interest rate and a target interest rate. For discussions of rules such as this, see Matthew B. Canzoneri, Dale W. Henderson, and Kenneth S. Rogoff, "The Information Content of the Interest Rate and Optimal Monetary Policy," *Quarterly Journal of Economics* (November 1983) pp. 545–566 and Bennett McCallum, "Interest Rate Pegging and Price Level Determinancy," *Journal of Monetary Economics* (January 1986), pp. 135–159.

and changes in the target variable means that difficulties exist in implementing reactive rules as well.

At least two other potential difficulties exist in implementing a monetary policy where the Fed announces and follows a rule, whether it be a reactive rule or a simple mechanical rule that fixes the growth rate of money at a low level. The first is a technical problem in implementing a rule: Can the Fed effectively control the money supply? Recall from our earlier discussion in Chapters 3 and 4 that the Fed does not directly control the money supply but rather directly controls the monetary base. In this section we review the evidence on the Fed's ability to control the money supply.

Even if the Fed can effectively control the money supply, there is still another potential problem to implementing a rule. Although the Fed has at times announced its intention to adopt a rule, in practice the Fed has usually not actually carried out such a policy. We thus conclude this section by examining the recent divergence between what the Fed announces as policy and what it actually implements. Given this divergence, we then consider suggestions, such as a gold standard, for imposing a fixed, low monetary growth rate on the Fed.

Lags and Difficulties in Specifying Feedback Rules

To implement an effective reactive monetary rule that targets a particular variable, say nominal GNP or prices, two pieces of information are important. First, the Fed should have a good estimate of the time it takes for a change in the money supply to affect the target. Second, the Fed should have a reasonable idea of what value the target variable would take in the future in the absence of the money supply change. For example, the calculations that are required to implement a reactive monetary rule that targets prices to achieve a rate of inflation precisely equal to zero are as follows:

1. The Fed calculates the number of months it takes for a 1 percent increase in the money supply to cause prices to rise by 1 percent, other things being equal. We will use the letter x to designate the number of months it takes before the full effect on prices of a money supply change occurs.

2. The Fed projects how prices will rise over the next x months if there is no change in the money supply. This projection takes into account anticipated changes in velocity and real GNP. In fact, we can see from the exchange equation (Equation 13.3) that this projection of the percent change in the price level over the next x months if the money supply is unchanged simply equals the anticipated change in velocity minus the anticipated change in real GNP. For instance, if velocity is anticipated to grow at an 8 percent rate over this time and real GNP is expected to grow at a 3 percent rate, then one can project a 5 percent growth in the price level if there is no change in the money supply.

3. To attain the goal of a zero inflation rate, the Fed will then reduce the money supply by an amount equal to the projected rate of inflation over

the next x months. In the above example, a 5 percent projected inflation rate, if the money supply is constant, will dictate reducing the money supply by 5 percent. This fall in the money supply, when coupled with the anticipated rises of 8 percent in velocity and 3 percent in real GNP, will achieve the goal of price stability, i.e., zero inflation, over the next x months.

One of the key features of the reactive monetary rule specified above is that there is a lag of x months between a monetary change and the time it affects prices. The rule may not achieve its goal of price stability if this lag between the change in the money supply and the change in the target is long and variable. Consider first how the length of a lag affects the effective implementation of reactive rules. If a substantial number of months passes before a change in the money supply fully affects prices, then the Fed must predict the level of prices far into the future. Predictions of future prices in the absence of any change in the money supply may be fairly accurate one month in advance but will be less accurate further in the future. To the extent that these projections are wrong, any monetary policy based on the projections will not lead to the desired outcome of stable prices.

Now consider how the variability in the lag between the change in the money supply and its effect on the target affects the effective implementation of reactive monetary rules. For example, let's say that while the average lag is six months, sometimes three months passes between the time the money supply changes and prices are affected; other times the lag is 12 months. Changes in the money supply will not achieve stable prices if the timing of their impacts is not known, as the following example suggests.

Assume that the Fed predicts deflation over the next six months due to an anticipated decrease in velocity. Seeking stable prices, the Fed increases the current growth rate in the money supply based on an *average* lag between a money supply change and price adjustment of six months. Assuming that the Fed has correctly anticipated velocity changes over the next six months, such a monetary change will still not achieve its goal of price stability if the actual lag differs from six months. For instance, if the effect of this particular money supply change on prices is felt a year rather than six months after its inception, the effect may occur at a time when the economy faces inflationary pressures. In such a case, the expansionary monetary policy not only will fail to avoid the deflation in the first half of the year but also will accentuate inflation in the second half of the year.

Monetarists use the existence of long and variable lags in the economy's response to money supply changes as an argument to counter the intuitive appeal of policy prescriptions that institute reactive rules targeting variables such as nominal GNP or prices. Due to such lags, a policy of a constant growth rate in the money supply might achieve a more stable inflation rate than a policy that constantly adjusts the growth of the money supply in anticipation of fluctuations in velocity and the full employment level of GNP that may or may not occur. The difficulties with a feedback rule are compounded when the timing of the future effect on prices of changes in the growth rate of the money supply is uncertain.

Can the Fed Control Monetary Aggregates?

If we ignore the potential problems in specifying feedback rules outlined above, we still face a potentially important problem in implementing monetary rules if the Fed cannot accurately control the money supply. In this section, we review the evidence on the Fed's ability to control the money supply.

Recall from our discussion in Chapter 5 that when we talk of the Fed determining monetary policy, the actual group that makes the key decisions concerning money supply changes is the Federal Open Market Committee (FOMC). The FOMC consists of the seven members of the Federal Reserve board of governors, plus five of the 12 Federal Reserve bank presidents. The FOMC usually meets eight times each year but may have a conference-call meeting to reevaluate monetary policy at any time.[30] The FOMC delegates the implementation of the monetary policy to the staff of the Open Market Desk at the Federal Reserve Bank of New York.

The Open Market Desk implements monetary policy by buying and selling federal government securities for the Federal Reserve system. We previously referred to this buying and selling of government bonds by the Fed as open market operations. Recall from Chapter 5 that when the Fed buys securities, the monetary base increases, typically in the form of increased bank reserves (vault cash plus deposits of private depository institutions at the Fed). When the Fed sells securities, the monetary base falls and bank reserves are reduced.

Although the Fed has direct control over the monetary base, the Fed does not directly control the money supply. The money multiplier links the monetary base and the money supply. As our analysis in Chapter 5 indicated, the money multiplier is determined by such factors as average reserve-to-deposit ratios and average currency-to-deposit ratios. To implement a policy of a constant rate of growth in the money supply, the Fed must anticipate and offset fluctuations in the money multiplier. Despite this potential difficulty, it is generally believed that the Fed can now control the money supply, at least on a quarter to quarter basis.[31]

In the 1980s, two changes concerning reserve requirements were made that strengthened the Fed's capability to control the money supply. The first change, which was instituted by the Monetary Control Act of 1980, made reserve requirements more uniform. Prior to this change, there was substantial

---

[30] The chairman of the board of governors is, by tradition, chairman of the FOMC. The president of the Federal Reserve Bank of New York is a permanent member of the FOMC. The other four memberships rotate annually among the presidents of the remaining 11 Federal Reserve banks. The one aspect of monetary policy that the FOMC does not control is the setting of the discount rate, which is done by the Federal Reserve board of governors.

[31] See McCallum, Footnote 2.

variation in reserve requirements for different types of deposits and for different depository institutions. Nonuniformity in reserve requirements is detrimental to monetary control since shifts between deposit accounts alter the average required reserve-to-deposit ratio across all deposits, and thus alter the money multiplier. As noted in Chapter 3, coincident with this change was the expansion of the definition of the money supply (M1) to include checkable deposits at all depository institutions, not just commercial banks.

A second recent change that has potentially improved the Fed's control of the money supply occurred in early 1984. At that time, the Fed instituted contemporaneous reserve requirements, which base required reserves on contemporaneous levels of deposits. Prior to this time, a lagged reserve requirements system was enforced in which required reserves were based on deposits two weeks earlier. Eliminating lagged reserve requirements made monetary control using monetary base components more precise.[32]

Will the Fed Follow Announced Rules?

The previous section indicates that implementing the monetarist policy prescription of a monetary policy rule is technically feasible. Over the last 15 years, policymakers at the Fed have often identified a constant growth rate of the money supply as the policy to follow. Yet the Fed has not in fact fully embraced such a monetarist policy, as a review of its actions indicates.

In 1975, Congress passed Concurrent Resolution 133, which stated that it was "the sense of the Congress" that the Fed should "maintain long-run growth of the monetary and credit aggregate commensurate with the economy's long-run potential to increase production." The resolution requested that the Fed "consult" Congress at regular intervals concerning its "objectives and plans" for monetary growth and "report to the Congress the reasons" for any departure from these monetary growth objectives. This congressional resolution might be interpreted as a monetarist monetary policy: a rule that restricted the growth rate of the money supply to the trend rate of growth in real GNP. Assuming a constant velocity, the outcome would be price stability.

The Fed initially objected to the resolution but subsequently pledged cooperation. For the next four years, however, the Fed, either knowingly or unknowingly, undermined the intent of the resolution in two ways. First, the Fed announced monetary targets for a variety of money supply measures and shifted attention back and forth from one measure to another, which confused Fed watchers about the direction of Fed policy. Second, each quarter the Fed announced the target growth rates for the different measures of the money supply using as a base the actual (not targeted) level of the money

---

[32] See McCallum, Footnote 2. The author notes in particular that using total bank reserves as an instrument for achieving a monetary target provides "a high degree of money stock control" given a system of contemporaneous, uniform reserve requirements.

supply of the prior quarter. This action by the Fed became known as "base drift" and meant that failures to achieve the target were buried in the base.

The typical way in which base drift occurred was the following. The Fed would announce target ranges for monetary growth at the start of the year. For instance, at the beginning of 1980 the Federal Open Market Committee announced a range of growth rates for M1 that would be acceptable during the current year. For instance, from the fourth quarter of 1979 to the fourth quarter of 1980, the Fed's target range of growth for M1 was 4.0 to 6.5 percent. Given that the actual fourth quarter value for M1 was $387.8 billion in 1979, the range of growth rates implied a range of target levels of M1 at the end of the year of between $403.3 billion and $413 billion. The midpoint of that range is $408.2 billion. The actual money supply level for the fourth quarter of 1980 was $416.8, so the Fed overshot its mark.

At the start of 1981, the Fed announced a new range for monetary growth for M1 of between 3.5 and 6.0 percent. No attempt was made to correct for the previous high rate of monetary growth. Instead, the planned growth of M1 for 1981 was projected from the previous high base level of $416.8 billion at the end of 1980 instead of from the target level of $408.2 billion. Given this base drift of $8.6 billion, even if the Fed had attained its target growth rate in the second year, money growth over the two-year period was still higher than the Fed initially intended for it to be. This example of base drift was not an isolated incident. As Carl Walsh reports, "the actual fourth-quarter level [of M1] was above the midpoint of the target range for seven of the ten years from 1976 to 1985. . . . These above target levels then formed the bases from which the subsequent target ranges were calculated."[33]

These actions by the Fed during the 1976 to 1985 period seriously weakened any credibility to the Fed's claim that it had adopted a policy rule of a low, constant rate of growth in the money supply. Federal Reserve economist Stephen Axilrod noted that "in the late 1970s, money target misses and evidence of accelerating prices eroded the market's confidence in the Federal Reserve's will" to maintain a noninflationary growth in the money supply.[34]

In an October, 1979 address to the American Bankers Association in New Orleans, Paul Volcker, at that time the newly appointed chairman of the Federal Reserve Board, announced what turned out to be a three-year period now referred to as the "monetary experiment." On average, even with base drift, monetary growth was reduced during this period, and inflation (in consumer prices) that was 12.5 percent in 1980 fell to approximately 4 percent in 1982. This general relationship between money supply growth and inflation was illustrated in Chapter 8 in Figure 8.3. The growth rate of

---

[33] Carl E. Walsh, "In Defense of Base Drift," *American Economic Review* (September 1986): 692.

[34] Stephen Axilrod, "U.S. Monetary Policy in Recent Years: An Overview", *Federal Reserve Bulletin* (January 1985): Vol. 71, pp. 14–24.

Figure 13.9   The Volatility of the Money Supply Measure: 1970–1987

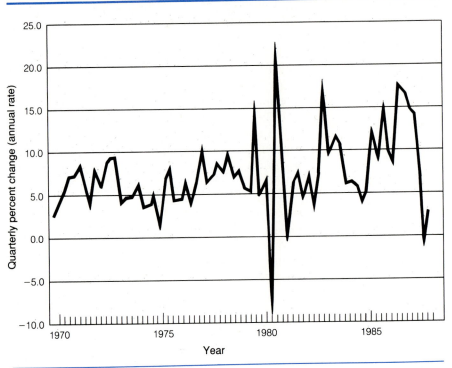

the money supply from quarter to quarter varied quite widely, however, during the 1979 to 1982 period, as is illustrated by Figure 13.9. In fact, the money supply was more volatile during this three years than in any earlier three-year period since the end of World War II.[35] This volatility of monetary growth substantially reduced the predictability of monetary policy in the short run, at least to those outside the Fed. Monetarists pointed to this volatility as evidence that the Fed's promise to follow a monetary rule was not pursued during this period. As a consequence uncertainty about future inflation rates increased.

In late 1982, the Fed publicly abandoned its intention to follow a rule of a fixed, low rate of growth in the money supply. The new monetary targets were vastly exceeded, suspended, and then new growth targets were announced that started from higher initial levels of the money supply. As Table 8.1 in Chapter 8 indicated, however, the period from 1982 to 1987

---

[35] See Milton Friedman, "Lessons from the 1979–1982 Monetary Experiment," *American Economic Review* (May 1984): 397.

was not one of rapid inflation, as there was a burst in the rate of growth in real GNP and velocity reversed its upward trend. According to James Tobin, during this period the Fed pursued a monetary policy "oriented to macroeconomic performance." As Tobin explains, "The Fed has had in mind a desired track, or range of tracks, of real GNP, unemployment, and prices, and has sought by its sequence of operating targets for nonborrowed [bank] reserves to keep the economy on track. This has meant tightening reserve supplies when recovery seemed overexuberant and easing them when it appeared to be stalling."[36]

At the time this book was written, the Fed appeared to be continuing its embrace of discretionary monetary policy, or of "doing the right thing at the right time." This view is evidenced by the following excerpt from the Federal Reserve's Report to Congress, submitted February 24, 1988:

> For 1988, the [Open Market] Committee set ranges of 4% to 8% growth of M2 and M3 . . . While the Committee at this time expects that growth of M2 and M3 will be around the middle of their ranges, the outcome could differ if significant changes in interest rates are required to counter unanticipated weakness in aggregate demand or an intensification of inflation. In carrying out policy, the Committee will continue to assess the behavior of the aggregates in light of information about the pace of business expansions and the source and strength of price pressures, with attention to the performance of the dollar on foreign-exchange markets and other indicators of the impact of monetary policy.

It should be remembered that the inclusion of numerical ranges for M2 and M3 in the above report are there primarily because Congress mandated in 1975 that such figures be included in the Federal Reserve's report to Congress.

A Commodity Standard: Would It Achieve the Monetarist Policy Prescription?

The recent fear of runaway inflation that prompted the Fed to announce limits on monetary growth echoes past concerns. Economist Irving Fisher wrote in 1911 that "irredeemable paper money has almost invariably proved a curse to the country employing it?"[37] By that Fisher meant that if the creation of money by central banks is not disciplined by the commitment to redeem currency for gold (or some other commodity), the result will ultimately be runaway inflation and the collapse of the monetary system. Several ways to "discipline" monetary authorities have been suggested. One

---

[36] See Tobin, Footnote 11. See also P. A. Spindt and V. Tarhan "The Federal Reserve's New Operating Procedures," *Journal of Monetary Economics* (1987): 107–123. The authors suggest that the Fed behavior after 1982 can best be characterized as a form of borrowed reserves targeting.

[37] Irving Fisher, *The Purchasing Power of Money,* new. ed. (New York: MacMillan, 1929).

way is the aforementioned monetary rule, either in the form of general guidelines such as those just discussed, or more explicitly, Congressional legislation or a constitutional amendment that codifies rules that limit the Fed's ability to expand the money supply.

A second way to discipline monetary authorities might be to institute a monetary system that ties the money supply to some real commodity by specifying that all money issued is to be redeemable for this commodity at a fixed price. While any commodity can serve as a standard by which to define the value of a dollar, historically gold has been the most common. For instance, from 1879 to 1914 (prior to the creation of the Federal Reserve), legal tender in the United States was gold or its equivalent in gold-backed certificates of the federal government.

A gold standard essentially fixes the purchasing power of a dollar in terms of gold. For example, in the United States from 1879 to 1914, the price of one dollar was fixed at 0.0484 ounces of gold. Fixing the price of a dollar in terms of gold is equivalent to pegging the price of gold in terms of dollars (e.g., between 1879 and 1914 one ounce of gold cost $20.67). With a fixed dollar value of gold, the dollar prices of other commodities will change only if a change occurs in the relative prices of these other commodities *in terms of gold.* In the absence of these relative price changes, a gold standard has the effect of fixing or pegging the level of money prices.

At least two major problems exist with the attempt to institute a commodity standard, whether this standard is based on gold or some other commodity. First, such a standard requires that commodity stocks, for instance bars of gold, be kept locked away. A real cost exists to society of not being able to use the stocks since gold kept in the Fed's vaults is gold that cannot be used in items such as jewelry and electronic parts.

A second and more telling criticism of a gold standard is that it may not attain the goal of stable prices. A gold standard fixes the money price of gold, but it does not directly fix the money prices of other goods. The money prices of other goods will remain unchanged only if no change occurs in their price in terms of gold. If, for example, advances in technology in the agricultural sector lead to a substantial rise in the supply of agricultural goods, the prices of these goods in terms of gold will fall. Given a constant money price of gold, the money prices of agricultural goods will thus fall. Conversely, a drop in the demand for gold or an increase in its supply will lower the price of gold in terms of other commodities. With a fixed money price of gold, the money prices of other commodities will increase.

History provides evidence that price stability is not assured with a gold standard. Although the gold standard for the 1879 to 1914 period kept inflation at rates that were much lower than the inflation rates during the Civil War or the 1970s, the gold standard did not completely stabilize the price level. For example, the cost of living rose 40 percent between 1895 and 1912. Furthermore, as Robert Hall notes, "had the United States been on the gold standard [in recent years], there would have considerable inflationary pressure in 1968–1970, 1974–1976, and 1981 and crushing deflation in 1970–1974 and 1976–1980."[38]

A gold or commodity standard differs from a simple monetary rule in that it ties monetary growth to maintaining a constant commodity price. Note that this is but one specific type of the general approach to monetary policy known as reactive rules, in which the Fed commits itself to specific changes in the money supply in reaction to changes in a particular variable in the economy.

To the Point

POTENTIAL PROBLEMS IN IMPLEMENTING MONETARY RULES

- If there are long and variable lags between changes in the money supply and changes in the target variable, then reactive rules that specify how the money supply should change to maintain a certain level of a target variable may in fact be destabilizing.

- Although the Fed controls the monetary base, it does not have complete control over the money supply since the money multiplier can change. However, legislation in the 1980s has increased the Fed's control of the money supply.

- Although the Fed has announced intentions to control the money supply a number of times in the past 15 years, it has not followed monetary rules, choosing instead to pursue a more activist monetary policy.

13.5 OPTIMAL MONETARY POLICY IN THE MODIFIED NEOCLASSICAL MODELS

In the context of the neoclassical model, we have identified the goal of optimal monetary policy as a low, stable rate of inflation. The model with predetermined prices suggests a second goal of monetary policy—to maintain real GNP at its full employment level. No consensus exists on whether full employment is best achieved through a monetary rule or through a more activist monetary policy. The advocates of discretionary monetary policy argue that an increase in the money supply should occur in periods when

---

[38] Robert E. Hall, "Explorations in the Gold Standard and Related Policies for Stabilizing the Dollar," in *Inflation: Causes and Effects,* ed. Robert E. Hall, (Chicago: University of Chicago Press, 1982) p. 114. Note that the substantial changes in the relative price of gold during these periods that are implied by this statement may have been reduced somewhat if the United States had been on a gold standard.

either a nonmonetary contractionary demand-side shock or cost-push inflation results in prices being set at a level too high to maintain full employment. The monetarists, who advocate a monetary rule, respond that unpredictable timing in the short-run impact on output of monetary policy changes means that discretionary changes in the growth rate of the money supply do more harm than good.

We now examine optimal monetary policy in the context of the modified neoclassical macroeconomic models that generate a short-run upward-sloping aggregate supply curve. The Phillips curve trade-off between inflation and unemployment, developed in Chapter 12, illustrates the resulting relationship between the actual rate of inflation (π), the expected rate of inflation for the current period (π_c^e), the unemployment rate (U), and the natural rate of unemployment (U_n). It takes the form

$$\pi = \lambda(U_n - U) + \pi_c^e \tag{13.5}$$

where λ is a positive constant.

Recall the previous discussion that the Fed abruptly reduced the growth rate of the money supply during the 1979 to 1982 period. The Fed engaged in this policy in order to reduce inflation, but an adverse side effect was a fall in the actual inflation rate below what had been expected for the current period ($\pi < \pi_c^e$), and consequently, as predicted by Equation 13.5, an increase in unemployment above the natural rate ($U > U_n$).

In the modified neoclassical model that assumes "sticky" money wages, inflationary expectations above actual inflation lead to labor agreements that fix money wages at a level too high for full employment. In the modified neoclassical model with incomplete information, inflationary expectations above the actual rate of inflation means that workers, in evaluating the acceptability of money wages, underestimate the real wages offered and thus supply less labor. In either case, actual inflation below the rate that is expected is accompanied by reduced employment and unemployment above the natural rate. In line with this explanation, by 1982 the unemployment rate reached its highest level in the post–World War II era.

The Fed, of course, realized that this reduction in the rate of growth in the money supply would likely result in higher unemployment even though they denied it. "In 1979 when Mr. Volcker moved to cut inflation by controlling M1, 'there wasn't any question that the board knew that recession would follow,' said ex–Fed Governor Philip Coldwell." Yet in 1979 when Mr. Volcker announced the new policy of targeting the monetary aggregates, his response to a reporter who asked if the change would lead to slower growth and higher unemployment was "I don't think it will have important effects in that connection."[39]

---

[39] *Wall Street Journal*, 6 January 1988, p. 14.

Countercyclical Monetary Policy: Conditions for Success

Summarizing the previous discussion, a contractionary demand-side shock leads to higher unemployment because it lowers inflation relative to that expected by the private sector. In the case of the 1979 to 1982 period, a key source of the demand shock was the Fed, which lowered the growth rate of the money supply in order to reduce inflation. Yet there have been other instances when a contractionary demand shock was not instituted by the Fed. When this happens, expansionary monetary policy can counter the contractionary demand shock and reduce the actual unemployment rate toward the natural rate. As Equation 13.5 indicates, for such countercyclical monetary policy to work, it must increase the rate of inflation *relative to* what was expected.

In the context of the modified neoclassical model, several conditions are important for successful countercyclical monetary policy:

1. Monetary authorities are able to project when a change in the growth rate of the money supply will impact aggregate demand.

2. Monetary authorities are able to forecast what the future conditions in the economy would be in the absence of a monetary policy change.

3. The effect of the countercyclical monetary policy action is not fully reflected in the expectations of inflation formed by private agents.

Let's review the potential difficulties in meeting these three conditions for successful countercyclical monetary policy.

We already mentioned two of the conditions in our previous discussion of the requirements for the successful implementation of reactive monetary rules: (1) the lag between a monetary policy change and its impact on the economy must be neither so variable that the timing of policy impacts cannot be projected accurately, (2) nor so long that an accurate forecast of potential future problems so far in the future is unlikely. Let's assume that conditions 1 and 2 are met: The Fed forecasts a future demand shock not expected by private agents and correctly times a money supply increase to counteract the shock. However, if the third condition is not met, successful countercyclical monetary policy is still not possible. That is, if private agents recognize this change in monetary policy and fully incorporate its effect on future prices when forming their expectations of inflation, then the monetary policy change will not offset the future demand shock.

This policy ineffectiveness proposition, discussed in Chapter 12, assumes rational expectations, where individuals use all available information in forming expectations of future prices. In particular, individuals use current monetary policy actions in forming their expectations of future prices. As we discussed earlier, this policy ineffectiveness proposition also assumes that individuals' predictions of the effects of monetary changes on the economy are similar to those of the modified neoclassical model.

Lucas critique: A theory that points out that examining the past impact of policy changes does not necessarily give one the ability to predict future effects of policy changes.

The potential difficulties involved in meeting the third condition cited above raise questions about the Fed's ability to pursue an effective countercyclical policy in the context of the modified neoclassical model. In addition, earlier in this chapter in our discussion of lags in implementing reactive monetary rules, we discussed some of the difficulties of meeting the first two conditions. It is no easy task for the Fed to know the length of time between a policy change and its effect on the economy or for the Fed to forecast accurately the future state of the economy. In the next section, we consider a theory known as the **Lucas critique**—a subtle reason that has been suggested as an explanation of why the Fed may have difficulty forecasting the effect of policy changes. We close with an examination of how pressures on the Fed to pursue a particular activist policy can be counterproductive.

The Superiority of Rules: The Lucas Critique

In our discussion of lags, we have seen that effective discretionary monetary policy requires that the Fed be able to predict with some accuracy when the effects of a monetary change will occur. To predict when the effects of any policy are felt, the Fed must be able to predict how the private sector reacts to that policy. To estimate the reactions of private agents, monetary authorities can look at how those agents behaved in the past, perhaps by using an econometric model to estimate past responses. Economist Robert Lucas has pointed out, however, that estimates based on past behavior are likely to be misleading when it comes to predicting future behavior.[40]

Lucas contends that the economic decisions of private agents depend, in part, on their perceptions and expectations of present and future government policies. If these policies are changing over time, so will the behavior of private individuals. In this case, the past behavior of the private sector provides only a partial ability to predict their future behavior. If monetary authorities use past behavior to predict future behavior, they will then obtain misleading estimates of how private agents will react to a change in monetary policy, and discretionary policy based on these faulty estimates may well be destabilizing. According to Lucas, the best way to predict behavior is to provide individuals with a stable environment in which to make their decisions. That is, the government should act in consistent, predictable ways. In terms of our preceding discussion, Lucas believes that the government should follow well-known, predictable policy rules.

Lucas believes that there is no solution to this fundamental dilemma for discretionary policy in the near horizon: "The ability to forecast the consequences of 'arbitrary' unannounced sequences of policy decisions . . . appears to be beyond the capability not only of the current [econometric] models, but of conceivable future [econometric] models as well. . . . In short, it appears that policymakers, if they wish to forecast the response of citizens, must

---

[40] Robert E. Lucas, Jr., "Econometric Policy Evaluation: A Critique," in *The Phillips Curve,* (Carnegie-Rochester Conference Series, 1976), pp. 41–42.

take the latter into their confidence." Expressed differently, the Lucas critique is an argument for adopting a monetary rule, for Lucas would interpret a rule as nothing more than "policymakers taking citizens into their confidence."

Political Pressures, Monetary Policy, and Time Inconsistencies

Up to this point, our discussion on the difficulties of carrying out successful activist monetary policy has stressed the potential operational difficulties involved in policy implementation. We have ignored the political pressures to which the Fed is often subjected. As some observers correctly point out, however, these political pressures can be quite important. Some argue that these pressures have led the Fed to consistently adopt inappropriate behavior. As economist William Poole states: "Our government makes the same monetary policy mistakes over and over again. These mistakes are not just the Federal Reserve's 'fault': the Fed is often subject to very considerable political pressure to pursue policies along lines known to be mistaken from past experience."[41]

If Poole is correct, why would the Fed ever behave in this manner? One explanation is that our political system favors policies that result in short-run gains, even if there are substantial long-run costs to these policies. With elections every two, four, or six years, politicians are concerned with rather short time horizons, which may cause them to seek stop-gap measures to improve the economy's performance. For example, the Phillips curve tells us that by generating surprise inflation today, the government can lower unemployment below the natural rate. Thus officeholders may benefit by pursuing an expansionary aggregate demand policy today. Although the policy will generate costs in the future—when it raises inflationary expectations—politicians may heavily discount those costs. Such short-run behavior appears to be politically beneficial. Economist Ray Fair finds that "voters look back between about six and nine months regarding the real growth rate and about two years regarding the inflation rate. This rather short horizon leaves room for an administration to manipulate the economy to increase the changes of its party getting reelected."[42]

A more charitable explanation of why policymakers consistently choose inappropriate discretionary policy does not presume that they ignore the future costs. Upon weighing all future costs and benefits, policymakers may still find it rational to increase the rate of inflation even though it only temporarily lowers the unemployment rate below the natural rate. However, if the private sector understands this well-intentioned policy of the government, then this policy will not succeed in lowering unemployment below the natural rate.[43] In other words, as we can see from Equation 13.5, when

---

[41] See Poole, Footnote 25.

[42] Ray C. Fair, "The Effect of Economic Events on Votes for President: 1984 Update," NBER Working Paper No. 2222 (April 1987), p. 12.

[43] Robert J. Barro and David B. Gordon, "A Positive Theory of Monetary Policy in a Natural Rate Model," *Journal of Political Economy* (August 1983).

rational individuals correctly forecast the inflationary policy of a rational government, expected inflation will equal actual inflation (that is, $\pi_c^e = \pi$) and the unemployment rate (U) equals the natural rate (U_n).

Policymakers who follow an optimal discretionary policy at each point in the future will end up with unemployment that is not lower but an inflation rate that is higher than optimal. Thus period by period optimal decision-making turns out in fact not to be optimal: This is called the time inconsistency problem. As Kydland and Prescott state: "The reason that such [discretionary monetary policies] are suboptimal are not due to myopia . . . . Rather, the suboptimality arises because there is no mechanism to induce future policymakers to take into consideration the effect of their policy, via the expectations mechanism, upon current decisions of agents."[44]

Is there a way out of this apparent dilemma? Some economists argue that if policymakers are allowed to engage in discretionary policy, then there is not. The only way out is for policymakers to restrict themselves from engaging in such behavior. That is, they must adopt policy rules from which they cannot deviate. Other economists respond that even with all the potential problems, there is still a strong case for an activist monetary policy in stabilizing the economy at full employment.

SUMMARY

One's stand on the controversy over appropriate or "optimal" monetary policy depends, in large part, on how one views the economy. If one takes the long-run view of the neoclassical model, the only potential role for monetary policy is to influence the inflation rate. In this context, optimal monetary policy has one simple goal—to achieve price stability. For some, achieving this goal means adopting a simple monetary rule that fixes the growth rate of the money supply. If one supports a monetary policy of reactive rules, then rules will dictate how the money supply will change in reaction to a predicted change in the target, be it nominal GNP or some price index.

In the short run, when prices are inflexible, monetary policy changes can potentially stabilize the economy at the full employment level of real GNP. This expands the goal of monetary policy, allowing it not only to stabilize prices but also to offset demand-induced fluctuations in real GNP, so as to mitigate the length and severity of the accompanying periods of high unemployment. For instance, if a fall in autonomous investment means that predetermined prices are set too high—which results in output below the economy's potential—then those who advocate discretionary monetary policy would have the Fed expand the money supply to stimulate production.

---

[44] See Finn E. Kydland and Edward C. Prescott, "Rules Rather than Discretion: The Inconsistency of Optimal Plans," *Journal of Political Economy* (June 1977).

There is the question of whether the Fed can successfully accomplish such a stabilizing role if the lags between monetary changes and the response of the economy to such changes are long and variable. Monetarists believe that the Fed cannot, and they argue that the appropriate monetary policy in the short run, as in the long run, is a monetary rule. To the monetarists, discretionary monetary policy is destabilizing. Critics of the monetarists counter that the economy is buffeted by nonmonetary demand shocks and cost pressures that can result in instances of prices being set too high. In such cases, these critics believe that the Fed should assume an activist role to restore full employment. Although nonmonetarists accept that the Fed's attempts to "fine tune" the economy are not without risk, they believe that lost production and high unemployment are greater evils that may result if the Fed follows a simple monetary rule.

The modified neoclassical macroeconomic models provide an alternative view of the short-run behavior of the economy in which short-run output fluctuations occur as a result of errors in forecasting price changes. The Philips curve summarizes this view, indicating that an unemployment rate above the natural rate reflects actual inflation below that which is anticipated. In this context, the ability of discretionary monetary policy to avoid swings in unemployment above the natural rate requires more than simply overcoming the potential problems of long and variable lags. Monetary authorities must also institute monetary changes whose effects have not been anticipated by private agents, so that these effects have not been incorporated into their expectations of inflation.

LOOKING AHEAD

In this chapter, we looked at optimal monetary policy in the context of various macroeconomic models. The next chapter provides a more in-depth look at the other major government macroeconomic policy tool—fiscal policy. Just as there are implementation problems due to lags that result in ill-timed effects of monetary policy changes, so too are there such problems with fiscal policy. An even larger issue concerning fiscal policy is that it often results in the creation of debt. The next chapter discusses the interaction between monetary and fiscal policy and investigates the impact of deficits on money supply growth.

KEY TERMS

Discretionary monetary policy, 505
Monetarist, 506
Monetary rule, 510

Cost-push inflation, 516
Reactive rule, 529
Lucus critique, 544

REVIEW QUESTIONS

1. In the text, we showed that the real return to holding money is simply $-\pi$, where π is the rate of inflation. Interpret this result.

2. Are there any real economic costs to having a high and variable inflation rate? If so, what are they?

3. If it were desired that there be a constant rate of growth in the money supply over time how would the Fed go about generating this? Would there be any technical difficulties in creating this constant rate of monetary growth? Are these difficulties usually much of a problem?

4. Has the Fed ever followed a policy of announcing targeted rates of constant growth in the money supply and sticking to these targets? Is the Fed's behavior after the Concurrent Resolution 133 an example of such a policy? What about the "monetary experiment" of 1979?

5. What do we mean by a monetary rule?

   (a) Distinguish between a monetary rule and discretionary monetary policy.

   (b) What are the arguments for and against a monetary rule? For and against discretion?

   (c) Distinguish between a monetary rule and a reactive monetary rule. Do you think a reactive rule will overcome the difficulties inherent in a monetary rule and monetary discretion?

6. The United States was on a gold standard from 1879 to 1914.

   (a) Explain how a gold standard works.

   (b) Under what conditions will a gold standard tend to assure price stability? When will it fail to achieve price stability?

   (c) Do you think monetarists tend to favor the re-establishment of a gold standard? Why or why not?

7. Give examples of some things that would cause velocity to change.

   (a) If the money supply is growing at a constant rate, what effect will changes in velocity have on inflation? What about supply shocks?

   (b) If our goal is a stable, low inflation rate, wouldn't it make sense to simply target the money supply to the price level?

8. According to the neoclassical model, macroeconomic demand shocks lead to changes in the price level. According to the model with pre-determined prices, macroeconomic demand shocks result in changes in output. Monetarists suggest that monetary instability is the major cause of such demand shocks, either directly or through induced changes in velocity.

   (a) What does the exchange equation tell us about the relationship between the money supply, velocity, and nominal GNP?

   (b) How can monetary instability affect velocity?

9. What factors do monetarists see as important in causing the Great Depression?

   (a) How do nonmonetarists explain the Depression?

   (b) How do these different views fit into the debate concerning rules versus discretion?

10. At times, it has been said that economics is still more of an art than a science. To the extent that this is true, does this bolster the argument in favor of a monetary rule or monetary discretion? Why?

11. Monetarists arguing in favor of a monetary rule advise against adjusting the money supply to offset macroeconomic demand shocks. Does this mean that they think changes in the money supply will have only insignificant effects on the economy?

12. According to a *Wall Street Journal* article, Milton Friedman "complains that people still don't agree with the monetarists' principal recommendation: a requirement that the Fed produce _____ regardless of fluctuations in prices, interest rates or employment." Fill in the blank.

13. Do nonmonetarists believe that the Fed will never make mistakes if allowed to pursue a discretionary monetary policy? If they do not, what argument do they give for allowing the Fed discretion?

14. Why does successful countercyclical discretionary monetary policy depend on the Fed being able to forecast demand shocks that the private sector cannot forecast?

15. The successful implementation of discretionary monetary (as well as fiscal) policy depends on decision makers predicting to some extent how private agents will react to policy changes.

   (a) Explain the Lucas critique.

   (b) Relate this critique to our discussion of the Phillips curve in Chapter 12.

16. With elections every two, four, or six years, politicians often have rather short time horizons. Given what we know about the short-run and long-run Phillips curves, do you think that political considerations can lead to problems when politicians are allowed to engage in discretionary policymaking? What happens if the public takes into account the incentives facing politicians? How does this consideration apply to the debate on rules versus discretion?

17. Let's say that due to a boycott of South African products, the supply of gold on world markets falls and the result is a rise in the price of gold in terms of other goods. Assuming there is only one other good, apples, then this means that the price of gold rises in terms of this second good, say from one to two apples.

   (a) If the money price of gold were to be kept at $20, what would be the implied change in the money price of apples?

   (b) If purchases of the two goods were of equal quantities (say, 10 units each) before the price change, what change in the price level does the above information imply? (Use base-year quantities as weights.)

(c) According to the neoclassical model, what monetary policy would have to be pursued to maintain a constant money price of gold in light of the rise in the relative price of gold?

18. According to the April 22, 1988 *Wall Street Journal*, "monetary policy makers look at a wide range of economic and financial information . . . . [Federal Reserve] Governor Angell, a farmer, a banker, and an economist, has long held that monetary policy should aim at stabilizing commodity prices."

(a) Consider a simple economy producing only two goods—the "commodity" (wheat) and a "service" (haircuts). Let's assume the price of wheat was $10 per bushel, and the price of a haircut was $5, so that the relative price of wheat was two haircuts per bushel. Last year five bushels of wheat were harvested and ten haircuts performed. Assuming last year is the base year, what was real GNP last year?

(b) Let's say that due to an abundant harvest, the supply of wheat rises from five to six bushels this year. The annual production of haircuts remains equal to ten. What is real GNP this year? What is the percentage change in real GNP (this year compared to last year)?

(c) Write down the exchange equation. Define any symbols.

(d) Assume real money demand depends only on real GNP, as computed in parts (a) and (b), and is independent of changes in the interest rate. Further, take the neoclassical view of how the economy adjusts to macroeconomic shocks. Then according to the exchange equation, if the nominal supply of money is held constant, what does the above change in wheat production imply? Be precise.

(e) According to part (d), what monetary policy would achieve stability in the price level? Ignore any effects of changes in relative prices that might accompany the increase in wheat production.

(f) Assume that, as a result of the abundant harvest, there is a fall in the price of wheat in terms of haircuts to one haircut per bushel of wheat this year from the two haircuts per bushel price of last year. If the money price of wheat were to be kept at $10, what would be the implied change in the money price of haircuts? (Recall that the price of haircuts last year was $5.) Would there be inflation, deflation, or no change in the general level of prices if the policy was one of stabilizing "commodity prices"?

(g) If one were to pursue the monetary policy outlined in part (e) of a money supply growth that lead to a stable overall price level, then the change in relative prices indicated in part (f) would suggest that the money price of haircuts would (higher, lower, the same), and the money price of wheat would be (higher, lower, the same).

(h) When comparing the stable price level outcome of part (g) with the (higher, lower, the same) price level suggested by Angell's policy of stabilizing commodity prices (i.e., wheat prices in our simple example), what is implied is that Angell would argue for a (greater, lesser, the same) rate of growth in the money supply.

(i) In light of our discussion of "optimal" monetary policies, which one of the three characterizations of monetary policy would you use to describe Governor Angell's approach?

Chapter 14

Fiscal Policy and the Debt

Ever since it was decided that anarchy was too costly a state to suffer, there has been government. And ever since the creation of governments, there have been taxes. During the Roman Empire, when the emperors took a census, they were less interested in how many people were under their aegis and more interested in how many people could effectively be taxed. Yet even though government spending and taxes existed, fiscal policy did not. We often associate changes in taxes with fiscal policy, but the two are separate. Fiscal policy is the explicit attempt by government to influence the economy in a certain direction, by manipulating either taxes or government expenditures, or both.

Manipulating taxes and government spending to alter and redirect the course of the economy is relatively new. Traditionally, taxes have had the more limited role of financing the activities of government—from defense spending to public services to public works. Many people associate the first efforts to use taxation and government spending to direct the economy with the New Deal and Franklin D. Roosevelt's administration during the 1930s.

Today, an important outgrowth of New Deal policies is the widespread acceptance of government deficits as a means of stimulating the economy.[1] Since the government relaxed efforts to continuously balance the budget, however, some public officials have expressed concern over a growing public

---

[1] A second legacy of the New Deal is still very much evident today. The Works Progress Administration (WPA) put people to work building post offices, libraries, bridges, and a host of other structures. A perusal of cornerstones in your hometown will more than likely turn up evidence of these efforts.

debt. It would be an exaggeration to suggest, however, that such a concern equals that in earlier times. For instance, few current politicians would write, as did Thomas Jefferson, that "I place economy among the first and most important of republican virtues, and public debt as the greatest of the dangers to be feared."[2]

This chapter discusses the government's spending, taxing, and borrowing behavior in terms of its role in attaining certain macroeconomic goals. The chapter opens with a review of the evolution of the role of governments in recent years, at both the Federal and local levels. Then we discuss various types of fiscal policy. Like monetary policy, fiscal policy options range from simple rules (e.g., a balanced budget amendment) to reactive rules (e.g., a system of taxation in which a deficit-financed tax cut occurs when nominal GNP falls) to pure discretionary fiscal policy (e.g., specific contemporaneous acts of Congress to change taxes and spending to stimulate or restrain the economy).

Since fiscal policy often leads to government deficit spending, the final two sections of the chapter examine various measures of the size of the debt and its impact on interest rates, investment, inflation, money growth, and long-term real economic growth. In the appendix to this chapter, we look at wage and price controls, another government macroeconomic policy tool that is neither a monetary nor a fiscal action.

14.1   RECENT CHANGES IN THE ROLE OF GOVERNMENT IN THE ECONOMY

By 1601, England had adopted the Elizabethan Poor Laws, which established a public responsibility to care for the poor, whereas in the United States prior to the 1930s, the government played a minor role in the economy. In fact, the federal government did not adopt a comprehensive package to deal with the poor until the Wagner Act of 1935, which established the social security system. The Great Depression spawned not only the Wagner Act but also the noted theories of economist John Maynard Keynes. Keynes' work, in indicating the effect of "public works" on employment and output, laid the theoretical foundation for fiscal policy as a stabilization tool.[3] The Depression came to an abrupt halt with the outbreak of World War II. The unemployment rate fell from 17.2 percent in 1939 to 1.9 percent in 1942. During the war, government officials gave little thought to what caused the Depression and how to avoid such an occurrence in the future.

---

[2] If Jefferson were alive today he might shudder at the brobdingnagian proportions the national debt has assumed. Actually, we don't know if Jefferson would shudder, or necessarily think the national debt is too high. We just wanted to use the word brobdingnagian.

[3] John Maynard Keynes, *General Theory*, Harcourt, Brace & World, Inc. (New York, 1964) p. 116–117.

After the war ended, Congress turned its attention to domestic problems and passed the Employment Act of 1946. This resolution—the first true statement of a goal for fiscal policy in the United States—stated that it was the "responsibility of the federal government to . . . provide maximum employment, production, and purchasing power." The Employment Act expressed the philosophy that the government should play an active role in achieving such economic goals as full employment, stable prices, steady growth in real GNP, and a balance of trade. To encourage this activist role, the Employment Act instructed the president to present an annual economic report to Congress and established the Council of Economics Advisers as part of the White House staff.

U.S. Government Outlays in the Twentieth Century

Coincident with the federal government pursuing an active fiscal policy has been an increase in total government spending as a proportion of gross national product. At the beginning of this century, total government spending amounted to less than 10 percent of GNP (6.1 percent spent by state and local governments and 3.2 spent by the Federal government), with the largest expenditures going toward education, followed by highway construction and maintenance. As Table 14.1 indicates, by 1987 total government expenditures had risen to 35 percent of GNP.

Table 14.1 illustrates not only the twentieth century trend toward greater total government outlays in the United States but also the rise in federal outlays relative to state and local governments since 1929. In 1929, federal spending equaled approximately 25 percent of total government spending. In 1987, total federal government spending had risen to over 61 percent of total government outlays, and equaled 21.5 percent of GNP, up from 2.4 percent in 1929. Table 14.1 makes clear the steady increase in the federal government's role in the economy.

Recall from Chapter 4 that total government outlays include both purchases of goods and services and transfer payments. Only the former reflect the direct use of resources by the government, however. Transfer payments simply redistribute income across households. In order to better understand government's changing role in the economy, let's examine how the division of government spending between goods and services and transfer payments has changed over the past 60 years.

Changes in the Composition of Government Outlays: The Rise in Transfer Payments

The change in the composition of government outlays between purchases of goods and services and transfer payments has been just as dramatic as the rise in federal government outlays. In 1902, expenditures on health, education, and welfare equaled less than 2 percent of the federal budget. By 1986, such payments made up over 50 percent of the federal budget,

Table 14.1   **Government Outlays as a Percentage of U.S. GNP in Selected Years**

Year	Federal	State and Local	Total*
1929	2.4	7.5	9.1
1933	6.2	12.9	19.1
1940	9.2	9.3	18.4
1950	13.5	7.8	21.3
1960	17.0	9.7	26.6
1970	18.1	13.2	31.3
1980	19.3	13.3	32.6
1985	22.1	13.0	35.1
1987	21.5	13.5	35.0

Source: Economic Report of the President (1988).
*Note that the figures are total government outlays, which include not only government purchases of goods and services but also transfer payments. Federal outlays do not include grants-in-aid to state and local government, since these are counted as part of the outlays by state and local governments.

and close to 35 percent of the total outlays of federal, state, and local governments combined.

Figure 14.1 breaks down total government outlays into expenditures on goods and services and transfer payments for the period 1950 to 1985. Transfer payments are further divided into interest payments on government debt and payments associated with programs for redistributing income such as social security, Medicaid, unemployment insurance, and food stamps.

For the period 1950 to 1987, Figure 14.1 indicates the changing division of government outlays between purchases of goods and services (e.g., national defense and education), transfer payments (e.g., social security and unemployment insurance benefits), and net interest payments on government debt.[4] Although total government purchases of goods and services in 1987 as a percentage of GNP was 5 percentage points less than it was in 1967, total government outlays have risen primarily due to the increase in federal transfer payments.

For instance, between 1967 and 1987 federal government transfer payments (including interest payments but excluding grants-in-aid to state and local governments) more than doubled, from 6 percent to 12.4 percent of GNP; state and local government transfer payments (including interest payments) rose from 1.2 to 1.8 percent of GNP. Note that the increase in interest payments on the federal debt starting in 1977 exacerbated the rise in federal transfer payments, while the fact that state governments reaped higher interest *earnings* as net holders of financial assets lessened the rise in state and local transfer payments.

---

[4] Net interest payments exclude interest payments by the federal government to state and local governments, which on net hold a positive amount of federal debt, as well as interest payments made to federal government agencies.

Figure 14.1   **Various Government Outlays as Percent of GNP**

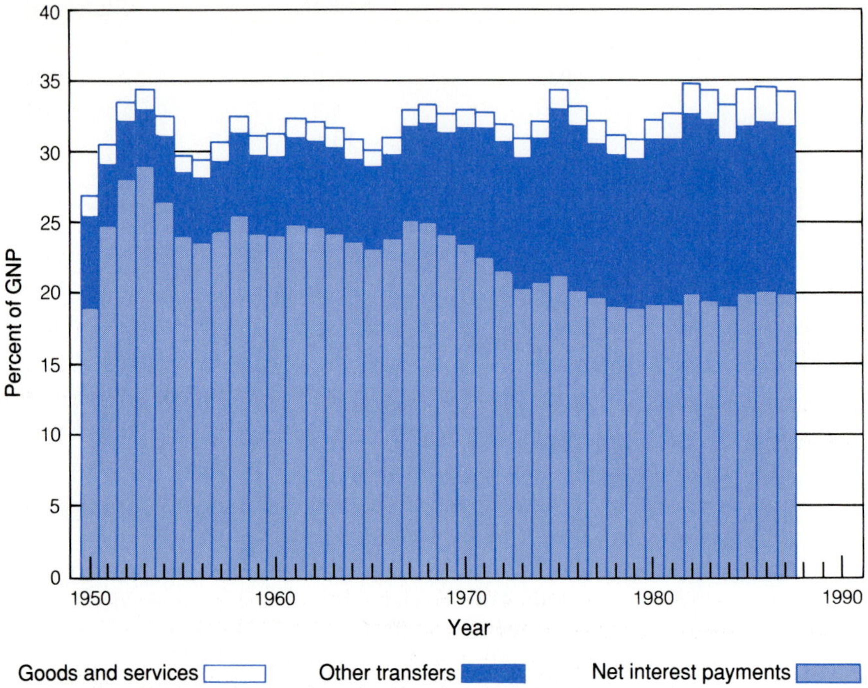

Goods and services ☐   Other transfers ■   Net interest payments ▨

Total government outlays can be broken down into purchases of goods and services and transfer payments. Transfer payments are separated into interest payments on government debt and other payments such as social security and unemployment insurance.

Source: Economic Report of the President (1987).

The rise in government outlays has concerned enough people both in and out of Congress that there has been some impetus for imposing discipline on the spending of Congress. The next section explores the macroeconomic implications of two of these suggestions.

14.2   TWO SIMPLE FISCAL POLICY RULES

In our discussion of optimal monetary policy in Chapter 13, we contrasted the simple monetary rule championed by monetarists with two alternatives: (1) reactive rules that introduced some automatic money supply response by the Fed to changing economic circumstances and (2) pure discretionary monetary policy, in which the Fed did not precommit to any particular rule for changing the money supply. The options for fiscal policy can also be divided into simple rules, reactive rules, and discretionary fiscal policy. Our discussion of fiscal policy starts by examining the motivation for and implications of two simple fiscal policy rules. These two simple fiscal policy rules are a balanced budget amendment and trust fund accounting.

Public Choice and the Expanding Size of Government

In the nineteenth century, political economist Frederic Bastiat expressed a cynical view of government when he argued that "the state is the great fiction by which everybody tries to live at the expense of everybody else." Bastiat, writing in 1850, felt that the absence of a strong central government in the United States and the freedom from government intervention it afforded was an important source of potential growth.[5]

In recent years, the philosophical descendants of Bastiat have argued that inherent in the political process is a bias toward ever-growing government spending, as everyone "tries to live at the expense of everybody else." Two Nobel economists, George Stigler and James Buchanan, have suggested that some government spending arises for the following reason: Politicians back spending proposals to win support from members of the special interest groups who receive government support; in so doing, few votes are lost as the general electorate often does not object to the small increase in their taxes required to pay for such programs. The general electorate may object even less if taxes are not changed and the increased spending is financed by borrowing. Consequently, those who oppose such spending proposals often are fewer in number and less vocal than those who would increase spending.[6] The area of economics devoted to the study of such political behavior is referred to as **public choice economics**.

Public choice economics:
The area of economics devoted to the analysis of political behavior.

The belief that natural voting patterns have resulted in an inexorable rise in government spending in general, and in government deficit spending in particular, has led some to suggest the need to exert fiscal discipline through a fixed set of rules that limit spending. One way suggested is to strictly limit the size of the government as a proportion of GNP. Another indirect form of fiscal discipline is to ensure that any spending increase imposes the immediate cost of higher taxes. With respect to the second form of discipline, two specific rules have received considerable attention of late:

---

[5] Dean Russell, *Frederic Bastiat: Ideas and Influence* (The Foundation for Economic Education, 1969).

[6] An example of special interest groups gathering forces to support a program is the National Dairy Association's fight in the early 1980s to continue price supports for dairy products. When the Reagan administration announced that it was thinking about cutting dairy price supports, the Dairy Association responded by handing out over $1.3 billion during the next six months, much of it to legislators who represented urban districts. In the ensuing vote, these congressional representatives overwhelmingly supported the continuance of dairy price supports even though its cost their constituents in the form of higher milk prices.

the balanced budget amendment and a trust fund rule.[7] We explore each of these in the next section.

Balanced Budget Amendments and Trust Fund Accounting

Many people associate the 1987 Gramm-Rudman Bill with a balanced budget amendment, although it does not strictly amend the constitution. There have been a number of calls for an actual balanced budget constitutional amendment over the years, but the Gramm-Rudman Bill is the closest Congress has come to date. Gramm-Rudman called for the Federal government to balance its annual budget by the year 1993. Balancing the annual budget means equating government spending with tax revenues, so that there is no change in the size of the debt. Achieving a goal such as this most likely would require both an increase in tax revenues and a decrease in spending.

The history of the Gramm-Rudman Bill illustrates the difficulties of achieving a balanced budget. At the outset, the Reagan administration ruled out a tax increase as the means to a balanced budget and attention shifted to cuts in spending. The resulting Gramm-Rudman Bill stipulated "across-the-board" cuts in certain spending programs if Congress failed to meet yearly deficit targets through 1993, when the deficit target is to be zero.[8] However, prior to passage of the bill, strong protests were lodged against cutting certain areas of spending, notably social security and Medicare. Consequently, as reported in the *Wall Street Journal*, the final 1987 Gramm-Rudman bill specified that if cuts in spending had to be made, "all of the cuts would come from only about 20 percent of the $1 trillion federal budget and, except for defense, those are the parts that have been pared most severely in the past. Fully four fifths of the budget is exempted from Gramm-Rudman."[9] This implies significant cuts in the nonprotected programs if a balanced budget is to be achieved by spending reductions.

The Gramm-Rudman Bill illustrates a second problem in achieving a balanced budget. Tax revenues and expenditures vary automatically with fluctuations in the economy. The government must project various scenarios of GNP and associated levels of revenue collection and expenditures each year in order to determine how much budget cutting or "revenue enhancement"

---

[7] The discussion to follow concerns the budgetary decisions of the federal government, for most state and local governments already have constitutional bylaws that require most expenditures to be financed solely by current tax levies. State and local governments often can issue debt to finance certain capital expenditures such as bridges and schools, however.

[8] An earlier version of the Gramm-Rudman Bill, passed in 1986, had 1991 as the target for a balanced budget. However, this bill empowered the General Accounting Office (GAO) to cut programs without returning to Congress for approval. Increasing and decreasing spending is a function of the legislative branch of government. Thus Gramm-Rudman took power that, according to the constitution, lies solely within the legislative branch of government. Not surprisingly, the Supreme Court ruled in the summer of 1986 that this part of the Gramm-Rudman Bill was unconstitutional. As a consequence, the bill was stripped of its power to implement spending cuts to achieve a balanced budget, requiring the new bill in 1987.

[9] *Wall Street Journal*, 20 October 1987, p. 72.

(read: tax increase) will be required to arrive at a balanced budget. If these projections are incorrect, then adjustments must be quickly made and agreed upon to maintain a balanced budget.

A second proposal to impose fiscal discipline is to set up "trust fund accounts" for various programs. The revenues raised from specific taxes would be placed in accounts that are earmarked for certain types of expenditures. The amount spent on a specific government program would then be limited by the size of its trust fund. The highway trust fund, which earmarks revenue collected from taxes such as the federal gasoline excise tax for the construction and maintenance of the interstate highway network, is an example of a trust fund. The Social Security program also began as a trust fund. However, legislated increases in coverage and benefits during the 1970s and 1980s committed spending beyond projected revenues from the social security tax.

Although a balanced budget amendment and a trust fund both impose fiscal restraint, an important difference exists between them. A trust fund, unlike a balanced budget amendment, does not strictly limit spending in a particular category to equal the amount of revenue collected for that category in a particular year. If spending exceeds revenue in a given year, the program can draw on the trust fund up to the amount in the fund.

A balanced budget amendment and a trust fund resemble the monetarist rule of constant growth of the money supply in that both fiscal policy rules restrict the power of the authorities to react to the current state of the economy. But as we see in the next section, many people argue that the government should react to the current state of the economy, and pursue an active fiscal policy. Such individuals believe fiscal policy is important in achieving a healthy economy.

To the Point

THE SIZE OF GOVERNMENT AND SIMPLE FISCAL POLICY RULES

- In the twentieth century, the size of government at all levels has grown steadily. Total government spending is some four times larger than in 1929, with most of that growth coming at the federal level. Within federal government spending, most of the increase is in transfer payments, which only since 1966 have doubled as percent of real GNP.

- Proponents of the area of economic study known as public choice suggest that the very nature of government lends itself to rising government spending. Proponents of any spending bill will be more vocal than its opponents because the benefits of spending are concentrated on a few, while the costs are less apparent, particularly if spending is financed by borrowing.

- To limit what some see as excessive growth in government spending, strict spending rules have been suggested. The balanced budget amendment restricts government expenditures so that they do not exceed tax revenues. Trust fund accounting establishes special funds for particular expenditures.

14.3   MORE ACTIVIST FISCAL POLICIES

Proponents of a balanced budget rule and trust fund accounts believe that these policy rules will limit spending by Congress and thus limit the overall size of government. Opponents argue that such policies will cause macro-economic instability. For instance, a rule for a continuously balanced budget would require government spending to fall when the economy faces a downturn since income and thus tax receipts would fall. It is feared that the required reduction in government spending would lead the economy into further decline. Opponents of a balanced budget rule often point to President Herbert Hoover's attempt to balance the budget in 1932 by raising tax rates as a contributing factor to the prolonged length of the Great Depression.

Even though most balanced budget proposals have an escape clause that allows movement away from a balanced budget in the event of an economic downturn, opponents of simple fiscal policy rules such as a balanced budget amendment point out that the process may be too slow. Because any reversal in spending patterns would be cited by many as an attempt to overturn the intent of a balanced budget, it faces inevitable delays.

Rather than seeking a policy that predetermines government spending and tax collections regardless of the state of the economy, critics of balanced budget amendments want at a minimum rules that allow taxes and government spending to react to the state of the economy. The fall in tax revenues and consequent budget deficit that accompanies a fall in income exemplifies such a "reactive" fiscal policy rule. A second example of a reactive fiscal policy rule would be an automatic rise in taxes when inflation increases that leads to a lower deficit, or possibly a government surplus.

Reactive Fiscal Policy Rules: Bracket Creep and Automatic Stabilizers

An increase in the rate of inflation can lead to fiscal policy changes that serve to dampen aggregate demand. For instance, a progressive tax system can lead to an increase in net real taxes as a reaction to inflation if tax brackets are not indexed to inflation. This phenomenon is known as bracket creep. Bracket creep means that inflation pushes individuals into a higher tax bracket, thereby increasing the real amount of their taxes.

For example, suppose an individual earns $30,000 per year and pays $4,500 or 15 percent of income in taxes, leaving a real disposable income of $25,500. Now suppose further that 10 percent inflation occurs and that the individual's salary increases to keep pace with inflation. The individual's new salary is $33,000. In order to have the same real purchasing power, after-tax income will have to be $28,050 (25,500 + (.10) · 25,500 =

28,050). For this to be the case, the individual will have to still pay only 15 percent of total income in taxes, or $4,950 (33,000 − 4,950 = 28,050). But with a progressive tax system, an increase in income automatically results in an increase in the tax rate as individuals are moved into higher tax brackets. For instance, if the tax rate on income above $30,000 were 28 percent, then the individual with the new income of $33,000 will pay $5,340 in taxes [($30,000 · .15) + (3,000 · .28) = 5,340]. Thus the individual's after-tax income has fallen below $28,050 to $27,660 (33,000 − 5,340 = 27,660).

By moving individuals into a higher tax bracket, inflation results in lower real after-tax income. If individuals have less real income, it means that net real taxes have increased. Thus in many respects a progressive income tax leads to contractionary fiscal policy in reaction to inflation.

Part of the tax package passed in 1981 called for indexing both tax brackets and exemptions starting in 1985. This means that if 10 percent inflation occurs, all tax brackets will increase by 10 percent, as well as the deduction for personal exemptions. When filling out their taxes for the 1985 tax year, individuals could deduct $1040 for each individual exemption as opposed to $1000 in the previous year. This higher deduction reflected the 4 percent inflation of the previous year. The Tax Reform Act of 1986 reduced the number of different tax brackets to two, which also reduced the amount of bracket creep. At the same time though, tax indexation was temporarily eliminated. Indexation is scheduled to be re-introduced in 1988 and 1989.

As we have just seen, a progressive tax rate system in which tax brackets are fixed in dollar values gives rise to bracket creep. Bracket creep is an example of a reactive fiscal policy rule that dampens inflation by automatically increasing real net taxes. A second example of a reactive fiscal policy rule is a rule that would stimulate the economy by automatically reducing real net taxes if there is a fall in real GNP. Such a link between net taxes and real GNP actually exists in current tax laws for two reasons. First, reliance on a tax system that levies taxes based on income means that lower income reduces total tax revenues. At the same time, a decrease in real GNP also automatically raises government transfer payments, such as unemployment compensation and welfare benefits. Thus net taxes (total taxes minus transfer payments) fall when real GNP falls. Similarly, increases in real GNP raise total tax revenues and lower transfer payments, which automatically increases net taxes. Income taxes and government transfer payments such as unemployment compensation are referred to as **automatic stabilizers** because they lead to automatic decreases (increases) in net taxes when real GNP decreases (increases).

Automatic stabilizer: Income taxes and transfer payment programs that automatically lead to decreases (increases) in net taxes when income decreases (increases).

Automatic stabilizers are considered reactive fiscal policy rules since changes in income taxes and government transfer payments occur automatically without discretionary legislation and these changes act to moderate fluctuations in income. Automatic stabilizers dampen the rise in income and prices in response to an increase in output demand and limit how much income and prices fall in response to a decrease in output demand. To understand why, consider how the multiplier works if net taxes are related to income. (If you want to refresh your memory, multiplier calculations first appeared in Chapter 10.)

To calculate the simple multiplier, we start with the condition for output market equilibrium:[10]

$$Y = C^d + I^d + CCA + G^d + X^d - Z^d$$

This equation is simply an expression equating output and output demand (the sum of consumption demand, gross investment demand, government demand, and net export demand). In Chapter 6, we introduced a linear consumption function of the form $C^d = a + b \cdot (Y - CCA - T)$, where a and b are positive constants, with b less than one since it represents the marginal propensity to consume, and where T denotes net real taxes. Substituting this expression into the condition for output market equilibrium, we obtain:

$$Y = a + b \cdot (Y - CCA - T) + I^d + CCA + G^d + X^d - Z^d$$

Let's now assume that net taxes T are a constant fraction t of real output Y. Substituting tY for net taxes T and solving for the equilibrium output Y, we obtain

$$Y = [1/(1 - b + bt)] \cdot (a + I^d + G^d + X^d - Z^d) + CCA$$

As indicated by the above equation, the simple multiplier is now $1/(1 - b + bt)$. A change in output demand—for example, due to a change in government demand (G^d) or investment demand (I^d)—will lead to a change in equilibrium output equal to $1/(1 - b + bt)$ multiplied by the change in output demand.

The simple multiplier in the equation above is smaller when taxes change with a change in income. To see this, note that if taxes are independent of income changes then the simple multiplier will be $1/(1 - b)$, and a marginal propensity to consume (MPC) of .8 will mean a multiplier of 5 [$5 = 1/(1 - .8)$]. However, if a \$1 fall in income lowers taxes by, say, 25 cents ($t = .25$), then a marginal propensity to consume of .8 means a multiplier equal to 2.5 $\{1/[1 - .8 + (.8 \cdot .25)]\}$. When taxes change with income, these simple multiplier calculations indicate that an initial \$10 reduction in output demand will lead to a \$25 fall in income, rather than a \$50 fall in income.

Discretionary fiscal policy changes, in which the government explicitly implements a tax or spending change to counter a downturn or to slow down an overheated economy, stand in contrast to the simple reactive fiscal policy rules reflected in automatic stabilizers. The observations of an increase

---

[10] Recall from Chapter 10 that the actual change in equilibrium income depends both on the magnitude of the shift in the *IS* curve (given by the simple multiplier analysis we consider below), the shape of the *IS* curve, and the shape of the *LM* curve. Only if the *LM* curve is horizontal will the simple multiplier predict the actual change in equilibrium income. Otherwise, the actual change will be less.

in deficit spending during a downturn and a surplus during a period of unsustainable growth in output do not tell us that the government is pursuing discretionary fiscal policy, however, since the existence of automatic stabilizers would by themselves produce such events. In the next section, we introduce the full employment budget as one approach to measuring the direction of discretionary fiscal policy, an approach that in essence nets out the effects of automatic stabilizers on government spending and net taxes.

The Full Employment Budget

Full employment budget: A budget that indicates what government expenditures and revenues will be if the economy is at full employment.

In the early 1960s when Walter Heller, Arthur Okun, and the other members of the President's Council of Economic Advisers were advocating a tax cut, they introduced as a reference point a measure reflecting what spending and net taxes would be if there were full employment. This reference point is now known by several different names—the high-employment budget, the natural employment budget, and the **full employment budget**. Inherent in each of these terms is the recognition that the state of the economy influences both the government's expenditures and receipts. In order to measure accurately the thrust of discretionary fiscal policy, we net out the cyclical component to obtain the cyclically adjusted, or full employment component. The cyclical component accounts for the effect that changes in real GNP have on government spending and net taxes due to the reactive fiscal policy rules (automatic stabilizers). What is left is known as the full employment or structural budget.[11]

Figure 14.2 illustrates how the actual budget deficits as a percent of GNP tend to automatically change in the same direction as the unemployment rate, one measure of business fluctuations. If a cyclical downturn occurs in the economy, deficits tend to increase or surpluses to shrink. As we have discussed, this happens because tax revenues decline with the fall in income and certain government outlays, such as unemployment compensation, rise with a fall in real GNP and the accompanying increase in the unemployment rate.

The full employment budget measures the amount by which government spending will exceed (or fall short of) tax revenues if actual real GNP equals estimated full employment (potential) real GNP. A full employment budget deficit occurs if, at full employment, government spending is projected to exceed taxes. A full employment surplus means that, at full employment, the government is projected to be withdrawing more from the private sector in the form of taxes than it would be spending.

Even though we may witness a deficit, if the full employment budget is in surplus, then discretionary policy is not stimulating the economy. Instead, a full-employment budget surplus is exerting what is sometimes called **fiscal**

---

[11] According to Frank de Leeuw and Thomas M. Holloway, "Cyclical Adjustment of the Federal Budget and Federal Debt", *Survey of Current Business* 63 (December 1983): 25–40, the term "structural" budget was first introduced by the administration in its discussion of the U.S. Budget for fiscal year 1964.

Figure 14.2   Budget Deficits and Fluctuations in the Unemployment Rate

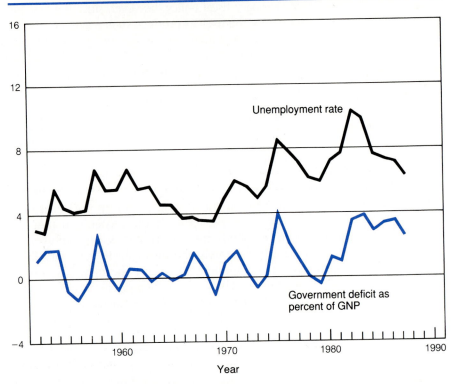

Note that much of the fluctuations in the deficit as a percent of GNP are related to changes in the state of the economy, as reflected by changes in the unemployment rate.

Source: Economic Report of the President (1987).

Fiscal drag: A situation that occurs when the fiscal policy of the government is restrictive as indicated by the fact that current tax and expenditure programs would result in a full employment surplus.

drag on the economy. The term fiscal drag suggests that the fiscal policy of the government is holding the economy back, which is indicated by the fact that the current tax and expenditure programs will result in a full employment surplus.

The full employment budget, and the related full employment surplus or deficit, are two basic measures of the direction of discretionary fiscal policy. An increase in the full employment deficit, indicating an increase in cyclically adjusted government expenditures and/or a fall in cyclically adjusted government net taxes, is a signal of stimulative fiscal policy. In Chapter 13, we discussed the monetarists' view of the Great Depression of the 1930s, according to which a dramatic fall in the money supply during the 1929 to 1933 period was the root cause of the drop in output and high unemployment rates. It must also be noted, however, that during the 1931 to 1933 period the full employment deficit declined to the extent that by 1933 there was actually a full employment surplus.[12] Simply looking at the actual deficits that existed during this period does not uncover this underlying contractionary discretionary fiscal policy, an outgrowth of President Herbert Hoover's preoccupation with a balanced budget.

A more recent example occurred during the first two quarters of 1981 when there was a significant reduction in the full employment deficit due to an increase in cyclically adjusted tax revenues as well as a fall in the rate of increase in cyclically adjusted government expenditures.[13] During roughly this same period, the monetary authorities were slowing the rate of growth of the money supply significantly, thus compounding the fiscal restraint. Many economists believe that this combination of restrictive fiscal and monetary policy was the cause of the sharp downturn the economy took in 1982.

We have discussed two examples, the early 1930s and the early 1980s, when contractionary fiscal policy had a restrictive influence on the economy. Yet this is not the traditional role one expects for discretionary fiscal policy. Rather, it is normally thought that discretionary fiscal policy should be used to head off downturns. In the 1960s, this became known as the "fine-tuning" role of fiscal policy; it was thought that discretionary fiscal policy could be used to "fine-tune" the economy and eliminate the roller coaster of recessions and inflations experienced in the past. The popular press asked the question, "Is the business cycle dead?" The experiences of the 1970s and 1980s, however, indicate that there is still some question concerning government's ability to tame the economy through discretionary fiscal policy. In the next section, we look at some of the problems of implementing discretionary fiscal policy.

Discretionary Fiscal Policy: The Timing Problems

The two people often associated with discretionary fiscal policy are Walter Heller and Arthur Okun. As successive chairmen of the President's Council of Economic Advisers in the 1960s, these two men directed the efforts to avoid, through discretionary fiscal policy, economic downturns such as the one that the Kennedy administration inherited in 1960. Upon leaving office, Walter Heller expressed confidence about our newfound ability to direct the course of the macroeconomy: "Change has brought a new look not just to economic process but to economic policy. Gone is the countercyclical syndrome of the 1950s. Policy now centers on gap closing and growth, on realizing and enlarging the economy's noninflationary potential."[14]

Heller's optimistic words leave us questioning how the inflation and

---

[12] E. Cary Brown, "Fiscal Policy in the Thirties: A Reappraisal," *American Economic Review* (December 1956).

[13] See de Leeuw and Holloway, Footnote 11.

[14] Walter Heller, *New Dimensions of Political Economy* (Cambridge, Mass.: Harvard University Press, 1966), p. vii.

unemployment of the 1970s and 1980s ever materialized. Part of the answer, as we saw in Chapter 9, is that some real shocks occurred during this period. For instance, the recessionary period of 1974 to 1975 has at its root supply-side disturbances. Part of the answer also comes from the realization that carrying out fiscal policy is not as easy as it first appeared in the early 1960s. Like the effective use of countercyclical discretionary monetary policy, many of the difficulties in implementing successful fiscal policy stem from problems in correctly timing fiscal policy changes. Timing problems come under the general rubric of "lags."

Recognition Lag. If fiscal authorities are going to use fiscal policy effectively as a countercyclical tool, they must be able to recognize the need for action sufficiently early. This is complicated by the fact that government policymakers must be certain that a movement in real GNP and unemployment actually indicates a new trend in the economy, not just a short-term blip. If fiscal authorities, like monetary authorities, react too quickly, they may exacerbate rather than stabilize the ups and downs in the economy.

In September 1974, President Gerald Ford decided it was time to attack the problem of rising prices. He proposed a tax increase to take some spending power out of the economy. (He also proposed that individuals wear buttons and ties with WIN—Whip Inflation Now—printed on them.) Four months later, the economy had begun what turned out to be a sharp downturn and the policies that Ford had proposed in September were all reversed. That Ford did not recognize in September that the economic expansion was petering out indicates the difficulties in identifying changes in the direction of the economy. Fortunately, in this case the legislation Ford called for was not immediately enacted, or the fiscal policy would have accentuated the ensuing downturn. However, this second lag—the "legislative lag"—between recognition and implementation is often detrimental to effective fiscal policy.

Legislative Lag. Fiscal policy usually requires legislative action. It literally takes an "act of Congress" to initiate discretionary fiscal policy. A long time may pass before Congress actually takes any action to implement a policy change. Congressmen and senators may attempt to attach riders onto a bill to protect projects in their home district from cutbacks, or they may take the opportunity to try to secure large projects for their home districts. Any bill must pass both the House and Senate and then be signed by the president. In the absence of a consensus for immediate action, a bill may be slowed down in many ways.[15] While Congress is debating the pros and cons of various policies, trends in the economy do not wait.[16]

---

[15] For an excellent presentation of the effectiveness of a filibuster to delay a bill, see Jimmy Stewart in *Mr. Smith Goes to Washington,* a Frank Capra film.

[16] The legislative lag of fiscal policy contrasts with monetary policy. When monetary authorities see a need for action, the time until they institute a change in policy can be fairly short since the Open Market Committee convenes often.

Walter Heller was instrumental in convincing President Kennedy that a tax cut was the key to stimulating the economy in the early 1960s. Accordingly, Kennedy went to Congress in 1962 and asked for a tax cut. After much debate and restructuring, the tax cut finally passed during the Johnson administration in 1964. By 1966, there was much talk in the newspapers of the economy "overheating" under the dual pressures of government spending on Johnson's Great Society anti-poverty programs and the Vietnam War. A surtax was proposed under the Johnson administration in 1966, but again due to legislative lags the surtax was not passed until 1968.

Fiscal policy legislative lags are not always as long as those described above. During President Reagan's first term, tax cuts and other changes in the tax laws were passed within one year of his taking office. In contrast, passage of the tax reform act in 1986 followed a lengthy period of legislative debate. Some might argue, however, that this tax package, along with the Gramm-Rudman balanced budget bill, are less a reflection of countercyclical fiscal policy and more a reflection of structural changes in the way government functions.

Implementation Lag. Passing legislation for a fiscal policy change does not mean immediate implementation of that change. For instance, the public works programs that were popular in the 1930s involved long delays in starting a specific project once the enabling legislation was passed. (Additionally, delays may occur in stopping these projects. If a construction project such as a bridge is started and the economy finds itself coming out of a downturn, we would not want to be up the creek by building a bridge that only spans half a river.) However, in some situations, a tax cut or increase can be implemented in a matter of weeks. With a tax cut, for example, the government can send a new schedule for withholding taxes to all employers that takes effect in a matter of weeks. Employers enter the new tax schedules into their computers, and fiscal policy goes into action.

The Life-Cycle Hypothesis and Fiscal Policy Effects

The existence of legislative and implementation lags does not necessarily eliminate the effect of a planned fiscal policy change on current output demand. For instance, a call for expansionary fiscal policy action (a tax cut or an increase in government spending) can lead to an immediate increase in household current consumption demand, even though the enabling legislation will not be passed and implemented for several years. The reason is that the planned fiscal policy change can lead households to anticipate higher future disposable income.[17]

---

[17] The higher future income can reflect an increase in disposable income that comes from future tax cuts or the general increase in future income stimulated by future increases in government spending or cuts in taxes. Naturally, as we saw in Chapter 8, if households also correctly anticipate the subsequent taxes required to service the debt, a tax cut will not affect consumption. This is what we referred to as the Ricardian equivalence theorem.

According to the view of household consumption behavior suggested by the life-cycle and permanent income hypotheses (which were introduced in Chapter 6), an anticipated increase in future disposable income will cause an increase in current consumption demand. Similarly, if firms anticipate higher output demand as a result of the planned expansionary fiscal policy, this can induce an immediate rise in investment demand as well. This may explain why in the early 1960s, even though there was more than a two-year lag between the proposal and the actual implementation of the tax cut, the tax cut was considered by many as instrumental in leading to an immediate expansion of aggregate demand and greater economic growth.

In contrast, if individuals perceive a fiscal policy change, for instance a tax cut, to be temporary, the life-cycle and permanent income hypotheses suggest there will be little effect on consumption. Recall that according to these hypotheses, household consumption spending depends on an average of current and anticipated future income, called "permanent income" by Milton Friedman. A temporary tax cut has little effect on current consumption demand since it has little effect on permanent income. The 1968 surtax is a classic example of the ineffectiveness of a tax change perceived as temporary by the public. At the time of its imposition, officials announced that the tax increase was only temporary. Thus household permanent income was affected only slightly, causing households to reduce their consumption spending by only a small amount. As mentioned in Chapter 11, it has been estimated that temporary tax changes affect expenditures by only 20 to 60 percent as much as tax changes perceived as permanent.[18]

In summary, the life-cycle and permanent income hypotheses suggest that proposed discretionary fiscal policy actions can have immediate effects on output demand even though there are lags in legislating and implementing discretionary fiscal policy. However, these hypotheses weaken the predicted effect on output demand of *temporary* fiscal policy changes, in particular temporary tax changes.

As we now well know, the government financing constraint tells us that government spending must equal tax revenues plus borrowing. Thus increases in government spending not financed through increased taxes result in higher deficits, as do tax cuts not accompanied by equal reductions in government spending. In fact, the major controversy around the tax bills of 1981 and 1986 concerned how the changes in tax rates would affect revenue collection and the deficit. The large deficits generated by the shortfalls in revenue collection heightened concern about the long-run effects of government borrowing on economic growth. We examine this issue in the next section. We begin with a question: What is the appropriate measure for determining the "burden of the debt?" We will see that as the government's debt has grown in recent years, economists have developed new measures that show that the "true debt" is not really as large as the published figures indicate.

---

[18] Alan Blinder, "Temporary Income Taxes and Consumer Spending," *Journal of Political Economy* (February 1981), pp. 26–53.

To the Point

ACTIVIST FISCAL POLICY: REACTIVE RULES AND DISCRETIONARY POLICY

- Opponents of balanced budget amendments and trust fund rules point out that such policies can cause macroeconomic instability. Rather than strict rules, they advocate rules that automatically react to the state of the economy. Income taxes and unemployment insurance payments, often called automatic stabilizers, are examples of these reactive rules.

- Because of automatic stabilizers, a contraction in the economy will lead to an automatic reduction in net taxes and an increase in the deficit. It is thus often difficult to tell the thrust of government fiscal policy. The full employment budget tells us what spending and taxes would be if the economy were at full employment. If there is a full employment deficit, then fiscal policy is expansionary, while a full employment surplus indicates fiscal drag.

- Besides reactive fiscal policy rules, such as automatic stabilizers, Congress may enact discretionary fiscal policies. These are special programs of spending and taxation that are aimed at a specific macroeconomic crisis in the economy.

- There is debate about whether discretionary fiscal policy can be an effective countercyclical tool. Because of recognition, legislative, and implementation lags, the time between the need for a fiscal policy action and the time when it actually goes into effect may be too long to counteract a downturn.

14.4 ASSESSING THE IMPACT OF THE GOVERNMENT DEBT

Periodically a small item shows up in newspapers reporting that Congress has raised the ceiling on the national debt. Long ago, Congress established a limit on the size of the national debt, but on numerous occasions it has been called upon to raise that limit. In the spring of 1986, Congress balked at raising the ceiling. The newspapers were then filled with stories about how the federal government would grind to a halt if Congress did not raise the ceiling. As one might expect, Congress eventually raised the debt ceiling. Nonetheless, the size of the debt remains a major concern of most legislators and their constituents.

The Debt to GNP Ratio

How large is the national debt? That depends on how the debt is measured. The most commonly cited measure is the nominal value of the debt. When

Congress raises the debt ceiling, it extends a ceiling that is measured in nominal or dollar terms. Raising the debt ceiling has been a common occurrence in recent years. In fiscal year 1976, the total federal debt was $631.9 billion. Ten years later, the federal debt had ballooned to over two trillion dollars, a more than three-fold increase.

These startling figures on the federal debt lack perspective, however, because they do not take into account either increases in the price level (which reduce the real debt) or increases in real GNP (which increase the economy's capacity to service the debt). One common way of putting the national debt into perspective is to divide the nominal debt by nominal GNP. Recall that nominal GNP equals real GNP times the GNP deflator. Thus when we divide the nominal debt by nominal GNP, we obtain a ratio of the real debt to real GNP.[19] This ratio not only takes into account changes in the average price level, but it also adjusts for changes in the economy's real productive capacity. Figure 14.3 indicates how the debt to GNP ratio has changed since 1915.

Despite recent concern about the size of the debt, Figure 14.3 shows that the current debt to GNP ratio pales in comparison to what it was after World War II, as the bulk of war expenditures were financed by the sale of bonds. The debt to GNP ratio peaked at 1.30 during that time, which meant that debt equaled 130 percent of GNP. After the war, the ratio fell steadily, and by 1974 it had bottomed out at .32. (Even the Vietnam War did not cause the debt to GNP ratio to rise.) In 1975, the debt to GNP ratio turned slightly upward again as a result of the deficits of the Ford administration, but it was not until 1982 that it climbed significantly. By the end of 1987, it had risen back to over .50, a level it had not reached since the late 1950s.

Figure 14.4 illustrates a breakdown of federal debt by holder—private investors, the Federal Reserve, and government accounts—since 1952. As the figure indicates, the bulk of Federal debt is held by private individuals. The portion of debt held by the Federal Reserve and in government accounts was less than 30 percent of total federal debt in 1987.

Even if we allow for the growth in real GNP over time, therefore, government indebtedness has grown significantly in recent years, and this rise has largely been an increase in the debt holdings of private investors. Nevertheless, as Figure 14.5 indicates, by international standards the indebtedness of the government sector in the United States is not all that large, being only about average for industrialized countries.

A second type of adjustment to the federal debt is to measure the debt at market value instead of par value.[20] At the time that a bond is issued, its coupon payment and par, or face, value are set according to current

---

[19] Specifically, nominal debt (the price level P times real government debt D_g) divided by nominal GNP (the price level P times real GNP Y) is $P \cdot D_g / P \cdot Y$ or simply D_g/Y, the ratio of real government debt to real GNP.

[20] Robert Eisner and Paul Pieper, "A New View of the Federal Debt and Budget Deficits," *American Economic Review* (March 1984): Vol. 74, p. 11–29.

Figure 14.3 The Federal National Debt to GNP Ratio

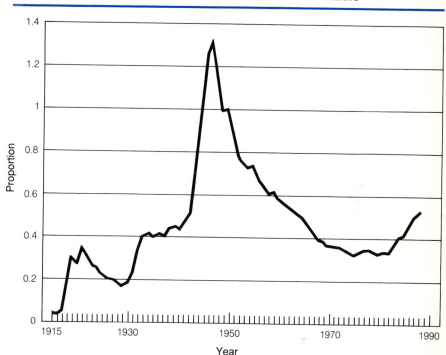

Following World War II, the debt to GNP ratio fell until the 1980s, when large deficits contributed to a sizeable increase in the debt.

Source: *Economic Report of the President* (1988) and *U.S. Statistics: From Colonial Times to 1970.*

interest rates. For instance, a bond with a perpetual annual coupon payment of $10 will have a par value of $100 if the market interest rate is 10 percent when the bond is issued. Recall from Chapter 3 that the $100 price is the present value of this perpetual stream of coupon payments ($100 = $10/.10).

When a bond is issued, its market value and its face value coincide. If the market rate of interest subsequently changes, so will the market value of previously issued bonds. For example, if the market rate of interest rises to 12 percent, then the market value of a bond offering a perpetual stream of $10 annual coupon payments will fall to $83.33. (At the higher interest rate, the $10/.12 or $83.33 amount, if set aside, would match the $10 per year coupon payment of the bond.) Although the bond was issued with a face value of $100, the bond's market value, and thus the actual indebtedness of the issuer of the bond, has fallen due to the increase in the interest rate.

When government debt figures are published, they reflect the par value of the government's obligations. Robert Eisner and Paul Pieper note that "if the debt were overwhelmingly in very short-term securities, or if interest

Figure 14.4   **A Breakdown of Federal Debt by Holder**

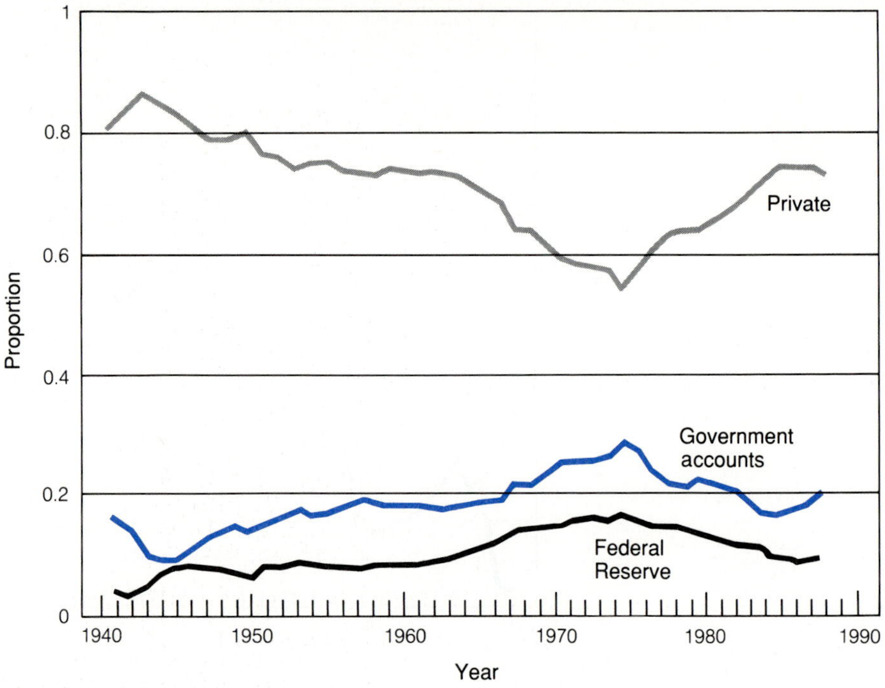

The bulk of the Federal debt is held by private individuals.

Source: Economic Report of the President (1988).

rates did not change much over the life of securities, the difference between par and market values would be small. Particularly in [the 1970s], neither of these conditions was met. Interest rates soared and market values of outstanding fixed securities collapsed."[21] As a result, Eisner and Pieper estimate that the 1980 market value of all United States government securities was under 93 percent of the par value. Naturally, the fall in interest rates between 1980 and 1987, other things being equal, reduced this gap between the market and face value of the debt.

A third adjustment to put the Federal debt into perspective, which has been suggested by Eisner and Pieper, is to subtract out the value of the tangible assets owned by the government—buildings, land, sewer systems, and the like—as well as financial assets. There is a question as to what market value to place on these assets, since a ready buyer for many of these assets, such as bridges and highways, is not available. Nevertheless, when the cost-derived value of these assets is counted, Eisner and Pieper find

---

[21] See Eisner and Pieper, Footnote 20.

Figure 14.5 A Comparison of Government Debt by Country

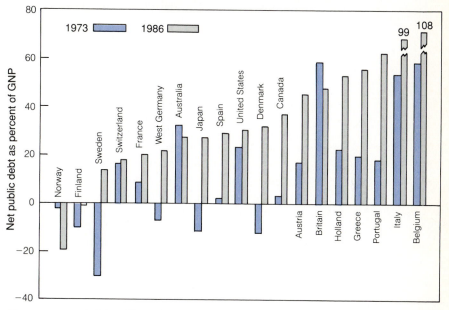

Figures are net debts (financial liabilities minus government financial assets). Note that although the debt as a percent of GNP rose in the United States between 1973 and 1986, so too did the debt of other countries. The average debt rose from 17 percent of GNP in 1973 to 33 percent in 1986 for all industrial countries.

Source: OECD.

that the government's net worth has, in fact, steadily increased since World War II.

The implication of the adjustments to the federal debt suggested above is that the federal debt is not as great as the gross dollar figures would indicate. In addition, it should be noted that the recent experience of state and local governments is not similar to that of the federal government. In fact, local governments have consistently run a surplus since 1966, and state and local governments are, on balance, net creditors.[22] Thus *total* government indebtedness has been rising less rapidly than we would think merely by looking at the rise in the debt of the federal government.

---

[22] It is interesting to note that the surpluses of state and local governments were growing during this period. For instance, during the 1983 to 1986 period, the annual surplus of state and local governments averaged more than $50 billion, while it averaged less than $35 billion from 1980 to 1982, approximately $20 billion from 1975 to 1979, and less than $8 billion from 1970 to 1975.

The Interest Payment to GNP Ratio

We noted previously that one useful measure of the debt is the size of the real debt relative to the economy's productive capability. This debt to GNP ratio indicates the portion of GNP required to retire the entire debt in one year. Although the debt to GNP ratio provides some perspective on the relative size of the debt, it is unlikely that the entire debt would ever be retired in a single year. A more realistic scenario is a policy of covering the interest payments on the debt, or "servicing the debt." Just as we can compute a measure of the cost to retire the debt in terms of proportion of GNP it takes to retire the debt, we can compute a measure of the cost of the debt in terms of servicing that debt.

As Figure 14.6 indicates, interest payments on the federal debt as a percentage of GNP hovered between the 1 and 2 percent mark until 1980. Since then, interest payments on the debt as a percentage of GNP have more than doubled.

Two factors have contributed to the recent rise in interest payments as a percentage of GNP. The first is the increase in the debt to GNP ratio itself. Other things being equal, a higher debt requires greater interest payments. The second contributing factor is an increase in interest rates. The federal government resembles any other borrower in that it must pay the market rate of interest when it borrows. The high market interest rates that existed during the late 1970s and early 1980s would have led to a higher government interest payment even if the debt to GNP ratio had remained constant. The high interest payments on the government debt generated by the simultaneous occurrence of high interest rates and large government deficits led to such a growth in government interest payment during this period that "if this [growth in interest payments] were to continue unchanged until the year 2013, the federal government would be forced to borrow or tax the equivalent of the entire gross national product simply to service its existing debt."[23]

Servicing the Debt: The Real Effects

Although our discussion indicates that servicing the debt has taken an ever-increasing share of GNP in recent years, we must be careful when we speak of the "burden of the debt on future generations of Americans." In one sense, no "real" costs exist to servicing the debt. At least for public debt held by Americans, we owe the debt to ourselves. Remember that interest payments are a form of transfer payments. If the government were to raise taxes to finance the higher interest payments, total taxes net of transfer payments (net real taxes) would be unaffected. While some individuals would pay higher taxes, the additional tax revenues would go to other individuals who held the government bonds. Since households' net real taxes

---

[23] John B. Carlson and E. J. Stevens, "The National Debt: A Secular Perspective," *Economic Review of the Federal Reserve Bank of Cleveland,* Third Quarter, (Cleveland, 1985), p. 11.

Figure 14.6 **Interest Payments on Federal Debt as a Percent of GNP**

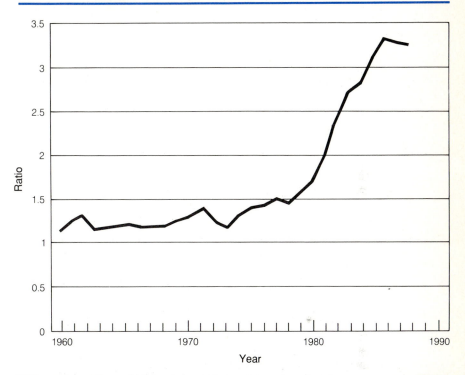

With a rising debt and higher interest rates, interest payments as a percent of GNP doubled in the 1980s compared to that of the 1960s and 1970s.

Source: Economic Report of the President (1988).

are unaffected, the spending capacity of households would not be directly infringed upon by payments required to service the debt.

In the late 1970s and early 1980s, however, total real tax collections did not rise to pay for the real increase in interest payments and other transfer payments that occurred during this time. If total tax receipts do not increase, then the increase in interest payments on the debt and other transfer payments means a reduction in net taxes. As a consequence, either government borrowing must increase or there must be a cut in government purchases of goods and services. During this period, the adjustment was predominantly an increase in borrowing, and as we have seen this substitution of borrowing for taxes can have real long-run effects. There is a shift out of investment to consumption which, as we discussed in Chapter 8, can have adverse consequences for the size of the future capital stock and thus the future productive capacity of the economy.

A real effect of servicing the debt can occur even if tax revenues are increased to offset higher interest costs, leaving net taxes unchanged. The reason for this is that the way taxes are levied can have real effects. For instance, suppose that the increased interest payments are financed through a tax on investment purchases by businesses. This will reduce the incentives to invest, with the result being a lower future capital stock and less growth in real GNP. In contrast, if higher taxes are levied on household consumption, then this effect on the future capital stock may be reversed, as the tax, if it encourages saving, will lead to increased investment.

Another "real" cost of servicing the debt arises from the fact that United States households do not hold all the government issued debt. In recent years, foreigners have acquired an increasing proportion of the debt, as evidenced by the fact that United States capital inflows have exceeded capital outflows. In order for the balance of payments to balance, this means that the United States has acquired more goods and services abroad than it has shipped to foreign countries, as evidenced by the recent large United States trade deficits.

In the future, the United States will have to pay back the foreign loans by sending more goods abroad than we receive in return. In other words, when the United States borrows today from foreigners, it must pay back in the future with real goods. To the extent that foreigners hold part of the national debt, future interest payments to service the debt can no longer be viewed as an internal redistribution of funds among United States households. Future tax dollars flowing abroad constitute a real cost to future generations of United States residents. It is the current generation that reaps a gain of not fully paying for government spending. Thus with foreigners purchasing government debt, there is an intergenerational transfer of the burden of running the government.[24]

Inflation and Changes in the Real Debt

We discussed earlier that what matters in determining the magnitude of public indebtedness is the real, and not the nominal, value of the government's debt. The debt to GNP ratio is one measure of how the real debt changes in relationship to real GNP. In this section, we examine the effect of inflation on the size of the real debt. Since inflation serves to reduce the real value of the debt over time, it is like a tax that is used to retire debt, or an "inflation tax." To clarify this discussion, let's determine the exact amount by which the government's real indebtedness changes in any year.

Recall that we use the term A_g^s to denote real government borrowing,

---

[24] As discussed in the next section, had the government financed its spending by taxing or borrowing solely from United States citizens, the real cost would have been incurred by the current populace in the form of lower consumption or investment.

or the real flow supply of financial assets, in the current period. This government borrowing causes the real value of the debt to increase. Inflation, however, causes the real value of the debt to fall. Let $\overline{D}_g$ denote the real value of government debt outstanding at the end of the last period and let π denote the inflation rate. Then the reduction in the government's indebtedness due to inflation can be approximated by $\pi \cdot \overline{D}_g$, the product of the inflation rate and the real value of debt outstanding at the end of the last period. For example, if the real value of the debt outstanding at the start of the period is \$100 billion, then a 5 percent inflation rate ($\pi = .05$) reduces the real value of the debt by approximately \$5 billion.[25]

Summarizing the above discussion, the net change in the government's real debt during the current period equals the amount the government borrows minus the reduction in the real value of the debt that occurs through inflation. That is, the net change in the debt, $D_g - \overline{D}_g$, is given by the expression

$$D_g - \overline{D}_g = A_g^s - \pi \cdot \overline{D}_g \qquad (14.1)$$

where D_g is the real market value of government debt at the end of the current period. This equation indicates that the real indebtedness of the government falls due to inflation (the term $-\pi\overline{D}_g$ in Equation 14.1). What is critical to recognize is that this result is the outgrowth of government bonds that stipulate fixed money payments. If these bonds had stipulated interest payments indexed so as to increase with inflation, then the real interest payments would be independent of the interest rate. In this hypothetical case, inflation would have no effect on the government's real debt.

Equation 14.1 highlights an interesting alternative interpretation of government deficits. Up to this point, we have identified a government deficit with a positive current borrowing ($A_g^s > 0$). However, Robert Eisner suggests that if "inflation and rising interest rates reduce the real value of government debt more than the nominal deficit raises it, there is no real deficit. Indeed, the inflation tax . . . converted supposed Carter administration and initial Reagan deficits into real surpluses."[26] In terms of Equation 14.1, during the late 1970s and early 1980s, the rise in real debt due to deficit spending (A_g^s) often was more than offset by the fall in real debt outstanding due to inflation ($\pi \cdot \overline{D}_g$). For example, from the end of 1979 to the end of 1980, the federal government debt in nominal terms grew by approximately 7 percent, reflecting a \$61.3 billion deficit. At the same time, however, the inflation rate as measured by the implicit price deflator, was close to 10 percent over this period, so that the real value of the debt fell.

---

[25] To be exact, the real value of the debt at the end of the current period would be $\overline{D}_g/(1 + \pi)$, so that the change in the real debt is $[\overline{D}_g/(1 + \pi)] - \overline{D}_g$ or $[-\pi/(1 + \pi)]\overline{D}_g$ which we approximate by $-\pi\overline{D}_g$.

[26] Robert Eisner, "How Big a Budget Deficit, and So What?," *Wall Street Journal*, 9 September 1987.

To the Point

GOVERNMENT DEBT: ITS GROWTH AND IMPACT

- Although the national debt is at an all-time high in nominal terms, debt as a percent of GNP fell steadily from the end of World War II until the late 1970s. The debt to GNP ratio—a ratio that indicates the fraction of GNP required if the entire debt were to be retired in one year—has climbed since then.

- In order to measure the proportion of GNP that goes to servicing the debt, we can look at interest payments on the federal debt as a percentage of GNP. These payments stayed between 1 and 2 percent of GNP until 1980. Since then, interest payments on the debt as a percent of GNP have more than doubled.

- When the debt is held by domestic households, there is no real burden on future generations to service the debt since interest payments simply transfer income across households. However, the fact that foreigners have acquired substantial holdings of United States government debt means some of the future interest payments will go to foreigners, not to other United States households.

- Inflation lowers the real value of the debt while current deficits increase the real value of the debt. During inflationary periods, the real indebtedness of the government may fall even if the government runs a current budget deficit.

14.5 ASSESSING THE IMPACT OF DEFICIT SPENDING

The previous section has looked at issues related to the debt. In this section, we examine the impact of a deficit. Recall from our discussion in Chapter 3 on stocks and flow variables that while the debt is a stock variable, the deficit is a flow variable. In other words, while the size of the debt can be measured at any point in time, say July 1, 1989, the deficit is measured over a period of time, say during the year 1989.

The debt and deficit are related, as we saw in the prior section, since a deficit ($A_g^s > 0$) results in an increase in the size of the debt ($D_g - \overline{D}_g$). As we will see in this section, unlike the effects of servicing the national debt, there are significant resource allocation questions associated with the creation of debt through running a deficit.

Deficit-Increasing Tax Reductions, Interest Rates, and Crowding Out

High deficits cause great concern primarily because they may lead to higher interest rates, which in turn cause firms' investment spending to fall. To assess how an increase in government borrowing affects the economy, we must first know the reason for that increase. Recall from our earlier discussion of the government financing constraint that government spending on output (G^d) is financed either by net taxes (T) or through the sale of financial assets (A^s_g) to households, private depository institutions, and the Federal Reserve.[27] That is, $G^d = T + A^s_g$. Thus government borrowing can increase either because the government increases its spending on output or because it reduces net taxes.

Suppose that the increase in the government deficit is due to a tax cut. As we saw in Chapters 8 and 11, the rise in government borrowing increases the demand for loanable funds, as shown in Figure 14.7(a) by the shift to the right in the demand for loanable funds curve from LF^d_0 to LF^d_1. At the same time, households put part of their increased disposable income into saving, as shown by the shift to the right in the supply of loanable funds curve from LF^s_0 to LF^s_1.

As this figure indicates, the increase in the demand for loanable funds by the government to finance the tax cut exceeds the increase in the supply of loanable funds by households because part of the tax cut goes toward increased household consumption of goods and services. The resulting upward pressure on the interest rate leads to a rise in the equilibrium interest rate from r_0 to r_1. In the money market, the higher interest rate causes an excess supply of money at the original levels of real GNP and prices, as shown in Figure 14.7(b). According to the aggregate budget constraint, the excess supply of money means an excess demand for output. The excess demand for output is directly attributable to the rise in consumption demand induced by lower taxes.

An excess demand for output at the original output level Y^* and price level P_0 means the aggregate demand curve has shifted to the right. Figure 14.8 illustrates this increase in aggregate demand by the shift in the aggregate demand curve from AD_0 to AD_1. The real effects on the economy now depend on three considerations. The first is whether the economy starts at full employment or at less than full employment. In Figure 14.8, we assume that the original level of real GNP (Y^*) is the full employment level. The second consideration is whether we take the short-run or long-run view of economy-wide adjustments to demand-side shocks. In Figure 14.8, one short-run view is captured by the upward-sloping aggregate supply curve of the modified neoclassical models (see Chapter 12), while the long-run view is reflected by the vertical aggregate supply curve of the neoclassical model (see Chapter 7). The third consideration is whether individuals anticipated

---

[27] As our discussion in Chapter 4 indicated, by substituting in the financing constraint of depository institutions, we could separate government's new issues of financial assets into those sold to the nonbank public, those sold to the private depository institutions, and those sold to the Fed. The sum of the last two comprises part of the change in the money supply. The last one alone comprises part of the change in the monetary base. We say "part of" since the monetary base and the money supply also change if the Fed buys previously issued government bonds.

Figure 14.7   The Impact of a Deficit-Financed Tax Cut

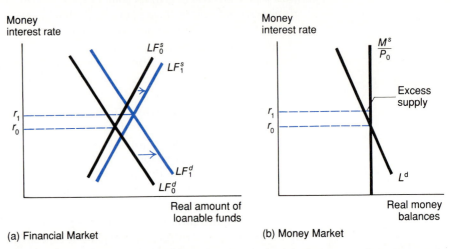

(a) Financial Market   (b) Money Market

A tax cut with no change in government spending requires an increase in government borrowing equal to the fall in taxes. This increased borrowing is shown by the shift to the right in the demand for loanable funds curve from LF_0^d to LF_1^d. Households allocate only part of the increase in current disposable income that accompanies a tax cut toward saving in the form of the supply of loanable funds. Thus as shown in part (a), the shift to the right in an increased supply of loanable funds curve from LF_0^s to LF_1^s is less than the shift in the demand for loanable funds. As a consequence, the interest rate that clears the financial market rises from r_0 to r_1. At the higher interest rate, as part (b) indicates, there is an excess supply of money at the original levels of real GNP and prices.

the tax change and incorporated the long-run effect of the change into their expectations of price changes. We assume they did not. As Figure 14.8 indicates, the short-run effect of the demand shock is then shown by the movement along the upward-sloping short-run aggregate supply curve $AS_{short\text{-}run}$ from point A to point B. In the long-run, the price level rises further, to P_1.

In addition to the rise in the interest rate due to the direct effect of increased government borrowing, as was shown in Figure 14.7(a), the interest rate also rises as a result of the increase in prices, as the rise in the price level reduces the real money supply and thus the real supply of loanable funds. A deficit-increasing tax cut thus leads to a shift away from the production of investment goods and toward the production of consumption goods, as the higher interest rate caused by the tax cut reduces firms' investment. Firms' borrowing to finance investment has been crowded out by the increased government borrowing. A consequence of the reduced investment is that there will be a lower capital stock in the future. Thus the deficit means not only that future generations inherit a higher government debt but also that they inherit an economy with a reduced productive capacity.

Figure 14.8 **The Short-Run and Long-Run Effects of a Tax Cut Starting from Full Employment**

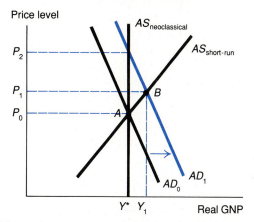

A cut in taxes, with no change in government spending, leads to excess demand in the output market at the initial levels of prices and output. The result is a rightward shift in the aggregate demand curve from AD_0 to AD_1. In the short run, the price level rises from P_0 to P_1 and real GNP rises from Y^* to Y_1. In the long run, prices fully adjust, rising to P_2 and real GNP returns to Y^*, the full employment level of output.

This view is substantially modified if we assume that the economy starts at less than full employment rather than full employment. In this case, as our analysis in Chapters 10 and 11 indicates, an increase in aggregate demand can lead to an increase in real GNP rather than a rise in prices. There are then two reasons why investment will not fall by as much as predicted above. First, the rise in the interest rate that dampens investment will not be as great. Since prices do not rise, there is not the increase in interest rates that would accompany a fall in the real supply of money. Second, if firms view the increase in current output as implying greater future sales, then there is an offsetting impetus increases investment.

Thus although the tax cut still results in some rise in the interest rate that would reduce investment, the simultaneous increase in output can stimulate investment, as our discussion of the accelerator model in Chapter 10 indicated. In addition, the tax cut offers immediate benefits in terms of increased output and employment.

Ricardian Equivalence Revisited

If a cut in income taxes leads solely to an increase in households' supply of loanable funds with no change in consumption, then a deficit-financed reduction in taxes will not affect interest rates, investment, or anything else in the economy. As we discussed in Chapter 8, the hypothesis that a borrowing-financed reduction in taxes does not affect the interest rate even in the face of strong credit demands by the government is known as the Ricardian equivalence theorem.

To refresh your memory, Ricardo reasoned that individuals will save more today when the government borrows to finance its current spending if they recognize that the tax payments required to service the debt will rise in the future. Although the cut in current taxes increases current disposable income, households recognize that their permanent disposable income remains unchanged. The present value of the taxes that households will have to pay in the future rises by an amount exactly equal to the increase in government borrowing today, which in turn just equals the reduction in current taxes. As a result, the borrowing-financed reduction in taxes will not affect household consumption demand. Households will simply use their current tax savings to purchase the new bonds that the government issues. Thus households meet government's increased demand for loanable funds with an equal increase in the supply of loanable funds. Interest rates do not rise because of the increased deficit.

While Ricardo recognized the theoretical possibility that the substitution of government borrowing for current taxes might leave the interest rate unaffected, he did not actually believe this would happen. Today, however, a number of economists subscribe to the Ricardian equivalence theorem not just as a theoretical possibility, but as a description of the real world. We have previously cited the recent work by Evans that finds no causal link between deficits and interest rates.[28] The Evans study is but one of several that fails to link high deficits with high real interest rates.[29] Yet in another study, Gregory Hoelscher finds "strong evidence that larger deficits are associated with higher long-term interest rates."[30]

The brunt of the evidence seems to be that everything else (including government spending) the same, an increase in the deficit has little impact on interest rates, and thus a deficit will not reduce investment substantially. Although some researchers attribute this negligible rise in the interest rate to Ricardian equivalence, our discussion of fiscal policy in an open economy suggests an alternative explanation for the small rise in the interest rate. We saw earlier (Figure 7.9 in Chapter 7) that the supply of loanable funds curve is flatter in an open economy than in a closed economy, as a rise in the United States interest rate attracts capital from abroad. An increase in the deficit and the accompanying rise in the demand for loanable funds will not

---

[28] Paul Evans, "Do Large Deficits Produce High Interest Rates?", *American Economic Review* (March 1985): Vol. 75, pp. 68–87.

[29] See Angelo Marasco and Allan Meltzer, "Long and Short-Term Interest Rates in a Risky World," *Journal of Monetary Economics* (November 1983): 485–518; John Makin, "Real Interest, Money Surprises, Anticipated Inflation, and Fiscal Deficits," *Federal Reserve Bank of San Francisco Economic Review* (Summer 1983): 31–45; and Charles Plosser, "Government Financing Decisions and Net Returns," *Journal of Monetary Economics (May 1982): 325–52.*

[30] Gregory Hoelscher, "New Evidence on Deficits and Interest Rates," *Journal of Money, Credit, and Banking* (February 1986): 1.

cause much of a rise in the interest rate if the supply of loanable funds curve is relatively flat. In this case, the increase in consumption induced by a tax cut leads not so much to a fall in investment as to a fall in net exports, as the increased capital inflows lead to an appreciation of the dollar.

There are other reasons for the inability to find a strong direct relationship between the government deficit and the real interest rate. One may be the fact, discussed earlier in this chapter, that it is difficult to obtain a proper measure of the government's debt. It also may partly reflect the fact that deficits are accompanied by accommodating increases in the money supply that hold real interest rates down, at least in the short run. We look at this possibility in the next section when we examine the relationship between the deficit and the rate of monetary growth in more detail.

Government Deficits and Inflation: Is There a Link?

In the autumn of 1974, the country had been experiencing relatively high inflation for the preceding two years. Congressional candidates across the country felt a need to explain this high inflation. While the oil supply shock was one often-cited culprit, many claimed that large government deficits were a second source of the inflation. Some went so far as to suggest that simply limiting government deficits, either through lower spending or higher taxes, would solve the inflation problem.

In earlier chapters, we analyzed the effects of an increase in the government deficit. We saw that an increase in government spending generates excess demand in the output market, which can lead to higher prices. In terms of the exchange equation, if an increase in the deficit leads to an increase in the interest rate, velocity increases. If the economy begins at full employment, then the increase in the velocity means a rise in the price level. Although an increase in government spending can lead to rising prices by raising velocity, much of the inflation experienced by the United States and other countries is related to changes in the money supply. However, the deficit may be instrumental in causing inflation if changes in the money supply are the result of government deficits. We explore this potential link in the next section.

Deficits and Accommodating Monetary Policy. In our discussion of crowding out, we saw that increased deficit spending may led to increased interest rates. In order to prevent the interest rate from rising, monetary authorities may increase the money supply concurrently with the increase in government spending. In the context of the model with predetermined prices, such an accommodating monetary policy can prevent the interest rate from rising and thus reinforce the expansionary effect of higher government spending. Figure 14.9 indicates the effects on output of coordinated expansionary monetary and fiscal policy using *IS-LM* analysis.

An increase in the deficit, whether due to a tax cut or a rise in government spending, shifts the *IS* curve to the right from IS_0 to IS_1 in Figure 14.9. If

Figure 14.9   An Increase in Government Spending with Accommodating Monetary Policy

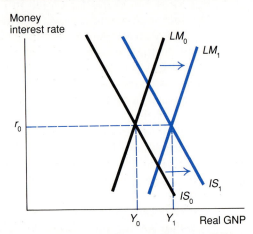

With an increase in government spending, the *IS* curve shifts to the right from IS_0 to IS_1. By increasing the money supply, the Fed can engineer a shift in the *LM* curve from LM_0 to LM_1. As a consequence, the interest rate remains unchanged and the increase in equilibrium real GNP exceeds what it would have been had there been no change in the money supply.

there is no change in the money supply, the interest rate will rise. In order to prevent this rise in the interest rate and in the process reinforce the expansionary thrust of the fiscal policy, the Fed may increase the money supply. If the money supply is increased sufficiently, the shift to the right in the *LM* curve will keep the interest rate constant, as is shown in Figure 14.9 by the shift in the *LM* curve from LM_0 to LM_1.

Although a policy of accommodating deficit-financed increases in government spending with an increase in the money supply may be effective in lowering the interest rate in the short run, the policy cannot keep the interest rate permanently lower once full employment is reached, because prices will then adjust. Our analysis of the neoclassical model tells us that in the long run a higher level of deficit-financed government spending causes the interest rate to rise whether the Fed increases the money supply or not. The only thing that increases in the money supply do in the long-run is to raise the general level of prices.

The Evidence on the Relationship Between Money Growth and Deficits. If the monetary authorities typically respond to an increase in the deficit by increasing the money supply ("monetizing the deficit"), we would expect a close correlation between deficits and money growth to exist. Several economists have tried to determine whether an empirical relationship does exist between the deficit and the growth rate of the money supply.

At the conclusion of World War II, United States monetary policy had no other purpose but to accommodate fiscal policy in the manner illustrated by Figure 14.9. Through the 1950s, the Fed and the Treasury had an informal agreement that the monetary authorities would attempt to keep interest rates low, so that when the government ran a deficit, it could finance that deficit at low interest rates. Furthermore, by increasing the money supply to keep the interest rate low when the government ran a deficit, the Fed could, at least when output was below its full employment level, prevent the "crowding-out effect" of expansionary fiscal policy.

This working relationship would lead us to expect a close correlation between deficits and the growth rate in the money supply during the 1950s. Since deficits were not very large during this period, however, the evidence is inconclusive. During the deficits of the 1970s, an interest rate target was one of the goals of the Fed, suggesting at least a partially accommodative monetary policy. However, two economists have found no significant relationship between money and debt growth in the United States.[31] Since 1979, the Fed has for the most part stated its goals in terms of monetary growth targets, placing less weight on interest rate targets.

Some recent research in the area of deficits and money growth on an international basis finds for a sample of ten industrialized countries "little evidence that government debt growth in excess of real growth is either related to money growth or permanently related to inflation over periods of a decade or less."[32] Thus for the United States as well as other industrialized economies, little support exists for the contention that government deficits lead to higher inflation by inducing monetary authorities to increase the monetary growth rate.

Government Deficit Spending: The Use of Public Funds and Crowding Out

If the rise in the deficit finances increased government spending rather than a tax cut, the adverse effect on private investment is clear in the context of the neoclassical model. At the new equilibrium, a higher interest rate reduces investment and consumption, as increased government demand takes the place of private spending. Thus the disposition of real GNP shifts away from private investment spending toward government spending.

---

[31] Robert Barro, "Comment From an Unreconstructed Ricardian" *Journal of Monetary Economics* (August 1978): 569–81; William A. Niskanen, "Deficits, Government Spending and Inflation," *Journal of Monetary Economics* (August 1978): 591–602.

[32] Aria Protopapadakis and Jeremy Siegel, "Is Money Growth Related to Government Deficits? Evidence from Ten Industrialized Economies," Working Paper No. 86-11, Federal Reserve Bank of Philadelphia, May, 1986.

Even if deficit spending reduces private investment, however, it does not necessarily follow that the future capital stock of the economy will be reduced as a result. Whether this occurs depends on how government spends the newly raised funds. If the government invests in capital goods such as roads, dams, bridges, or education, the future productive capability of the economy may even be increased by such deficit spending. In contrast, if the government incurs a large deficit to subsidize congressional lunches, then this has the likely effect of reducing the future capital stock.

A disquieting note in this area is the trend of government spending during the last several decades. While government spending has been rising in the last 20 years, spending by the government on capital as a share of total government spending on goods and services has been falling.[33] This is not to say that government spending that is not on capital items necessarily reduces the welfare of future generations. During World War II the national debt more than quadrupled in a four-year period. Even though most of the increased government expenditures did not serve to raise the stock of capital in the nation, few would argue with the importance of these expenditures.

In summary, the neoclassical model predicts that an increase in borrowing-financed government spending must crowd out an equal amount of private spending, which may reduce the future capital stock depending on how the government spends the money raised by borrowing. Our conclusions change, however, if we do not subscribe to the neoclassical model. In the neoclassical model, output is entirely determined by "supply factors," so that if the government purchases more output, less is available for other uses. This is not the case in the predetermined price model, which is characterized by real GNP below the full employment level. According to this model, a borrowing-financed increase in government spending can increase total output in the economy without much (if any) private spending being crowded out.

SUMMARY

Along with the growth in the size of the federal government in the last 50 years has come the understanding that government spending and taxation affect the macroeconomy. Many believe that government has rightfully assumed its new-found role of attempting to maintain the economy at full employment through fiscal policy. Such corrective fiscal policy encompasses both the automatic stabilization of reactive rules, such as net taxes that automatically fall when real GNP falls, as well as discretionary fiscal policy, where the government enacts legislation to raise spending or reduce taxation to counteract downturns in the economy. Enacting effective discretionary fiscal policy is not easy because of lags in recognizing problems in the economy, responding

---

[33] Charles R. Hulten and George E. Peterson, "The Public Capital Stock: Needs, Trends, and Performance," *American Economic Review* (May 1984): Vol. 74, 166–73.

with appropriate and acceptable legislation, and implementing tax cuts or spending increases.

Economists concerned by the growth in government have argued for fiscal policy rules, such as a balanced budget amendment or trust funds. These rules essentially eliminate fiscal policy as a macroeconomic stabilization tool. Since arguments in favor of such rules often use as justification the recent rapid rise in deficit spending at the federal level, we must understand not only the changes in the government debt that have occurred but also the implications that these changes have for the macroeconomy.

One measure of the debt that provides perspective on its size is the debt to GNP ratio, for this indicates what fraction of GNP it would take to retire the debt in one year. A second, related measure is the ratio of the interest payment on the debt to GNP, for this indicates what fraction of GNP it takes to simply service the debt each year. Currently, less than 5 percent of the GNP is used to service the debt. Although interest payments are predominantly transfers among households, the fact that foreigners hold increasing amounts of United States government debt means that some of these transfers are intergenerational transfers. Interest payments to Americans can also have real effects since they necessitate current or future tax increases that can distort incentives to work, save, and invest.

Although servicing the debt per se may not have substantial real effects, there are real effects to changes in the debt, or deficits. The neoclassical model tells us that deficits, whether due to reduced taxes or increased spending, can lead to less private investment, which reduces the future capital stock and thus the productive capacity of the economy. There are several potential qualifications to this predicted effect of deficits on investment and the capital stock, however. For a deficit-financed tax reduction, the Ricardian equivalence doctrine suggests that substituting borrowing for taxes may not affect the interest rate. For a deficit-financed spending increase, the change in total investment includes not only the fall in private investment but also the potential increase in investment by the government. Finally, if the economy is at less than full employment, tax cuts or increased government spending lead not only to higher deficits but also to an expanding economy that offers the immediate benefit of a higher GNP as well as an environment that can stimulate investment.

One thing not directly attributable to deficits is sustained inflation. Deficits can contribute to sustained inflation if they induce the monetary authorities to expand the money supply. The evidence, however, does not indicate a historically strong link between deficits and monetary growth.

LOOKING AHEAD

An understanding of the character of the labor market is important to an analysis of macroeconomics, for employment determines real GNP in the short run. We have not yet examined the workings of the labor market in detail, in particular the relations between the employed, the unemployed, and those outside the labor force. We turn to this topic in the next chapter.

KEY TERMS

Public choice economics, 557   Fiscal drag, 564
Automatic stabilizer, 561
Full employment budget, 563

REVIEW QUESTIONS

1. What has happened to total spending by United States state and local governments and the federal government during the past 50 years? What has happened to the division of total government spending between the federal government and state and local governments?

2. What do we mean by government transfer payments? Give some examples of transfer payments. What has happened over time to the division of total government outlays between spending on goods and services and transfer payments.

3. Why has George Stigler argued that in the very nature of the political process there is a bias toward ever-growing government spending?

4. What are the key features of the Gramm-Rudman Bill? What pressures gave rise to this bill? Are all government outlays subject to Gramm-Rudman cuts if required to meet deficit targets?

5. Two types of proposals have been suggested to impose fiscal restraint on the federal government: those calling for a balanced budget amendment and those calling for trust fund accounting.

    (a) How would a balanced budget requirement or the establishment of trust funds for various programs tend to impose fiscal discipline?

    (b) In what ways would a balanced budget requirement and trust funds differ?

    (c) In what ways are a balanced budget requirement and trust funds analogous to the monetary rule that the money supply grow at a constant rate?

    (d) What arguments have been given against balanced budget and trust fund rules?

6. What do we mean by automatic stabilizers?

    (a) Give some examples of automatic stabilizers.

(b) In what sense are automatic stabilizers examples of fiscal policy rules?

(c) According to the macroeconomic model with predetermined prices, an initial change in autonomous spending causes real GNP to fall. Recall that the multiplier indicates the total change in real GNP caused by a unit change in real autonomous spending. What effect does the existence of automatic stabilizers have on the multiplier? Why?

7. The effective use of discretionary fiscal policy as a stabilization policy requires that fiscal policy changes be timed correctly so as to have the desired effects on output demand at the appropriate times. The more unpredictable and the longer are the lags involved in using fiscal policy, the more difficult will this timing problem be. Discuss the various lags involved in the implementation of discretionary fiscal policy.

8. In 1975, Gerald Ford announced a $50 tax rebate, urging everyone to take the money and go out to dinner as his and Betty's guest. If Ford felt he had to urge people to do this, what was he anticipating people were going to do with their $50? How would people's reaction to the rebate change if they were to anticipate the rebate as occurring periodically rather than a one-time affair? Why?

9. What do we mean by the full employment budget? What information does it tell us?

10. Why is the nominal value of the national debt not a very useful figure? Discuss the ways of obtaining a more informative debt measure.

11. If the government borrows today, it will have to assess tax payments to pay the interest on the debt in the future.

(a) Will these taxes per se constitute a burden on future generations? Why or why not?

(b) Is there any reason to believe that just the act of levying the taxes will impose a real cost in the future?

12. Suppose that the government enacts a borrowing-financed reduction in taxes.

(a) According to the neoclassical model, what will be the effect on interest rates and private investment spending? Why?

(b) How is your answer to (a) affected if the Ricardian equivalence theorem holds? Why?

(c) Now suppose that the government enacts a borrowing-financed increase in real spending. What will happen to interest rates and private investment spending? How is your answer affected if households anticipate the future taxes stemming from the increased borrowing?

13. Can increases in real government spending permanently affect the inflation rate? Why or why not?

14. What do we mean by the inflation tax? How does the inflation tax work?

    (a) On what assets does the inflation tax accrue?

    (b) Is there any limit to the revenue that can be raised from ever higher inflation? If so, where does this limit come from?

15. If there is an unanticipated increase in inflation, what happens to the real interest payments that the government makes on the debt it has issued? If the government's real spending and borrowing in the current period do not change, what happens to the real amount of net taxes that the government collects? Do taxpayers gain at the expense of bond-holders? Why or why not?

    (a) What do you think will happen to the interest that the government will have to offer on the new bonds that it issues?

    (b) Suppose that at the time it issues bonds, individuals anticipate correctly that inflation will increase in the future. What effect does this higher anticipated inflation have on the real interest payments that the government will have to pay out? Why? What happens to the inflation tax that the government will collect? Why?

16. From the point of view of efficient resource usage, are there any real gains from the government raising revenue through the inflation tax? Are there any real costs?

Wage and Price Controls

An area of public policy that is neither monetary nor fiscal policy is a system of economy-wide wage and price controls. The most recent experience in the United States with wage and price controls occurred during the Nixon administration. On August 15, 1971, President Nixon announced on national television that all wages and prices would be frozen at their current levels. A general wage-price freeze is the same as a price ceiling applied to all products in the economy. A wage-price freeze is put into effect because policymakers determine that the equilibrium price level is rising too fast. Consequently, they freeze prices below the equilibrium price level. A number of problems ensue from such a policy, however.

First, the price freeze causes shortages in some markets. If a price ceiling is set below the equilibrium price for a market, the quantity demanded for the good in that market will exceed the quantity supplied. A shortage will result, and the market will resort to some form of non-price allocation such as waiting in line, giving preferential treatment to certain customers, or trading on the black market. When a general wage-price freeze is enforced, shortages will not occur in every market since the level at which prices are frozen will be sufficient to clear certain markets. In those markets where the price level is not market-clearing, the problem of shortages will appear. Furthermore, the longer prices are frozen, the more shortages will appear, since fewer prices will be market-clearing. Frozen prices no longer serve to clear markets because of a second problem with a general wage-price freeze: It does not get at the root cause of inflation.

When the money supply and velocity combine to grow at a faster rate than the growth of real GNP, prices rise. Wage and price controls do not get at the cause of inflation, they only contain the symptoms. The underlying cause of the inflation still exists, but with wage and price controls, no way exists to monitor the strength of forces causing inflation. With prices frozen, the obvious signal—rising prices—that inflationary forces are too strong is obscured. Thus inflationary pressure builds so that when price controls are lifted, prices often skyrocket.

Price controls that mask signals of inflationary pressures are analogous to the cortisone shots an athlete takes for a knee injury. The pain that the athlete experiences is a signal sent by the body not to use that knee. The shot of cortisone masks the pain but does not deal with the real problem in the knee that causes the pain. The athlete may continue to feel no pain while severe damage is being done to the knee. Inflation is like a pain being sent out as a signal about the economy. If the symptom is stifled, it will not be possible to know the strength of the forces that lead to inflation, nor the extent of the damage.

Walter Heller, former chairman of the Council of Economic Advisers, suggested that wage and price controls were an effective means to control inflation if they were accompanied by moderate monetary and fiscal policies. Subsequently, an opponent of this theory noted that this was like saying a curse would kill a flock of sheep if you accompanied it with a large dose of arsenic. Yet, this is perhaps too vitriolic a reply, for there can be a role for wage and price controls in dampening inflationary expectations that are out of line with actual conditions.

According to the modified neoclassical models of Chapter 12, we have seen that a curtailing of aggregate demand to dampen inflation can also in the short-run lead to a fall in real GNP. Recall that behind this fall in real GNP are forecasting errors, in particular individuals overestimating actual inflation. If wage and price controls convince individuals to immediately reduce expectations of inflation, then these forecasting errors could be eliminated, or at least mitigated. The result would be that a policy to reduce inflation by restricting aggregate demand could be successful while avoiding, or at least moderating, the temporary period of high unemployment that otherwise would accompany a fall in aggregate demand.

The U.S. economy has had little experience with wage and price controls and the subsequent problems they cause. In many Eastern European countries controlled prices are a way of life, as is waiting in line. Soviet authorities hold out their low inflation rates as an example to the world of how well their system works. They do not, however, discuss the cost of time lost waiting in lines, nor the costs arising from shortages and the lack of availability of goods. The *Wall Street Journal* reported that, according to a Soviet educator in the Soviet publication *Pioneer,* there exists a reason other than price controls as to why the shelves in Soviet stores are always empty while those in capitalist countries are full.

> People in capitalist countries do not earn enough money to buy such products and therefore they remain on the shelves. The income of the Soviet people has been rising steadily so that they can now afford to buy everything they desire. It is the buying power of the Soviet people that keeps the store shelves empty.

Part Five

Special Topics: Labor Market, Money Market, and International Trade and Finance

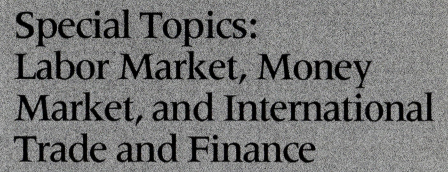

Chapter 15

The Labor Market: Job Search, Layoffs, and the Natural Rate of Unemployment

IN examining the factors determining real GNP, employment, and the price level, we have drawn several important conclusions. In the short run, due to "sticky" prices and incorrect price expectations, real GNP and employment can deviate from their full employment levels. Such deviations will not persist indefinitely, however, because prices ultimately adjust to excess demands and supplies in order to clear all markets, and individuals ultimately learn the actual levels of prices. In other words, in the absence of macroeconomic demand or supply shocks, real GNP and employment tend toward their long-run equilibrium levels.

As we discussed in Chapter 7, long-run equilibrium does not imply the absence of unemployment. The labor market is in a constant state of flux, with voluntary quits, new entrants, and layoffs in declining industries. Since unemployed workers do not have complete information on job vacancies and on how wages vary across employers, workers searching for jobs typically experience periods of significant unemployment. Consequently, some unemployment is "natural," or consistent with long-run equilibrium in the labor market. In fact, most unemployment is "natural," not cyclical. The upward trend in unemployment during the 1970s and 1980s was due primarily to increases in the natural rate of unemployment—which has been estimated to have risen at least two percentage points from 1960 to 1985, from approximately 4 to 6 percent.[1]

We do not mean to imply that cyclical unemployment is unimportant. From 1971 to 1987, when the natural unemployment rate averaged approximately 6 percent, the actual unemployment rate ranged from a low of 4.9 percent in the boom year of 1974 to a high of 10.1 percent in the recession year of 1982. Thus there were times during this 17-year period when cyclical unemployment rose to as much as 4 percent of the labor force (assuming a natural unemployment rate of approximately 6 percent), and other times when the actual unemployment rate was slightly below the natural rate, indicating that the cyclical component of the unemployment rate was negative. In all but four of these 17 years, however, the unemployment rate hovered between 5.6 and 7.7 percent.

In this chapter, we systematically examine the factors that lie behind the natural rate of unemployment. We begin with a simple stock-flow model of the labor market in order to define the **equilibrium unemployment rate** as depicted by Figure 15.1. At any moment, workers enter the pool of unemployed workers because they have quit or have been fired or laid off from their jobs or because they have just entered the labor force. Similarly, individuals continuously leave this pool of unemployment because they have located acceptable jobs or have been recalled to prior jobs, or because they have dropped out of the labor force. In the absence of macroeconomic shocks, these movements of workers into and out of the pool of the unemployed determine a long-run equilibrium, or natural, unemployment rate—a rate at which the flow into the unemployed ranks equals the flow out.

An important determinant of the natural unemployment rate is the speed with which unemployed workers locate acceptable jobs. This in turn depends on their job-search behavior. Although an unemployed worker might quickly become employed by taking the first job available, stopping the job search may cost the worker another job that offers a higher wage. The unemployed worker must balance the expected cost to remaining unemployed and looking for an acceptable job against future expected gains to finding a better job by continuing to search. As we will see, job-seekers do this by picking a **reservation wage**—the minimum wage offer that they would find acceptable—that balances out the costs and gains to continued search. In addition to determining a reservation wage, a job-seeker must decide how intensely to search for a job. These choices—the reservation wage and intensity of search—together with employers' hiring activities, determine the exit rate from unemployment to employment.

Milton Friedman has stated that the natural unemployment rate "is not a numerical constant but depends on 'real' as opposed to monetary factors—

Equilibrium unemployment rate: The rate at which the flows into unemployment equal the flows out of unemployment.

Reservation wage: The minimum wage offer that a job-seeker finds acceptable.

---

[1] These numbers are cited by Lawrence Summers, "Why Is the Unemployment Rate So Very High near Full Employment," *Brookings Papers on Economic Activity* Washington, D.C. (1986), p. 340.

Figure 15.1   The Flows Into and Out of Unemployment

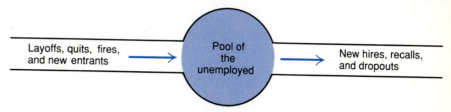

Flowing into the pool of the unemployed are workers who have quit or have been fixed or laid off as well as new entrants into the labor force. Flowing out of the pool of unemployed are workers who have found new jobs or have been recalled to prior jobs, as well as those dropping out of the labor force. When the flow in equals the flow out, the number of unemployed workers is constant.

the effectiveness of the labor market, the extent of competition or monopoly, the barriers to or encouragements to working in various occupations, and so on."[2] Various government policies are among the "real" factors affecting the natural unemployment rate. In the context of the stock-flow model of unemployment, we examine the effect on the natural unemployment rate of government policies such as the unemployment insurance program and minimum wage legislation.

In Chapter 12, we discussed the long-term employment relations that exist between workers and employers. In this chapter, we expand upon this discussion to show how, given long-term employment relations, temporary reductions in output demand can lead not only to adjustments in hours, but also to temporary layoffs. Since temporary layoffs in response to seasonal fluctuations in demand constitute an important source of the movement of workers into the unemployed ranks, they are important in determining the natural unemployment rate. We conclude the chapter by discussing how involuntary unemployment may arise because employers cannot monitor the performance of their workers without a cost.

15.1   THE NATURAL RATE OF UNEMPLOYMENT: A STOCK-FLOW ANALYSIS

Workers continually move both between employment and unemployment and into and out of the labor force. These labor market flows are quite

---

[2] Milton Friedman, "Nobel Lecture: Inflation and Unemployment," *Journal of Political Economy* (June 1977) p. 458.

substantial in number.[3] As you might expect, the unemployment rate grows when the number of individuals entering unemployment exceeds the number leaving unemployment. The size of the unemployment pool falls when the number of individuals escaping unemployment exceeds the number entering the ranks of the unemployed. If the number of workers leaving unemployment equals the number entering, then the number unemployed does not change and the unemployment pool is in equilibrium. In the section that follows, we look at what factors determine the size of an equilibrium pool of unemployed workers. We then focus on a particular equilibrium unemployment rate, namely the natural rate of unemployment. As we see it, the natural unemployment rate is the equilibrium unemployment rate that occurs in the absence of macroeconomic shocks.

Labor Market Stocks and Flows: A Simple Example

We begin our analysis by considering only movements between employment and unemployment, ignoring for the moment movements into and out of the labor force. We will consider a hypothetical labor market composed of 100 million workers. At any given time, a stock of unemployed workers and a stock of employed workers exists. It is important to recognize, however, that over time the stock of unemployed workers is not made up of the same individuals; rather, continuous exchanges, or flows, occur between the stocks of unemployed and employed workers.

Employed workers become unemployed by quitting or being laid off their jobs, or by being fired. On average, approximately 80 percent of the flow into unemployment from the employed ranks comes from "involuntary" layoffs and dismissals, a fraction that increases in recession years.[4] Conversely, unemployed workers become employed either by searching for and finding a job or by being recalled from a layoff by a previous employer.

Suppose that each month 2 percent of employed workers become unemployed, while 18 percent of unemployed workers become employed. Our

---

[3] See Michael R. Darby, John C. Haltiwanger, and Mark W. Plant "The Ins and Outs of Unemployment: The Ins Win," NBER Working Paper No. 1997 (August 1986) and James Poterba and Lawrence Summers, "Reporting Errors and Labor Market Dynamics," *Econometrica* (November 1986): 1319–1338. The authors provide recent evidence on flows. Information for an earlier period is the following: Stephen Marston notes that the "the flow of workers in and out of unemployment each month is always far greater than the increase in the number of the unemployed. For example, during the [mid-1970s] business contraction, when the unadjusted unemployment rate rose from 4.2 percent (October 1973) to 9.2 percent (June 1975), unemployment rose by an average of 231,000 workers per month. But during the same period, 2.7 million workers became unemployed on average every month, more than eleven times as many as the net increase." (Stephen Marston, "Employment Instability and High Unemployment Rates," *Brookings Papers on Economic Activity* Washington D.C. (1976) p. 169.

[4] Although quite a few workers quit their jobs in any given month (with quits being especially prevalent among workers with relatively little job tenure), most do not quit until they have located alternative employment. Thus most job quitters move directly from one job to another without experiencing a spell of unemployment.

assumptions about the labor market and the flows between unemployment and employment are then

The flow per month from unemployed to employed = .18 × (number unemployed)

The flow per month from employed to unemployed = .02 × (number employed)

Given the above assumptions on the rates of flow into and out of the unemployed pool and a labor force of 100 million workers, we can determine what division between unemployed and employed will result in stable (equilibrium) levels of unemployment and employment. In our example, equilibrium results when 90 million workers are employed and 10 million are unemployed. The next section will show how these numbers can be calculated. For the moment, let's see why they represent the equilibrium numbers of unemployed and employed.

With 90 million employed and 10 million unemployed, the flow into unemployment just equals the flow out of unemployment, which means that no net change occurs in the number employed or unemployed. The flow into unemployment equals 1.8 million workers since we have assumed that 2 percent of employed workers become unemployed each month (1.8 million = .02 × 90 million). The flow out of unemployment also equals 1.8 million since 18 percent of the 10 million unemployed workers find employment each month (1.8 million = .18 × 10 million).

If the initial numbers of employed and unemployed differ from the equilibrium levels of 90 million and 10 million, respectively, both levels will change over time toward the equilibrium of 90 million employed and 10 million unemployed. For instance, suppose that the number employed initially equals 95 million, with 5 million unemployed. In the first month, 2 percent, or 1.9 million, of the employed workers will become unemployed and 18 percent, or .9 million, of the unemployed workers will become employed. Since the flow into unemployment exceeds the flow out of unemployment by 1 million, at the end of the month the number unemployed will rise to 6 million and the number of workers who are employed will fall to 94 million. This adjustment process will continue until unemployment rises and employment falls to their respective equilibrium levels of 10 million and 90 million.[5]

An Equilibrium Unemployment Rate

If individuals move between employment and unemployment at constant rates, the equilibrium levels of employment and unemployment exist which, when reached, will tend to persist over time. In our example, the equilibrium

---

[5] In our example, we start with employment above the equilibrium level and unemployment below the equilibrium level. As a consequence, the level of unemployment rises and the level of employment falls until equilibrium is reached. If we start with employment below and unemployment above their equilibrium levels, then over time unemployment will fall and employment will rise until equilibrium is achieved.

levels of unemployment and employment were 10 million and 90 million, respectively. The equilibrium rate of unemployment therefore equals 10 percent, or 10 million unemployed divided by a labor force of 100 million. Below we obtain a general method for determining the equilibrium unemployment rate.

Let α denote the fraction of employed workers who become unemployed each month, and let β denote the fraction of unemployed workers who become employed each month. (In our example, we set α and β equal to .02 and .18, respectively). In addition, let E denote the number employed at the beginning of the month and U the number unemployed. This means that the number of employed workers who become unemployed during the month equals $\alpha \cdot E$, and the number of unemployed workers who become employed equals $\beta \cdot U$. Recall that the net change in the unemployment level during the month is the difference between the number entering unemployment and the number escaping unemployment. In our present notation, the difference between $\alpha \cdot E$ and $\beta \cdot U$ indicates this net change.

At the equilibrium unemployment and employment levels, the flows into and out of unemployment will be equal, or

$$\alpha \cdot E = \beta \cdot U \qquad (15.1)$$

In order to solve for the equilibrium number employed and unemployed, we need one further piece of information—the fact that the number of employed workers plus the number unemployed equals the total labor force. Letting L denote the total number of workers who are in the labor force (in our example, L is 100 million), we have $L = E + U$. Solving for the number employed (E), we then have

$$E = L - U \qquad (15.2)$$

In other words, the number of workers employed simply equals the difference between the total number who are in the labor force and the number who are unemployed.

Substituting the expression for the number employed (Equation 15.2) into Equation 15.1, we obtain

$$\alpha \cdot (L - U) = \beta \cdot U \qquad (15.3)$$

Solving Equation 15.3 for the number unemployed, we find that the equilibrium unemployment level is given by

$$U = [\alpha/(\alpha + \beta)] \cdot L \qquad (15.4)$$

Finally, recall that the unemployment rate equals the number of unemployed workers divided by the number of workers in the labor force. Thus we can obtain the equilibrium unemployment rate by dividing both sides of Equation 15.4 by L. Letting U_e denote the equilibrium unemployment rate, we have

$$U_e \equiv U/L = \alpha/(\alpha + \beta) \qquad (15.5)$$

In other words, the equilibrium unemployment rate is equal to the fraction of employed workers who become unemployed each month (α) divided by the sum of the fractions of employed workers who become unemployed that month and unemployed workers who become employed that month ($\alpha + \beta$).

The Effects of Labor Force Entry and Exit on an Equilibrium Unemployment Rate

Up to this point in our analysis of the equilibrium unemployment rate, we have focused on the flows between unemployment and employment. We have ignored the other type of flow affecting the unemployment rate—the flow into and out of the labor force. (Recall that an individual is considered out of the labor force if that person is neither employed nor unemployed.) Individuals are considered new entrants if they are entering the labor force for the first time and reentrants if they entered before and subsequently withdrew. Employed workers leaving the labor force include both permanent retirees and individuals who withdraw temporarily, such as those leaving to raise a family or return to school. Unemployed workers also leave the labor force because they cannot find acceptable jobs; they are often referred to as discouraged workers.

One estimate of these flows for the period between 1977 and 1982 indicates that each month 1.2 percent of the employed became unemployed and .7 percent of the employed exited the labor force. Among those unemployed, 18.6 percent became employed each month while 8.8 percent dropped out of the labor force. Finally, of those not in the labor force, 2.3 percent entered the labor force each month.[6] Figure 15.2 illustrates the various types of labor market flows, taking labor market entry and exit into account.

As this figure indicates, essentially all individuals entering the labor force experience a spell of unemployed job search.[7] For some, this period of search is sufficiently short that it is never recorded as unemployed. While the government surveys households once each month, many individuals enter the labor force and find employment within the four weeks between surveys.[8]

Let's incorporate the effects of labor market entry and exit into our derivation of the equilibrium unemployment rate. Recall that we have denoted

---

[6] James Poterba and Lawrence Summers, "Reporting Errors and Labor Market Dynamics," *Econometrica* (November 1986): 1332.

[7] We say, "essentially all" since there are a few individuals who are coaxed out of retirement or from raising a family by an attractive job offer that they did not seek out. These few individuals go immediately from out of the labor force to employed status with no intervening spell of unemployment.

[8] In addition, some college seniors who find a job that begins upon graduation become employed without a recorded spell of unemployment. Although they engage in a lengthy job search prior to employment, their response to the household survey question concerning their activities identifies school, rather than job search, as their primary activity. Thus prior to employment they would be recorded as out of the labor force.

Figure 15.2   **Labor Market Flows**

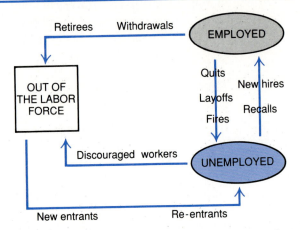

The chart illustrates the various labor market flows between employment, unemployment, and nonparticipation in the labor force.

the flow from employment to unemployment by $\alpha \cdot E$ (quits, fires, and layoffs). To get the total flow into unemployment, we must add the flow of workers entering the labor force. Letting N denote the number of individuals not participating in the labor force and ϕ the fraction of nonparticipants who enter unemployment each month, the total flow into unemployment is $\alpha \cdot E + \phi \cdot N$.

The flow of workers out of unemployment into employment is $\beta \cdot U$, consisting of unemployed workers who find new jobs or who are recalled to former ones. To obtain the total flow out of unemployment, we must add to this the flow of unemployed workers who drop out of the labor force. Letting δ_u denote the fraction of unemployed workers who drop out of the labor force, the total flow of workers out of unemployment equals $(\beta + \delta_u) \cdot U$. In equilibrium, the flow into unemployment equals the flow out, or

$$\alpha \cdot E + \phi \cdot N = (\beta + \delta_u) \cdot U \qquad \textbf{(15.6)}$$

In addition, in equilibrium the number of individuals entering the labor force $(\delta \cdot N)$ equals the number exiting the labor force, from both the ranks of the employed and the unemployed. Letting δ_e denote the fraction of employed workers who leave the labor force every month, the total flow of workers out of the labor force is $\delta_u \cdot U + \delta_e \cdot E$. Equating the flow of workers into the labor force with the flow out, we obtain

$$\phi \cdot N = \delta_u \cdot U + \delta_e \cdot E \qquad \textbf{(15.7)}$$

Substituting Equation 15.7 into Equation 15.6, we have in equilibrium that

$$\alpha \cdot E + \delta_u \cdot U + \delta_e \cdot E = (\beta + \delta_u) \cdot U \tag{15.8}$$

Flows from employed and out of   Flows to employment and out of the
labor force into unemployment   labor force from unemployment

As before, we can now obtain an expression for the unemployment rate by substituting the expression for the number employed (Equation 15.2) into Equation 15.8. After doing so and rearranging, we find that the equilibrium unemployment level is given by[9]

$$U_e \equiv U/L = \alpha^*/(\alpha^* + \beta) \tag{15.9}$$

where α^* equals $\alpha + \delta_e$, the total rate at which workers flow from the employed ranks, either to unemployment or out of the labor force.

Equation 15.9 tells us that besides depending on the rates at which employed workers move from unemployment to employment (β) and from employment to unemployment (α), the equilibrium rate of unemployment also depends on the rate at which employed workers drop out of the labor force (δ_e). With everything else remaining the same, an increase in the rate at which employed workers drop out of the labor market (δ_e) causes the unemployment rate to rise (since a higher δ_e means a higher flow rate out of the stock of employed and thus a higher α^*).[10] Later in this chapter, we will see that differences in dropout rates among demographic groups has been an important factor leading to their different unemployment rates.

The Natural Rate of Unemployment as an Equilibrium Unemployment Rate

In the absence of macroeconomic shocks, there is a natural rate at which workers flow from the employed ranks to the condition of being out of the labor force. This flow is made up of those temporarily withdrawing from the labor force as well as retirees. Similarly, in the absence of macroeconomic

---

[9] To derive Equation 15.9, first rearrange Equation 15.8 to obtain
$$(\alpha + \delta_e)E = (\beta + \delta_u - \delta_u)U$$
Simplifying by letting $\alpha^* = (\alpha + \delta_e)$ and noting that $\delta_u - \delta_u = 0$, we can rewrite this equation as
$$\alpha^* \cdot E = \beta \cdot U$$
From Equation 15.2, we can substitute the labor force L minus the number unemployed U for the number employed E. The result is
$$\alpha^* \cdot (L - U) = \beta \cdot U$$
Solving for the number unemployed, we have
$$U = (\alpha^* \cdot L)/(\alpha^* + \beta)$$
To obtain the equilibrium unemployment rate, we now simply divide by the labor force L, with the result being Equation 15.9.

[10] While the rate at which unemployed workers drop out of the labor force (δ_u) and the rate at which nonparticipants enter unemployment (ϕ) do not affect the unemployment rate, changes in these variable do alter the number unemployed and the number in the labor force. An increase in ϕ raises both the equilibrium labor force and the number employed, leaving the unemployment rate unchanged. Similarly, a reduction in the rate at which unemployed individuals drop out of the labor force raises both the equilibrium labor force and the number employed.

shocks, there is a natural rate at which workers flow from unemployment to employment (new hires and recalls) and from employment to either unemployment (layoffs, quits, and fires) or out of the labor force. Letting δ_e, β, and α denote these natural rates at which workers move from employment to out of the labor force, from unemployment to employment, and from employment to unemployment, respectively, Equation 15.9 defines the associated natural unemployment rate. The natural unemployment rate is that rate toward which the economy gravitates to in the absence of macroeconomic shocks.

Equation 15.9 makes good intuitive sense as a formula for the natural unemployment rate. Assume for the moment that no one exits the labor force from the employed ranks ($\delta_e = 0$). Then if no employed workers ever become unemployed in the absence of a macroeconomic shock ($\alpha = 0$), the natural unemployment rate will be zero, a result we would expect.[11] Furthermore, the greater the rate at which workers naturally flow from the employed ranks either to unemployment or out of the labor force (α^*), is relative to the rate at which they leave unemployment for employment (β), the higher will be the natural unemployment rate.[12]

Unemployment Dynamics During Recessions and Recoveries

We now know that the natural movements of workers between employment, unemployment, and nonparticipation will generate over time a natural equilibrium unemployment rate as defined by Equation 15.9. This equilibrium unemployment rate that the economy tends to in the absence of macroeconomic shocks is called the natural rate. In reality, the rates at which workers flow between employment and unemployment and into and out the labor force are not constant, however, which causes the unemployment rate to fluctuate from its natural level.

In times of recession, for example, more employers are laying off workers and fewer employers are hiring. Consequently, the flow from employment to unemployment (α) exceeds the norm while the reverse flow from unemployment to employment (β) falls short of the norm. With job losers outpacing job finders, unemployment rises. In contrast, the unemployment rate falls during a recovery since the workers who find jobs outnumber those who lose them.

In summary, then, our stock-flow model provides a useful framework for viewing changes in unemployment around the natural rate. The natural unemployment rate is the unemployment rate that we would observe the

---

[11] Note that if δ_e is greater than zero, there will be a positive natural unemployment rate even if no employed workers ever became unemployed ($\alpha = 0$). The unemployed will be made up of those entering unemployment from out of the labor force, who will just balance those exiting the labor force from the employed ranks.

[12] To see this, we can rewrite the expression for the natural unemployment rate as $1/[1 + (\beta/\alpha^*)]$.

economy tending to in the absence of macroeconomic shocks. In terms of the analysis in Chapter 12, this "absence of macroeconomic shocks" implies that the expected rate of inflation equals the actual rate of inflation. Thus an alternative way of defining the natural rate is that rate of unemployment that prevails when expected and actual inflation coincide.

At any point in time, the natural unemployment rate is an average of widely divergent unemployment rates across various demographic groups. In the case study that follows, we use the labor market stock-flow analysis to examine the source of these divergent unemployment rates.

Case Study

DIFFERENCES IN UNEMPLOYMENT RATES AMONG DEMOGRAPHIC GROUPS

The variations in the overall unemployment rate due to booms and recessions appear minor when compared to the variations in unemployment rates among economic groups. Table 15.1 presents data on the unemployment rates of various demographic groups by age, sex, and race in March, 1988. The patterns indicated are similar to those of other years: Unemployment rates are especially high for teenagers and decline with age, nonwhite unemployment rates are more than twice those for whites; and the unemployment rate for females is frequently slightly greater than that for males. Some of the highest unemployment rates—those for nonwhite teenagers—range between 30 and 40 percent.

Our stock-flow analysis of the labor market helps to explain the different unemployment rates among demographic groups. A group's unemployment rate is high either because unemployed workers in that group take a long time to obtain employment (β is low for them), because after becoming employed they have a high probability of becoming unemployed again (α is high), or because they frequently quit their jobs to pursue nonlabor market activities (δ_e is high). Much research has been conducted on how each of these considerations applies to three demographic groups: young workers, women, and nonwhites.

An interesting feature of the figures in Table 15.1 is that as the age of the group considered increases, the medium duration of unemployment among the unemployed in the group rises. Although this suggests it takes a longer time for more mature workers to locate employment (β is lower), older workers have lower unemployment rates. The reason for this apparent paradox is that younger workers have a weak job attachment. Not only do teenagers frequently leave employment and the labor force (δ_e is high), but they also frequently move from employment to unemployment due to quits and layoffs (α is high). These high rates of turnover account for higher

Table 15.1   The Unemployment Rate by Demographic Groups (March 1988)

	Unemployment Rate	Employed as Percent of Population	Duration of Unemployment		
			Percent under 5 weeks	*Percent over 15 weeks*	*Median number of weeks*
Age					
16–19	16.5	49.6	55.8	13.3	4.5
20–24	9.1	77.0	43.7	24.2	6.7
25–54	4.5	82.7	33.3	34.1	9.7
55–64	3.2	55.3	26.2	38.5	11.6
65+	2.6	11.4	38.2	27.1	7.5
All	5.6	65.2	38.9	28.2	8.0
Sex					
Male	5.7	75.3	35.1	31.3	9.2
Female	5.5	56.0	44.3	23.8	6.4
Race					
White	4.7	65.5	39.0	28.1	7.9
Nonwhite	11.5	62.8	38.2	28.6	8.6

Source: U.S. Bureau of Labor Statistics, *Employment and Earnings*, April 1988. The duration data are not seasonally adjusted.

unemployment rates for teenagers as compared to mature workers even though they have shorter spells of unemployment.[13]

The difference in turnover between the young and the old has implications not only for unemployment but also for job tenure. Specifically, individuals with a higher probability of leaving employment will on average have shorter job tenure. As noted by Christopher Ruhm in a recent study of male heads of households, "holders of 'short' jobs are 4.7 times more likely to experience unemployment than those with more than ten years seniority."[14] During cyclical downturns, however, this situation changes. Workers with substantial tenure in former jobs make up a much larger proportion of cyclical fluctuations in employment and unemployment. As Ruhm suggests, one reason for this is provided by "the recent work considering the role of recessions in redistributing labor across sectors of the economy. Since high tenure workers are relatively immune from transitory demand shocks, we might expect short tenure workers to bear the brunt of temporary fluctuations in demand. Large scale cutbacks and plant closures occurring during recessions would then impact workers higher up on seniority ladders, increasing their share of

---

[13] See Marston (p. 183), Footnote 3, and Poterba and Summers (p. 1332), Footnote 3.

[14] Christopher J. Ruhm, "Job Tenure and Cyclical Changes in the Labor Market," *Review of Economics and Statistics* (May 1987): 373.

unemployment. This effect will be strengthened if recessions are 'unbalanced,' hitting declining sectors especially hard."[15]

Up until recently, women's lower labor force attachment resulted in higher unemployment rates than for men. For instance, in the 1970s, Stephen Marston found that "the high rate at which employed women leave the labor force [δ_e in our model] is the main factor in the higher unemployment rates they experience . . . None of the other flow rates adds much to women's unemployment rates."[16] Even in the early 1980s, evidence existed that women's job tenure was "substantially shorter than men's, on the average. Only about one-quarter of all women over the age of 30 [were] employed in jobs which will last over twenty years, whereas over half the men over 30 [were] holding these near-lifetime jobs."[17]

As changes occurred in women's work expectations, however, their labor force attachments have become stronger. Coupled with a typically shorter duration of unemployment than males (a higher β), the result is that by 1988 female unemployment rates were at or below those of males. The growing similarity between male and female labor force attachments is illustrated by surveys of young women between ages 14 and 21. When asked whether they expected to be working when they were 35, only 27.5 percent of young white women and 55.6 percent of young black women answered in the affirmative in 1968. In actuality, about 70 percent ended up working at age 35. Presented with the same question in 1979, 71.7 percent of young white women and 85.9 percent of young black women expected to be working at age 35.

In anticipation of their greater likelihood of working, young women today are acquiring increased training. While in 1965 about 42 percent of bachelor's degrees were earned by women, in 1985 that figure had risen to about 51 percent. Similarly, the percentage of master's degrees earned by women rose from approximately 32 percent in 1965 to about 50 percent in 1985. More striking, the percentage of doctoral degrees earned by women rose from about 11 percent in 1965 to 35 percent in 1985 while the percentage of professional degrees rose from about 2 percent to 32 percent. In light of women's increased training, we can expect further increases in their commitment to the labor force.[18]

The high unemployment rate of nonwhites stems from two sources. First, nonwhites have a high probability of moving from employment to

---

[15] Ruhm (p. 378), Footnote 14. This phenomenon was discussed in Chapter 9 when we looked at sectoral shifts in labor demand as an example of a "supply-side" disturbance.

[16] See Marston (pp. 179 and 182), Footnote 3. Poterba and Summers report similar qualitative findings.

[17] Robert Hall, "The Importance of Lifetime Jobs in the U.S. Economy," *American Economic Review* 72 (September 1982): 716.

[18] The source for the data on women's expectations of working and the percentage of degrees they earn is the *Economic Report of the President* (1987).

unemployment. In terms of our stock-flow model, they have a high probability of moving from employment to unemployment (a high α). In addition, unemployed nonwhites face somewhat poorer job prospects (a low β), as suggested in part by the longer median duration of unemployment for nonwhites than for whites.

The overall unemployment rate simply equals a weighted average of the unemployment rates for the various demographic groups, where a group's weight is the fraction of all workers in the labor market belonging to that group. As a result of the increasing labor force participation of women and the increasing proportions of the nonwhite and teenage populations, the composition of the labor force by age, sex, and race has changed significantly over the last several decades. For example, between 1960 and 1980, the female proportion of labor force participants grew from about 33 percent to 43 percent, the nonwhite proportion increased from about 11 percent to 12 percent, and the teenage proportion grew from about 7 percent to 9 percent.

Interestingly, the increase in labor force participation by women is not unique to the United States, as Table 15.2 indicates. Other developed countries have similar experiences, as the following table indicates.

During the 1970s and early 1980s, increased participation in the labor force by women, the young, and nonwhites meant an increase in labor force groups that at that time had relatively high unemployment rates. This was an important reason for the rise in the natural unemployment rate during the 1960s and 1970s. As noted earlier, the natural unemployment rate increased from about 4 percent in the late 1950s to over 6 percent in the 1980s. At least one percentage point of this increase was due to the changing composition of the labor force.[19]

To the Point

THE EQUILIBRIUM UNEMPLOYMENT RATE

- The equilibrium unemployment rate is that rate of unemployment at which the flow into the unemployed ranks equals the flow out. The flow into the unemployed ranks consists of quits, fires, and layoffs from the employed ranks and new entrants and reentrants from those not in the labor force. The flow out of the unemployed ranks consists of new hires and recalls to the employed ranks and dropouts from the labor force.

- In equilibrium, the unemployment rate equals $\alpha^*/(\alpha^* + \beta)$, where α^* equals $\alpha + \delta_e$, the total rate at which workers flow from the employed ranks either to unemployment or out of the labor force, and β is the rate at which the unemployed find employment.

---

[19] James Tobin, "Stabilization Policy Ten Years After," *Brookings Papers on Economic Activity* Washington, D.C. (1980).

Table 15.2   **Labor Force Participation Rate of Women over 16**

	1975	1984
Australia	43	44.6
Canada	44.4	53.5
Japan	45.7	49
Sweden	55.2	61.5
United States	46.3	53.6
West Germany	38.3	41*

* 1983, not 1984.
Source: Patrick McMahon, "An International Comparison of Labor Force Participation Rates, 1977–84, *Monthly Labor Review* (May 1986).

- Higher turnover (a high α^*) for younger workers, women, and blacks is one reason why these groups have had higher unemployment rates. The unemployment rate for blacks is also higher because the rate at which they find employment is lower (a low β).

15.2   JOB SEARCH BY THE UNEMPLOYED

We have seen that the rate at which unemployed workers become employed (β) is an important determinant of the natural rate of unemployment. We now turn to an examination of the "job search" behavior of the unemployed worker, since it is an important determinant of the likelihood of an unemployed worker finding employment in any given period.

Each job-seeker begins a job search by first making two decisions: the minimum acceptable wage offer (the reservation wage) and the amount of time to devote to searching for a job each period (search intensity). This section examines what determines the reservation wage and search intensity. We also explore how the reservation wage and search intensity determine the likelihood of an individual escaping unemployment in any period (β) and thus the average duration of unemployment.

Job Search and the Reservation Wage

Workers generally have some knowledge about the wages that various employers offer and the existence of job vacancies, information usually acquired from newspapers or employment agencies, or by talking to friends. Because their information is imperfect, however, unemployed workers do not know the exact locations of job vacancies for which they are qualified or the wages and other employment conditions attached to the various job openings. In order to find employment, therefore, workers must go through the time-consuming and costly process of seeking out and contacting various employers. When an employer makes an employment offer to the worker, the worker must decide whether to accept the offer or to continue searching for a better one.[20]

If an unemployed worker accepts the first employment offer, such an action may mean giving up the chance of finding a more attractive employment offer elsewhere. At the same time, if an unemployed worker sets standards that are too high, the job search may continue for too long a time. Not only will a worker incur explicit search costs during an extensive job search, but the worker will also be foregoing the potential wages of any rejected wage offer. Exactly how should a worker decide when to accept an offer and quit searching?

The Net Gain to Search.   To answer this question, let's consider the following example. Suppose that an unemployed worker can generate one employment offer each week. During the week, the worker incurs an explicit search cost c_e, which includes things such as telephone and transportation expenses. Since searching for a job is usually a stressful task, the worker incurs a second cost, the value of leisure time lost, which we will denote as c_t. Thus $c = c_e + c_t$ denotes the explicit and time costs of search.

Offsetting these two costs to search are several gains to search. One is the potential payment of unemployment compensation, denoted by UI, that this worker receives during each week of unemployment. A second gain is derived from the anticipated wage the worker will receive if an acceptable job is located. The minimum wage that the job searcher will accept is the *reservation wage* (W_r). The worker rejects any wage offer below W_r and accepts any wage offer equal to or greater than W_r. Since it is possible that the wage offer accepted will exceed the reservation wage, the worker expects that the wage accepted will be above the reservation wage. We will let W_a denote this expected wage that the worker anticipates upon having located a wage above the reservation wage.

For simplicity, let's suppose that once a worker accepts an employment offer, he stays on the new job forever, thus earning a perpetual stream of wages. From our discussion of perpetuities in Chapter 3 we know that the present value of a perpetual stream of wage payments equals the wage divided by the interest rate. Since W_a denotes the average across the wages

[20] Labor economists have devoted a great deal of attention to the problem faced by the unemployed worker engaged in the process of job search. Early papers in the search literature include George Stigler, "Information in the Labor Market," *Journal of Political Economy* (October 1962) pp. 94–105 and Armen Alchian, "Information Costs, Pricing, and Resource Unemployment," in Microeconomic Foundations of Employment and Inflation, Edmund Phelps, ed., (W. W. Norton & Co., New York, 1970). Our analysis in the text follows more closely the discussion in Dale Mortensen, "Job Search, the Duration of Unemployment, and the Phillips Curve," *American Economic Review* (December 1970) Vol. 70, pp. 847–862, and John J. McCall, "Economics of Information and Job Search," *Quarterly Journal of Economics* (February 1970) Vol. 84, pp. 113–126.

that the worker finds acceptable, we can compute the expected gain to locating an acceptable job as the present value of the average acceptable wage, or W_a/r.[21]

Taking account of both the cost and gains to search, if the worker successfully locates an acceptable wage offer during the week, the expected net gain is given by

$$NG_{success} = -c + UI + W_a/r$$

The net gain to successful search equals the current unemployment insurance benefits (*UI*) plus the discounted value of future wage payments on the new job (W_a/r) minus search costs (*c*).

The search during the week may not be successful, however. If the individual does not find acceptable employment by the end of the current week, then the search process repeats next period. In this case, the individual still incurs the search costs (*c*) and receives unemployment benefits (*UI*) this period. In addition, the searcher can anticipate the prospect of successful search in the future, summarized by *NG*, the net gain to search next week. Thus the net gain to failed search in the current period is given by

$$NG_{failure} = -c + UI + NG/(1 + r)$$

where the expected net gain to unemployed search next week (*NG*) is appropriately discounted by $1/(1 + r)$.[22]

Letting θ denote the probability that the worker escapes unemployment in any week, the worker's expected net gain to unemployed search this week (*NG*) is simply the probability of finding employment this week multiplied by the net gain to successful search in the current week plus the probability of not finding an acceptable wage offer this week $(1 - \theta)$ multiplied by the net gain from failed search in the current week. That is,

$$NG = \theta \cdot NG_{success} + (1 - \theta) \cdot NG_{failure} \qquad \textbf{(15.10)}$$

Substituting the expressions for the net gain to successful and unsuccessful search this week into Equation 15.10, we obtain

$$NG = -c + UI + \theta \cdot W_a/r + (1 - \theta) \cdot NG/(1 + r) \qquad \textbf{(15.11)}$$

Although Equation 15.11 may look overwhelming, it has a straightforward interpretation.[23] To get the expected net gain to unemployed search, we must subtract out the search costs (*c*) that the worker incurs in the current week and add the unemployment compensation *UI* received. We assume that a week of search will generate an acceptable employment offer with probability θ (an acceptable offer has a wage equal to or above the worker's

---

[21] In order to simplify the analysis, we do not explicitly take account of the fact that the gain to working should be net of the value of the worker's leisure.

[22] Since our time dimension is in weeks, the interest rate *r* is defined for one-week intervals.

[23] Students familiar with the mathematical technique of dynamic programming may recognize that Equation 15.11 is an example of Bellman's equation.

reservation wage). The worker will then earn a stream of wages with an expected present value of W_a/r. There is a probability $1 - \theta$ that the offer will not be acceptable, in which case the worker will remain unemployed and will receive the discounted expected net gain to search next week of $NG/(1 + r)$.

The Choice of the Reservation Wage. How should the worker choose a reservation wage in order to maximize the expected net gain to search? The answer to this question is deceptively simple: The present value of the reservation wage should just equal the expected net gain to continued search. In other words, the reservation wage should be chosen such that when a wage offer is rejected, it is because its present value is below the discounted net gain to continued search, $NG/(1 + r)$. Conversely, a wage offer that is accepted will have a present value above the discounted gain to continued search. If a wage offer equals the reservation wage, then the worker is indifferent between continued search or accepting employment. Algebraically, the reservation wage is such that $W_r/r = NG/(1 + r)$. Rearranging this expression to obtain an expression for the net gain to search, $NG = W_r(1 + r)/r$, and substituting this expression for NG in Equation 15.11, we obtain

$$(1 + r) \, W_r/r = -c + UI + \theta \cdot (W_a/r) + (1 - \theta) \cdot (W_r/r) \quad \textbf{(15.12)}$$

By rearranging the terms, we can rewrite Equation 15.12 as

$$MC \equiv c - UI = \theta \cdot (W_a - W_r)/r - W_r \equiv MG \quad \textbf{(15.13)}$$

Equation 15.13 has a useful interpretation in terms of marginal cost (MC) and marginal gain (MG). The left side of the equation—the sum of explicit and time costs to search minus unemployment benefits—can be considered the marginal cost to searching one more week. The right side of the equation indicates the marginal gain to continued search if a wage offer equal to the reservation wage W_r were received. The reservation wage is chosen so that having received a wage offer equal to the reservation wage, the marginal gain to continued search just equals the marginal cost. Given a wage offer equal to the reservation wage, the marginal gain to rejecting employment and continuing to search is the expected increment in the present value of wage income from continued search, $\theta(W_a - W_r)/r$, net of the wage foregone in the current period, W_r.

Figure 15.3 illustrates the choice of the optimal reservation wage. The horizontal axis shows the unemployed worker's possible wage offers. The downward-sloping line MG is the right side of Equation 15.13; this line represents the marginal gain to continued search having received the wage offer W. The downward slope reflects the fact that a higher offer reduces the marginal gain to continued search, since it reduces the expected increment in wage income to continued search $\theta(W_a - W)/r$ and increases the foregone earnings in the current period W.

In Figure 15.3, horizontal line MC denotes the marginal cost to continued search. The worker's reservation wage W_r is that wage offer at which the

Figure 15.3   **Marginal Gain, Marginal Cost, and the Reservation Wage**

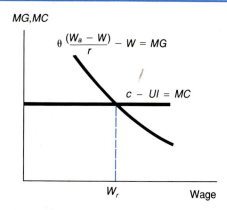

The choice of a worker's reservation wage is such that the marginal gain (*MG*) realized by searching one more period rather than accepting the wage offer equals the marginal cost to searching one more period (*MC*). The reservation wage equals W_r in the figure.

marginal gain to continued search equals the marginal cost. For wages below the reservation wage, the marginal gain to continued search exceeds the cost, so these wages are rejected. For wages equal to or above the reservation wage, the gain to searching one more week is equal to or falls short of the cost, so such wage offers are accepted.

Search Intensity and Other Determinants of the Likelihood of an Employment Offer

Up to this point in our analysis, we have assumed that the unemployed worker gets exactly one job offer each period. Thus the worker only decides on a reservation wage. The real world is more complex than this, however, with unemployed workers often unable to generate one wage offer each period. The likelihood that a worker receives a wage offer depends both on how hard the worker looks and on the search behavior of employers. Let's take these considerations into account and modify our search model.

We will use τ to denote the probability that an unemployed worker obtains a job offer in any period. The worker can increase the likelihood of a job offer in any period by searching more intensively. This means that in addition to choosing a reservation wage, the unemployed worker must also decide how intensively to search for a job.

As with the choice of the reservation wage, the worker chooses search intensity to equate marginal cost and marginal gain. The marginal cost of searching more intensively is simply the increase in cost necessary to increase the probability of obtaining an offer. These increased costs take the form primarily of foregone leisure and increased effort. The marginal gain to increased search intensity comes from finding an acceptable offer more quickly.

The search behavior of employers also plays an important role in whether or not an unemployed worker obtains a job offer. The likelihood of a job offer (τ) is directly related to the number of employers seeking to fill job vacancies. If a job-seeker visits an employer with no job vacancies, then no employment offer will be forthcoming. The existence of a vacancy at a particular employer does not ensure an offer of employment, however. An employer with a vacancy typically will not offer employment to the first applicant interviewed but will screen a number of applicants prior to making any wage offer. One study found that on average employers screen approximately eight applicants before making a wage offer.[24] Therefore without knowledge of the minimum qualifications an employer requires of a successful job applicant, a job-seeker has one chance in eight of being offered a job if a vacancy exists.

In sum, the rate at which unemployed workers find job offers (τ) depends on search activity by both sides of the market. Not only does the job-seeker's search intensity affect the likelihood of escaping unemployment in any period, but the rate at which job-seekers find positions also depends heavily on employers' search activity.

The Reservation Wage, Search Intensity, and the Expected Duration of Unemployment

Having characterized an unemployed worker's optimal search strategy, we can determine how a worker's search behavior affects the likelihood of escaping unemployment in any period. The probability that a worker will find employment in any period equals the probability that the worker obtains a job offer multiplied by the probability that the worker will accept a job offer. A job-seeker controls the likelihood of obtaining employment through choices of both search intensity and the reservation wage; the higher the search intensity, the greater the likelihood of obtaining a job offer; the lower the reservation wage, the higher the likelihood of accepting a job offer. Historical evidence bears out these predicted effects of intensity and reservation wage on subsequent labor force status.[25]

Aggregating across workers, we can interpret how unemployed search behavior affects the natural rate of unemployment. In general, if workers

---

[24] John M. Barron, Dan A. Black, and Mark A. Loewenstein, "Employer Size: The Implications for Search, Training, Capital Investment, Starting Wages, and Wage Growth," *Journal of Labor Economics* (January 1987), pp. 76–89.

[25] One study of the monthly flows from unemployment to employment concludes that the time per period devoted to search and the relative reservation wage significantly affect the employment probability in the direction predicted by the model of search behavior. See John M. Barron and Otis Gilley, "Job Search and Vacancy Contacts: A Note," *American Economic Review* (September 1981): Vol. 71, p. 750–751.

search more intensively or pick lower reservation wages, then the average likelihood of escaping unemployment increases, which means an increase in β, the fraction of unemployed who find employment each period. As Equation 15.9 indicated, this increased flow from unemployment to employment causes a lower natural rate of unemployment. For instance, in our previous example, if β increases by 10 percent from .18 to .198, with α^* equal to .02, then the unemployment rate falls from 10 to 9.2 percent.[26]

A simple link also exists between search behavior and the length of time a person is unemployed.[27] For example, suppose than an unemployed worker searches sufficiently hard that the worker is certain of finding a job vacancy within one period. Suppose further that the worker will accept any wage offer (that is, the reservation wage is close to zero). Then the worker will accept the first employment offer and be employed in exactly one period.

If the worker's search intensity is lower or the reservation wage is higher, then the probability that the worker will become employed in any period drops, say to 1/2. In this case, the worker can expect to be unemployed for two periods. An even lower search intensity or higher reservation wage results in a lower probability that the worker will leave unemployment in any period, and thus a longer expected unemployment spell. For example, if the probability that the worker will obtain an acceptable offer is 1/4, then the worker can expect to be unemployed for four periods.

To the Point

JOB SEARCH BEHAVIOR AND THE DURATION OF UNEMPLOYMENT

- An unemployed worker seeking a job decides on a reservation wage (the minimal wage offer that is acceptable) and on search intensity (the time and effort spent each period locating employment offers). Both decisions are based on weighing the marginal gains and costs.

- The reservation wage equates the marginal gain and cost to continued search. Since the marginal gain to continued search decreases with increases in the wage offer received, any wage offer below the reservation wage will be rejected (the marginal gain to continued search exceeds the marginal cost) while any wage above the reservation wage will be accepted (the marginal gain to continued search is less than the marginal cost).

- Search intensity is increased up to the point where the marginal cost,

---

[26] Recall that the equilibrium unemployment rate is given by $\alpha^*/(\alpha^* + \beta)$. Thus if $\alpha^* = .02$ and $\beta = .18$, the equilibrium unemployment rate is .10 or 10 percent. If $\beta = .198$, this rate falls to $.02/(.02 + .198) = .0917$ or 9.2 percent.

[27] In fact, the expected duration of unemployment for a given worker is simply $1/\tau\theta$, the inverse of the probability that the worker will leave unemployment in any period. The student familiar with probability theory might note that the number of periods the worker is unemployed is a random variable with a geometric probability distribution with a mean of $1/\tau\theta$.

primarily time costs, of searching more intensively equals the marginal gain that comes from finding a wage offer more quickly.

- The expected duration of unemployment depends inversely on search intensity and directly on the reservation wage. In addition, the extent of search by employers for new workers will affect the expected duration of unemployment.

15.3   SOME EFFECTS OF GOVERNMENT POLICIES ON THE NATURAL RATE OF UNEMPLOYMENT

As we noted in the introduction to this chapter, the natural unemployment rate depends on real, not monetary, factors. The natural unemployment rate is not fixed and immutable, however. In fact, various government policies affect the natural unemployment rate in very real ways.

Unemployment Insurance, Search, and the Natural Unemployment Rate

In Chapter 9, we noted that an increase in unemployment insurance benefits raises the natural rate of unemployment and leads to a fall in aggregate supply. With the search model we have just developed, we can take a more analytical view of the effects of the unemployment insurance benefits program.

An increase in unemployment insurance benefits (*UI*) affects search behavior in two important ways. First, since increased benefits lower the marginal cost to continued search, they raise recipients' reservation wages. The cost to continued search falls, so workers will turn down some wage offers that they would have accepted when unemployment benefits were lower. Figure 15.4 illustrates how increased unemployment insurance benefits affect the reservation wage. The marginal cost of continued search shifts down from MC_0 to MC_1 and consequently the reservation wage increases from W_{r0} to W_{r1}.

The second effect of increased unemployment compensation on search behavior is to reduce workers' search intensity. Since higher unemployment compensation reduces the difference between what an individual receives while employed as opposed to unemployed, less of an incentive exists to locate job offers. In fact, one study estimated that recipients of unemployment insurance devote on average 20 percent less time to job search than do the unemployed who do not qualify for unemployment insurance benefits.[28]

---

[28] John M. Barron and Wesley Mellow, "Search Effort in the Labor Market," *Journal of Human Resources* (Summer 1979): 14, pp. 389–404.

Figure 15.4   The Effect of Increased Unemployment Compensation on the Reservation Wage

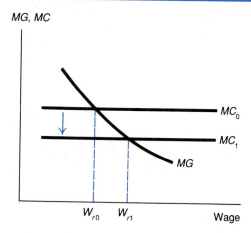

An increase in unemployment insurance benefits reduces the marginal cost to searching for employment one more period from MC_0 to MC_1 and leads to an increase in the reservation wage from W_{r0} to W_{r1}.

Since unemployment insurance raises reservation wages and reduces search intensity, it results in a reduced probability that an individual will escape unemployment in any given period. One study estimated that the probability of an individual obtaining employment in the subsequent period falls by 30 percent if the individual is receiving *UI* benefits.[29] As Equation 15.9 showed, a lower β (the fraction of unemployed workers who become employed each period) implies a higher natural rate of unemployment.

Although our discussion indicates that higher unemployment insurance benefits alter search behavior so as to increase the natural rate of unemployment, there are a number of previously mentioned gains to unemployment insurance programs. For instance, in Chapter 9 we mentioned the fact that unemployment insurance, by financing the job search of workers who might otherwise have difficulty in undertaking the costly task of finding a suitable job, can improve the matching of workers to particular jobs. In Chapter 14, we noted the role of unemployment insurance as one of the government programs that helps to stabilize the economy in the wake of macroeconomic demand shocks. The fall in output that accompanies a fall in demand in the short run is less severe because as income and employment fall, government unemployment insurance payments rise, providing an automatic fiscal policy stimulus.

[29] John M. Barron and Wesley Mellow, "Changes in Labor Force Status Among the Unemployed," *Journal of Human Resources* (Summer 1981): 16, p. 435.

Minimum Wage Legislation and the Natural Unemployment Rate: The Interaction of Search Between Employers and Job-Seekers

Minimum wage legislation is another government policy with potential effects on the natural unemployment rate. Beginning with the Fair Labor Standards Act of 1938, the government has specified a minimum wage that certain workers must receive. When first enacted, minimum wage legislation applied to approximately 43 percent of all workers. The legislation has expanded over time to cover more workers, and by 1975, coverage peaked at close to 85 percent. As a result of a 1978 court decision that eliminated most state and local government employees from coverage, however the percentage of workers covered has fallen to under 80 percent.

Over time, Congress has steadily increased the minimum hourly wage from its initial level of $.25 in 1938. It reached $.75 in 1950, $1.60 in 1968, $2.65 in 1978, and $3.35 in 1981. At the time of the writing of this book, legislation is pending to raise the minimum wage from $3.35 to $4.65 on January 1, 1991 and to $5.05 on January 1, 1992. As these changes make clear, the minimum wage is set in nominal, not real, terms. When we are considering economic behavior, however, it is not the nominal minimum wage by itself that is important, but the nominal minimum wage relative to the price level or to other wages. For instance, while the nominal minimum wage did not change between 1981 and 1987, the minimum wage divided by the level of consumer prices—the real minimum wage—fell by 20 percent. Similarly, for employers considering whether to hire skilled workers at high wages or unskilled workers at the minimum wage, the minimum wage relative to other wages matters. For the period from 1981 to 1987, the minimum wage as a percent of the average hourly wage (excluding overtime) in manufacturing fell from 43 percent to 35 percent.

Holding prices and other wages constant, a decrease in the minimum wage raises employment because it increases employers' incentives to hire unskilled, low-productivity workers. This especially affects the employment of teenagers. Researchers have estimated that a 10 percent decrease in the real minimum wage causes approximately a 10 percent increase in teenage employment.[30] The employment of workers in their early twenties also appears to be affected by the minimum wage. No clear effect exists concerning the employment of older workers, however. These findings can be explained by the fact that the minimum wage legislation puts a lower limit on wages only for the less productive younger workers (workers without much training).

While a fall in the real minimum wage increases the employment of

[30] See Charles Brown, Curtis Gilroy, and Andrew Koehn, "The Effect of the Minimum Wage on Employment and Unemployment," *Journal of Economic Literature* (June 1982): 20, pp. 487–528.

young workers, it decreases their equilibrium unemployment rate. Since a lower real minimum wage induces employers to increase their hiring, the number of job vacancies rises, making it more likely that a young worker will find an employment offer during a period of search (i.e., a higher τ). This causes the fraction of the unemployed who find a job each period to increase (i.e., a higher β), which results in a lower natural rate of unemployment, as Equation 15.9 indicates.

Government Training Programs

The persistence of high unemployment rates for youth and minorities at the same time that there is strong demand for skilled workers has led both economists and politicians to look for ways to stimulate employment and training opportunities for the disadvantaged and inexperienced. By the end of 1979, a number of programs were in place aimed at stimulating the private sector to provide additional training for the unskilled. While most of these programs were later curtailed or eliminated during the Reagan administration, it is useful to consider the types of government actions that have been suggested as capable of reducing unemployment through training.

By the end of 1979, some programs aimed at reducing unemployment through training included the following:

1. Targeted Jobs Tax Credit (TJTC)—A program that provided a tax credit for hiring certain categories of workers, such as economically disadvantaged youth (ages 18 to 24), veterans, ex-convicts, and the handicapped.

2. Comprehensive Employment and Training Act's On-the-job Training contracts (CETA-OJT)—A program in which local prime sponsors contract with private employers to hire and train workers referred to them by CETA.

Studies of the effect of these programs suggest that, at least to some extent, workers hired under such programs substitute for workers who otherwise would have been employed. However, one study did find a rise in overall employment. Specifically, for every five workers subsidized, total employment rose by one worker.[31] Part of the relative ineffectiveness of employment subsidies in creating jobs could be traced to simple ignorance of the program. For instance, one survey of employers indicated that fewer than 20 percent were familiar with the TJTC program, and only one half were familiar with the CETA-OJT programs.[32]

---

[31] John Bishop, ed., *Subsidizing On-the-job Training: An Analysis of a National Survey of Employers,* National Center for Research in Vocational Education (Ohio State University, 1982).

[32] John Bishop and Mark Montgomery, "Firm Familiarity With Employment Subsidies," in Bishop, Footnote 31.

15.4 FIRM-WORKER ATTACHMENTS, IMPLICIT CONTRACTS, AND TEMPORARY LAYOFFS

In the appendix to Chapter 5, we discussed the importance of hiring and training costs for employers' hiring and dismissal decisions. These hiring and training costs make it cheaper for employers to retain current workers, who have already been trained, than to hire new ones. Consequently, when employers are faced with a temporary drop in the demand for their output, they are reluctant to dismiss their current workers. Employers also offer higher wages to their experienced workers to reduce the rate at which they quit.

Hiring and training costs thus provide one incentive for long-term relations between employers and workers. A second incentive arises because employers know the capabilities of experienced employees. Employers will usually prefer a long-term employee who is a known quantity to a new worker of unknown ability.[33]

We turn now to an examination of the implications of long-term employment relations regarding "temporary" layoff policies. A layoff is considered temporary, as opposed to permanent, if the laid-off worker is subsequently recalled by the employer. Temporary layoffs in the face of transitory or seasonal fluctuations in the demand facing specific employers contribute to the natural unemployment rate, since the natural rate of unemployment depends on the rate at which the employed become unemployed (α).

Implicit Contracts and Temporary Layoffs

By age 40, approximately 40 percent of all workers are in a job that they will keep for at least 20 years.[34] Long-term employment relations encourage the development of certain employment rules that maximize the joint gains of employers and their workers. If there is a transitory demand shock, workers are more willing to be temporarily laid off, secure in the knowledge that they will be recalled when output demand recovers. Similarly, if employers know that their laid-off workers will be available for recall when output returns to a normal level, then they will be willing to lay off workers when output demand temporarily falls. Such an employment policy maximizes the joint gains of employers and workers because it has employees working more when the relative demand for their output is higher. When output

---

[33] This argument, and its implications for promotions, job assignments, and fires, is developed in John M. Barron and Mark A. Loewenstein, "On Employer-Specific Information and Internal Labor Markets," *Southern Economic Journal* (October 1985): 52, pp. 431–445.

[34] See Hall, Footnote 17.

demand falls and work time consequently has a lower payoff, it benefits all if workers take more leisure time.[35]

Only some of the agreements between employers and workers concerning compensation, job duties, and employment policies are written out explicitly. Many agreements between employers and workers are informal and implicit. This is due primarily to the prohibitive cost to all parties of developing a list of all possible contingencies and specifying rules for responding to them. These contracts that involve shared, informal understandings on how employers and employees will act in response to various contingencies are termed "implicit contracts." You might well ask how such contracts are enforced if they are not written down. Both workers' and employers' reputations depend on their past actions. Thus although an employer might find it momentarily advantageous to deviate from an implicit understanding with workers, such a deviation will cost the employer in the future. If an employer acquires a reputation for breaking implicit contracts, that employer will have difficulty retaining workers and hiring workers in the future.

Temporary Layoffs and Unemployment Insurance

As we discussed earlier, unemployment insurance programs increase the natural rate of unemployment because they reduce job search intensity and increase reservation wages. Unemployment insurance programs affect the natural unemployment rate in another way. An employer's employment policies take into account not only the demand for the employer's product and the preferences of employees toward leisure, but also quirks in government programs such as the unemployment insurance program.

Two features of the unemployment insurance program have encouraged employers and employees to use temporary layoffs.[36] First, although the taxes that an employer must pay to fund unemployment insurance benefits depend on the employer's past layoffs, these taxes only partly reflect the unemployment insurance benefits that the employer's workers received. In addition, until 1987 some unemployment benefits received by workers were not subject to federal taxation. These two features of the unemployment insurance program induced greater use of temporary layoffs than would have otherwise occurred.

When an employer lays off a worker today, the worker can collect unemployment benefits from the unemployment insurance fund. These funds come from taxes on employers. The amount that an employer pays into the fund often does not change with changes in the level of payments that the

---

[35] A number of papers exist in the economics literature—often referred to as the "implicit-contract" literature—that analyze optimal employment policies given long-term attachments between employers and workers and a fluctuating output demand for a firm's product.

[36] See Martin Feldstein, "The Effect of Unemployment Insurance on Temporary Layoff Unemployment," *American Economic Review* (December 1978): 68, pp. 834–846.

employer's workers have received from the unemployment insurance fund, however. In other words, employer contributions to the unemployment insurance fund are "imperfectly experience rated," or not based exactly on past layoff experience. This implies that with a layoff, the subsequent increase in the employer's unemployment taxes can be less than the payment that the laid-off worker receives.

In essence then, the unemployment insurance fund subsidizes an additional layoff, thereby increasing the joint gains to employers and workers of using more layoffs when demand is low. Although it is not clear precisely how these gains are divided between the employer and employees, the layoff rate will be higher. A similar argument applies if unemployment benefits received by workers are not subject to federal taxation, as was the case until the Tax Reform Act of 1986 (implemented in 1987). The joint gains to adopting a more liberal layoff policy are then positive since more worker compensation can take the form of unemployment compensation rather than wages, which means that the total income taxes paid by workers will be lower. Thus with the change that made unemployment insurance subject to federal taxes in 1987, we should expect to see some fall in the amount of temporary layoffs.

We must realize that the unemployment insurance fund per se does not encourage temporary layoffs. Rather, the peculiar features of the administration of the unemployment insurance fund encourage the excessive use of layoffs.[37] How significantly has the system affected layoff unemployment? One estimate is that the incentive provided by the average level of unemployment insurance benefits has been responsible for approximately one half of all temporary layoff unemployment.[38] Another study on the topic found that "the layoff unemployment rate would have been about 30 percent lower if the subsidy to unemployment caused by the current unemployment insurance system had been eliminated."[39]

Implications for the Natural Unemployment Rate

Earlier in this chapter, we discussed how the natural unemployment rate is determined by the rates at which workers flow into and out of employment and unemployment. Layoffs account for much of the movement between employment and unemployment, and most layoffs are temporary in that they end with workers returning to their original employers. It has been estimated that about 75 percent of those laid off return to their original employers. Among all persons classified as "unemployed job losers," temporary layoffs account for 50 percent of all unemployment spells.[40]

Given the long-term attachments between employers and workers, it is

---

[37] See Robert Topel, "On Layoffs and Unemployment Insurance," *American Economic Review* (September 1983): 73, pp. 541–559.

[38] See Feldstein (p. 834), Footnote 36.

[39] See Topel (p. 551), Footnote 37.

[40] See Feldstein, Footnote 36.

not surprising that most layoffs are temporary. An employer has an incentive to recall laid-off workers before hiring new ones, and workers have an incentive to wait for recall. The wage that a laid-off worker receives if he returns to his former employer probably exceeds any potential alternative wage offer since the original employer has already invested in training costs. Laid-off workers also receive unemployment compensation. Consequently, a worker on temporary layoff has a higher reservation wage and searches less intensively for alternative employment. This combination makes the worker unlikely to find and accept an alternate job.

Layoffs add to the flow out of the stock of the employed into the stock of the unemployed. Many of these workers will not be hired by those employers experiencing a temporary high demand because neither the employers nor the laid-off workers want to incur the necessary training costs. Instead, most of the laid-off workers will remain unemployed until their original employers recall them. For these reasons, temporary layoffs are one important factor contributing to the natural rate of unemployment.

15.5 EFFICIENCY WAGES AND THE POSSIBILITY OF INVOLUNTARY UNEMPLOYMENT

Up to this point in the chapter, we have been examining unemployment that is ''natural'' or consistent with labor market equilibrium in the absence of macroeconomic shocks. A positive natural rate of unemployment occurs not because aggregate output demand is too low, but because of incomplete information on job vacancies and wage offers coupled with the continuous entry and exit of workers into the labor market. Constant changes in the relative demands for employers' output that lead to periodic temporary layoffs also contributes to the natural unemployment rate.

In the last few years, researchers have argued that powerful forces exist that cause ''involuntary'' unemployment. This research has become known as the ''efficiency wage models of unemployment.''[41] This involuntary unemployment argument is as follows. Suppose that employers find it costly to measure the work effort their employees provide. Some workers, knowing that their employer may have difficulty monitoring their work effort, would avoid duties or shirk responsibility. To induce workers not to do this, employers must devote resources to monitoring employees, and either reward those not shirking or punish those found to be putting forth too little effort.

---

[41] An influential paper in the literature is Carl Shapiro and Joseph Stiglitz, ''Equilibrium Unemployment as a Worker Discipline Device,'' *American Economic Review* (June 1984): 74, 433–444. For a discussion of the various papers in the literature, see the survey by Janet Yellen, ''Efficiency Wage Models of Unemployment,'' *American Economic Review* (May 1984) 74, pp. 200–205 and the paper by Lorne Carmichael, ''Can Unemployment Be Involuntary: Comment,'' *American Economic Review* (December 1985): 75, pp. 1213–1214.

The efficiency wage models focus on the punishment of firing workers caught shirking. In this case, higher wages make this policy more effective in discouraging worker shirking since higher wages raise the costs of being fired. Even though some workers might be willing to work at a lower wage than an employer is currently offering, the employer will not want to hire them. Without the incentive of a higher wage, the newly hired workers would shirk too much while on the job. The outcome is that those employed are paid a wage above the wage that the unemployed are willing to accept. Thus there is "involuntary" unemployment in that some unemployed workers say they are willing to work at lower wages than paid current employees but employers are not willing to hire workers at these lower wages.

Although the efficiency wage models of unemployment put forth an interesting explanation of unemployment, it is unclear how much unemployment they explain. Some have pointed out that employers can often select more efficient ways to induce workers not to shirk. For instance, they can make new workers pay "entrance fees," which they would forfeit if caught shirking. Since such entrance fees would be subtracted from the wages that workers would otherwise receive, workers would be discouraged from shirking during their early periods of their employment. Another way suggested to discourage shirking is to allow workers to have the rights to the benefits of a pension plan only after a certain number of unblemished years of service. In either case, however, there is a potential moral hazard problem facing employers.[42] Employers may fire workers even though they have not been shirking in order to appropriate their workers' "entrance fees" or retirement funds.

Two other points should be made concerning the efficiency wage model of involuntary unemployment. First, the unemployment the model explains is not really involuntary. Even though workers say they would work at a lower wage, some really are not willing to work, since they would shirk if not monitored. Second, the unemployment that the model explains is primarily noncyclical. For example, suppose that aggregate demand falls in the economy, which causes the aggregate price level to fall. At first glance, the efficiency wage model seems to predict that unemployment will rise. After all, wouldn't the demand for labor fall, and wouldn't employers be unwilling to lower the money wages they offer, resulting in decreased employment and higher unemployment? The answer is not necessarily. The efficiency wage model predicts that employers will be unwilling to lower real wages, but not nominal wages. In fact, employers will ultimately lower the nominal wage by exactly the proportion of the reduction in the price level in order to leave real wages, and hence employment, unchanged.

---

[42] Carl Shapiro and Joseph Stiglitz, "Can Unemployment Be Involuntary? Reply," *American Economic Review* (December 1985): 75, p. 1215–1217.

SUMMARY

With the labor market in a constant state of flux, some unemployment is "natural." The natural unemployment rate is determined by the natural rates at which workers flow between employment and unemployment and into and out of the labor force in the absence of macroeconomic shocks. For instance, a rise in the flow of workers from employment to unemployment increases the natural rate. Unemployment rates vary across demographic groups due to differences in the flows between unemployment and employment. The primary cause of higher unemployment rates for young workers is their weaker labor force attachment as indicated by high flow rates from employment. The high unemployment rate for nonwhites primarily reflects not only a higher flow rate from employment to unemployment but also a lower flow rate from unemployment to employment.

Search behavior is a key element affecting the flow from unemployment to employment. An unemployed job-seeker must decide two things: the minimum acceptable wage offer, or reservation wage, and the amount of time to devote to job search each period, or "search intensity." A higher reservation wage or a lower search intensity lessens the likelihood of an individual escaping unemployment. The likelihood that an unemployed worker will find employment is also related to the number of employers searching to fill job vacancies. Thus the search choices of both the unemployed and employers are key in determining the natural rate of unemployment.

Job-seekers select reservation wages that equate the marginal cost and the marginal gain to searching one more period. Unemployment insurance reduces the marginal cost of search, which leads to higher reservation wages. Search intensity also is chosen to equate marginal cost to marginal gain. The marginal cost to more intensive search is primarily the increased leisure foregone and the increased effort necessary to increase the probability of obtaining an offer. The marginal gain to increased search intensity comes from finding an employment offer more quickly.

Since an increase in unemployment insurance benefits lowers the marginal cost to continued search, it not only raises recipients' reservation wages, but it also leads to reduced search intensity. Thus increased unemployment insurance benefits increase the probability that an individual will not escape unemployment in any given period, thereby raising the natural rate of unemployment. In contrast, the minimum wage increases the natural rate of unemployment by reducing the hiring activity of employers, making it less likely that a young worker will find an employment offer during a period of search.

Hiring and training costs provide incentives for long-term employment relationships between employers and workers. These shared, informal understandings on how employer and employee will act in response to various contingencies are called "implicit contracts." Temporary layoffs accompany these long-term implicit contracts. The unemployment insurance system encourages temporary layoffs since neither the employers nor the employee bear the full cost of an additional layoff.

LOOKING AHEAD

This chapter has examined one important market in the economy, the labor market. The next chapter examines in more detail a second important "market" in the economy, the money market. On the demand-side, we explore the role that the nonsynchronization of payments and receipts plays in generating a demand for money. On the supply-side, we develop a more complete view of the money multiplier that explicitly accounts for changes in desired holdings of reserves on the part of private depository institutions as well as changes in the desired holdings of currency by the nonbank public.

SUMMARY OF KEY EQUATIONS

Equating flows to and from unemployment

$$\alpha \cdot E + \phi \cdot N = (\beta + \delta_u) \cdot U \qquad (15.6)$$

Equilibrium unemployment rate

$$U_e \equiv U/L = \alpha^*/(\alpha^* + \beta) \qquad (15.9)$$
$$(\alpha^* = \alpha + \delta_e)$$

Optimal reservation wage

$$c - UI = \theta \cdot (W_a - W_r)/r - W_r \qquad (15.13)$$

KEY TERMS

Equilibrium unemployment rate, 596
Reservation wage, 596

REVIEW QUESTIONS

1. Explain how the constant movements of workers into and out of the state of unemployment determine a "natural" rate of unemployment.

2. Suppose that there are 200 million people in the labor force. Each week, 14 percent of unemployed workers become employed either by searching for and finding a job or by being recalled from layoff. Two percent of employed workers become unemployed by quitting their jobs, being laid

off, or being dismissed. Suppose that 20 million workers are initially unemployed.

(a) What is the initial unemployment rate?

(b) How many workers are initially employed?

(c) Ignoring movements into and out of the labor force, trace out the time path of employment and unemployment.

(d) What is the natural unemployment rate?

3. Let α denote the proportion of employed workers who become employed every week, let δ_e denote the fraction of employed workers who leave the labor force every week, and let β denote the fraction of unemployed workers who become employed every week.

(a) Assuming that these parameters $(\alpha, \beta, \delta_e)$ will occur in the absence of macroeconomic demand or supply shocks, what is the natural rate of unemployment equal to?

(b) What effect does an increase in β have on the natural unemployment rate? Interpret this effect.

(c) What effect does an increase in δ_e have on the natural unemployment rate? Interpret this effect.

(d) Let ϕ denote the proportion of nonparticipants who enter unemployment every week. What effect does an increase in the natural level of ϕ have on the equilibrium labor force, the equilibrium number of employed and unemployed, and the natural unemployment rate? Interpret these effects.

4. Indicate how the unemployment rate varies across the various age, sex, and race groups in the labor force. Discuss the major reasons for the different unemployment rates of the different demographic groups.

5. The proportions of labor force participants who are female, nonwhite, and teenagers grew between 1960 and 1980. What effect has this had on the natural unemployment rate? Why?

6. Discuss the job-search problem faced by an unemployed worker. What constitutes the net gain to continued search? The net cost?

(a) What do we mean when we talk about a worker's reservation wage?

(b) How should a worker choose a reservation wage?

7. Illustrate the unemployed worker's choice of the optimal reservation wage.

(a) Show the effect that an increase in unemployment insurance has on your answer. What happens to the worker's reservation wage? What happens to the expected length of time that the worker remains unemployed? What happens to the expected wage that the worker will get when employment is accepted? Why?

(b) Suppose that each week an unemployed worker pays a fee to an employment agency to help him locate employment. Show the effect that an increase in this fee has on the worker's choice of the reservation wage. What happens to the expected length of the worker's unemployment spell? What happens to the expected wage that he will receive when he locates acceptable employment?

(c) Suppose the interest rate rises. Show the effect on the unemployed worker's reservation wage. Interpret this effect. In what sense does search by the unemployed worker represent an investment in his human capital?

8. Milton Friedman has said that the natural rate of unemployment "is not a numerical constant but depends on 'real' as opposed to monetary factors." Explain this statement.

9. What types of factors lead to long-term employment relations between employers and their workers? How important are these long-term employment relations?

10. What do we mean when we speak of "implicit contracts" between firms and workers? What forces give rise to such contracts? How are they enforced?

11. The unemployment benefits that unemployed workers receive are paid for by taxes assessed on employers.

(a) What do we mean when we say the employer contributions to the unemployment insurance fund are "imperfectly experienced rated"?

(b) How does this affect the number of layoffs that any employer will choose in a week? Will workers agree to the employers' policy? Why or why not?

(c) Some types of businesses offer jobs that are more prone to layoff. How is the mix of businesses and jobs affected by imperfectly experienced rated unemployment insurance? Why?

(d) Discuss the implications for the natural rate of unemployment.

(e) From the point of view of resource allocation, what are the benefits and costs of unemployment insurance?

12. A May 1979 *Monthly Labor Review* article by Joyanna Moy reports that a number of Japanese firms "loan" excess workers "for a specified period of no longer than 6 months to enterprises experiencing current labor shortages. The workers maintain their affiliation with and receive their full wages from the lending company. The borowing company usually pays temporary-worker wages to the lending company and the difference in wages plus benefits is made up by the lending employer."

(a) What are the advantages of the lending arrangement described above to the lending and the borrowing firm?

(b) What effect do you think the practice described above has on labor turnover in Japan?

(c) Discuss the implications of the lending arrangements for the natural rate of unemployment.

13. How do "efficiency wage models" explain unemployment?

(a) Is the unemployment in these models really "involuntary"? Why or why not?

(b) Can efficiency wage models explain cyclical unemployment?

Chapter 16

The Money Market: Money Demand and Money Supply

AN inescapable conclusion from the macroeconomic analysis presented in this book is that money plays a central role in determining the economy's overall performance. The crucial role played by money is highlighted by the exchange equation developed in Chapter 8. In obtaining this equation, we noted that we could express real money demand as $L^d = k \cdot Y$, where k denotes the ratio of real money balances demanded to real GNP. Equating this expression for the real quantity of money demanded to the real quantity supplied (M^s/P) and rearranging, we obtained the exchange equation:

$$M^s \cdot V = P \cdot Y \qquad (16.1)$$

where the term V equals $1/k$ and represents the desired ratio of real GNP to real money balances. We called V the velocity of money. Remember that by money we mean the M1 measure of money—that is, individual holdings of checkable deposits and currency.

The exchange equation tells us that any change in *nominal* GNP must be accompanied by either a change in the nominal money supply (M^s) or a change in velocity (V). However, changes in velocity merely reflect underlying changes in real money demand relative to real GNP. We can thus conclude that any change in nominal output will be accompanied by either a change in the supply of money or the demand for money.

Given their importance, it is worthwhile to study money demand and supply in more detail than we have had a chance to do so far. We thus begin this chapter with a more thorough analysis of the underlying determinants of the money demand function. In particular, we consider the maximization problem facing a household deciding how much of its wealth to hold in the form of money and how much to hold in the form of interest-earning financial assets.[1] By holding more wealth in the form of money, the household can reduce transaction costs, but at the cost of reduced interest earnings on financial assets. As we will see, the solution to a household's maximization problem yields a determinate form for the money demand function. Following our discussion of money demand, we look at some empirical estimates of the demand for money function in order to see if the evidence is consistent with the theory. In addition, we look at the behavior of money demand during the Great Depression and examine the relationship between expected inflation and money demand.

Next we turn our attention to the supply of money. We extend our earlier discussion of money supply determination by explicitly incorporating into the analysis the holding of currency by households and the holding of excess reserves by depository institutions. We demonstrate how we can solve for the money multiplier in terms of the currency-to-deposit ratio, the required reserve ratio, and the excess reserve ratio. We then show the importance of these considerations for the Great Depression and conclude by discussing the behavior of the currency-to-deposit and excess reserve ratios in more recent years, with particular emphasis being placed on the effects of federal deposit insurance.

16.1 THE DEMAND FOR MONEY: AN INVENTORY APPROACH

In Chapter 6, we indicated that households' demand for real money balances is positively related to real GNP and inversely related to the interest rate. We now examine this relationship more carefully. Specifically, we consider the maximization problem confronting a household deciding how much of its wealth on average to hold in the form of money during a period and how much to hold in the form of interest-earning financial assets.[2] By holding more wealth in the form of money the household can reduce its transaction costs during the period. Of course, the cost of holding more wealth in the form of money is the interest earnings that are lost because of the household's

---

[1] Recall that for simplicity we are assuming that money holdings do not earn any interest. Thus while r is the interest rate offered by financial assets such as bonds, the interest rate offered by money is zero. The assumption that money does not earn interest is innocuous. We could instead simply interpret r as the difference between the interest rate offered by financial assets and that offered by money; the analysis with respect to the choice between money and financial asset holdings would be unaffected.

[2] For the moment, we continue to ignore the possibility that households hold part of their wealth in the form.

reduced holdings of financial assets. In choosing its optimal money holdings, the household weighs these two considerations against one another.

It is important to realize that although our discussion of money demand throughout this book refers only to households, counted in household money demand are the desired money holdings of other participants, in particular firms. We lump the money demands of others in with households because the factors determining the demand for money by others such as firms parallel those determining the demand for money by households. Firms also have to balance the reduction in transaction costs from increased cash holdings against the lost interest from reduced asset holdings.

The model of money demand that we present in this chapter is similar to those found in the seminal papers by William Baumol and James Tobin.[3] This line of analysis has become known as the "inventory approach" to money demand in order to indicate that the problem facing a household in deciding how much money to hold is similar to that facing a firm in determining how much of a good to keep on hand in the form of inventories. The gain to a firm in holding larger average inventories of goods stems from the reduction in transaction costs associated with restocking when supplies are exhausted. Thus transaction costs include the costs of ordering, shipping, and processing new goods. The cost of holding increased inventories of goods stems from the cost of the higher borrowing required to finance their acquisition. Optimal inventory holdings are such that these transaction and interest costs are appropriately balanced against each other. As we show below, the same principle applies to a household's (or a firm's) optimal money holdings.

The Nonsynchronization of Receipts and Expenditures

The "representative" household receives income as payment for the labor and capital inputs that it provides. Let α denote the fraction of income Y used to purchase output for consumption.[4] Households are usually not paid continuously over time but rather receive payments at discrete points in time. Thus let N denote the number of times that the representative household is paid each period. For example, if a period is equal to a year and the

---

[3] William J. Baumol, "The Transactions Demand for Cash: An Inventory Theoretic Approach," *Quarterly Journal of Economics* 66 (November 1952): 545–566 and James Tobin, "The Interest-Elasticity of Transactions Demand for Cash," *Review of Economics and Statistics* 38 (August 1956): 241–247. Extensions of the inventory-theoretic approach to money demand include Merton H. Miller and Daniel Orr, "A Model of the Demand for Money by Firms," *Quarterly Journal of Economics,* 80, (August 1966): 413–435, Anthony M. Santomero, "A Model of the Demand for Money by Households," *Journal of Finance,* 29 (March 1974): 89–102, and Herschel I. Grossman and Andrew J. Policano, "Money Balances, Commodity Inventories, and Inflationary Expectations," *Journal of Political Economy,* 83, (December 1975): 1093–1112.

[4] Of course, α will generally depend on the amount of taxes that has to be paid to the government as well as the interest rate. Furthermore, given a linear consumption function with a positive vertical intercept, α will decline with Y. We will ignore these considerations since they are not important for our current analysis.

household is paid monthly, then N is equal to 12. For convenience, let us assume that the household's income receipts are spread evenly across the N paydays.

A household's expenditures will generally not coincide perfectly with its income receipts. The household is therefore confronted with a problem. It will have to keep some money on hand in order to pay for its expenditures, but this is costly since it means that the household gives up the chance to hold interest-earning financial assets. A possible solution to this problem may be for the household to keep all of its wealth in the form of financial assets and then to sell off these assets when it needs to purchase consumption goods. Obviously, though, the transaction costs associated with this course of action are likely to be prohibitive.

Suppose that the household purchases consumption goods continuously at a constant rate over time, so that during each period between paychecks it purchases $\alpha Y/N$ units of consumption goods. Thus if P denotes the average price level, the household will need to set aside exactly $P\alpha Y/N$ dollars from each paycheck at the start of each period in order to pay for its consumption purchases during the period. The household's problem is to decide how to divide this amount between money holdings and holdings of financial assets during the course of each period.

One possibility, illustrated in Figure 16.1(a), is for the household to immediately convert its entire paycheck into money and then to continuously draw down on its money holdings until the next payday. As part (a) indicates, the household's money holdings will therefore initially be equal to $P\alpha Y/N$ when it is paid at time 0. These money holdings fall continuously over time as the household uses them to purchase consumption goods. Money holdings are finally exhausted at time T, at which time the household will receive its next paycheck.

A second possibility, illustrated in Figure 16.1(b), is for the household to initially convert only half of its paycheck into money and put the remainder into financial assets. In this case, the household will initially (at time 0) have money holdings of the amount $(1/2)(P\alpha Y/N)$. These initial money holdings will be exhausted at time $T/2$, at which time the household converts the remaining financial assets into money. It then continuously draws these money holdings down to finance consumption purchases until the next pay period.

A third possibility, illustrated in Figure 16.1(c), is for the household to convert only one third of its initial paycheck into money and to put the rest into financial assets. Thus the household's initial money holdings are equal to $(1/3)(P\alpha Y/N)$. These money holdings are exhausted when the period between paychecks is one third over (at time $T/3$). At this time, the household sells off $(1/3)(P\alpha Y/N)$ dollars worth of financial assets. It uses this money to finance consumption purchases until the period between paychecks is two thirds over. The household then sells off its remaining $(1/3)(P\alpha Y/N)$ dollars worth of financial assets and uses this money to finance consumption purchases until the next paycheck at time T.

Figure 16.1   The Time Pattern of Money Holdings

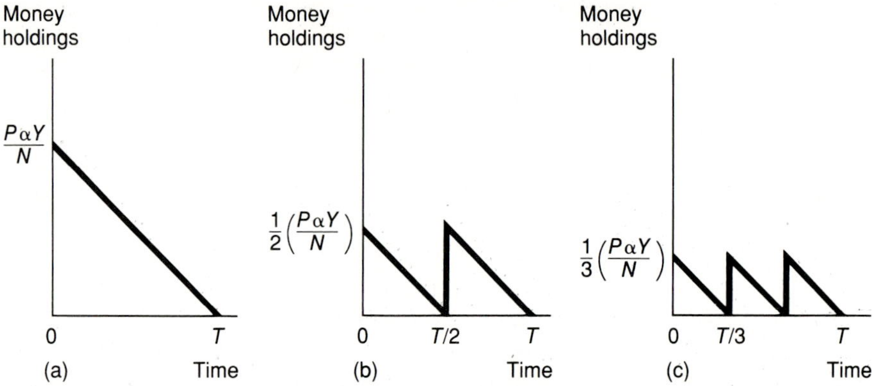

In part (a), the household immediately converts its entire paycheck into money and draws on these money holdings until the next payday. In part (b), the household initially converts only half of its paycheck into money and puts the remainder into financial assets. The household's initial money holdings are exhausted when the period between paychecks is half over. At this time, the household converts its remaining financial assets into money. In part (c), the household initially converts only one third of its paycheck into money. It converts financial assets into money twice—when the period between paychecks is one third over and when it is two thirds over.

Optimal Money Management

The examples above illustrate an important point: by incurring the transaction cost of additional conversions from financial assets into money, households can reduce their average holdings of money, thereby increasing their interest earnings on financial assets. For example, in the case where the household converts its entire paycheck immediately into money, its initial money holdings are $P\alpha Y/N$ and its money holdings at the end of the pay period are zero. Since the household's money holdings decline at a constant rate, the household's average money holdings are $(1/2)P\alpha Y/N.$[5] If the household initially puts one half of its paycheck into financial assets and thus incurs the cost of selling off financial assets when the pay period is half over, then its average money holdings are $(1/4)P\alpha Y/N.$[6] Finally, if the household initially converts

---

[5] Of course, since the household behaves the same way each period between paychecks, its average money holdings during the year are the same as its average money holdings during each period between paychecks.

[6] Note that at time zero, money holdings are $(1/2)P\alpha Y/N$ and at time $T/2$, money holdings are 0, so that average money holdings from time zero to time $T/2$ are $(1/4)P\alpha Y/N$. Similarly, average money holdings are $(1/4)P\alpha Y/N$ from time $T/2$ to time T. Thus during the entire period from time zero to time T, average holdings must also be $(1/4)P\alpha Y/N$.

only one third of its paycheck into money holdings and twice incurs the cost of selling off financial assets, then its average money holdings are $(1/6)P\alpha Y/N$.

By now the pattern should be clear. In general, if each period between paychecks the household makes n conversions into money, then its average money holdings, M, are given by

$$M = (1/2n)P\alpha Y/N \tag{16.2}$$

Given a money interest rate equal to r, the interest earnings that the household loses because it holds money instead of financial assets is therefore $r(1/2n)P\alpha Y/N$. Dividing by the price level P, we obtain the household's interest losses in real terms namely, $r(1/2n)\alpha Y/N$. Note that this amount falls as n rises. That is, by increasing the number of times that it converts financial assets into money, the household can reduce its average money holdings and thus reduce the interest it foregoes on financial assets. In deciding how often to convert from financial assets into money, the household must compare this interest gain from lower average money holdings with the cost of additional conversions into money.

We will use b (for brokerage charge) to denote the real cost incurred by the household each time it converts its paycheck or financial assets into money. This brokerage or transaction cost includes not only explicit brokerage charges but also, perhaps more importantly, the expense in trouble and time in making the conversion. Note that if the household makes n conversions into money, then the total real transaction cost it incurs is simply bn.

The household wants to minimize the sum of the transaction costs it incurs when it converts financial assets into money and the interest cost it foregoes by holding money instead of financial assets. The solution to this problem is illustrated in Figure 16.2. In interpreting this figure, note that transaction costs rise by b for each additional conversion. In the graph, the marginal cost curve (MC) denotes this marginal cost of an additional conversion.

Although additional conversions cause transaction costs to rise because of brokerage fees, additional conversions reduce forgone interest costs since they lower average money holdings. In Figure 16.2, the marginal benefit curve (MB) indicates the increase in interest earnings achievable for each one-unit increase in the number of conversions. The marginal benefit to an increase in conversions falls with additional conversions because, as the household makes more conversions into money, the reduction in its average money holdings that it is able to achieve by making an additional conversion becomes smaller. This falling marginal benefit may be seen from Equation 16.2. For example, when the household increases the number of its money conversions from one to two, its average money holdings fall from $(1/2)P\alpha Y/N$ to $(1/4)P\alpha Y/N$, resulting in a gain in real interest earnings of $r(1/4)\alpha Y/N$. But when the household increases the number of its money conversions from two to three, its average money holdings only fall from $(1/4)P\alpha Y/N$ to $(1/6)P\alpha Y/N$, so that the gain in the form of increased real interest earnings is only $r(1/12)\alpha Y/N$.

Figure 16.2   The Optimal Number of Conversions into Money

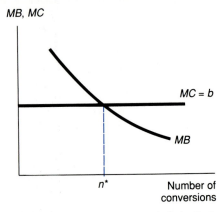

The optimal number of conversions into money (n^*) is that number at which the marginal benefit from an additional transfer into money holdings—the increase in the household's real interest earnings because of its lower average money balance holdings—just equals the marginal cost of an additional transfer—the real brokerage cost (b).

As Figure 16.2 indicates, the optimal number of conversions into money (n^*) is that number at which the marginal benefit from an additional transfer into money holdings—the increase in the household's real interest earnings because of its lower average money balance holdings—just equals the marginal cost of an additional transfer—the real brokerage cost (b).

Using calculus, we can solve for n^* explicitly. The total cost that the household would like to minimize is given by

$$C = r(1/2n)\alpha Y/N + bn \qquad (16.3)$$

To find the number of conversions that minimize this total cost expression, we can differentiate this expression with respect to n and set it equal to zero. We obtain

$$dC/dn = (r(1/2)\alpha Y/N)(-1/n^2) + b = 0 \qquad (16.4)$$

Solving for n now yields the optimal number of money conversions. Thus

$$n^* = (r\alpha Y/2bN)^{1/2} \qquad (16.5)$$

Having found the optimal number of conversions into money, we also know the average money balances that the household chooses to hold. From Equation 16.2, the household's (average) nominal demand for money balances (M^d) is given by

$$M^d = (1/2n^*)P\alpha Y/N \qquad (16.6)$$

Dividing Equation 16.6 by the price level P, we obtain the household's real demand for money

$$L^d = (1/2n^*)\alpha Y/N \tag{16.7}$$

Substituting the value of n^* obtained in Equation 16.5 into Equation 16.7 yields an explicit form for (average) real money demand

$$L^d = (b\alpha Y/2rN)^{1/2} \tag{16.8}$$

This result is often referred to as the square root rule for the demand for money, and reflects the general character of solutions for inventory models of money demand.

Finally, letting $k = (1/2n^*)\alpha/N$, we can rewrite our money demand equation (Equation 16.7) in a more familiar and more compact form:

$$L^d = k \cdot Y \tag{16.9}$$

Note that Equation 16.9 is identical to Equation 5.14 in Chapter 6. As we noted in Chapter 6, the parameter k is simply the ratio of the amount of real money balances demanded to real GNP (or, equivalently, the ratio of nominal money balances demanded to nominal GNP). All we have done here is to show how k is determined by households' optimal management of their portfolios if the only motive for holding money is to facilitate transactions.

Factors Affecting the Demand for Money

Equation 16.8 allows us to explicitly examine the factors that affect real money demand, such as the interest rate, brokerage charges, and real income. Note, however, that a change in the price level is not a factor affecting real money demand. Since a change in the price level alters neither the marginal gain (the increase in real interest earnings) nor the marginal cost (the real brokerage charge, b) of an additional conversion of financial assets into money, the household's optimal number of conversions into money (n^*) is unaffected, which means that the ratio of real balances demanded to real GNP (k) will not change. As can be seen from Equation 16.6, nominal money balances demanded change by the same proportion as the price level. Although an increase in the general price level causes households to want to increase their nominal money holdings in order to finance their higher nominal expenditures, real money balances demanded are not affected.

Recall that in Chapter 6 we argued that an increase in the interest rate makes it more costly for households to hold wealth in the form of money balances, thereby causing the demand for money to fall. How does this effect show up in our inventory model of money demand? A higher interest rate raises the marginal benefit to a household of making an additional conversion from financial assets to money since the resulting reduction in average money balances yields a higher gain in interest earnings. As Figure 16.2 suggests, the resulting shift up in the marginal benefit curve would cause the optimal number of conversions from financial assets to money (n^*) to increase. The higher n^* translates into a lower desired ratio of money balances to income (k), and thus a lower demand for money, as indicated by Equation 16.8.[7]

In contrast, an increase in the brokerage charge (b) that a household incurs when it converts financial assets into money causes its optimal number of conversions from financial assets to money to fall, which translates into an increase in the demand for money. In the late 1970s and 1980s, the advent of automatic tellers and discount brokers likely reduced the "brokerage charge" to converting financial assets to money. Other things being equal, this reduced brokerage charge would reduce the demand for money and hence increase velocity.

Finally, consider the effect of an increase in real income Y. Associated with an increase in Y is an increase in household consumption spending, which means that households will hold more money in order to finance their higher expenditures. In fact, if the number of times that households choose to convert financial assets into money were unaffected by an increase in real income, then the value of k in Equation 16.9 would not change, which means that real money balances would increase by the same proportion as real income, Y.

However, k is affected by the increase in income. With the increase in their real consumption expenditures, households find it worthwhile to make more conversions from financial assets into money.[8] In terms of Figure 16.2, the increased income and consequent higher consumption expenditure raises the marginal gain to additional conversions from financial assets to money. This causes the optimal number of conversions from financial assets to money to rise, which means that k, the ratio of real income to real money balances, falls. Expressed differently, an increase in household income and expenditures makes it more worthwhile to devote more time and effort to portfolio management in order to economize on money balances. The increase in the number of conversions from financial assets to money and consequent reduction in k means that although an increase in real income causes money demand to rise, desired real money balances rise by a proportion that is smaller than the increase in real income.[9] Economists sometimes refer to this result as indicating economies of scale in money management.

---

[7] Differentiating the expression for the demand for money obtained in Equation 16.8 with respect to the interest rate, r, we see that a 1 percent change in the interest rate results in a one-half percent change in real money demand in the opposite direction. In other words, the interest elasticity of money demand is $-1/2$.

[8] Note that we are holding constant real brokerage fees b. It may be the case, however, that an increase in income raises the value of time to households. To the extent that brokerage charges include time costs, the result would be an increase in b that, as we have seen, would by itself lower the number of conversions.

[9] We can show that money demand does indeed rise by referring to the expression for money demand obtained in Equation 16.8, namely, $L^d = (b\alpha Y/2rN)^{1/2}$. Differentiating money demand with respect to real income, we see that a 1 percent change in Y causes a one-half percent change in money demand. That is, the income elasticity of the demand for money is $1/2$.

The Aggregate Demand for Money

Our inventory model of money demand provides a justification for the assumptions in Chapter 6 about money demand in the economy. For convenience, our analysis here has focused on the behavior of the "representative household." We have seen that the amount of real money balances that this household demands depends positively on the household's real income (Y) and inversely on the money interest rate (r) and the real brokerage charge (b). Of course, the aggregate demand for real money balances in the economy has these same properties since we obtain the aggregate demand for money by adding up the amounts demanded by all individual households.[10]

The aggregate demand for money differs from the individual household's demand for money in one important respect, however. The individual household's money demand has a sawtooth pattern (as illustrated in Figure 16.1). However, aggregation smooths this pattern out since the timing of income receipts and money payments varies across households.

It is also worth reiterating that we include the money demand of firms with households. In reality, firms are important demanders of money. However, since the same basic considerations that apply to households' money demand also apply to firms' money demand, we lose nothing of importance by focusing our discussion on the demand for money by households.

Integer Constraints on the Number of Conversions from Financial Assets into Money

Thus far we have simplified our analysis of money demand by allowing the variable n to take on any positive value whatsoever, thereby ignoring the fact that n must really be an integer (1, 2, 3, etc.) because in reality a household can only convert its paycheck and financial assets into money an integer number of times. This assumption is less innocuous than may appear at first glance. In fact, the constraint that n be an integer increases the likelihood that some households may choose to immediately convert their entire paycheck into money, putting none of it into financial assets.[11]

For example, consider a household whose real monthly expenditures are equal to $1500 (which means that the household's real yearly expenditures are $18,000). If the annual interest rate is 12 percent, will the household choose to hold any portion of this amount in the form of financial assets? If the household initially converts half of its monthly paycheck into financial assets and then converts this amount into money balances when a month is half over, its average monthly holdings of real financial assets will be equal to $750/2 or $375 (note that this corresponds to part (b) in Figure

---

[10] You may remember that since our discussion has concerned the representative household, we let Y denote both aggregate income in the economy and the income of that household.

[11] This point was first made by Robert Barro, "Integer Constraints and Aggregation in an Inventory Model of Money Demand," *Journal of Finance* 31 (March 1976): 77–88.

16.2). Since the monthly interest rate is 1 percent (12 percent divided by 12), the household's monthly real interest earnings will amount to $3.75. Thus the household will be willing to incur the cost of putting some of its monthly paycheck into financial assets only if the real brokerage cost is $3.75 or below. Expressed differently, if the real brokerage cost is greater than $3.75, then all households with monthly expenditures below $1500 will convert their monthly paycheck immediately into money and put none of it into financial assets to be converted into money at some later point during the month.

The previously derived results concerning the effects of changes in income and interest rates on the demand for real balances do not hold for households whose real expenditures are sufficiently low that they choose to immediately put their entire paycheck into money. A small increase in real income now results in an equiproportionate increase in these households' money demand. The income elasticity of money demand is now one instead of 1/2. And a small change in the interest rate will have no effect on these households' money demand.[12]

In summary, integer constraints on the number of times that financial assets can be converted to money modifies our analysis of money demand. Naturally, in obtaining the aggregate demand for money we add up money balances demanded by all households. Thus the income and interest elasticities of aggregate money demand are the average of the elasticities of those households whose incomes are sufficiently high that they choose to initially put part of their paychecks into financial assets and those whose incomes are sufficiently low that they choose to convert them immediately into money balances.[13]

16.2   THE DEMAND FOR MONEY: ADDITIONAL CONSIDERATIONS AND EMPIRICAL EVIDENCE

In this section, we consider possible extensions to our money demand model and examine some of the empirical evidence with respect to the demand for money. We begin by discussing the effect on money demand of uncertainty by households as to the timing and size of their receipts and payments. Next

---

[12] These statements are modified to the extent that a rise in income or the interest rate induces some individuals to begin to convert money to financial assets.

[13] In Footnotes 7 and 9, we noted that those households whose incomes are sufficiently high that they choose to make more than one conversion from their paychecks and financial assets into money have money demand income and interest rate elasticities of 1/2 and −1/2, respectively. Since households who put their entire paychecks immediately into money have money demand income and interest elasticities of 1 and 0, the income elasticity of aggregate money demand is predicted to be between 1/2 and 1, while the interest elasticity is predicted to be between 0 and −1/2.

we consider the evidence concerning the direction and size of the income and interest elasticities of money demand. We conclude the section with a discussion of the relationship between expected inflation and the demand for money.

Uncertainty About Receipts and Payments

Besides taking account of integer constraints, there is another way of extending our money demand model to make it more realistic. We have made the rather strong assumption that households know the timing and the size of their payments and receipts with certainty. Naturally, however, uncertainty about payments and receipts should affect households' demand for money. If households (and firms) are uncertain about the timing and the size of their income receipts and payments, then there is a chance that they will not have sufficient money on hand to make some desired purchases. They therefore will hold money simply to guard against the costs of becoming illiquid. Taking uncertainty into account does not vitiate our preceding analysis of money demand. Our prediction that the demand for real money balances is positively related to real income and inversely related to the interest rate still holds. We have simply identified another factor that may affect the demand for money balances—a households' uncertainty about their receipts and expenditures. The greater this uncertainty, the greater will be the amount of money that is demanded.

As a practical matter, it seems likely (and the evidence suggests this) that variations in the degree of uncertainty concerning receipts and payments are generally sufficiently small so as not to cause significant changes in the aggregate demand for money. However, there have been some specific episodes during which increased uncertainty may well have had quite important effects on money demand, the most notable of these being the Great Depression. Milton Friedman and Anna Schwartz have estimated that from 1929 to 1933 the ratio of real money balances demanded to real GNP rose by almost one third.[14] It is almost certainly the case that the increased uncertainty accompanying the onset of the Great Depression contributed significantly to this increase in money demand. As Friedman and Schwartz note, the "major virtue of cash as an asset is its versatility. It involves a minimum of commitment and provides a maximum of flexibility to meet emergencies and to take advantage of opportunities. The more uncertain the future, the greater the value of such flexibility and hence the greater the demand for money is likely to be."

---

[14] Milton Friedman and Anna J. Schwartz, *A Monetary History of the United States, 1960–1967,* (Princeton University Press, Princeton, N.J. 1963): p. 302. Instead of couching their discussion in terms of money demand, Friedman and Schwartz refer to the "income velocity of money." As noted at the beginning of this chapter, and elaborated on in the next section, velocity is simply the ratio of nominal income to money demand or $1/k$.

Empirical Evidence on the Demand for Money

Consistent with our theory, empirical estimates indicate that the demand for money is indeed a real demand, as the amount of nominal balances demanded appears to be proportional to the price level. As is also predicted by the theory, the evidence shows that the demand for real money balances is inversely related to interest rates and positively related to the level of real income.

With respect to the relationship between the demand for money and interest rates, David Laidler indicates that "if we consider the United States over the period 1892–1960, the elasticity of demand for money M2 with respect to a short-term rate of interest appears to have varied between -0.12 and -0.15 and, with respect to a long-term rate of interest, between -0.2 and -0.6. (If M1 is used instead, the relevant elasticities are -0.17 to -0.20 and -0.5 to -0.8, respectively.)."[15] Stephen Goldfeld estimates the demand function for M1 from 1952 through 1973 and finds an income elasticity of about 0.56 and an interest rate elasticity of -0.19.[16]

The Long-Run Behavior of Velocity

One of the most striking features of velocity was its continuous upward movement from the end of World War II until the early 1980s. This increase in velocity was not only continuous, but it also was quite substantial. For example, from the mid-1950s to 1983, the velocity of money had more than doubled from about three to over six.

The postwar increase in velocity can be readily explained in light of our preceding discussion. As noted above, the velocity of money is simply the ratio of real GNP to real money demand. Thus saying that the velocity of money is rising is exactly the same as saying that individuals are economizing on their money balances relative to income. Several factors have been responsible for this.

First, real income has grown over time. According to our inventory model of money demand, these increases in real income induce individuals to economize on their money balances, thus resulting in reductions in k in Equation 16.9. Second, interest rates rose substantially in the postwar era. This upward trend in the general level of interest rates has been referred to

---

[15] David Laidler, *The Demand for Money: Theories and Empirical Evidence* (Second Edition, Harper and Row, New York, 1977), p. 133.

[16] The "income elasticity of money demand" refers to the percent change in the amount of money demanded that results from a 1 percent change in income. These elasticities are long-run in nature; they indicate the percent changes in real money demand that will be caused by changes in real income and interest rates given that individuals have time to fully adjust. Short-run money demand elasticities may be considerably smaller. According to Goldfeld's estimates ("The Case of the Missing Money," *Brookings Papers on Economic Activity*, no. 3, 1976: 683–730), the short-run (one quarter) income and interest rate elasticities of money demand are .18 and $-.06$, respectively. In addition, we should point out that the interest rate variables that Goldfeld uses in his regression equations are short-run rates, that is the rates on time deposits and commercial paper.

many times throughout this book (see, for instance, Figure 1.4). The market interest rate on treasury bills was 0.4 percent in 1945, 2.9 percent in 1960, 6.5 percent in 1970, and 10.6 percent in 1982. Our money demand model tells us that this increase in interest rates causes money demand to fall and thus velocity to rise. The subsequent fall in velocity during the 1982–1987 period can be attributed in part to the reversal of this trend, as interest rates fell during this period.

While an inverse relationship between interest rates and money demand is well documented and helps explain some of the changes in money demand, and thus velocity, that have occurred, innovations in financial markets and banking are also important factors that have affected velocity. Some of these innovations, especially those occurring in the late 1970s and the early 1980s, were triggered by the rise in interest rates in conjunction with the prohibition by law of interest payments on demand deposits.

The Banking Acts of 1933 and 1935 prohibited the payment of interest on demand deposits. Although depository institutions could not make explicit interest payments on their checking accounts, they could offer implicit interest by not assessing depositors full service charges or by giving away free gifts such as toasters or dishes. It has been estimated that implicit interest in the form of service charge remissions on demand deposits increased from about 1.5 percent in 1950 to approximately 2.5 percent in 1968.[17] Of course, there are limits to the implicit interest that depository institutions can efficiently provide. When interest rates rose to high levels in the late 1970s, it became increasingly difficult for regulated institutions to compete for funds by offering implicit interest payments. After all, how many toasters can a family use?

One consequence of banks being prohibited from paying interest on checking accounts was that new financial intermediaries offering "money substitutes" which paid some interest arose during the 1970s.[18] Not only did new financial intermediaries arise, but existing depository institutions offered new accounts as a way of getting around the prohibition of interest payments on checking accounts. In particular, negotiable order of withdrawal (NOW) accounts started to arise in the mid-1970s. The accounts were first offered by savings and loan associations in New England. The NOW accounts functioned for all practical purposes as checking accounts.

---

[17] Robert Barro and Anthony Santomero, "Household Money Holdings and the Demand Deposit Rate," *Journal of Money, Credit, and Banking,* May 1972: 397–413.

[18] Up until 1980, commercial banks not only were prohibited by law from paying interest on checking accounts but also the Federal Reserve's Regulation Q limited the interest rates that could be paid on time and savings deposits. Similarly, the Federal Home Loan Bank set ceiling rates on deposits at savings and loan associations. As a result, when interest rates rose, individuals not only moved out of demand deposits, but they also moved out of other deposits as well. Some of these funds were simply shifted into money substitutes such as money market funds while others were used to purchase financial assets directly. The movement of households away from deposits and toward the direct holding of financial assets is called disintermediation (as opposed to intermediation). The Banking Reform Act of 1980 called for all Regulation Q interest rate ceilings on both checking and savings accounts to be gradually phased out between 1980 and 1985.

The Monetary Control Act of 1980 gave formal legal approval to these accounts and made them available nationwide. As we mentioned earlier, NOW accounts are today considered to be part of M1 and general purpose and broker/dealer money market accounts have become part of M2.[19] Money market mutual funds hold various short-term securities as assets and offer deposit accounts against which checks can often be written. Invented only in 1973, their assets had grown to over $200 billion by the end of 1982. Shifts by individuals out of demand deposits (M1) into money market funds (M2) or other similar assets show up as an increase in the velocity of M1. In the case study that follows, we will look at how economic circumstances in the 1970s and early 1980s led to shifts out of components of M2 back into M1, thus reversing the trend of an increasing M1 velocity.

Other innovations that help explain the general increase in the velocity of money over the last 30 years are improved methods of financial management. Technological advances, in particular the increased and improved use of computers, have been partly responsible for such improvements in financial management. These improvements would appear in our model of money demand as reductions in b, the real cost of conversions between financial assets and money. This causes individuals to economize on their money balances; in Equation 16.9 k falls and the velocity of money rises.

One final important innovation is the increasingly widespread use of credit cards. Credit cards offer an alternative to holding money as a way to meet unanticipated payments. Consequently, the increased acceptance of credit cards has contributed to the fall in money demand and rise in velocity during this period. Note, however, that the use of a credit card does not eliminate the demand for money, since the payment of credit card bills still requires money holdings.

Case Study   THE MISSING MONEY

Macroeconomists have devoted a substantial amount of effort toward studying the demand for money, effort that has not been without reward. In fact, until the events of recent years, the behavior of money demand was thought to be fairly well understood. As Robert Gordon observed, "Slightly more than a decade ago, the demand for money was one of the least controversial topics in macroeconomics, both in its underlying theory and in the stability and plausibility of coefficient estimates."[20] As we noted above, consistent with the theory, empirical estimations of the money demand function indicate

---

[19] Institution-only money market funds are included in M3, but not M2.

[20] Robert Gordon, "The Short-Run Demand for Money: A Reconsideration," *Journal of Money, Credit, and Banking* (November 1984): 403–434.

that the demand for real balances is inversely related to interest rates and positively related to the income level. For example, with data from 1952 to 1973, Steven Goldfeld used ordinary least squares regression analysis to estimate the following equation for the current quarterly real demand for M1:

$$L^d = c + 0.127 \cdot Y - 0.0412 \cdot r_d - 0.018 \cdot r_c + 0.0676 \cdot (\overline{M}/P) \quad \textbf{(16.10)}$$

where c is a constant term, Y is real GNP in the current quarter, r_d is the current interest rate on time deposits, r_c is the current interest rate on commercial paper, and $(\overline{M}1/P)$ is the level of real money balances in the preceding quarter.[21] As predicted by our theory, the estimated coefficient for real GNP is positive while the interest rate coefficients are negative.

Given values of the explanatory variables on the right side of the above regression equation, we can obtain a prediction for the real demand for money in subsequent periods. If the money demand function is stable, then the predicted value for money demand should not be too different from actual money demand. Up until the mid-1970s, estimated money demand equations similar to Equation 16.10 predicted money demand quite accurately. However, things changed sometime around 1974. For as Goldfeld notes, ''The equation performs extremely poorly when extrapolated beyond the period of fit . . . the equation consistently overpredicts the demand for real money balances.''

A fall in money demand corresponds to an increase in velocity. As may be seen from Figure 16.3, the velocity of money (using the M1 measure of the money supply) rose substantially from 1960 to 1981. While much of the increase in velocity over this period can be explained by increases in real income (assuming an income elasticity of money demand less than one) and interest rates, Equation 16.6 cannot explain a good part of the increase, especially that occurring in the mid- and late 1970s.

Money demand equations such as Equation 16.10 overpredicted the demand for money (M1) because they did not control for the financial innovation occurring in the 1970s that led individuals to shift out of the liquid assets (currency and demand deposits) counted in the M1 measure of money. This phenomenon is referred to as the ''case of the missing money.'' Michael Dotsey has used the volume of electronic funds transfers as a proxy for the state of financial innovation.[22] By including this variable in the estimation of the money demand equation, Dotsey obtained a money demand function that was stable before and after the mid-1970s. Dotsey interprets this result as indicating that individuals reduced their demand for the liquid assets counted in the M1 measure of money supply in the 1970s

---

[21] Steven Goldfeld, footnote 16, p. 686. All the variables in the regression equation are expressed in natural logarithms. Their coefficients can thus be interpreted as elasticities.

[22] Michael Dotsey, ''The Use of Electronic Funds Transfers to Capture the Effect of Cash Management Practices on the Demand for Demand Deposits,'' *Journal of Finance* (December 1985): 1493–1504.

Figure 16.3   The Velocity of Money

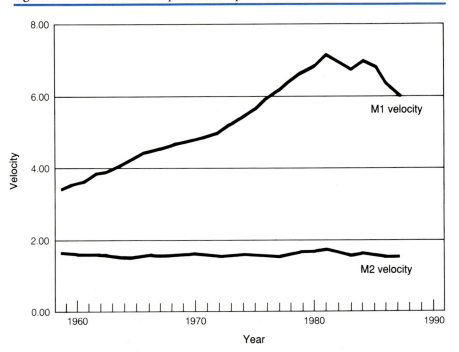

The velocity of money, which equals the ratio of nominal GNP to the money supply, fluctuates less when the broader M2 measure of the money supply is used than when the M1 measure is used.

because financial innovations (proxied by an increase in the volume of electronic funds transfers) permitted a shifting of assets into time and savings deposits, which are only included in the M2 measure of the money supply. Figure 16.3 supports this view, as velocity using the M2 measure of the money supply was fairly stable during the 1970s.

A similar story can help explain the 1980s. During that period, a reversal took place as the demand for assets counted in the M1 measure of the money supply rose and velocity computed by using the M1 measure of the money supply fell. This was caused in part by the introduction and increased use of interest-paying checkable accounts, such as the NOW and ATS accounts, that were counted in M1 and now paid interest. Individuals shifted back into these new checkable deposits from assets such as time and savings deposits, which were only included in the M2 measure of the money supply. As Figure 16.3 indicates, in the 1980s these financial innovations resulted in a fall in M1 velocity, but again M2 velocity was relatively stable.

The unstable velocity of the last few years has some potentially important policy implications. As we pointed out in Chapter 13, with an unstable velocity, a simple monetary rule involving a constant rate of growth in M1 will not be successful in achieving a steady rate of growth in nominal GNP. Nonmonetarists would thus use our recent episode of a changing M1 velocity to support their argument against following a simple monetary rule. In contrast, monetarists might argue that instead of concentrating on M1, the evidence of the 1970s and 1980s suggests that it may make more sense for the monetary authority to focus on a broader monetary aggregate such as M2 whose velocity appears to be more stable.

Alternatively, instead of focusing on a monetary aggregate that can only be controlled indirectly, one might argue that the Fed should concentrate on the rate of growth of the monetary base, something it can directly control. The end effect on M1 and M2 growth will in turn depend on individuals' preferences toward holding assets that are part of M1 or part of M2, something with which the Fed need not concern itself. In a period, like the current one, of significant changes in the banking system—changes brought on in part by deregulation—a policy of targeting the monetary base would seem to preserve the rationale behind Friedman's original monetary rule, namely that the Fed's behavior should be known and predictable in order to minimize potential destabilizing effects on the economy.

Expected Inflation and Money Demand

Notably absent from our discussion of the factors determining households' demand for money has been the expected rate of inflation. Yet a higher inflation rate makes it more costly to hold money balances since it means that an initial amount of money balances will be worth less at any time in the future because it will be able to purchase less output. Why then does the inventory model of money demand not predict that an increase in the expected inflation rate will cause households' demand for money to fall?

Recall that we have assumed that households can hold wealth in only two ways: as money balances or as holdings of financial assets. A higher inflation rate means that any nominal asset will be worth less in the future. Thus not only will it be more costly to hold money balances, it will also be more costly to hold financial assets. Since the attractiveness of money relative to financial assets is unaffected, households' optimal money management (as summarized by the variable n^*) is unaltered. Consequently, the inventory model of money demand predicts that a change in the expected rate of inflation will not *directly* affect households' desired real money holdings.

There is, however, one indirect way in which a change in the expected rate of inflation can affect money demand. In Chapter 8, we saw that an increase in the expected inflation rate causes an increase in the inflation premium incorporated into nominal interest rates, so that equilibrium interest rates rise. The increase in money interest rates in turn leads to a reduction in households' real demand for money balances.

A second way in which a change in expected inflation can alter real money demand arises if we now expand the options available to households for storing wealth to include holding inventories of commodities. During periods of high inflation, we often see households acquiring inventories of goods that hold their value with inflation, such as gold, art, rare coins, oriental rugs, silver, and real estate. These inventory holdings replace not only money holdings but also financial asset holdings denominated in money terms, such as bonds.

In extreme cases of inflation, known as hyperinflations, bond markets tend to dry up since it is often too costly for borrowers and lenders to agree to long-term contracts when inflation is very high and variable. However, individuals sometimes adapt to quite high inflation rates by linking the future payments specified in long-term contracts to price indexes. For example, indexed bonds were used in Brazil and Israel during the 1980s, countries where the rate of inflation was in triple digits. In the case of hyperinflations such as that of Bolivia in the 1980s, however, inflation is so high that even indexed bonds are impractical. As a consequence, households tend to hold a substantial part of their wealth in the form of commodity inventories instead of financial assets or money.

It is relatively simple to apply our inventory model of money demand to an analysis of money demand when households must choose between holding wealth in the form of money balances and in the form of inventories of goods. The opportunity cost of holding wealth in the form of real money balances rather than in the form of inventories of commodities is the depreciation that occurs in these real balances because of inflation. Thus the cost of holding a dollar of real money balances is simply the expected rate of inflation (as opposed to the interest rate when the alternative to holding money was holding financial assets). An increase in the expected rate of inflation will therefore reduce the demand for real money balances.

Because it is so costly to hold money balances during hyperinflationary periods, households and firms devote a greal deal of time and effort to finding ways that enable them to reduce their holdings of money balances. For example, firms begin to pay their workers more frequently. Instead of paying them monthly, firms pay workers weekly, daily, or even more frequently as occurred in Germany in the post–World War I era. As is clear from Equation 16.2, such an increase in the number of times that households are paid (N) enables them to reduce their real holdings of money.[23]

Phillip Cagan examined the demand for real money balances during seven different European hyperinflations occurring between World Wars I and II.[24] His results are consistent with our predictions. Specifically, Cagan

---

[23] In addition to the direct negative effect that an increase in N has on households' real money balances, an increase in N also causes households to reduce n^*, which has a positive effect on their real money holdings. From our result in Equation 16.8, we know that the first effect dominates the latter.

[24]Phillip Cagan, "The Monetary Dynamics of Hyperinflation" in *Studies in the Quantity Theory of Money*, ed. Milton Friedman (Chicago: University of Chicago Press, 1956). Cagan's requirement for a hyperinflation was that prices rise by at least 50 percent per month (which translates with compounding into a yearly inflation rate of almost 1300%). The seven hyperinflations he

estimated that on average during all of these hyperinflations a 10 percent increase in the expected rate of annual inflation led to a 3.9 percent reduction in the demand for real money balances.

Consumption and Money Demand: The Implications

Up to this point, we have presumed that real money demand depends on real GNP, with real GNP being used to represent the total transactions in the economy. While this view is widely accepted, some have suggested the level of consumption would be a better proxy.[25] The argument is that households' demand for money, like consumption demand, should be related to permanent income, with transitory changes in income having little effect on real money demand. However, since permanent income is not directly observable, consumption is taken as a proxy for permanent income. In support of this proposition, several studies have found that consumption or other measures of permanent income more accurately predict money demand.[26]

One interesting implication of money demand being a function of consumption is that a decrease in taxes may now be contractionary. This somewhat surprising result can be made clear if we explain it in terms of an *IS-LM* framework. Recall that the standard effect of a cut in taxes is to shift the *IS* curve to the right, as a higher disposable income leads to an increase in consumption demand at each level of income. This is shown in Figure 16.4 by the shift to the right in the *IS* curve from IS_0 to IS_1. With no other change, the result will be the standard one. In the short run at existing prices, real GNP will rise along with a higher interest rate.

But now consider what will happen if the rise in consumption demand also leads to an increase in real money demand. In this case, the *LM* curve shifts upward and to the left. To see this, note that at the original level of interest rate and income the increase in money demand leads to an excess demand for money. Equilibrium in the money market now requires a higher interest rate at each level of income as shown by the shift up in the *LM* curve in Figure 16.4 from LM_0 to LM_1. In Figure 16.4, we have presumed a shift to the left in the *LM* curve sufficiently large so that it more than offsets the shift to the right in the *IS* curve. Under these circumstances, the tax cut leads to a fall in real GNP from Y_0 to Y_1.

---

looked at were Austria, January 1921–August 1922; Germany, September 1920–July 1923; Greece, January 1943–August 1944; Hungary, July 1922–February 1924 and July 1945–February 1946; Poland, April 1922–November 1923; and Russia, December 1921–January 1924.

[25] For instance, James M. Holmes and David J. Smyth, ''The Specification of the Demand for Money and the Tax Multiplier,'' *Journal of Political Economy* (January/February, 1972): 179–185 and N. Gregory Mankiw and Lawrence H. Summers, ''Money Demand and the Effects of Fiscal Policies,'' *Journal of Money, Credit, and Banking* (November 1986): 415–429.

[26] These studies include those cited in the preceding footnote as well as John P. Judd and John L. Scadding, ''The Search for a Stable Money Demand Function,'' *Journal of Economic Literature* (September 1982): 993–1023.

Figure 16.4   Effects of a Tax Cut When Money Demand Depends on Consumption

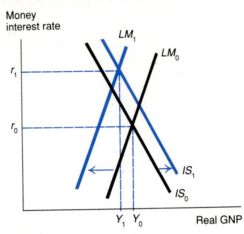

With a cut in taxes, consumption increases and the *IS* curve shifts to the right from IS_0 to IS_1. Assuming money demand depends directly on consumption, the cut in taxes and resulting higher consumption leads to increased money demand. In order to maintain equilibrium in the money market, the interest rate must increase at each level of output. This is shown by the shift to the left in the *LM* curve from LM_0 to LM_1. We have depicted the case where the shift to the left in the *LM* curve exceeds the shift to the right in the *IS* curve, so that the tax cut leads to a fall in real GNP from Y_0 to Y_1.

One case in which this unexpected result may have, in fact, occurred is the 1981 tax cut. As Mankiw and Summers report, "The increase in the unemployment rate from 7.5 percent in January 1981 to 10.8 percent in December 1982 does not suggest a large stimulative effect of tax cuts." In addition, Mankiw and Summers find evidence that the tax cut affected velocity as predicted. (Note that if a tax cut leads to a lower output, a lower level of velocity will result.) As they report, "M1 velocity declined by 1.7 percent between the fourth quarter of 1981 and the fourth quarter of 1982."[27] Naturally, as we have seen, the major deregulation of the depository institutions during this time, as well as the possible effect of restrictive monetary policy, also helps to explain this decline in velocity.

To the Point

PROPERTIES OF THE MONEY DEMAND FUNCTION

- An increase in the price level results in an equiproportionate increase in the demand for nominal money balances.

---

[27] Mankiw and Summers (p. 428), Footnote 25.

- An increase in the real cost of converting financial assets into money causes the quantity of money demanded to increase. An increase in the interest rate causes the quantity of money demanded to fall.

- An increase in real income results in an increase in the amount of money balances demanded.

- The more uncertain that households are regarding the timing and the size of their income receipts and payments, the greater is the demand for money.

- If the options available to households for storing wealth are expanded to include holding inventories of commodities, then higher expected inflation can be shown to reduce money demand as households shift from money holdings to holdings of real assets.

16.3 THE SUPPLY OF MONEY: A FURTHER ANALYSIS OF THE MONEY MULTIPLIER

In Chapter 5, we saw that a $1 increase in the stock of high-powered money sets off a deposit creation process, thereby leading to a greater than $1 increase in the money supply. We termed this increase in the money supply that results from a $1 increase in the monetary base the money multiplier. After making a couple of simplifying assumptions, we were able to solve for the multiplier. In fact, we showed that if households do not change their holdings of currency and depository institutions do not change their holdings of excess reserves, then the money multiplier is equal to the reciprocal of the required reserve ratio. In this section, we show how we can solve for the multiplier under more general conditions.

Open Market Purchases, Currency Holdings, and Excess Reserves

To see the effect that currency holdings by households (or firms) and excess reserve holdings by depository institutions have on the money multiplier, we will return to the example in Chapter 5 that we used to illustrate the deposit creation process. Recall that we assumed that the Federal Reserve bought $10 worth of government bonds from a bond dealer. For variety, we will now assume that the purchase of government bonds by the Fed is from Bank A instead of the bond dealer. The result, illustrated in Table 16.1 as Step 1, is a $10 reduction in Bank A's financial asset holdings and, as seen in Chapter 5, a $10 increase in its reserve holdings. Since Bank A's deposits have not changed, Bank A's excess reserves have increased by $10.

The effects of loaning this money to firm XYZ, which wants $10 in order to purchase a punch press, are shown as Step 2 in Table 16.2. Bank A's deposits increase by $10, as do its financial asset holdings.

Table 16.1   **The Deposit Creation Process: Step 1**

	Assets		Liabilities	
Federal Reserve	Financial assets (bond purchase from Bank A)	+10	Reserves of depository institutions	+10

	Assets		Liabilities	
Bank A	Reserves	+10		
	Financial assets (bond sale to Fed)	−10		

Table 16.2   **The Deposit Creation Process: Step 2**

	Assets		Liabilities	
Bank A	Financial assets (loan to XYZ)	+10	Deposits (XYZ's deposit)	+10

Firm XYZ borrows the $10 so that it can purchase a machine, which it pays for by writing a check. In Chapter 5 we had assumed that the seller, Bodine's Machines, deposited the entire amount of the check in its account at Bank B. Bank B then credited Bodine's account and sent the check to the Fed; the Fed credited $10 to Bank B's reserve account and subtracted $10 from Bank A's reserve account.

Now let us modify our analysis by assuming that Bodine does not want to hold all of its money in the form of deposits, but instead wants to hold some in the form of currency. Specifically, let us assume that Bodine's desired currency-to-deposit ratio is .25. That is, Bodine wants to hold 0.25 dollars in currency for every dollar that it holds in the form of deposits. Thus instead of depositing the entire $10 check at Bank B, Bodine will only deposit $8 and will keep $2 in the form of increased currency holdings. Of course, Bank B still sends the check to the Fed, which still clears it by crediting $10 to Bank B's reserve account and subtracting $10 from Bank A's account. These effects are summarized in Step 3 of Table 16.3.

In Step 3, deposits at Bank B increase by $8 instead of $10 since Bodine converts part of its check into increased currency holdings of $2. This $2 increase in currency holdings means there is a $2 reduction in depository institutions' reserves. In giving Bodine $2 in currency, Bank B has to draw down on its vault cash, which is part of its reserve holdings. Thus total

Table 16.3   **The Deposit Creation Process: Step 3**

	Assets		Liabilities	
Bank A	Reserves (transferred to Bank B)	−10	Deposits (reduction in XYZ's deposit B)	−10

	Assets		Liabilities	
Bank B	Reserves (transfer from Bank A minus $2 reduction in vault cash)	+8	Deposits (Bodine's deposit)	+8

	Assets		Liabilities	
Federal Reserve			Reserves of depository institutions	−2
			Currency held by households	+2

reserves in the bank increase by only $8. Of the initial $10 increase in depository institutions' reserves stemming from the Fed's original open market purchase, $2 has leaked out of the private banking system into increased household currency holdings.

Assuming as before that the required reserve ratio is .10, Bank B's required reserves have now increased by $.80—the $8 increase in deposits multiplied by .10, the required reserve ratio. Bank B therefore has excess reserves of $7.20, which it is free to loan out if it so desires. In our earlier analysis, we assumed that depository institutions chose not to hold any additional excess reserves. There are times, however, when depository institutions will choose to hold on to some extra excess reserves. Suppose, therefore, that Bank B's desired excess reserve to deposit ratio is .02. Then in addition to the $.80 increase in reserves that it is required to hold, Bank B will also want to hold an extra $.16 as excess reserves (.02 × $8). Consequently, of its initial increase in excess reserves of $7.20, Bank B will only choose to loan out $7.04. Since Bank B's purchase of financial assets is financed by the creation of deposits, this results in a $7.04 increase in the money supply. This is shown as Step 4 in Table 16.4.

As before, the deposit creation process will continue until no depository institution has excess reserves that it wants to loan out. Assuming that all households have a desired currency to deposit ratio of .25 and that all depository institutions have a desired excess reserve to deposit ratio of .02,

Table 16.4   The Deposit Creation Process: Step 4

	Assets		Liabilities	
Bank B	Financial assets	+7.04	Deposits	+7.04

Table 16.5   The Deposit Creation Process: Final Outcome

	Assets		Liabilities	
Combined private depository institutions	Reserves Financial assets	+$3.24 23.76	Deposits	+$27.02

	Assets		Liabilities	
Federal Reserve	Financial assets	+$10	Reserves of depository institutions	+$3.24
			Currency held by households	+6.76

the total effects on both the combined balance sheets of depository institutions and the balance sheet of the Federal Reserve is shown as Step 5 in Table 16.5.

When the deposit creation process is complete, deposits in the banking system will have increased by $27.02 and currency in the hands of households will have increased by $6.67. We will show below how to obtain these results, but for now let us simply verify them. Note first of all that depository institutions' required reserves have increased by $2.70—the $27.02 increase in deposits multiplied by the required reserve ratio of .10. Actual reserves have, however, increased by $3.24, the initial $10 Fed purchase of bonds minus the $6.76 increase in households' currency holdings. Depository institutions' excess reserves have thus increased by $.54—the $3.24 increase in actual reserves minus the $2.70 increase in required reserves. Depository institutions are just content to hold these additional excess reserves since their deposits have increased by $27.02 and their desired excess reserve to deposit ratio is .02 (i.e., $.54 = .02 × $27.02).

Since deposits have increased by $27.02 and currency holdings have increased by $6.76, the total increase in the money supply is $33.78. The money multiplier is therefore 3.378, which is smaller than the multiplier of 10 that we obtained when households did not increase their currency holdings and depository institutions did increase their holdings of excess reserves.

Below we show how we can derive a general formula for the money multiplier that takes into account possible currency holdings by households and excess reserve holdings by depository institutions.

An Expanded Analysis of the Money Multiplier

As noted above, the money multiplier tells us the increase in the money supply (M^s) that results from a $1 increase in the monetary base, or high-powered money, (H). In order to derive this multiplier in the more general context in which households hold currency and depository institutions hold excess reserves, suppose that the monetary base changes by ΔH dollars (as the result, for example, of an open market operation by the Fed). As we have seen, this will set off a process of financial asset purchases and deposit creation until deposits in the banking system have risen sufficiently that depository institutions are just content to hold their additional reserve holdings.

The first step in deriving the money multiplier is to note that the eventual increase in depository institutions' excess reserve holdings is simply the difference between the increase in actual reserve holdings minus the increase in required reserve holdings, or

$$\Delta(\text{excess reserves}) = \Delta(\text{reserves}) - \Delta(\text{required reserves}) \quad \textbf{(16.11)}$$

Next note that increases in the monetary base can take only two forms: increases in depository institutions' reserve holdings and increases in households' currency holdings. That is,

$$\Delta H = \Delta(\text{reserves}) + \Delta(\text{currency}) \quad \textbf{(16.12)}$$

From Equation 16.12, we see that the eventual increase in depository institutions' reserve holdings is simply the increase in the monetary base minus the increase in households' currency holdings. In other words, $\Delta(\text{reserves}) = \Delta H - \Delta(\text{currency})$. Substituting this result into Equation 16.11, we obtain

$$\Delta(\text{excess reserves}) = \Delta H - \Delta(\text{currency}) - \Delta(\text{required reserves}) \quad \textbf{(16.13)}$$

The change in depository institutions' required reserves is simply the change in deposits multiplied by the required reserve ratio. Thus letting rr denote the required reserve ratio (as we did in Chapter 5) and letting ΔD denote the change in deposits,

$$\Delta(\text{required reserves}) = rr \cdot \Delta D \quad \textbf{(16.14)}$$

Similarly, letting cd denote households' currency to deposit ratio,

$$\Delta(\text{currency}) = cd \cdot \Delta D \quad \textbf{(16.15)}$$

Substituting Equations 16.14 and 16.15 into Equation 16.13 then yields

$$\Delta(\text{excess reserves}) = \Delta H - cd \cdot \Delta D - rr \cdot \Delta D \quad \textbf{(16.16)}$$

The deposit creation process stops when depository institutions are just content to hold their increased excess reserve holdings. Thus if we let er

denote depository institutions' desired ratio of excess reserve to deposits, the deposit creation continues until

$$er \cdot \Delta D = \Delta(\text{excess reserves}) \qquad \textbf{(16.17)}$$

Substituting Equation 16.17 into Equation 16.16, we see that the deposit creation process comes to a halt when

$$er \cdot \Delta D = \Delta H - cd \cdot \Delta D - rr \cdot \Delta D \qquad \textbf{(16.18)}$$

Finally, using Equation 16.18 to solve for the change in deposits, ΔD, we find that

$$\Delta D = [1/(er + rr + cd)]\Delta H \qquad \textbf{(16.19)}$$

Having found the eventual change in deposits resulting from the change in the monetary base of the amount ΔH, it is now an easy matter to find the changes in currency holdings and the money supply. Since households' currency-to-deposit ratio is cd, the increase in currency is simply cd multiplied by the increase in deposits. That is, substituting Equation 16.19 into Equation 16.15 gives us

$$\Delta(\text{currency}) = [cd/(er + rr + cd)] \cdot \Delta H \qquad \textbf{(16.20)}$$

Since the increase in the money supply is simply the increase in deposits plus the increase in currency, we have

$$\Delta M^s = \Delta(\text{currency}) + \Delta D$$
$$= [cd/(er + rr + cd)] \cdot \Delta H + [1/(er + rr + cd)]\Delta H \qquad \textbf{(16.21)}$$
$$= [(cd + 1)/(er + rr + cd)] \cdot \Delta H$$

Recalling that money multiplier is the increase in the money supply per dollar change in the monetary base, we see from Equation 16.21 that the money multiplier is given by

$$\Delta M^s/\Delta H = (cd + 1)/(er + rr + cd) \qquad \textbf{(16.22)}$$

This result is consistent with our example above in which the currency-to-deposit ratio was .25, the required reserve ratio was .10, depository institutions' desired excess reserve ratio was .02, and the money multiplier turned out to be 3.378.

In interpreting Equation 16.22, note that the money multiplier must be greater than one since the ratio of depository institutions' reserves to deposits ($er + rr$) is less than one. Note also that, as expected, increases in either the required reserve ratio (rr) or depository institutions' desired excess reserve ratio (er) lead to a reduction in the money multiplier.

In addition, an increased currency-to-deposit ratio on the part of households (cd) also leads to a lower money multiplier since it means that there will be increased leakages of the monetary base out of the banking system's reserves into currency. For instance, in our example if cd rises from .25 to

.3, the money multiplier will fall from 3.38 to 3.10 (that is, from 1.25/(.02 + .1 + .25) to 1.3/(.02 + .1 + .3).[28]

16.4 THE SUPPLY OF MONEY: CHANGES IN THE MONEY SUPPLY WHEN THE MONETARY BASE IS CONSTANT

We have just shown that every $1 change in the monetary base gives rise to a change in the money supply of $(cd + 1)/(er + rr + cd)$ dollars. This means, of course, that given a monetary base or high-powered money of H, the money supply M^s is given by

$$M^s = [(cd + 1)/(er + rr + cd)] \cdot H^{[29]} \qquad (16.23)$$

From this equation we see that the money supply is determined by the monetary base (H), households' average currency-to-deposit ratio (cd), the required reserve-to-deposit ratio (rr), and the average excess reserve-to-deposit ratio (er). In this section, we examine the behavior of the currency-to-deposit and excess reserve ratios over time and consider the consequent effects on the supply of money.

The Experience During the Great Depression

Most changes in the money supply are caused by changes in the monetary base. There have been certain occasions, however, when changes in currency-to-deposit and reserve-to-deposit ratios have led to significant changes in the money supply, the most notable the Depression.

As we discussed earlier, depository institutions play a crucial role as financial intermediaries, transforming the financial assets issued by firms and government into more liquid assets—deposits—that households find appropriate

---

[28] To show formally that an increase in the currency-to-deposit ratio (cd) causes the money multiplier to fall, differentiate the money multiplier with respect to cd to obtain $(er + rr - 1)/(er + rr + cd)^2$. This expression is negative since $er + rr$ is less than 1, as noted in the text.

[29] Recall that when we talk about the "money supply," we are referring for the most part to M1, which consists of currency and checkable deposits. The broader measure, M2, consists of M1 plus savings accounts, small time deposits, money market funds, and mutual funds. Although the same basic considerations that affect the supply of M1 also affect the supply of M2, the analysis is more complicated for M2 since M2 consists of a number of different assets that are supplied by a variety of institutions. In determining the supply of M2 or of an even broader monetary aggregate, we would need to take into account the simultaneous demand and supply decisions of each institution and of the public with respect to the various types of financial assets. This type of "general equilibrium analysis" of money supply determination may be found in Anthony Santomero and Jeremy Siegel, "A General Equilibrium Money and Banking Paradigm," *Journal of Finance* (May 1982) Vol. 37, pp. 357–371.

for their needs. This financial intermediation is made possible by the existence of economies of scale in lending and borrowing.

On the lending side, the sheer size of the depository institution's portfolio allows it to reduce risk through diversification. On the borrowing side, only a small fraction of depositors will generally ever want to withdraw their deposits at any one time. Furthermore, for a large number of depositors, this fraction is usually quite predictable. Thus depository institutions can hold portfolios that are relatively illiquid and still be able to satisfy sudden demands for cash on the part of individual depositors.[30]

Of course, a depository institution will run into trouble if its customers become concerned about its ability to convert deposits into currency. Such concern will result in a "run on the bank" as customers rush to withdraw their deposits while they still can. However, since the bulk of its portfolio is in the form of relatively illiquid financial assets, the depository institution will not be able to meet the simultaneous demand for currency by a large number of depositors, even if its financial asset holdings are sound ones. Consequently, it will be forced to suspend at least temporarily, and possibly permanently, the privilege of making cash withdrawals from deposits.

Banking panics occur when there is a widespread fear on the part of the public that depository institutions will fail. From 1867 until the Depression, the most severe panics occurred in 1873, 1884, 1890, and 1893, and 1907.[31] These panics provided much of the impetus for the creation by Congress of the Federal Reserve System in 1913 as the "lender of last resort." It was hoped that this and other powers given the Fed would enable it to promote monetary stability. However, as we noted in Chapter 13, the worst banking panics in our history occurred during the years 1930 through 1933. Milton Friedman and Anna Schwartz argue that instead of making these panics less severe, the existence of the Fed made them more severe. Rather than taking corrective measures of their own, banks waited for measures by the Fed, measures which did not materialize.

Banking panics have two related, but conceptually distinct, effects on the overall money supply. First of all, the desire of households to hold a greater fraction of their money in the form of currency and less in the form of deposits translates into an increase in households' currency-to-deposit ratio. This increase in the currency-to-deposit ratio was especially significant during the Depression. In August 1929, this ratio was about .17 or 17 percent. By March 1933, it had risen to approximately 41 percent.[32] From Equation

---

[30] Recall from Chapter 3 that an asset is said to be liquid if it can be quickly converted into cash at little cost. Many of the financial assets held by depository institutions take the form of specialized loans to businesses and consumers. Such loans tend to be illiquid because they are often difficult and costly to evaluate.

[31] See Friedman and Schwartz, Footnote 14.

[32] The ratios in the text were calculated by dividing currency held by the public by demand deposits at commerical banks; the data on both currency and demand deposits were obtained from Friedman and Schwartz. Other currency deposit ratios behaved similarly. For example, the ratio of currency to demand and time deposits at commercial banks rose from an average of 9.3 percent in 1929 to 23 percent by March 1933.

16.18 we see that an increase in the currency-to-deposit ratio causes the money supply to fall. Friedman and Schwartz estimate that other things being equal, the fall in the currency-to-deposit ratio from 1929 to 1933 would have resulted in a 37 percent fall in the money supply.

The increased currency demands by households that are associated with banking panics generally affect depository institutions' desired reserve holdings. "Whenever the public has shown distrust of banks by seeking to lower the deposit-currency ratio [that is, raise the currency-deposit ratio], banks have reacted by seeking to strengthen their reserves."[33] In the terminology of our above analysis, depository institutions' desired excess reserve to deposit ratio (*er*) increases during a banking panic. In order to be able to meet potentially sudden and large cash demands by depositors, depository institutions hold a greater fraction of their assets in the form of reserves and a smaller fraction in the form of financial assets.

From August 1929 to March 1933, the ratio of commercial bank reserves to all deposits rose from about 7.6 percent to 11.9 percent.[34] According to Equation 16.18, an increase in depository institutions desired excess reserve ratio causes the money supply to fall. Friedman and Schwartz estimate that if other things are held constant, the increase in the reserve-to-deposit ratio from 1929 to 1933 would have produced a 20 percent decline in the money supply.

In Chapter 13, we discussed the important macroeconomic consequences of the banking panics from 1929 to 1933 and the resulting increases in the currency-to-deposit and reserve-to-deposit ratios. All told, the money supply fell by 35 percent from 1929 to 1933 and nominal income fell by an even larger percentage. In 1936 and 1937, as the economy was in the recovery process, the Fed doubled reserve requirements. As indicated by Equation 16.23, other things being equal, a rise in the required reserve ratio (*rr*) reduces the money supply. In fact, due to the increase in the required reserve ratio the money supply did fall during this period even though the monetary base was rising.

Federal Deposit Insurance and the Recent Behavior of the Currency-to-Deposit and Excess Reserve Ratios

The banking panics of the Great Depression stimulated a great deal of banking legislation, the most important of which was the creation of the Federal Deposit Insurance Corporation (FDIC) and the Federal Savings and Loan Insurance Corporation (FSLIC) in 1934 to insure deposits at commercial banks and savings and loan associations, respectively. Federal deposit insurance has resulted in a drastic reduction in the number of bank failures that occur. Friedman and Schwartz note two reasons for this.[35] First, "bad" banks are

---

[33] See Friedman and Schwartz (page 685), Footnote 14.

[34] The ratio of reserves to demand deposits rose from 14.3 percent to 21.4 percent.

[35] See Friedman and Schwartz (p. 440), Footnote 14.

seldom permitted to fail if they are insured. Instead, they are reorganized under new management or merged with a good bank. Second, the knowledge on the part of small depositors that they will be able to realize their deposits even if their bank should experience financial difficulties prevents the failure of one bank from producing "runs" on other banks that could result in even "sound" banks closing their doors.

Because the institution of federal deposit insurance has essentially eliminated banking panics, the currency-to-deposit ratio now exhibits much greater stability, no longer displaying drastic short-run changes such as those that occurred during the Depression. Naturally, going hand-in-hand with the more stable currency-to-deposit ratio on the part of households is a more stable desired excess reserve ratio on the part of depository institutions.

Not only have fluctuations in the excess reserve ratio become relatively minor as a result of the elimination of banking panics, but depository institutions' excess reserves have not come close to the high levels they reached in the 1930s. In fact, since 1970 depository institutions' excess reserve holdings have been especially low, averaging less than 1 percent of total reserves. (In the 1930s, the ratio of excess reserves to total reserves averaged 37 percent, in the post–World War II era, they have not exceeded 6 percent). To a large degree these low excess reserve holdings are a reflection of the very high interest rates that have prevailed in recent years as well as of an efficient federal funds market that allows banks to exchange reserves for short periods.[36] Higher interest rates on financial assets raise the cost to depository institutions of holding assets in the form of idle reserves, thereby inducing them to economize on their reserve holdings.

Before concluding the discussion in this section, it should be pointed out that the increased money supply stability brought about by federal deposit insurance has not come without some cost since the insurance provides depository institutions with an incentive to choose more risky portfolios than they otherwise would. Although the funds for the deposit insurance are obtained by assessing a small levy on the deposits of insured banks, the insurance premium (per dollar of deposits) that a depository institution pays is fixed and independent of the riskiness of its portfolio.

To prevent depository institutions from choosing portfolios that are too risky, it may therefore be necessary to place restrictions on the assets that they are allowed to hold.[37] As John Kareken notes, "When deposits are risky, depositors insist on being compensated for assuming greater risk. And by their insistence they discourage some risk-taking. When, however, deposits are risk-free, depositors do not insist on promised rates of return that vary with the riskiness of banks' balance sheet. So if the government has made depositors a solemn (and, rarer, credible) promise that whatever happens

---

[36] The interest rate on loans of reserves between banks is called the "federal funds rate."

[37] Of course, a possible alternative is for the FDIC to assess insurance premiums on the basis of its assessments of the riskiness of each bank's portfolio. However, obtaining a satisfactory measure of risk would be an extremely difficult, if not impossible, task.

they will be paid back, then there is only the government to discourage risk taking by banks."[38]

Furthermore, it may be necessary to examine depository institutions on a regular basis in order to guarantee that they are in compliance with government banking regulations. Thus the FDIC and FSLIC are empowered by law to examine insured banks and savings and loan associations in order to monitor their behavior.[39] Not only is this regulation costly, requiring "armies of examiners" according to Kareken, but it is often imperfect, as demonstrated by the case of Franklin National Bank and more recently by the large numbers of high risk loans that some banks have made to lesser-developed countries.

Franklin National Bank was formerly the twentieth largest bank in the United States, with deposits of nearly $3 billion. In the 1960s Franklin made many high risk loans. As these loans went bad, Franklin turned to bond investments. However, these bonds fell in value as interest rates rose. Hoping to make up these losses, Franklin turned its attention to the foreign exchange market, speculating heavily in both foreign currencies and foreign currency futures. This too turned out to be quite unsuccessful; during the first half of 1974 alone the bank lost $45.8 million on these transactions. Franklin canceled its second-quarter dividend in May 1974 and in the next four months deposit withdrawals exceeded $1.5 billion. The bank failed before the end of the year.

Although the Franklin National debacle appears to be an instance of regulators not scrutinizing bank activities closely enough, bank failures often occur for reasons other than mismanagement. The recent round of bank failures in the United States relates more to a change in economic activity in certain sectors than mismanagement. The number of banks losing money in 1986 rose to 2741, or approximately 20 percent of all banks.[40] By way of comparison only 4 percent of banks experienced losses in 1979. Even

---

[38] John Kareken, "Deregulating Commercial Banks: The Watchword Should Be Caution," *Federal Reserve Bank of Minneapolis Quarterly Review* (Spring-Summer 1981): 2. It may be noted that, formally, deposits are only insured up to a fixed amount, which is currently $100,000. Thus it would appear that banks have at least some creditors who would have a strong incentive to monitor their behavior. However, "in the way it has gone about its business, the FDIC has made it quite reasonable for (supposedly) uninsured creditors to be unmindful of what their banks are doing" (Kareken, p. 3). Banks are seldom permitted to "fail." Instead, the FDIC has handled most bank failures by arranging for a solvent bank to purchase the good assets of a failed bank to assume the liabilities of the failed bank as partial payment, a practice known as purchase and assumption. This, of course, means that in practice there are no "uninsured" creditors. For further discussion of this point, see Stanley C. Silverberg, "Implications of Changes in the Effective Level of Deposit Insurance Coverage," *Proceedings of a Conference on Bank Structure and Competition* (Federal Reserve Bank of Chicago, 1980).

[39] In addition, national banks are subject to examination by the Comptroller of the Currency, state banks are subject to examination by their state banking commissions, and member banks are subject to examination by the Federal Reserve System. In practice, the various agencies have worked out agreements to minimize duplicate examination.

[40] George Gregorash, Eileen Maloney, and Don Wilson, "Crosscurrents in 1986 Bank Performance," *Chicago Economic Perspectives* (May/June 1987): 23–35.

though many banks suffered losses or failed, there was wide variance across the country. For example, banks in the Kansas City and Dallas Federal Reserve districts had the poorest performance in 1986. This reflects their heavy concentration in loans in agriculture (Kansas City) and energy (Dallas). One might argue that having loan portfolios so heavily into volatile and declining areas is a form of mismanagement, but it is certainly a different situation than the case of Franklin National.

To the Point
PROPERTIES OF MONEY SUPPLY AND THE MONEY MULTIPLIER

- The supply of money is equal to the product of the money multiplier and the monetary base.
- The money multiplier is affected by households' currency holdings and depository institutions' excess reserve holdings. Increases in households' currency-to-deposit ratio and depository institutions' excess reserve ratio cause the money multiplier to fall.
- Banking panics, such as those that occurred during the Depression, cause the currency-to-deposit and excess reserve ratios to rise, resulting in a lower money multiplier and money supply if other factors are held constant.

SUMMARY

In this chapter, we have expanded on our earlier analysis of money demand and money supply. Using the "inventory model of money demand," we were able to obtain a specific form for the money demand function that related the demand for money inversely to the interest rate and directly to real brokerage costs and to real income. These predictions are consistent with available evidence.

The demand for money also depends on individuals' uncertainty concerning the state of the economy. The more uncertain that individuals are about the timing and the size of their receipts and payments, the greater will be their demand for money. It is this factor that seems to be responsible for the large increase in money demand during the Depression. From 1929 to 1933, the ratio of real money balances demanded to real GNP rose by about one third, and, equivalently, velocity fell by one third.

Two other factors that influence money demand are innovations in financial management, particularly the development of money substitutes, and changes in expected inflation. An increase in expected inflation indirectly affects money demand since higher expected inflation can lead to increased nominal interest rates, which in turn cause the demand for money to fall.

Furthermore, an increase in expected inflation will directly reduce money demand as households shift their wealth into inventories of real commodities.

The money multiplier is determined by the currency-to-deposit ratio and the excess reserve ratio. An increase in depository institutions' excess reserve ratio leads to a reduction in the money multiplier. An increase in households' currency-to-deposit ratio also leads to a lower money multiplier since it results in increased leakages of the monetary base out of the banking system's reserves into currency holdings by households. These changes in the money multiplier imply changes in the same direction in the supply of money.

Changes in the currency-to-deposit ratio and the excess reserve ratio had especially important effects during the Depression. The worst banking panics in our history occurred between 1930 and 1933; during this period both the ratio of currency to demand deposits and the ratio of excess reserves to deposits rose substantially. These two factors together were responsible for the approximately 35 percent reduction in the money supply occurring between 1929 and 1933.

The banking panics of the Great Depression led to the creation in 1934 of the Federal Deposit Insurance Corporation (FDIC) and the Federal Savings and Loan Insurance Corporation (FSLIC) to insure deposits at commercial banks and savings and loan associations, respectively. Because the institution of federal deposit insurance has essentially eliminated banking panics, the currency-to-deposit and excess reserve ratios now exhibit much greater stability.

LOOKING AHEAD

In the final chapter of this book, we take an expanded look at macroeconomics in an open economy. Up to this point, we have analyzed the foreign sector assuming flexible exchange rates. Yet, lengthy periods of time have passed when exchange rates have not been freely determined by market forces. Instead, governments have publicly intervened in foreign exchange markets to fix, or peg, exchange rates at particular levels. Even in today's world of predominately flexible exchange rates, instances occur when governments privately attempt to determine exchange rates by intervening in the foreign exchange market. We turn now to the history of such government intervention and the implications for macroeconomic analysis.

SUMMARY OF KEY EQUATIONS

Optimal number of conversions

Linear money demand function

where $k = (1/2n^*)\alpha/N$

$$n^* = (r\alpha Y/2bN)^{1/2} \qquad (16.5)$$
$$L^d = k \cdot Y \qquad (16.9)$$

Money multiplier

Money supply

$$\Delta M^s/\Delta H = (cd + 1)/(er + rr + cd) \qquad (16.22)$$

$$M^s = [(cd + 1)/(er + rr + cd)] \cdot H \qquad (16.23)$$

REVIEW QUESTIONS

1. Explain the factors involved in an individual's decision regarding how much wealth to hold in the form of money balances. What is the gain to holding more wealth in the form of money? What is the cost?

2. Suppose that Mr. Stilt's consumption expenditure is $500 every month. Suppose that he purchases consumption goods at an even rate during the month.

   (a) Suppose that Mr. Stilt initially converts exactly half of his paycheck into money and puts the rest into financial assets. Depict graphically the pattern of his money holdings during the course of the month.

   (b) What are Mr. Stilt's average monthly holdings equal to? What are his average yearly money holdings equal to?

   (c) Suppose that the interest rate rises. How will this affect Mr. Stilt's money demand decision? Illustrate the resulting effect in your diagram to (a). What happens to his average money holdings?

3. Illustrate graphically how the marginal cost and marginal gain of an additional transfer into money holdings during a period determine an individual's optimal number of conversions from financial assets into money.

   (a) Show the effect that an increase in the interest rate has in your diagram. Explain this effect.

   (b) What are some of the costs to transacting between financial assets and money? How would the development and increased availabiity of automatic teller services affect this cost? Illustrate the resulting effect of the development of automatic tellers in your diagram above. What is the consequent effect on the individual's desired money balances? Why?

4. "An increase in real income results in an increase in desired money demand, but by a less than proportionate amount." True of false? Explain.

5. What effect do you think that increased uncertainty about the future has on households' demand for money? Why? What happened to the demand for money during the Depression? Is this consistent with your answer?

6. Explain the relationship between money demand and the income velocity of money. What has happened to the income velocity of money over time? What are the reasons for this?

7. "An increase in inflation does not affect the relative gains to holding money and financial assets. It therefore will not lead to any change in households' desired money holdings." True or false? Explain.

8. Suppose that the number of times that a household is paid during the year rises. Assuming that everything else is held constant, what happens to the household's average money holdings?

   (a) We generally observe that firms pay their workers more frequently during hyperinflations. Is this result consistent with your answer?

   (b) Why do individuals continue to use money during hyperinflations?

9. Explain how the money multiplier is affected by holdings of currency by households and holdings of excess reserves by depository institutions.

10. Suppose that the household currency-to-deposit ratio is .20, the required reserve ratio is .10, and depository institutions' desired excess reserve ratio is .02.

   (a) What is the money multiplier equal to?

   (b) If the monetary base is $100 million, what will the money supply be equal to?

   (c) If households' desired currency deposit ratio rises, what will happen to the money multiplier? To the money supply? Why?

11. What is meant by the term "financial intermediary"? In what sense do depository institutions serve as financial intermediaries? Give some other examples of financial intermediaries.

12. Depository institutions generally hold only a small fraction of deposits in the form of reserves.

   (a) What do depository institutions do with the deposits they receive if they do not hold them as reserves?

   (b) Why do depository institutions generally not have to hold much of their deposits in the form of reserves.

   (c) What danger do depository institutions and their depositors run if they do not hold many of their deposits in the form of reserves? Until the creation of the FDIC, deposits at banks were not insured. Why were depositors willing to hold money in the form of deposits at banks?

13. Discuss the role played by the banking panics in the early 1930s in causing changes in the money supply and contributing to the Depression. The Federal Reserve System was created as the "lender of last resort." However, Friedman and Schwartz argue that the Federal Reserve made the banking panics of the 1930s more, not less, severe. What arguments do they give for this?

14. The FDIC and the FSLIC were created in 1934 to insure deposits at commercial banks and savings and loan associations.

(a) What effect has this had on the stability of the currency-to-deposit ratio? Why?

(b) What effect has this had on depository institutions' excess reserve holdings?

(c) Has the establishment of the FDIC and the FSLIC affected the riskiness of the portfolios that depository institutions choose? Why or why not?

15. What effect does a reduction in depository institutions' desired excess reserve ratio have on the money supply? Why? What effect will an increase in the interest rate have on depository institutions' desired excess reserve ratio? Why? Throughout the text, we have assumed that the money supply is independent of the interest rate. In light of your answers, how should we modify this assumption?

16. Up until 1980 only commercial banks that were members of the Federal Reserve System were subject to the Fed's reserve requirements. Banks with federal charters were required by law to be a member of the Federal Reserve System. Membership was optional for banks with state charters. In 1948, almost half of all state banks were members of the Federal Reserve System. By 1980, this figure had fallen substantially. Can you give an explanation for this?

17. "The demand for money is a demand for real balances." True or false? Explain.

Chapter 17

International Trade and Finance

Throughout this book, when we have analyzed an economy's adjustments to macroeconomic shocks, we have incorporated a foreign sector with flexible exchange rates. In some respects, however, our discussions of the open economy have been incomplete. For one thing, up to this point we have not examined why nations engage in trade. Yet the existence of foreign trade is one of the primary reasons there is a market for foreign exchange. Thus we begin this chapter with an example that isolates the fundamental basis for trade. Ths example shows how comparative advantage means that countries can gain from trade. These gains from trade benefit all of the countries involved.

Although up to now we have presumed flexible exchange rates, nonflexible exchange rate regimes have been prominent throughout history. The second section of the chapter examines the past use of this alternative to flexible exchange rates, focusing on the international gold standard prior to World War I and the Bretton Woods fixed exchange rate agreements of 1944 to 1973.

The third section of the chapter reviews the effects of macroeconomic demand shocks when exchange rates are flexible. This review serves to highlight the heretofore neglected role of flexible exchange rates in isolating an economy from the macroeconomic policies that its trading partners pursue. The review of flexible rates also provides a starting point for examining some recent issues in international macroeconomics, including the macroeconomic effects of government intervention in the foreign exchange market. Even though we nominally operate with a system of flexible exchange rates today, central banks at times intervene in the foreign exchange market, fixing exchange rates and stabilizing currency prices. We conclude the chapter by examining how central bank intervention can effectively fix foreign exchange rates.

17.1   COMPARATIVE ADVANTAGE AND TRADE

Between the start of the depression and 1950, international trade was stagnant. Since the early 1950s, however, trade between countries has become increasingly important to the international community. Table 17.1 presents data on the imports and exports as a percent of GNP for five key industrial countries, sometimes referred to as the Group of Five. The table highlights several interesting features of recent trade across countries. First, and this may surprise you, Japan was not the leader in exports as a fraction of GNP in 1986. Rather, Germany leads in this category, with 27 percent of total GNP produced for export compared with close to 11 percent for Japan and the United States.

A second feature highlighted by Table 17.1, and one we discussed at the outset of this book, is the large gap in 1986 between U.S. exports and imports as a percent of GNP. This large U.S. trade deficit shows up as trade surpluses for many of the U.S. trading partners, in particular for Japan and Germany. Finally, Table 17.1 documents that for the Group of Five, trade has become a more important aspect of commerce since the 1950s.

Since increased trade engenders a growing interdependence across countries, it is important to understand why trade take place between countries. As we show below, the gains from trade arise from the fact that every country is the low-cost producer of some goods, something that may surprise you. For instance, you may believe that Korea or Japan can produce every

Table 17.1   Exports and Imports as a Percent of GNP

		United States	Germany	United Kingdom	France	Japan
1950	Exports	4.3	11.4	22.3	15.6	11.4*
	Imports	4.1	12.7	22.9	14.6	10.5
1970	Exports	5.6	22.6	22.3	15.2	11.3
	Imports	5.4	20.6	21.4	14.9	10.2
1986	Exports	11.1	27.0	19.3	17.2	10.7
	Imports	14.7	21.3	22.8	17.9	6.5

* Figure is for 1955.

Source: Various issues of *International Financial Statistics*, International Monetary Fund.

good more cheaply than the United States. Suppose for purposes of illustration that in the United States five laborers can produce either five bushels of corn or one computer while in Japan the same number of workers can produce either ten bushels of corn or five computers. Because Japanese workers can produce more of either corn or computers than United States workers, is it not the case that Japan is the low-cost producer of both corn and computers? The answer is no; in fact, the United States is the low-cost producer of corn, while Japan is the low-cost producer of computers. Let's examine why.

The Concept of Comparative Advantage

Table 17.2 shows the production potentials for Japan and the United States in our hypothetical example. Note that 5 units of labor in Japan yields either 10 bushels of corn or 5 computers. Thus if Japan uses 5 units of labor to produce 5 computers, it foregoes producing 10 bushels of corn. So in real terms, the cost of producing one computer in Japan is two bushels of corn. On the other hand, 5 units of labor in the United States can produce either 5 bushels of corn or 1 computer. Thus the real cost of one computer in the United States is 5 bushels of corn, for that is what must be foregone to produce the computer. Therefore as Table 17.2 indicates, Japan is the low-cost producer of computers.

Comparative advantage: A country is said to have a comparative advantage in the production of a good if that country is the low cost producer of the good.

Let's now examine the cost of producing corn. Since in the United States 5 workers can produce either 5 bushels of corn or 1 computer, the cost of producing 1 bushel of corn is 1/5 of a computer. In contrast, Japan's cost of producing a bushel of corn is 1/2 of a computer. Therefore the United States, not Japan, is the low-cost producer of corn.

This example illustrates our earlier claim: in comparing any two countries, each country has a **comparative advantage** in the production of some goods. In our two-good example, neither country can be the low-cost producer of both goods; each has a comparative advantage in producing one of the two goods.

Table 17.2   An Example of Two Differing Production Potentials

	Corn per 5 Units of Labor (bushels)	Computers per 5 Units of Labor	Computer Cost (corn foregone)	Corn cost (computers foregone)
Japan	10	5	2 bushels of corn	1/2 of a computer
United States	5	1	5 bushels of corn	1/5 of a computer

The Gains from Specialization in Production and Trade

Since Japan has a comparative advantage in producing computers and the United States has a comparative advantage in producing corn, both countries can gain by specializing in production and trading with each other. The United States specializes in the production of corn, while Japan specializes in the production of computers. In order to consume goods other than just those it produces, the United States will export corn and import computers; Japan will export computers and import corn. The end result is that the two countries together have more of both computers and corn.

To see how specializing according to comparative advantage results in both more computers and corn, let's trace through a numerical example. Assume that prior to trade Japan and the United States each are allotting 50 workers to corn production and 50 to computer production. As Table 17.3 indicates, the result is that Japan prior to trade produces 100 bushels of corn and 50 computers, while the United States produces 50 bushels of corn and 10 computers. In sum, then, Japan and the United States produce 150 bushels of corn and 60 computers.

If Japan now follows its comparative advantage and specializes in producing computers, it could shift, say, 10 workers out of corn production into the production of computers. As Table 17.3 indicates, the result will be 10 more computers produced at a cost of 20 fewer bushels of corn. In contrast, producing according to its comparative advantage means that the United States will shift from the production of computers to the production of corn. Let's say 30 workers are shifted into corn production, so that the United States increases corn production by 30 bushels at the expense of 6 fewer computers being produced. Table 17.3 reports the new situation when each country switches more of its labor resources to the production of the good that it has a comparative advantage producing. What is critical to note is that such specialization according to each country's competitive advantage can result in more of both corn and computers being produced. In our example, total production is now 160 bushels of corn (80 in each country) and 64 computers (60 in Japan and 4 in the United States).

It should not be surprising that total output can rise when countries specialize according to their comparative advantage. What is simply occurring is that production of each good is being switched to that country where the good can be produced at the lower cost (in terms of other goods foregone). Since total output increases with specialization, trades can be devised that make individuals in both countries better off—that is provide them with more of both goods. Table 17.3 illustrates one such trade, with 8 computers exported from Japan to the United States in exchange for 24 bushels of corn exported from the United States to Japan.

There is an often heard opinion that importing "cheap foreign goods" reduces our standard of living. What is wrong with this statement? After all, we do import "cheap foreign goods." That is the nature of trade: Each country exports the goods it has a comparative advantage in producing and

Table 17.3 **The Gains from Specialization in Production and Trade**

	Japan		United States	
	Corn	Computers	Corn	Computers
Initial position prior to trade	100	50	50	10
After specialization according to comparative advantage	80	60	80	4
Hypothetical trade	24 (import)	8 (export)	24 (export)	8 (import)
After trade	104	52	56	12

imports those that can be produced at a lower cost in other countries. In our example, the United States would be importing Japanese computers that had an effective price of 3 bushels of corn (24 bushels for 8 computers or 3 bushels per computer), which is below the 5 bushel cost of domestic computers. Importing "cheap goods" does not, however, reduce our standard of living, but *raises* it. By enabling us to buy some goods abroad more cheaply than they can be produced at home, trade allows us to raise our per capita consumption of all goods. The same is true for the countries with which we trade.

Why then do individuals argue for quotas that restrict the quantity of imports, or for tariffs that impose a tax on imports? If foreign trade is beneficial, why would some people want to block or restrict it? The reason should be clear from our example; the emergence of trade means that some individuals who are employed producing goods that can be made more cheaply elsewhere will lose their jobs and have to search for alternative employment. In our example, specialization means that individuals in the United States who are initially employed producing computers will have to find alternate employment. Thus the increased trade imposes retraining and job search costs on those individuals who are displaced by foreign imports. So, not *everyone* may gain from trade, even though trade increases the total amount of goods available for consumption in the economy. Those individuals who were formerly producing goods that are now imported, often suffer an actual loss in income. Part of this loss reflects the time it takes individuals to reallocate their labor resources to other pursuits. Another part of the loss is the lower wages that displaced workers may be reemployed at, which among other things may reflect the fact that such workers lose the return to specialized training they acquired in their former jobs.

The fact that trade has occurred between countries throughout recorded history is indicative of its benefits. In early times, most exchanges across countries were conducted through barter. As trade became more complex and sophisticated, precious metals became the standard unit of exchange. This, however, introduced an element of instability into domestic economies. For with precious metals backing domestic money supplies, international trade that shifted holdings of gold and silver among countries had repercussions on domestic economies. In the next section we explore the history of international trade and finance from the gold standard at the turn of the century to the fixed exchange rates after World War II and, finally, to the current regime of flexible exchange rates.

17.2   A HISTORY OF INTERNATIONAL TRADE AND FINANCE

When discussing the open economy throughout this book, we have presumed that exchange rates are flexible. In a regime of flexible exchange rates, the prices of one currency in terms of other currencies are determined through the interaction of demand and supply in the foreign exchange markets; governments do not intervene to maintain a particular set of exchange rates. This does not mean that in a flexible exchange rate system governments never enter the foreign exchange markets. In fact, even in flexible exchange rate systems, governments buy and sell their currencies to influence exchange rates. What a flexible exchange rate system really means is that governments have no publicly announced goal of fixing exchange rates at specified levels.

Although flexible exchange rates are now common, this is a relatively recent phenomenon. It was only in 1973 that countries who were members of the International Monetary Fund (IMF) agreed to a system of flexible exchange rates. Previously, there had existed two types of international monetary regimes that involve fixed exchange rates. Prior to World War I, a gold standard was the basis for international exchange. Following the Bretton Woods meetings of 1944, a monetary regime was instituted that fixed exchange rates against the U.S. dollar. Participating nations agreed to help maintain these exchange rates in the face of international financial crises. This regime was dissolved in 1973. Let us now examine how each of these two fixed exchange rate systems worked and discuss the events that led to the system of flexible exchange rates under which the world monetary order now operates.

The International Gold Standard

Before national currencies were established, money consisted primarily of precious metals. Clam shells, stones, and other artifacts also served as money, but gold and silver dominated as "commodity" money. If an individual from England wanted to purchase an item from an individual in France, the two individuals would have worked out a price, specifying payment in some amount of gold or silver. With the introduction of national currencies came the need to establish exchange rates between various currencies. If an English merchant wanted to buy goods from a French merchant, an international banker would exchange a certain number of pounds for a certain number of francs. This established an exchange rate between the two currencies.

From the 1870s until 1914, an international gold standard served to fix exchange rates among western countries. Nations fixed a value for their money in terms of gold and stood ready to buy or sell gold at that price. This resulted in a system of fixed exchange rates among nations. For example, let's say the United States agreed to pay 1/20 of an ounce of gold per United States dollar. If France agreed to pay 1/100 of an ounce of gold per French franc, then 1/20 ounces of gold would cost five francs. Thus an exchange rate of one dollar to five francs was automatically established.

Many in the financial world, as well as advocates of nonintervention in the economy on the part of government, found the international gold standard attractive because it imposed automatic market forces to counteract alleged inflationary tendencies of governments. The noted Scottish economist and philosopher David Hume described these automatic forces in terms of the specie-flow adjustment mechanism.[1]

The Specie-Flow Adjustment Mechanism

The specie-flow adjustment mechanism describes how a trade imbalance (trade surplus or deficit) can be eliminated over time even though a gold standard exists and thus exchange rates are fixed. This adjustment process to eliminate trade imbalances depends on the link between the gold reserves held by a country and its money supply.[2] We will show how this specie-flow adjustment process works to eliminate an imbalance in the balance of payments in the two-country context of, say, Great Britain and the United States. Remember from Chapter 3 that the balance of payments indicates the net demand for a country's currency associated with the country's balance of trade and its international capital flows.[3]

Let's suppose that for some reason a deficit exists in Great Britain's balance of payments. For example, the deficit could be the result of a spurt

---

[1] Specie is the general term for gold or other metal used as money.

[2] Some economists have pointed out that the link between a country's gold reserves and its money supply may have been tenuous in some historical cases since nations under a gold standard often backed only a small fraction of their total money supply with gold. For instance, the Bank of England in the late nineteenth century kept gold in reserve that equaled only 2 to 3 percent of the money supply. In the analysis that follows we abstract from such considerations, simply accepting that under a gold standard a tie exists between a nation's gold reserves and its money supply. A more complete description of the role of the Bank of England during the gold standard period prior to World War I is contained in Michael G. Rukstad, *Macroeconomic Decision Making in the World Economy* (Chicago: Dryden Press, 1986), pp. 380–399.

[3] More precisely, we obtain the balance of payments by summing together the net balances on the current and capital accounts.

in the inflation rate in Great Britain, which raises the prices of British goods relative to U. S. goods at the established exchange rate. As we discussed in Chapter 13, because the money prices of goods in general are rising while the money price of gold is held constant, inflation under a gold standard implies a fall in the relative price of gold. One reason for a fall in the relative price of gold could be an increase in the supply of gold.

Figure 17.1 indicates the shift to the right in the supply of pounds curve from $S_{£0}$ to $S_{£1}$ that will result as British importers seek to purchase increased quantities of the now relatively cheaper U. S. goods. Simultaneously, the demand for pounds falls as U. S. importers reduce their purchases of the now relatively more expensive British goods. The figure illustrates this decreased demand by a shift to the left in the demand curve from $D_{£0}$ to $D_{£1}$.[4] The outcome is an excess supply of British pounds in the foreign exchange market of amount AB at the fixed exchange rate of $1/E_0$ dollars per pound.

In order to eliminate its balance of payments deficit, the British central bank must buy up the excess supply of pounds in the foreign exchange market with its reserve holdings of gold. In essence, therefore, Great Britain will send some of its gold reserves to the United States. Given the link between gold reserves and the money supply, the fall in Great Britain's gold reserves will cause its money supply to fall. As the exchange equation indicates, the fall in the money supply will in turn cause a reduction in Great Britain's nominal GNP. As we have seen in our previous discussions of the exchange equation, this fall in nominal GNP can take the form of a fall in prices or a fall in real GNP or both. The neoclassical model suggests that in the long run the effect will in large part be simply a fall in prices. In the short run, however, at least part of the fall in nominal output may reflect a decrease in Great Britain's real GNP.

Whether the adjustment in Great Britain's nominal GNP takes the form of a fall in prices or a fall in output, the result in the foreign exchange market is the same—an elimination of the original excess supply of pounds. A fall in British real income restricts British purchases of all goods, including foreign goods. The reduction in British imports in turn decreases the supply of pounds in the foreign exchange market. Lower prices make British products more competitive in world markets. This causes British exports and thus the demand for pounds in the foreign exchange market to increase. In addition, the lower British prices make U. S. goods less attractive to the British, so that British imports and thus the supply of pounds in the foreign exchange market fall. By raising the demand for pounds and reducing the supply, a downward adjustment in British prices thus eliminates the British balance of payments deficit, as does a fall in British real GNP.

In the United States, the inflow of British gold reserves causes changes that also help to eliminate the excess supply of pounds in the foreign exchange market. With higher gold reserves, the U.S. money supply expands and U.S.

---

[4] We first explained the effects of increased domestic inflation on the supply of and demand for the domestic currency in Chapter 8.

Figure 17.1   Intervention in Foreign Exchange Markets Under an International Gold Standard

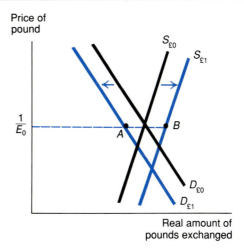

With an increase in the supply of pounds from $S_{\pounds0}$ to $S_{\pounds1}$ and a fall in the demand for pounds from $D_{\pounds0}$ to $D_{\pounds1}$, there exists an excess supply of pounds in the foreign exchange market of AB at the exchange rate $1/E_0$. The shifts in supply and demand might be due to an outburst of inflation in Great Britain, which has the effect of raising the prices of British goods relative to U.S. goods at the established exchange rate $1/E_0$. Great Britain can offset the deficit under an international gold standard by buying up AB pounds in exchange for gold reserves.

---

prices and income thus rise. Higher U.S. prices and real income increase the U.S. demand for British goods and thus raise the demand for pounds. Simultaneously, higher U.S. prices reduce the British demand for U.S. goods and lower the supply of pounds.

The process we have just described illustrates how the specie-flow adjustment mechanism automatically eliminates an initial balance of payments deficit. Inflation in Britain that leads to a British balance of payments deficit causes a flow of gold reserves out of Great Britain and into the United States. The resulting money supply changes—the British money supply falls while the U.S. money supply rises—causes changes in prices and income in the two countries that eliminate the initial balance of payments deficit.

Two key features of the specie-flow adjustment process deserve further mention. First, the adjustment process involves a reduction in the British money supply that, according to the neoclassical model, causes prices to fall, thereby partly offsetting the initial burst of inflation. Thus those who fear inflation when governments are left unchecked see an advantage to the specie-flow adjustment mechanism in that it automatically places external limits on inflation.

Second, the specie-flow adjustment process clearly illustrates how the fixed exchange rate system inherent in an international gold standard ties together the economies of various countries. An inflationary shock that raises prices in one country is transmitted to other countries. Inflation in Great Britain, via its adverse effect on Britain's balance of payments, leads to international transfers of gold (or foreign currency reserves, as under the Bretton Woods system discussed below) to other countries. Similarly, a contractionary shock that lowers prices and real income in one country is transmitted to other countries. Arguments are often made against fixed exchange rate systems for just this reason: Fixed exchange rate systems do not insulate a country from price and income fluctuations that occur elsewhere in the world; unlike the case with flexible exchange rates, such fluctuations abroad are transmitted to the home country.

At the outbreak of World War I in the summer of 1914, the international gold standard ceased to exist; gold was no longer used to settle foreign accounts. By the early 1920s, exchange rates for most currencies were determined in the market and there was thus a short period of flexible exchange rates such as that in existence today. In the mid-1920s, there was an attempt to reinstitute an international gold standard and the accompanying fixed exchange rate system. That attempt was doomed by the outbreak of the worldwide depression in the early 1930s.

As exports fell for all nations due to the worldwide depressions, a number of countries attempted to stimulate their exports by devaluations. A devaluation increases demand for exports by lowering the prices of a country's goods in foreign markets. In addition, demand for domestically produced goods is enhanced by the fact that a devaluation increases prices of imports. These attempts to stimulate employment at home through devaluation are referred to as "beggar-thy-neighbor" policies, policies that attempt to increase employment in the domestic country at the expense of other countries.

Beggar-thy-neighbor policies during the period included not only currency devaluations but also increased tariffs on imported goods and quotas. For example, the U. S. Congress enacted the Smoot-Hawley Tariff Act in 1930, which imposed an average tax on United States imports equal to almost 60 percent of their value. The typical outcome of beggar-thy-neighbor policies by one country is that other countries retaliate, and all countries end up losing. When one country devalues or imposes tariffs and quotas, others respond in kind and total trade falls. This outcome characterized the early 1930s; by 1933 total trade between countries had fallen by more than 50 percent of its level in the late 1920s.[5] The lost gains from trade contributed to and magnified the worldwide contraction of the 1930s.

As a result of the competitive devaluations and other beggar-thy-neighbor policies, the gold standard was abandoned between 1929 and 1933 by 35 countries, including the United States, the United Kingdom, and Japan.

---

[5] See Charles Kindleberger, *The World Depression* (Berkeley: University of California Press, 1973), p. 172.

Significant revisions in the international monetary arrangements were not formally instituted until after a meeting among nations in Bretton Woods, New Hampshire, in 1944.

The Bretton Woods Agreement

In 1944, an international monetary conference took place at Bretton Woods, New Hampshire, which established the International Monetary Fund (IMF) to supervise the institution of fixed exchange rates. This fixed exchange rate system was different from that under the international gold standard, however. With an international gold standard, the exchange rate between two countries is fixed because each country fixes the price of its currency in terms of gold.

Under Bretton Woods, the United States agreed to fix the price of its currency in terms of gold, while all other countries agreed to fix the price of their currencies in terms of the U.S. dollar. Furthermore, these countries did not have to honor their currencies with payments of gold upon demand; instead of holding gold they could hold reserves in the form of other currencies. Between 1944 and 1973, most nations held U.S. dollars as their primary reserve currency, with British pounds sterling the distant second.

Due to its position in 1944 as the leading economy in world trade, as well as the major holder of gold reserves, the United States assumed a unique obligation under the Bretton Woods agreement. Since the United States agreed to maintain its currency at a fixed price in terms of gold, the United States was actually the only country to support a gold standard with respect to its foreign transactions.[6] Specifically, the United States agreed to fix the price of a dollar at 1/35 of an ounce of gold (or 1 ounce of gold equalled $35), and to convert its currency freely into gold when foreign governments requested it.

Although countries agreed to fix exchange rates under the Bretton Woods agreement, they nevertheless sometimes found it necessary to make adjustments in these rates, with adjustments occurring most frequently in the exchange rates of lesser developed countries. In fact, of the 21 major industrial countries that signed the Bretton Woods agreement, all but two—the United States and Japan—had changed the par value of their currency by 1971. Twelve of the 21 countries devalued their currency more than 30 percent against the dollar. Under a fixed exchange rate regime, downward and upward adjustments in the price of a currency are not termed depreciations and appreciations of the currency but **devaluations and upward revaluations**. The demise of the fixed exchange rate system in 1973 may actually have begun in 1967, when Britain devalued the pound. Let's examine the 1967 British devaluation in order to clarify the mechanics of the fixed exchange rate system.

Devaluation and upward revaluation: In a fixed exchange rate system, a devaluation is the reduction in the supported price of a currency; an increase in the supported price is termed an upward revaluation.

---

[6] Domestically, U. S. citizens had not been able to exchange U.S. dollars for gold since 1934.

The British Experience: An Example of Devaluation Under Fixed Exchange Rates

From the time of the Bretton Woods conference to 1967, the British pound had been devalued only once, in 1949. In the 18-year period after 1949, the pound came under attack several times, but Britain always stood ready to support the price of the pound in international markets at the fixed rate of $2.80 per pound.

Balance of Payment Deficits and Currency Support. Suppose that the $2.80 price of a pound set in 1949 was an equilibrium price. Figure 17.2 depicts this equilibrium: The demand curve for pounds $D_{£0}$ intersects the supply curve for pounds $S_{£0}$ at the exchange rate of $1/E_0$ or $2.80 per pound. In Chapter 6, we discussed the forces that determine the demand for and supply of a currency. Whenever Great Britain exports more goods abroad or foreigners invest in more British financial assets, the demand for pounds increases. Whenever Great Britain imports more goods or invests in more foreign financial assets, the supply of pounds increases.

Figure 17.2 shows a shift to the right in the supply of pounds curve, which may have been caused by an increased attractiveness of foreign goods to the British. At the original exchange rate of $1/E_0$ dollars per pound (E_0 pounds per dollar) there was now an excess supply of pounds, which exerted downward pressure on the value of the pound. In order to maintain the original exchange rate $1/E_0$, Great Britain had to stand ready to buy pounds with other currencies, much as it would have to stand ready to buy back its currency with gold under a gold standard. That meant that in essence Britain had to shift the demand curve for pounds to the right to $D_{£1}$ in order to keep the currency valued at $2.80 per pound (that is, $1/E_0$).

That is exactly what Great Britain did in 1967. The British central bank used its reserve holdings of foreign currency to buy up the excess pounds in the foreign exchange market. However, in the absence of the downward adjustment in the price of the pound required to eliminate the excess supply of pounds, Great Britain experienced a persistent balance of payments deficit, which in one month (October 1967) equalled almost $300 million, or roughly 107 million pounds.

Great Britain's ability, like that of any other country, to prop up the price of its currency when the market dictated otherwise was not infinite, but limited by the extent of its reserve holdings of other currencies, primarily the dollar. As the number of foreigners presenting pounds for payment increased, British reserves declined, and the impending crisis came nearer. Eventually, the British defense of the pound had to stop, and the price of the pound had to fall. In terms of Figure 17.2, if the demand for British pounds is $D_{£0}$ in the absence of efforts by the British government to support its currency, then the price of the pound in international markets falls from $1/E_0$ to $1/E_1$.

Figure 17.2 A Fixed Exchange Rate and the Pressure to Devalue

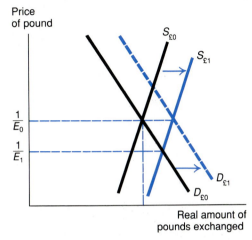

With a shift to the right in the supply of pounds curve from $S_{£0}$ to $S_{£1}$, the price of a pound falls from $1/E_0$ dollars to $1/E_1$ dollars in the absence of government intervention in the foreign exchange market. If Great Britain uses its holdings of foreign currency to purchase AB pounds each period, this effectively shifts the demand for pounds curve from $D_{£0}$ to $D_{£1}$ and will maintain a constant exchange rate.

Speculative Fever with Fixed Exchange Rates. If the price of the pound in terms of other currencies falls, then by definition the value of the other currencies rises. International currencies are like any other asset: Individuals want to hold those assets that will appreciate in value and to sell those assets that will fall in value. A currency that is about to be devalued is no different. The 1967 devaluation of the pound lowered its dollar price from $2.80 to $2.40. If individuals had known that the devaluation was about to occur, they would have sold off all their holdings of pounds. Let's illustrate why with an example. Suppose that you have 100 pounds that can be sold at the current "fixed" exchange rate of $2.80 per pound. If you sell all 100 pounds, you can take the $280 you gained from selling the pounds and after the devaluation buy the pounds back for $2.40 each. After the devaluation, you will therefore be able to buy 116.67 pounds with your $280 (280/2.40). By knowing about the impending devaluation and acting accordingly, you can increase your holdings of pounds by nearly 17 percent.

Not surprisingly, authorities about to devalue a currency strive to keep information about that devaluation a secret. Otherwise, speculators will act in a way that will increase the pressure for devaluation. In Figure 17.2, we indicated that increased attractiveness of foreign goods led the British to increase the supply of pounds from $S_{£0}$ to $S_{£1}$. If we add in speculators who are selling off British pounds hoping to turn a quick profit, the supply curve of pounds will shift even further to the right. A pound that had been overvalued before speculation will now be even more overvalued. Thus the devaluing country must not let its intentions be known. It appears that the British bungled the 1967 devaluation in this respect, however.

The Saturday Night Massacre. The British devaluation of 1967 was referred to by *The Economist* as a "botched panic-stricken flight from an overwhelmed [value]."[7] In order to understand this claim that the government had mismanaged the devaluation, we must look back to three years earlier when Prime Minister Harold Wilson of the liberal Labour party took office. The Labour party was elected largely because of the $2 billion payments deficit of the previous year of conservative government rule. Wilson had to decide whether Great Britain would accede to the pressure on the pound and devalue. Before he took office, Wilson warned the House of Commons that "devaluation would be regarded all over the world as an acknowledgement of defeat, a recognition that we are not on a springboard but a slide."[8]

Both the pressure on the pound and the efforts by the Wilson government to forestall devaluation continued over the first three years of his administration. In 1965, the government boosted taxes, curbed credit outflows, and engaged in austerity measures aimed at holding down prices to make exports more attractive to foreigners. In July 1966, a wage-price freeze was instituted, in hopes of halting the inflation that continued to erode the British export position and that contributed to its balance of trade deficit. By November 1967, however, the previous month's record trade deficit of $300 million made a devaluation seem inevitable.

Once devaluation seemed inevitable, most analysts advocated a swift devaluation, for speculation would lead the supply of pounds to increase, forcing the central bank to buy up more pounds to keep the exchange rate fixed. As *The Economist* reported, "[Once] sterling had reached an obviously untenable position, every day's delay in devaluing has meant merely further losses to reserves—and has also meant that the eventual devaluation would have to be bigger, and have to cause even more disturbance to the world monetary system."[9]

In the last two weeks before the devaluation, a round of pound selling took place that made the previous October payments deficit seem small in comparison. In an attempt to avoid retaliatory devaluations by its trading partners, Britain let the world know about its half-hearted decision to devalue the pound.[10] When the information on these consultations leaked out, the

---

[7] *The Economist*, 25 November 1967.

[8] *Time*, 24 November 1967.

[9] *The Economist*, 25 November 1967.

[10] If a devaluation is sprung on trading partners by surprise, those countries may retaliate with their own devaluations. In fact, the previous time Britain devaluated (under Clement Attlee in 1949), reducing the price of the pound from $4.03 to $2.80, 23 nations followed by devaluing their own currencies.

serious selling of the pound started. In the week before the devaluation, the British government alone purchased more than half a billion dollars worth of pounds in the foreign exchange market—nearly twice the trade deficit of the previous month.

Prime Minister Wilson came on the BBC on the last Saturday in November, 1967 (interrupting the movie *Midnight Lace* with Doris Day) to announce that Britain was devaluing the pound from $2.80 to $2.40. The repercussions were swift and varied. Some of the British press attacked Wilson because he had devalued, others because he had waited so long. The United States and many other Western powers were generally supportive. Ireland, Denmark, and Brazil all immediately devalued their own currencies to protect their trade positions against Great Britain. Over the long run, the British devaluation marked the beginning of the demise of the Bretton Woods fixed rate system.

Flexible Exchange Rates, Dirty Floats, EMS, and the Louvre Agreement

Following the British devaluation of 1967, upward revaluations and devaluations of "fixed" exchange rates became more common. For instance, in August 1969, large balance of payments deficits, due largely to speculators who viewed the French franc as overvalued, forced France to devalue the franc (against the dollar) by approximately 11 percent. Two months later, West German marks, which were viewed as undervalued, experienced an increase in demand that led to an upward revaluation of the mark against the dollar by approximately nine percent. By 1971, large U.S. balance of payments deficits led many to expect the U.S. dollar to be devalued. Exchange rates against the dollar remained fixed, however, because foreign central banks were buying up the flood of dollars in the foreign exchange markets and adding to their dollar reserves. However, central banks were becoming less willing to buy up dollars in order to keep the price of the dollar from falling.

In August 1971, President Nixon feared that foreign central banks might try to convert their nearly $35 billion of dollar reserves into gold, while the U.S. had gold reserves worth only $10 billion. Thus on a Sunday night, August 15, 1971, President Nixon made the following statement in a televised address: "I have directed Secretary Connally to suspend temporarily the convertibility of the dollar into gold or other reserve assets, except in amounts and conditions determined to be in the interest of monetary stability and in the best interests of the United States."[11] In December of the same year, finance ministers and central bank officials of the major industrial nations who met in Washington devalued the dollar against such currencies as the Japanese yen, the German mark, and the Swiss franc. The new exchange rates lasted less than 15 months, however. In February 1973, the dollar was

---

[11] From the text of President Richard M. Nixon's August 15, 1971, announcement of changes in economic policy, as made available by the White House.

devalued again, and countries such as Germany and Switzerland stopped their efforts to support the dollar. Within a month, the majority of the world's trade was among nations with floating, or flexible, exchange rates.

The current era of flexible exchange rates that began in March 1973 has not kept governments from attempting to influence exchange rates on occasion. A flexible exchange rate regime simply means that governments make no public announcements about fixing currency prices at specific levels. The term **dirty float** is often used to describe foreign exchange markets characterized by suspected government intervention. This means that even though exchange rates are supposed to be floating freely, governments buy and sell their own currencies in order to influence the value of their currency in the foreign exchange markets.

Dirty float: A foreign exchange market characterized by suspected government intervention to influence floating exchange rates.

Examples abound of government intervention in foreign exchange markets during the current period of flexible exchange rates. Vice President Walter Mondale headed a trade delegation to Japan in January 1977 in part to complain that Japanese officials were engaged in a policy of a dirty float. (In this case, it was alleged that Japan was selling yen and buying dollars in order to keep the price of the yen down, making Japanese exports less expensive in foreign markets.) C. Fred Bergsten, an economist who accompanied Mondale, is reported as saying "we knew what the Japanese were doing, and we told them to knock it off."[12] A more recent example of government intervention occurred in 1986: "For the third consecutive day, Britain's central bank intervened to support the pound, perhaps averting a sharper plunge. Paul Temperton, an economist at Merrill Lynch & Co.'s London unit, estimated the Bank of England spent between $200 million and $300 million yesterday to prop the pound."[13]

In addition to these examples of individual countries unilaterally intervening in exchange markets, there have been both public and private agreements among groups of countries to maintain exchange rates at certain levels. An example of a public agreement is the creation in 1979 of the European Monetary System (EMS). The EMS agreement required that each country's central bank maintain its currency within established ranges. Each bank was required to use its own international reserves to maintain demand for its currency and thus protect the value of its currency. Since the EMS agreement publicly fixed exchange rates, it resembles the fixed exchange rate system of Bretton Woods, albeit the exchange rates are fixed only within certain ranges and the countries involved are limited to European nations. In practice, the EMS has forced the noninflationary policy of Germany to be adopted by traditional inflationary countries such as France and Italy in order that they avoid a fall in the value of their currency against the German mark.

In addition to public agreements to maintain exchange rates among various countries, there are also private agreements. For instance, in early

---

[12] Quoted in Michael Moffitt, *The World's Money* (New York: Simon and Schuster, 1983), p. 134.

[13] *Wall Street Journal,* 26 September 1986.

1987 a group of seven key industrial nations—known as the Group of Seven or G-7, it included the United States, Japan, France, Great Britain, West Germany, Canada, and Italy—met in Paris at the Louvre. The resulting "Louvre Accord" set secret ranges over which exchange rates could fluctuate; the participating governments—the signatories to the agreement—agreed to keep the prices of currencies within these ranges through appropriate intervention in the foreign exchange markets. In essence, an agreement such as this to manage the exchange rates is an example of a dirty float among consenting countries.

We now turn to a review of the international repercussions of macroeconomic demand shocks in both the long run and short run in an open economy with flexible exchange rates. With this as our background, we then examine a number of important short-run issues so far neglected. These include (1) the short-run impact of exchange rate movements on the trade balance when exports and imports are unresponsive to price changes—the J-Curve; (2) the coordination of macroeconomic policies across countries to minimize adverse effects of monetary and fiscal policy changes on exchange rates, exports and imports; and (3) the tremendous volatility of exchange rates after the move to flexible exchange rates in 1973. We conclude the chapter by considering the effects of demand shocks when there is government intervention to manage exchange rates.

To the Point

TRADE AND EXCHANGE RATE REGIMES

- Total output can rise when countries specialize in production according to their comparative advantage and engage in trade. In this case, production of each good is carried out by that country where the good can be produced at the lowest cost (in terms of other goods foregone).

- Trade between countries involves the exchange of currencies. Until 1973, two types of international monetary regimes that involved fixed exchange rates were prevalent. Prior to World War I, a fixed exchange rate system based on a gold standard existed. Following the Bretton Woods meetings of 1944, a monetary regime was instituted that fixed exchange rates against the United States dollar.

- A system of flexible exchange rates has existed since 1973. A flexible exchange rate system simply means that governments do not intervene in the foreign exchange market to maintain exchange rates at specific, publicly announced levels.

- The current era of flexible exchange rates has not kept governments from attempting to influence exchange rates on occasion. The term dirty float is often used to describe foreign exchange markets characterized by suspected government intervention (on the demand or supply side of foreign exchange markets) to influence floating exchange rates.

17.3   A REVIEW OF MACROECONOMIC SHOCKS WITH FLEXIBLE EXCHANGE RATES

We now review some of the effects of monetary and fiscal policy changes in an open economy with flexible exchange rates. An important point that will emerge from our discussion is that demand-side shocks affecting only prices or real GNP may alter the extent of international trade but not net exports. In contrast, policy shocks or other demand-side shocks that affect the interest rate can have real effects on net export demand.

Price Changes and the Maintenance of Purchasing Power Parity

We can summarize how price changes affect exchange rates in one sentence: If we consider two countries, the country with the lower inflation rate will tend to have an exchange rate that is appreciating at a rate approximately equal to the difference between the inflation rates of the two countries. For instance, if the inflation rate in Japan equals zero, while in the U.S. it is 10 percent, then the yen will appreciate (its price in terms of U.S. dollars will rise) at a rate equal to the difference between the two inflation rates, or 10 percent, *other things being equal.* Note we are not saying that only differences in inflation rates lead to exchange rate movements, just that this is one factor that will cause exchange rates to change over time.

In Chapter 8, we referred to this pattern of changes in foreign exchange rates as *relative purchasing power parity.* Purchasing power parity means that, other things being equal, foreign exchange rates vary in order to maintain constant *relative* prices. An example will help to illustrate how flexible exchange rates lead to purchasing power parity.

Suppose that the original exchange rate between the United States and Japan is 100 yen to $1. If 10 percent inflation occurs in the United States, but there is no change in the yen price of Japanese goods, then the price of U.S. goods *relative* to Japanese goods will rise for Japanese consumers. At the original exchange rate, the Japanese will reduce their planned purchases of U.S. goods. This means there will be a reduction in the demand for dollars in the foreign exchange market. Figure 17.3 illustrates this reduction in the demand for dollars as a shift to the left in the dollar demand curve in the foreign exchange market from D_0 to D_1.

The figure also shows that inflation in the United States leads not only to a reduction in the demand for dollars in the foreign exchange market but also to an increase in the supply of dollars from S_0 to S_1. At the initial exchange rate E_0, the dollar prices of Japanese goods have not changed, while inflation in the United States has caused the dollar prices of U.S. goods to rise. As U.S. consumers seek to buy more Japanese goods at the original exchange rate, the supply of dollars in the foreign exchange market increases.

With flexible exchange rates, the foreign exchange market adjusts to higher inflation in the United States by causing the price of the U.S. dollar

Figure 17.3   **The Effect of U.S. Inflation on the Foreign Exchange Market**

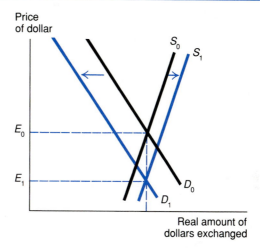

At the original exchange rate E_0 and with an inflation rate higher in the United States than in Japan, the relative prices of U.S. goods for the Japanese will rise. This lowers the demand for dollars, as shown by the shift to the left in the demand for dollars curve from D_0 to D_1. In addition, at the initial exchange rate a higher inflation rate in the United States will reduce the relative prices of Japanese goods for Americans. The shift to the right in the supply of dollars curve from S_0 to S_1 shows the resulting increase in the supply of dollars. The fall in the exchange rate from E_0 to E_1 restores equilibrium in the foreign exchange market.

to fall. Naturally, this depreciation of the dollar causes the price of the yen to increase, or appreciate. In fact, with 10 percent inflation in the United States, everything that has a dollar price increases by 10 percent, including the price of yen; Japanese goods with the same yen prices now have dollar prices that are 10 percent higher. Since U.S. goods have prices that are 10 percent higher as well, relative prices remain unchanged. At the new equilibrium exchange rate, U.S. consumers can purchase the same amount of Japanese goods as before. Similarly, Japanese consumers can purchase the same amount of U.S. goods. Although U.S. goods now have higher dollar prices, they have the same *yen* prices, since the price of a dollar has fallen by 10 percent. In this way, purchasing power parity is maintained.

The Effects of Interest Rate Changes

Unlike price changes, interest rate changes affect trade between countries in very real ways. For instance, suppose that the United States has a high interest rate due to an increase in government deficit spending. High interest rates in U.S. financial markets increase the attractiveness of U.S. assets such as treasury bills and United States corporate bonds in comparison to foreign assets. Thus rising interest rates increase the quantity of loanable funds that foreigners supply in U.S. financial markets. The higher domestic rates also reduce purchases of foreign securities by individuals in the United States.[14]

Figure 17.4 shows how these changes will affect the dollar in the foreign exchange market. The influx of capital into the U.S. financial markets will cause the demand for dollars to increase from D_0 to D_1. The reduced capital outflow of U.S. dollars to foreign financial markets will cause the supply of dollars to decrease from S_0 to S_1. As Figure 17.4 indicates, this will result in the dollar appreciating from E_0 to E_1.

The increased price of the dollar caused by the high U.S. interest rate will have two important effects. First, it will discourage foreign purchases of U.S. goods, which will cause U.S. exports to fall. Second, an appreciating dollar reduces the relative cost of foreign goods to U.S. citizens, thereby causing U.S. imports to rise. In sum then, the increased price of the dollar causes net export demand to fall.[15]

In the early 1980s, high U.S. government deficits coincided with high interest rates, and the effect was as described above. From the third quarter of 1980 to the second quarter of 1984, the dollar appreciated 40 percent against an index of other currencies. Exports fell from 10.1 percent of U.S. GNP in the third quarter of 1980 to 6.1 percent in early 1984 while imports rose from 7 percent to 12.5 percent of GNP. The balance of trade fell from a surplus of $57 billion (1982 dollars) in 1980 to a deficit of $84 billion in 1984, and there was a corresponding increase in net capital inflows.

Income Changes and Net Exports

Recall from Chapters 9 and 10 that when prices are inflexible, we can summarize the effects of macroeconomic demand shocks with the *IS–LM* graph. The *IS–LM* graph shows how a change in output demand will change both output and the interest rate. We have already seen that interest rate changes affect exchange rates and trade. As we will see in this section, income changes also affect exchange rates, imports and exports, but not net exports.

In an open economy, increases in income lead to increases not only in purchases of domestically produced output but also in purchases of foreign goods. Thus U.S. imports rise with increases in income. The increase in imports causes the supply of dollars in the foreign exchange market to increase, which Figure 17.5 shows as a shift to the right in the dollar supply curve from S_0 to S_1.

---

[14] Similar changes in international capital flows would take place if there were a fall in the foreign interest rate (r_f) or an increase in the expected rate of change in the price of the dollar (θ^e).

[15] Recall from our discussion in Chapter 8 that this effect on net export demand means that a positive aggregate demand shock causes a smaller increase in the equilibrium interest rate in the open economy than in the closed economy.

Figure 17.4   The Effect of a Rise in the U.S. Interest Rate on the Foreign Exchange Market

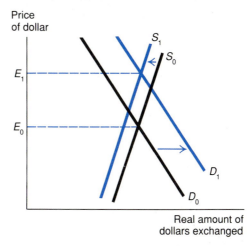

With an increase in the U.S. interest rate, U.S. capital inflows increase (as the shift to the right in the demand for dollars curve from D_0 to D_1 shows) and U.S. capital outflows fall (as the shift to the left in the supply of dollars curve from S_0 to S_1 shows). As a consequence, the dollar appreciates from E_0 to E_1. The rising price of the dollar discourages U.S. exports and encourages U.S. imports. Thus when exchange rates are flexible, high U.S. interest rates cause U.S. net exports to fall.

The figure also illustrates that the increase in the supply of dollars causes an excess supply of dollars at the initial exchange rate E_0, which causes the price of the dollar to fall to E_1. The reduced price of the dollar causes imports and thus the quantity of dollars supplied to fall. At the same time, exports and the quantity of dollars demanded rise. (These two changes are shown graphically by movements down the dollar supply and demand curves.)

At the new equilibrium, the increase in the quantity of dollars demanded exactly equals the net increase in the supply of dollars.[16] Since capital flows are unaffected, this means that the net increase in U.S. imports must exactly equal the increase in U.S. exports, so that net export demand is unaffected. Thus with flexible exchange rates our multiplier analysis remains unaffected by introducing international trade. Even though the increase in income caused by expansionary government policies leads to a depreciation of the dollar and an increase in the volume of trade among countries, the income adjustment alone does not cause *net* exports to change.

Remember, however, that when we take into account the effects of

---

[16] Note that the net increase in the supply of dollars equals the increase in import demand stemming from the initial increase in income minus the reduction in import demand caused by the fall in the price of the dollar.

Figure 17.5   The Effect of an Increase in U.S. Income on the
              Foreign Exchange Market

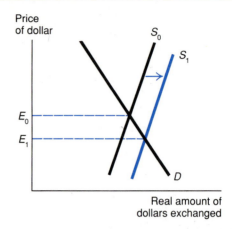

An increase in U.S. income leads to a rise in imports at existing exchange rates, and thus a shift to the right in the supply of dollars curve from S_0 to S_1. As a consequence, the dollar depreciates from E_0 to E_1. This fall in the price of the dollar serves to stimulate U.S. exports and to discourage U.S. imports. At the new foreign exchange market equilibrium, the net increase in U.S. imports accompanying the income change exactly equals the increase in U.S. exports, so that net export demand is unaffected.

interest rate changes induced by demand-side shocks, short-run net exports are affected by demand-side shocks. Furthermore, since the *IS* curve for the open economy is flatter than that for the closed economy, we know that in the short run monetary policy changes have a greater impact on real GNP in an open economy, while changes in fiscal policy have less of an effect on real GNP.

To the Point

FACTORS POTENTIALLY INFLUENCING EXCHANGE RATES AND TRADE

- Changes in price levels across countries affect exchange rates. Countries with lower rates of inflation will have their currencies appreciate. Other things being equal, the result is no change in relative prices and thus no change in exports, imports, or net exports.

- Changes in rates of return to lending abroad versus lending domestically will affect exchange rates and trade. For instance, an increase in U.S. interest rates will lead to an increase in net capital inflows and thus an appreciation of the dollar. This rising price of a dollar will result in a rise in U.S. imports, a fall in U.S. exports, and thus fall in U.S. net exports.

- Differences in rates of growth in real GNP across countries affect exchange rates and trade. For instance, an increase in U.S. real GNP relative to real GNP in foreign countries will lead to an increase in imports. The resulting depreciation of the dollar will lead to an offsetting rise in U.S. exports, so that U.S. net exports do not change.

17.4 IMPORTANT SHORT-RUN ISSUES IN INTERNATIONAL ECONOMICS

Exchange rates move quickly to clear the foreign exchange markets. So far we have assumed that the underlying real variables, in particular exports and imports, respond quickly as well to changes in the real exchange rate. This means that a depreciation leads to an improvement in the trade balance (exports minus imports) as the real dollar value of exports rises and the real dollar value of imports falls. However, the adjustment of exports and imports to relative price changes is often incomplete in the short run. One consequence, as we discuss below, is that a depreciation can actually worsen the trade balance in the short run. This is the so-called J-curve phenomenon.

A second primarily short-run issue of importance with respect to international activity is how macroeconomic policies of one country impact a second country. As we see below, macroeconomic policies that have an impact on the interest rates of the initiating country can have real impacts on other countries, as interest rate changes affect international capital flows, leading to changes in exchange rates and net export demand. Similarly, a country's policy-induced income changes can, in the short run, affect the net export demand of its trading partners when we take into account the so-called J-curve phenomenon.

Given that the policy decisions of one country can have an impact on other countries, a potential role emerges for the coordination of macroeconomic policies across countries. The topic of macroeconomic policy coordination is the third short-run issue we consider. The final issue examined is the extent to which short-term speculation in foreign exchange markets can lead to excessive fluctuations in exchange rates given flexible exchange rates.

The J-Curve

We have already noted that high U.S. interest rates, among other factors, caused the value of the dollar to appreciate by over 50 percent against an index of other currencies from 1981 to 1985. This appreciation alone increased the dollar prices of U.S. goods to foreigners by over 50 percent while reducing the dollar price of foreign goods to U.S. buyers. As one would expect, exports fell (by 7 percent) and imports rose (by 38 percent) over this period. As a consequence, by 1985 U.S. net exports were equal to − 108.2 billion (1982) dollars and the balance of trade deficit was equal to 3 percent of GNP.

Starting in the first quarter of 1985, there finally appeared to be some relief in sight as the value of the dollar began a precipitous decline. By the end of 1987, an index of the value of the dollar against the currencies of major industrial foreign countries indicated that the dollar had fallen back approximately to its 1981 level. Coincident with this fall in the dollar was a substantial increase in real exports, as one would expect since a depreciation reduces the costs of exports to foreigners. Exports, which averaged an annual rate of 367.3 billion (1982) dollars in the first two quarters of 1985, rose to an average of 370.9 billion (1982) dollars for the first two quarters of 1986 and rose again to $405.5 billion for the first two quarters of 1987. By the last quarter of 1987, exports were running at an annual rate of $453.8 billion.

Yet although the depreciation of the dollar during the 1985 to 1987 period led to an increasing level of exports, the U.S. balance of trade did not improve because there was a substantial rise in U.S. imports from 1985 to 1987 rather than the fall that would be expected with a depreciation of the dollar and consequent rising cost of imports to U.S. buyers. Real imports rose from an annual rate of 461.6 billion (1982) dollars in the first two quarters of 1985 to an annual rate of $580.1 billion for the last two quarters of 1987. Real imports grew so much that by the end of 1987 the trade deficit was not reduced from its level at the end of 1985.

The fact that the depreciation of the dollar did not immediately lead to an improvement in the balance of trade deficit highlights the potentially surprising short-run impact of a depreciation. Let's see why a depreciation in a country's currency may not immediately lead to an improvement in a country's balance of trade. In the process, we derive the **J-curve**, which describes the situation where the trade balance actually initially worsens with a currency depreciation.

J-curve: A curve that indicates a situation in which a depreciation of a country's currency can initially result in a worsening of that country's trade balance.

Suppose that the current exchange rate between the U.S. dollar and the British pound sterling is $1 = (1/2)£. At that exchange rate, suppose that we import 400 British tweed caps that cost 2£ each, or $4. We thus supply $1600 in the foreign exchange market. At the same time, let's suppose that Great Britain imports 700 bottles of fine Idaho champagne from the United States. Assuming that this champagne sells for $2 per bottle, the British will demand $1400 in the foreign exchange market to finance their purchases of champagne. With the United States supplying $1600 and Great Britain demanding $1400 at the current exchange rate, there is a $200 trade deficit.

In Figure 17.6, we have drawn short-run supply and demand curves for the dollar that capture only the demands and supplies that flow from imports and exports, respectively. In addition, as we discuss below, these supply and demand curves have unusual shapes because we assume no change in the quantities of imports and exports in response to changes in the exchange rate. The $200 excess supply of dollars is depicted in Figure 17.6 at the exchange rate (1/2)£ per dollar by the line segment AB. This

Figure 17.6   A Balance of Trade Deficit in the Foreign Exchange Market

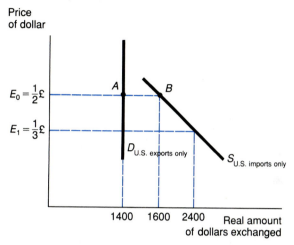

At the exchange rate of $1 = (½)£, the United States imports 400 tweed caps at 2£ per cap, thus supplying $1600 in the foreign exchange market. Great Britain purchases 700 bottles of Idaho champagne at $2 per bottle and demands $1400 in the foreign exchange market. At the initial exchange rate, there is a $200 trade deficit. The supply and demand curves for dollars are drawn under the extreme short-run case where demand elasticities of exports and imports are assumed to be zero. Note that for the supply curve, a price elasticity of demand for imports less than one (such as zero) means that the short-run supply of dollars curve has a negative slope. A depreciation of the dollar to $1 = (⅓)£ thus increases the trade deficit. This initial detrimental effect of a depreciation of the dollar on the trade balance is shown by the J-curve.

balance of trade deficit will be matched by an equal surplus on the capital account, arising from a net $200 demand for dollars by central banks (U.S. or foreign) or by private foreign investors.

Let's say that the dollar now depreciates from $(1/2)£$ per dollar to $(1/3)£$ per dollar. The depreciation of the dollar means that Idaho champagne is cheaper and we would expect the British to quaff more. However, let's take the extreme case and assume that the quantity of exports demanded is unchanged even though the cost to the British of U.S. champagne has fallen (the $2 bottle of champagne falls in price from 1£ to 2/3£). This extreme case captures the idea that the fall in the quantity of champagne demanded may not be great in the short run. Given the unchanged export demand, the quantity of dollars demanded remains unchanged at $1400. This result is shown in Figure 17.6 as a vertical demand for dollars curve.

Remember that a depreciation of the dollar necessarily means an appreciation of the pound. In our example, the pound appreciates from $2 = 1£ to $3 = 1£. The appreciation of the pound means that British tweed caps cost more and we would expect U.S. citizens to buy fewer caps. However, let's again take the extreme case in which the quantity of imports is unchanged. Because the pound has appreciated by 50 percent, so too has the dollar price of a 2£ tweed cap risen by 50 percent, from $4 to $6. If we assume that in the very short run U.S. buyers do not cut back on their purchases of tweed caps at all, then the quantity of dollars supplied on the market will *rise* when the dollar depreciates (the pound appreciates), from $1600 ($4 × 400) to $2400 ($6 × 400). This extreme case is shown in Figure 17.5 by the negatively sloped supply of dollars curve.

We have just seen a depreciation of the dollar that left the quantity of dollars demanded unchanged at $1400 but increased the quantity of dollars supplied from $1600 to $2400. In this example, a depreciation of the dollar results in a worsening of the balance of trade, as the balance of trade deficit rises from $200 to $1000, as shown in Figure 17.6. However, this is a short-run effect because we assumed little change (in our extreme example, no change) in either the quantity of imports or exports demanded. The responsiveness of quantities demanded to the price changes tends to rise over time, as individuals make more substantial changes in expenditure patterns when given time to adjust. Thus one would eventually expect a depreciation to reduce a deficit. Over time, a depreciation and resulting lower prices of exports will stimulate exports; at the same time, the higher prices of imports implied by a depreciation will lead to significant reductions in imports as individuals have time to adjust their buying patterns and domestic producers have time to gear up the production of goods that can be substituted for imports.

Figure 17.7 shows how the initial increase in the deficit caused by a depreciation lessens over time as individuals begin to shift their buying patterns in light of the changes in relative prices. This is known as the *J*-curve phenomenon due to the shape of the curve indicating the path of the trade balance over time in response to an initial depreciation of the dollar.

What we observed in the United States from 1985 to 1987 was that the depreciation of the dollar did worsen the trade deficit, as the deficit rose in 1986. As the *J*-curve predicts, however, the trade deficit did finally appear to start falling by 1988.

The question that perplexes some economists is why the extensive depreciation of the dollar in the 1985 to 1987 period did not lead to a more immediate and significant reduction in the U.S. trade deficit. The "short run" of the *J*-curve phenomenon seemed to be fairly long. It has been suggested that U.S. consumers had developed such an affinity for foreign goods that a slow change in buying patterns in response to higher prices was to be expected. Others have suggested that it takes time for U.S. producers to fill the gap in producing goods that are initially imported. Thus in the short run an increased demand for domestically produced substitute goods may result primarily in a bidding up of the prices of these domestic goods, thereby softening the negative impact of higher foreign prices on the quantity of imports demanded.

Figure 17.7 The *J*-curve Phenomenon

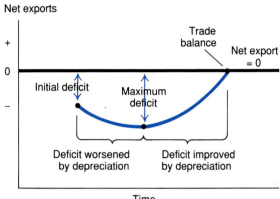

If the United States starts with an initial deficit, a depreciation of the dollar will initially increase the deficit. As time passes, demands for imports and exports become more responsive to the price changes implied by the depreciation of the dollar. Thus the trade deficit will eventually decline.

Flexible Exchange Rates: Do They Insulate the Economy from Foreign Shocks?

We have focused on the effects of domestic macroeconomic shocks in an economy with flexible exchange rates. Now let's examine the effect on the domestic economy if a second country experiences a macroeconomic shock. Do flexible exchange rates insulate an economy from foreign macroeconomic shocks? For instance, is the U.S. economy affected by a change in government spending in West Germany or a change in monetary policy in Japan? If economies are "integrated" in the sense that policy decisions in one country affect the economic activity of its trading partners, then coordination of macroeconomic policy across countries becomes important. At the same time, if flexible exchange rates insulate countries from one another's policies, then flexible exchange rates can substitute for international macroeconomic policy coordination. In fact, in light of the increasing inability of countries to coordinate their policies in the years just prior to 1973, this was one argument used to support a shift to flexible exchange rates in 1973.

As it turns out, whether flexible exchange rates insulate an economy from foreign policy shocks depends in part on the time period under consideration and in part on the nature of the foreign policy shock. For instance, take the long-run view of the neoclassical model and consider a change in one country's monetary policy. In this case, flexible exchange rates do insulate one country from such a policy change in a second country. This is the purchasing power parity argument we discussed in Chapter 8. For example, if Japan reduces the rate of growth of its money supply, the resulting lower rate of inflation in Japan will lead only to a lower exchange rate for the dollar. As a consequence, relative prices between Japan and the United States will remain the same, and there will thus be no change in U.S. exports and imports.

Note, however, that the macroeconomic policies of one country can have real effects on a second country if such policies affect international capital flows. Examples of such policies are (1) a fiscal policy change—for example, the deficit-financed reduction in taxes initiated by the Reagan administration in the 1980s or (2) a contractionary monetary policy—for example the reduced growth rate of the U.S. money supply in the late 1970s and early 1980s. Expansionary fiscal policy will lead to higher U.S. interest rates in both the short and long run. In the short run, the model with predetermined prices predicts that contractionary monetary policy will also lead to higher real interest rates.

A rise in U.S. interest rates induces Americans to shift from purchases of foreign financial assets to the now more attractive U.S. financial assets. Thus there is a reduction in the supply of dollars in the foreign exchange markets. The higher U.S. interest rate also causes U.S. capital inflows from foreigners to increase, and thus increases the demand for dollars in the foreign exchange market. The resulting appreciation of the dollar may initially raise U.S. net exports if buying patterns are unresponsive to changes in relative prices (the *J*-curve phenomenon for an appreciation). However, over time the appreciating dollar will tend to reduce U.S. net exports, as United States exports fall and United States imports rise. From the point of view of foreign countries, the expansionary U.S. fiscal policy ultimately stimulates their economies by raising net exports. At the same time, however, the higher U.S. interest rate siphons loanable funds to the United States, resulting in higher interest rates and thus reduced investment in foreign countries.

To reiterate, the macroeconomic policies of country A will not affect economic activity in country B if the policies affect only country A's prices and if exchange rates are flexible. In contrast, policy changes that alter international capital flows have an impact on net export demand and thus on real economic activity in other countries. As we have just seen, this occurs if the policy change alters the real interest rate in the country initiating the change.

There is a second less obvious route by which one country's policies can affect international capital flows and thus a second country's economic activity—namely, when one combines the short-run impact of policy changes on income with the *J*-curve phenomenon. For instance, consider a decrease in the rate of growth of the money supply in Japan that in the short run lowers real income in Japan. With lower income in Japan, Japanese demand for U.S. goods will decrease. At the initial exchange rate, the fall in the demand for dollars in the foreign exchange market that accompanies the reduction in Japanese demand for U.S. goods means that there is an excess supply of dollars. As a consequence, the dollar depreciates.

In the long run, a depreciating dollar will restore the balance between the demand for and supply of dollars by increasing net U.S. exports demand: A falling value of the dollar raises U.S. exports and thus the quantity of dollars demanded in the foreign exchange markets, while it reduces the real value of U.S. imports and thus the quantity of dollars supplied in the foreign exchange markets. At the new, lower, long run equilibrium value of the dollar, there is therefore no change in net export demand.

However, as our discussion of the *J*-curve phenomenon indicates, in the short run the depreciation of the dollar may reduce, not increase, U.S. net exports. What this means is that as the dollar depreciates, the initial gap between the quantity of dollars demanded in the foreign exchange markets associated with U.S. exports and the quantity of dollars supplied associated with U.S. imports widens. Without an offsetting increase in the demand for dollars or fall in the supply of dollars in the short run, the dollar would go into a free fall. But the fall in the dollar is typically limited by changes in international capital flows.

One source of these international capital flows is government intervention in the foreign exchange market to limit the fall in the dollar. For instance, the Japanese central bank can decide to purchase U.S. financial assets (A_{for}^d rises), thus increasing the demand for dollars in the foreign exchange markets. A second source of these offsetting international capital flows is through the actions of private speculators who anticipate that the dollar has fallen so far that it will rise over time as U.S. exports and U.S. imports eventually adjust to the change in relative prices. The anticipated future appreciation of the dollar makes U.S. dollar denominated assets more attractive; as occurs with a higher U.S. interest rate, the effect is to encourage net capital inflows ($A_{\text{for}}^d - AF_h^d$), and thus increase the demand for dollars and reduce the supply of dollars in the foreign exchange market.

Whether through government intervention or speculation, the result is that the fall in U.S. net export demand ($X^d - Z^d$) caused by lower growth in Japan is offset by an increase in U.S. net capital inflows ($A_{\text{for}}^d - AF_h^d$), so that the real demand for dollars equals the real supply of dollars at the new, presumably lower, dollar exchange rate. The fall in U.S. net export demand reduces output demand in the United States economy and leads in the short run to a fall in U.S. income. In other words, the short-run impact of Japan's contractionary policies has been transmitted or "exported" to another country.[17]

The Potential Role for International Macroeconomic Policy Coordination

In our above discussion, we detailed how the macroeconomic policies of one country can impact a second country. For instance, in the short run,

---

[17] In the long run, the depreciation of the dollar will stimulate U.S. exports and reduce U.S. imports, and U.S. net export demand will return to its original levels.

an expansionary fiscal policy that increases income and interest rates in the initiating country can raise the net exports of its trading partners, improving their trade balances and stimulating their economies. In other words, the benefits of one country's expansionary policies can be spread to other countries.

The above scenario indicates that a country initiating expansionary policies to improve its economy also stimulates the economies of its trading partners, but experiences a worsening trade balance as part of the price for doing so. This negative aspect of an expansionary policy can be avoided, however, if countries act together. For instance, in a two-country world, if both countries agree to pursue expansionary fiscal policies, then both can experience increased production and employment with no change in their trade balance. The increase in each country's income resulting from its expansionary policy will lead to higher imports. If imports rise by the same amount in both countries, then the trade balance for each (exports minus imports) will be unaffected, although total trade between the two countries will rise.

Similarly, interest rate effects can be offsetting if countries coordinate their policies. For example, if both countries pursue expansionary fiscal policies, interest rates in both countries will rise. This means that the return to lending abroad *relative to* lending domestically need not change for lenders in either country. Thus international capital flows may be unaffected if policies are coordinated.

The coordination of macroeconomic policies between countries seems a desirable route to follow. Yet coordination between countries is not that common. One reason for this is that countries tend to have different objectives. For instance, it has been said that West Germany may be more eager than the United States in seeking policies that will limit inflation. This means that West Germany may not want to join with the United States and other countries in expansionary policies if they fear possible inflationary consequences.

The second reason why coordination has not been pursued more actively is not related to differences in national goals but rather to perceptions of how the macroeconomy behaves. As we have seen already, there are a number of differing models of the macroeconomy, models that differ in their predictions concerning the impact of policy changes.[18] Policymakers in different countries appear at times to subscribe to different models of the macroeconomy. Naturally, this makes successful cooperation difficult. In point of fact, if the policymakers in the various countries base their actions on conflicting models, then depending on the realities of the economy, the end result may be a situation worse than what may have occurred had no cooperation taken place.[19]

---

[18] Some of these differences are discussed in Ralph Bryant and Dale Henderson, eds., *Empirical Macroeconomics for Interdependent Economies* (Washington D.C.: Brookings Institution, forthcoming.) The authors report on the simulated effects of some carefully specified policy changes for 12 leading econometric models of the world economy.

[19] Two papers make this point: Jeffery Frankel and Katherine Rockett, "International Macroeconomic Policy Coordination When Policy-Makers Do Not Agree on the True Model," *American Economic Review*, vol. 78 (June 1988), pp. 318–340 and Jeffery Frankel, "The Sources of

The impact that such differences in national goals or perceptions of how the macroeconomy operates can have on limiting coordinated macroeconomic policies is magnified if the benefits to coordination are not great to begin with. Although in principle coordination seems desirable, empirical estimates suggest that the likely gains are small because the effects of policy in one country on the economies in other countries tend to be small. In particular, the evidence does not find that the monetary expansions of one country have consistent real effects on trading partners, an observation not at all unexpected if one takes the neoclassical view of monetary policy effects. On the other hand, fiscal policy changes tend to have stronger cross-country effects, although still small. For instance, Stanley Fischer estimates that an increase in government spending by Europe equal to 1 percent of GNP improves the U.S. trade balance by only $5 billion in the second year after the policy change. This does not imply a substantial change in U.S. exports.[20]

Flexible Exchange Rates: Does Speculation Lead to Excessive Volatility?

When the world monetary regime shifted away from managed fixed rates to a flexible exchange rate regime in 1973, one of the objections to the change was that there would be substantial or, as some would say, "excessive" fluctuations in exchange rates. Substantial fluctuations in exchange rates introduce uncertainty with respect to future prices of traded goods and thus can reduce the total amount of international trade.

A key source of potential exchange rate fluctuations is significant changes in private international capital flows as individuals speculate on how exchange rates will change. Speculation involves individuals buying those currencies that are anticipated to appreciate and selling those currencies that are anticipated to depreciate. Such speculation in currencies can be destabilizing if it causes exchange rates to temporarily deviate from their underlying value. The deviations in the exchange rate that result from such speculation are known as **speculative bubbles**. Let's see how speculative bubbles might emerge by looking at an example of speculation in tulip bulbs. We then turn to the recent experience concerning the behavior of the dollar to see if the fears of excessive fluctuation due to speculation are well-founded.

Speculative bubble: Occurs when speculation causes the price of an asset (currency, gold, etc.) to temporarily deviate from its underlying value.

The existence of speculative bubbles is well-documented in history. In sixteenth-century Holland, the price of tulip bulbs was bid up enormously in what is now referred to as "tulipomania." Although the tulip bulbs were initially purchased for their beauty, eventually speculators bought tulip bulbs only because they believed that someone would turn around and buy that bulb from them at a higher price. This is sometimes called the "bandwagon"

Disagreement Among International Macro Models and Implications for Policy Coordination," NBER Working Paper, No. 1925 (May 1986).

[20] Stanley Fischer, "International Macroeconomic Policy Coordination," NBER, Working Paper, No. 2244 (May 1987).

effect, with rising prices leading individuals to anticipate even higher prices in the future. As with any bubble, a speculative bubble must eventually burst. Rapidly increasing prices fueled more speculation until the price of tulip bulbs reached a point vastly higher than what was justified on the basis of their "beauty value." As is typical of speculative situations, once the price of tulip bulbs started to decline, the fall was quick and precipitous.

This dramatic speculative bubble of the sixteenth century may have its counterparts today, as suggested by the rise and fall of real estate prices in Florida in the 1920s and, more recently, the rise and fall in the price of gold in the late 1970s. Many feel that the substantial variation in the value of the dollar between 1981 and 1988 is also an example of a speculative bubble, as surging net capital inflows to the United States led to the substantial appreciation of the dollar from 1981 to 1985. Let's examine the events of the 1980s to see if there is evidence of a speculative bubble.

There are a number of explanations for the appreciation of the dollar that do not rely on the "speculative bubble" approach. The relative political stability in the United States and high real interest rates made dollar-denominated financial assets an attractive investment in the early 1980s. Specifically, Jeffrey Frankel and Kenneth Froot have found that the short-term real interest rate differential between the United States and foreign countries substantially explains the dollar appreciation through 1982.[21] Proxies for the real interest rate differential on long-term instruments suggest that the dollar remained a good investment up through 1985. It thus appears that a major part of the rise in the dollar can be explained by fundamentals such as interest rate differentials instead of speculation, and thus the run up of the dollar does not have the markings of solely a speculative bubble.

According to Milton Friedman, speculative bubbles, and the resulting excessive swings in the prices of assets (be they tulip bulbs, gold, or currencies) are likely to be rare. The reason is that when the bubble bursts, and price falls, the speculators holding the asset will bear large losses. This is a powerful incentive not to speculate unless one strongly believes that the direction of change in the underlying price of the asset is in his favor. In such cases, speculation would generally not result in prices deviating wildly from trend. As Friedman observes, "People who argue that speculation is generally destabilizing seldom realize that this is largely equivalent to saying that speculators lose money, since speculation can be destabilizing in general only if speculators on the average sell when the currency is low in price and buy when it is high."[22]

Friedman's idea that speculation is not destabilizing has received some support with respect to exchange rate movements. Frankel and Froot report

---

[21] Jeffrey Frankel and Kenneth Froot, "Explaining the Demand for Dollars: International Rates of Return, and the Expectations of Chartists and Fundamentalists" (Paper delivered at Modeling Exchange Rates in Agricultural Trade Models, Lake Tahoe, California, July 23–26, 1986).

[22] Milton Friedman, "The Case for Flexible Exchange Rates," in Milton Friedman, ed., *Essays in Positive Economics* (Chicago: Chicago University Press, 1953).

that "a current increase in the spot [current] exchange rate itself generates anticipations of a future decrease . . . which should work to moderate the extent of the original increase. Speculation is stabilizing."[23] In contrast, Stephen Marris and Paul Krugman conclude that the dollar was on an irrational bubble path during the early 1980s.[24] To quote Krugman in 1985: "It appears that the market has simply not done its arithmetic, and has failed to realize that its expectations about continued dollar strength are not feasible." Krugman's claim that the dollar was overvalued turned out to be right, as the dollar subsequently plummeted. In sum, there is disagreement concerning the likelihood of speculative bubbles, and the evidence on the recent run-up and subsequent decline in the dollar is itself mixed.

To the Point

SHORT-RUN ISSUES IN INTERNATIONAL ECONOMICS

- In the short run, a depreciation in the dollar may worsen the balance of trade if exports and imports are not responsive to the depreciating dollar. If the price elasticity of demand for imports is less than one, then in the short run a depreciation of the currency means an increased supply of dollars. Without a large offsetting increase in exports (and resulting increase in the demand for dollars), the outcome will be a widening of the gap between the dollar value of imports and exports. This short-run phenomenon is referred to as the *J*-curve.

- The domestic economic policies of one country can affect other economies. Policies that affect a country's rate of inflation, interest rate, or growth in real GNP relative to other countries can affect exchange rates and trade. If countries engage in international policy coordination, such as simultaneously pursuing expansionary fiscal policy, then changes in exchange rates and the balance of trade between the countries can be avoided.

- A key potential source of exchange rate fluctuations is a significant change in private international capital flows as individuals speculate on how exchange rates will change. Speculation involves individuals buying those currencies that are anticipated to appreciate and selling those currencies that are anticipated to depreciate. Such speculation in currencies can be destabilizing if it causes exchange rates to temporarily deviate from their underlying value. Deviations in exchange rates that are the result of such speculation are known as speculative bubbles.

---

[23] Jeffrey Frankel and Kenneth Froot, "Using Survey Data to Test Standard Propositions Regarding Exchange Rate Expectations," *American Economic Review* 77 (March 1987): 151.

[24] Stephen Marris, "Deficits and the Dollar: the World Economy at Risk." *Policy Analysis in International Economics* (Washington: Institute for International Economics, 1985). Paul Krugman, "Is the Strong Dollar Sustainable" in *The U.S. Dollar—Recent Developments, Outlooks, and Policy Options* (Federal Reserve Bank of Kansas City, 1985), pp. 103–133.

17.5   SOME MACROECONOMIC IMPLICATIONS OF GOVERNMENT INTERVENTION IN FOREIGN EXCHANGE MARKETS

One often hears talk of a currency being "overvalued" or "undervalued" in the foreign exchange market. Such statements, which are often used to justify government intervention in the foreign exchange market, imply that there is some "true" value for the dollar that is better known by some outside observer or policymaker than the market. Yet sometimes, as was the case recently, the dollar may be "overvalued" or "undervalued" because central banks are secretly entering the foreign exchange markets to affect the prices of currencies.

The experience of the early 1980s indicates the importance of such intervention. The U.S. was concerned about the intervention of the Japanese central bank to hold down the price of the yen, since such an action stimulated Japanese exports and put U.S. products at a disadvantage in Japanese markets. Then AFL-CIO president George Meany articulated the fear that if such inroads into the American manufacturing base continued, we would be reduced to a nation that would shine each other's shoes for a living. The Reagan administration through a series of discussions and the threats of severe import quotas, put pressure on the Japanese to allow the yen to reach its natural level.

We will now incorporate into our macroeconomic analysis the possibility that central banks sometimes intervene in foreign exchange markets to fix exchange rates. We will consider the implications of two different interventions by a central bank in the foreign exchange markets. The first, which is what happened with Japan, occurs when the central bank enters on the supply side, selling its own currency in exchange for foreign currency. The second occurs when the central bank enters on the demand side, buying its own currency in exchange for its holdings of international reserves, such as foreign currency. The first type of intervention induces a depreciation in a country's currency; the second type typically forestalls a currency depreciation. Both actions are done in an attempt to hold exchange rates at levels different from those which the market would otherwise dictate.

Intervention to Induce a Depreciation

Let's consider the impact of an intervention by the Japanese central bank (the Bank of Japan) to reduce the price of the yen. One way for the Japanese central bank to intervene is by selling yen for dollars in the foreign exchange market, thereby increasing the supply of yen (or equivalently, increasing the demand for dollars). Figure 17.8 illustrates the effect of the Japanese central bank's intervention in the foreign exchange market for yen.

According to this figure the depreciation in the yen induced by Japan's

Figure 17.8   An Intervention in the Foreign Exchange Market

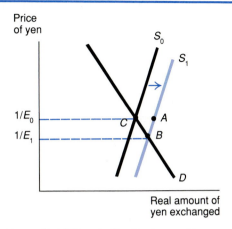

The sale of Japanese yen for dollars in the foreign exchange causes the supply of yen to rise from S_0 to S_1. As a consequence, the price of the yen falls from $1/E_0$ to $1/E_1$. This depreciation of the yen implies an appreciation of the dollar.

central bank intervention in the foreign exchange markets eventually leads to a fall in the quantity of yen supplied (from point A to point B), reflecting a decrease in Japanese imports. The depreciation also leads to a rise in the quantity of yen demanded (from point C to point B), reflecting an increase in Japanese exports. Thus the induced depreciation of the yen ultimately leads to an increase in Japan's net exports. From the point of view of the United States, this induced depreciation of the yen (appreciation of the dollar) results in a fall in net export demand, as U.S. exports to Japan fall and U.S. imports from Japan rise.

The macroeconomic effect of the fall in U.S. net exports, like other reductions in output demand, is a reduction in U.S. prices and output. The accompanying rise in Japanese net exports leads Japanese prices and output to increase, however. Thus this intervention is sometimes referred to as a "beggar thy neighbor" policy to remedy unemployement. When we discussed the British devaluation of 1967, we noted that the British let the world know of their plan before actually devaluing.[25] One of the reasons they did this was precisely because the devaluation increased British net exports at the expense of net exports of other nations because the devaluation lowered the relative price of British goods. Remember, not all of Great Britain's trading partners accepted the devaluation with equanimity—as in fact, Ireland, Den-

---

[25] Of course, the British devaluation was different from the case discussed here in that the British devaluation lowered the price of the pound to its true market value whereas in the example above, the Japanese central bank acted to push the price of the yen below its market value.

mark, and Brazil immediately devalued their own currencies in an attempt to avoid a trade deficit with Great Britain. Thus Great Britain's attempt to reduce the relative prices of its exports and raise the relative prices of its imports was countermanded by retaliatory devaluations on the part of some of its trading partners.

Intervention to Avoid a Depreciation

More common than government intervention to depreciate its currency is government intervention to avoid devaluing its currency. In October 1978, the dollar was battered in international markets because of the relentless pressure of inflation at home. As the prices of U.S. exports rose and the relative prices of imports fell, the balance of trade fell from a surplus of $9 billion in 1975 to a deficit of over $30 billion in 1977. The trade deficit led to a devaluation of the dollar in international markets. In the second half of 1977, the dollar fell by approximately 10 percent against the West German mark and Japanese yen and by almost 10 percent against the Swiss franc.

From August 1977 to January 1978, the Federal Reserve sold approximately $1.74 billion worth of foreign currency (demanded dollars in the foreign exchange market) in an attempt to forestall the inevitable depreciation of the dollar.[26] Figure 17.9 illustrates the effect of such an intervention in the foreign exchange market for the dollar. The demand for dollars curve D_1 reflects the Fed's sale of foreign currency (purchase of dollars). Without the Fed's intervention, the demand for dollars would be lower (the curve would be D_0), and the price of the dollar would be lower (E_0 instead of E_1). The Fed's intervention essentially increases the demand for dollars curve from D_0 to D_1.

Behind the Fed's demand for dollars in the foreign exchange markets is a supply of foreign currency to finance the Fed's purchases. Thus a policy of intervention by the Fed to avoid a depreciation cannot be maintained indefinitely; the Fed has a limit on foreign reserves available to sell in international markets.

Domestic Monetary Policy, Fixed Exchange Rates, and Sterilization

We now know that when a central bank intervenes to prop up its currency, it does so by selling foreign currency (buying its own currency). Let's examine how this intervention affects the monetary base and, via the money multiplier, the domestic money supply. As Table 17.4 indicates, a sale of foreign currency that leads to a reduction in the Fed's total assets must be accompanied by an equal reduction in the Fed's outstanding liabilities.

---

[26] Estimated by Michael Rukstad (*Macroeconomic Decision Making in the World Economy*, Chicago: Dryden Press, 1986).

Figure 17.9   **An Intervention in the Foreign Exchange Markets to Avoid Depreciation**

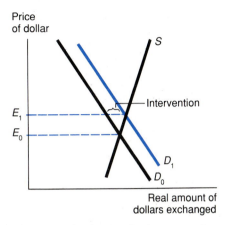

The Fed's purchase of dollars in the foreign exchange markets maintains the higher demand curve for dollars (D_1). Without such purchases, the demand for dollars curve would be D_0 and the dollar would have a lower value (E_0 instead of E_1).

In this table, we assume that the Fed intervenes in the foreign exchange markets by selling off $2 billion worth of its international reserves (foreign currency). At the same time, let's assume the Fed does not engage in open market operations, so that its holdings of financial assets remain unchanged. From the balance sheet, we thus know that the Fed's $2 billion purchase takes $2 billion of its liabilities "out of circulation." In other words, the liabilities of the Fed—bank reserves plus currency in the hands of the nonbank public—are reduced by $2 billion. Because these liabilities constitute the monetary base, the $2 billion fall in international reserves causes the monetary base to decrease by $2 billion.

Table 17.4   **The Balance Sheet of the Federal Reserve**

Assets	Liabilities	
Financial assets	Currency in hands of the nonbank public	
International reserves ($-$$2 billion)	Vault cash	Monetary base ($-$$2 billion)
	Deposits of depository institutions at Fed	

Recall from Chapter 5 that the domestic money supply equals the monetary base multiplied by the money multiplier. When the monetary base falls because of an attempt by the Fed to avoid a depreciation of the dollar, the domestic money supply also falls. In this way, the Fed's maintenance of a particular exchange rate has dictated a particular domestic monetary policy. Specifically, the Fed's actions to avoid a depreciation of the dollar have led to a restrictive monetary policy.

The consequent corrective forces are similar to those occurring under an international gold standard. The restrictive monetary policy that accompanies the loss of international reserves leads first to a reduction in income and then, over time, to lower prices. The reductions in income and prices ultimately eliminate the deficit in the balance of payments that had initially put downward pressure on the dollar. If the source of the initial balance of payments deficit is excessive monetary growth, then the attempt to maintain a fixed exchange rate will exert a countervailing force for monetary restraint.

When we examine Table 17.4, we see that the loss of international reserves associated with propping up one's currency need not result in the monetary base falling. If the Fed engages in open market operations to purchase financial assets at the same time that it is selling international reserves, then the net result can be a change in the Fed's portfolio of assets. The Fed can hold more financial assets and fewer international reserves. In a sense, these open market purchases allow the Fed to "sterilize" its intervention in the foreign exchange market leaving the monetary base, and thus the money supply, unaffected.

Sterilization: A process in which central bank intervention in foreign exchange markets is counteracted by appropriate open market operations in domestic financial markets in order to leave the money supply unchanged.

This **sterilization** process can break the link between balance of payments deficits that result in a loss of international reserves and reductions in the monetary base that restrict money supply growth. The finite amount of international reserves that a central bank holds still limits the extent to which it can intervene in the foreign exchange markets, however. Thus governments trying to avoid a depreciation have sought other methods to protect the exchange rate, methods that do not depend on the level of foreign reserves that their central bank holds.

Case Study

CENTRAL BANK INTERVENTION TO SUPPORT THE DOLLAR

Earlier we noted that the dollar appreciated in the foreign exchange markets in the early 1980s, reached its peak in the first quarter of 1985, and then began falling sharply. In an effort to lend stability to the foreign exchange markets, the finance ministers and central bank governors of the so-called Group of Seven (which includes the United States, Japan, West Germany, Great Britain, France, Italy, and Canada) met in February 1987 and agreed to the "Louvre Accord." Stating that exchange rates were about right (at that time the dollar was equal in value to 153 yen and to 1.82 marks), the officials agreed that their governments should adjust economic policies in order to maintain stable currencies.[27]

The foreign exchange market did not appear to share the finance ministers' belief that exchange rates were about right; throughout the year the private supply of dollars continued to exceed the demand. In order to limit the fall in the price of the dollar, central banks intervened heavily in the foreign exchange market. The experience is summarized in an interview with Milton Friedman, who noted that in 1985 foreigners reduced the rate at which they were buying U.S. financial assets. This reduction in capital inflows into the U.S. led to a fall in the dollar's price. However, Friedman continues on to note:

> In 1987, we had a different situation. Governments adopted the policy of trying to peg the exchange rate. I don't know what the right price of the dollar is, and no one else does either.
>
> Governments decided that they were smarter than the market. It was price-fixing. Japan and Germany are buying the dollar. But they aren't fools—not unmitigated ones, anyway. They aren't spending their own money; they're spending their citizens' money.[28]

Our previous discussion in this section showed exactly how these actions by central banks could forestall depreciations in the value of the dollar: Purchases of dollars by Japanese, German, and British central banks and sales of foreign reserves by the Fed all have the effect of shifting the demand for dollars curve in the foreign exchange market to the right. Note that the dollar purchases by foreign central banks meant that foreign citizens were still financing our trade deficit, albeit now they were financing it indirectly through the actions of their central banks (whereas earlier they had been financing the American trade deficit directly through private purchases of U.S. financial assets).

The central bank intervention in the foreign exchange market following the 1987 Louvre Accord was massive, with *The Economist* estimating that central banks had bought up $90 billion by October 1987. These dollar purchases showed up as increases in these banks' foreign reserve holdings during the year. Thus from January to November 1987, the West German central bank's foreign reserve holdings increased in value from $51.6 billion to $76.3 billion while those of the Japanese central bank increased from $42 billion to $77.6 billion.

---

[27] In September 1985, after the dollar had already started falling, the ministers from five of the G-7 countries had met in New York and announced that the dollar was overvalued. At the time of this meeting the dollar was equal in value to 240 yen and 2.84 marks, down from its February highs of 261 yen and 3.47 marks.

[28] *Wall Street Journal*, 28 December 1987.

As demonstrated by Great Britain's ill-fated attempt to prop up the pound in 1967, it is unlikely that central banks can indefinitely maintain currency prices at levels different from those dictated by the market. For example, in the case of the dollar, this would have meant that foreign central banks would have to continue buying large quantities of dollars in the foreign exchange market, something which they would eventually become unwilling to do. However, the question still remains whether central banks can intervene in foreign exchange markets so as to offset private fluctuations in the currency demands and supplies, thereby reducing volatility in the foreign exchange market. Economists are divided on this point.

For example, John Williamson of Washington's Institute for International Economics and Marcus Miller of Britain's Warwick University argue that governments should agree on mutually consistent real exchange rate targets.[29] After agreeing on the targets, central banks should use monetary policy (involving a combination of interest rates and foreign exchange intervention) to keep exchange rates within 10 percent of the targets. Such a policy it is argued will enable policymakers to reduce exchange rate instability caused by speculative runs that have little to do with underlying economic fundamentals.

Other economists doubt that central bank intervention will be successful in stabilizing foreign exchange markets. Friedman argues that central banks do not have the knowledge required for such stabilization. Others have pointed out that government intervention may well increase rather than reduce speculation in the foreign exchange markets since in forming expectations of foreign exchange rate movements individuals will have to forecast manipulative measures of government officials. With respect to the recent period of foreign exchange market instability, this very consideration led University of Rochester economist Karl Brunner to note that "Every time [Treasury Secretary] Jim Baker opens his mouth, policy changes."[30]

The debate concerning the advisability of government intervention in the foreign exchange markets notwithstanding, central banks were not able or were unwilling to prevent sharp reductions in the price of the dollar during 1987. By the end of the year, the dollar had fallen in value to 127 yen (a post–World War II record low) and to 1.63 marks. Furthermore, the volatility in the foreign exchange market appears to have been fundamentally related to the stock market crash of October 1987. One cannot fail to notice

---

[29] John Williamson and Marcus Miller, "Targets and Indicators: A Blueprint for the International Coordination of Economic Policy" (Institute for International Economics, September 1987). Our discussion here is based on a summary of the paper that appeared in The Economist, 26 September 1987.

[30] *Wall Street Journal,* 28 December 1987. Interestingly, James Hamilton argues that similar problems emerge with the gold standard: "Despite governments' legal assurances that they are committed to a gold standard, speculators never perceive the terms of gold parity as immutable." (p. 20) Hamilton provides evidence that the gold standard exacerbated rather than ameliorated the volatility of capital flows during the late 1920s and early 1930s, thereby contributing to the Depression. See James Hamilton, "Role of the International Gold Standard in Propagating the Great Depression," *Contemporary Policy Issues,* vol. 6, no. 2 (April 1988).

that the crash was immediately preceded by squabbling among U.S. Treasury Secretary James Baker and other foreign ministers about the appropriate value of the dollar and the appropriate policy actions that should be taken to achieve that value. Harvard economist Martin Feldstein, former Chairman of the President's Council of Economic advisers, has argued that portfolio investors were concerned that the Fed would engage in a restrictive monetary policy in its attempt to prop up the dollar:

> Dollar levitation through incantation and sterilized intervention is no longer feasible. For a very short while earlier this year it was possible to slow the dollar's decline by vague declarations of currency accords and by threats of currency intervention. When that failed, the central banks turned to actual massive exchange-market intervention that temporarily frightened speculators and portfolio investors.
>
> But it soon became clear that the only way to keep the dollar from falling was to raise U.S. interest rates abroad. That increase in our interest rates and the fear that the Fed would push interest rates higher whenever the dollar came under attack played a central role in triggering the stock market crash.[31]

Feldstein makes the important point that intervention in the foreign exchange market can dictate domestic monetary policy. This point received considerable attention during the foreign exchange and financial market volatility of late 1987 and early 1988. For example, in October *The Economist* noted that "some of the central banks' foreign exchange transactions are feeding through as faster money supply growth in Japan and West Germany."[32] And speculating on the future course of monetary policy in an editorial, the *Wall Street Journal* asked:"Will the Fed lower interest rates to stimulate investment? Will it boost the money supply to check unemployment? Will it raise interest rates to defend the dollar?"[33]

Trade Restrictions

A government can prevent a balance of payments deficit and staunch the outflow of international reserves by imposing costs on importers. For example, a nation experiencing a balance of payments deficit can impose taxes on imports in the form of tariffs. By making imported goods more costly, the supply of a country's currency in the foreign exchange market will fall. When the supply of a currency falls, there is upward pressure on its price.

Other trade barriers exist that restrict imports and put upward pressure on the price of a currency (i.e., offset pressures for depreciation). Japan maintains a variety of nontariff barriers against imports. These include import quotas for many agricultural products and "red tape" barriers for manufactured

---

[31] "Budget Card Tricks and Dollar Levitation," *Wall Street Journal*, 1 December 1987.

[32] *The Economist*, 9 October 1987.

[33] *Wall Street Journal*, 9 February 1988.

goods, such as more stringent inspection requirements for imported goods than for Japanese products. According to the Council of Economic Advisers, "if [these trade restrictions] were removed, the yen would depreciate and increased Japanese imports in the currently protected sectors would be offset by reduced deficits or increased surpluses elsewhere."[34]

It is not only the Japanese who set up trade barriers. As reported in *The Economist*, "According to a study reported by the World Bank . . . 21 percent of industrial-country imports from poor countries were covered by 'hard-core' nontariff barriers in 1986. . . . Hard-core nontariff barriers include devices such as outright prohibitions, quotas, voluntary export restraints." While international trade barriers had fallen from the end of World War II through the mid-1970s (with the average level of tariffs on manufactured goods being reduced from 40 percent to under 10 percent), "since the mid-1970s the trading system has seen an explosion of new kinds of protection."[35] Since 1974, the United States has adopted trade barriers against a variety of products including carbon steel, nonrubber footwear, color televisions, cars, prepared mushrooms, wood shingles, laptop computers, and semiconductors.[36] Of perhaps greater importance, at the time of this writing the Senate and the House of Representatives had just passed and President Reagan just signed a more comprehensive trade bill.[37]

Although governments often find it politically expedient to impose trade restrictions of the sort described above, economists often argue against such policies, pointing out the economic costs that they impose. As we discussed at the beginning of this chapter, trade between countries is usually mutually beneficial since it enables the trading partners to specialize their production according to their comparative advantage. A country imposing trade restrictions that lower the volume of trade thus can impose economic costs on itself as well as its trading partners.

SUMMARY

In this chapter, we have examined the reasons for and the effects of international trade, the events leading up to the recent adoption of flexible exchange rates,

---

[34] *Economic Report of the President* (February 1983), p. 56.

[35] *The Economist*, 26 September 1987.

[36] It was perhaps France who adopted the most novel trade barrier. According to the October 9, 1987 issue of *The Economist*, "France perfected the bureaucratic approach to trade restraint. It decided to curb an invasion of Japanese VCRs by instructing that all shipments should be processed at a small customs post in Poitiers—hundreds of miles inland from the ports at which they were landed. With only a little ingenuity, it was possible to spend months checking a single lorry-load of VCRs for whatever it is that customs officials check for."

[37] Also of interest is the fact that protectionism was a major plank in the platform of erstwhile presidential candidate Richard Gephardt.

and a comparison of the effects of macroeconomic shocks when exchange rates are flexible and when they are fixed by government intervention in the foreign exchange market. The role of international trade is essentially the same as that of trade within a country. It is a means by which countries can gain through specialization in the production of goods for which they are the low-cost producers.

The international gold standard is one example of a fixed exchange rate regime. A second example is the Bretton Woods agreement. An examination of the fixed rate system initiated by the Bretton Woods agreement makes clear the difficulties inherent in attempting to fix currency prices. When governments do not allow the market to determine exchange rates, imbalances in the foreign exchange market are ultimately corrected by automatic realignments in individual economies. More specifically, an imbalance of payments sets off an international transfer of reserves that can lead to changes in domestic money supplies. Such monetary changes cause price and income levels to adjust. This, in turn, leads to realignments in the demands and supplies of currency in the foreign exchange market that restore equilibrium at the fixed exchange rate. Under an international gold standard, these adjustments are accomplished automatically through the specie-flow adjustment mechanism. Other attempts to fix exchange rates, whether publicly (i.e., the Bretton Woods agreement) or surreptitiously (i.e., a dirty float), impose similar restraints on domestic monetary policy.

Flexible exchange rate regimes give countries some latitude to pursue independent macroeconomic policies. If one country chooses a faster rate of monetary growth than a second country, this will be accommodated by a depreciation of the currency of the country with the greater inflation rate. The depreciation of the currency serves to maintain constant relative prices and purchasing power parity among countries. Generally, flexible exchange rates insulate a domestic economy from macroeconomic shocks that affect prices or real GNP in other countries. Interest rate changes in a country do have real effects on that country's trading partners, however. For example, a reduction in interest rates in Germany will be accompanied by a rise in international U.S. capital inflows that will cause the dollar to appreciate, leading to a reduction in U.S. exports and an increase in U.S. imports.

KEY TERMS

Comparative advantage, 669
Devaluation and upward revaluation, 677
Dirty float, 682

J-curve, 690
Speculative bubble, 697
Sterilization, 704

REVIEW QUESTIONS

1. Consider two countries, Fredonia and El Dorado. In a given year, the countries can produce the following different combinations of goods X and Y.

Fredonia		El Dorado	
Good X	Good Y	Good X	Good Y
50	100	150	100
100	80	200	90
150	60	250	80

   (a) In terms of good Y, what is the cost to Fredonia of producing one unit of X? In terms of good X, what is the cost to Fredonia of producing one unit of Y?

   (b) In terms of good Y, what is the cost to El Dorado of producing one unit of X? In terms of good X, what is the cost to El Dorado of producing one unit of Y?

   (c) What good does El Dorado have a comparative advantage in producing? What good does Fredonia have a comparative advantage in producing?

   (d) Which good do you expect Fredonia to produce and which good do you expect El Dorado to import?

2. "The workers in foreign countries are willing to work for next to nothing. As a result, foreigners can produce everything cheaper than we can. We simply cannot compete in anything." Evaluate this statement.

3. Consider a country that is currently suffering a balance of trade deficit. As a possible solution to the deficit, it is suggested that tariffs be imposed on foreign goods that are imported.

   (a) Assuming that there are flexible exchange rates, show the effect that enacting this policy has on the foreign exchange market. What happens to the foreign exchange rate?

   (b) What happens to the volume of trade?

   (c) What happens to the country's balance of trade deficit? Does it improve? Explain your answer.

4. In the text, we claimed that trade between two countries is mutually advantageous to both.

   (a) Why is this so?

   (b) If trade is mutually advantageous, why are there so many individuals who are in favor of restricting trade?

5. How would an international gold standard establish fixed exchange rates?

6. In the text, we stated that an international gold standard introduces automatic market forces that would counter possible inflationary tendencies on the part of governments—a process known as the specie-flow adjustment mechanism. How does it work? Another feature of the international gold standard, like any fixed exchange rate regime, is that it makes the domestic economy more susceptible to disturbances in foreign economies. Why is this?

7. Suppose that the central banks of several countries agree to maintain fixed exchange rates.

   (a) If the U.S. government makes an open market purchase, what will happen to the U.S. money supply? According to the neoclassical model, what will happen to the price level?

   (b) Show the resulting effect in the foreign exchange market. At the initial exchange rate, is there an excess supply of or demand for dollars?

   (c) What can the Federal Reserve do to maintain the exchange rate at the fixed level? If it does this, what happens to the monetary base? Why? What happens to the money supply?

   (d) How does the Fed's balance sheet compare with what it was before the Fed made the initial open market purchase?

   (e) Instead of the Fed taking action to maintain the exchange rate, let's assume that foreign central banks can intervene in the exchange markets. To maintain the initial exchange rates, will these foreign banks have to buy or sell dollars? What will happen to the monetary base in their countries?

   (f) What will happen to their money supplies? What will happen to their price levels?

   (g) In light of your answers here, evaluate the following statement: "Inflationary monetary policies in one country will be exported abroad." Will your answer change if exchange rates are flexible?

8. Discuss the key features of the Bretton Woods system. Although this system required only the United States to fix its currency in terms of gold, is it true that the prices of other currencies in terms of gold were in fact fixed? Why or why not?

9. In our discussion in the text, we saw that when exchange rates are fixed at levels that individuals view as untenable, speculation will increase the pressure for exchange rate adjustments. Specifically, in the hopes of earning profits individuals will sell currencies that they expect to be devalued and purchase those that they expect to be revalued, thereby increasing the pressure for devaluation and revaluation. One of the arguments that has been advanced against a flexible exchange rate system is that speculation makes exchange rates very volatile, which in turn increases the risks of individuals engaged in foreign trade.

(a) Suppose that speculators believe that the West German mark is currently undervalued. What will they do as a consequence? What will happen to the price of the mark?

(b) Suppose that it turns out that speculators were wrong; the mark is not undervalued initially. What will happen to the price of the mark? Will speculators have earned profits or losses? Has speculation increased or decreased the volatility of the foreign exchange rate?

(c) Suppose that it turns out that the speculators were right; the mark is initially undervalued. Will the speculators have earned profits or suffered losses? Will speculation have increased or decreased volatility in the foreign exchange market? Why?

(d) Should we expect speculators who are consistently wrong to continue to operate for a lengthy period of time? Why or why not?

(e) Based on your answers above, do you think that speculation will lead to increased or decreased stability in the foreign exchange market?

10. One way that individuals can reduce the risks associated with currency conversions is to buy foreign currency in the futures market. For example, suppose that an American dealer promises to pay a German producer 20,000 marks next year for a good to be delivered to him next year. On the basis of this contract, the American dealer enters into a contract to sell the good to someone in the United States for a specified number of dollars. If the American dealer does not enter into the futures market, then his dollar profit next period will depend on whether the mark appreciates or depreciates in terms of the dollar. To eliminate this risk, he can enter into the foreign exchange market and buy 20,000 marks to be delivered to him next year. Suppose that the current price of a mark is $(1/E)_0$ dollars. Let r denote the interest rate and suppose that speculators expect the price of a mark to appreciate by ϕ percent. What will be the dollar price today of a mark to be delivered in one year? (Hint: think of how many dollars a speculator thinks he will need today to buy one mark one year from now if he invests the dollar today at the current interest rate and then buys the mark in one year at the future exchange rate. Arbitrage will drive speculators' expected profit to zero).

11. What do we mean by the term "dirty float"?

12. What do we mean by "beggar thy neighbor trade policies"? Which of the following would be examples of such policies? Explain why or why not.

(a) An act by a central bank to induce a depreciation in its currency.

(b) An act by a central bank to induce an appreciation of its currency.

(c) The imposition of import quotas.

13. "Flexible exchange rates insulate a domestic economy from disturbances in foreign economies." True or false?

14. Suppose that our balance of trade account with another nation is negative.

   (a) Does this mean that our net exports are positive or negative?

   (b) If there is no central bank intervention in the foreign exchange market, is our balance on the capital account with this other nation positive or negative?

   (c) What are individuals in the other nation getting in exchange for the goods and services they are selling us?

   (d) Now suppose that the foreign country's central bank is intervening in the exchange market to keep the price of its currency below what it otherwise would be. Is the foreign central bank buying or selling dollars in the foreign exchange market?

   (e) Now what is the foreign country getting in exchange for the goods and services it is selling us?

   (f) Will the foreign central bank be willing to maintain its intervention in the exchange market forever? Why or why not?

   (g) Should we mind if the foreign central bank maintains its intervention in the exchange market forever?

15. Suppose that for some reason real GNP in Fredonia falls (assume no change in the interest rate in Fredonia).

   (a) What happens to Fredonia's demand for our goods?

   (b) Show the effect on the demand for and supply of Fredonian pesos in the foreign exchange markets.

   (c) If the exchange rate is to remain fixed at its initial level, will central banks have to buy or sell Fredonian pesos?

   (d) Assuming that the exchange rate remains fixed at its initial level, what happens to Fredonia's net export demand for U.S. goods?

   (e) Suppose that there is a flexible exchange rate regime between Fredonia and the United States. What effect does the reduction in Fredonian real GNP have on U.S. net export demand? Why?

16. In the text we noted that politicians in the United States and elsewhere frequently find it politically expedient to impose trade barriers. Such barriers are often called for in the name of "fairness" and it has been suggested that they may be a means of reducing the currently large U.S. trade deficit.

   (a) Suppose that Congress imposes a 5 percent tariff on all imports. What will be the effect on import demand?

   (b) Illustrate the consequence on the equilibrium price of the dollar in the foreign exchange market.

   (c) Is the policy successful in lowering the trade deficit? What is the effect on the volume of trade between the United States and other countries?

   (d) Which United States citizens gain from the tariff? Which ones lose?

17. During the recent period of dollar weakness in the foreign exchange markets, some argued that to induce foreigners to continue purchasing U.S. financial assets, central banks would have to intervene in the foreign exchange market and prevent the dollar from sliding further.

   (a) How is the rate of return realized by a foreigner on a U.S. financial asset related to changes in the price of the dollar?

   (b) In deciding whether to purchase a U.S. asset, does a foreign buyer care about past changes in the price of the dollar or expected future changes in the price of the dollar?

   (c) Can you think of an argument why central bank intervention to prop up the price of the dollar might discourage rather than encourage capital inflows into the United States?

18. Recall that the real price of a foreign good in terms of a domestic good tells us the amount of the domestic good that must be given up to purchase a unit of the foreign good. This relative price depends on the price of the foreign good abroad, the exchange rate, and the money price of the domestic good. *The Economist* (April 8, 1988) gathered data on the price of a Big Mac in 17 countries. These prices are presented in the table below.

Country	Price of Big Mac in local currency	Dollar exchange rate (March 28, 1988)
Australia	1.95 Australian dollars	1.36
Belgium	90 Belgian francs	34.80
Britain	1.19 pounds	0.54
Canada	2.05 Canadian dollars	1.24
Denmark	22.75 Danish kroner	6.36
France	17.30 francs	5.63
Hong Kong	7.65 Hong Kong dollars	7.80
Ireland	1.22 Irish pounds	0.62
Italy	3,300 lire	1,229.00
Japan	370 yen	124.00
Netherlands	4.85 fl	1.86
Singapore	2.80 Singapore dollars	2.00
Spain	285 pesetas	111.00
Sweden	18.50 Swedish kronor	5.89
United States	2.39 dollars	
West Germany	4.10 Deutschmarks	1.66
Yugoslavia	2,300 dinars	1,400.00

The third column of the table presents the dollar exchange rates prevailing on March 28, 1988, the time of *The Economist's* Big Mac survey. By way of example, the table indicates that a dollar could be exchanged for 111 Spanish pesetas in the foreign exchange market. Equivalently, one peseta was worth .9 cents ($= 1/111$). Determine the value of Big Macs abroad in terms of Big Macs in the United States.

19. Suppose the same good is produced in two countries. Tell why in the absence of frictions such as transportation costs and government restrictions (which include such things as tariffs and quotas), arbitrage should guarantee that the same good sells for the same price in both countries. The condition that the same good have the same price in different countries is sometimes referred to as *absolute purchasing power parity* in order to express the notion that the purchasing power of a currency in terms of the amount of a good that can be purchased is the same whether the dollar is used to buy a good here or abroad.

   (a) Based on your computations for problem 18, are the prices of foreign Big Macs equal to that of an American Big Mac?

   (b) How can you explain the reason for your result in part (b)?

   (c) What do we mean by relative purchasing power parity? Compare this with absolute purchasing power parity.

Glossary

Accelerator Model: A model that predicts that the level of net investment demand depends directly on changes in output. When output accelerates, that is when the change in output gets larger, investment demand rises. (Chapter 10)

Aggregate Budget Constraint: A constraint that is obtained by summing the constraints faced by each of the individual participants in the economy. It indicates that the excess demands in the various markets in the economy must sum to zero. (Chapter 4)

Aggregate Demand Curve: A curve that depicts all combinations of output and price levels associated with equilibrium in the output, financial, and money markets (closed economy) or the output, financial, money, and foreign exchange markets (open economy). (Chapter 7)

Aggregate Supply Curve: A supply curve that depicts combinations of price levels and real GNP that reflect the underlying relationship between employment and the price level determined by the labor and other input markets. (Chapter 7)

Automatic Stabilizer: An automatic fiscal policy change that partially counters the impact on the economy of changes in autonomous spending. Automatic stabilizers serve to moderate fluctuations in income by reducing the size of the multiplier for changes in autonomous spending. (Chapters 11 and 14)

Autonomous Change: A change in a variable such as investment or consumption demand that is not induced by a change in variables to be determined by the analysis, such as the current interest rate or income level. (Chapter 9)

Balance of Payments: The difference between the private demand for and supply of dollars in the foreign exchange markets. (Chapter 3)

Balance of Payments Accounts: A record of U.S. international transactions. Included in the balance of payments accounts are the balance of trade (exports minus imports) and international capital flows. (Chapter 3)

Balance of Trade: The difference between exports and imports. (Chapter 3)

Bank Reserves: Reserves held by depository institutions either as vault cash or as deposits at the Federal Reserve. Reserves held by private depository institutions to meet reserve requirements set by the Fed are termed required reserves. Reserves held in excess of required reserves are termed excess reserves. (Chapter 5)

Bond: A contract between a borrower and a lender that specifies the terms of a loan agreement. (Chapter 3)

Business Cycle: Alternating periods of contractions and expansions in economy-wide output. (Chapters 9, 11, and 12)

Capital Consumption Allowance: The measure of the extent of capital depreciation that is reported in the National Income and Product Accounts. *See* Depreciation. (Chapter 2)

Capital Inflow: The purchase of U.S. financial assets by foreigners. Associated with a capital inflow is a demand for dollars by foreigners in the foreign markets. (Chapter 3)

Capital Outflow: The purchase of foreign financial assets by the United States. Associated with a capital outflow is a supply of dollars by Americans in the foreign exchange markets. (Chapter 3)

Commercial Paper: Short-term bonds that mature in less than one year and are issued by large corporations. (Chapter 3)

Comparative Advantage: An advantage that a country is said to have in the production of a good if that country is the low cost producer of the good. (Chapter 17)

Consumer Price Index: An index used to measure changes in the level of consumer prices. (Chapter 2)

Consumption Expenditures: Household purchases of final output. Household consumption is the sum of purchases of durable and nondurable goods. (Chapter 2)

Consumption Function: The relationship between total household consumption spending and the total disposable income of all households. A linear form of the consumption function proposed by Keynes is $C^d = a + b \cdot (Y - CCA - T)$, where a and b are positive constants, C^d is consumption demand, and $Y - CCA - T$ is real disposable income. (Chapter 6)

Corporate Bonds: Long-term financial assets that have a maturity of more than ten years and are issued by firms. (Chapter 3)

Corporate Notes: Long-term debt instruments issued by firms that have a maturity of between one year and ten years. (Chapter 3)

Cost-Push Inflation: Inflation that is induced by rising costs such as higher wages or increases in the price of oil. (Chapter 13)

Coupon Payment: The fixed dollar amount paid to the holder of a bond each period prior to its maturity. Zero-coupon bonds pay no coupon; they promise only a lump-sum payment on maturity. (Chapter 3)

Crowding Out: A situation where increases in one component of spending, such as government spending, crowds out other components of spending, such as investment and consumption spending, in the output market. The reduction in private spending occurs in response to an increase in the interest rate. (Chapter 8)

Deflation: *See* Inflation.

Demand Shocks: Changes in variables such as autonomous investment or consumption demand, as well as monetary and fiscal policies changes, that affect aggregate demand. (Chapter 9)

Depository Institutions: Institutions that encompass not only private depository institutions such as commercial banks, savings and loan associations, and credit unions but also the Federal Reserve. (Chapter 4)

Depository Institution Financing Constraint: A constraint that equates the depository institutions' real flow demand for financial assets (A_b^d) to the change in the real supply of money $(M^s - \overline{M})/P$. (Chapter 4)

Depreciation: The loss of value in a capital good as it wears out with use or becomes obsolete. The national income accounts' measure of depreciation is called the capital consumption allowance (CCA). (Chapter 2)

Depreciation of a Currency: A fall in the price of a currency in terms of other currencies. A rise in the price of a currency is termed an appreciation of the currency. (Chapter 6)

Devaluation: In a fixed exchange rate system, the reduction in the supported price of a currency. An increase in called the supported price is termed an upward revaluation. (Chapter 17)

Dirty Float: A foreign exchange market characterized by suspected government intervention to influence floating exchange rates. (Chapter 17)

Discretionary Fiscal Policy: Changes in fiscal policy initiated at the discretion of government policymakers. These changes contrast with automatic stabilizers, which tie changes in government spending and/or net taxes automatically to changes in such variables as real GNP. (Chapters 11 and 14)

Discretionary Monetary Policy: A monetary policy that involves changes in the money supply made purely at the discretion of the Fed. These changes in the money supply each period are an attempt by the Fed to achieve such goals as full employment, price stability, low and stable interest rates, a trade balance or surplus, and stable exchange rates. (Chapter 13)

Disposable Income: Total output (Y) minus the capital consumption allowance (CCA) and total net taxes (T). (Chapter 4)

Endogenous Variables: Variables such as prices, real GNP, and the interest rate, that are to be determined by the analysis. (Chapter 8)

Equilibrium Unemployment Rate: The unemployment rate at which the flows into unemployment equal the flows out. (Chapter 15)

Excess Reserves: Reserves held by private depository institutions in excess of required reserves. (Chapter 4)

Exchange Equation: An equation derived from equilibrium in the money market. The exchange equation can be expressed as $M^s \cdot V = P \cdot Y$. (Chapter 8)

Exogenous Variables: Variables such as government spending and the money supply that are not determined by the analysis. Exogenous variables are taken as given. (Chapter 8)

Expected Rate of Inflation (π^e): The rate of inflation expected to occur in the future. (Chapter 5)

Expected Real Rate of Interest: The nominal interest rate minus the expected rate of inflation. This rate is referred to as the "ex ante" real rate of interest. (Chapter 3)

Exports: The goods and services produced by an economy that are sold to foreigners. (Chapter 2)

Financial Assets: Assets such as stocks and bonds that provide a future monetary flow. (Chapter 3)

Firm Financing Constraint: A constraint ($I^d = A_f^s$) indicating that firms' desired net investment purchases (I^d) must be financed by their real supply of financial assets (A_f^s). In other words, firms' investment demand is constrained by the amount of funds raised through the issuance of new financial assets. (Chapter 4)

Fiscal Drag: A situation that occurs when the fiscal policy of the government restricts aggregate demand, which is indicated by the fact that current tax and expenditure programs would result in a full employment surplus. (Chapter 14)

Fiscal Policy: The government's decisions concerning its choices of real spending on output, net real taxes, and the real supply of government bonds. (Chapter 4)

Fisher Effect: A theory stating that the money interest rate will increase by an amount equal to the increase in the expected inflation rate. (Chapter 8)

Flow Variable: A variable that is measured over a period of time. Examples are the real output produced in the economy over a year (real GNP), the real dollar value of financial assets issued during a particular year in the primary market, and the amount of capital equipment purchased by firms in a given year (real investment spending). (Chapter 3)

Foreign Exchange Rate: The price of one country's currency in terms of the currency of a second country. (Chapter 3)

Foreigner foreign exchange constraint: A constraint that indicates that the sum of foreigners' demand for U.S. goods and services (U.S. exports, X^d) and for U.S. financial assets (A_{for}^d) equals their real supply of foreign currency (FC^s). (Chapter 4)

Fractional Reserve Banking System: A banking system in which private depository institutions hold only a fraction of their deposits as reserves. (Chapter 5)

Frictional Unemployment: Unemployment associated with the typical flow of new entrants into the labor market and quits, as well as permanent layoffs reflecting a change in the composition of output produced by the economy. Sometimes a distinction is made between frictional and "structural" unemployment with structural unemployment reflecting the unemployment that results from changes in the production of output across firms reflecting a long-run change in the composition of aggregate output. *See* Natural Unemployment Rate. (Chapter 7)

Full Employment: A level of employment that occurs at that output predicted by the neoclassical model. All corresponding unemployment is frictional. (Chapter 7)

Full Employment Budget: A budget that indicates what government expenditures and revenues will be if the economy is at full employment. (Chapter 14)

General Equilibrium Analysis: An examination of simultaneous equilibrium in all the markets in an economy. (Chapter 7)

GNP Deflator: The price index used to measure changes in the overall level of prices for the goods and services that make up the gross national product. It is sometimes referred to as the implicit GNP deflator since it is implicitly defined by the ratio of nominal to real GNP. (Chapter 2)

Government Financing Constraint: A constraint that equates real government spending (G^d) to real net taxes (T) and real government borrowing (A_g^s). (Chapter 4)

Government Purchases of Goods and Services: Those purchases made at all governmental levels (federal, state, and local). Does not include government transfer payments. (Chapter 2)

High-Powered Money: Another term for the monetary base. (Chapter 5)

Household Budget Constraint: A constraint that equates the sum of consumption and saving ($C^d + S$) to households' real disposable income ($Y - CCA - T$). (Chapter 4)

Household Foreign Exchange Constraint: A constraint that equates households' real demand for foreign currency (FC^d) to the sum of import demand (Z^d) plus households' real desired purchases of foreign financial assets AF_h^d. (Chapter 4)

Human Capital: Investments in activities such as schooling, on-the-job training, medical care, and job search that raise monetary and psychic income by increasing workers' productivity. (Chapter 9)

Imports: Goods and services that are produced abroad and purchased for domestic consumption. (Chapter 2)

Income Effect: A higher wage means that the individual can choose to increase both the amount of output he/she purchases and the amount of leisure he/she enjoys. If leisure is a normal good, then this income effect induces the individual to work fewer hours—that is, supply less labor and demand more leisure. There is also a substitution effect associated with the change in the wage. (Chapter 6)

Incomplete Information: Information that is not complete regarding changes in prices. When workers do not fully anticipate price changes, the result is an upward-sloping aggregate supply curve. (Chapter 12)

Inflation: A rise in the general level of prices; deflation is a fall in the general level of prices. (Chapter 2)

Interest Rate: The specified charge per dollar per period that borrowers pay or lenders receive. (Chapter 3)

International Capital Flows: The sale and purchase of financial assets across different countries. Foreign purchases of U.S. financial assets are referred to as U.S. *capital inflows,* since they reflect the inflow of funds associated with foreigners' purchases of U.S. financial assets. Private international capital outflows associated with U.S. purchases of foreign financial assets are referred to as U.S. *capital outflows,* since they reflect the outflow of funds associated with U.S purchases of foreign financial assets. (Chapter 3)

Intertemporal Substitution Hypothesis: A hypothesis indicating that labor supply responds positively to transitory increases in the real wage and the real interest rate. (Chapter 6)

Investment: The purchase of final output by firms. Investment consists of nonresidential fixed investment (spending by firms to construct new plants and purchase machinery and other capital equipment), residential fixed investment (spending for the construction of new homes and apartments) and net inventory investment (the change in the stock of raw materials, parts, and finished goods held by firms in inventory). (Chapter 2)

Involuntary Unemployment: A type of unemployment that occurs in the predetermined price model when workers cannot find employment at prevailing wages. (Chapter 10)

IS Curve: A curve that depicts all output-interest rate combinations consistent with equilibrium in the output market. (Chapter 10)

J-Curve: A curve that indicates a situation in which a depreciation of a currency can initially result in a worsening of that country's trade balance. (Chapter 17)

Keynesian Cross Diagram: An illustration of equilibrium in the output market in terms of firms producing a quantity equal to output demand. (Chapter 10)

Labor Demand: *See* marginal product and value of the marginal product of labor.

Labor Force: Consists of all individuals who are either employed or unemployed. (Chapter 2)

Labor Productivity: The amount of output per work hour. (Chapter 2)

Laffer Curve: A curve depicting the relationship between the income tax rate and total tax revenues. Above some critical tax rate, increases in the tax rate reduce total tax revenues due to the negative effects on taxable income. (Chapter 9)

Law of Diminishing Marginal Return: A law stating that as more units of labor are added to a fixed amount of capital, the resulting increases in output tend to diminish. It is the reason for the downward-sloping labor demand curve. (Chapter 5)

Life-Cycle Hypothesis: Proposed by Franco Modigliani, this hypothesis, like the permanent income hypothesis, examines the implications of the fact that households care about consumption over their lifetime. In such analysis, consumption demand depends directly on anticipated future income as well as current income. (Chapter 6)

Liquidity Trap: Arises in a hypothetical situation in which the response of money demand to a change in the interest rate is extremely high, implying a nearly flat *LM* curve. (Chapter 11)

LM Curve: A curve that depicts all output-interest rate

combinations consistent with equilibrium in the money market. (Chapter 10)

Loanable Funds: The suppliers of new financial assets (firms and government) are demanders of loanable funds. The demanders of these financial assets (households, depository institutions, and foreigners) are the suppliers of loanable funds. (Chapter 5)

Lucas Critique: Proposed by Robert Lucas, this theory points out that examining the past impact of policy changes does not necessarily give one the ability to predict future effects of policy changes. Lucas contends that the economic decisions of private agents depend, in part, on their perceptions and expectations of present and future government policies. If these policies are changing over time, so will the behavior of private individuals. (Chapter 13)

M1: A measure of the money supply consisting of currency, travelers checks, and checkable deposits held by the nonbank public. M1 counts assets that can be *directly* used to purchase goods and services. (Chapter 3)

M2: A measure of the money supply consisting of all assets included in M1 plus all assets that can be quickly converted into a medium of exchange. M2 provides a broader measure of the money supply than M1 since it also counts noncheckable savings accounts at depository institutions, small time deposits (less than $100,000), money market deposits, and mutual funds. (Chapter 3)

Macroeconomics: The branch of economics that studies the determinants of such aggregate economic variables as total output, employment and unemployment, the level of prices, interest rates, and foreign exchange rates. (Chapter 1)

Macroeconomic Shock: A change in an exogenous variable. These changes can come either from the private sector or the public sector. Some examples of private sector shocks are a reduction in firms' investment demand and an increase in households' consumption expenditures. Public sector macroeconomic shocks include unexpectedly large deficits or a change in the pattern of monetary growth. (Chapter 8)

Marginal Product of Capital (*MPK*): The increase in output associated with a one-unit increase in capital, other inputs being held constant. (Chapter 5)

Marginal Product of Labor (*MPN*): The increase in output associated with a one-unit increase in the employment of labor, holding other inputs constant. The marginal product of labor curve constitutes firms' demand for labor curve. (Chapter 5)

Marginal Propensity to Consume (*MPC*): The ratio of the increase in households' real consumption demand to the increase in their real disposable income. The marginal propensity to consume is positive but less than one. (Chapters 6 and 10)

Marginal Propensity to Save (*MPS*): The ratio of the increase in households' real saving to the increase in their real disposable income. The marginal propensity to save is positive but less than one. The marginal propensity to save plus the marginal propensity to consume equal one. (Chapter 6)

Maturity: The length of time before the repayment of a bond's principal. (Chapter 3)

Monetarist: A proponent of the belief that the Fed should base current money supply changes on previously stated rules. (Chapter 13)

Monetary base: Also referred to as high-powered money. The sum of currency held by the nonbank public and bank reserves (vault cash and deposits of private depository institutions at the Fed). (Chapters 4 and 5)

Monetary Policy: Decisions relating to actions by the Federal Reserve (the U.S. central bank) that determine the rate of change in the money supply. (Chapter 4)

Monetary Rule: A monetary policy that commits the Fed to a fixed rate of growth in the money supply. It is a monetary policy advocated by economists known as monetarists. (Chapter 13)

Money: A medium of exchange, a store of value, and a unit of account. In the United States, M1 and M2 are two measures of the money supply. (Chapter 3)

Money Multiplier: The ratio of the total change in the money supply to an initial change in the monetary base. In the simple case where the change in the monetary base is solely in the form of bank reserves and depository institutions hold no excess reserves, the money multiplier is $1/rr$, where rr is the required reserve-to-deposit ratio. (Chapter 5)

Mortgages: Bonds that finance the construction of new homes, as well as farm and business property. Mortgages are long-term loans secured by real estate. (Chapter 3)

Multiplier: In the context of the predetermined price model, an indication of the change in equilibrium output caused by each $1 change in autonomous spending. (Chapter 10)

Municipal Bond: Long-term debt obligations issued by local governments. (Chapter 3)

National Income and Product Accounts: The official U.S. government statistics on GNP and its various components. These figures are compiled by the U.S. Department of Commerce. (Chapter 2)

Natural Rate of Unemployment: The rate of unemployment associated with the neoclassical model. It consists solely of frictional unemployment. (Chapter 7)

Net Exports: The difference between exports and imports. (Chapter 2)

Net Investment: Gross investment minus the capital consumption allowance. Net investment is a measure of the change in the capital stock. (Chapter 2)

Net National Product: GNP minus the capital consumption allowance. (Chapter 2)

Net Real Wage [(1 − t)(W/P)]: The money wage after taxes divided by the level of output prices. The net real wage measures the after-tax amount received by a unit of labor in terms of real goods and services. (Chapter 6)

Neutrality of Money: The fact that a change in the money supply has no long-run effect on real variables. This result is predicted by the neoclassical model. (Chapter 8)

Nominal Gross National Product (GNP): The current market value of all final goods and services produced by an economy in a specified period of time. (Chapter 2)

Non-market-clearing Prices: In the predetermined price model, the setting of output prices at a level such that firms cannot sell all they desire at existing prices. (Chapter 10)

Open Market Operations: The buying and selling of government bonds by the Federal Reserve. Such activity alters the size of the monetary base. (Chapter 5)

Participation Rate: The proportion of the noninstitutionalized population over age 16 in the labor force. (Chapter 2)

Perfect Foresight: Refers to expectations that turn out to be completely accurate. (Chapter 11)

Permanent Income Hypothesis: Proposed by Milton Friedman, this hypothesis suggests that consumption is based on an individual's perception of permanent income. It is similar to the life-cycle hypothesis. According to the permanent income hypothesis, transitory or temporary changes in real disposable income have little impact on consumption. (Chapter 6)

Perpetuity: A financial instrument that yields a perpetual stream of payments. (Chapter 3)

Phillips Curve: A curve depicting the relationship between inflation and unemployment. (Chapter 12)

Present Value: The amount that one is willing to give up today in order to obtain a future sum. That amount depends on the interest rate and the number of years until the sum is obtained. The present value of $1 to be received n years from now given an annual interest rate r equals $1/(1 + r)^n$. (Chapter 3)

Price Index: A ratio of the expenditure on a basket of goods and services in some given year to the expenditure in some base year. Three important price indexes for the U.S. economy are the GNP (implicit price) deflator, the consumer price index (CPI), and the producer price index (PPI). (Chapter 2)

Primary Financial Market: The financial market in which newly issued assets are traded. This market, unlike the secondary market, concerns flow variables. (Chapter 3)

Production Function: The relationship between a firm's output and its capital and labor inputs. (Chapter 5)

Public Choice Economics: The area of economics devoted to the analysis of political behavior. (Chapter 14)

Purchasing Power Parity: A condition indicating that flexible foreign exchange rates tend to vary so as to maintain constant relative prices. In considering two countries, purchasing power parity means that the country with the lower inflation rate tends to have an exchange rate that is appreciating at a rate approximately equal to the difference in inflation rates between the two countries. (Chapter 8)

Quantity Theory of Money: A theory that assumes velocity is stable, so that changes in money supply will result in equiproportionate changes in nominal GNP. *See* Exchange equation. (Chapter 8)

Rational Expectations: Expectations formed by using all available information, including how anticipated monetary and fiscal policy changes will affect future demands, supplies, and thus equilibrium prices. (Chapter 11)

Reactive Rules: A rule that specifies in advance how government policies will change based on new information on the state of the economy. One example of a reactive monetary rule is to have the growth in the monetary base, and thus in the money supply, automatically adjust whenever the growth of nominal GNP deviates from its trend. Another reactive rule would have the Fed commit itself to holding the CPI to a preannounced target and adjust the monetary base, and thus the money supply, accordingly. (Chapter 13)

Real Business Cycles: Fluctuations in real output related to supply shocks such as oil disruptions. (Chapter 9)

Real Exchange Rate ($P_f/(P \cdot E)$): A measure of the real amount of domestic goods and services that must be given up to obtain a foreign good. The real exchange rate for U.S. goods is $(P \cdot E)/(P_f)$. (Chapter 6)

Real Gross National Product: Nominal gross national product adjusted for price changes. It is a measure of the total output of goods and services produced by the economy each year in terms of base year ("constant dollar") prices. (Chapter 2)

Real Money Demand (L^d): Households' desired holdings of real money balances. It is equal to their nominal money demand at the end of the period divided by the price level. (Chapter 4)

Real Rate of Interest: The nominal or money rate of interest minus the rate of inflation. This rate provides a measure of the real cost to borrowing, or the real gain to lending. (Chapter 3)

Real Wage: The money wage divided by the level of output prices. The real wage measures the payment for a unit of labor in terms of real goods and services. (Chapters 2 and 5)

Recession: A period showing a fall in real GNP, typically spanning at least two quarters. A severe recession, such as that which occurred in the early 1930s, is called a depression. (Chapter 2)

Rental Cost of Capital: *See* User cost of capital. (Chapter 5)

Required Reserves: Reserves held by private depository institutions to meet reserve requirements set by the Fed. (Chapter 4)

Reservation Wage: The minimum wage offer that a jobseeker finds acceptable. (Chapter 15)

Ricardian Equivalence: A theory stating the possibility

that deficit financing is equivalent to taxation. Named after the noted early nineteenth-century economist David Ricardo. (Chapter 8)

Secondary Financial Market: The financial market in which financial assets that have been previously issued are traded. (Chapter 3)

Speculative Bubble: Speculation feeding on itself that causes the price of an asset (currency, gold, etc.) to temporarily deviate from it underlying value. (Chapter 17)

Sterilization: A process that occurs when government intervention in foreign exchange markets is counteracted by appropriate open market operations in domestic financial markets in order to leave the money supply unchanged. (Chapter 17)

Sticky Wages: Money wages that do not quickly adjust to changes in labor demand or supply. Sticky wages can result in an upward-sloping aggregate supply curve. (Chapter 12)

Stock Variable: A variable that is measured at a specific point in time. For example, at any point in time the real dollar value of previously issued financial assets is a stock variable. Other examples are the amount of capital in the economy and the amount of money in the hands of households. (Chapter 3)

Substitution Effect: A higher wage increases the gain to working an additional hour and thus leads individuals to substitute labor for leisure. This direct effect between the wage and labor supply is referred to as the substitution effect. There is also an income effect associated with a change in the wage. (Chapter 5)

Supply-Side Economics: The argument that a reduction in taxes raises the rewards to work, save, or invest and can thus lead to increased real output, and to lower inflation and interest rates. (Chapter 9)

Supply Shocks: Changes in variables such as oil supply, weather, technology, strikes, or government policies that affect aggregate supply. (Chapter 9)

Term Structure of Interest Rates: The relationship between interest rates on bonds that are similar in all characteristics except maturity. (Chapter 3)

Transfer Payments: Government outlays such as social security payments and interest payments on government debt that simply involve the redistribution or transfer of income among households. (Chapter 2)

Treasury Bills: Bonds issued by the federal government with maturities ranging from 3 months to one year. They are considered to have no possibility of default and are thus sometimes referred to as risk-free. (Chapter 3)

Treasury Bonds: Bonds issued by the federal government that have maturities longer than ten years. (Chapter 3)

Treasury Notes: Bonds issued by the federal government that have maturities of between one and ten years. (Chapter 3)

Unemployment Rate: The number of unemployed workers expressed as a fraction or percentage of the total number of workers in the labor force. (Chapter 2)

Unintended Inventory Accumulation: A situation that firms experience when output demand falls short of actual production. In contrast, if output demand exceeds actual production, firms experience unintended inventory decumulation. (Chapter 10)

User Cost of Capital: The expected cost to use or "rent" capital; it equals $(P_k/P)(r - \pi^e + d)$. The user cost of capital rises with an increase in the interest rate r and the rate of depreciation of capital d; it falls with an increase in the expected rate of inflation π^e and rise with an increase in the real price of capital P_k/P. (Chapter 5)

Value of the Marginal Product of Labor ($P \cdot MPN$): The marginal product of labor multiplied by the price of output. It defines the increase in revenue from the employment of one additional unit of labor. The value of the marginal product of labor curve is a firm's demand for labor curve when demand is plotted against the money wage. It is downward-sloping due to the law of diminishing marginal product of labor. (Chapter 5)

Velocity of Money (V): The average number of times the money supply turns over per year in transactions involving the purchase of final output. In equilibrium it is the ratio of real GNP to real money demand. *See* Exchange equation. (Chapter 8)

Zero-Coupon Bonds: *See* Coupon payment. (Chapter 3)

Author Index

Topic Index

Guide to Symbols